THE OXFORD
COMPANION TO
MUSICAL INSTRUMENTS

THE OXFORD COMPANION TO
MUSICAL INSTRUMENTS

WRITTEN AND
EDITED BY
Anthony Baines

Oxford   New York
OXFORD UNIVERSITY PRESS

*This book has been printed digitally and produced in a standard specification
in order to ensure its continuing availability*

OXFORD
UNIVERSITY PRESS

Great Clarendon Street, Oxford OX2 6DP

Oxford University Press is a department of the University of Oxford.
It furthers the University's objective of excellence in research, scholarship,
and education by publishing worldwide in

Oxford New York

Auckland Bangkok Buenos Aires Cape Town Chennai
Dar es Salaam Delhi Hong Kong Istanbul Karachi Kolkata
Kuala Lumpur Madrid Melbourne Mexico City Mumbai Nairobi
São Paulo Shanghai Singapore Taipei Tokyo Toronto

with an associated company in Berlin

Oxford is a registered trade mark of Oxford University Press
in the UK and in certain other countries

Published in the United States
by Oxford University Press Inc., New York

ISBN 0-19-311334-1

Jacket illustration: detail from *Still Life with Violin*,
by Amédée Ozenfant. © DACS 1992.
Photo: Giraudon/Bridgeman Art Library.

CONTENTS

INTRODUCTION

This book has its origins in a suggestion from the publishers, made shortly after the appearance of the *New Oxford Companion to Music* (1983), that the material in that work bearing on musical instruments might form the basis for a compact reference work on the instruments themselves—that is, leaving aside electric and the vast field of electronic instruments, on which materials by Richard Dobson, originally intended to form part of the present work, have appeared as a separate volume.

Many of the original *NOCM* articles will be seen again, little changed save where fresh discoveries or viewpoints across the intervening years have called for a revision. A few have been substantially rewritten, however, while many articles that described several or many different instruments of a family or class have been split up into separate entries for direct consultation—though it has seemed preferable not to impose a rigorously consistent scheme throughout, and not a few of the original collective entries have been judged better left practically as they were.

Makers of instruments not being entered individually, an Index to those cited in the course of articles is included at the end of the book, showing the entries in which their names appear.

One would expect this book to be primarily concerned with instruments of our own ('Western') traditions. One would also certainly expect due attention to those of further afield ('non-Western'). Here the editor acknowledges great reliance on the right to draw freely—be it verbatim or not—on the expert contributions to the *NOCM* on the music of different major world regions or cultures. Some general observations on the instruments of each, along with a list of those which are entered individually, will be found under: AFRICA, AMERICAN INDIAN, CHINA AND KOREA, INDIA, JAPAN, MIDDLE EAST, PACIFIC ISLANDS, and SOUTH-EAST ASIA. Correct orthography in foreign instrument names is not always strictly followed, diacritics being omitted in many cases (e.g. *vina*) where the word is well known in English without them.

The contents of this one-volume Companion are necessarily selective, with entries of a controlled total number calculated to provide a guide to names and terms most likely to be met in literature, musical or general. As the offspring of a larger Companion the book in no way sets out to be compared with Sibyl Marcuse's comprehensive Dictionary of almost 30 years ago or the invaluable three-volumed *New Grove Dictionary of Musical Instruments*. Rather, the present work provides a run-down of the sort of things that a musical instrument can be—or better said (to follow Karl Izikowitz in the title of his work of 1934 on the Americas), 'musical and other sound instruments', subscribing to a long tradition in general accounts of instruments to sidestep commitment as to what is indisputably 'musical' and what is, by intention and use, definitely not. A few of the present entries cover instruments made for producing sounds which, even if of a musical quality, may never yet have served music in any direct capacity whatsoever.

Musical technicalities are taken no further than should be easily understood by the general reader. A rather large quantity of musical notes (C D E, etc.) will, however, be found among the entries. It is of course perfectly possible to pursue a valid and creative interest in musical instruments without knowing a note of music; but a reader who has this knowledge may wish to know of an instrument 'how do you tune it?', 'how deep does it go?', and other such things so simply said in notes, until it may come to a question of distinguishing notes in different octaves: of the seven Cs on the piano, for instance, which C is meant? There are at present two competing systems, both with roots in the Middle Ages:

Ex. 1.

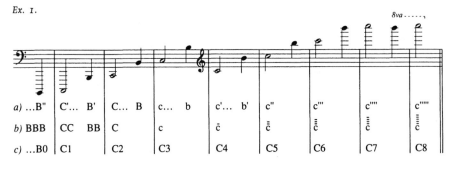

i. Old German tradition, normal through the times of Praetorius (Ex. 1*b*; a German may still speak of 'the three-stroked D', i.e. *d'''*, and so on). It was later tidied up by Helmholtz (Ex. 1*a*), becoming standard also in Britain for works on instruments, including this one.

2. France, Italy: notes named *do* (in France originally *ut*), *ré*, *mi*, etc., formerly with cumbersome ancient octave designations derived from the Guidonian hexachords ('A la mi re', etc.) but early in the present century modernized with numbers, the tuning A (*a'* in Ex. 1*a*) becoming la⁴, and the bottom C of the piano do°. In 1960 the American Standards Institute adopted the same numbering system but affixed to the familiar note letters A B C, etc. (Ex. 1*c*). In Britain there has grown a strong movement to follow the same practice.

FURTHER READING

For author references in or appended to articles see Works Cited (at the end of the book), where full titles are given under authors' names. (NB: It has to be admitted that although new books are welcomed every year, there are still categories of instrument on which the literature is decidedly thin when it comes to the authoritatively informative kind of book that one is looking for.)

In the matter of articles in periodicals, the quantity now reached among those devoted to instruments, in English alone, is such that in order to guide non-specialist readers to a firm start without needing vast space, the course taken here is to allow three journals, each noted for wide subject coverage, to speak for the progress of instrument research over the recent years, namely *The Galpin Society Journal*, *Early Music*, and the *Journal of the American Musical Instrument Society*; for details see Works Cited.

A. B.

London, 1991

ACKNOWLEDGEMENTS

The editor wishes to thank the following writers for articles taken over from the *New Oxford Companion to Music* or containing material adapted from sections of such articles for the purposes of the present Dictionary.

Francis Baines (Hurdy-gurdy, Viol, and many other stringed instruments)
Pearle Christian, Michael Burnett (Steel Band)
Jonathan Condit (Korea)
James Dalton (Organ)
Ian Gammie (Guitar)
Michael Lowe (Lute)
Elizabeth Markham (Japanese Music)
Helen Myers (African Music, Pacific Islands, South-East Asian Music)
Julian Pilling (Accordion, etc.)
Alec Roth (Indonesia)
James Tyler (Cittern)
D. R. Widdess (Indian Music)
Rembrandt Wolpert (Chinese Music)
M. J. Wright (Bells, Handbells).

ABBREVIATIONS

Amer.	American
Arab.	Arabic
arr.	arranged by
b.	born
c.	*circa* (about)
cent.	century
d.	died
ed.	editor; edited by
edn.	edition
EM	*Early Music*
Eng.	English
esp.	especially
facs.	facsimile
fl.	*floruit* (flourished)
Fr.	French
Ger.	German
Gk.	Greek
Grove	*The New Grove Dictionary of Music and Musicians*
GSJ	*Galpin Society Journal*
Hung.	Hungarian
incl.	including
It.	Italian
K.	Köchel (catalogue of Mozart's works)
Lat.	Latin
L. H.	left hand
lit.	literally
MS(S)	manuscript(s)
n. d.	no date
NOCM	*The New Oxford Companion to Music*
orch.	orchestrated by
Port.	Portuguese
pron.	pronounced
publ.	published
repr.	reprint(ed)
rev.	revised
R. H.	right hand
Ru.	Russian
Sp.	Spanish
trans.	translation; translated by
Turk.	Turkish
*	cross-reference to another article, in which the reader will find more information

PICTURE CREDITS

Accademia Filarmonica, Verona: cornett, pl. 1a; Ashmolean Museum, Oxford: cittern, pl. 1, English guitar, pl. 1.

Barnes & Mullins Ltd., London: mandolin, pl. 2; Bate Collection, Oxford: basset horn, pl. 1, bassoon, pl. 2, clarinet, pl. 1f, clarinet, pl. 2, recorder, pl. 1, saz, pl. 1; B. T. Batsford, London: Japan, pls. 1 & 2 (from F. T. Piggott, *The Music and Musical Instruments of Japan*); Bayerische Staatsbibliothek, Munich: Renaissance instruments, pl. 1; Deben Bhattacharya, Paris: India, pl. 1; Biblioteca Nazionale Marciana, Venice: fiddle, pl. 1; Bibliothèque Nationale, Paris: trombone, pl. 2; Bodleian Library, Oxford: medieval instruments, pl. 1 (MS Bodley 264, fol 188ᵛ); Boosey & Hawkes Ltd., London: glockenspiel, pl. 1, sousaphone, pl. 1, tuba, pl. 1, vibraphone, pl. 1; photo Max Yves Brandily, Paris: harp, pl. 3; John F. Brennan, Oxford: organ, pl. 1; British Library, London: fiddle, pl. 2, hurdy-gurdy, pl. 1; British Museum, London: aulos, pl. 1; Alexandr Buchner, Prague: bagpipe, pl. 1.

CEDRI, Paris: accordion, pl. 1; Cliché des Musées Nationaux, Paris: serpent, pl. 1.

Deutsches Museum, Munich: clavichord, pls. 1 & 2.

Raymond Elgar, Bexhill: double bass, pl. 1.

Gemeentemuseum, The Hague: horn, pl. 2, lute, pl. 2; Germanisches Nationalmuseum, Nuremberg: lute, pl. 3, piano, pl. 1, viola d'amore, pl. 1.

Billy Reed Hampton: Appalachian dulcimer, pl. 1; Photo Ernst Heins, Amsterdam: gamelan, pl. 1; Hobgoblin Music, Crawley: rebec, pl. 1; T. W. Howarth & Co. Ltd., London: oboe, pl. 1.

Illustrated London News: friction drum, pl. 1.

Estate of Jean Jenkins: lute, pl. 4 (from J. Jenkins and Olsen, *Music and Musical Instruments of Islam*, 1976); Foto Jobst, Klingenthal: Wagner tuba, pl. 1.

Karl-Marx-Universität, Musikinstrumenten-Museum, Leipzig: cornett, pl. 1b, racket, pl. 1; Korean Overseas Information Service: Korea, pl. 2; Kunsthistorisches Museum, Vienna: recorder, pl. 2; Kunstsammlungen Veste Coburg: bandora, pl. 1.

LAVIGNAC—Editions DELAGRAVE—PARIS: fiddle, pl. 3, kemancha, pl. 1, mrdanga, pl. 1; Martin Lessen, Rochester, NY: keyed bugle, pl. 1 (photo Smithsonian Institution); Bill Lewington Ltd., London: clarinet, pl. 1a–e, flute, pl. 1; Lyon & Healy Harps, Inc., Chicago, Illinois: harp, pl. 1.

Metropolitan Museum of Art, New York: lyre, pl. 1 (Fletcher Fund, 1956), square piano, pl. 2 (Rogers Fund, 1975); Marian and Tony Morrison, South American Pictures, Woodbridge, Suffolk: panpipe, pl. 1; Museo del Prado, Madrid: shawm, pl. 1; Museum für Völkerkunde, Leipzig: South East Asia, pl. 1.

National Army Museum, London: military band, pl. 1; National Bank of Greece: lira, pl. 1 (from F. Anoyanakis, *Greek Popular Musical Instruments*, 1979); National Museum of Finland, Helsinki: kantele, pl. 1; *Nice Matin*: pipe and tabor, pl. 1 (photo Vincent Tivoli); Nordisk Rotogravyr Stockholm: Middle East, pl. 1 (from Tobias Norlind, *Musikinstrumentens Historia*, 1941).

Paxman Ltd., London: horn, pl. 1; Pitt Rivers Museum, Oxford: Northumbrian bagpipes, pl. 1, sheng, pl. 1, vina, pl. 1, zither, pl. 3; Popperfoto, London: saung, pl. 1, South East Asia, pl. 2; Premier Percussion Ltd., Leicester: drum set, pl. 1, timpani, pl. 1.

Alec Roth, Durham: bonang, pl. 1; Royal College of Music, London: cello, pl. 1, chitarrone, pl. 1, tromba marina, pl. 1; Royal Tropical Institute, Amsterdam: drum, pl. 1 (photo Felix van Lamsweerde); Russell Collection of Early Keyboard Instruments, Edinburgh University: virginal, pl. 1.

The Edward F. Searles Musical Instrument Collection; given by Edward S. Rowland, Benjamin A. Rowland, Jr., George B. Rowland, Daniel B. Rowland, Rodney D. Rowland, and M. A. Swedlund, in memory of their father, Benjamin Allen Rowland (courtesy, Museum of Fine Arts, Boston): regal, pl. 1; The Selmer Company, L.P.: trumpet, pl. 1; Shrine to Music Museum, University of South Dakota: trumpet, pl. 2; Smithsonian Institution, Washington: square piano, pl. 1; Society for Cultural Relations with the USSR: lute, pl. 5; Sotheby's: cornet, pl. 1, double flageolet, pl. 1, harpsichord, pl. 2, oboe, pl. 2, slide trumpet, pl. 1, spinet, pl. 1, zither, pl. 2; Steinway & Sons: piano, pl. 2; *The Straits Times*: nose flute, pl. 1.

Tameside Local Studies Library: brass band, pl. 1; *The Telegraph* Colour Library: sound sculpture, pl. 1; J. Thibouville-Lamy & Co., London: autoharp, pl. 1.

VAAP, Moscow: bandura, pl. 1; Victoria and Albert Museum, London: virginal, pl. 2; H. Roger Viollet, Paris: military band, pl. 2.

Warwickshire Museum: lute, pl. 1; Mrs Bliss Wiant: China and Korea, pl. 1, qin, pl. 1 (from Bliss Wiant, *The Music of China*, n.d.).

Zentralantiquariat der Deutschen Demokratischen Republik, Leipzig: pluriarc, pl. 1 (from B. Ankermann, *Die afrikanischen Musikinstrumente*, 1901, repr. 1976).

A

Accordion (the smaller types better known as 'melodeon'; Fr.: *accordéon*; Ger.: *Akkordeon, Ziehharmonika*; It.: *fisarmonica*; Ru.: *garmonika*; Sp.: *acordeón*). *Free-reed instrument held between the hands, with finger buttons ('button keys') or piano-style keys for the melody played by the right hand, and for the left hand, buttons (or spoon-shaped keys) giving bass notes and chords. The left hand, which works the bellows, is passed through a strap to be able to draw them outwards, fanwise (Pl. 1), as well as press them inwards. The name, from Ger. *Akkord*, 'a chord', appears first in a Viennese patent by Cyril Demian and his sons in 1829, alluding to this provision of ready-made chords, then new, and a distinguishing mark of accordions of all types in contrast to *concertinas.

1. *Single or double action.* Each melody button controls, basically, two metal reeds, one speaking on the press, the other on the draw of the bellows. They are riveted on either side of a rectangular metal plate (A in Fig. 1) with a slot under each reed; the plates are glued over compartments in a long wooden reed-box projecting into the interior of the bellows. A reed vibrates only when air flows in the direction first on to the reed, then through the slot in the plate. Air flowing in the opposite direction would merely bend the reed away without vibration. A leather (or plastic) flap is therefore placed over each slot on the opposite side from the reed, to prevent wastage of wind in this way. The reed B (Fig. 1), attached on the outside of the plate, speaks on the press; C is the flap which prevents air then reaching the other reed (invisible, on the underside of the plate) which speaks on the draw,

when a similar flap (on the underside below B) prevents air flowing past reed B.

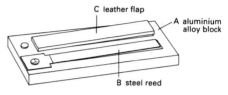

Fig. 1.

(a) *Single action.* The original action (Melodeon, British chromatic accordion, 2 and 3 below). The two reeds of a pair give different notes, in most cases adjacent notes of a major scale; an octave of the scale needs four buttons only—e.g. C, E, G on the press, D, F, A, B on the draw. Melodies therefore require short to-and-fro movements of the bellows, bringing a rhythmic briskness especially effective in dance music.

(b) *Double action.* (Piano accordion, Continental chromatic accordion, 4 and 5 below). Both reeds give the same note, which therefore sounds whichever way the bellows move, and favours music of more sweeping character.

With either action the pairs of reeds are often duplicated or further multiplied for various effects, e.g. slightly off-tuned to give a 'beat' tremolo, or to sound in octaves. Register knobs or tabs on the outside then move slides to bring in or shut off the additional ranks of reeds as desired, and may be marked by a code using two horizontal lines: a dot between them signifies normal pitch; above them,

Pl. 1. Melodeon accompanying violin for folk music, Ireland.

an octave higher; below, the octave lower. Dots above and between may stand for 'oboe' effect, and in all three positions for 'cello'. Two dots in the same space signifies 'tremolo'.

Every accordion has an air-release button for the left thumb, opened when filling or exhausting the bellows without playing a note or chord.

2. Melodeon. Very popular for folk music. The simplest form has a single row of melody buttons for the scale of C, or often G, D, or A. The low dominant is duplicated (as on a diatonic *harmonica) to give a complete dominant harmony on the draw. Two spoon-shaped keys for the left hand give the bass note and chord of the tonic on the press, the dominant on the draw. Older melodeons had brass reeds but now they are steel.

A common addition is another row of melody buttons, and corresponding left-hand keys, for playing in the key a fifth or fourth higher (Pl. 1), e.g. in G and D, popular in Britain, or on the Continent F and C, sometimes with in addition a half-row for accidentals ('club' model) or, rarer, four or five rows in keys a fifth apart ('helicon bass', popular in Yugoslavia for instance). Though one normally plays on one row at a time, extra rows offer useful alternative fingering, a 'press' note becoming available also on the 'draw'. Though very rhythmical in effect, the in-and-out action for the scale makes the simpler melodeons less suitable in 6/8 time, so that in Ireland, for jigs, and Italy, for the *Saltarello*, a chromatic instrument, or one with a half-row giving alternative fingerings, is most usual. A popular name in Italy is *organetto* (the instruments said to have been first made in that country by Paolo Soprani of Castelfidardo in Marche, *c.*1860).

3. British chromatic accordion. This corresponds to the chromatic harmonica in that it adds to the single-row melodeon a second row of buttons giving notes a semitone higher (or lower). Therefore, if playing in other than the basic key, other fingering patterns have to be learnt; yet quick dances can be played with great speed and clarity. Players tend to ignore the bass on these instruments since makers' tradition is to supply this for the basic tonality only. There may also be *three* rows of buttons a semitone apart, in B, C, and C♯; once the technique of playing across the rows has been mastered this instrument provides one of the finest accompaniments to country dancing, and is particularly popular in Scotland. Large and heavy 43 × 20 cm. (17″ × 8″), it was developed around 1946; Jimmy Shand has been perhaps its best-known player. There is a row of tabs by the treble keyboard to bring into play extra reeds for 'sharp tremolo', 'flat tremolo', upper and lower octaves, and combinations of these. The bass side resembles that of the piano accordion (see 5, below) with 120 buttons and double action.

4. Continental chromatic accordion. A double-action instrument, held by many to provide an ideal fingering for an accordion. In France it is the accordion of the celebrated 'musette' school. The basses and chords are the same as on a piano accordion. The right hand has buttons, three rows being the essential, the buttons arranged on the system shown in Fig. 2. Those of each row are separated by a minor third, and those in a slanting line from left (top) to right by whole tones. All tonalities are covered by three fingering patterns: one being for the major keys of A, C, E♭, F♯, the ascending scale in all four of these keys being fingered ('1' being the index): 1 2 3 2 3 4 3 4. Corresponding patterns cover the other two groups each of four major keys. Larger instruments add two more rows, duplicating the lower two of Fig. 2. With five rows one pattern suffices for every key. There is also a reversed scheme known as 'B fingering', much in favour in Germany.

BELLOWS

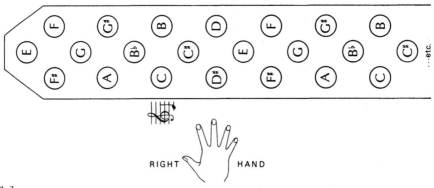

RIGHT HAND

Fig. 2.

5. *Piano accordion.* Double action is here essential since each key of a piano-style keyboard must always sound its own note and no other. The chords and bass notes are however made with buttons, and the sizes of the instrument are customarily reckoned by the number of them—up to 120 (occasionally more), those with fewer than 32 being usually regarded as children's models. With 120 bass buttons, the keyboard will cover 3½ octaves from *f*, with up to 11 tabs for different registers. Some of these registers are achieved by means of tone chambers giving the effect of bassoon, violin, bandoneon (see CONCERTINA, 4), etc., as well as the various tremolo and octave groupings. The bass buttons, for the left hand, are laid out in six rows, proceeding by fifths along each row. From the nearest to the bellows the rows are: 'counter-bass' (the sequence of fifths a third different from that of the fundamental bass); fundamental bass; its major chord; minor chord; dominant seventh; and diminished seventh. Each chord is basically (i.e. until octave coupling is brought in) of three notes, made from a set of reeds tuned to a chromatic series from *g* to *f♯'*. The button for a given chord pushes a metal bar within the casing carrying three pins which move stiff wire rods which in turn rotate the required three out of a set of 12 long thin rods running longitudinally from one end of the case to the other, one for each chromatic note. Links from these then lift the pallets which allow air to pass through the required reeds (the system somewhat recalling the 'roller board' used in tracker-action organs; see ORGAN, Fig. 4).

A piano accordion of the present kind was advertised in the 1911 catalogue of Mariano Dallapé (founded c.1876), of Stradella, near Milan, though he made no claim to have invented it. Some of the larger models now have 'free bass' buttons, for playing melodies or counterpoints in the bass, these buttons following the arrangement of the right-hand buttons of the continental chromatic accordion (4, above). Such 'free bass accordions' greatly enlarge the scope for new compositions for accordion.

6. *Electronic piano accordions.* These are of two kinds. One has normal bellows and reeds, with a switch by which the keys will control an electronic tone generator (a single-oscillator divider, adjustable for tuning the reeds) plus effects and so on; the reeds and the electronics can be used separately or together, e.g. for the left hand to give a bass guitar sound with the chord buttons giving guitar sound. The other kind is fully electronic, with a similar electronic tone generator; the bellows do not pump air but serve to control loudness (with swell, etc.).

7. *Early accordions.* Examples from shortly after the 1829 Viennese patent are in narrow rectangular shape, very light to hold in the hand, with ten round pearl-covered right-hand keys and two simple push-valves for the left. Rather similar in shape is the French accordion made from the 1840s, once

much exported (and still advertised in France up to the First World War). This is often seen as an antique, called 'flutina', one of its old trade names. On it were laid the foundations of the 'musette' school. Delicately made, of inlaid mahogany with mother-of-pearl keys, it is often pitched in A with a second row of keys for the semitone below. The tonic is on the draw (not the press) and there are two left-hand buttons as on the simple melodeon.

8. *Repertory.* As with so many of the instruments newly invented in the 19th century, the solo and ensemble repertory is largely written by, or for, the leading artists themselves. Tchaikovsky, however, included the accordion in his Orchestral Suite of 1883; Berg, in *Wozzeck* (1921); Prokofiev, in his Cantata of 1936; Charles Ives, Virgil Thomson, and Roy Harris in various works; also Hindemith, Gerhard, and later composers such as Musgrave (in her Clarinet Concerto).

Acoustic. The rapid ascendancy of electric and electronic instruments in many fields has led to a frequent need to distinguish non-electric or non-electronic forms of an instrument—keyboard, percussion, etc., as well as guitar—as 'acoustic'.

Acoustics of musical instruments. The present book is mostly about instruments as one sees them, silent or being played. One would like to add 'and how one hears them', thus taking the matter straight into acoustics, as the science of musical instruments, a subject which however, over the years, has grown into a complex of physics, mathematics, and psychology, advanced to a degree that puts an up-to-date summary far beyond the present scope. There are, however, matters, often treated under elementary or basic acoustics, which enter repeatedly when describing instruments and can still be looked at usefully, though with due allowance for the considerable simplifications involved, as see the following entries: BEATS AND DIFFERENCE TONES; CAVITY RESONATOR; CENTS; FORMANT; HARMONIC SERIES; HERTZ; PARTIALS; PITCH; TEMPERAMENT. Also (percussion instruments): GLOCKENSPIEL, 5; PERCUSSION, 3; TIMPANI, 5; TUBULAR BELLS, 2; XYLOPHONE, 2; (stringed instruments): BOW, 1; HARMONICS; MONOCHORD; STRINGED INSTRUMENTS, 1; (wind instruments): CROSS-FINGERING; OVERBLOWING; STOPPED PIPE; WIND INSTRUMENTS, 1, 3.

Benade 1976; Campbell and Greated 1987; Hall 1980; Helmholtz 1875; Rayleigh 1877; Taylor 1976; Wood 1930; etc.

Aeolian harp (from the Greek god Aeolus, the Keeper of the Winds). Instrument with strings which, when the instrument is placed outside or in the opening of a window, are sounded by the wind, producing a vague, changing harmony. It has a soundbox up to one metre (3′) long, placed vertically or horizontally and wide enough for a dozen or so gut or wire strings (not too thin) to be stretched along it over a low bridge near each end. The strings, of the same length, are all tuned to the same fairly deep note, but are graded in thickness.

It is still not clear how it works, but it seems the air-stream, as it passes a string, sheds eddies which tend to shake the string from side to side, and when the eddy frequency comes near to a harmonic frequency of the string, this will vibrate at that harmonic. As the wind speed fluctuates, different harmonics will come to the fore, and with strings of different thicknesses, a different harmonic pitch from each. Since all are tuned to the same note, the sum result is a chord, rising and falling bodily up and down the harmonic series as the wind speed varies. With faster wind the thinner strings may vibrate in the region above the eighth harmonic, where harmonics lie a tone apart or less, adding a strange flavour to the sound. Some models have a second set of strings tuned an octave lower, to thicken the chord.

The Aeolian harp has been known from at least the 17th century, when Athanasius Kircher drew attention to it (1650) (it corresponds to 'aeolian bows' of the Far East, hung in trees). It became very fashionable in Europe in the first part of the 19th century, and is frequently mentioned in the poetry of Coleridge and Shelley. Georges Kastner, in Paris, wrote an extensive monograph on the instrument (1848).

Aeolsklavier. See CLASSIFICATION, 1. Several other inventions, also of around the 1820s with names beginning 'aeol-', were *free-reed instruments with keyboard.

Aerophone. One of the main classes in modern *classification of instruments: almost entirely wind instruments but including such as *bull-roarer and *buzz-disc.

Africa. South of the Sahara, lands of bewitching music in which instruments play their due share: instruments many of which have continued to hold true to forms going back to the earliest traceable cultural strata; others developed from such forebears into complex forms found nowhere else, while yet others have sprung into existence as pure inventions no less uniquely African. Further are those, mostly with more limited distributions, that have entered the continent from outside, or so it is presumed in the absence of historical data from times perhaps as remote as Egyptian Antiquity; or of Arab or European origin, likewise to find a place beside those of the foundation cultures. Towering over all is the drum, or rather, the symphony of drums with other associated percussion, the voices, and the dance, in which the genius for rhythmic complexity is manifest as a foremost hallmark of African music, as well as the driving force behind its influence from the New World upon our lives in the West, even where here reduced to elementary patterns in plain common time.

1. *Types of instruments:* (a) *Idiophones.* Rattles: strung shells, nuts, etc., shaken or worn; gourd, basketry, often used in pairs of contrasting pitch (cf. *maracas), also types with external beads (in Ex. 1, *axatse*, and see CABAZA). Scrapers: notched stick etc., and notches cut in a *musical bow or a drum. *Slit drums, often as *talking drums. *Xylophone, with from two bars upwards. Bells: wood or metal, with clapper or struck on the outside, single or double bell (as in Ex. 1, *gankogui*, and see AGOGO BELL). Lamellaphones (*sansa) of plucked tongues, usually iron, a uniquely African instrument. Also, and to a greater extent than is usual in the West, rhythmic employment of domestic and other objects that come ready to hand ('improvised instruments').

(b) *Drums.* From rudimentary, of gourds, clay pots, tin cans, with skin membrane drawn over the opening; to drums carved in wood in all shapes (see DRUM, 4), played with sticks or hands, with sounds of contrasting timbre and pitch (Ex. 1), and shells or jingles often attached, adding buzzing sounds.

(c) *Stringed.* *Musical bows (mouth bow, gourd bow): *Gora (bow with blown vibrating quill). *Pluriarc (bows combined in one instrument). Harp: arched harps (see HARP, 10a), mostly north of the Equator. *Lyre, mainly East Africa to Ethiopia. *Kora ('harp-lute') with perpendicular notched bridge, West Africa. *'Ground instruments', over a pit in the ground. *Idiochord zithers, for self-accompanying songs and sung poetry characteristically with short figures continually repeated; 'harp-zither', West Africa (see MVET). Stick-zither (see SESE). Fiddles, popular, with one to three strings.

(d) *Wind.* Flutes: chiefly end-blown, often notched, and with three to four holes (see FLUTE, 7); carved wood or horn whistles, often, like the flutes, played in ensembles (see NANGA). Horns: ivory, antelope horn, gourd, etc., side-blown, again often in ensemble; longer types (trumpets) of wood, cane, gourd. Reed instruments: fewer, some of Arab extraction, as Hausa *algaita* (see SURNA). Also an aerophone, *bull-roarer, still whirled in initiation rites in the Congo.

2. *Rhythms.* As one single illustration, Ex. 1 is adapted from a transcription of the *Nyayito* funeral dance of the Eve people of Ghana made by A. M. Jones (1959; see also NOCM, i. 30–4 by Helen Myers). The excerpt begins at the point where the drums (hand-beaten) enter. Shortly preceding this, the song and the hand-claps have already begun, and the iron double bell *gankogui* (played with a wooden beater) has set up the co-ordinating 'time-line' which continues throughout with metronomic regularity, along with a rhythm from the bead rattle *axatse*. The master drummer, on the large drum *atsiméuu*, enters with a standard pattern associated with this dance (the text underlays

Ex. 1. Ghana (Eve), Nyayito funeral dance, short extract from point where the drums enter (adapted from NOCM 32–3, transcription after. Jones 1959)

indicate the drummers' mnemonic syllables identifying different pitches and types of stroke); his first entry, a rhythmic phrase of 5 + 7, an 'additive' rhythm to which the smaller drums *sogo* and *kidi* give a standard reply. The smallest drum *kagang* starts a simple pattern in cross-rhythm to the iron bell and repeats it through the whole piece.

It would be easy enough in Western notation to transcribe all the parts in a matching 12/8; but such vertical arrangement would not reflect the perception of the African players, who hear each rhythmic part independently (e.g. 5/8 etc. of the master drum while others play a 6/8), and with the time-line as an unceasing reference point. The syncopation, the superimposition of additive rhythm, and the relentless time-line, all combine in the excitement and drive of African music, in a quality that West African musicians call 'hot'; the hotter the rhythm, the better the performance.

Ankermann 1901; Brandel 1961; Hyslop 1975; Jones 1959; Kirby 1934; Söderberg 1956; Tracey 1948; Wachsmann in Trowell 1953.

Afuche. See CABAZA.

Agogo bell. Afro-Brazilian and Afro-Cuban metal percussion instrument used in some Latin-American dance music and by school percussion groups. Two small conical bells of blackened thin metal, soldered down the sides, are joined by a metal loop for holding while striking on the outside with a metal rod. The larger bell, *c.*15 cm. (6″) long, stands a little beyond the other for convenience in striking them alternately, and may sound a fifth lower.

The parent instrument, the West African double iron bell (*agogo*, *ngongi*, etc.) is forged and soldered from a single length of iron sheet, then bent over for the two bells to stand level. It is often a leading rhythm instrument in dances, as see AFRICA, Ex. 1, here named *gankogui*. Another common type of African iron bell is the single bell with an iron-rod clapper like that of a European *cowbell.

Aïda trumpet. See TRUMPET, 3*c*.

Ajaeng. The long zither (*c.*1 metre or 3′) of Korea on which the strings are 'bowed' with a rosined stick of forsythia wood. The right-hand end, near which (as with other long zithers of the Far East) the player sits, is raised up (see CHINA AND KOREA, Pl. 2, centre front). The stick is held with the forefinger above (rather as one holds a dart) and produces deep, full 'rasping' sounds from the seven strings (silk, nylon) pentatonically tuned. Each string has a movable bridge of 'inverted Y' form (as on *zheng, *koto). Uses: court orchestra; folk ensembles.

There is a Chinese mention from about the 10th century AD of a zither, *yazheng*, sounded with a bamboo strip, the *ajaeng* being a surviving form. There are also modern Chinese versions (*mingzheng*,

etc.), but said to be better known abroad than in China itself.

Akkordzither. See AUTO-HARP.

Ala bohemica (or 'Bohemian wing'). Some strange stringed instruments known only by medieval Czech pictures (Buchner 1957) were apparently in Latin writings named *ala*: a long soundbox, held high against the left shoulder, with a set of long strings and (usually) a set of shorter strings fanning out near the top, both hands plucking.

Albisifono. See ALTO AND BASS FLUTE, 2.

Alboka. See HORNPIPE.

Alghaita. See SURNA.

Algoza (or *alghoza*). A duct flute or flageolet of northern India, of wood, or of cane often painted in bands of colour, and with a recorder-like beak at the blowing end. Around 35 cm. (14″) long, it typically has five holes, and a narrow 'window' giving a reedy sound easily overblown to higher notes. Characteristically the player (commonly a shepherd) plays on two at once, holding them separately one in each hand (leaving the lowest holes open) whereupon they will beat together with a bright, almost fiddle-like sound.

Alphorn. Properly the long wooden horn of Switzerland, but the name usefully serves to embrace similar traditional instruments made by other European herdsmen for directing their animals—from Scandinavia across to parts of Russia, Romania, and Czechoslovakia, and also formerly the Black Forest and Thuringia in Germany and the Vosges in France, with their own name in each region (e.g. Romania, *bucium*). The horn is made by sawing or splitting in half the trunk of a young fir or other suitable tree, carving out each half and reuniting them under an airtight binding of bark or roots to form a long tube. The shape of the bore varies from conical to almost cylindrical. Often in the Alps and Carpathians a tree is chosen which curves at the base of the trunk for the horn to curve upwards at the wider end (Pl. 1). In many regions the instrument is also built in the folded shape of a trumpet. The mouthpiece may be simply a cavity carved in the narrow end (see CORNETT, 4) or it may be made separately; the player's lips vibrate as they do with brass instruments. The length of the tube, from 4′ to 16′ (*c.*120 cm. to 5 m.) or more, allows a good number of natural harmonics to be sounded in calls and tunes—up to the sixth harmonic with a short alphorn, or to the twelfth or higher with the 12′ horn well known in Switzerland (i.e. with the same tube-length as an orchestral F horn).

Ex. 1.

8 10 11 12   11   6

The antiquity of the instrument is not known, but alphorns 11' long (some 335 cm.) are mentioned by a 16th-century Swiss writer, and one of its calls is met in Rhau's *Bicinia Gallica* of 1545; see Ex. 1. Familiar later borrowings include (for more, see Hyatt King 1945): Beethoven, finale of Sixth Symphony (the *Kuhreigen* or *ranz des vaches*, 'cattle call', here given to the clarinet); Rossini, *Guillaume Tell* Overture (first phrase of the cor anglais solo, also from a Swiss *ranz des vaches*); Brahms, finale of First Symphony (the horn tune, with an F♯ representing the 11th harmonic); and Wagner, *Tristan und Isolde*, the second shepherd's call in Act 3, sometimes performed on the *tarogato, though for this call Wagner had a straight wooden instrument made (*Holztrompete*) of which at least one opera house has preserved an example: a brass section in the middle carries a whole-tone piston valve, making the fast notes of the call somewhat easier for an orchestral brass player.

Pl. 1. Shepherds with alphorns. Romania.

In other parts of the world may be found long trumpets of wood or giant grasses, the largest in South America (*clarin, *erke, *trutruca).

Althorn. See ALTO HORN, also CLAVICOR.

Alto. In France the viola, or in brass bands the alto saxhorn (TENOR HORN). For other 'alto' members of an instrument family, see entries under the main name except those below.

Historically 'alto' and 'bass' both derive from 15th-century Latin *contratenor altus* ('high contratenor') and *contratenor bassus* ('low'), 'contratenor' itself having arisen to name a third part

added to the 'superius' and 'tenor' parts, similar in range to the tenor and intertwining with it. Four-part polyphony then brought the distinction between high and low contratenors which has led to 'alto', 'bass', and other abbreviated forms like Italian *contralto*, the former French *haute-contre* ('high contra'), while Eng. 'countertenor' has dropped 'altus'. In designating instruments, 'alto' began to enter British usage (from It. or Fr.) only during the 19th century, in place of 'tenor' which is still often retained where 'alto' is used elsewhere (e.g. *recorder, *tenor horn).

Alto and bass flute. 1. *Alto flute* (Fr.: *flûte contralto en sol*). See FLUTE, Pl. 1d. Built in G, a fourth below the flute, the lowest note, written *c'*, sounds *g* (in unison with the violin G string). Length, 87 cm. (34″); bore, from 24 to 26 mm., i.e. wider than the 19 mm. of the flute by close to the ratio 4:3 of the interval of a perfect fourth. Tone, unmistakable, full, languidly haunting in all registers. In regular manufacture, it is needed in three famous orchestral works of the years 1911–16: Ravel (*Daphnis and Chloé*), Stravinsky (*Rite of Spring*), and Holst (*The Planets*, here named 'Bass flute' after British practice at the time). The alto flute has since been important again in many of Britten's works for the stage, and in compositions by Boulez and Stockhausen, and is frequently scored for in music for television.

It was invented by Boehm, and in his later years became his 'favourite' instrument, mainly for its distinctive tone, suited to music in what he called 'song style' (Boehm 1871; see FLUTE). He transcribed for the alto flute, with piano accompaniments, slow movements from Mozart's and Beethoven's piano works, Schubert *Lieder*, and so on, creating the interest which first led makers in London and Paris to list the instrument in their catalogues.

2. *Bass flute*. An octave below the flute, with lowest note *c*. Useful for flute societies (playing music entirely for flutes). The 130-cm. (*c*.52″) tube is made manageable by a bend in the upper part (as FLUTE, Pl. 1e), bringing the player's left hand some 50 cm. (20″) nearer to the lips than were the tube wholly straight (latterly the ordinary Boehm flute has been available with similar 'bent head' to suit small beginners). For other bass flutes see FLUTE BAND.

Boehm built a bass flute; but better known and more often mentioned in instrument history is the design of a Milan player, who named it after himself 'Albisifono' (*c*.1910): also of metal with

Boehm-system keywork, but held straight downwards, having at the top a T-shaped head with the mouth-hole in the centre of a short horizontal cross-piece closed with a cork at each end—an arrangement perhaps following that also Italian invention of not long before, the *Giorgi flute. Mascagni scored for it in *La Parisina* (1913). The idea has recently been revived in a design by the American flautist Pierre-Yves Artaut.

3. *Bass flute* (Renaissance). See FLUTE, 5.

Alto clarinet. In E♭, a fifth deeper than the clarinet, with up-turned metal bell (as on the *bass clarinet) and short curving crook to take the mouthpiece. It looks like CLARINET, Pl. 1c, but a little shorter. Used in the larger military and concert bands in America and France, also in all-clarinet ensembles. In British bands it was displaced in the early 20th century by the saxophone, but can still be found in antique shops, with the old Albert-system fingering. In France and the USA there have also been models with a wooden bell pointing downwards as on the clarinet.

When invented in Paris, *c.*1810, by Ivan Müller, it was built in F, which for a long time lasted as alternative to E♭. The *basset horn is also in F but sounds down to low F in actual sound, a note which neither type of alto clarinet can reach (the part for alto clarinet in F in the published score of Stravinsky's *Threni*, requiring this note, therefore calls for a basset horn).

Alto fagotto. See TENOROON.

Alto horn. American name of the valved brass instrument in E♭ corresponding to the British *tenor horn and French *saxhorn alto*. The equivalent instrument in Germany is *Althorn*.

Alto trombone. See TROMBONE, 5b.

American Indians. 1. *Ancient civilizations.* Early instrument categories familiar to all peoples inhabiting similar environments across the globe (see EARLY EVOLUTION, 1)—instruments such as rattles, drums, flutes—were known equally to the Old Civilization of South and Central America from the early classic period *c.*500 BC, attaining high levels of craftsman's ingenuity and artistic design, up to the time when the course of indigenous development betrays at least to some degree the influence of the *conquistadores*.

From Peru are silver rattles on long handles, and small bells, some of wood; drums, both upright, with single head, and portable, played with both hands on two heads; and in Mexico, the upright drum on legs, *huehuetl*, and the two-note tongued slit-drum ('log-drum', *teponatzli). Virtually the only melodic instruments were flutes and panpipes (*antara, siku*; see PANPIPE, 2 and Pl. 1): in Peru end-blown flutes, plain or notched (*quena) of clay,

or the bones of slain prisoners; and duct flutes (*pincullo). In Central America, duct flutes, as the pottery 'Aztec flute', spreading out at the bottom; zoomorphic vessel whistles including those ingenious masterpieces of the potter's craft, the 'whistling jars' (a jar containing water connects through a pottery tube into another jar which has a small vessel-whistle concealed in a figure moulded at the top). Wood or pottery trumpets from Peru are of clay coiled in a small circle, and with well-formed integral cup-mouthpiece; and conch (*pututu*), natural or in fancy designs in pottery. Of stringed instruments (such as *musical bow) there are no ancient visible signs.

2. *The present.* The greatest variety of instruments is in South and Central America; yet some of the most unusual are in the North.

(a) *Idiophones.* Strung rattles of bones, hooves, and (in the North) teeth, beaks, claws; gourd and basketry rattles (*maracas); clashed sticks (especially North); *scrapers; *slit drums, in South America often in groups, for signalling in the tropical forest; *stamping tubes (South); rubbed turtle shell. Some others may be African introductions.

(b) *Drums.* Single-headed: most characteristic of the North; upright and bowl ('kettle') drums, clay or wooden, played with a stick. A curious feature in both Americas is that some drums are part-filled with water while in use (not strictly a *'water drum'), either before the skin is tied on or afterwards through a hole in the side, the object being apparently to make the sound carry better. Double-headed: frame drum (see DRUM, 4e), North.

(c) *Stringed.* Musical bow (mouth bow, plucked or rubbed with a stick), formerly south to Patagonia, north to Alaska, in central areas with reinforcement from Africa; *Apache fiddle. Hispanic, guitars (including many small; see GUITAR, 5; HARP, 8.

(d) *Wind.* Flutes, still by far the chief wind instruments: notched flutes (*quena) in the South, also transverse (Andes, north to Colombia); panpipes of every description (see PANPIPE, 1a–e); duct flutes include giant ritual flutes (see FLUTE, 8a) and numerous others (pincullo, *anata; in the North *Apache flute); whistles of all kinds (bone, etc.), including vessel-flutes of a fruit shell, etc. (some blown as *nose flute) for imitating bird song, etc. Reed instruments: some most unusual *reedpipes (Brazil, Guyana) and all-wooden *reed-horns (British Columbia). Trumpets: cane, coiled bark, etc. (see TRUMPET, 8 a–c). Also *bull-roarer, in the South now often a plaything but also used by shamans from the Plains southward.

Collaer [1967]; Densmore 1927; Harcourt 1925; Haefer 1975; Izikowitz 1934; Stevenson 1959; Vega 1943.

American Musical Instrument Society. An international organization founded in 1971 'to promote the study of the history, design, and use of musical instruments in all cultures and from all periods'. It holds annual meetings, and its important Journal, *JAMIS*, is published annually, obtainable through membership of the Society (AMIS Membership Office, The Shrine to Music Museum, Vermillion, South Dakota 57069, USA).

American organ. See REED ORGAN.

Anaconda. See SERPENT, I.

Anata (or *tarca*). South American wooden duct flute (see FLUTE, 7c) of the Gran Chaco region of Argentina, made by the method of halving the wood from end to end to hollow out the bore, then reuniting to shape the exterior (here in combinations of square, octagonal, or round shapes) and piercing six fingerholes. Lengths from 22 to 65 cm. (9"–2'), and played especially during Carnival. (See also AMERICAN INDIANS.)
Vega 1943.

Angelica (or Angel lute). A kind of lute of the period *c.*1650–1750, unique in having all the strings tuned to a diatonic scale, for playing mostly on the full, resonant sound of open strings—though, as noticed at the time by *Talbot, best in slow pieces, in which discords from the undamped strings are least apparent. Of 16 single gut strings tuned from *D* to *e'* in naturals, the six longest run from a high pegbox, as in an archlute: a fine example by Tielke, Hamburg, one of some six preserved, is 127 cm. (50") tall. The neck was fretted, the first fret needed for accidentals, and up to the fifth fret for playing on the top string up to *a'*, the highest note met in pieces for angelica contained in contemporary manuscripts. (See also LUTE.)
Pohlmann 1968.

Angklung. I. Indonesian instrument of swinging bamboo tubes (Fig. I) suspended in a light upright frame with a wide bamboo forming the base. There are three or two tubes, their upper parts cut to a tongue-shape through which they are suspended to swing to and fro. At the bottom each is closed by a knot below which are cut two small prongs to guide the tube in a slot in the base tube. When the instrument is given a sideways push, or shaken sideways, setting the tubes swinging, the prongs strike the ends of the slots with a clatter accompanied by *stopped-pipe notes from the air vibrating in the tubular portions, each of which is cut to measure half the length of the one beyond it, so that their air notes sound in octaves. The sum effect is most attractively musical.
A dozen or so angklungs can make up a set, played by a group of performers, and tuned to give, between them, five-note scales to form the basis of a village *gamelan.

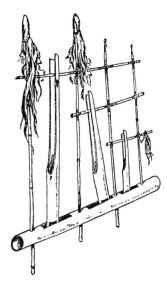

Angklung, Fig. I.

In Chicago, *c.*1900, Deagan brought out for the variety stage a huge chromatic angklung with steel tubes in two diatonic ranks a semitone apart, mounted one above the other in a metal frame eight feet tall. An example is in the Shrine to Music Museum, South Dakota (see COLLECTIONS, 5).

2. 'Angklung' can in East Java mean an instrument in which similarly shaped bamboo tubes are played like a xylophone: see CHALUNG. (See also GAMELAN.)
Kunst 1949.

Angular harp. See HARP, 10b.

Antara. Panpipe of Peru and neighbouring countries (see PANPIPE, 2).

Antique cymbals. See CYMBAL, 4.

Antiquity. The condensed table lists principal types of musical instruments of the Ancient World in order of earliest known appearances, in art or actual remains, in Mesopotamia and Egypt: a sequence that broadly continues eastward to India, and in the West to Greece, Etruria, and Rome, with the addition of the organ (*hydraulis, c.*250 BC); see also BIBLICAL INSTRUMENTS.
Farmer 1957; Michaelides 1978; Hickmann 1961; Wegner 1963; Fleischhauer 1964; Rimmer 1969a; *Sachs 1940. Also *collections, London, Paris; see Hickmann 1949.

TABLE I.

BC	Mesopotamia	Egypt
2600	arched harp (HARP, 10a) lyre (LYRE, 2) reedpipe (divergent, REEDPIPE, 2; AULOS)	temple clappers, early *sistrum arched harp end-blown flute (NAY) reedpipe (parallel)
2000	vessel rattle frame drum (DRUM, 4e) angular harp (HARP, 10b) long lute (LUTE, 7)	barrel drum (DRUM, 4b) lyre
1500	angular harp (horizontal) cymbals, small	sistrum (rods) frame drum angular harp long lute reedpipe (divergent) short trumpet (TRUMPET, 7)

Anvil (Fr.: *enclume*; Ger.: *Amboss*; It.: *incudine*). The clinking of the forge has been called for by composers from Auber (*Le maçon*, 1825) to Britten (*The Burning Fiery Furnace*); well-known instances are by Verdi, *Il trovatore* (gypsy smiths, Act 2); Wagner, *Das Rheingold* (the famous transition to the Nibelung forge, with 18 anvils sounding F in three different octaves behind the scene); Walton, *Belshazzar's Feast* (four strokes for the God of Iron). For *Rheingold* some German opera houses have employed genuine anvils, others elsewhere heavy steel plaques over 2.5 cm. or 1 inch thick ('anvil plates'). For a single anvil, a steel lamina from a lorry spring or steel brake-drum has proved an effective substitute.

Apache. Of the Indians of this name in North America. 1. *Apache fiddle*, a wooden tube with one horsehair string stretched over a narrow slit along the tube and played with a short bow (whether an adaptation of the violin bow to some forgotten type of *idiochord zither, no one knows for certain). 2. *Apache flute* ('lover's flute'): a duct flute of the 'roofed' kind (see FLUTE, 7c), the voicing window roofed by a tied-on saddle-like piece carved in wood.

Apollo lyre. See LYRE-GUITAR, 2.

Appalachian dulcimer. A fretted zither (see ZITHER, 2), indigenous to Kentucky and Alabama, where it accompanies songs, ballads, and square dances. The long soundbox, of walnut, maple, etc., typically has the shape shown (Pl. 1). It is placed across the knees with the tuning end over the left knee. Down the centre is a raised fret-board, placed over openings cut in the pine soundboard underneath. Three steel strings (some may be paired) run from tuning pegs to a bridge at the extreme right. Under the first string (that nearest the player), are 14 metal frets placed diatonically for a major scale of two octaves starting on the dominant (the keynote is therefore at the third fret; Fig. 1, top line). The melody is played on this first string tuned, say, to g', by pressing it to the frets with a 'noter', a short cane stick held thumb uppermost in the left hand. The other strings are 'drones' tuned to the first string and the fifth below (G and C). All are gently sounded together with a plectrum of turkey or goose quill cut to a long point and held in the right hand (the fret-board usually being recessed at the striking point); alternatively, finger-picks can be used so that the drones may be struck independently in accompaniment rhythms. The frets will serve minor tunes without altering the drones by raising the melody string to B♭ (bringing C to the first fret for C minor; Fig. 1, second line), or the string may be raised to C for C Mixolydian (with B♭, third line), or lowered to F for C Dorian (with E♭, B♭, the C now at fourth fret, see bottom line), the drones sounding the same notes throughout.

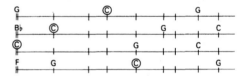

Fig. 1. Tuning the melody strings to different notes (*shown left*) for playing in different modes with diatonic fretting.

Much is due to Jean Ritchie for bringing the instrument to wide notice in the USA and beyond (Ritchie 1963). She was taught to play it by her grandfather in the Kentucky mountains, where the dulcimer was made by local craftsmen from the 18th century onwards, mainly from the 1890s. No doubt it had a parent among fretted zithers brought in from northern Europe; but nothing more definite is known of its origin.

Pl. 1. Appalachian Dulcimer by Billy Reed Hampton (1982).

Arch-cittern. See CETERONE.

Arched harp. Term for harps, ancient, African, and Asian, composed of a skin-covered soundbox and a curving wooden 'neck', the strings crossing the space between them. See HARP, 10a and Pl. 5 (Africa); SAUNG, Pl. 1 (Burma).

Archlute. One of the forms of lute which have bass strings (diapasons) running from a second pegbox: see LUTE, 3.

Arcicembalo. See KEYBOARD, 4 (microtonal keyboards).

Arco (It., Sp.; Fr.: *archet*). Bow of a stringed instrument.

Arghul. Double *reedpipe of the Near East, with one pipe a long drone: see ZUMMARA.

Armonica. see HARMONICA.

Arpa (It., Sp.: 'harp'). *Arpa doppia*: see HARP, 9b.

Arpanetta. See SPITZHARFE.

Arpeggione. A bowed guitar (cross between a guitar and a cello) invented by the Viennese guitar-maker J. G. Staufer in 1823. He called it 'guitare d'amour'. The following year Schubert wrote for it the Sonata in A minor with piano (D 821); he called the instrument 'arpeggione', and this became its recognized name after the work was published in 1871. It is cello-sized with arched belly and bridge, but a guitar outline and no soundpost. Six strings, tuned as in the guitar, pass over 24 metal frets giving a fingered compass up to the *e'''* above the treble staff. A Tutor written by V. Schuster (for whom the Sonata was written) gives it the name 'guitarre-Violoncell'. The Sonata has been recorded by Klaus Storck on an original arpeggione in the Berlin collection. The sound, while superficially cello-like, is distinctively crisp and clear in the high register, less full in the lower.

Askaules (Ancient Gk.). See BAGPIPE, 7.

Aulos. Today in Greece (pron. 'avlos') a folk flute of various kinds. But in Ancient Greece (apart from a general meaning of 'pipe') a reed instrument and particularly the pair of slender pipes played together by one musician, by far the most important kind of musical wind instrument through Western Antiquity (in Latin, *tibia*; see BIBLICAL INSTRUMENTS, 1f), heard at public and private feasts and ceremonies of every kind, and in Greece also in the theatre, leading the chorus. (It is for poetic euphony that in later literature 'aulos' has generally been translated 'flute' rather than 'pipe'.)

Pl. 1. Aulos and crotala (*see* CLAPPER, 4). British Museum, vase E.38.

1. *Greek aulos* (Pl. 1). Each hand separately holds a pipe with a detachable wooden swelling socket at the top for holding the reed, a double reed of early form (see REED, 5; whether a single reed (REED, 3), was also used remains uncertain). The original pair of maple-wood pipes in the British Museum (the 'Elgin aulos', recovered from a tomb of the 5th century BC along with unique remains of a tortoiseshell lyre) seem fairly typical in size, 35 and 31 cm. (14″ and 12″) long as they stand without their reeds. Each has five holes in front, neatly undercut, and one for the thumb on the back midway between the first two in front. Trials with replicas have suggested sounds in the contralto voice range. Many vase paintings show the player's cheeks puffed out; in others a strap round the face stops them from doing so (Pl. 1), perhaps as an aid to blowing the reeds forcefully (it is not shown with female players). Greek sources give no clear indications as to the scales and compass of the pipes; and on the question of how the two pipes functioned together, they say absolutely nothing. In paintings the hands appear mostly to be doing the same thing; yet beyond this we may bear in mind the sheer variety of techniques that have since existed on double *reedpipes over the Mediterranean and Black Sea areas (e.g. in Sardinia the *launeddas, this name itself probably deriving from 'aulos').

Several of the Roman-period remains have metal sleeves over the holes, evidently to be turned to shut off certain holes and change the scale. Also favoured in Rome were 'Phrygian auloi', with an upturned horn-like bell on the left-hand pipe, which is sometimes much longer than the other.

2. *Monaulos* ('single pipe'). Best known by narrow cane pipes from Hellenistic Egypt, 25 to 45 cm.

(10–18″) long, with about eight fingerholes, comfortably close together, and often two thumbholes, the lower of them placed between the fourth or fifth in front (compare the present Japanese *hichiriki). Some actual double reeds have been found with them (Brussels *collection).

3. *Plagiaulos* ('transverse pipe'). Several preserved pipes, some bronze, are cast with a side projection which seems intended to take the reed, for holding the pipe like a transverse flute.

'Aulos' could cover pipes of a flute kind (as in the organ, *hydraulis) but evidence for actual flutes or flageolets, apart from the panpipe, is peculiarly sparse from Greece or Rome. (See also ANTIQUITY.)

Auto-harp. A kind of *zither (Pl. 1) providing simple ready-made chords and used by many folk-singers. The shallow soundbox, about 33 cm. (21″) long with a curve on the far side, is placed flat on the lap or held nearly upright, sloping side to the right. It carries some 36 metal strings tuned (with a key) to a scale that may be chromatic. The transverse bars ('chord bars') are held above the strings by a coil spring at each end. Each bar has felt pads which, when the bar is pressed down by the left hand, silence all the strings that are not required for the chord stated on the label on the bar (or marked by a number). The strings are sounded by the right hand, usually for thumb and first two fingers. Having struck a chord, one can continue the tune on individual strings until the next chord. Among the many techniques special to the auto-harp in folk music, the right hand will maintain a brisk rhythm with the picks over a group of strings, unchanging

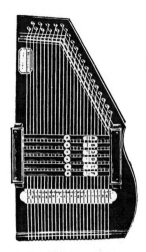

Pl. 1. An early German auto-harp.

while the left hand moves to a different chord bar for the answering harmony. Players, especially latterly, have also tuned to a diatonic scale, for playing on the strings with both hands ('open chording'), dispensing with the chord bars.

The auto-harp was invented in the 1880s, as *Akkordzither*, in Germany, it is said by K. A. Gütter of Markneukirchen, an instrument for the home. It has since been above all in America, from the 1920s, that improvements have brought its wide popularity. A *chord zither can be of similar shape but without the chord-bars.

Aztec flute. See AMERICAN INDIANS, 1.

B

Bach trumpet. A 20th-century term; see TRUMPET, 2a.

Baglama (or *baǧlama*). One main form of the Turkish lute *saz. In Greece (*baglamas*) a small type of *bouzouki.

Bagpipe (Fr.: *cornemuse*, etc.; Ger.: *Sackpfeife*; It.: *cornamusa, zampogna*, etc.; Ru.: *volynka*; Sp.: *gaita*). For especially complex species see separately: MUS-ETTE (France); NORTHUMBRIAN BAGPIPES, I; UIL-LEANN PIPES (Ireland); and ZAMPOGNA (Italy).

A bagpipe is sounded by reeds to which wind is fed by arm pressure on a flexible bag (in most traditions of sheep- or goatskin). This is kept filled with air from the mouth or, not infrequently, from small bellows strapped to the waist and to the other arm. A bagpipe with only one pipe is an extreme rarity, virtually all having at least two. Of these, one is the 'chanter' with fingerholes for playing melodies, and any others are usually 'drones' sustaining single notes. Bagpipes are or have been indigenous from the Atlantic coast of Europe as far east as the Caucasus and from Tunisia to India, almost everywhere different, made on regionally distinctive lines by local craftsmen. International interest in folk music has, however, brought most species into the open through festivals and record-ings, through which their diverse typology and musical qualities can be appreciated. They are by no means all as powerful in sound as the well-known Scottish bagpipe: some are heard at their best in a small parlour.

1. *Construction and compass.* The principal com-ponents are illustrated in Fig. 1a by a relatively uncomplicated species, the Spanish *gaita gallega* of Galicia in its common form with one drone only. Into openings in the bag (1), with its cover of woven cloth, are tied turned wooden sockets or 'stocks' which hold the pipes (here of boxwood), protect the reeds from contact with the bag, and allow quick removal of a pipe for attention to the reed. The blowpipe (2) by which the bag is inflated has a leather flap-valve to prevent air flowing back when the bag is pressed. The chanter (3) has a conical bore and, as usual with the bagpipes of Western Europe, a double reed (see REED, 4), shown detached. The drone (4) has a single reed (see REED, 2) and is built in cylindrically bored sections with sliding joints for putting the note in tune with the chanter. In this example from Spain, as with many others, the drone sounds two octaves below the chanter's principal keynote. A bagpipe is by no

means easy to learn to play well, much experience being needed in adjusting the reeds to respond equally to pressure and in maintaining steady air supply through the moments when the bag is replenished from the mouth or bellows.

The compass of a chanter is rarely more than nine notes, since as a rule it is not overblown to the second octave (though on several species it is possible to do this), nor can the music be articulated with the tongue as on other wind instruments; yet so far from proving a disadvantage, bagpiping owes much of its vigour to articulation with the fingers, for example separating notes by 'cutting' (grace-notes) or quick interpolation of a low note which merges with the sound of the drone so as not to be perceived. To expedite these techniques, chanters are often played with largely 'covered fingering', i.e. as far as possible lifting only one finger, or two, for each note and keeping the rest down.

2. *Bagpipes in Britain:* (a) The 'Great Highland Bagpipe' (Gaelic: *piob mhór*), shown in Fig. 1b, is now known almost the world over. It today has pipes of African blackwood, with three drones (bass, tuned *A*, and two tenors, *a*) thrown over the left shoulder; the Scottish piper often walks to and fro while playing. The chanter keynote is *a'* and its bottom note is a tone lower. The third degree in traditional tuning (written *c''* or *c''♯*) typically sounds just below C♯ while the fourth is a somewhat sharp D; a similar pattern holds at the fourth above (F♯ and G). The Highland is the only bagpipe with a large repertory peculiar to itself in print, usually showing the elaborate gracings (as in Ex. 1). Leading this are the impressive laments and, above all, *piobaireachd* or, as Walter Scott anglicized it, 'pibroch', developed from *c.*1500 and disseminated throughout the Highlands by the MacCrimmon family, hereditary pipers to the MacLeods of Dun-vegan, where there was a college of piping in the 18th century.

'Pibroch' is the *ceól mòr* ('great music') of the Highland pipe, comprising a very highly developed form of theme (or ground, *urlar*) and variations (involving intricate grace-note patterns). Ex. 1 shows the opening of an *urlar* which has been hailed as one of the finest single-line melodies in European music—the 'Lament for the Children' by Patrick Mòr MacCrimmon (*c.*1595–*c.*1670).

The lighter types of bagpipe music, broadly classed as *ceól beag* (the 'small music'), embrace marches, airs, and dances such as the strathspey and reel. The regimental band of pipes and drums

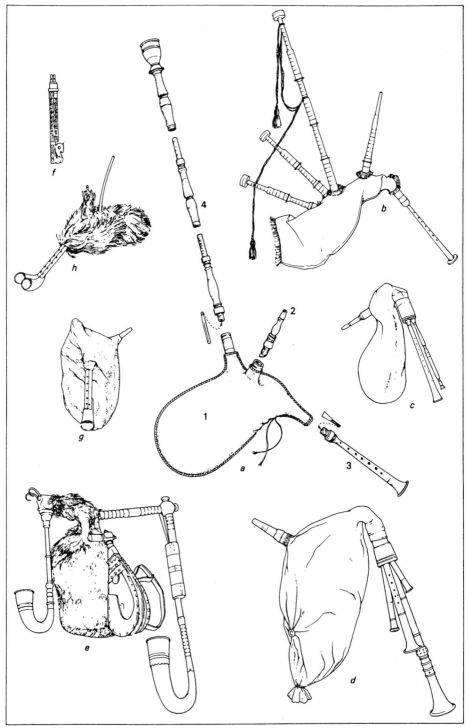

Fig. 1. (*a*) Spain (Galicia); (*b*) Scottish Highland; (*c*) France, bass drone not shown; (*d*) Italy; (*e*) Czechoslovakia (Bohemia); (*f*) Hungary (showing chanter only); (*g*) Greece (Karpathos); (*h*) Tunis.

Ex. 1. Opening of a famous *urlar* by Patrick Mòr MacCrimmon

grew up following the first official employment of a piper among Highland companies in 1745.

For learning the tunes, a practice chanter may be used. This has a narrow cylindrical bore, so that it sounds much softer than the proper chanter and deeper; it is blown through a *wind-cap. A well-known Tutor has been Logan's (1923).

(b) Some modifications of the Highland bagpipe include the Irish war-pipe introduced in about 1910, inspired by a description and illustration in Derrick's *Image of Ireland* (1581) and nothing to do with the widely known Irish *Uilleann pipe. It has been played in Northern Ireland and by some of the Irish regiments in bands with drums; the 'Brian Boru' model has four keys on the chanter to extend the compass upwards and downwards. There are two drones (A, a) or three (A, e, a). These pipes have latterly been mainly superseded by the Scottish instrument.

(c) 'Border pipe' is a recent term used to cover the former Scottish 'Lowland pipes'; also the now revived Northumbrian 'half-long pipe'; these are bellows-blown, with three drones of which one may sound the fifth, e.g. A, e, a as above. All are held in a single drone-stock, and the chanter is narrower and less penetrating than in the Highland. They date from the 18th century, and may be related to a general type of mouth-blown two-drone bagpipe which was widespread across Europe from the 16th century onwards, well known from pictures by Dürer, Bruegel, and others, with the drones often, by their size, tuned to a deep fifth, producing in modern reproductions a very warm, mellow effect. Such could well be the bagpipe referred to in 'The Battel' in *Lady Nevell's Virginal Book*, 1591 (see VIRGINAL, 4). Whether the Lancashire, Derbyshire, and Lincolnshire bagpipes occasionally mentioned up to the 18th century were or were not similar is now quite unknown. Today in England may be heard a useful 'old English' bagpipe which the player makes himself, with one (bass) drone.

3. *France and Spain.* (a) *Central France. Cornemuse, chabrette* ('little goat'), or, in Auvergne, *musette.* Recognized by the flat, rectangular chanter stock which holds, alongside the chanter, a small drone (*petit bourdon*), often silent (with no reed and stopped up). The bass drone (omitted in Fig. 1c) too may be silenced when playing bourrées together with the *hurdy-gurdy, which itself provides drones. Bellows are often used. Varieties of this type of

bagpipe once, it seems, ranged over France from the Pyrenees to Normandy, also Belgium, where the *muse-au-sac* was played by shepherds up to 1900 and has been revived by folk-music groups.

(b) *Brittany.* The *biniou*, small, with chanter and drone both sounding an octave higher than in other Western bagpipes; it is always played in duet with a folk oboe, *bombarde*, which joins in at the repeats, playing the tune an octave lower. There was a move, after 1945, to supplant the *biniou* by the Scottish bagpipe and form marching bands.

(c) *Spain.* The *gaita* (Fig. 1a) is native to northeastern Spain (Galicia, Asturias) and also northern Portugal. It is a thriving popular instrument, often played with side drum for dances. As frequently with European bagpipes, the end of the drone, outwardly turned to a bottle shape, is internally an ovoid or spherical cavity with terminal orifice no wider than the bore of the tube. This rounds out the sound of the drone note; but also, if the forefinger be laid across this orifice and smartly removed after a quick squeeze on the bag, the drone reed will go silent (e.g. for testing the chanter on its own), and keep so until pressure is relaxed and then built up normally.

(d) *Mallorca and Menorca. Xirimía* (Sp.: *chirimia*), with a large drone stock which holds the bass drone between two smaller drones which are dummy. It is related to Catalan bagpipes which became extinct after the 19th century but whose name, *cornamusa*, goes back to the 14th—as in the *cornamusa ab lo bordo* ('with the drone') described at the Aragon court in 1390.

4. *Italy.* *Zampogna, native to South Italy and Sicily, with two chanters played in harmony and mostly (not all) using double reeds throughout. In northern Italy, the *piva* or *cornamusa*, played within living memory in Lombardy and Liguria, was of the general Western European kind with single chanter and one or two drones, all in separate stocks, and the drones with single reeds, as Fig. 1a. (See also BOMBARDE, 2.)

5. *Central and Eastern Europe.* Bagpipes here differ from those of the West in having a cylindrically bored chanter which is sounded with a single reed similar to that of the drones. The bore width is small (around 7 mm.) as though following ancient use of natural materials like elder or crane-bone.

Pl. *1*. Bagpiper, southern Poland.

The sound, with the attenuated second harmonic due to the cylindrical tube, tends to a humming quality with less 'edge' than in the West, yet to all ears unmistakably a bagpipe.

(a) Poland, *koziol* (Pl. 1) ('goat'), and Bohemia, *dudy* or *gaida* (Fig. 1e); also formerly played in neighbouring parts of Germany, as the *Dudelsack* or *Bock*. The angled bass drone usually rests upon the player's shoulder to hang down behind, ending in a large upturned bell of cowhorn or brass. Bellows are much used, and the instrument typically accompanies violin and clarinet, the bagpipe contributing its own version of the melody while providing the support of its drone below.

(b) Hungary and Slovakia (*dude*), the Ukraine (*volynka*), and Romania (*cimpoi*): the chanter has two parallel bores in one flat piece of wood (Fig. 1f). One bore is for the melody; the other has a small extension and only one hole, which is opened and closed by the little finger to sound a drone which swings between the keynote and the dominant below. There is a normal bass drone and in Hungary bellows may be used. Bartók had a high regard for its tradition and examined its technique in great detail.

(c) Macedonia, Bulgaria (*gajda*): a single chanter ends with an obtuse angle carved from horn. In Bulgaria a country wedding is said to be nothing without the *gajda*, on which long dances are played with consummate virtuosity. In Dalmatia and Bosnia, the *diple* (or *mih*, or in Istria, *piva*), also has parallel bores in one piece of wood, but no separate drone. It is also played without the bag (see DIPLE).

(d) In Sweden, also Estonia and Latvia (USSR), rescued on the point of extinction, are country bagpipes with a short stubby chanter, a bass drone lying across the thigh, and sometimes a smaller drone at the fifth above.

6. *Primitive bagpipes*. These have pipes of cane, nearly always two tied together or placed together in a carved-out cradle-like piece of wood often called a 'yoke'. A cowhorn bell is usually fixed over the ends of both pipes together (Fig. 1g). They are really bagpipe versions of the *hornpipe, and are heard in some of the Aegean Islands, in Crete (*tsabouna*, etc.) and in the north-east corner of Turkey (*tulum*); also in Armenia (*parakapzuk*), Georgia (*stviri*), the Mari and Chuvash republics of the Soviet Union, and in Malta (*zaqq*). The fingerholes are sometimes the same in the two pipes (the fingers spread across both), the two pipes often slightly off-tuned for a tremulant effect. Otherwise, one pipe may have a single hole which the lowest finger opens and closes for an 'alternating drone' on two notes a tone apart while the other pipe sounds the melody; or one pipe may have only two, or three, holes for making traditional two-part effects on the two pipes together. The bagpipes from North Africa (*zukra*, etc.) to the Persian Gulf have unison pipes, very often with a small horn bell on the end of each (Fig. 1h).

7. *Early history*. The only reliable evidence for a bagpipe in Antiquity is where Dio Chrysostom mentions (in Greek) a contemporary ruler who was reputed to be able to pipe (*aulein*) both with the mouth and with a bag under the armpit. This must be Nero, confirming what Suetonius, using the word *utricularius*, says about this emperor's aspirations as a musician. The Greek word *askaules* (literally 'bag-piper') also occurs, as in Martial. After this is an unreliable, fanciful account under the name 'chorus', but no creditable news of a bagpipe until the 12th century, when the treatise

of John Cotto has the word *musa*, which certainly meant a 'bagpipe' in the following century. The drone is first mentioned—'muse au grand bourdon'—in Adam de la Halle's pastourelle *Le jeu de Robin et de Marion* of *c*.1280 (the bass drone is 'grand bourdon' in France to this day). Pictures from that time show many different types, few of them exactly matching any played today. Nor were they by any means confined to rustics, for they were also played at tournaments and suchlike events. They became less prominent during the later 14th century as the wealthier classes took their main pleasure in polyphonic music, to which bagpipes are naturally less suited. There were nevertheless some strong survivals on the higher social levels, not only in the Scottish Highlands but also in France, where the *musette was professionally played at court in the 17th century and became a minor cult there for part of the 18th.

Baines 1960; Bartók 1976; Brussels Museum *Bulletin* 1976, 1978; Cannon 1988; Chassaing 1983; Collinson 1975; MacDonald 1803, repr. 1971; Partridge and Jeal 1977; Rehnberg 1943 (with Eng. summary).

Balaban (or *duduk*; Turkish, *mey*). A cylindrical wooden pipe sounded with a very large double reed, played in north-east Turkey, northern Iran, and in the USSR across to Dagestan on the Caspian Sea. From *c*.28 to 40 cm. long (11 to 16″), it has seven fingerholes plus a thumb-hole, and gives a rich, mellow tone, deep for its size (since it behaves as a *stopped pipe) deeper and less strident than that of the popular *surna (a shawm) and suitable for indoor music. Often, like the *surna*, it is played in pairs, both with *circular breathing and one sounding a drone. A similar instrument in China is the *guan*, also (in *Sachs's terminology) a *'cylindrical oboe' and ultimately descended perhaps from the *monaulos* type of instrument of Late Antiquity (see AULOS, 2). The names *balaban* and *daduk* are also given in some regions to double-pipes resembling the *zummara*.

Picken 1975, MEY; Vertkov 1963.

Balafon (or *bala*, etc.) One of the many African names for the *xylophone.

Balalaika. The Russian stringed instrument with a triangular body. It has a thin neck with 16 frets (up to 31 frets in all) and three strings of which the main melody string, the first, is of steel and normally tuned to *a′*, with the other two, of gut or nylon, a fourth lower (both *e′*). These last are partly played 'open' as a drone, and partly stopped with the thumb. The right hand typically thrums the strings with the forefinger, but the strings are also plucked individually. Ex. 1 (from the Tutor by M. Ignateev) is the start of a beginner's exercise on a Russian folk-song: ⊓ downwards stroke, V upwards. For a balalaika orchestra there have been since 1888 larger sizes down to a contrabass over

five feet tall, with a spike at one corner to rest on the floor like a double bass.

Ex. 1.

Similar sizes are now made of the *domra* (from 'tambura'), an older Russian long lute (see LUTE, 7) now revived after a long period of extinction. This, also three-stringed (or now often four-stringed, tuned as the mandolin), has a rounded body, as had the balalaika itself when first depicted in the 18th century (with gut strings and diatonic frets). The triangular form is also met (and may have originated) in the Central Asian *dombra* of the Kazakhs, here with two strings.

Ballad horn. A former British mainly amateur brass instrument with three valves, made from *c*.1856 by Distin (London), then by Boosey & Co. up to the First World War. It is circular, made in models with the bell pointing upwards, forwards, or downwards. The pitch is C (a tone above the *baritone) so that melodies can be played directly from the printed song copy without transposition. Usually a B♭ crook was supplied for playing from band parts if desired. The ballad horn was well enough received for Rudall Carte & Co. to reply with a similar 'Voice' or 'Vocal horn'.

Webb 1984.

Bamboo pipes. See FLAGEOLET, 4.

Bandola, bandolín, bandalón. Names for various pear-shaped, flat-backed plectrum instruments of Spain and Latin America, in general looking like a flat-black mandolin—which in Spain may become written with the initial 'b', *bandolín*—but in stringing and tuning closer to the *bandurria. Like this, they serve in South America largely for playing the melody, with much tremolando, and accompaniment of guitars, both small and full-size. In Colombia, and in Chile (though now rarer there), a bandola may have six metal courses, the upper ones triple, the others double, and tuned in (or mostly in) fourths, bandurria-style; but in Venezuela are four-course varieties, some single-strung. *Bandolón* denotes larger instruments of similar kind, tuned an octave or so lower, with multiple courses running from a rather massive pegbox over a short, wide, bandurria-like neck.

Bandoneon. The large, square-ended type of German concertina, most famous for its place in tango orchestras of Argentina: see CONCERTINA, 5.

Bandora (or pandora). Plucked instrument of the late Renaissance, large-sized, deep-pitched, metal-strung, and played with plectrum or fingers. It was said to have been invented in London in 1562 by the well-known lute- and viol-maker John Rose, and was much used in English music up to the late 17th century, also spreading to Europe. It could equal or exceed the present guitar in size, with a flat-backed body built with wavy outline (Pl. 1, at the far end of the table). The *orpharion also had this shape, perhaps derived from the scallop shell which bore Venus (goddess also of harmony) from the waves. (A three-lobed outline is met in some museum instruments which were long thought to be original bandoras but appear to be late reconstructions following an untrustworthy drawing in the 18th-century French *Encyclopédie*; see FAKES AND FORGERIES.)

The bandora has fixed metal frets, and these, the nut, and bridge were usually set obliquely in a way that gives extra length to the lower strings. There are six double courses of strings, the first five tuned as those of the first five of the present guitar but a fifth lower (thus from *a* down to *D*). The sixth course was (in England) tuned a tone below these (*C*) and a seventh course was added early on a fourth below that. The music, in tablature, includes numerous solo pieces of the decades round 1600, most of them contained in lute MSS; with the voice, as in Barley's *A new Booke of Tabliture for the Bandora* (1596); and with other instruments, notably the *Consort Lessons* (i.e. pieces for performance) by Thomas Morley (1599) and by the lutenist Philip Rosseter (1609). These six-part settings of favourite airs are for violin (the tune), flute, lute (a virtuoso part), cittern, bandora, and bass viol (the bass line). The bandora fills in the harmony below the cittern: Ex. 1, from Morley, gives its opening bars in 'Go from my window', the part (here 'pandora') transcribed at sounding pitch from the six-line tablature, of which the first chord is shown on the left of the example. Cittern and bandora are seen together in Pl. 1, with violin and (here apparently) bass violin. Possibly they have part-books of the *Lessons* before them while a fifth player is arriving through the door and the sixth has not yet turned up. The *Lessons* are believed to have been written in the first place for the very expert City of London Waits—possibly the musicians seen in action, with the required instruments, in the well-known 1597 painting of the marriage of Sir Henry Unton (London, National Portrait

Pl. 1. A Musical Society, engraving (1612) by Simon de Passe; (*left to right*) cittern, violin, bandora, and bass viol.

Gallery). In a modern edition of Morley (Dart 1957) the lute part, of which the complete original is lost, is reconstructed from other settings of the pieces.

Ex. 1.

Bandura. A popular Ukrainian instrument looking like a large lop-sided lute and held almost vertically on the lap (Pl. 1). The body, with a back shaped rather like a shallow basin, bulges out on the treble side and, across this, up to 36 metal strings (called *pristrunki*) fan out to tuning pins placed round the edge, which has a thick rim to hold them. These are chromatically tuned melody strings, plucked by the right hand. Over the short neck run six or more bass strings, mostly plucked by the left hand.

Pl. 1. Ukranian bandura players.

The bandura, going back to the 18th century, formerly accompanied minstrels' songs and ballads, but its ringing, harp-like tone is now heard in popular orchestras. There was also, played mostly in the first half of the 19th century, the *torban* or 'Russian theorbo' (or 'gentleman's bandura'), in appearance like a *theorbo and again with *pristrunki*, here diatonic (as in older banduras), as well as fretted strings and long bass strings. Bandura and *torban* are both said to have been brought to Russia by Italian musicians early in the 17th century (there is, in fact, a Paduan instrument of

c.1590, now in Vienna, with similar treble strings, perhaps related to the *pandora* which the lutenist Piccinini later (1623) named as having been his invention; see also POLYFANT).

Bandurria. A small Spanish plucked instrument (Pl. 1) heard in popular music, especially in southern parts of the country, playing the melody over the accompaniment of the guitar, usually with a very fast tremolando made with the plectrum. Pl. 1 shows a bandurria of traditional form (today, longer, wider models have come into use). The small body is relatively deep-sided (around 7.5 cm. or 3″), while the short string-length of barely 26 cm. ($10\frac{1}{2}$″) allows the first of the six double courses of strings (today metal) to be tuned up to high a''. The other courses are tuned progressively downwards in fourths (each at the 5th fret in unison with the open course above) down to $g\sharp$, the leading-note for a basic scale of A major, continued on to the higher frets up to a'''.

Pl. 1. Bandurria from a Theodor Stark catalogue, German (c. 1900).

The name 'bandurria' goes back to the 14th century and a form of the instrument is briefly described by Bermudo (1555), but only from the 18th century are there full details, much the same as today. Another of its accompanying instruments in Spain, tuned in the same way but an octave lower, is the *laúd*—not a lute (as the word also means) but flat-backed, with oval or wavy-sided body, often two wavy soundholes, and metal strings.

Bangu (or *pan-ku*). Chinese drum on a tripod stand; see *gu*, 2.

Banjo. Stringed instrument of Afro-American origin with a soundbox consisting of a calfskin vellum or plastic membrane stretched over a hoop, the 'rim', now usually of laminated wood.

1. *Construction.* The rim used to be carried on an extension of the banjo's long neck, called the 'perch-pole', passing diametrically across the rim below the membrane. This is now generally replaced by a steel rod. The membrane or 'head' (A in Fig. 1) is ready-supplied with a flesh-hoop (B), and is pressed down by the metal tension hoop (C), tightened by 24 or so hooks (D) arranged circumferentially, each drawn down by a hexagonal nut underneath the fixed bracket (E). The head, instead of resting directly on the top of the rim in the older manner, now usually rides over a metal 'tone ring' (F), introduced by Gibson, in the USA, and since made to many different designs.

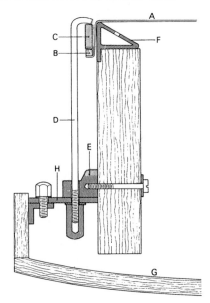

Fig. 1. Typical cross-section of banjo.

Usually there is also a wooden resonator (G), a kind of circular tray attached by screws to a metal flange (H) carried on the hook brackets. The resonator serves not only to project the sound forwards (through holes in the flange) but also to reflect air vibrations back on to the head, increasing the sustaining power. The strings pass over a low bridge placed on the membrane at a point as far from the 12th fret (the octave fret) as this is from the nut. There are generally 22 frets altogether. The strings are now steel, but until recently silk and gut were normal, save for a steel first string. The string-length (from nut to bridge) of a full-size banjo is about equal to that of the guitar.

2. *G Banjo* (the normal five-stringed banjo). Of various tunings, the 'C tuning' is the main one. The first four strings are then tuned: d', b, g, and c (the music, however, is written an octave higher, as with the guitar). In 'G tuning' the c is raised to d. The fifth string (uppermost as the banjo is held) has three-quarters the length of the rest and is pegged at the side of the neck near the fifth fret, and tuned to g' (thus higher than the first string), sounding only that note; the name 'G banjo' refers to this string.

The strings are struck mostly with the right-hand thumb and first and second fingers. In 'folk' styles ('Bluegrass', etc.) this is done mainly with the nails, picking the strings individually, interspersed with chords sounded by brushing the strings with the backs of the nails. The short fifth string is struck with the right thumb in idiomatic ways, typically between beats as a kind of high 'drone'. In jazz, with its regular successions of plectrum chords, this 'thumb string' is not touched or may be omitted ('plectrum banjo'). Though replaced by the guitar from around the end of the 1920s it has since returned to popularity especially in 'traditional jazz', in which its vigorous sound has been badly missed by many.

3. *Origins.* The original 'banja' made by slaves on the New World plantations—mentioned in the Antilles in 1678 and in Maryland in 1754—was a simple lute of half a gourd on a stick with a sheepskin nailed on: it may have been remembered from West Africa, where the name 'bania' has still been reported. After growing adoption by the white population from the 1820s it became made also in wood, the latter leading to the banjo with plain wooden hoop and tuning pegs, and no frets, which many players continue to cherish as the classic form of the instrument. The short fifth string may have been in use well before the celebrated touring minstrel J. W. Sweeney from Virginia popularized it by perhaps the 1840s, by which time William Boucher, of Baltimore, was a prominent maker.

4. *Zither banjo.* The metal hoop and metal frets followed in the 1880s, and soon partly steel stringing and geared tuning. With a wooden resonator added this newer banjo came to be described in Europe as 'zither banjo', sometimes with four strings for playing with a plectrum, or, if with five, the short string leads to the main tuning head through a small hole in the neck.

5. *Tenor banjo.* A variety first introduced as a doubling instrument for cellists in hotel and theatre

orchestras to play the chords in foxtrots and the like; it has four strings tuned in fifths to the same notes as the viola and is still popular among some players. The 'seven-string' banjo is a British variety now almost forgotten, with two extra strings.

6. *Banjolele or banjo ukulele*. A 'banjo mandolin' similarly adapts a banjo-like construction to the mandolin.

Bansuri (or *bānsurī*). Transverse flute of North India, corresponding to the *kural* (*kulal*, or *murali*) of the South: of plain, smooth bamboo, with the length of a fife or twice that, 80 cm. (32"); it has seven fingerholes, plus a vent hole below, of similar size, but some varieties have only six holes. The *bansuri* dates in India from the first century AD at the latest, associated especially with the god Krishna, who is often depicted playing it. In the North, it is now heard most in Bengal and Bihar. Soloists play in classical styles using the longest size, over $2\frac{1}{2}$ octaves range, sliding the fingers for vocal-style *glissandi*; among them are, and have been, great celebrities.

Baraban. Russian: 'drum'.

Barbitos. One of the lyres of Ancient Greece. See LYRE, 2*b*.

Baritone. Valved *brass instrument built in the key of B♭ an octave below the ordinary *trumpet or *cornet. In many countries it is one of two distinct brass instruments at this pitch.

1. *Britain*. The baritone of the *brass band (see BRASS BAND, Pl. I) has narrower tubing and bell than the *euphonium, and serves principally as an essential background instrument in the ensemble. It is the same in France (*baryton*), where the euphonium is called '*basse*' (short for *saxhorn basse*).

2. *America*. The baritone (in full, 'baritone horn') is here the instrument that plays the same leading part in a *military or concert band that the euphonium plays in Britain. Makers offer a choice in dimensions (wide-bore models sometimes listed as 'euphonium') and the bell is often curved round to face the audience. In times back to the Civil War, when brass bands were most popular in the USA, two distinct instruments were used as they are in Britain: 'tenor horn', corresponding to the British baritone, and 'baritone horn' to the euphonium.

3. *Germany*. Two corresponding species: the narrower-bore named *Tenorhorn*, and the wider-bore *Bariton*, both with rotary valves and built either in normal format (*Tuba-form*), or oval (*Ei-form*) with the bell pointing more to the side, as for instance illustrated in *Wagner tuba. A rare orchestral appearance is where the *Tenorhorn* opens Mahler's Seventh Symphony with a solo (played in

other countries preferably on the narrower-bore of the instruments where there are two kinds).

4. *Italy and Spain*. Again, correspondingly, (It.) *flicorno tenore* and *baritono* (or *basso*; (Sp.) *fiscorno* (similarly), words apparently deriving from German *Flügelhorn* (*Flugel horn).

Baritone oboe. See BASS OBOE.

Baroque. 1. *The term*. This was introduced first by art historians in Germany in the 1880s, followed later by literary historians likewise to cover the period roughly from the late 16th century to the early 18th. Music historians have used it (rarely before the 1920s) to cover *c*.1600–1750, the main period of the *continuo—though from *c*.1700 running into the period known to art history as 'rococo' (succeeded by 'classical' *c*.1770).

A 'baroque' instrument today (as the term is met in programmes or recordings) may be an original or reproduction from this period or, especially with wind instruments, one of later 18th-century date (from which many more originals are preserved, not too different in sound and technique from the genuinely baroque); or with violins, an instrument which has survived in or been restored to its original state (see VIOLIN, 7*a*, *c*) or is newly built in conformity and played in baroque manner with a contemporary type of bow and little or no vibrato. Many schools of music now give tuition on baroque instruments, stringed and wind, and normally restricted to students who have already qualified on the modern instruments.

2. *Contemporary works*. Among the more important on instruments are:

Bismantova 1677, etc., facs. edn. 1978 (for sections on the recorder, etc., see Castellani 1977).

Speer 1687, 1697 (the first of the little German books on instruments containing tunings and fingering charts, as also Majer, Eisel (see below)).

*Talbot *c*.1695 (the richest English source mentioning all instruments).

Bonanni 1722 (for the numerous Plates, though omitting the often important text, see Harrison and Rimmer 1964).

Prelleur 1731, repr. 1965.

Majer 1732, facs. repr. 1954 (a very similar work is Eisel 1738).

Next, three major works:

Quantz, Johann Joachim (1697–1773), *Versuch einer Anweisung die Flöte traversiere zu spielen* (Berlin, 1752; Eng. trans. Reilly 1966, 1985). (The work, by the flute teacher and composer to Frederick the Great, deals not only with the flute and with interpretation and ornamentation, but also in turn with each section of the string orchestra down to the *Contraviolist* (double bass), the keyboard continuo, and ensemble performance generally.)

Bach, Carl Philipp Emanuel (1714–88, second son of J. S. Bach), *Versuch über die wahre Art das Clavier zu spielen* (Berlin, 1753–62; Eng. trans. Mitchell 1949).

Mozart, Leopold (1719–87, father of the great composer), *Versuch einer gründlichen Violinschule* (Augsburg, 1756; see VIOLIN).

Donington 1973.

Barrel drum. General term for drums of barrel-like shape. See DRUM, 4*b* (ii).

Barrel organ (with fair organ, barrel piano). Barrel organs are pipe organs with the keyboard replaced by a rotating cylinder ('barrel') armed with projections which raise levers to admit air to the pipes. From the mid-19th century the barrel began to give place to punched cards joined in an endless band (see 5 below). 'Barrel organ' eventually became a familiar name for a barrel piano (6).

1. *The barrel*. In English domestic and church barrel organs of the 18th and 19th centuries, the barrel, of wood, may be up to 1 m. (3') long, lying horizontally, turned by a handle which, save in large instruments, simultaneously works the bellows placed underneath. The barrel is first marked round its circumference with lines, one for each note and spaced at regular intervals in alignment with a row of hook-like metal levers mounted in a fixed frame to actuate the pallets which admit air to the pipes. Into the marked lines are inserted pins or (for the longer notes) bridges of flat brass wire, each placed to trip its corresponding lever at the correct moments as the barrel rotates.

In most of these barrel organs a single major scale suffices, sometimes with one or two accidentals included. More important is to provide for a change of tune. If not too long, one tune can immediately follow another. But normally the marked lines for the first tune are spaced out to leave room for pinning other tunes between. To change the tune the barrel is shifted a little along its axis to bring a fresh set of pins in alignment with the actuating

levers (a system already described in a 9th-century Arabic treatise). Nine or more tunes are thus accommodated on the English barrels. Alternatively, the marked lines can spiral round the barrel, the axle of which then has a screw thread at one end so that while rotating it moves continuously in the opposite direction to the spirals and the tunes follow each other automatically. Most organs were supplied with at least three alternative barrels, stored in the bottom of the case. The church barrel organ marks a purely English development, the oldest date claimed being 1700, at Peak Forest, Derbyshire; the latest, 1879, at Ash Priors, Somerset. Altogether some 80 still existed in 1967 out of some 500 whose earlier existence in churches is recorded. One of the last to remain in regular weekly use was a Bryceson Bros. of *c.*1810, in the tiny church of Shelland, Suffolk.

As with other pipe organs, ranks of pipes simultaneously sounding an octave, etc., above the main rank fill out the sound: the Shelland organ having besides open and stopped diapasons, a principal (4'), twelfth, fifteenth (two'), and tierce (seventeenth; see ORGAN, 2). A domestic instrument may have only a stopped diapason with octave and fifteenth, but also a percussion section of drum, cymbals, and triangle operated through extra pins in the barrel.

The most frequent tunes on the barrels are 'Old Hundredth', 'Evening Hymn' (Tallis's Canon), 'Hanover' (Croft, often listed on the barrel as 'Old 104th'), and 'Portuguese Hymn' (*Adeste fideles*). Many barrels include a march, 'Rule, Britannia', or a piece from Handel, for use as a voluntary. As an example of the barrel-organ pinner's claim to equal the best 'live' performance, Ex. 1 shows the melody (omitting the sparse harmony) of the 'Old 104th Psalm' as transcribed from a small anonymous early 19th-century domestic organ. The profusion of small ornament is typical, while a keen eye will observe that in bar 8 the lack of C♯ on the organ made a correct mordent (matching bar 4) impossible.

Ex. 1.

2. *Bird organs* (*or* serinettes, *from the Fr. for 'canary'*) *and 'flute clocks'*. The former, also hand-turned, could be placed on the lap for playing high-pitched tunes to encourage a caged bird to sing and perhaps learn to repeat; many were made in Mirecourt (Vosges) and were still sold in the 1840s. Earlier barrel mechanisms, from the late 17th century, were turned by weights or clockwork, and often embodied in a clock. Haydn wrote 30 pieces (since published) for clockwork organ-clocks with small barrels, made by Niemecz, a priest in the service of Prince Esterházy. Mozart in his last years wrote three pieces variously titled 'for an organ-mechanism (*Orgelwerk*) in a clock', or 'for a barrel of a small organ'. Later, in the 19th century, manufacture of *Flötenuhren* ('flute-clocks') became centred in the Black Forest, producing all from cuckoo-clocks to complex orchestrions (see 4 below).

3. *Early street organs*. These first appeared, early in the 18th century, as the small portable, hand-turned pipe organ later known in France as *orgue de Barbarie* (which a theory of later times held to be after an early maker in Modena named Barberi). It was carried on a strap round the neck, or stood on one leg with a cloth to keep the rain off and a monkey to take the pennies. With improved road surfaces, the organ was carried on wheels, often on an old perambulator chassis. The organs were mostly built by Italians living in Paris, Berlin, or other northern capitals.

4. *Orchestrions* (mechanical orchestras). These are large barrel organs with pipes and percussion for imitating an orchestra. They originated in Germany in the late 18th century, driven by weights. Some imitated the orchestra also visually, with automata playing violins, etc., one being the Panharmonicon made in Vienna by Leonard Maelzel, brother of the better-known J. N. Maelzel, inventor of the *metronome. Beethoven originally wrote *Wellingtons Sieg* (1813) for this instrument. The Maelzels were, by 1829, settled in Boston, Mass., where they built a mechanical orchestra composed of 42 automata, playing overtures by Mozart, Spontini, and others.

An especially notable orchestrion in the light of modern developments in music was the Componium (1821) of the Dutch inventor D. N. Winkel, which could compose its own variations on a given theme. Now preserved in the Brussels *collection, it has two barrels, each with the theme pinned on the far left. To the right are the pins for seven variations, in every case leaving two bars silent between every two which are pinned. Both barrels rotate continuously, and the missing bars of any one of the eight tunes of one barrel can be substituted by bars from any of the eight on the other, the barrels being moved laterally under a clockwork 'computer'.

5. *Change to punched cards. Fair-ground organ.* A technical breakthrough, from the 1840s, was to replace the barrel by the punched-card principle, adapted from the Jacquard weaving loom (first patented in France in 1801). With looms, the band of cards, resembling a book folded zigzag, is drawn down at each press of a pedal for a card, with its pattern of holes, to face the end of a set of horizontal rods or 'needles', spring-loaded so that wherever there is a hole the needle moves forward (to operate a loom heddle) and is afterwards pushed out by the hole as the card moves down for the next to take its place. A fair organ, in which the 'book' of cards (or perforated paper roll) is fed in continuous movement, has been of two kinds. If 'with keys' (e.g. a '50-key organ'), levers corresponding in function to the loom 'needles' enter the holes to operate mechanically the air-admission to the wooden pipes, and are pushed away as the holes pass on: a method that reached perfection in the still well-known fair and dance 'steam' organs of Gavioli, Paris, from near the end of the 19th century. If 'keyless', the action is wholly pneumatic; air is drawn through the holes as they match those in a fixed 'comb', the air entering them operating small bellows which in turn open the pallets under the pipes: a method, bringing less wear on the paper, first thought of in Paris in the 1840s and becoming from the late 1870s very widely used (also with free reeds, *organette*) and later made in the USA by Wurlitzer. Such organs, intended to be enjoyed visually as well as listened to, were rich in ornament, with the fronts colourfully painted, a percussion box on each side (side drum on the left, rattled on by two little sticks side by side, and bass drum and cymbals on the other); girl figures striking little bells, light bulbs blazing. A competitor in Paris was Charles Marenghi, with organs 8 m. (27′) long and in Antwerp, Mortier (up to 1938). The master of the famous Dutch Street organ, Carl Frei, ran his works at Breda until 1944, some organs incorporating a carillon. After demand fell, a society was formed in Holland in 1954 to preserve the remaining instruments (two among them still using barrels), and their export abroad is now prohibited. For the merry-go-round at fairs the 'book organ' remains a favourite despite electronic competition, and firms like Chappa in London supply new books, or paper rolls, to keep the music up to date. There are fine collections of such organs, as in Britain at Thursford, Norfolk, while some very successful organs heard in the streets today are home-made throughout.

6. *Barrel pianos*. These, turned by handle, began to be made in Italy in the late 18th century; at first small, then, from the 1880s, resembling an upright piano and placed on a two-wheeled cart. They were still made and played almost entirely by Italians until, after 1922, Mussolini, concerned for the dignity of his nation, recalled all Italians engaged in street music. Apart from these, a noted English maker of the early 19th century was John Hicks

(London and Bristol), who made small portable models. Later there were barrel pianos driven by powerful clockwork motors for installation in dance halls and amusement arcades, along with automatic violins played with small resined wheels.

Bedos de Celles 1778, repr. 1936; Cockaygne 1971; Langwill and Boston 1967; Ord-Hume 1978.

Baryton. Bowed instrument of the period 1640–1820, used mainly in Austria and Germany. It is a kind of bass *viol with the addition of up to 20 wire strings which run behind the neck. They are primarily *sympathetic strings but are exposed at the back so that they can be plucked with the left thumb to supply occasional bass notes to the music played on the six (or seven) bowed strings. An ornamental grille beside the fingerboard conceals the wires from the front. The earliest-known music for the baryton, in a German manuscript of the 1660s, is written in tablature with the wire strings numbered downward from the note *d*. More famous is Prince Nicholas Esterházy's devotion to the instrument (he had one by Stadlmann, now preserved in Budapest), resulting in a manuscript collection of short pieces including at least 175 by Haydn: *Divertimenti a tre per il pariton* [baryton], *viola e violoncello*. These introduce the wire strings only sparingly, indicated by numbers below the staff. They have been recorded by Riki Gerardy of the Esterházy Baryton Trio.

There are early possible connections with England in a kind of viol with wire strings for the thumb, said to have been liked by James I. It was intended for playing 'lyra way' (see LYRA VIOL). Another name for the German baryton is *viola di bordone*.

Fruchtmann 1962.

Bass. As an instrument, normally the *double bass, or in *brass and *military bands, a *tuba. For 'bass' instruments of other families, see under the main word with the exceptions below. For the origin of the term 'bass', see ALTO.

Bassanelli. An obscure late Renaissance family of double-reed wind instruments. *Praetorius (1619) illustrates them and ascribes their invention to one of the celebrated Bassano family of instrument makers in Venice, perhaps c.1582 (Selfridge-Field 1976). In an Italian manuscript work of c.1600 (Virgiliano) they are called *armilloni*. No instruments have yet been found to match these *bassanelli*, said to have sounded softer than *shawms.

Bass bar. An internal component of the violin, etc. (see VIOLIN, 2).

Bass clarinet (in It. often *clarone*). An octave below the clarinet, this is also of wood, but with an upturned flared metal bell and, at the top, a cylindrical S-curved metal crook (neck) for the mouthpiece (see CLARINET, Pl. 1d). Held vertically between the knees, it is carried on a sling or in some designs supported on a metal spike. Required in numerous orchestral works, it is played by one of the clarinet section (see ORCHESTRA, 1b). Its music is written in the treble clef, at an octave and a tone above the actual sound, the written range being fully that of the clarinet—and see 1, below, for extra bottom notes. Exceptionally it is written in the bass clef (see TRANSPOSING INSTRUMENTS). For clarinets of yet deeper pitch, see CONTRABASS CLARINET.

1. *Design and keywork*. The reed is of about tenor *saxophone size but a fraction narrower. The bore width varies, being generally somewhat more than twice that of a clarinet for the sound to tell well, especially in the bass register. The keywork makes the fingering the same as on the clarinet, save that two 'speaker' keys are usual, and in many older models (many still in use) these are operated by two separate keys for left thumb, changing from one to the other on passing from d'' to e''. On most modern designs there is only one thumb key, the two vents automatically changing over as the right-hand third finger is lifted. Wagner frequently scores for 'bass clarinet in A' with prominent use of its low E (sounding C♯). Hence it is necessary for the normal instrument (in B♭) to have extra length and an extra key in order to produce this note. But this is not all. In Germany after Wagner's time a bass clarinet descending to the written low C came locally into manufacture to become the standard form of the instrument in Russian orchestras. Many works by Prokofiev and Shostakovich demand these lower notes—the low C sounding in unison with the bottom B♭ of the bassoon—and as a result many bass clarinettists elsewhere have adopted this extended model, now available from the French clarinet-makers, to be able to fulfil the intentions of these composers. The instrument shown in CLARINET, Pl. 1, has this extended compass.

2. *Orchestral character*. When, early in the time of Berlioz, a fully efficient bass clarinet became available to bands and orchestras, the orchestral wood-wind section was already fixed in its basic constitution with bassoons its sole deeper voice. It took some time before, with later Romantic composers, the bass clarinet began to make frequent appearances in the orchestral score, with an often memorable effect. Wagner, in *Tristan und Isolde* and the *Ring*, makes it one of his primary wind voices, with long and solemn solo passages such as had never been written for any deep wind instrument of the orchestra. Outside opera, Franck's D minor Symphony could be cited as demonstrating particularly well the instrument's curious ability to imbue the entire woodwind with its strange purring quality when allotted the bass of the harmony. Like the clarinet itself, its diminuendo can be taken to the point of virtual silence (then depriving listeners from hearing the notes at all, as often happens

when the bass clarinet is called upon where Tchaikovsky once writes a very difficult *ppppp* for bassoon).

3. *Early bass clarinets*. Several designs appeared in the late 18th century, experimental only, for no known music requires them (though there are earlier parts for 'bass *chalumeau', of appearance still unknown). Most early types were built (first perhaps by Grenser, Dresden, 1793) with a 'butt joint' like that of the bassoon, with compass down to the low C or D. Notable are some American examples of 1810–15 made (presumably for wind bands) by Catlin and others of Hartford, Connecticut, where they are now preserved; some were advertised under the name 'Clarion' (Eliason 1983). The modern instrument, along with the first entry into the symphony orchestra, dates from the 1830s, when Sax in Brussels and Buffet in Paris arrived at practically the present format, and Meyerbeer wrote for it an obbligato of virtuoso proportions in his opera *Les Huguenots* (1836).

Bass drum. (Fr.: *grosse caisse*; Ger.: *Grosse Trommel*; It.: *gran cassa*, *tamburo grande*; Ru.: *baraban bolshoi*; Sp.: *bombo*). There are two main forms: the big orchestral and band drum, normally placed or carried with the heads facing sideways; and the smaller bass drum of the popular *drum kit, placed with one head facing the player, to be struck by a foot-pedal.

1. *Orchestral bass drum*. In Britain up to 100 cm. (40″) wide with shell 30 cm. (12″) deep; in America and on the Continent, less wide but deeper. The shell is of laminated wood, metal, or fibreglass, and the drum is placed on a folding stand—or pivoted in a metal frame in order to be tilted horizontally for performing rolls literally as demanded, for instance, by Berlioz. The beater has a felt-covered end about 8 cm. (3″) wide, and is struck away from the centre of the drum with a glancing blow and damped with the other hand to accord with the written note-value. The roll is made on the same head using two beaters; or, if playing in the old way with a cymbal attached to the drum (see CYMBAL, 2), a double-ended beater can be used, making rolls with one hand by rotating the wrist.

2. *Military bass drum* (see BRASS BAND, Pl. 1, centre front). The drum traditionally has (like a military side drum) three small brass feet on one of the hoops, for resting the instrument safely on the ground during a halt. It is carried on the march over a 'drum apron' of leather or of sheep- or leopardskin. One hand strikes close to the centre, to give the step clearly. The other hand fills in and adds to the spectacular effect. On signals from the Drum Major's staff the bass drummer gives the 'double tap' at the approach of the next double bar for the band to cease playing or change to the next tune. In the USA, a band may now use two

or more bass drums of different sizes, tuned to contrasting pitches.

3. *Small bass drum*. Jazz brought in the small bass drum, supplied with a drum kit, around 55 cm. (22″) in diameter and 35 cm. (14″) deep. It is kept steady by two metal spurs and struck with a sprung foot-pedal (see DRUM KIT, Pl. 1; the invention has been credited to a black drummer, Dee Dee Chandler, *c*.1895). There is usually a damper-pad inside to deaden the sound so that the foundation beat is heard distinctly. Often it is played with the second head removed, or cut with a hole, and a cushion placed in the shell to deaden the sound further.

4. *Gong drum*. So called because it is single-headed, this dates from the 1850s and some British orchestras still prefer it: percussionists say that it offers certain advantages in control of the sound, but on the other hand the single skin is liable to give out an undesirably definite pitch. Gong drums are now also made in smaller sizes for school music.

5. *Earlier forms*. The bass drum was developed after the 18th-century introduction of *Turkish music. The Janissary drum was itself a not particularly large but deep-shelled drum, resembling deeper types of the present Turkish *davul, and was struck on both heads: the mounted drummer slinging it at a slant over the left thigh, striking the right head with a stout hooked stick, and the left with a slender wand, reaching back with the wrist resting on the rim of the drum. The early European versions are made with a shell very long compared with the diameter of the head ('long drum'). Diameters were then increased until by the period following Waterloo a 'bass drum' (as it was by then called) is wider than deep, e.g. *c*.75 × 55 cm. (30″ × 22″), a very large drum. Still it was usually played in a 'Turkish' manner, with a leather-padded beater for the right hand, and for the left—if not a second beater—a short besom-like switch, in Germany called *Rute* or *Ruthe* (visible in MILITARY BAND, Pl. 2, bottom right). In written parts, notes with tails downwards (or written in the lower octave: see TURKISH MUSIC, Fig. 1) indicate the beater, and with tails upwards (or in the higher octave) the switch: see for example the part in Haydn's 'Military Symphony'. After the switch went out of use, it was later revived, first in light and dance orchestras for steam-train imitations, and then occasionally in the full orchestra, e.g. by Mahler in the third movement of his Second Symphony.

6. *Other forms*. As a folk instrument, a bass drum is widely essential over Latin America (*bombo*), and, no doubt here of military origin, takes part in every country festival in Portugal, named *Ze-Pereira* ('Joseph Pear-tree'). This is played with two sticks, one padded, the other thin and plain. The Orangeman's 'Lambeg drum' in Northern Ireland is

Basset clarinet, Ex. 1.

another, very big and violently struck with two canes for hours on end in the streets.

Basse de musette. A name given in many collections (or in German, *Musettenbass*) to a peculiar type of conical double-reed tenor-pitched instrument of about twice the length of an oboe but much thicker and wider and with a coiled crook for the reed. Examples are mostly from churches in the region of Berne, Switzerland, where it is supposed that in the 18th century they supported the chant. The keys, which cover the first and third holes for each hand, in many cases bear a not-understood mark, 'I.IR'. See also *Heckelphone*.

Basset (from It. *bassetto*). An old term employed chiefly in Germany from the 16th century onwards, broadly denoting a 'small bass'. See DOUBLE BASS, 5c; RECORDER, 4; SHAWM, 1.

Basset clarinet. Modern name for a clarinet, in B♭ or in A, with compass extended down to the written low *c* as on the *basset horn. In the 18th century Anton Stadler, for whom Mozart wrote (see CLARINET, 4c), used this extension and Mozart writes these lower notes for B♭ clarinet in *La clemenza di Tito*. Occasionally in the 19th century an instrument was fitted with a lower joint lengthened by approaching 15 cm. (6″) and with the requisite extra keys in order to perform especially the 'Parto, parto' aria in this work (Ex. 1). It has since been demonstrated, from internal evidence of the music itself, that Mozart must have written down to C also in the Quintet and Concerto, both for A clarinet. The autographs of these works have never been found, but some recent editions have optionally restored the low notes in the likely places, and some soloists, among them notably Alan Hacker, have had the instrument lengthened to play them; it is then called a 'basset clarinet'. (Note in Ex. 1 how the passage written in the bass clef is put an octave lower, as in basset horn and French horn music.)

Basset horn (It.: *corno di bassetto*). One of the clarinet family (see CLARINET, Pl. 1c), pitched in F, a fourth below the B♭ clarinet, and extended in range down to the written low *c*, sounding the low

F of the bass voice. It is made today principally for works of Mozart and Richard Strauss which include it. 'Basset' ('little bass') alludes to its deep notes; 'horn' no doubt to the curved shape of early models.

1. Construction. As well as with the upturned metal bell illustrated (CLARINET, Pl. 1c), the basset horn is also made with a straight-downwards wooden bell like that of the clarinet itself. The bore is normally kept fairly small (narrower than that of an *alto clarinet) for the important upper register to preserve a fluent expressiveness equal to that of a clarinet, though of a deeper, more subdued quality. The instrument is supplied in standard Boehm system by most major clarinet manufacturers, the keys for the bottom four semitones being usually allotted, or at least partly, to the right thumb.

2. History and repertoire. The basset horn seems to have originated in Germany or Austria about 1760, a time when clarinets were still being built with two keys only (see CLARINET, 4a). To these were added on the basset horn, curved in a 'sickle' shape covered in leather (see COR ANGLAIS, 2), a key for the written low *f* and, on the back for the thumb, one for the bottom *c*, with no notes in between. To save overall length the low C key acts on a flat piece of wood in which the tube twice reverses direction, then leading to a brass bell pointing downwards, as in Pl. 1, here showing the following classic 'angled' model in two straight joints connected by a short 'knee'. Soon the note *e* was provided for (as in examples by the makers Mayrhofer), and then *d*; but the two intervening semitones remained normally omitted. Mozart occasionally writes these two semitones, but it has been demonstrated that they are just possible by cross-fingering with the existing D and C keys. In all he used the basset horn in some 20 works, ending with the Requiem, in which basset horns and bassoons are the only woodwind.

Up to the 1830s German regimental bands often included a pair of basset horns to play the middle parts, while a continuing vogue for the instrument among clarinet virtuosos is pleasantly commemorated in Mendelssohn's two *Konzertstücke*, Op. 113 and 114. Still made in Germany, chiefly

Pl. 1. Basset horn by Grenser, Dresden (*c.* 1790).

for Mozart's operas, it was already available to Strauss when he composed *Elektra* (1909). He used it last in the Wind Sonatina of 1945. Others have written for it since, including Stockhausen, exploiting the entire possible compass of four complete octaves.

Basset Nicolo. *Praetorius gives 'Nicolo' as the name for a tenor *shawm with one key and lowest note *c*. But his illustration, captioned 'Bassett: Nicolo', shows a kind of straight-built tenor *crumhorn with four keys. Various explanations have been offered.

Bass flute. See ALTO AND BASS FLUTE.

Bass guitar. 1. *Electric bass guitar.* See GUITAR 9.

2. *Older meaning.* A guitar which has besides a normal set of guitar strings, a set of seven or so 'basses' tuned in diatonic order (like the 'diapasons' of many lutes), struck with the thumb to provide a bass to the chords played on the main strings. There are rare 17th-century examples with bass strings running from a high pegbox as in a *theorbo, and there exist pieces of music (e.g. of 1659 in Italy) for *chitarra tiorbata* (Pinnell 1979). But in the

later designs the basses run over a second (unfretted) neck which diverges from the main neck at a small angle, with the tuning machines or pins at the top. The soundbox is appropriately somewhat widened. The instrument has been used in Russia and Central Europe since the 19th century in popular music and is now traditional in the Viennese 'Schrammel quartet' (see CLARINET, 4*d*). See also HARP-GUITAR, 3.

Bass horn. Name of certain derivatives of the *serpent, made through the first 40 years of the 19th century and used mainly in bands.

1. *In England.* Of brass or copper, composed of two tubes meeting at the bottom in a narrow V about 85 cm. (34″) tall. The wider leads up to a flared bell 20 cm. (8″) across. The narrower has six fingerholes formed as projecting brass chimneys, and a long swan-necked crook for a cup mouthpiece. There are four (or three) closed keys, and the lowest note is *C*. Invented, it is said, before 1800 by a French refugee serpentist, Frichot, it gives sounds in some respects clearer than those of the wooden serpent, which it often came to replace in bands on the bass part (sometimes headed for it 'Corno Basso') until both were replaced by the *ophicleide.

A design having tube-length twice as long, with the idea of facilitating the technique by dispensing with the need to sound fundamentals, was the 'Basso Hibernicon', invented by an Irish clergyman, Cotter, in 1823 and made in London by the leading wind-instrument maker Thomas Key. In the Yorkshire Music Festival of 1835 it appeared in the orchestra beside four serpents and three ophicleides. A unique example is in the Bate *Collection, Oxford.

2. *In Germany.* Through the same period, the name *Basshorn*, or *Englisches Basshorn*, covered various versions of, or improvements on, the wooden *basson russe* (see SERPENT, Pl. 2), used in band and orchestral parts which may equally be headed 'Serpent', as also in works by Mendelssohn and by Wagner (*Rienzi*). See also CIMBASSO.

Bass lute. A large 16th-century lute with body length around (69 cm. (27″), one-third bigger than in an average lute) and string length *c.*90 cm. (35″), tuned a fifth lower than the lute (or perhaps also a fourth lower) and used for deep accompaniments to the voice or other lutes until superseded by instruments of the *chitarrone* type. Examples are very rare, the instruments having usually been converted into *theorbos, etc. A fine one by Magnus Stegher, Venice, is in the Bologna *Collection.

Bass oboe. Instruments pitched an octave lower than the oboe have been made experimentally from *c.*1700 (one by Denner exists). The later French 'hautbois baryton' designed by Brod *c.*1825 has since remained in manufacture on demand (by

Marigaux, for example). The bulb bell at first pointed upwards, later downwards, and the bottom note sounds *B*. British oboists have termed it the 'bass oboe', but it is not clearly remembered whether in *The Planets* Holst envisaged this (as named in the score) or the *heckelphone, a more powerful instrument, for the Bass Oboe part, which in exposed places is cued in other wind parts lest no bass oboe be procurable.

Bassoon (Fr.: *basson*; Ger.: *Fagott*; It.: *fagotte*; Ru.: *fagot*; Sp.: *fagote, bajón*). The tall woodwind instrument with a conical bore and played with a double reed (see REED, Fig. 3*f*). In height 134 cm. (4½'), it is held slanting upwards to the player's left, cradled in the left hand while the right presses the lower part to the thigh. From the curved metal crook or 'bocal' (from the French word) on which the reed is placed, the tube leads through four separate 'joints', reversing direction at the bottom to total just over 275 cm. (9'). A white ring at the top (ideally of ivory) is a German tradition, the current standard bassoon following the design of Heckel, of Biebrich, near Wiesbaden (Pl. 1*b*, showing the 'hand-rest' for the web of the right hand, another German feature). The bassoon has been a regular member of the orchestra since the beginning of the 18th century, when, along with the oboe, it made up the orchestra's first woodwind section. For its historical predecessor, also with a doubled-back tube, see DULCIAN. For the larger 'double bassoon' see CONTRABASSOON (and for rare smaller sizes, TENOROON).

1. *Construction*. Fig. 1 shows the four joints, omitting detail: 1, crook; 2, the wing joint, so called from the sideways thickening through which the three left-hand fingerholes are drilled slantwise (Fig. 1*b*) to spread them out on the inside without exceeding finger-span on the outside; 3, 'butt', oval in section to contain two parallel tubes connected at the bottom by a metal U-tube concealed under a protecting metal cap; 4, 'long joint', ascending to 5, the 'bell'. The weight is taken by a sling round the neck, leaving the thumbs free, for both play a very active part in the technique, having 12 or more keys to control between them. Instead of the sling some players prefer a 'seat strap' (hooked to the bottom cap and sat on) or a cello-like spike. This is mainly because the instrument, with its mechanism, weighs more than it once did—though even so, many players take up the bassoon at a very early age, and using a sling in the traditional way (in the 18th century, one would hang it by a ribbon loop to a button of one's frock coat). Reeds can be purchased, made by specialist reed-makers; otherwise, players make their own.

2. *Compass and registers*. Indicated in Ex. 1 to the left of the outlined box are the lowest notes down to *B♭'*, emitted through the long joint and bell and controlled mainly by the left thumb: a bass extension of the main compass inherited (down to

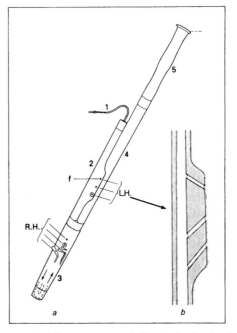

Fig. 1. (*a*) Bassoon, view as held, omitting hand-rest and most of the keys. The first hole emits the note *f*. (*b*) Section of wing joint.

C) from the old dulcian. Within the boxed area the notes are made with the same fingering, or very nearly so, as the corresponding notes of the oboe an octave and a half higher: the two instruments lie technically a twelfth apart (the same interval at which the cello stands below the violin); the dotted line marks the transition from fundamentals to overblown octaves. Then, continuing the tenor register above *d'*, the fingering is at once more complicated—for details, see OVERBLOWING—up to the classical top note *a'*, and on to *c''* and *d''*, very rarely higher up to *e''*. Unlike our modern oboes the bassoon uses no octave key but has merely a small hole near the base of the crook, which is closed in the lower registers by a 'crook-key' for the left hand.

In the classical orchestra especially the bassoon holds a unique position, not only as the chief solo

Ex. 1.

melodic voice in the tenor range (so notably, expressing every mood, in the works of Beethoven), but equally as the all-purpose melodic 'octave doubler', blending, without asserting its individuality, at the octave below with any of the smaller woodwind or equally with the violins. In the later German Romantic works the bassoon becomes overshadowed as a soloist by the horn, though it was for the instrument as developed in Germany in (or practically in) its present standard form that it rose to new peaks in the symphonies of Tchaikovsky and Sibelius.

3. *Systems:* (a) The Heckel system goes back substantially in its present form to *c.*1870, Heckel (founded 1836) continuing to be the leading maker though others in Germany have high repute, as Püchner, and in the USA, Fox. Made in maplewood, the wing and smaller bore of the butt are lined with ebonite to resist moisture. Two of the fingerholes have ring mechanisms: for hole 3 the ring serves to make two semitones (c♯ and e♭) obtainable with the same thumb key; for hole 5, the purpose is to tune the high g', otherwise too flat. The standard keywork has 21 keys altogether, but there may be more (e.g. a key to facilitate high d''). On the butt several keys are worked from the opposite side, by pins running through the wood between the two bores of this joint. (Wagner and some others later have written low A' for bassoon, but it has been exceedingly rare to oblige them with an extra-long bell and extra key especially for this note.)

(b) The French bassoon (Pl. 1a: chief maker Buffet-Crampon, Paris, founded 1836) is made in dark rosewood (with no white ring on top) and is used by nearly all players in France and still by a few in Britain, where—as in Italy and Spain—it was the regular bassoon up to the 1930s. Debussy, Elgar, and Puccini all wrote for this or very similar instruments. In the USA, where the German system has predominated for longer, the Buffet bassoon was in use up to this same time in the Boston Symphony Orchestra (Raymond Allard the principal player). Its distinctive, very human sound will be at once recognized in a French orchestra, though latterly the German bassoon has begun to appear, its sound being more certain to 'cut through' in an orchestra equipped with other German-style wind, brass especially. Important differences in the lower-register fingering are (left-hand holes shown on the left; 'O', hole open): B♭ and b♭ both ●●●●○● as a necessary alternative; c♯ ●●○●○○ G♯ key (and c♯', without this key); e (third space) ●○○○●● ; f♯ ○○○●●● F key. (For higher notes, see OVERBLOWING.)

(a)

(b)

Pl. 1. (a) French system, front; (b) German system, front and back.

Older models similar to the French, by Mahillon (Brussels), Boosey (London), etc. were also in professional use in Britain in the 1930s, and up to quite recently many school orchestras depended on them; they cost scarcely more than an oboe or clarinet (whereas today the price of a bassoon can be around three times that of a good-quality oboe). They can sound very sweet—only with the strongest 'military model' reed might the instrument give more buzz than note.

4. *Early bassoons.* Developments from the 1630s (Mersenne) eventually led, probably by the 1660s and first in France, to the present three joints and form of crook which brings the instrument to an elegant playing position, no longer clutched to the body as the old dulcian had been. The earliest known examples are however German (some by Denner; see CHALUMEAU, 2), all with ornamental turning not unlike that on the contemporary oboe, but later, by the 1730s, given up in favour of plainer lines. The brass keys are two on the butt (F, G♯, corresponding to the keys of the oboe) and two on the long joint (D and bottom B♭, with a plain thumb-hole between them for C): thus the lowest fifth of the compass remains diatonic (cf. the *short octave of keyboard instruments) though F♯ and E♭ can be cross-fingered. At the time of Mozart's Concerto (1774) four-keyed bassoons were still made; Pl. 2 shows the later F♯ key (right thumb) and E♭ (next to the D key, long joint). The rest of the fingering is quite like that of the present French bassoon and, with a suitable crook (sometimes hard to find, and usually with no small hole in it) and reed (wider or longer than modern), brings no technical problems in works of the period, in which original instruments or reproductions are now often heard (among some favourite old makers, Porthaux (Paris), Grenser (Dresden), Milhouse (Newark on Trent, from 1788 London), each country true to its traditional basic model. The sound in general is warm and friendly, perfectly matched to the milder orchestral dynamics of the time, while it was quite usual for one or two bassoons to double the cellos and basses in works that have no separate bassoon parts in the score.

By the time of Beethoven's unsurpassed orchestral writing for bassoon (for example, in the Violin Concerto), eight or nine keys were usual, and the English instruments had replaced the old 'wavy' bell profile by one slightly evased, giving louder low notes. In England also single-reed ebony mouthpieces were made (like small saxophone mouthpieces no doubt for use by bandsmen trained on the clarinet; such are obtainable also today, with a reed *c*.11 mm. (4¼″) wide and barely longer than that of the smallest piccolo clarinet, and work efficiently enough in a marching band.

In Paris, from the 1820s, Savary brought the eight-keyed bassoon to such perfection, by degrees adding further keys, that his instruments were still being played by leading professionals in London in

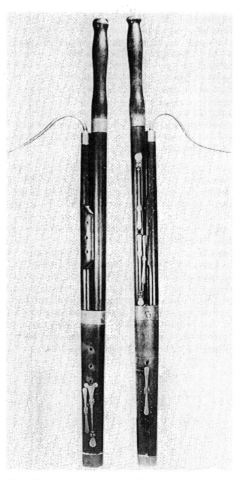

Pl. 2. Bassoon by Kusder, London, late 18th century, front and back.

the early 20th century along with the newer French models. In Germany, however, the Mainz player Carl Almenraeder (1786–1843) announced (1825) a new design which by 1831 he was producing in Biebrich in conjunction with J. A. Heckel: a bore evenly conical through all joints instead of varying from joint to joint as previously; new locations for many of the holes and keys; and abolition of all but one of the lower-register cross-fingerings—but retaining the deep-drilled, narrow fingerholes, which bring to the bassoon its somewhat compressed, 'closed-in' tone character by a filtering out of the higher partials of notes that issue through those holes. They also tend to bring tonal inequalities more noticeable than on other woodwind instruments; yet searches for a more rational layout using full keywork (e.g. a 'Boehm-system' bassoon tested in France in the 1860s) or electronic control of the note-holes (Brindley and others later) have hitherto failed through altering the bassoon's traditional sound almost beyond recognition.

5. *Repertory.* The bassoonist's purely solo repertory is largely outweighed by its part in chamber music and in concertos for several instruments, e.g. the quintets for piano and wind by Mozart and Beethoven, and the *sinfonie concertante* by Haydn and Mozart. Solo pieces from the Baroque include Galliard's six sonatas (for bassoon or cello, but clearly written for the bassoon); numerous concertos by Vivaldi (not easy to bring off); and a rather dull Sonata in F minor by Telemann. The chief classical concertos are Mozart's K. 191, Weber's Op. 75 and his Introduction and Hungarian Rondo, Op. 35 (originally for viola and very charming); and one by Hummel. Good later works include Glinka's *Trio pathétique*, with clarinet and piano; sonatas by Saint-Saëns and by Hindemith, both of whom wrote solos for most wind instruments; Elgar's Romance, Op. 62 (an endearingly personal work); and above all Poulenc's Trio (1926) with oboe and piano. Nor should one forget the lighter side: Dan Godfrey's Humorous Variations on 'Lucy Long' was featured in the first of the Queen's Hall Promenade Concerts in 1895 and still brings the house down.

Camden 1962; Halfpenny 1957; Joppig 1988; Langwill 1965; Weber 1825, 1828 (on Almenraeder's improvements). Also Baines 1957 (with list, p. 361, of most important past tutors).

Bass trumpet. Best known in Wagner's *Ring*, in which it plays an important and thrilling role, the orchestral bass trumpet is built in B♭ or C, an octave below the ordinary B♭ trumpet, of which, to the eye, it is a large version, with three (or four) valves. There is also a long Continental tradition of military bass trumpets, beginning during the Napoleonic wars with plain natural instruments for cavalry bands, in B♭ and also in the E♭ below (tuba pitch), and used for their few available notes to fill the harmony below the natural trumpets. The low E♭ bass cavalry trumpet especially remains much in use (in France, Holland, etc.), built in three coils, looking like a large bugle. Valved versions, made from the 1820s, have become rarer, though the *tromba bassa* in B♭ may still be seen in large Italian military bands. Wagner must have known of these instruments, but, while there is no question over the sounding pitch of his Bass Trumpet parts (written 'in E♭', 'in D', etc., see TRANSPOSING INSTRUMENTS: BASS TRUMPET), there is still some mystery over the basic pitch he originally envisaged this valved instrument to be built in.

Bass viol. The bass instrument of the *viol family, often known as 'viola da gamba'. Also, in Britain an old-fashioned popular name for the *double bass. In New England, from the 1790s to the 1850s, a kind of large cello made, for accompanying church choirs, under this name or 'church bass'; many were made by Abraham Prescott, of Deerfield,

New Hampshire (d. 1858). In collections they are generally described as 'New England Bass Viol'. Some have 5 strings, and often the sides of the body are glued into grooves cut in the back and belly (examples in US National Museum, Washington, DC).

Bass violin (or *basse de violon*). The name up to the end of the 17th century of the instrument since known as the *cello. Up to a few generations ago, the cello was still often spoken of among violin connoisseurs as a 'bass' (as the *viola was known as the 'tenor').

Beats and difference tones. Certain phenomena that may be recognized when two musical notes are sounded together.

1. *Beats.* Interference between two soundwaves that differ by only little in frequency results in a wave-form in which the ear perceives a regular pulsation in loudness of sound known as 'beats'. For example, two strings or pipes giving Middle C, not in exact unison but one making, say, 262 vibrations per second (*Hz) and the other 261: It follows from the difference of one vibration in every second that the ear registers one beat per second as the two waves come into coincidence and heighten their combined amplitude. Were the lower frequency reduced to 260.5 Hz, the rate of beating would increase to 1½ beats per second (three beats to every two seconds); or if to 257 Hz, five beats per second. Beyond this the rate soon becomes too fast for individual beats to be distinguished and a roughness ensues until eventually beats vanish and the ear perceives two notes a semitone or so apart, as in this example C and B (the latter, 247 Hz).

Beats of around five per second are made use of in various instruments to produce a tremolo sound, e.g. between two reeds in an accordion (the degree of detuning required becoming less in higher octaves, where frequencies run into higher figures leading to greater numerical differences which unless diminished would produce an undesirably fast beat). Also, in tuning keyboard instruments, beats provide an important means of checking the octaves and the tempering (see TEMPERAMENT) of fifths and thirds. Although beats of mistuned consonances are a specialized study which reveals much about the neural processing of sounds, it appears that, in a very simplified model, though the notes themselves making the interval do not beat, their partials (harmonics) do; with a fifth, for example, the third partial of the lower note is the same as the second partial of the upper, and if these do not form a perfect unison they will beat, and give an experienced tuner a good indication of the desired departure from a pure (beatless) interval. (For 'beat' as a baroque musical ornament, see FLUTE, 4a).

2. *Difference tones.* Two frequencies that lie a pure interval apart, such as a fifth or a third, are both

integral multiples of a common fundamental; and if the pitch of that fundamental is not too low to sound a recognizable note, it may become heard when the original two notes are played together on an instrument or on two of similar kind (recorder players often notice it). It is a 'difference tone' since its frequency is the difference between those of the notes played (e.g. a' 440 Hz and e'' 660, difference $220 = a$; or a' and $c\sharp''$, pure major third, difference now $110 = $ low A). The audible fundamental in such cases is held by scientists to be a subjective phenomenon, the residue arising in the hearing system along with numerous further possible weaker 'combination tones' scarcely consciously noticed. The whole subject has become one of extreme psychological and mathematical complexity. See also ORGAN, 3b (acoustic bass).

Becken. Ger.: 'cymbals'.

Beganna. The larger type of Ethiopian lyre; see LYRE, Pl. I.

Bell. Church bell, tower bell (Fr.: *cloche*; Ger.: *Glocke*; It., Sp.: *campana*; Ru.: *kolokol*). For other bells, see AGOGO BELL, BELL CHIME, CARILLON, CHIME, COWBELL, HANDBELLS, SLEIGHBELL (pellet bell), TUBULAR BELL (and for church bell imitation, also BELL PLATES).

1. *Bell founding.* The massive bells of the Western nations are struck sometimes on the inside, other times on the outside, with a wrought-iron beater which in the case of Big Ben in London is said to weigh more than 200 kg., a fifth of a ton. Hung high in a tower, their tremendous sound energy carries above other buildings to be heard afar and without injuring the ears of people passing close below. As with all fine cymbals and gongs also, the bells are cast in bronze: 'bell metal' is of around 77 parts copper to 23 of tin, poured into a mould of which the core is of bricks covered with loam. The 'cope' (outer mould) is of cast iron, covered with loam and with the inscriptions or decoration impressed on the surface in reverse. Both moulds are polished, and after coating with graphite, are assembled and clamped for pouring the metal. An older, pre-19th-century method is to build upon the core, having greased it, a 'false bell', also of loam, giving the outer form; this also greased, the cope is made upon it and, when all is hard and dry, removed for chipping off the 'false bell'; the cope is then buried in earth upside down, the core replaced, and the metal poured.

In Britain there are now two major founders and they work in close concert. The Whitechapel Bell Foundry, formerly Messrs Mears and Stainbank, has been there since 1570: Big Ben (1859) in the Clock Tower of the Houses of Parliament is among its famous bells. John Taylor & Co. of Loughborough, founded in the 19th century, has among its products the ring of 12 at St Paul's Cathedral

in London, with Great Paul (1881), the largest bell in Britain.

For a bell to sound a given note, makers go by experience aided by their own tables for diameters, heights, and thicknesses (especially of the thick 'sound-bow', where the bell is struck). The pitch varies approximately inversely as the diameter; and with large bells of the normal shape a rough comparative guide to pitch is the cube root of the weight (Big Ben, $c.13\frac{1}{2}$ tons, though nearly twice as heavy as Great Tom (1680) at Christ Church, Oxford, sounds only a third deeper, about f); smaller bells however are likely to be relatively thicker in proportion to size and to sound higher than this simple reckoning would suggest. Among some 29 existing very large bells estimated to be heavier than Big Ben, 20 are in Europe, the six heaviest being in the USSR, reaching 170 tons (this excludes the giant broken bell of 1733 which stands in the Kremlin, with a sound-bow 60 cm. (2' thick); three of the others are in the USA (the largest in the Riverside Church, New York City, 1931, over 18 tons and 3 m. (10') wide), and six in the Far East, including one of the oldest bells in the world, in Korea, AD 771, 275 cm. (9') tall, five times the weight of Big Ben, and of the oriental 'beehive' (non-flared) shape, struck on the outside by a horizontally suspended wooden beam moved like a battering ram. In Europe, casting of bells had begun in Italy by the 8th century, using the 'lost wax' method, and replacing monastery bells forged in iron (rather like cowbells) up to 30 cm. (1') tall—before which, in antiquity, there are only known bronze or pottery bells, small enough to be shaken in the hand.

2. *Bell overtones.* As one well knows, a bell gives out other pitches at the same time as the main strike note: the 'tierce' at the interval of a third above (often nearer a minor third than major); a short-lasting fifth and octave above the strike note, perhaps less easy to hear; and, far below, a deep 'hum note' up to an octave below the 'tierce'. They arise from different modes of vibration having certain analogies with those of a cymbal (see PARTIALS, 7b) but with a complex distribution of mass which makes physical analysis of the behaviour difficult, while the strike tone itself has often been considered to be a 'resultant' existing only in our hearing system. Normally on the Continent (save for carillon bells) the overtones are not carefully tuned after casting: little can be more stirring than the random mingling of their pitches, hues, and durations as they fill the square below in a symphony of pure bell sound. On the other hand, for carillons and in Britain for change-ringing (see below), musical clarity is obtained by 'bell tuning': with the bell mouth-upwards, it is thinned inside at specific antinodal latitudes—originally by hammer and chisel; now, with the bell rotating, by a vertical milling cutter and the aid of an electronic pitch-meter—to flatten partials selectively

(or if metal is removed close to the rim, sharpen them) until they are heard at precise musical intervals in relation to the strike note. For an example, the tenor bell of the ring at Amersham, Bucks., recast by Taylor in 1983, can be heard to give out a clear e' (hum), e'' (strike), g'' (tierce), b'' (less distinct), and a shrill e'''.

3. *Methods of Sounding*. (*a*) *Chiming*. This, the most used method on the Continent, is where a bell swings through an angle, generally under 180 degrees; when the angle is wider, it is 'tolling'. The clapper, being suspended inside the bell at a point which is well below the 'headstock' which carries the bell itself, swings faster than the bell, and on the return swing gains on the bell to touch this as it rises. To swing the bell for chiming, the rope need be attached only to an arm projecting at right angles from the headstock.

(*b*) *Clocking*. This is chiming by means of a 'clock hammer' generally placed on the outside; or the bells may be sounded by ropes attached to the clappers themselves, as brought to great heights in Russia, with a single man controlling in his two hands the ropes from five or more large bells just above him.

(*c*) *Ringing*. This is where the bell is balanced upside down and swung through a full circle. It is made possible, and with least effort, by passing the rope round the flanged circumference of a large wheel, a method first introduced in the 16th century. It enables the ringer to time accurately the moment of the stroke, impossible with chiming, and making possible change-ringing.

4. *Change-ringing*. This numerical system of ringing a peal of bells in a constantly changing order is peculiarly English, but has spread to the former Dominions and the USA. The idea arose in Elizabethan times but was suppressed under the Puritans, so that its main history began with the Restoration, as a secular hobby combined with the duty of ringing for the Sunday services and for special engagements, notably weddings. The principles are first described in the *Tintinnabula* (1668) by C. R. Fabian Stedman, a Cambridge printer who had joined the Ancient Society of College Youths (founded in London in 1637); he followed this work nine years later with his comprehensive *Campanologia*.

A ring of bells may comprise from five to 12 bells, usually tuned to a major scale; the majority of rings in England include six. The bells are installed by the bell-hanger in an iron frame and are aligned in different directions to even out the stresses on the tower. Each of the hemp ropes leads from a spoke of the wheel to the circumference, thence down to the ringing chamber below, where the rope bears a fluffy, coloured grip or 'sally' up to 1 m. (3') long. From the rest position (Fig. 1*a*), the 'hand-stroke' starts the rotation, the sally falling to the floor, then swiftly rising; the ringer, with

the free end of the rope, then checks the swing (the bell having sounded once) as the next 'up' position (Fig. 1*b*) is approached. Then, at the correct moment, the rope is pulled for the 'back-stroke', on which the bell returns and the sally falls then rises by the smaller distance which returns it to position as in Fig. 1*a* (the bell having again sounded once). A necessary device is the ash-wood 'stay' fixed to the gudgeon (pivot) of each bell: should the bell more than just overtop the 'up' position, this stay, then pointing downwards, moves a horizontal beam or 'slider' against a fixed stop. This allows the bell to rest upright when ringing is not in progress; but the stay is also calculated to break should the momentum of the bell be so great that suddenly to check it might cause serious damage to the suspension.

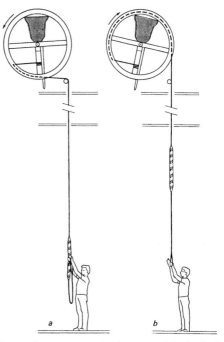

Fig. 1. Change-ringing; (*a*) the start and (*b*) the finish of the bell's trajectory.

Originally a ring was sounded from the smallest bell to the largest, this sequence being called 'Rounds'. Simple changes in the order were then made by varying the order of striking pairs of bells on the instructions of the master ringer (1, 2, 3, 4,; 2, 1, 4, 3; 2, 4, 1, 3; etc.). This system of 'call change', still practised in parts of Britain, grew in the early 17th century into what is now called 'change-ringing'. The total number of different changes obtainable is found by multiplying the number of bells thus: on three bells, $3 \times 2 \times 1 = $ six changes; on six bells, $6 \times$ five $\times \ldots \times 1 = 720$; on eight bells, 40,320 changes. The ringers' aim is, starting from Rounds, to ring as many changes, with no repetition, as time permits, finally coming back to Rounds. There are many thousands of ways of producing the changes, from the simple changing of pairs as above. If it is desired to ring changes on an odd number of bells, it is usual for the largest bell (the tenor) to be rung at the end of every sequence. This gives a sense of rhythm and completeness to the ringing and is preferred by many. Such 'odd bell-ringing' is called by a general name of Doubles on five bells, because two pairs change each time; Triples on seven bells (three pairs change); Caters on nine bells (four pairs change); and Cinques on 11 bells (five pairs change). The corresponding terms for 'even bell-ringing', with all of the bells changing, are Major on eight bells (as eight bells are invariably tuned to a major scale); Minor on six bells; Royal on ten bells; and Maximus on 12 bells. In addition to this general description each different method will have a name of its own—Grandsire Triples, Plain Bob Major, Cambridge Surprise Royal, for example.

The standard performance is a peal of at least 5,000 changes, all different and taking about three hours. Lesser lengths of changes are called Touches, Quarter-peals, etc. Because of improvements in bell engineering in recent years, it has been possible for one band of ringers to ring the whole extent of 40,320 changes on eight bells, without stopping and without repetition, and entailing more than 20 hours' continuous ringing, even on light bells.

Each year most ringing societies send representatives to a meeting of the Central Council of Bell Ringers, set up in 1891 and publisher of *The Ringing World*, weekly, founded 1911.

5. The powers of bells. The protective powers assigned to bells are well known. The 'passing bell', tolled to protect the soul of the dying from evil spirits; the ringing of the church bell to avert pestilence, still reported from Greece in the present century; the blessing of the bells (of a new set) by the bishop, continuing in Catholic churches (though in this connection not only bells, for not long ago in Malta custom required a priest to be summoned by a family to bless the new piano. Among mottoes inscribed on bells, one from the 15th century runs '*Vivos vico—mortuos plango—fulgura frango*' (calling the living to church, lamenting the deceased, breaking up the lightning; referred to by Schiller in *Das Lied von der Glocke*). The guardian of a chapel in the Tyrol had to watch for thunderstorms and then ring the bell for the other churches in the valley to take it up (magic and practical expediency going hand in hand). And to these mottoes may be added '*festa decoro*', marking the joyous occasions—weddings, national thanksgivings—when the bells are specially rung today.

Morris 1951; Price 1983; Westcott 1970; Wilson 1965.

Bell (of a wind instrument) (Fr.: *pavillon*, literally 'tent'; Ger.: *Schalltrichter*, 'sound funnel'; It.: *padiglione*; Sp.: *pabellón*). The flared end of a wind instrument. With brass instruments it serves an important acoustic purpose; with woodwind, such as oboe or clarinet, less so. In some scores (e.g. of Mahler) one may find in the wind parts the direction *Schalltrichter auf!* or *pavillon dans l'air*, for the player to raise the bell to project the sound directly forwards for added dramatic effect in fortissimo.

Bell chime. A term used, like *gong chime, where a set of bells, not tower bells, and often small, constitutes an instrument, normally played by a single person. The Chinese bell chime, *bianzhong* (*pien-chung*) has from eight to 24 bells, struck on the outside, of equal size but different thickness; extremely accurate tuning methods for them were known from antiquity. The chime is used in Confucian ritual music, as are also bells *bozhong* (*po-chung*) hung individually (see CHINA AND KOREA, 1*a*).

Bell harp. Now a rare curiosity, this has wire strings tuned to a scale and plucked with the thumbs while holding the instrument vertically and swinging it in the two hands to produce undulations in the sound. It has been known in two forms: by John Simcock of Bath from 1763 under the name 'English Harp' (later 'bell harp'); and a hundred years later as made, for example, by Richard Cook, London, from 1864, named 'Fairy Bells'.

Most preserved examples are of the latter type: rectangular, *c*.60 cm. (2′) tall, with eight or more strings running in the space between a strong wooden base-board, and a cover-plate that leaves the tops of the strings exposed for plucking. Say there are eight strings: the four higher-tuned are for the right thumb, the others for the left, with the peculiarity that in each group of four the shortest string lies closest to the centre-line of the instrument, the rest following thus (for a tuning in the key of C):

C D E F / C (upper) B A G.

To descend the scale the right thumb proceeds outwards from C (upper) to G, then the left thumb continues in the opposite direction from F to low C. (The plan is clearly exhibited by the oblique slots in the cover-plate which give access to the tuning pins.) The purpose of the arrangement is nowhere stated; but it possibly had some link with change ringing (see BELL, 4); at least some past owners of the Fairy Bells were themselves ringers, though by the early 20th century the instrument had made entries into popular musical entertainment.

Bell lyra. A glockenspiel mounted vertically for use in marching bands. See GLOCKENSPIEL, 4.

Bell plates. For imitating church bells: thick square or rectangular plates of steel or aluminium alloy up to 1 m. (3′) high and 3 mm. thick, hung on a stand. They were in use in theatres by early in the

20th century. Struck with a felt-covered mallet, they now sound pitches from *c* upwards. For special problems, as the four deep bells required by Wagner in *Parsifal*, see CHIME.

Bell tree (or 'bell tower'). An upright rod with handle at the bottom carries small inverted bowls of metal (or for children, coloured plastic) of graded size, one above the other. They may be separated, with the smallest on top (Christmas tree effect), or overlapping, the largest on top (allowing a tinkling glissando by running the beater down the whole set). See SISTRUM, Fig. 1b. There have also been small keyboard versions with the bells mounted on a horizontal axis.

'Bell tree' is also a name for 'Jingling Johnny' (Fr.: *chapeau chinois*; Ger.: *Schellenbaum*), frequently carried in military bands through the 19th century (sometimes later): a staff furnished with small bells or pellet-bells, with a brass crescent on top and a pair of horse-tails below. A souvenir of the 18th-century 'Turkish Music', it can be seen in *military band, Pl. 2. The *bell lyre has since succeeded it.

In Japan, the *suzu*, with tiers of pellet bells attached to a handle, is shaken in one hand at Shinto ceremonies and dances.

Bell wheel. Originally, from the 10th century, a dozen or more bells attached round the circumference of a large wheel mounted high on a church wall or in the tower, turned by a rope on feast days or at the Elevation. Later (15th–18th centuries) as an adjunct to the organ, the wheel turned by the organ bellows, chiefly in Germany (*Zimbelstern*, lit. 'star of bells'). There have been experiments to revive it.

Beme (byme, Early Eng.). A trumpet or war-horn, as in Psalm 98: 'with steven [voice] of bemes ledand-like to se[e]; with steven of beme horned that be'—for the Latin *'in tubis ductilibus* [of beaten metal] *et voce tubae cornea*' [ox-horn].

Bend. Guitarists, while or before making a note with the left hand on the fret, may pull (bend) the string sideways, raising the pitch through tightening it, then letting it return; and if continued while the string still sounds, it makes all kinds of vibrato. Hence 'bending' a note, now a recognized term in electronic music also, in which its imitation can be important. The technique figures prominently as an expressive device again in plucked instruments elsewhere, as in India (*sitar, *vina). On wind instruments an early jazz expression, 'dinge', has signified a corresponding effect made with the lips while blowing.

Bendir (or *bendair*). Frame drum of North Africa, chiefly Berber, looking like a large *tambour with a hoop *c*.20 cm. (8″) deep, without jingles but with a gut snare under the wide goatskin head, which is played on close to the rim with the fingers of both hands. The name seems to derive from Spanish *pandero* ('tambourine').

Bersagliers horn. See BUGLE, 3.

Biblical instruments. To know what the musical instruments named in the Bible actually were is made difficult by the almost complete absence of an ancient Israelite iconography, while written accounts from other sources are few and from far later times than the books of the Old Testament, in which are most of the references to instruments.

1. *150th Psalm*. The problems can best be put by going through the names as they occur in the 150th Psalm, which gives nearly all the important ones, listed below in these styles: 'English', Authorized Version of 1611; (Latin), the Vulgate: *Hebrew*.

(a) 'Trumpet' (*tuba*): *shofar. The ram's horn (in Jeremiah 51, 'last trump'); or else *ḥatzoṭzerah*, the metal trumpet (the silver trumpet described in Numbers 10) which may at first have resembled the short Egyptian instrument (see TRUMPET, 7). Psalm 98 names them both, translated in the Latin (see Beme), and by Wycliffe (who began his translation in 1378): 'in trumpis betun out with hamer, in vois of a trumpe of horn' (see also BEME). Occasionally the Hebrew has *keren*, 'horn' in a more general sense, as in Joshua 6 (Fall of Jericho) along with *shofar*.

(b) 'Psaltery' (*psalterium*): nebel (*nevel*). Greek writings point to a harp (vertical angular: see HARP, 10b; PSALTERIUM) but whether *nebel* meant this in earlier times cannot be established. In three psalms (from 33 onwards) *asor*, 'ten', comes next to it but not clearly as to whether referring to ten strings on a *nebel* or to some different instrument.

(c) 'Harp' (*cithara*): kinnor. A lyre, quite likely (to judge especially from a Philistine vase of *c*.1000 BC) of a kind known from Egypt, square-bodied, with asymmetrical arms, held forwards (see LYRE, 2).

(d) 'Timbrel' (*tympanum*): tof. Without doubt a frame drum (see DRUM, 4e), like a tambourine without jingles, played in antiquity especially by the womenfolk (Exodus 15, Judges 11), and in the psalm paired with 'dance' (chorus): *machol*. (In some 14th-century psalters, Lat. chorus is misunderstood as 'croud', *crwth.)

(e) 'Stringed instruments' (*cordae*): minnim, 'strings'.

(f) 'Organ' (*organum*): 'ugab. Meaning unknown. In Genesis and in Job, both of early date, 'ugab is preceded by *kinnor* and is translated in the Greek Septuagint by 'psalterion' or 'psalmos' (singing), becoming 'organa' in Psalm 150, evidently in the Greek sense of 'instruments'. It is purely a supposition of modern times that the Hebrew word refers to wind instruments (and that the 'u' vowel points to some flute). The English Revised Version replaced 'organ' by 'pipes'. Elsewhere both English versions put 'pipes' for (tibiae): ḥalil, which can with some confidence be understood as a reed-pipe; probably a double pipe (see AULOS), an instrument of public rejoicing (1 Kings 1) or lamentation (Jeremiah 48), as compare in the New Testament, Greek *auletai*, translated 'minstrels' in Matthew 9.

(g) 'Cymbals' (cymbala): mtziltayim (metziltayim). From 'to clash'. Important Temple instruments along with *nebel* and *kinnor*. The word is qualified in two ways, (i) 'loud' (benesonantes): shem'a, 'clear'; (ii) 'high-sounding' (jubilationis): teru'ah, 'harsh', or 'noisy'. Bronze cymbals c.10 cm. (4") in diameter have been excavated in the region of Israel, in some instances a pair joined by a fine chain. A question is whether the psalm points to different sorts or to different ways of sounding. Also possibly *idiophones are 1 Samuel 18, 'instruments of music' (sistrum): shalishim, meaning unknown; and 2 Samuel 6, 'cornets' (sistrum): mnaanim, from 'to shake'.

2. *Book of Daniel*. The instruments listed in this Book as those at the court of Nebuchadnezzar, and named in Aramaic, have presented translators with a desperate task (e.g. Engl. 'sackbut' (trombone) for the word *sabbeca*, perhaps denoting a kind of harp). Modern scholarship has brought forward various solutions (Sachs 1940).
Sendrey 1969.

Bīn. The North Indian *vina*.

Biniou. The bagpipe of Brittany. See BAGPIPE, 3b.

Bin-sasara. Japanese strung clapper, and one of the exotic sound-makers that were introduced to Western percussion by Carl Orff and are now manufactured for school ensembles. Up to 100 thin wooden plaques about 7 cm. (2½") long and 2.5 cm. (1") wide are strung by their ends on a cord with a hard-grip at each end. By these the instrument is held up in a 'horseshoe', while a deft movement of the hands makes the plaques clatter against each other in fast sequence in one direction and then in the other. It is associated with a village 'snow festival' along with flute and barrel drum. (*Sasara* is a general word for rattles; see JAPAN, 1a).

In Europe a folk instrument somewhat similar is a string of 15 to 20 wooden plaques, likewise manipulated with both hands, met in Russia, also in Portugal, where again it is sounded at winter festivals.

Bird calls and lures. See WHISTLES AND BIRD CALLS.

Bird organ. See BARREL ORGAN, 2.

Biwa. The classical Japanese lute, in shape resembling the Chinese *pipa*, from which it derives, but at once distinguished today in having only four or five high frets, whereas in a *pipa* the frets are very numerous and extend over the belly. (For the quite different Japanese long lute, see SHAMISEN.)

The pear-shaped body is shallow in depth and usually has two small crescent-shaped soundholes. It flows into the short neck, carved in the same piece and joined to a turned-back pegbox for four or five deep-tuned strings (silk, gut, nylon) struck with a large triangular wooden plectrum (*bachi*).

There are several varieties. Closest to the instrument introduced from China in the 8th century is the metre-long *gakubiwa* of the court music (see JAPAN, Ex. 1). The strings are tuned to the required mode, several of which put the first three strings in fourths (and the 4th string variously below). Smaller (c.70 cm., 28"), is the *heikebiwa*, derived from an older *mosobiwa* to which blind priests chanted Buddhist legends, and long associated with performance of the popular epic, the 'Tale of the Heikin' (on a medieval interclan feud'; the strings may be tuned in the pattern *g d B G* and are tensioned by the finger pressing between the frets, giving flexibility to the pitch of notes. The *satsuma biwa* (named from a province) arose in the 19th century, c.90 cm. (3') with five frets and played with the widest type of biwa plectrum, often struck also against the wooden belly.

Bladder and string. See BUMBASS.

Bladder-pipe (Ger.: *Platerspiel*). Mainly a historical instrument (13th–16th centuries) though sometimes still sold at fairs in Europe in small versions for children. Basically a simplified relative of the bagpipe, with a pig's bladder (or rubber balloon) tied to enclose the reed instead of a bag, and kept inflated by blowing into a short tube, pressing the bladder to the mouth to maintain air pressure. In some early pictures the pipe has a curved crumhorn-like end, or the holes appear to be made in an ox-horn. The present toy versions have an *idioglot single reed, though it is possible that a double reed was once used. It was chiefly a popular or folk instrument but perhaps not entirely so (a bladder can be deodorized with ammonia, then kept pliable with brine). Some true bagpipes use an animal's bladder for the bag, placing it under the arm, i.e. not as with a bladder-pipe in the above senses.

Blockflöte. Ger.: *recorder.

Blown gong. The name given by Jaap Kunst, the great authority on Indonesian music, to the *gong bumbung* (or *gumbang*): a bamboo instrument blown to produce a deep sound as a village substitute for the large gong of a *gamelan. The wide bamboo, about 60 cm. (24") long and 10 cm. (4") wide, is stopped at the lower end by a septum. The open end is blown into through a much narrower bamboo introduced into it, while at the same time singing a deep note with a vibrato, in all with a gong-like effect (so it is said).

Bo (or *po*; Chinese, 'to strike').

1. A cymbal.

2. *Bofu* (*po-fu*), a barrel drum (see DRUM, 4*b*) of Confucian ritual.

3. *Bozhong* (*po-chung*), a type of temple bell.

Boatswain's pipe. See WHISTLE, 2.

Bocal. See CROOK, 1.

Bock. See BAGPIPE, 5*a*.

Bodhrán (Gaelic, pron. 'borán'). Irish *frame drum, since the 1950s popular in folk music. It is like a large, deep tambourine, without the jingles, held by a rope, or crossed wires, attached across the inside. The other hand strikes the skin with a wooden beater knobbed at the ends, twisting the wrist. By varying the stroke, and pressing skin underneath with the holding hand, a variety of sounds are produced. Before its present popularity it was a little-known folk instrument of the west of Ireland (perhaps first made from a winnowing tray), used in the Christmas-tide 'hunting the wren', an old custom formerly known also in France and the Isle of Man.
Such 1985.

Boehm system. Term for the fingering system of the modern *flute and *clarinet, derived from Theobald Boehm's invention (1832) for the flute (see FLUTE, 4*c*). The chief identifying feature is the arrangement by which the right-hand first finger makes the note F, not as on earlier and 'simple system' models, F♯. The saxophone too has this arrangement, but since it has had no other it is not described a 'Boehm system'. For rarer applications, see OBOE, 3*c*, and, a special adaptation, FLAGEOLET, 3.

Bogen (Ger.). 1. Bow of a stringed instrument.

2. Of brass instruments, see CROOK, 2.

Bogenklavier. See GEIGENWERK.

Bombarde. 1. The 14th- and 15th-century French and English word for an alto-pitched shawm (see SHAWM, 2). The name was probably borrowed from the artillery bombard, a kind of mortar. In Germany the word 'bombarde' became corrupted to 'Pommer', though some 17th-century scores have 'bombardo' (see SHAWM, 1*b*).

2. In France, 'bombarde' continues to denote a double-reed instrument, namely the small shawm-like bombarde which today accompanies the bagpipe in Brittany (see BAGPIPE, 3). It is about 33 cm. (13″) long, usually with small detachable bell and often an open key for the right little finger, closed for the bottom note *b♭'*. It is now also produced industrially, with white plastic tips. In Liguria and some neighbouring parts of Italy a similar 'bombarda' accompanied a bagpipe ('cornamusa') up to the early 20th century—as in the south a corresponding instrument is regularly seen (see ZAMPOGNA, 2).

Bombardon. A former military-band name for the *tuba, still often seen in Britain in printed band parts. Deriving from 'bombarde' (see BOMBARDE, 1) the name is met in Germany from the 1820s for various bass cup-mouthpiece instruments, as *bass horn or *ophicleide, then, from *c.*1835, valved predecessors of the tuba itself. In Italy, the diminutive, *bombardino*, means the *euphonium.

Bombo (Sp., Port., 'drum'). Familiar name for a *bass drum, or in folk music (as all over Latin America and the West Indies) for a drum which is generally larger than a *caja* (*caisse*, 'side drum') and struck with one, or two, beaters with padded ends.

Bonang. Indonesian gong-chime, a main instrument of the *gamelan. The brightly polished, deep-sided gongs ('kettles') (Pl. 1) rest boss upwards in

Pl. 1. Bonang.

two parallel rows, the five to seven gongs of a row placed upon two cords which run the length of a low wooden stand. The gongs of the row further from the player are tuned to a scale an octave above the nearer row, though to facilitate fast playing across the octave, gongs an octave apart are mostly placed not directly opposite each other. They are struck on the boss with a pair of sticks wound with string. The gongs of a bonang are much the same in overall dimensions, but differ in the width of the flat annular part which immediately surrounds the boss. Most of the vibration takes place in this ring, and its width is a main determinant of the pitch.

In the gamelan, two bonangs form a pair, placed at a right angle to each other, with one player to each: the lowest note of the larger, *bonang barung*, is an octave below that of the smaller, *bonang panerus* or *peking*, so that (since each covers two octaves) their ranges overlap by an octave. Since a gamelan may play music in two different scale-systems, *slendro* and *pelog*, a *barung* and a *peking* are required for each system, and are placed beside one another in two L's.

Bones. As folk instruments, traditionally dried rib bones from cooked beef. Commercial varieties are made of rosewood or hard plastic some 15 cm. (6") long, almost flat in section and slightly curved, and comprise a pair for each hand. One bone is gripped between first and second fingers and held still across the palm; the other, held between second and third fingers, is struck against the first while shaking the wrist. Songs and dances can be accompanied very expertly (even making deliberately contrasted pitches), the bones having been popular instruments since long before the Victorian association with troupes of 'black' minstrels.

Played in the same way, of similar size and a pair in each hand, are hardwood boards (see CASTANETS, Fig. 1*b*), each cut with a wide V notch near one end to fit between the base of the fingers. In Spain and Portugal they are called 'castanets', elsewhere 'clappers'. In Swiss schools, children may make them to play at Carnival time while singing a special song. They are clearly related to 'the bones', and are sometimes in fact carved from beef bones.

Bongos. Among the percussion instruments of Latin American dance music—*claves, *guiro, and *maracas—are three single-headed Afro-Cuban drums, bongos, *conga drum, and *timbales, now modernized and manufactured with screw-tensioning, etc. They are also used (especially bongos) to some extent in rock music and modern compositions. The bongos are a pair of small hand-played drums, 15 to 20 cm (6–8"). in diameter, joined together for placing between the knees or on a stand (Fig. 1*a*). The shells are often coopered in two woods of contrasting hue, such as maple and elm. The heads, traditionally of goatskin, can be tuned about a fourth apart. Rapid extemporized rhythmic patterns are played with fingers, thumb, or the whole hand, on or away from the rims—as with *tablas, and many other hand drums.

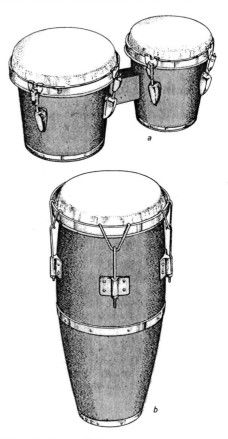

Fig. 1. (*a*) Bongos; (*b*) Conga drum.

Boobams (the name an inversion of 'bamboos'). Percussion instrument of definite pitch devised in recent years in the USA, at first for studio music but now entering the orchestral percussion required in modern works. Made up of measured lengths of bamboo or substitute material up to 10 cm. (4") wide, each has one end covered by a tensioned plastic membrane, struck by the fingers or a soft-headed beater. The heard pitches of the notes are determined by the lengths of the tubes, the instrument behaving in this respect as a 'struck *aerophone' (cf. STAMPING TUBE). The tubes are placed vertically in a diatonic row, e.g. of two octaves from *f* upwards, with a separate row for the sharps.

Border pipe. See BAGPIPE, 2c.

Bourdon (Fr.; Ital., Sp.: *bordone, bordón*). In Romance languages the general meaning is of a deep buzzing sound, as in French where it means 'bumble bee' (this insect's wings setting up a frequency of around 200 Hz, the pitch of tenor *g*, more or less; a gnat may buzz about an octave higher). In musical senses it can denote: a deep-tuned string of a stringed instrument (see CRWTH; FIDDLE, 2); the drone of a *bagpipe or *hurdy-gurdy; a deep *organ register; the largest *bell in a belfry; the snare of a *drum; or in the West Indies a *stamping tube. In 15th-century England, the three parts in vocal music were 'treble, mean, and burdon', where we would now say 'treble, tenor, and bass'. The word may be of Low Latin onomatopoeic origin.

Bouts. In the body of a violin, cello, etc., the outward-bulging parts are the 'upper' and 'lower bouts', and the inward curves between form the 'middle' or 'centre bouts' (from 'bout' in an old sense of a 'bend' or 'fold').

Bouzouki (from Turk.: *bozuk*). Greek stringed instrument of popular music since the rise, at the end of the 19th century, of the *rebetiko* music in the Aegean seaports. It is now also widely manufactured elsewhere, following the impact of Greek café music and films. It is a metal-strung plectrum-played lute, a metre (yard) long and belonging to the large family of long lutes (see LUTE, 7), the neck being very long compared with the size of the body.

The pear-shaped, round-backed body is built up from ribs, and in the course of the 20th century has come to embody much of the technology of the *mandolin, and latterly of the *guitar, with plastic scratch-plate on the belly, plastic ornament elsewhere, a fingerboard extended on to the belly, fixed metal frets up to 26 in number, and geared tuning. As with the mandolin, there are now models with flat backs, often preferred in Western-style folk music, in which the bouzouki is quite often seen. Also, instead of the Greek three courses of wire strings tuned in the pattern *d' a d*, there are generally four courses tuned as the first four strings of the guitar (or a tone lower) and of about guitar-string length, for easier interchangeability.

Greek playing is very agile, with introductory flourishes vigorously performed in the mood which suits the song to follow. Earlier in the 20th century the instrument was still built like the Turkish *saz, with deep body and tied wire frets for playing in modal scales.

Anoyanakis 1979.

Bow (Fr.: *archet*; Ger.: *Bogen*; It., Sp.: *arco*; Ru.: *smychok*). Of a stringed instrument, that by which a string is put in sustained vibration. See also MUSICAL BOW (a bow with bow-string here forming the instrument itself).

1. Action. A *violin bow may have up to 200 strands of hairs selected from the tails of horses, by tradition white (a visual preference). The hairs have a natural surface of flat scales pointing away from the root yet the bow, having been rosined, works equally in both directions of movement, owing to the myriad specks of rosin which adhere to the hair. Under the microscope they can be seen as close-packed glittering yellow particles.

The string, deflected by the bow, then slips back over it, repeating the cycle at the frequency of the note (dependent on the length, tension, etc.; see STRINGED INSTRUMENTS, 1)—for as one knows, the pitch of the note is practically independent of the bow speed (else there could be no such thing as a violin). The string can slip back while still in contact with the bow owing to the great reduction in frictional force once two surfaces are moving in opposite relative directions ('dynamic friction' as opposed to the 'static friction' when there is no relative motion, as when the string is moving with the bow). But looking at the matter in more detail, it was long ago demonstrated (e.g. Helmholtz 1875) that there is more to it than a simple displacement and recovery under the force of tension. The angular discontinuity given to the string (deflection) passes along the string to the ends following a parabolic path (not straight to the ends as with a plucked string), changing sides on the return, during which the string commences a fast slip-back occupying a shorter time than the deflection (a 'sawtooth' wave-form). The physics proves extremely complex (involving relative velocities of bow and of lateral motion of the string at each instant in the cycle), while not all authorities are wholly agreed over every detail.

The bow is moved across the string at or close to a right angle (a 'straight bow'). This also avoids risk of exciting in the string longitudinal (as opposed to transverse) vibration resulting in a squeak.

2. Types of bow. Fig. 1 shows four of the many types of bow that have been or still are used. In (*b*)—found in Asia and shown in early medieval pictures—the stick, roughly bow-shaped, is grasped by the handle, normally palm upward if the fiddle is held downwards (like a *viol) or palm downward if held upwards like a violin. In (*a*) again in Asia, and in various forms in early Europe, the stick, often straight or nearly so, has the hank of hair loosely attached and then tightened while playing by the fingers of the bowing hand. The next (*c*) is an example of a 'baroque' violin bow (see VIOLIN, 6a), a product of great advances in design and craftsmanship, with a finely tapered stick of 'snake-wood' (*Brosimum aubleti*), almost straight or slightly arched upwards, and a 'pike' head. The 'frog' at first rested in a slot in the stick for the hair to be tightened with fingers or thumb, but tensioning by drawing the frog back with a screw came in during the 18th century. When the hair is tightened, the stick arches more. The modern form of bow (Fig. 1*d*) developed gradually from the mid-18th century, and was finally determined in the work from 1775 and onwards of François Tourte (1747–1835) in Paris, with John Dodd in London and Wilhelm Cramer (not a maker but a player, who came to live in London) arriving at similar results at about the same time. It is commonly distinguished from the older bow as the 'Tourte bow'. The stick is of Brazil wood, *Caesalpina echinata* (the dye-wood, also sold as 'Pernambuco wood', lighter than snakewood), given an inward curve by heat. In the frog (normally of ebony, sometimes ivory) the hair is wedged in a recess, and kept there by a 'slide', where another wedge spreads the hair flat. On screwing back the frog, the two opposite points of attachment of the hair are brought closer together and the stick begins to straighten out.

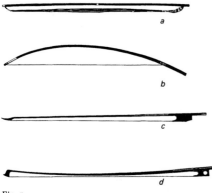

Fig. 1.

An important technical difference between use of the older outcurved or straight bow stick and of the later incurved one arises when it comes to pressing on the string with the upper part of the bow. With the old bow, bending the hair over the string draws the ends of the hair closer together, to which the stick answers by arching further in the thinner part, bringing the point and the frog closer together. With the new bow, on the other hand, where bending the hair first acts towards straightening the stick, the distance from the far end of this to the frog is scarcely changed on pressing harder, while the ends of the hair are brought closer by relatively very little. Consequently the effect of greater bow pressure on the string becomes dissipated through flexure of the stick far less in the new bow than in the older. Many kinds of accentuation, attack, and *crescendo* that are made with the new bow are difficult or barely possible with the old. Conversely, the limitations of the old can bring a sensitively singing style of bowing which is part and parcel of the 'baroque' violin playing with which audiences have today grown increasingly familiar.

For a summary of the different ways of bowing on the violin, see VIOLIN, 5*c*. A good bow is prized no less than a good instrument—cellists have been known to say even more so. The names of great bow makers are as renowned as those of the great instrument makers, and there are great collectors of violin bows alone.

A violin or other bow is occasionally employed to sound instruments other than strings: modern music may call for a cymbal or vibraphone to be sounded with a cello bow, bowing on the edge or end. See also NAIL VIOLIN and MUSICAL SAW.

3. *First appearance of bowing.* Antiquity has left no evidence whatever of bowing strings. This is first seen in a few pictures of the 10th century AD from Byzantium, and from Spain, in a Mozarabic Apocalypse of pre-950. From the same time is the earliest written allusion to bowing, in the Arabic treatise of Al Farabi (d. *c*.950) of Baghdad (Erlanger 1930): the *rabāb*, on which 'strings are drawn over strings'. One view (Bachmann 1964; see FIDDLE) is that the practice had arisen among horse-rearing peoples of Central Asia, who today preserve legends of the magical origin of the fiddle, the 'steed' of the shaman, master of the spirits, as he journeys from our world to the upper and lower spheres. We find features common to all fiddles across Asia— particularly how (see FIDDLE, 1) the notes are almost always made simply by pressing on the tight string (i.e. not against the solid neck or a fingerboard)—which point to a departure from the ancient tradition of plucked instruments even to the extent that one could see the bowed stringed instrument as having come into existence quite independently from the beginning in its remote homelands.

Strings have also been sounded simply with a stick or plant stem, resined or moistened, as in China from well before the bow is mentioned (see AJAENG), or as where an old street fiddler continues to play the violin with every shred of hair worn away leaving nothing but a rosin-covered stick. (Also without hair are the rosin-covered wheels of the *hurdy-gurdy, mechanical violins, and friction keyboard instruments: see GEIGENWERK.) See also VIOLIN, FIDDLE.
Bachmann 1964; Boyden 1965, 1980; Erlanger 1930; Retford 1964.

Bowed lute. A modern expression often met to cover the term 'lutes' where used in the general sense of stringed instruments which are composed of a body and a neck, and are played with a bow (and thus including the violin). See classification, 3*b* (i). Alternatively, as in this book, 'fiddle' may serve in the same sense.

Bowed lyre (bowed harp). Modern term for some folk instruments, distantly related to the *crwth, played up to the beginning of the 20th century in Karelia (Finland) and Estonia (USSR), and now enjoying some revival among folk music groups.

They are often of long rectangular shapes, played on the knee. Of the two to four horsehair strings, the melody string is stopped with the backs of the fingers through openings in the body, other strings sounding a drone, all being bowed together. See also GUE (Shetland Isles, formerly).

Andersson 1930; Panum 1941.

Bowed psaltery. A modern instrument developed in Germany from the 1930s, chiefly for school music. The 50-cm. (20″) long soundbox in the shape of an isosceles triangle can be placed on a table or held in one hand, resting the short side against the body. The 25 wire strings run to tuning pins placed along both of the long sides: 15 on one side tuned to a diatonic scale of two octaves, and 10 on the opposite side for the sharps. A lightweight arched bow is held in the centre and finds the required string in the space between its tuning pin and the next pin above. To pass from one string to another the bow is lifted to clear the pins, so that the playing is detached, though not too audibly so, since the sound from the undamped strings rings on.

Bowed zither. Several kinds were produced from 1823 onwards by Austrian and Bavarian *zither manufacturers and may now be found as antiques. Placed flat on a table (like a zither) and played with a violin or special bow, they have wire strings, three or four, passing over a zither-type fingerboard with 29 metal frets. Early models are heart-shaped or triangular, with the fingerboard down the middle. Later designs (as the *Streichmelodeon*, 1856) roughly imitate the shape of the violin and are tuned as this, but with a difference that, when placed on the table with the tuning machines on the left, the lowest-tuned string comes on the far side (whereas with a violin it would be on the near side). The 'trumpet zither' has a metal horn on the neck, which itself is hollow. The *Philomele* (Munich, c.1850) most closely approaches the violin, being held up like one, with the strings in violin order, though retaining the fretted fingerboard. See also PSALMODIKON; LANGELEIK, 3 (FIDHLA).

Brass band. A band composed wholly or mainly of brass instruments with percussion, in contrast to a *military or concert band, in which woodwind instruments take equal place.

1. *The British brass band* (Pl. 1). The great majority of bands are members of the National Brass Band Club, under the rules of which the players are strictly amateur, only the conductor or trainer being permitted the status of a professional musician. Each band aims to muster the standard instrumentation as laid down by the rules of the band contests, with approximately 25 players in all. The Salvation Army has the second greatest number of bands, over 1,000; they use the same instruments but have no rule regarding how many players should make up the band.

(*a*) *Instruments.* The instruments are as follows, all the brass parts, save for the bass trombone, being transposing so that the fingering for the written notes (see VALVE, 1) is the same for all of the eight different kinds of valved instrument.

E♭ *soprano cornet* (sounds a third higher).

B♭ *cornets* (sounding a tone lower). Four parts, normally with three players on the solo part, two on the second, and two on the third. The 'Repiano cornet & flugel' part is shared by one cornet and one *flugel horn, playing together or solo as marked. 'Repiano' is the brass band form of the word *ripieno*. The other brass instruments, apart from the trombones, are those which have the bell pointing upwards (historically they derive mainly from the family of *saxhorns). There is normally one player per part save where noted.

E♭ *tenor horn* (or, for short, 'horn') (three parts, sounding a sixth lower than written). The smallest of these instruments, played with a deep vase-shaped mouthpiece.

B♭ *baritone* (two parts, sounding a ninth lower). Pitched as the *euphonium, but with a slimmer appearance owing to the narrower bore, suited to filling the harmony above the bass; played with a cup-shaped mouthpiece.

Trombones (three parts as in the orchestra; the 1st and 2nd, however, have the parts transposed as for the baritone). The bass trombone is the only non-transposed wind part, and was up to recent years always played on the G bass trombone (see TROMBONE, 4).

B♭ *euphonium* (one part, sounding a ninth lower; sometimes two players). With wide dimensions, the euphonium is suited both to the bass line in its upper octave and to solo passages in the tenor register: the 'cello' of the band.

E♭ *bass* (sounds an octave and a sixth lower; usually two players). The smaller of the two *tubas.

B♭ *bass* (sounds two octaves and a tone lower; one or two players). Usually called 'BB♭ Bass'; the larger tuba.

Drums (bottom space in the music, bass drum; 2nd space, cymbals; 3rd space, side drum. Two players).

(*b*) *Rise of the band, and contests.* The bands began in Lancashire; the Stalybridge Old Band, founded in 1814, is claimed as the first of the working men's bands, though it was not (in those pre-valve days) a brass band but composed on the lines of a small military band, with clarinets and keyed bugle playing the melodies. Published band arrangements, largely transcriptions of operatic numbers, appeared in the 1840s, and entirely for brass instruments. The first British Open Brass Band Championship was in 1853, in Manchester; the first National Championship in 1900 in London, at the Crystal Palace (burnt down in 1936) when there were over 20,000 bands in the country.

Pl. 1. The Stalybridge Band (c. 1904). Among the instruments visible; upper left, euphonium, tenor horn, flugel horn, and on far right, back row, baritone. In front, E♭ and (the larger) BB♭ basses.

The following were the obligatory test pieces for the two British Championships over the years 1974–8:

British Open Championship: Gilbert Vintner, 'James Cook'; Elgar Howarth, 'Fireworks'; Percy Fletcher, 'An Epic Symphony'; G. Bailey, arr. Frank Wright, 'Diadem of Gold'; Berlioz, arr. Wright, 'Benvenuto Cellini Overture'.

National Championship: Malcolm Arnold, 'Fantasy for Brass Band'; Robert Farnon, 'Une Vie de Matelot'; Eric Ball, 'Sinfonietta for Brass Band, The Wayfarer'; Edward Gregson, 'Connotation for Brass Band'; Arthur Bliss, arr. Eric Ball, 'Checkmate'.

2. *Other countries*. In the USA, the Boston Brass Band was founded in 1835, after which the bands rose to a peak of popularity in the years 1860–80. In Australia, the army bands are all brass. In France a *fanfare* may include saxophones as well as brass, while in many countries the outdoor music which English-speaking visitors always refer to as a 'brass band' will most likely include clarinets also.

Russell and Elliott 1936.

Brass instruments (Fr.: *cuivres*; Ger.: *Blechblasinstrumente*; It.: *ottoni*; Ru.: *mundshtuchnye instr.*; Sp.: *instrumentos a boquilla*). The instruments of this large family are sounded by vibration of the player's lips, which are placed against the rim of a metal mouthpiece of cup or vase shape to form a small aperture controlled from the sides of the mouth. The airflow makes the lip surfaces vibrate (widening and narrowing the aperture in alternation) at frequencies determined by the muscles in conjunction with the strong feedback from the various modes of vibration aroused in the air-column of the instrument.

1. *The mouthpiece*. This is normally turned from a casting. Fig. 1 shows the external taper of the stem, to fit into the reverse-tapered socket of the instrument, while internally, the stem normally expands conically (the 'backbore').

The primary determinant of tone-colour, so strikingly different through the brass instruments, lies in the length and profile of the tubing; yet each requires its particular shape and size of mouthpiece cup as history has evolved it in conjunction with the tube-form itself. A width of around 17 mm. is average for *trumpet, *cornet, *flugel horn, and also for the *horn. The brilliant sound of the trumpet (prominent upper partials in the tone) is made with the shallowest cup (Fig. 1a), average depth 10 mm.; the darker sound of the horn (few partials in its normal mellow tone) with a cup more than twice as deep (c). Trombones and tubas, playing normally in lower registers, use cups wider and deeper in proportion (b, trombone). The larger size allows wider lip apertures favouring amplitude

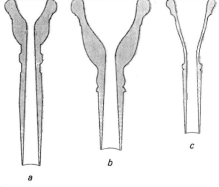

Fig. 1.

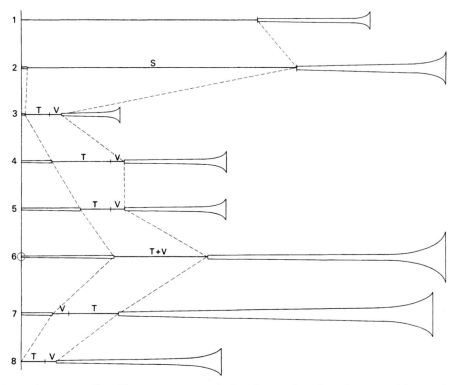

Fig. 2. Specimen profiles of brass instruments with the tube straightened out (T, tuning slide, V, valves). Cylindrical sections are indicated by a single line. 1. Natural trumpet. 2. Trombone (S, slide). 3. Piccolo trumpet. 4. B♭ trumpet. 5. Cornet. 6. B♭ horn. 7. Euphonium. 8. Flugel horn.

of vibration at low frequencies. The horn, however, has been developed in design to produce strong low notes with its mouthpiece no wider than a trumpet's. Clearly there is more to these matters than a simple relation of shape and size to the sounds produced: modern science has gone deeply into questions of resonances within the mouthpiece cup as well as through the instrument itself up to the bell, and led to explanations of a complexity that precludes any attempt at a summary in brief (see ACOUSTICS—Benade; Campbell and Greated).

2. *The tube.* Fig. 2 shows diagrammatically how the typical tubings of various instruments would appear if straightened out: for clarity, cylindrical sections are indicated by a plain line; conical sections, and the hyperbolic bell section, in profile.

(*a*) No. 1. A pure example of what is known as 'cylindrical bore': a baroque trumpet, a 'natural' instrument (having no valves). This bore, with its relatively short bell section, is historically associated with trumpets and also with trombones (2), though modern trombones have a longer bell expansion, accounting for over 40 per cent of the total when the slide is not extended. In most modern trumpets (3, 4), and in the cornet (5), the expansion takes

up half the total; and there is a tapered section (the 'mouthpipe') at the beginning of the tube. With a cornet the taper is long enough and (from smaller width by the mouthpiece) steep enough to bring a distinctive shade of sound.

As to the width of the cylindrical tube, it will be found that roughly the same internal diameter in the region of 10–12 mm. holds throughout Fig. 2 between the two zigzag lines (save for being often larger today among the deeper instruments). This can probably be put down to the fact that up to the 18th century most makers of brass instruments were primarily trumpet-makers, with their big routine job of brazing over a mandrel length after length of tubing, brass or silver, of the width required for trumpets, then produced in quantity for ceremonial and military uses. The same-sized tubing would later be a first choice for the cylindrical parts of other instruments, notably the horn.

(*b*) The French horn, straightened out in No. 6, might at first, early in the 18th century, have a true 'conical bore' which expands gently all the way to the flared bell (see HORN, 4*a*). The great feature, however, is the very small initial width at the mouthpiece socket (ringed in the diagram), far smaller than in any other brass instrument and taking a narrow-stemmed mouthpiece, crucial elements in the recipe for the magic of horn sound. From the mid-18th century onwards, *crooks and tuning slides, and then valves, have necessarily introduced a considerable length of trumpet-width cylindrical tubing, but with barely noticeable effects upon the quality. The horn remains in musical effect 'conical', just as the trumpet (4) still counts as 'cylindrical', though both are, in build, in their different ways 'cylindro-conical'.

(c) Nos. 7 and 8 illustrate a very different series of conical-bore instruments, mainly post-classical band instruments—flugel horn (8), tenor horn, baritone, and euphonium (7), and the tuba—all of them derived in some measure from the *bugle. The bore expands throughout save where interrupted by the valves, and begins at the mouthpiece socket with a full trumpet width or more. The tube thus becomes very wide, especially with euphonium and tuba, containing a large volume of air in relation to length—recalling the ancient cowhorn from which the bugle itself derives. The tone-colours are round and bland and the instruments are capable of great carrying power; as a band approaches from the distance the euphonium is likely to be the first to reach the ears after the bass drum.

Table I shows the comparative pitch and approximate tube-length of the various brass instruments. The outlined areas give the tonality range of the natural trumpet and horn (baroque/classical period) obtained by means of the different *crooks; see also HORN, 6b.

The brass are wind instruments in which the bell is vitally important, acting in conjunction with the mouthpiece to establish resonances over a *harmonic series which the lips can then select from: a matter on which brass-playing absolutely depends. Every note is emitted through the bell—save in the minority of former types which have keys covering holes down the side (see KEYED BUGLE; KEYED TRUMPET; OPHICLEIDE) and are on that account rather more difficult to sound at greatest volume on all notes. The bell is formed to a flared profile that is either hyperbolic by design, or approximates to this through a maker's empirical scheme for proportioning the widths at the different points to the distance back from the rim. A wide conical tube can itself act as a bell without necessarily developing into a flare, as in some old designs of tuba and bugle.

3. *Making and maintenance.* Brass tube used to be made from sheet metal (originally obtained from 'battery mills') of average thickness 0.5 mm., bedded round an iron mandrel, soldered with spelter, and filed and polished. In 20th-century manufacture, seamless drawn tube has been available, and bell flares may be spun from a brass disc over a steel former. Yet the old method is also still in use for bells, cutting from sheet as marked on a template. For a strong seam as the bell widens, the meeting edges are generally cut with square teeth which are interlocked before soldering and filing; often it is necessary to insert a gusset to fill the space towards the wide end where the edges do not meet. The rim itself is finally strengthened with

TABLE I.

Tube-length to nearest foot	Pitch (open fundamental)	(a) Cylindrical bore	(b) Horn bore	(c) Wide conical bore
2′	b♭	Piccolo B♭ trumpet		
3′	f	F trumpet		
	e♭	Soprano cornet		Soprano flugel
	d	D trumpet		(continental)
4′	c	C trumpet		
	B♭	B♭ trumpet, cornet		Flugel horn, Bugle
6′	G			Bugle (USA)
	F	Former F trumpet	F alto horn, Tenor cor	
	E♭	Cavalry trumpet		Tenor (alto) horn
	D	Baroque trumpet		
8′	C	Bass trumpet		Ophicleide (or B♭)
	B♭′	Bass trumpet (military)	Trombone B♭ horn	Baritone, Euphonium, Tenor Wagner tuba
12′	G′		G bass trombone	
	F′		F bass trombone F horn	F tuba, Bass Wagner tuba
	E♭′			E♭ tuba and Sousaphone
	D′		Trompe de chasse	
16′	C′			C tuba ('CC')
	B♭″		Contrabass trombone	B♭ tuba ('BB♭') and Sousaphone

a strong wire lapped into the rim, or with a flat 'garland' on which the maker used often to stamp his name.

Tapered sections of the tube (as on the left in Fig. 2) are made over a tapered steel mandrel, bedding the tubing down on to this by pushing through a graded series of holes in an iron plate, then smoothing. The various bends and 'bows' (U-bends, in the USA 'crooks') are made while the heated tube is filled with molten lead. The parts are then assembled using soft solder (though not for the valves) to facilitate dismantling for repairs. The most common damage incurred in use, namely dents, is traditionally made good by shaking steel balls ('dent balls') inside the tube against the dent; or if in the bell, with a suitable mallet, then planishing. Jammed-in mouthpieces or slides can be troublesome problems (if the application of oil inside and out fails); but in the larger cities there will be an expert repairer possessing special mouthpiece extractors and so on. (See Brand 1942; Springer 1976.)

4. *Basic playing techniques.* We may first look at a familiar 'natural' instrument, the bugle. With its tube-length of around 130 cm. (51″) it has a harmonic series based on a fundamental of B♭ (see Table 1). As with many brass instruments the fundamental itself is not used. The bugler sounds harmonics 2 to 6, shown in Ex. 1 in the traditional notation which transposes the series into the key of C (see TRANSPOSING INSTRUMENTS). He 'pitches' each note in turn: that is, he hears the note in advance in his head, then tightens the lips to the degree, learnt from the first days of tuition, by which they vibrate at each required frequency.

Ex. 1.

Valves are a means—the trombone slide is another—for filling in the compass chromatically by making instant changes to the tube-length without interfering with the emission of all notes through the bell. For their basic fingering, see VALVES, 1.

5. *Other brass instruments.* One cannot hope to enter every kind of brass instrument that ever existed, such as many ephemeral valved designs of the 19th century, unsolved mysteries from the 18th, and all the brass (or bronze, etc.) species of antiquity and of non-Western cultures. Entries are as follows: (Western brass): ALTO HORN, BALLAD HORN, BARITONE, BASS TRUMPET, BOMBARDON, BUGLE, CIMBASSO, CLARINO, CLAVICOR, COACH HORN, CORNET, CORNO, DUPLEX, EUPHONIUM, FLUGEL HORN, HELICON, HORN, HUNTING HORN, KEYED BUGLE, KEYED TRUMPET, MELLOPHONE, OPHICLEIDE, POST-HORN, RUSSIAN HORN, SAXHORN, SLIDE TRUMPET, SOUSAPHONE, TENOR COR,

TENOR HORN, TENOR TUBA, TROMBA, TROMBONE, TRUMPET, TUBA, VALVED TROMBONE, WAGNER TUBA; (Non-Western and ancient): BEME, BUCCINA AND CORNU, BUYSINE, KARNA, LITUUS (with CARNYX), LUR, NAFIR, OLIPHANT, SRINGA; and for the Roman *tuba*, TRUMPET, 7*b*; (In addition, instruments likewise sounded with the lips but not of brass): ALPHORN, BASS HORN, CLARÍN, CONCH, CORNETT, COWHORN, DIJERIDU, ERKE, FINGERHOLE HORN, ROZHOK, SERPENT, SHOFAR, TRUTRUCA, VACCINE; also HORN, 8, TRUMPET, 8.

Bahnert *et al.* 1958; Baines 1976; Carse 1939; and see under individual instruments.

Bratsche. Ger. *viola.

Brazilian tambourine. See JINGLE RING.

Brian Boru pipes. See BAGPIPE, 2*b*.

Bridge (Fr.: *chevalet*; Ger.: *Steg*; It.: *ponticello*). The component of a stringed instrument which transfers string vibrations to the soundboard. It may be a 'movable bridge' (as on the *violin); or it is a 'fixed bridge' (as on a *lute). In some instruments the strings are tuned by individual movable bridges, as in the Far East, *long zither. For a rare 'upright bridge' with side notches for the strings, see KORA, an African instrument. For meanings of 'bridge' on keyboard instruments, see STRINGED INSTRUMENTS, 5.

Bronze drum. An Oriental cult instrument of the Bronze Age onwards, wholly of bronze, known over Eastern Asia from Burma to South China and Indonesia. Rarely now in use, it is a heavy cylinder with concave sides, open at the bottom, with a flat circular top of thinner metal which is struck. The width varies from about 45 cm. (18″) up to 120 cm. (4′), the sides somewhat deeper. The parts are separately cast in stone moulds, the sides in two semicircular halves brazed together, the top then added. Characteristically the centre shows a star pattern and the rim bears cast toads (animals whose changes in skin colour can betoken a change in the weather). Suspended by a rope, the top rests vertically, to be drummed on in rain-making and funeral rites.

Buccin. An early 19th-century trombone for military bands, made on the Continent up to c.1830, with the bell in a wide curve ending in, as it was termed, a 'dragon's head'.

Buccina and Cornu. Ancient Roman instruments of horn kinds.

1. *Buccina* (more properly *bucina*). Any small blowing horn from a swineherd's cowhorn to versions, sometimes in bronze, used in the army, at first for camp signals and the like, later (from the 1st century AD) as the regular instrument of certain branches of the army, notably cavalry, in which it

came to be referred to by various writers as 'lituus' (after the name of the older Roman non-military hook-belled *lituus, by this time no more in use). For the Roman trumpet, tuba, see TRUMPET.

2. *Cornu* (lit. 'horn' in all senses of the word). Especially a curving bronze horn, Etruscan by origin, of two main forms, both held by a wood or bronze cross-bar with the bell pointed forwards: the smaller, a regular military instrument, curved in over half a circle; and the larger and later (well known by examples from Pompeii in the Naples museum), with tubing prolonged into more than an open circle bringing the bell high above the player's head (some 3.3 m. or 11′ of tube altogether). The last is depicted especially in amphi-theatre scenes along with the *hydraulis (organ), perhaps signalling the course of events. Both kinds used cast mouthpieces with very shallow cups *c.*25 mm. wide. Nothing is known of the sounds they made.

3. *Confusion between the names.* There has long been confusion arising from what has recently been shown (Meucci 1989) probably to have been a copyist's error placing bucina and cornu in reversed order in a passage in Vegetius, *Epitoma rei militaris* (4th century AD). This has led to the *cornu* often up to the present time being called a 'buccina'. The *cornu* itself was revived under the name *tuba curva* in Revolutionary France, scored for in music by Gossec and later by Cherubini. Sax made a valved version, *sax-tuba*, for sounding on the stage in Halévy's opera *Le Juif errant* (1852).

Bucium. Romanian *alphorn.

Bugariya (*bugarija*, Yugoslavia). See TAMBURITSA.

Bugle (Fr.: *clairon*; Ger.: *Signalhorn*; It.: *corno da segnale*, but often spoken of as *tromba*; Ru.: *gorn*; Sp.: *corneta*).

1. *British bugle.* Of copper, brass-mounted, or plated brass. (For its notes, see BRASS INSTRUMENTS, Ex. 1). The British military calls include Regimental Calls, Field Calls, and Routine Calls, all published in *Trumpet and Bugle Sounds for the Army* (HMSO). Marches for Corps of Drums (bugles with drums) are available from publishers, and, from instrument suppliers, the traditional tasselled cords for the bugle, green or tricolour. In Britain the bugle is normally built in B♭ to the old Sharp Pitch (see PITCH, 3). For playing with other instruments at standard pitch a 'low-pitch shank' is obtainable, about 7 cm. (3″) long and inserted between bugle and mouthpiece.

2. *American bugle.* In the USA 'bugle' covers, besides the B♭ bugle, the Army Regulation bugle, also termed 'field trumpet': built in G and usually with one valve ('Piston bugle') which lowers by a fourth to D to make part of a scale possible. In Ex. 1 tails up show the notes available with the valve at rest,

and tails down with it lowered; the *c″* (bracketed), being a seventh harmonic, lies rather flat. Such a valve had also been used in Europe, best known on the Italian *Tromba per fanfare per Bersaglieri* ('Bersaglieri horn'), brought out in 1861. Baritone and other larger bugles with or without the valve are made in the USA for playing tenor or bass parts in bugle bands; see MILITARY BAND, 3.

Ex. 1. Sounding pitch, with harmonics numbered.

3. *History.* The bugle goes back to the Seven Years War (1756–63), when Hanoverian Jäger Companies (sharpshooters) took over from the hunting field the large semicircular metal horn of the *Flügelmeister* ('wing master'), carried by a leather cross-strap, and the first instrument to bear the name *Flügelhorn*, though in the army, *Halbmond* ('half-moon'). The English in turn adopted it for the Light Infantry as the bugle horn, normally built in D, a third above the present bugle. About 1800 it was remodelled in one-looped form (retained in the *keyed bugle) pitched in C, or B♭ as now. The present two-loop form came in after the Crimean War, though on the Continent the single loop (adopted from the British after the Napoleonic wars) is still often preferred. Some of the calls go back to the *Halbmond* days. The first notes of the Last Post are older still, taken from a cavalry trumpet call at least as old as the 16th century. The opening of Suppé's *Light Cavalry* quotes the bugle version of the old Austrian Retreat for the trumpet. A rich collection of calls of various European armies is in the Appendix of Kastner's *Manuel générale de musique militaire* (1848). Latterly, Britten required the bugle itself in *Noye's Fludde*.

Buisine (or buysine, from Lat. *buccina). A frequent name in Old French literature for the medieval long trumpet (see TRUMPET, 3), or sometimes a long, curved metal horn. From *buisine* comes Ger. *Busune*, later *Posaune*, at first meaning 'trumpet', then 'trombone'.

Bukai. See FRICTION DRUM, 2.

Bull-roarer (or thunderstick, whizzer, etc.; Fr.: *rhombe*; Ger.: *Schwirrholz*). A flat piece of wood, typically 15 to 30 cm. (6–12″) long and tied, through a hole at one end, to a long string with which it is whirled round above the head. The wood thereupon rotates, generating disturbances of pressure in the air which impinge on the ear as a roaring or screaming sound. The wood may be tapered towards the ends and is often notched along each side (in which case the instrument may be found easier to sound: to the inexperienced, the bull-roarer is not as simple as it looks). In *classification it comes under 'Free aerophones'.

Western countries have known the bull-roarer during the present century chiefly as a toy (Haddon 1898). But among primitive societies it may still be an important ritual instrument, representing the voice of ancestors during male initiations, or for weather and other magic. Among the Navajo Indians of North America it is said to be most potent when made from a pine which has been struck by lightning. In South America a few generations ago a man walking through the Amazon forest would take it with him as protection against evil spirits. It must be one of man's earliest ritual noise-makers, probably going back to the Upper Palaeolithic and possibly derived from some hunting or scaring implement of earlier still. It was swung by the Ancient Greeks (*rhombos*) in Corybantic rites, and up to a century ago in rural parts of Europe for protection against thunderstorms.

The bull-roarer appears in chamber music in Henry Cowell's *Ensemble* for five strings and two thundersticks.

Bumbass. The name, from German, conveniently serves to embrace a number of old or newer instruments of popular music-making. The most usual form has consisted of a tall pole and a single string, usually of gut, stretched along it to pass over a resonator—an inflated pig's bladder (the 'bladder-and-string' of earlier centuries) or a tin can, or wooden box or small drum. The string is jarred into deep-pitched vibration by rubbing with a notched stick or bow. Cymbals and jingles are often attached in top. A German exporter's catalogue of the 1890s thus describes how the bumbass is played: 'like a Double Bass without however fingering the String. While playing the Instrument is struck down upon the floor in time with the Music, thus causing the Cymbal and Bells to ring, while the drawing of the Bow across the String brings forth a sound similar to the roll of a Drum.'

A variant of the 20th century is the 'tea-chest bass', an imitation double bass: a tall flexible stick is fastened to one side of the upside-down chest and a string is stretched from the top to the centre of the chest; the string is plucked while the stick is flexed to vary the tension and pitch.

Bush bass (Australia). See LAGERPHONE.

Buzz disc (Ger.: *Schwirrscheibe*). Now a toy well known in practically every continent, and in Asia as far as the Bering Strait. The small disc (of wood, bone, tin, an old coin, etc.) is pierced with two holes close to and equidistant from the centre. The string is led through these and knotted in a long loop, passed round both hands. The disc is swung round to wind up the string which, on moving the hands apart, rapidly unwinds to spin the disc, making a whirring noise from air disturbance caused by a slight wobble of the disc. Momentum then winds up the string again, to continue the sound. The buzz disc (sometimes made with a serrated edge) is thought to be as ancient as the *bull-roarer, possibly evolved from some early noise-maker used in luring prey but subsequently serving in ritual and magic.

C

Cabaza (or *cabaça, cabaza afuche*). Afro-Brazilian rattle with external beads, used in Latin-American dance music, at first for the samba. In its original form, a rough-surfaced tree-gourd (*Crescentia*) with handle attached and, round the outside, a network of small beads threaded together (see MARACAS, Fig. 1c) to be rustled with the other hand between striking the instrument on the palm or fingers. Modern forms (also called *afuche*) have, instead of the gourd, a wooden cylinder with a covering of dimpled metal, and the beads are steel.

In West Africa the beaded rattle is important, for example joining the iron bell (see AGOGO BELL) in the basic rhythm of a dance: see AFRICA, Ex. 1, here named *axatse*. Some such rattles have snake vertebrae for the beads. (For the tubular type of samba rattle, see CHOCALHO.)

Caisse, caixa, caja. Respectively Fr., Port., Sp.: 'drum', usually a *side drum (snare drum), as in Fr. *caisse claire*, or a folk-music drum of some similar size. The same words, *caisse*, etc. are used for the soundbox of a stringed instrument.

Calung. See CHALUNG.

Cammerton, Chorton (Ger.: 'chamber pitch', 'choir pitch'). German baroque terms: *Cammerton* covered tuning pitches used in concert music; *Chorton* for a higher pitch met in organs and church music. See PITCH, 2 for assessment of their values in relation to modern pitch (the one lower, the other higher than this; the two were generally regarded at the time as for practical purposes a tone apart). As a result, in a Cantata by Bach, for example, the organ part is often written in a different key from the others. Earlier meanings of the terms described by *Praetorius (1619) are not as yet fully understood.

Campanelli (It.: 'little bells'). In orchestral scores, normally the *glockenspiel. In *Madam Butterfly*, the *campanelli giapponesi* are the little bells given the little falling motif on the third C and E in Act I at the marriage, playable on glockenspiel.

Canon. See PSALTERY, 1.

Cantigas de Santa Maria. See MEDIEVAL INSTRUMENTS, 2.

Capotasto (from It., literally 'head fret'; Sp.: *cejilla*).

1. A wood, metal, or plastic bar, plain or padded, that can be secured across the neck of a fretted instrument—guitar, banjo, etc.—behind a fret which is to serve temporarily as a nut, in order to play in some higher key while keeping the same fingering that the player is accustomed to with the instrument in its plain state. The device can be kept in place with elastic or a screw tightened on the back.

2. In a grand piano, a felted bar or 'capo d'astro' often fixed above the strings a small distance beyond the tuning pins, acting as a downwards-pressing nut and eliminating the risk of a sharp blow on a key tending to lift the strings.

Carillon. A set of bells, up to 70 or more, installed in a tower for playing music, either automatically on the hour (and usually its halves or quarters), or, disengaging the mechanism, from a keyboard. Belgium and Holland have long been the most famous countries for carillons, some 70 existing today in Belgium with an average among the bigger carillons of 45 bells apiece, individually weighing from several tons down to barely 6½ kg. (14 lbs.). During the 20th century a great number have come into use in the USA (some with a compass of up to five octaves) and in Britain and the Commonwealth also. (For electric carillons replacing bells by metal tubes or rods, see CHIME.)

The automatic mechanism uses a rotating drum like that of a *barrel organ, first of wood, later brass, and bearing steel pegs of several types, to engage levers which pull down the wires leading up to the bells above. The drum of the cathedral carillon at Mechelin (Malines), made in 1736, has a diameter of 4.6 m. (15′) and a length of over 2 m. (6′). It operates on 90 levers and plays eight tunes during the hour, each tune calling for only a small amount of revolution of so huge a barrel, one full turn giving all eight tunes.

Modern instruments, however, use an endless band of perforated plastic rather like a player-piano roll. Metal fingers running over the plastic as it is unwound make electric contact through the perforations to energize a solenoid striking apparatus. Rapid passages, crescendo and diminuendo, and even long-held chords (produced by a sort of tremolo motion) are possible on a carillon, and the simpler keyboard fugues and sonatas can be played. Bach wrote some tunes for the carillon of one of his employers, the Prince of Anhalt-Cöthen.

The manual keyboard, with stout rod-like keys for playing the bells by hand alternatively to actuation by cylinder, came in after about 1480, the earliest actual example being in Bruges (1532). There may also be a pedal board.

Carillon bells, rather thinner than swung tower bells and struck with less force, are carefully tuned for the partials to sound harmonious. Average weights have been quoted as: note g, 5,500 kg. (5½ tons); g', 675 kg.; g'', 110 kg.; g''', 23 kg. (50 lbs.): the cube roots of these figures roughly halving for each octave upward (see BELL, 4). The diameters for these notes range from $c.$200 to $c.$27 cm. (8–10″).

The carillon grew from the mid-14th-century use of a pair of bells to sound the hours, struck by puppets ('quarter jacks') and then, as further bells were added, by mechanisms for playing tunes (in the Low Countries, *voorslagen*) which called attention to the first stroke of the hour, and were in use in Brussels and Louvain by 1381. Carillon building reached its greatest period in the 17th century, when the most celebrated makers were the Hemony brothers (b $c.$1609 and 1619) of Zutphen, Netherlands, and finally Amsterdam. Some hundred of these bells exist, along with arrangements of tunes of all kinds for the *voorslagen*, noting which were especially liked. From the 18th century a decline set in, followed by a recovery in the years after 1945, with the relearning of partly forgotten technology and revival of the mean-tone tuning used by the Hemony brothers and their contemporaries.

There are schools of carillon-playing at Mechelin, and at the Curtis Institute, Philadelphia. Birmingham University has held a course in campanology, the science and art of the carillonneur, as an optional part of the Mus.B. degree.

Price 1933; Rice 1926.

Castanets (Sp.: *castañuelas*; It.: also *nacchere*). 1. *True castanets*. Each hand wears a pair of shells made in boxwood, walnut, rosewood, ebony, etc. but not, apparently, in chestnut (Sp.: *castaño*). The wood is first turned to a shape like that of a spinning top, then halved and carved to make the two matching shells, which, on coming together, do not wholly close the hollows, allowing a sound from the air inside to be heard as well as the higher 'click' from the wood. Each shell has two holes for the cord, which is twice looped over the thumb or middle finger (Fig. 1a). The shells are thus suspended over the palm, the tension of the cord keeping them slightly apart for the fingers to play on the outermost shell. By using successive fingers the sounds can follow very rapidly. Spanish dancers distinguish between the 'male' castanet worn on the left hand and the 'female' on the right, the former giving a lower pitch through being hollowed more widely. This castanet is struck on the beat, generally with two fingers together. The other makes quicker sounds within the beat using separate fingers (Ex. 1). Castanets have been known in Spain from the Middle Ages, and in southern Italy for perhaps as long; some believe they were

brought originally by the Phoenicians. Some in southern Italy are so small, barely 2.5 cm. (1″) across, that they are worn on the back of the finger and shaken by the dancer, their diminutive hollows giving a high, crisp sound.

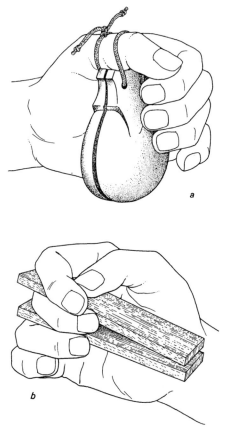

Fig. 1.

Ex. 1.

2. *Handle castanets.* The two shells are laced to the end of a handle, usually with between them a fixed shell hollowed on both sides. Such are likewise met as folk instruments, used in some countries alongside the preceding type for ritual noise-making as in Holy Week. They are well known too as a normal orchestral and percussion band substitute for true castanets, being easy to seize quickly and simpler to play. Rhythms are executed by shaking and striking on the free hand, though this makes accurate rhythmic figures difficult to control.

(Another method is to attach the castanets flat beside each other over a wooden block, the upper shell sprung up, to be played on with the fingers.) A further type has a pair of shells at each end of a handle, and there are toy versions with the shells attached by leather hinges.

3. *Flat 'castanets'*: small flat boards, a pair for each hand, in Spain and Portugal also called 'castanets' or elsewhere 'clappers'. See Fig. 1b; for the method of playing, see BONES.

4. *'Iron castanets'* (*or qaraqib*). Seen in Morocco, these are pairs of forged plates, cymbal-like at each end, and loosely joined at one end by a string. One pair is held in each hand for clashing in the dances of the Gnawi sects originally from West Africa.

Cavalry trumpet. See TRUMPET, 3a.

Cavaquinho. The popular Portuguese small guitar, in length c.52 cm. (20"), with four strings (gut, wire, etc.), strummed with the top string tuned as high as possible in a tuning of the same pattern as the first four of the guitar or, frequently, with the first string a note lower. There are many different regional designs, and in Madeira the name is often *machete*. There used also to be a larger, five-stringed form called *cavaco*.
For small guitars in general, see GUITAR, 5.

Cavity resonator. A broad term relating to air resonance within a hollow vessel or structure having one or more small outlets, such as an *ocarina, or with stringed instruments, a soundbox with soundhole. The name 'Helmholtz resonator' is often used, after the great German acoustician *Helmholtz (1821–94) who employed special glass resonators for measuring pitches contained in a musical sound (see PARTIALS).
The air vibrates, not with nodes and antinodes as in an air-column, but in one whole somewhat as though a reciprocating piston were acting upon it. The resonant frequency varies as follows: (i) Inversely as the volume of air; easily tested by blowing across the top of a bottle (an approximate test only, since the length and width of the neck enter into it): thus from empty to half empty, volume ratio $1 : 1\frac{1}{2}$, the note rises by $1 : \sqrt{2}$, i.e. by a diminished fifth (tritone); or from empty to one-quarter empty, by 2, an octave. (On hard blowing, the air in the neck, where energy is concentrated, may vibrate independently with a loud shriek.) (ii) With the square root of the area of the aperture (or sum of apertures, e.g. fingerholes). (iii) With the depth of the apertures, the greater, the lower the frequency, though if small, this factor may be ignored for a rough assessment.
Cavity resonance is important not only in the design of soundboxes (as see VIOLA, 6) but again in the handling of gourd and other attached resonators (as MUSICAL BOW, 3), and is chiefly

responsible for the recognizable pitch of such percussion instruments as *temple blocks, where the sound from the air inside greatly masks the brief sound from the struck wood itself.

Celempung (or *chelempung*). Javanese stringed instrument often used in the *gamelan; a kind of large zither with, under the strings, a tapering soundbox supported on four legs and sloping down to the narrower end where the player sits. The 13 or 14 pairs of metal strings, covering two octaves, pass over a high, slanting metal bridge and are plucked with both thumbnails, the fingers damping from below. Two instruments are required, ready-tuned for *pelog* and *slendro* respectively. The present construction is a development, incorporating European features, of a simpler original form perhaps distantly related to the Far-Eastern family of *long zithers. The *siter* is a smaller, higher-pitched variety, sometimes replacing the *celempung* or included along with it.

Celesta. Keyboard instrument with steel bars which rest on felt supports over individual wooden resonator boxes and are struck from above with felted hammers. Unopened it looks rather like a small *harmonium. The compass is written as *c* to *c''''*, but sounds an octave higher. A damper pedal is provided. Patented in 1886 by the Mustel family in Paris, many of whose instruments are still in use, it was heard by Tchaikovsky who then immortalized it in the 'Dance of the Sugar Plum Fairy'. Many have since used its gentle but immediately recognizable sound, notably Richard Strauss in *Der Rosenkavalier* and Bartók in *Music for Strings, Percussion, and Celesta* (1935).
Prior to the celesta, tuning forks had been struck from a keyboard in the Typophone of 1865—also patented by Mustel—which D'Indy scored for in *Le chant de la cloche* (1883). The *Dulcitone*, invented (it is said) in Scotland in 1880, similarly employs tuning forks and was quite well known as a soft-sounding domestic instrument up to the 1930s, though suffering a disadvantage that with wear the forks are apt to work loose and the notes respond unevenly.

Celestina. One of the 18th-century keyboard inventions for sounding the strings by friction: see GEIGENWERK. 'Celestinette' seems to have been the name of an earlier invention than this (by Mason, London, 1761) using a bow moved by the right hand. ('Celestina' is also a 19th-century 4' organ stop.)

Cello (short for 'violoncello', and the name used almost everywhere today, save in France, where it is always in full, *violoncelle*, and Ru.: *violonchel*; Sp.: *violoncelo*). Historically the bass of the violin family (see BASS VIOLIN). But over and above this, the vast range of the instrument—in solo works the note C may be sounded in five different octaves—

and its huge expressive powers render the cello the great solo instrument of the family after the violin itself.

1. *Dimensions.* The cello stands in pitch a twelfth below the violin, its strings tuned *a d G C*. From the front it looks very large by comparison but is in fact only a little over twice the size (on average 2.12 times), with body length 75.5 cm. (29¾″) and string length in proportion, 69 cm. (27″). Suiting the length, the basic fingering system of the cello (since the 17th century, at least) is with the fingers placed on four successive semitones. The widths of the body are in or near the same proportion as in a violin (though cellos vary here) but the sides can be nearly four times as deep, which, in conjunction with proportionately shorter and narrower f-holes, brings an internal air-resonance pitch around a twelfth deeper than in a violin, namely near *G*, though if the f-holes are on the wide side it can rise to above *A*.

The neck of a cello appears thin in comparison, needing only 5 mm. (0.2″) greater breadth at the nut for the four strings, but balanced visually by slightly out-pointed corners of the base of the pegbox with, on the back, a roundel-shaped button in which the fluting is continued (a feature also of some violas). The high bridge brings to the strings practically the same angle as on the violin as well as keeping the bow clear of the cello's broader waist when playing on the outer strings.

2. *Construction.* A cello is built in much the same way as a violin except that the softer wood of pear or poplar is sometimes used for the back and sides instead of maple. The front and back are carved to thicknesses 2 to 3 mm. greater in the centre than in a violin, while the bass-bar has dimensions of twice the size (and can sometimes be expertly adjusted to deal with a bad 'wolf note'). Most of the great Italian violin makers (see VIOLIN, 4) have left cellos—not quite all (the celebrated Guarneri 'del Gesù' being one doubtful case in this respect)—but 50 or more exist by Stradivari, who played a major part in establishing, at the beginning of the 18th century (to supersede previous more bulky models), the design on which the cello has since principally followed.

For small beginners there is the 'three-quarter' size cello (68 cm. (27″) or less in body length) or the 'half' size (down to 56 cm. (22″)), though the smallest can be difficult to obtain.

The spike or 'end-pin' of metal (or ebony with a steel core) which supports the cello off the floor has become standard equipment only in the 20th century. Before this, the instrument was normally supported on the calves of the legs (Pl. 1). Most players in ensembles specializing in baroque music have reverted to this older method. At the other extreme, a trend among solo cellists at the present time is to use a spike of increased length, following Paul Tortelier (1914–90); or as used by Mstislav Rostropovich (b. 1927), a spike with a bend in it,

which brings the cello into a position nearer to the horizontal whereby the weight of the bow falls more downwards on the strings as it does with the violin.

Signor Piatti

Pl. 1. The great cellist Alfredo Piatti (1822–1901); he holds the cello nearly upright, supported between the legs.

3. *Strings and playing.* Originally the strings were all of gut, with an overspun C string by the 18th century. Today most cellists use silver- or aluminium-covered gut for the lowest strings, while rope-cored steel for the A string can especially aid the soloist and will not break. Nylon-core, steel-covered strings have been gaining popularity, and all-steel stringing is not uncommon.

The bow is about 2.5 cm. (1″) shorter and some 25 per cent heavier than that of the violin, with the band of hair wider to about the same degree. The principles of bowing are, broadly speaking, similar (it is the viol that is bowed in opposite ways).

In the basic playing the fingers cover a minor third, e.g. on the D string, E to G. This is increased to a major third when required, always by 'back extension' of the first finger to make a whole-tone with the second, e.g. in A major, for the hand to stretch E to G♯. As no larger stretch is possible in the lower positions of the hand, the pupil is generally taught the scale of E♭ in the manner shown in Ex. 1, involving changes of position (moving the thumb) after the back extension for the initial tone. Soon the beginner learns to identify the multitude of fingering patterns on and across the strings, constantly used in playing even the simplest passages and instantly recognized by the experienced cellist when sight-reading, though they become boundlessly intricate with more difficult or soloistic music.

Ex. 1.

The downwards hold of the instrument makes it possible for the cellist to use 'thumb positions' of the left hand: the thumb is brought to the front and pressed to the string, usually two strings, to form the root for various positions reaching high up the strings. Where fingerings are marked in exercises, the sign ♀ denotes the thumb. The thumb is not normally used in this way below the halfway point along the string save in otherwise difficult double stops (constantly met) and to produce artificial harmonics by thumb and third finger.

Three clefs are commonly met in cello music—bass, tenor, and treble. In much older solo music, whenever a passage written in the treble clef follows one in the bass clef, the former (in treble clef) is written an octave higher than it sounds—a practice that arose presumably to give a better impression of 'ascent' to the eye.

4. *Stages in cello history: (a) Bass violin.* The bass of the violins seems to have been at first in Italy a quite small instrument tuned a fifth below the viola (as a bass recorder is below the tenor) and with three strings—like the others of the *viola da braccio family—the bottom string of the three tuned to a nominal F (Ganassi 1543) though by other accounts it had a fourth string ten years earlier. Its likeness at that time is seen, a rather small cello, in the angel frescos of c.1535 by G. Ferrari in the church at Saronno, near Milan.

The four-string tuning upwards from C as today is given in Germany also from these years (Gerle) and again by *Praetorius; but elsewhere the fourth string carries the original sequence of fifths downwards, to B♭'. This, with all strings tuned a tone lower than today, was retained to the end of the 17th century in France (the 'basse de violon'), England ('bass violin'), and sometimes Italy (here often **'violone'). It accounts for the low B♭ met in French works of Lully's time (and, at the low French pitch of the period, sounding even below modern A). Whichever the tuning, the instruments were large, with body-length up to 80 cm. (31½"), and are seen in pictures with the bow held either way, as now or with the palm uppermost. Essentially a strong instrument able to give the bass line

alone in countries where double basses were as yet almost unknown, it was recalled in England by Roger North (*Musicall Grammarian, c.*1728) as 'a very hard and harsh sounded bass, and nothing so soft and sweet as now' (i.e. the violoncello proper).

A minor point, particularly remarked on in the earliest French description (Jambe de Fer 1556), was a metal ring fixed in the back of the instrument for a hook or band by which it could be played standing. In the 18th century too, a hole for a ring may be found in the back: in pictures from many countries the cello is seen played on a sling in popular processions (as it still is, or equally the double bass, in folk music of Central Europe).

Very few of these large bass violins now survive in their original size, nearly all having been since 'cut down' to cello dimensions. This entails principally a refashioning of the upper and lower ends of the body, but necessarily leaving the centre bouts intact, whereby these can appear to a discerning eye somewhat long in proportion to the whole.

(b) Violoncello. This name (preceded in 1642 by *violoncino*) appears in the 1660s, in the early Italian solo literature, much of it written in Bologna during times when the solo repertory of the violin also was fast expanding. The diminutive form of the word 'violone' very likely (though no one of the time says so) arose with the reduced dimensions made feasible by availability of a metal-overwound bottom string to sound well with the shorter string-length (Bonta 1977). The smaller (today's) model seems to have been first seriously developed in the late 17th century, notably by Andrea Guarneri and Francesco Ruggeri (see VIOLIN, Table 1). Stradivari had continued to make to the older dimensions up to 1701 before turning to the smaller from 1707 onwards. (As with violins, the older cellos have since been given new necks: see VIOLIN, 7).

Two of the early cellist–composers are Degl' Antonii (unaccompanied *Ricercare* for cello or harpsichord, 1687) and Domenico Gabrielli (*Ricercari* for cello solo, 1689). The latter (named for 'violone', though the composer was listed as player of the 'violoncello') gives the tuning g d G C, writing up to the octave g'. This tuning, with the first string a tone lower than it is now, is specified again in various other Italian works of the period; also by Bach in one of the cello suites (see SCORDATURA).

(c) Classical developments. Real virtuosity on the cello can be said to have begun in the 18th century with the use of thumb positions, along with the present use of the four fingers by semitones. The cellist Francesco Alborea ('Franciscello', 1691–1739), who played in Italy and Austria, is often cited as one of the first to make them known. Two sonatas are attributed to him (ascending to d″ in range), and they feature the many double stops and arpeggiated chords across the strings which were to become so frequent in solo cello music. Two outstanding figures from later in the 18th

century are the brothers Duport, from Paris. The elder, Jean-Pierre (b. 1741), wrote sonatas reaching high a'''. He is the player behind Mozart's last quartets (K. 575, K. 589, and K. 590), known as the 'Cello Quartets' from the prominence given to the instrument. It was also the elder Duport who first performed Beethoven's early sonatas, Op. 5, in Berlin, with the composer at the piano. The younger brother, Jean-Louis, is celebrated for his detailed *Essai sur le doigter*, (1806), which laid a foundation for future cello fingering and remains a standard work.

Boccherini was a cellist and has left some of the finest works in the classical repertory. The best-known classical concerto, Haydn's in D, was once thought (less so today) to be partly by the composer's cellist-colleague Anton Kraft: the theory being that Kraft sketched the work and gave it to Haydn, who later completed it (after which, in the 19th century, Gevaert touched it up and added to the orchestration). The solo part seems to show off the most difficult things that Kraft could do—just as a century later Dvořák's Cello Concerto of 1895 incorporates many very similar passages, no doubt prompted by the composer's recital-colleague in the USA, the cellist Hanus Wihan.

Among famous names after the Duports are Romberg (1767–1841), the grand old man of the German school; the Belgian Servais (1807–66); and the Italian Piatti (1822–1901; Pl. 1), noted for his Method and also for pioneer work in reviving the baroque repertory with an edition of Marcello's sonatas. (Like many violinists of the time he is said to have applied vibrato only where he wished, not continuously as most have done since.) After 50 years came Pablo Casals (1876–1973), among whose greatest and most influential achievements was the bringing of the left-hand technique and its changing of position more into line with violin-playing than it had been traditionally (his cello was by Matteo Goffriller, Venice). Next came three near-contemporaries born between 1902 and 1906: Emanuel Feuermann of Austria and Gregor Piatigorsky of Russia, who both settled in the USA; and Pierre Fournier of France. After these there is the dominating figure of Mstislav Rostropovich, whom history will doubtless show to have been the greatest influence after Casals.

5. *Repertory*: (a) *Baroque*. A list (Cowling 1975) gives some 56 Italian composers of sonatas for cello and continuo, including Gaetano Boni (fl. first half 18th century), Pergolesi, Platti, and Benedetto Marcello (for cello or bass viol); from Vivaldi come six sonatas, some of them very fine works, and 27 concertos; and from Bach, the six unaccompanied suites (see also below, 6b), restored to the repertory by Casals.

(b) *Classical*. There are concertos and sonatas by Boccherini, Carl Stamitz, and Wagenseil; a second concerto by Haydn was discovered in 1961, in addition to the well-known one in D (see above,

4c). Sonatas include five by Beethoven: two in Op. 5; Op. 69; and two in Op. 102; also Variations, e.g. on an Aria from Mozart's *Magic Flute*. (For Schubert, see ARPEGGIONE.)

(c) *Romantic*. The main concertos of this period are by Schumann (Op. 129); two by Saint-Saëns (Op. 33 and Op. 119); Lalo; and Dvořák (Op. 104); also Tchaikovsky's Variations on a Rococo Theme, Op. 33. Among the sonatas are two by Mendelssohn (Op. 45 and Op. 58); Chopin (Op. 65); two by Brahms (Op. 38 and Op. 49); Grieg (Op. 36); and Rachmaninov (Op. 19).

(d) *20th-century*. These are very numerous, including Webern's Three Little Pieces, Op. 11; Debussy, Cello Sonata (1915); Bloch, *Schelomo*; Fauré, two sonatas (Op. 109 and Op. 117); Elgar, Cello Concerto, Op. 85, one of the finest; Ibert, unaccompanied sonata; and Ireland, Sonata. After these come works by Prokofiev, Shostakovich, and Martinů, as well as Britten's Cello Sonata and Cello Symphony (both written for Rostropovich) and three suites for unaccompanied cello. Also for unaccompanied cello are the sonatas by Kodály, Hindemith, and Xenakis (*Nomos*).

6. *Five-stringed cellos*: (a) *Bass violin*. Listed by *Praetorius is a large bass violin with a fifth string tuned to the F below the rest. In many subsequent pictures (as Dirk Hals's painting *The Cello Player*) we see the five-stringed instrument, rested on the ground and bowed palm upwards, but here more likely with the 5th string tuned above the others, to d' (as noticed in France; see Cyr 1982); such an instrument made in Ghent in 1717, with 81-cm. (32″) body is in the Brussels *collection. See also BANDORA, Pl. 1.

(b) *Bach's Sixth Suite for unaccompanied cello*. This appears in the manuscript (not an autograph) with the specification, 'with five strings', referring to the four of the cello plus one tuned to the e' above. (Legend has it that the suites were written for the player C. B. Linigke but this is by no means certain.)

(c) *Violoncello piccolo*. In nine cantatas, Bach scores for the *violoncello piccolo* as an obbligato instrument with a full cello compass. A later inventory from the Cöthen court lists two *violoncelli piccoli*, one of them with five strings made by Hoffmann, the chief maker of string instruments in Leipzig in Bach's time. The size of the 'piccolo' is nowhere stated, but also by Hoffmann are at least three small five-stringed cellos with an average body-length of 60 cm. (24″, like a half-size cello). These could just possibly be *violoncelli piccoli*, though still not necessarily the instrument intended for the Sixth Suite, which has no mention of 'piccolo' (though it has been well recorded using a five-stringed cello piccolo).

For 19th- and 20th-century enterprises to redesign the violin family, often incorporating a cello-tuned instrument of much enlarged size, see VIOLA, 6.

Bonta 1977; Cowling 1975; Ginzburg 1983; Pleeth 1982; Van der Straeten 1915, repr. 1971. For early works cited, see RENAISSANCE INSTRUMENTS, 3.

Cembalo (It.). Abbreviation of *clavicembalo*, the *harpsichord. In folk music it can mean other things, e.g. in Italy a tambourine.

Cencerro. It., Sp., *cowbell.

Cents. To express an interval between two notes or pitches accurately, the time-honoured method has been to use ratios, calculated or obtained from lengths measured on the string of a *monochord. The 19th-century British physicist Alexander Ellis then introduced the logarithmic system of 'cents', now in general use.

By equal temperament division of the octave (ratio $2:1$) into 12 equal semitones, the ratio for each semitone is that which when multiplied by itself 12 times comes to 2: i.e. the 12th root of 2, or 1.05946 (the square of this giving the ratio of a whole-tone; the cube, a minor third, etc.). Putting these into common logarithms, $\log 2 = 0.30103$ (for the octave ratio) divided by 12 gives the logarithm of the semitone ratio, 0.02509. Being awkward figures, they are multiplied to make the octave 1200 cents, and the semitone 100 cents, that is, by multiplying each logarithm by 3986 (1200 divided by log 2). The whole-tone is 200 cents, the minor third 300 cents, and so on, up through the chromatic scale. One-hundredth of a semitone is one cent.

To convert an interval into cents, find the frequency ratio of the higher note to the lower (e.g. for a simple example, the perfect fifth, ratio $3:2$, result 1.5). Multiply the logarithm of the result (here 0.1761) by the number 3986 (here giving 702 cents). Alternatively, find the logarithms of the two quantities in the ratio, subtract one from the other, and again multiply by 3986. Should the two notes be more than an octave apart, giving a result greater than 1200, subtract this number to transpose the interval within the octave. The minimum pitch difference which can readily be discriminated is of the order of 3 or 4 cents.

Ceterone (or arch-cittern). Late 16th- to 17th-century *cittern extended to carry a second pegbox (cf. THEORBO) for up to eight open bass strings. The fingerboard strings are tuned as in a cittern. Examples are very few, though there are many of the 18th-century French *arcicistre* (see ENGLISH GUITAR, 2).

Chabrette (or *cabrette*). See BAGPIPE, 3.

Chains. Large iron chains shaken with their lower ends on the floor or on a metal sheet. Schoenberg used them as an orchestral instrument in *Gurrelieder* (1911) at the climax of the Wild Hunt (written with tremolo signs in the part). Varèse and Havergal Brian have also used them.

Chakhē and crocodile zither. *Long zither of South-East Asia.

1. *Chakhē* (Thailand; in Kampuchea, *takhē*). A large, zither-like, instrument (see SOUTH-EAST ASIA, Pl. 2, left), $c.130$ cm. (50″) long, hollowed in wood, resting on the ground on ivory feet. The three strings, played with a plectrum, are two of gut (formerly silk) and one of brass, tuned in the pattern *a, e, A*. Attached to the bridge, they run to the pegs over 11 or 12 wooden frets which increase in height to the first, acting as the nut. Though also played solo the full, vibrant sound mainly contributes a deep register to ensembles.

2. *Crocodile zither.* The now-rare Burmese 'crocodile', *mi gyaun*, has a straight, rounded body 1 m. (3′) or more long, with open slot below, and carved with the beast's head at the plucking end, the tail at the other, and small feet underneath. The *chakhē* was also once made in this form, which perhaps has a distant predecessor in bamboo (see LONG ZITHER).

Chalumeau. Single-reed wind instrument of the first part of the 18th century, with a bore and mouthpiece that anticipated those of the *clarinet by 20 years or less. Seven original examples are known (Munich and Stockholm *collections), small instruments prettily made in boxwood: the soprano is under 22 cm. (9″) long, the tenor 24″, i.e. about equal to a sopranino and a treble *recorder respectively though going an octave lower than these, to *f* and *f*, owing to the combination of reed with cylindrical bore. On the back is a thumb-hole, and a second brass key, similar to the one in front and opening exactly opposite it, to make an 11-note compass from F to B♭ with a sound not unlike the low register of a small clarinet.

The name of the instrument is first met in 1687, in a German ducal order to Nuremberg for a set of four *Chalimo* along with a set of five *Hautbois* (oboes with bassoon), all new 'French' instruments (Heyde 1986a); yet there is no news of such an instrument at that time in France (where *chalumeau* meant a pastoral reedpipe or the chanter of a bagpipe)—though in England 12 years later was advertised a seven-hole 'Mock Trumpet', possibly some simple form with *idioglot reed (Dart 1953). Then, through the years 1706–35, are some 100 works written in Austria, Germany, and Italy with parts for chalumeau, usually two, the French word spelt in all sorts of different ways (*salmò*, etc.). First, Viennese operas by Fux, G. Bononcini, and others (these requiring the small-sized chalumeau); then cantatas by Telemann, concertos by Vivaldi, followed later by numerous works of Graupner, and finally two operas by Gluck in their original versions. Some of the works, back to 1707, include also a bass chalumeau, though we now have no proper idea what this looked like.

One of the surviving chalumeaux, a tenor, is by the great Nuremberg woodwind maker J. C. Denner (1655–1707), who was credited with having improved the instrument. How, is not stated: he may have created the set of different pitches, or added the keys, or have himself devised the cane reed tied over a separate wooden mouthpiece. He, or his son Jakob (1681–1785), then proceeded to invent the clarinet, giving the tenor-pitched chalumeau a complete upper register at the twelfth. In a few of the parts for chalumeau the note c'' occurs, being possible by 'leaking' the thumb-hole as in recorder playing (and just possible for this note on a clarinet); but to make an entire upper register, the 'leak' must be a smaller hole and higher up, in fact the speaker or register key, the crucial advance in the new invention, of which the earliest known appearance of the name, *clarinette*, is in a Nuremberg document of 1710 (Nickel 1971: 251).
Lawson 1981.

Chalung (or *calung*). Bamboo percussion instrument of Indonesia (West Java). Bamboo tubes, closed at one end (the other end sometimes cut to a tongue), are laid horizontally in a frame for playing with a beater like a xylophone. With two to 18 tubes it may be seen in village ensembles taking the place of the expensive *gong-chime. Western writers have termed it a 'tube xylophone', another example of which is the *grantang* of Bali. See also GAMELAN.
Kunst 1949, 1973.

Chamber organ. Mainly from the late 17th to the early 19th century, a pipe organ for a private house or concert room, built like a piece of furniture, tall cupboard or suchlike, with an iron pedal at the bottom to work the bellows. One manual. Pipes may include a stopped diapason, 8′, with a 4′ and 2′, and a mixture. Stops may be 'divided', to enable the right hand to play on one stop and the left on another (as with a *harmonium). Gilt dummy pipes may be in front. Many great organ builders made chamber organs, as Father Smith, and Snetzler, in 18th-century England, and a number in America. The German equivalent, *Positiv*, has a pedal board, for use also in churches where an organ was required that could be set up in some special position.
Wilson 1968.

Change-ringing. See BELL, 4.

Chanter. The melody pipe of a *bagpipe. Practice chanter, see BAGPIPE, 2*a*.

Chanterelle. The highest-tuned string of a *lute or *violin.

Charango. The South American (Andean) small *guitar with the body of an armadillo shell (sometimes pressed inwards before drying to give the semblance of a guitar waist), or else hollowed in wood or, in the towns, flat-backed. Known since the 18th century, very popular almost everywhere from North Chile to Peru. Five double or triple courses, now metal, typically tuned e'' e'', a' a', e' e'', c'' c'' g' g'. It is strummed with the fingers with much tremolando.

Chauk-loubat. Burmese; see DRUM CHIME.

Chekker (Old Fr.: *eschiquier*, lit. 'chessboard'). Some kind of stringed keyboard instrument mentioned first in 1360, last known in 1519, in France. Whether it was an early form of *clavichord or of *harpsichord is still in dispute (Barry 1985).

Chelys. An Ancient Greek name of the *lyre, from its body of a tortoise carapace. In Renaissance writings, often the *lute or the *viol.

Cheng. Chinese long zither: see ZHENG.

Cheng-cheng. Small cymbals of Bali; see GAMELAN, 2.

Chifonie. A medieval French name (variant of *symphonie*) for a precursor of the *hurdy-gurdy.

Chillador (Sp., 'screamer'). Popular small guitar of Chile, *c.*59 cm. (2′) long with five pairs of metal strings, plucked and thrummed in festive music. In Peru, also the *charango*, and in Mexico the *jarana.

Chime. 1. *As a tune.* A tune or motif played by church bells. The well-known chime of Big Ben is the 'Cambridge Chime' or 'Westminster Quarters'. It is said to have first been arranged in 1793 for Great St Mary's, Cambridge by Dr Crotch, by permutation of a descending phrase in the opening of 'I know that my Redeemer liveth' in Handel's *Messiah*. A favourite chime in Germany and the USA is the 'Parsifal Quarters', on the bell motif in Wagner's opera, which the composer knew from a peal of 1869 at Beuron Abbey.

2. *Electric chimes* (electric carillon). Much used, especially in the USA in place of church bells, these in most cases employ metal tubes (see TUBULAR BELLS). They are sounded electrically (programmed or from a keyboard) by solenoid with leather-tipped armature for the striking; the vibrations are received by microphone or by magnetic pickups to be amplified and fed to a loudspeaker. As with tubular bells, the main note heard, that to which the 'bell' is tuned, is given by the 4th mode of vibration (see PARTIALS, 1). In some designs the tubes are thinned at various points in order to

bring the pitch of neighbouring modes into consonance with the main note, to sweeten the sound (as in 'overtune tuning' see XYLOPHONE, 2).

3. *Rod chimes.* Slender steel rods, fixed at one end. Plain (non-amplified) rod chimes are well known in small striking clocks, the rod coiled in a spiral to save space. They have also been made as a compact substitute for tubular bells in musical education. Amplified rod chimes have been used in opera (from c.1931) for the *Parsifal* bells, striking with a light leather-covered beater. (Prior to this, Bayreuth at one time used very long thick piano wires stretched on a resonator and supported by gongs and tuba.)

4. *'Gong chimes', etc.* 'Chime' as applied to instruments of further kinds where they make up a tuned set (Fr.: *jeu*) played usually by one person: *drum chime (Burma), *gong chime (also *gamelan, *South-East Asia), stone chime (see LITHOPHONE), porcelain bowl chime (*jaltarang, India). Among bamboo and glass chimes occasionally demanded as modern percussion instruments are non-tuned lengths of the material hung in a loose bundle and sounded by rapidly clenching or agitating the bundle with the hands.
Peery 1948.

Chime bar (or 'resonator bell'). A metal bar like those used in a *glockenspiel but individually mounted over its own resonator, made mainly for use in schools. In the type most often seen the bar is held by two pins lengthwise over a tubular, brightly coloured plastic resonator which has a wide circular hole beneath the centre of the bar. The dimensions of the resonator are such that the air-cavity is in tune with the bar. If the hole is closed the bar becomes almost inaudible, so that if a card is moved about over the hole, a big vibrato can be made (the principle being in effect that of the *vibraphone). In another type, the resonator is a rectangular wooden box, again with a hole in the top, but better for placing a number of bars close together in a row to form a metallophone—or *xylophone, for chime bars are also available from Germany with wooden bars. Deep bass sizes are also made, tuned to notes down to *c* (the C below Middle C) and have been found valuable, held in the hand, in music therapy for the deaf, the vibrations being sensed through contact.

Ch'in. Chinese classic long zither without bridges. See QIN.

China and Korea. With their many close correspondences the instruments of these nations are summarized here together: 1, China; 2, Korea; also 3, Tibet.

1. *China.* NB: Instrument names are given in the current official *pinyin* system of romanization, adding in parentheses on first mention the older

forms familiar to the West hitherto. The main differences are in the consonants: *p, t, k* now in most cases written respectively *b, d, g* but '*pipa*' stays; old '*ch*' is now *q* or *j* (standing for two pronunciations of Eng. 'ch'); old *ch* is now *zh* (pronounced 'dj'); *hs* becomes *x* (of which the English pronunciation, 'ks', can faintly suggest 'hs'); and *tz* is now *z* (pronounced as in German).

Chinese musical instruments are traditionally classified into 'eight categories of sound' according to the material from which they are (or once were) made: metal, stone, clay, skin (drums), silk (strings), wood, gourd, and bamboo (the last two, along with clay, being wind instruments). They are rearranged below to follow the order of the four main classes in Western *classification. Nearly all the instruments are being made today, some more than others, and keeping to tradition save where modernization has set in, as with instruments for the modern Chinese orchestra and so on.

(a) *Idiophones:* (i) *Metal.* Bells: struck on the outside, *zhong* (chung), some large, hung in frames or towers, for ceremonial music; *bozhong*, c.50 cm. (20″) high, hung in individual frames, used in Confucian ritual music together with the *bell-chime, *bianzhong* (pien-chung); small handbells, *yinjing*, struck with a wooden stick, now only in monastic worship; pairs of small bells, *xing*, connected by a long cord to hit against each other with a high piercing sound owing to a slight difference in pitch, and popular in musical ensembles. Cymbals, *bo (po). Gongs, *luo*, single gong in theatre, ceremonial, and popular music, and see GONG-CHIME, 2 (*yunluo*). Iron chime, obsolete though not so in Korea (2a, below). (ii) *Stone* (see LITHOPHONE). Sonorous stone slabs, *qing* (ch'ing), and stone chime, *bianqing*. (iii) *Wood.* In Confucian ceremonies the beginning of each strophe of the music is marked by three strokes of a wooden hammer on the *zhu* (chu; in Korea ch'uk), an open-topped wooden box about 60 cm. (2′) wide with thick sloping sides, beaten in turn on the bottom and left and right sides. The end of a strophe is marked on the *yu*, a wooden tiger of about the size of the above, with bamboo teeth along its back, crouching on a wooden box: three beats on its head and three scrapes with a split bamboo over the bamboo teeth. The monk's 'wooden fish', *muyu* (see TEMPLE BLOCKS), in many sizes, is mainly to accompany Buddhist and Taoist chant. Clappers, in folk music and opera, of two or more pieces of hardwood tied together at one end with silk cord (two-piece, *banzi*, for military scenes in Beijing (Peking) opera; of six to nine pieces, *chungdu*, of sandalwood, etc.) Xylophone, *muqin*, of the Western type, frequently heard in Cantonese music.

(b) *Drums.* A huge variety, differing from province to province, with one or two skins attached with broad nails: for some main types, see QU (*ku*); also BO, for *bofu* (po-fu).

(c) *Stringed*. Zithers (see LONG ZITHERS), led in prestige by the **qin* (ch'in); *se*, many-stringed, now of little importance; **zheng* (cheng; Pl. 1, right), with individual movable bridges and very popular. Lute: **pipa*, large, pear-shaped; **yueqin* ('moon' ch'in), with circular body; **sanxian* (san-hsien; Pl. 1, second from left), three-stringed long lute (see LUTE, 7). Fiddle: **erhu* (Pl. 1, centre), one of the many varieties (in general, *huqin*) all played with the hair of the bow passed between the strings. Dulcimer: yangqin (see DULCIMER, 2). Three of these instruments appear in Pl. 1 along with a flute and (second from right) Mongol fiddle.

(d) *Wind*. (i) *Clay*. Vessel flute, **xuan* (hsuan); and many toy clay whistles. (ii) *Bamboo*. Transverse flute, **dizi* (tsi-tzü; Pl. 1, left), with vibrating membrane; end-blown flute, *xiao* (hsiao), a notched flute with the top largely closed by a knot in the cane. Double-reed, *sona* or *suona*, of the Asian shawm family (see SHAWM, 4), with numerous popular functions; **guan*, or *guanzi* (kuan-tzü), a **'cylindrical oboe'*, of much older Western Asian origin. (iii) *Gourd*. Free-reed mouth organ, **sheng*, one of the most ancient of Chinese instruments along with the vessel flute. (iv) *Others*. Not included in the ancient classification are the brass trumpets, **laba* (la-pa), a name sometimes used also for the *sona*.

2. *Korea*. Several instruments have a special interest through preserving types and usages that have been lost in China.

(a) *Idiophones*. Bells (see BELL, 1, for a huge early example) include the **bell chime pyonjong*. Cymbals, *chabara*. Gongs: large, *ching*; small and flat, *kkwaenggwar*. Iron chime of suspended rectangular plates, *panghyang*. Stone chime (Pl. 2, top right, and see LITHOPHONE), *pyongyong*, played together in the court orchestra with the bell chime and sounding an octave higher. 'Wooden fish', *moktak*. Clappers, *pak*.

(b) *Drums*. Barrel drum, *puk*, struck on the right head with a thick wooden stick, on the left with the hand; barrel drums with nailed heads and struck with soft-headed beaters, *chwago* (court orchestra) and *yonggo* (military band); hourglass drum, the large *changgo* (Pl. 2, on right) essential to most ensembles, struck on the horseskin right-hand head with a thin bamboo, and on the other, thicker, of cowskin, with the hand.

(c) *Stringed*. **kayagum* (Pl. 2, right) and **komun'go* (left), the long zithers: the *kayagum* corresponds to the Chinese *zheng*; the *komun'go* is considered the noblest of Korean instruments. Both take part in court music, as does the **ajaeng*, bowed with a stick. This last (centre of group), like the fiddle, *haegum*, is customarily classed with wind instruments, from its sustaining sounds. Dulcimer, *yanggum*, played with a single beater.

(d) *Wind*. Vessel flute, still part of an ancient Chinese ensemble at the semi-annual sacrifice to Confucius. Transverse flutes: *taegum* (Pl. 2), c.80 cm. (32"), with vibrating membrane; *tang-jok*, smaller, without membrane (court orchestra); notched flute, *tanso* (court chamber orchestra). Double-reed: **p'iri* (Pl. 2, centre rear), cylindrical, like the Chinese *guanzi*, and leading instrument in the basic traditional ensemble group with the fiddle, flute *taegum*, and drum *changgo*; *hojok*, shawm family, leading the military band and Buddhist instrumental music, with the long brass trumpet *nabal* and the conch alternating with long-held notes, and the cymbals, gong, and drum *yonggo*. Pl. 2 shows an instrumental ensemble of shamanist music of south-western Korea, in which are seen several of the instruments named.

3. *Tibet*. Popular instruments (many extending into Nepal, Bhutan, etc.) include a long lute, rather similar to a Kashgar **rabab*; fiddle, resembling the Chinese; dulcimer; bamboo transverse and duct flutes; a shawm resembling the Middle-Eastern **surna*. Buddhist monasteries have percussion and wind ensembles, with close instructions for performance preserved in written notations (Vandor 1973).

Pl. 1. China: an informal group (Wiant 1965): *left to right, di* (flute), *sanxian* (long lute), *erhu* (fiddle), *knur* (Mongol fiddle), *zheng* (zither).

Pl. 2. Korea: a sinawi ensemble: front row, *komun'go* (zither), *ajaeng* ('bowed' zither), *kayagum* (zither); behind, *haegum* (fiddle), *taegum* (flute), *p'iri* (cylindrical oboe), *changgo* (hourglass drum).

(*a*) *Idiophones.* Handbell. Cymbals, heavy, with high-domed bosses, clashed up and down (see CYMBAL, Fig. 1*d*).

(*b*) *Drums.* Two-headed frame drum *rnga*, on a stand or atop a pole. Rattle drum, *damaru*, of two human skulls joined at the crown, or their likeness carved in wood.

(*c*) *Wind.* Double-reed (shawm family) *rgya-gling*, the only melody instrument, large (over 50 cm., 20″) with wide metal bell, and ornamented with metal bands and often precious stones. Trumpets: *dung* (*dung-chen*), straight, conical, brass or copper, some three metres long, built in sections telescoped together after use to a mere *c.*50 cm.; a pair of them deliver deep drawn-out notes (chiefly the 2nd harmonic), preluding the slow chanting of the monks. Thighbone trumpet, traditionally from an executed man (or else of copper, with zoomorphic bell) sounding 'like the chilling howl of a wolf at dawn' (the two openings at the end of the femur were said to represent the nostrils of the mythical horse that conveyed the spirits of the departed). *Conch, heavily mounted in brass.

Chao Mei-pa 1969; *Lavignac* 1913, 'Chine et Corée' (by M. Courant); Picken 1957; Van Aalst 1884, repr. 1964; Wiant 1965.

Ching. In Korea a gong; Thailand, cymbals; China, *ch'ing* (now *qing*), sonorous stone (see LITHOPHONE).

Chirimía (Sp.), a *shawm, the name now met especially in Latin America from Colombia to Mexico, where the instrument is played in popular and religious festivals along with drums (though in Mexico it tends to be replaced by a trumpet or other instrument). A well-known form is of Guatemala, bored cylindrically but with a long conical staple through which it keeps the high pitch of a conical pipe and will overblow to the octave, though seldom done in practice (McNett 1960). 'Chirimía' can also mean, in Colombia, an ensemble composed of flute and drums.

The Catalan form of the word, *xirimía* (*xeremía*), can mean in the Balearic Islands a *reedpipe, and see BAGPIPE, 3*d*.

Chirula, chistu (or *txistu*). Basque and Gascon names of the tabor pipe; see PIPE AND TABOR.

Chitarra. It., '*guitar'.

Chitarra battente (It.). Often in museum literature a name for baroque five-course *guitars of the kind where the maker has chosen to construct a vaulted back (of ribs) instead of the more typical flat back. In Italy, however, it has denoted, from the 17th century to the present, a guitar, usually large, with ribbed back, a bend in the belly at the level of the low bridge (as with a Neapolitan *mandolin), and wire strings. As a folk instrument in Calabria today, there may be four courses of thin strings, rather slack, plus a shorter unstopped string (*scordino*) with its peg next to the 7th of the 10 frets. The tunings vary. The strings are strummed, largely unstopped, in vigorous, resonant close chords of tonic and dominant, enlivened by beating or rubbing the soundboard with the same hand (cf. 'long lutes' in Central Asia; see LUTE, 7*b*).

Tucci and Ricci 1985.

Chitarrone. A large, tall lute, mainly of the early 17th century. 1. *Chitarrone and theorbo.* During the last quarter of the 16th century in Italy, musical style was passing through a period of great change. In accordance with the humanistic interpretation of the nature of Ancient Greek music, composers began to ascribe greater importance to the solo voice and dramatic rendering of the text. With the development of the *basso *continuo, this called for instruments capable of giving a strong but relatively simple harmonic support to the voice, with particular emphasis on the bass line. Special types of lute were developed to provide for this.

Pl. 1. Chitarrone by Magno Dieffopruchar (Venice, 1608).

The most important was the chitarrone or *theorbo. Whether these two names indicate distinct instruments (the first name a remembrance of *kithara*, the ancient lyre) or whether they were synonymous is as yet impossible to tell. It is chiefly a convenience of our present age (encouraged in the matter by *Praetorius, 1619) to use the name 'chitarrone' for instruments of the tallest build (Pl. 1) and 'theorbo' for those which, though also large, are less tall. Both gain their height from the long unstopped bass strings (*diapasons). Instead of the turned-back head of classic lute construction, the main pegbox (for the stopped strings) stands almost upright, to be continued upwards to a second pegbox for the bass strings. In general there will be seen six or seven courses of stopped strings, single or double, and seven or eight single diapasons tuned diatonically.

Chitarrone, Ex. 1.

The most important feature that distinguishes these instruments from all other types of lute is the large size in relation to the pitches that a lute is tuned to: the length of the stopped strings is such that it becomes impossible to tune the top course (and likewise usually the second) to the required pitch, so it had to be an octave lower. Ex. 1 gives the normal 'A' tuning (see LUTE, 2b) for the theorbo; the string marked with an asterisk may also be tuned to chromatic notes, F♯ or E♭. Solo music in tablature for chitarrone or theorbo had to take into account this 'octave displacement' of the top two courses which leaves the third course as the highest tuned. (A well-known source of such music is J. H. Kapsberger's *Intavolatura di chitarrone*, Venice, from 1604.)

2. *Chitarrone, some details.* Up to more than 200 cm. (6½') tall, with a body-length of 71 cm. (28"), the upward extension to the main pegbox is canted at a slight angle for the diapasons to stand clear of the fingerboard courses—the diapasons reaching up to twice the length of the fingerboard strings (roughly as long as the lower strings of a harpsichord can be) and by some accounts strung with wire. Among the finest originals are those of Matteus Buechenberg (Rome), with the body ventilated by a 'triple' rose.

The name is first met in the description of the *intermedii* performed at a ducal wedding in Florence in 1589: one of its players was Antonio Naldi, who was later said to be its inventor. In Monteverdi's *Orfeo* (1607) nearly every number is headed as having on the continuo one chitarrone for a recitative and three for choruses, not all necessarily of the tall kind, and also telling us that one should not always expect a single player of one of these great lutes to suffice in an ensemble.

Smith 1979.

Chocalho (chocolo or 'shaker'). Tubular rattle of Brazilian origin, which entered Latin-American music along with the *cabaza, etc. Of bamboo, or now metal, c.40 cm. (16") long, with shot or such-like inside, the ends of the tube are closed, sometimes with parchment, for shaking longitudinally in one hand (for the samba in eight quavers to the bar). Milhaud uses it in *Saudades do Brasil* (1920). Similar rattles are met also as European folk instruments (as in Sicily where, made of cardboard, they are used for quieting infants), and again in New Guinea, shaken while dancing.

Chonguri. Popular long lute (see LUTE, 7) of Georgia (USSR). The body is round-backed, of ribs, with a pine belly of a characteristic outline like a lozenge with the sides rounded off, and a square-cut foot. Older instruments have a group of small

soundholes. Three nylon strings, variously tuned, run from a curving pegbox with side pegs; and there is a short fourth string pegged to the bass side of the neck (as in a *banjo), for continually sounding a 'drone' note an octave above the open note of the deepest main string. Played by women in accompaniment to the voice, and for dances, the *chonguri* has come to be heavily modernized and made in sizes down to bass for the folk orchestras.

Vertkov 1963.

Chordophone. In *classification of instruments the class name for stringed instruments. Included are *idiochord instruments, with 'strings' of bamboo slivers raised from the bark under tension.

Chord symbols. Through most of the 20th century a normal shorthand for chords constantly used in song and dance music, in jazz, and in popular genres since. For example, a pianist or guitarist would need to know only 'Am7 / D7 /' to accompany the first bar of 'Tea for Two' in the key of G. The following are the symbols as normally written (small variations are met) for the commonest chords, all here shown for illustration as based on C.

C (major chord); C6 (added sixth; add A); C7 (dominant seventh on C; add B♭); Cmaj7 (major seventh; add B); C9 (C7 plus D); C7 ♭9 (C7 plus D♭); C7♭5 (e.g. CEF♯B♭).

Cmi or Cm (minor chord); Cm6 (adding A); Cm7 (adding B♭).

Cdim or C° (diminished seventh, C E♭ F♯ A); Cm7 ♭5 (same with the A raised to B♭, e.g. C F♯ B♭ E♭ — famous as the 'Tristan chord' in Wagner).

Caug or C+ (augmented fifth, C E G♯); C7+ (C E B♭ G♯); and C9+ (with D).

A limitation with these simple symbols, that they do not specify inversions of chords, has been removed where necessary in rock and pop music for guitar by adding to the normal symbol an oblique stroke followed by the required bass note, e.g. 'C/G' (2nd inversion of C major). Similarly a symbol can show a bass note that is foreign to the chord itself as in 'C/B' (C chord with this bass descending) or such as Gm7/C (the chord as it were with a pedal C below). Higher in a chord a note can be added without producing a conventional seventh or ninth harmony, e.g. 'C add 9' (C major plus D but without B♭). Any number of chords thus freed from conventional harmony function can be expressed by symbols such as this, or by marking 'sus' ('suspended') before a note as in 'Csus4' (i.e. for the fingering to raise E to F). Details can be found in Rock and Pop Guitar Tutors.

Chord zither. The flat soundbox, in shape not unlike an *autoharp, has metal strings in two groups: the longer arranged for four-note chords (with an overwound string for the bass note of the chord), these played with the thumb; the shorter in chromatic sequence (or in a simple model, diatonic) for playing the melody with the fingers. There are many designs varying in details. The instrument can be played flat on a table, or held standing like an ancient lyre. Like the autoharp, the chord zither has been much used by folk-singers.

Chorton. See CAMMERTON, CHORTON.

Chorus (as naming an instrument). See BAGPIPE, 7; BIBLICAL INSTRUMENTS, 1d.

Chuniri. A stringed instrument, played (like the *chonguri) in Georgia, USSR, and somewhat suggestive of a bowed *banjo, it has a skin over a wooden hoop held on a long flat neck, with side pegs for two or three strings of black horsehair sounded with a simple, strongly outcurved bow. Like many other traditional few-stringed fiddles, a professional instrument for accompanying songs and recitations, and now also modernized, with bass sizes included.

Ciaramella. See ZAMPOGNA, 2.

Cimbalom. The large Hungarian dulcimer (see DULCIMER, 2).

Cimbasso. A name frequently met in Italian opera scores from c.1827 onwards, such as in Bellini's *Norma* (1831) and Verdi's up to and including *Aïda* (1870), for the wind part below the trombones. It was at first played on one of the several kinds of upright *serpent: A. Bertini's *New system for learning . . . all instruments* (London, 1837) gives the *Cimbasso* six holes, seven keys, and compass C to g' (Myers 1986: 134). By the mid century the parts were being played on *ophicleide or bombardon (early tuba), until Verdi, from *Otello*, expressed a preference for a deep valved trombone. After his time, Italian orchestras have used this or a tuba for these often very agile parts.

In 1959, Alexander Bros. of Mainz, to make all these parts playable on a slide trombone, brought out under the name 'Cimbasso' a bass slide trombone in F aided by two valves for the left hand: for the middle finger, lowering to D, for the thumb, to C, and both together, low B♭. Their use in conjunction with the slide enables all Verdi's parts to be played with some facility.

Cimpoi. See BAGPIPE, 5b.

Cinema organ. Like a church *organ this is a pipe organ with flue and reedpipes, but the ranks of pipes are organized on different principles and a large battery of percussion effects is incorporated. Made through the 1920s and 1930s, it is a development of the 'Hope-Jones Unit Orchestra' of

Robert Hope-Jones (1859–1914) and the Wurlitzer Company, and named by them 'Unit and Extension Organ' (see ORGAN, 6). The pipes are housed for preference in two chambers above the cinema proscenium along with the fan-blowers, and are electro-pneumatically operated from a console which can be raised and lowered by a lift. Each of the main ranks has the basic four-octave compass usually extended by an octave downwards and two octaves upwards, so that the same rank can furnish from 16-foot tone up to 2-foot, while mutation stops can be drawn from the same unit. There may be ten such ranks, allowing a great number of combinations selected by a huge array of stop keys arranged in a horseshoe round the three- or four-manual console, with pedals below. Many of the stop keys may have a 'second touch' (an extra push) to provide further combinations or bring in percussion and effects—drums, cymbals, glockenspiel, xylophone, vibraphone, carillon, sleighbells, weather effects, motor-horns, etc.—and with either single action (one impact) or reiterating (e.g. drum roll) as required.

The pipes speak at a pressure of some 15″, twice to three times the usual for a church organ, the pipes being voiced for powerful sound. The basic tone, that which in conjunction with a constant tremulant produces the characteristic 'cinema organ' sound, is the stopped flue rank *tibia clausa* (metal or wood) with wide dimensions and very high 'cut-up', giving the opening a square appearance instead of oblong. For adequate power, the bass of a tibia unit may use *diaphone pipes. Besides Wurlitzer there have been noted makers in the USA, also in Britain, France, and Germany.

Whitworth 1932, repr. 1981.

Circular breathing. A term introduced by American musicologists for the method, practised widely over the world, by which players of various wind instruments such as *reedpipe, *shawm, and *didjeridu avoid pausing to take breath through the mouth by inhaling through the nose to store air in the cheeks. As air is rapidly inhaled through the nose

(lowering the soft palate) the inflated cheeks are drawn in to propel the air held in them into the instrument before the soft palate is raised for resumption of normal blowing. The technique, well known to glass-blowers, may be learned while blowing through a straw into a bowl of water.

Cistre. Fr., 'cittern'; see also ENGLISH GUITAR, 2.

Cithara (from Gk. *kithara*). In classical Latin, a *lyre; in medieval Latin, generally a *harp, and so translated in the English Bible (see BIBLICAL INSTRUMENTS). In music of the Renaissance period where instruments are named in Latin, 'cithara' (or 'cythara') can mean the *cittern (as 'lyre', or 'chelys': Gk., 'tortoise', can mean the *lute).

Cither viol (Sultana). A bowed derivative of the 18th-century *English guitar, first made as an amateur novelty by the expert Dublin violin maker Thomas Perry in the 1760s, and later by others up to the 1820s. The body is vaulted and in the early models has 'flame' soundholes and an outline recalling a *viola d'amore. The stringing is that of an English guitar (but in single courses) with geared or watch-key tuning.

Cithrinchen. See CITTERN, 5a.

Citole and gittern. Two medieval instrument names, mainly of the period 1250–1350. There have been problems in identifying which instruments they respectively referred to. In pictures and carvings one sees small plucked string instruments with four or five strings which fall broadly into two kinds: in Fig. 1, *a* and *b* are variants of one, and *c* and *d* can be seen as variants of the other.

Older historians have generally seen in the rounded pear shape of Fig. 1*a* the prototype of the Renaissance *cittern (*e*), and in the incurved sides of *c* (see also MEDIEVAL INSTRUMENTS, Pl. 1), that of the Renaissance *guitar (*f*). For the instrument shown in Fig. 1*b* the name 'mandora' has been used, though this word was rare in the Middle Ages.

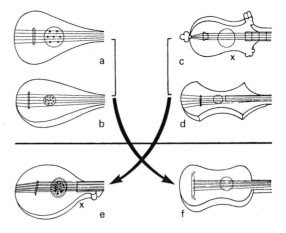

Fig. 1. Citole and gittern: shapes relating to the question of identification.

These identifications have been rigorously re-examined by Laurence Wright in his article 'The Medieval Gittern and Citole; a case of mistaken identity' (1977). The true connections, to summarize his argument very briefly, are marked in Fig. 1 by the arrows. The incurve marked 'x' in *c* ends up as the incurve 'x' in *e*, where vestiges of 'cusps' are often to be found. The unique early 14th-century instrument of type *c* preserved (in a subsequently altered state) in the British Museum is thus not a gittern, as was hitherto thought, but a citole. Wright then finds a chain of evidence to identify *a* with 'gittern'. By the 15th century 'gittern' in fact denoted a round-backed instrument with a resemblance in shape to a small lute (cf. Fig. 1*b*, and see Page 1980, Pl. II), and it is thought that the Spanish—with their perennial aversion to lute-like shapes—developed the guitar shape (*f*) quite independently of Fig. 1*c*, *d*, even though the back may not be flat but convex, built up from ribs. By the 16th century 'gittern' could mean the 4-course guitar.

Today it looks as though the new interpretations have won: where the older books say 'citole' (or 'mandora'), read 'gittern'; where they say 'gittern', read 'citole'.

Cittern (Fr.: *cistre*; Ger.: *Cister, Sister*. It.: *cetra, cetera*; Sp.: *cítara*). The main metal-strung plucked instrument of the 16th to the mid-17th century. It has a pear-shaped body (Pl. 1) with almost flat back, and very shallow sides which normally decrease in width from the neck to 2.5 cm. (1″) or less at the lowest end—the small volume of air contained serving to emphasize the cheerful, glistening tone from the thin wire strings (struck with the fingers or more usually a plectrum). The cittern is now available again in reconstructions, and can contribute immense life to an early music ensemble, besides possessing a solo repertory of its own.

1. *Strings.* These are steel for the higher tuned, brass for the lower, passing over a low bridge, to a wooden 'comb' or to hitch-pins at the bottom of the body. Tuning is by side pegs or pegs inserted into the front of the head. This has a carved finial, and underneath usually a carved hook which could be (Wright 1977) a vestige of the hole for the thumb characteristic of the head of a medieval citole (see CITOLE AND GITTERN, Fig. 1, here not showing the head). A thick fingerboard with fixed frets of metal or bone extends on to the belly, with (as on the Spanish *guitar) the octave fret where neck meets body. Most original citterns are Italian, and these have the thick neck cut entirely away under the bass side of the fingerboard, easing the position of the left thumb. A typical string-length is 45 cm. (18″, between guitar and *mandolin lengths) but some instruments are bigger and tuned deeper. (For the 'arch-cittern' with added bass strings, see CETERONE.)

Pl. 1. Cittern by Gasparo da Salò, Brescia, 2nd half 16th century, side and front.

2. *Tuning and tablature.* Ex. 1*a* shows the common Italian tuning of the 16th century, with six double courses of strings tuned in a 're-entrant' (zigzag) scheme. England used four courses, tuned as the first four of the Italian; France, also four courses, but the fourth put a whole tone lower and usually including triple courses with octaves (Ex. 1*b*). The music is written in tablature. Italian tablature, like Italian lute tablature, puts the first course on the bottom line and uses numerals for the frets (open string, 'O'). English uses the French system, first course on the top line and letters for the frets (open string 'a'): see Ex. 2, from Holborne (1597, which points distinctly to plectrum playing, no string being left out between two others in a chord). The French, for reasons not yet clear, omitted the fret following the third, so that this (lettered 'd') is followed a whole tone higher by the next, lettered 'e': see Ex. 3, noting how the melody is here played on the fourth course and therefore sounds in octaves (Ex. 1*b*). There may also be gaps in the fretting farther up the fingerboard, or small frets not reaching right across.

Ex. 1.

a

b

Ex. 2.

Ex. 3.

3. *Development of the cittern.* Descended perhaps from the medieval *citole, the cittern was developed in 15th-century Italy: pictorial evidence shows curious wooden blocks then serving as frets. The whole instrument except the belly was carved in one piece until construction in separate pieces, as in violin-making, was adopted by Italian makers from the mid-16th century, notably Girolamo Virchi of Brescia, said to have been a teacher of Gasparo da Salò (see VIOLIN, 4). A tribute to Virchi's craftsmanship, besides the superlative example of 1574 bearing his name (Vienna *collection), is a long-held ascription of two of his unsigned citterns to Stradivari. No English example is known to exist, though the cittern appears in numerous pictures (see BANDORA, Pl. 1).

4. *Repertory.* After the French tablatures of Guillaume Morlaye, Adrien Le Roy, and Simon Gorlier of the 1550s, outstanding publications include that of Paolo Virchi (1574, the date of the cittern made by his father, Girolamo—see above), those of the Fleming, Frederick Viaera, and, in London, Holborne's *Cittharn School* (1597) and Robinson's

Newe Citharen Lessons (1609), both including versions of many of the popular tunes. Many English collections for mixed ensembles also contain a part for cittern, for example Morley's *First Book of Consort Lessons* of 1599 (see BANDORA). (Today the name 'cittern' is often used by British folk groups for a type of 5-course flat-back *bouzouki.)

5. *Derivatives of the cittern.* See ENGLISH GUITAR (with the 18th-century French equivalent and Portuguese *guitarra*).

(a) *Hamburger Cithrinchen* ('little cittern', mentioned in England as 'bell cittern'). Best known as made by Joachim Tielke (1641–1719) of Hamburg, a master of decorative craftsmanship esteemed equally for his guitars and viols. The body, only some 28 cm. (11") long, has a bell-like outline, with a small extra rose near each outward point. The sides still narrow towards the bottom of the body and the neck is cut away on the bass side; but there are five double courses of strings, described as tuned like the upper five of a guitar.

(b) *Waldzither* (or *Halszither*, 'necked zither' as distinct from the later neckless *zither, the word 'zither' having originated as a dialect form of '*cister*'). While by the late 17th century the cittern had lost popularity elsewhere, modified forms of it continued to be made in Germany, some to survive in use into the 20th century, under these names, in South Germany and Switzerland, as a farmhouse folk instrument; a small German tutor for it was recently still in print, by Wobersin (n.d.). A noted former maker, Kram of Nuremburg, from c.1760, made it especially in arch-cittern style, with the body somewhat square in outline, and with four double courses plus up to nine basses, all strings of wire. In some of his examples the basses can be selectively raised by a semitone to suit different keys by turning a wooden cylinder attached below the upper head and armed with small brass nuts.

Dart 1948; Hadaway 1973; Tyler 1974; see also Baines 1966.

Clapper. General term for instruments made specifically for making some kind of clapping noise, such as the following few examples, among many.

1. Two pieces of wood, bamboo, etc., held one in each hand, as in *Japan, 1a, the clapper of the court music.

2. More frequently, two or more wooden pieces are loosely tied together through holes at one end, or hinged together, for flapping in one hand, as the orchestral *whip; Chinese theatre clappers (see CHINA, 1a); 'handle' forms of *castanets; innumerable varieties made as toys, bird-scarers, etc.; and large instruments of long hinged boards as formerly used on whalers ('Nantucket bell') and other vessels for calling the watch. For a 'strung clapper' with 20 or many more pieces strung to clatter together, known in Europe, but see especially SASARA (Japan), also *bin-sasara.*

3. 'Wooden-shoe clapper': the front of the sole is hinged, to be clapped against the rest by a string at New Year festivals, by a man disguised in Belgium as a bear, but as a goat in Romania—900 miles distant yet not far in terms of ancient folklore.

4. From Ancient Egypt are ivory or wooden tied clappers in the shape of a human hand and forearm, as if a ritual extension of hand-clapping. But the Graeco-Roman festival-dancer's *crotala* comprised two stick- or wedge-shaped plaques, a pair for each hand (see AULOS, Pl. I), very likely tied or hinged (rather than played like *bones, and see CASTANETS, Fig. 1b) though no good actual examples have yet been found which might settle the question.

5. In *classification of instruments, 'split idiophone' covers instances, mainly in South-East Asia, where one end of a bamboo stick is cut into two long prongs, which are struck on the arm for a brief rattling sound. See RATTLE, 2, for some European shaken instruments which might be regarded as forms of clapper.

Clarín. Old Sp. word for a *trumpet, sometimes for a *bugle. In Bolivia and Peru, now a long cane trumpet with cowhorn or metal bell and a mouthpiece opening in the side; sounded at church festivals. It can reach 2 m. (80") long, sometimes of two parallel tubes connected at the far end (bringing the mouthpiece next to the bell) or even three such tubes. In villages east of Ica (Peru) is a kind made from discarded tin canisters and up to 5 m. (16½') long, sounded with 'an ear-splitting bellow' along with drum and the flute *quena. See also ERKE.

Clarinet (similarly in other languages though in Italy sometimes 'clarino'; Ru.: *klarnet*; in 19th-century England often 'clarionet'). Invented in Germany at the beginning of the 18th century by Denner (the elder or the younger; see CHALUMEAU, 2), the clarinet is unique among wind instruments in obtaining its large, flexible musical compass through combination of a cylindrical tube (apart from the bell) with a vibrating reed, here a single reed attached over a mouthpiece (Fig. 1)—a combination which brings an acoustic behaviour analogous to that of a *stopped pipe, giving the instrument its unmistakable sound through strong predominance of odd-numbered partials in the tone, while it is to these harmonics that the fundamental scale is 'overblown' to carry the compass upwards, beginning with those at the interval of a twelfth above. Again in stopped-pipe manner, the fundamentals lie deep in relation to the size of the instrument: the clarinet, though of about the same length as the flute, can sound notes nearly an octave deeper. This size, 66 cm. (26") long, is that of the 'Bb clarinet', by far the most used: for other sizes and pitches see 4 below; and for much larger and deeper clarinets, ALTO CLARINET, BASSET HORN,

BASS CLARINET, and CONTRABASS CLARINET. In ethnographic studies the name 'clarinet' can denote any ancient or primitive *reedpipe that employs a single reed (see IDIOGLOT).

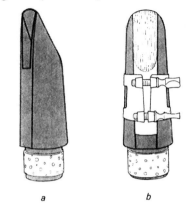

Fig. 1.

1. *Construction.* The clarinet today is of 'African blackwood' ('grenadilla') or for some lower-priced models, moulded plastic. The nickel-silver keywork is normally in 'Boehm system', as (Pl. 1b) recognized by (normally) five 'rings' in front and one ring behind. Apart from the mouthpiece it is in four parts: the short 'barrel' (which can be pulled out to counteract rising temperature); upper and lower joints; and flaring bell (just above which the 14.75- to 15-mm. bore starts to widen out). The reed (after a quick moistening between the lips) is secured over the slot in the mouthpiece, their ends matching, by the two-screw 'ligature'. It is then placed on the lower lip, drawn back over the teeth with the mouth closed firmly round the sides. Most players place the upper teeth directly on the sloping top of the mouthpiece, but some draw the upper lip back over the teeth as well. Reeds are sold in boxes of 10 or 25 labelled from 'soft' to 'hard', 'medium hard' being an average for orchestral work, 'medium soft' for a beginner (for materials and adjustments see REED, 3).

2. *Compass and registers.* The notes of the Bb clarinet sound a tone lower than written. Ex. 1 (p. 67), lower line (notes as written) compares the lower part of the compass with (upper line) that of oboe or saxophone, which both have a conical tube and overblow to the octave. The fundamental registers are indicated up to the first barline, followed by the upper registers; notes placed above each other require broadly speaking the same number of fingers to be put down. In each line the upper register embraces notes from d" to c'''. On the clarinet they are obtained by opening the thumb-key ('speaker' or 'register' key) while keeping the thumb-hole closed. Since on the clarinet these notes are 3rd harmonics, a twelfth above the fundamentals g to f, this leaves a gap to be filled

Pl. 1. Modern clarinets: (*a*) E♭ clarinet: (*b*) B♭ clarinet: (*c*) basset horn; (*d*) bass clarinet (to low C); (*e*) contrabass clarinet (b♭), all by Leblanc, Paris (except (*b*) by Yamaha of Japan); (*f*) a simple-system clarinet by Albert (Brussels, 1879).

from *g* to *c''*. For this, there is the thumb-hole, opened for *g'*; a small key (first finger) for *a''*; and the two lowest notes *e* and *f* (which on the other instruments serve merely to extend the compass downwards) are overblown with the speaker key to supply *b'* and *c''*. This gives the fingers that operate these keys a great deal to do, but far from impeding technique, the clarinet benefits from having two unusually extensive registers, which encourages performance of sweeping scales and

particularly those long arpeggios so idiomatic to the clarinet since the solo works of Mozart (when the instrument possessed only one key more than the four so far referred to).

Above *c'''* comes the high register, keeping the speaker key open: 5th harmonics, from *c♯'''* (5th harmonic of low A) up to *f♯'''*, for these raising the first finger; and so on: see OVERBLOWING for details. Through this high register the clarinet loses the grandeur of its two main registers although it

Ex. 1.

is extensively used. Technique has been much expanded of late, with quarter-tones and *"multiphonics'.

3. *Systems.* The 'Boehm system' clarinet was patented in Paris in 1844 (see 4d below) and has remained virtually unchanged since. Rarer models with six rings in front have also an extra key (right little finger) and a longer lower joint taking the compass down to written eb, to sound the bottom note of the clarinet in A (4, below) and needed by players, chiefly in Italy, who dispense with this, playing all parts on the Bb clarinet, transposing parts 'in A' a semitone lower at sight. Clarinets have also been made in brass, plated, but for some reason do not seem to sound as well as those of wood, ebonite, etc. 'Simple system' clarinets (or 'Albert system', Pl. 1f, after the former Brussels maker) have usually two rings in front (sometimes four) and no ring on the back. Though tonally they can be very pleasing, they are for normal purposes out of date, though some professional British players were using them up to the 1960s. In America they were common up to the time when many of the early jazz clarinettists were brought up on them. An advisable device (though many players have managed without it, and it is absent in Pl. 1) is the 'Patent C sharp' (the written c♯), recognizable by a second open-standing key low down on the left side of the lower joint and closed by the low F key, which here carries a small, a sharply angled arm.

In Germany and Austria more complex forms of Albert system have been used, with from four rings and 18 keys as played by Mühlfeld, whom Brahms wrote for, up to the present system by Oehler (Berlin). This has a mass of key-mechanism providing further alternative fingerings and improving the quality of some others. The German mouthpiece is more pointed than is normal elsewhere and the reed a shade narrower; the old, once universal, method is retained of tying on the reed with a long length of soft string.

4. *Clarinets in other keys.* (a) *A clarinet.* For orchestral and chamber music this is required as well as the Bb clarinet: about 4 cm. longer (71 cm. (28")), sounding a minor third lower than written, and normally played with the same mouthpiece, swapping it over according to whether the part states

'in Bb' or 'in A' (in Fr. and It., 'Sib' and 'La' respectively). The two instruments can be bought as a matched pair, though this is not essential. They sound almost identical (the A clarinet slightly mellower), the tradition being to write for A clarinet where the music or movement is composed in a sharp key. This arose as a necessity in the time of Mozart when it was mechanically impossible to play the clarinet fluently in keys much removed from its own natural key. Although with the modern keywork this no longer applies, the instrument still sounds musically at its best in tonalities not too distant from its 'home' key.

(b) *C clarinet.* Parts marked 'in C' are written for the C clarinet (c.60 cm. (23½")) long, much used in the past where the orchestral key is C or G. Through the 20th century such parts have normally been performed on the Bb clarinet, the player reading a tone higher, but the C clarinet is still manufactured and some players prefer it where Mahler and Richard Strauss, for example, have had its distinctively bright tone quality particularly in mind.

(c) *Eb clarinet* (or *clarinetto piccolo*, Pl. 1a). c.49 cm. (19¼") long, a fourth above the Bb clarinet and sounding a minor third higher than written. Present in every full military band, and in the orchestra occasionally scored for, for the sake of its quaint, 'chirpy' quality—as in Berlioz's *Symphonie fantastique* (Finale, where 'the loved one' is turned into a witch) and Strauss's *Till Eulenspiegel* (the hero in his mischievous mood). In the latter case the part is in fact written for the D clarinet, 2.5 cm. (1") longer and a semitone deeper, and obtainable today in France and Germany, but parts like that in *Till* are found to lie well on the Eb clarinet and are normally played on this, reading a semitone lower. The Eb clarinet was preceded in Beethoven's time by smaller F' clarinet.

(d) *Ab piccolo clarinet.* Manufactured in France and Italy for large military bands to give some support the highest register: 40 cm. (16") long, sounding from Middle C to the top Eb of the piano. Another small clarinet, in G, is the traditional wind instrument of the Viennese 'Schrammel Quartet' along with two violins and bass guitar.

5. *Earlier clarinets.* (a) *Baroque clarinet.* As first made by the Denners in Nuremberg: two keys only (the speaker, and the A key on the front, and c.50 cm. (20") long when built in D, the most typical key, giving in the upper register the same notes as the 'clarino' register of the contemporary trumpet, with a strong, bright tone to match. Originals are rather rare, but reproductions are now made and heard in early clarinet music including Handel's Overture in D with two horns, and concertos such as notably Molter's of the 1740s, which require astonishing execution up to the highest G, four lines above the staff.

(b) *Five- and six-keyed clarinet.* Clarinets with the present compass down to the written *e* were coming into general use by the 1760s, mostly in B♭ or C, in boxwood with ivory 'tips' and four or, by Mozart's time, five brass keys. These are usually square-ended, leathered underneath, and mounted on brass pins through raised blocks or bulges in the wood (Pl. 2). For low *f* there is a plain hole, high in position but deep-bored through the bulge in which the three lower keys are pinned. (English clarinets by 1800 add a long key on the upper joint for trills across the break between the registers. American-made five-key clarinets exist from *c.*1810 by Catlin, Hartford, Conn., with five keys.)

Pl. 2. A five-keyed B♭ clarinet by Cahusac, London, late 18th century (Bate Collection, Oxford).

The lower joint on these instruments is normally in two parts, the upper with the right-hand holes, the other bearing the lower keys; on some B♭ clarinets the upper part could be exchanged for a longer piece marked 'A' for playing as an A clarinet. Specimens of five- or six-key clarinets abound from all countries, for they continued to be played in local bands through much of the 19th century and, on the Continent, to be manufactured, often still in boxwood, as cheap export models.

Technically, the cross-fingerings required for semitones are excellent in the upper register, where they matter most in the music; the chief ones are (highest hole on left; '○', hole open):

f″	●●●●○●
f♯″	●●●○●●
g♯″	●●○●○●
b♭″	●○●○○○
c‴	○●○○○○

In the low register they are difficult to match to the other notes in strength and clarity, and can at first be a main problem in playing Mozart's works on a five-keyed clarinet, on which they can sound especially beautiful. (The middle *f♯′*: left hand, first and second fingers, thumb-hole open; *g♯′*: A key and thumb-hole closed; or else speaker key alone, or adding the second finger.)

(c) *Up to 13 keys.* Chiefly to help the low register further keys were becoming common from *c.*1810, added in various ways by the makers in different countries. Weber's two concertos (1811) were introduced by Carl Baermann with 10 keys. The 13 keys on which the subsequent 'Simple System' is based were credited to Ivan Müller, Paris, 1812, along with cupped keys and stuffed pads.

A widespread practice was to play with the reed uppermost, in France up to the 1830s, in England the 1840s, and in Italy sometimes (as at the Naples opera) to the end of the Second World War, apparently with no detectable effect on the performance as compared with the normal 'reed lowermost' method. This last seems to have been an alternative in Germany from the earliest (two-keyed) times, and to have been normal there by later in the 18th century; it was probably (it is not known for certain) the method used by Anton Stadler, for whom Mozart wrote his Clarinet Quintet and the Concerto (see BASSET CLARINET).

(d) *Boehm system.* In Paris, 1839, Louis-Auguste Buffet, with Klosé, clarinet professor at the Conservatoire, exhibited the *clarinette à anneaux mobiles* (i.e. rings), the patent following in 1844. The inventors' description continues '*d'après le système de M. Boehm*', the rings and the right-hand fingering being like those of Boehm's 1832 conical flute (see FLUTE, 4*c*; also OBOE, 4*d*). This clarinet came to be called 'Boehm system' during the 1860s. An original by Buffet, in C, is in the Bate *Collection, Oxford: of boxwood and brass, but otherwise hardly differing from the modern save in the more delicate keywork.

6. *Repertory.* Some early works are referred to above. The clarinet's important solo repertory begins with Mozart: Concerto, K. 622: Quintet, K. 581 (with strings); and Trio in E♭, K. 498 (with viola). Carl Stamitz wrote a good concerto, in E♭. From Beethoven we have the Trio, Op. 11 (with cello). Weber equals (some players say surpasses) Mozart in his two concertos, Op. 73 and Op. 74, and approaches him in the Concertino, Op. 26, and

(with piano) the *Grand duo concertante*, Op. 47. Lesser works include four concertos by Spohr; concertos by the Finnish player Crusell, from 1803; and Schumann's *Fantasiestücke*, Op. 73 (with piano).

The next summit comes with Brahms's two sonatas, Op. 121, 1 and 2. Some commendable works then include: Gade, *Fantasiestücke*; Saint-Saëns, Sonata, Op. 167; three sonatas by Reger (rather heavy); Busoni's Concertino, and also his *Elegie* (with piano); and Debussy, *Première rhapsodie* with piano. There are some splendid works by late Romantic British composers, including the sonatas by Stanford and Bax, and—the finest after Brahms—the Fantasy Sonata by John Ireland. There are noisy concertos by Milhaud and Copland, and pleasant sonatas by Hindemith and Poulenc. More unusual are Stravinsky's Three Pieces for clarinet solo (1919) and Berg's Four Pieces, Op. 5.
Brymer 1976; Halfpenny 1965; Kroll 1968; Rendall 1954, rev. 1971; Weston 1971, 1977; Willaman 1949. See also CHALUMEAU; Baines 1957; Carse 1939.

Clarinetto d'amore. A minor species of *c.*1750–1820, more than 30 examples known, usually with a bulbous bell and a short metal or wooden neck to take the mouthpiece. Pitched in various keys below the B♭ clarinet, usually in G or A♭, it seems to have been used mostly by soloists, for instance (as a French author said) in 'sad and lugubrious' pieces. It is hardly ever named in a score: J. C. Bach names it in some of his Mannheim works (as the opera *Temistocle*, 1772), but the parts are for instruments in low D, probably for *basset horns of an early type built in this deep key.

Clarino. 1. As a term in baroque and classical trumpet music, see TRUMPET, 4.

2. As a modern instrument, clarino (or clarion horn) is a spirally wound trumpet in 7′ D (the pitch of the baroque trumpet) that has been seen for some years in performances of baroque music. It was invented in Germany in 1959 by Finke on the basis of a coiled silver trumpet seen in the 1727 portrait of the Leipzig trumpeter Gottfried Reiche (see CORNETT). It has two small holes or 'vents' (and there may be others) normally covered by the fingers. The chief of these holes when uncovered causes the trumpet to sound the harmonic series of G, a fourth above its normal D series. The object is to produce the (sounding) *g″* and *b″* which are problematic eleventh and thirteenth harmonics on a D trumpet, as the unproblematic eighth and tenth harmonics of the G series. Such vents are now often provided on replica baroque trumpets of conventional baroque format, the holes here situated on the rear bow. See also POST-HORN, 2.

Clarion. The original, 14th–15th century, meaning of this word in France and England is far from being understood: a trumpet certainly, but how it differed from the ordinary trumpet of the era (see

TRUMPET, 5) in size, build, or style of playing, is nowhere clearly explained, though differences there definitely were, and very likely of such a kind that led to the Italian term *clarino* for high-register playing in trumpet. See also BASS CLARINET, 3, and (as organ 4′ reed stop) ORGAN.

Clarone (It.). See BASS CLARINET.

Clarsach. Gaelic, a harp. See HARP, 7.

Classification of instruments. The Ancient Greeks at first classified their musical instruments in what seemed an obvious way and as some peoples still do: those that were blown and those which were struck (including stringed instruments, then all 'struck' with fingers or plectrum). By the 2nd century AD (Nicomachus), the leading role of stringed instruments in music had led to their detachment from 'struck' (drums, cymbals) to give the since familiar 'Strings, Wind, and Percussion'.

The oldest Indian treatise on drama and music, from about the same time, recognizes, however (see INDIA), that there are involved in musical instruments substances of four main kinds: strings; air; membranes; and hard vibrating materials. Not until 1880 was a full classification on similar lines published in the West, by V.-C. Mahillon (1841–1924), founder of the great *Collection in Brussels. This was followed (Berlin, 1914) by the similar scheme of Erich von Hornbostel and Curt *Sachs which has since been standard; it puts the 'hard vibrators' first, under the title *Idiophones. Our instruments of Western music scarcely call for more rigorous classification than the old and traditional, and the Hornbostel–Sachs scheme does not revolve around them, though it can accommodate them; but the instruments from other fields benefit greatly, above all from a standard order for description, arrangement, and reference. The two authors were aware that their scheme had imperfections; but so would any other, and the best course, as now generally agreed, is to stick to theirs—especially since its terminology has begun to reach the general public through descriptions issued with recordings and the like (and is much used in the present work). A brief summary is therefore given below, with some examples of instruments or regions named in parentheses. The full classification uses the Dewey decimal system, carried up to eight or nine digits, but this has been used only by specialists.

Summary of the Hornbostel–Sachs classification of musical instruments:

1. IDIOPHONES (the substance of the instrument itself yields the sound).

(a) Struck. (i) Directly: by concussion (two or more complementary sonorous parts are struck together; e.g. rhythm sticks, castanets, pairs of cymbals); by percussion (the instrument is struck by a non-sonorous object; e.g. triangle, xylophone, bell).

(ii) Indirectly (without performing a movement of striking): by shaking (rattles); by scraping a notched or toothed surface (guiro); 'split idiophones' (see CLAPPER, 5).

(b) *Plucked* (jew's-harp, *sansa*, musical box).

(c) *Rubbed* (rubbed tortoiseshell, glass harmonica).

(d) *Blown* (*Aeolsklavier*, a German keyboard invention reported in 1822, with wooden rods blown from bellows).

2. MEMBRANOPHONES (the sounds are excited by a stretched membrane).

(a) *Struck drums*. (i) Directly struck: kettledrums; tubular drums (with subgroups further subdivided according to whether single-skin or two-skin): cylindrical (side and bass drums), barrel, double-conical (Indian *mṛdaṅga*), hourglass, conical, and goblet (e.g. *darabuka*); frame drums (similarly subdivided; e.g. tambourine, 'Shaman drum'). (ii) Indirectly struck: rattle and clapper drums (e.g. Asian 'monkey drum').

(b) *Friction drums*. (i) With a rubbed stick. (ii) With a rubbed cord (drum held still or drum whirled). (iii) Directly rubbed.

(c) *Singing membranes* (kazoos).

3. CHORDOPHONES (with a string or strings stretched between fixed points).

(a) *Simple chordophones or 'zithers'* (here in a general sense). The instrument consists solely of a string-bearer or of a string-bearer with a resonator (e.g. a gourd) which is not integral and which can be detached without destroying the apparatus. Each group divides into idiochord (string made in the material of the string-bearer, e.g. bamboo) and heterochord (the string is of a different material from the string-bearer). (i) Bar zithers (musical bows, stick zithers, Indian *vina*). (ii) Tube zithers (the string-bearer has a vaulted surface): either whole-tube (Madagascan *valiha*) or half-tube (Japanese *koto*). (iii) Raft zithers (canes are tied together in raft fashion). (iv) Board zithers (the string-bearer is a board, e.g. zither, dulcimer, piano). (v) Trough zithers (strings over a trough).

(b) *Composite chordophones*. The string-bearer and resonator are organically united. (i) Lutes (the strings are parallel with the soundboard; in some cases they are 'bowed lutes', e.g. fiddles): pluriarcs (each string has its own bow-shaped bearer, West Africa); yoke lutes (with arms and crossbar lying in the plane of the soundboard, e.g. lyres, crwth); handle lutes; pierced or 'spike' lutes (as in Asia); neck lutes (e.g. lute, sitar, guitar, violin). (ii) Harps (the strings lie in a plane perpendicular to that of the soundboard): open (no fore-pillar or column); arched (in Antiquity, Burma, Africa); angular (Antiquity, Caucasus); frame (with column, as in Europe). (iii) Harp-lutes (here denoting West African instruments with upright notched bridge, e.g. *kora*).

4. AEROPHONES (the air itself forms the vibrator in the primary sense).

(a) *Free aerophones*. The vibrating air is not confined by the instrument. (i) Displacement or non-interruptive (e.g. whip-cracking). (ii) Interruptive: idiophonic or reeds: concussion reed (with two blades, e.g. split grass stem), percussion reed (with one reed beating over a frame; found in British Columbia), free reed (one blade in a close-fitting slot; e.g. accordion), ribbon reed (stretched edgewise to air-stream); non-idiophonic (the interruptive agent is not a reed; e.g. siren, rotating plaque (as in the bull-roarer)). (iii) Plosive aerophones (e.g. pop-gun).

(b) *Wind instruments proper*. A vibrating air-column or air-mass is enclosed in the instrument. (i) Flutes (each group subdivided into open or stopped at lower end and further subdivided into with or without fingerholes): without duct: end-blown (*nay*, notched flute, panpipe), side-blown or transverse, vessel; duct flutes: external duct (Javanese *suling*), internal duct (recorder, ocarina). (ii) Reed instruments: double-reed, cylindrical (*hichiriki*, crumhorn), conical (shawm, oboe); single-reed, cylindrical (*zummara*, clarinet), conical (saxophone); free-reed (here only if with fingerholes (South-east Asia), otherwise placed in 4a, above). (iii) Trumpets (the player's lips vibrate): natural (each group divided into end- or side-blown; conch, trumpets, horns): chromatic (with fingerholes, keys, slide, or valves).

Complex instruments like bagpipes and organs are placed according to the components that may be considered as playing a leading part. This applies too in cases where two (or more) of the main classes are represented in one instrument, e.g. the tambourine: membranophone plus idiophone (the metal discs).

Electronic musical instruments had scarcely come into existence when the classification was drawn up, but for completeness (especially now that early types of electronic instruments have entered museum collections) there has since been provisionally added:

5. ELECTROPHONES.

(a) *Electro-acoustic*. Acoustic instruments functionless without pick-ups (electric guitars).

(b) *Electromechanical*. With tone-wheels (Hammond Organ).

(c) *Electronic*. The vibrations are generated by oscillators (electric organ, synthesizer).

Clavecin. Fr., *harpsichord.

Claves (Sp., literally 'keys'). Percussion instrument of Cuban origin and an essential rhythm instrument of Latin-American dance music, along with the scraper, *guiro, and rattle, *maracas. Of the two hardwood rods, 16.5 cm. (6½″) to 20 cm. (8″) long, one is held in the slightly cupped left hand, the two main nodal regions (the same as with a *xylophone bar) resting on the ball of the thumb and the index finger respectively while the hollow of the hand provides resonating space below. This rod is struck in the centre with the other rod held lightly in the right hand, whence players often speak of the 'clave' (the other rod being in effect a beater).

The claves are among the many popular percussion instruments introduced into concert works by Varèse and used since by Copland and Berio (*Circles*) among others.

Clavicembalo. It., *harpsichord.

Clavichord (Fr.: *clavicorde*; Ger.: *Clavichord, Klavichord*; It., Sp.: *clavicordo*. An early name, *manicorde*, is often met). Stringed keyboard instrument, one of the earliest, in use by the 15th century and in some countries into the early 19th. It is today again readily obtainable for all who like a small, quiet, and authentic instrument in the home for playing, for example, the keyboard music of J. S. Bach, who is said to have preferred the clavichord to any other keyboard instrument apart from the organ.

I. Construction. The clavichord is oblong like a *virginal or square piano, usually smaller (around 220 cm. or 4′ long, but some much larger). On raising the lid one sees the wooden key-levers and to their right a roughly square soundboard (Pl. 1).

The steel or brass strings, two to a note (the longest pair nearest the front) run from the tuning pins on the right, over the bridge glued to the soundboard (*c.*3 mm. thick or less), and thence directly to the hitch-pins on the left without passing over a second bridge or nut as the strings do in other keyboard instruments. Fixed upright in the end of each key (Pl. 2) is a brass blade or 'tangent' about 13 mm. (½″) tall. This strikes its pair of strings when the key is pressed and remains held against them so long as the key is held down. The part of the strings to the left of the tangent is prevented from vibrating by strips of soft cloth ('listing') interwoven between the strings (visible as white zigzags in Pl. 2, upper right-hand corner). The strings thus vibrate from tangent to bridge until, when the key is released and the tangent falls clear, the damping of the left-hand part by the cloth instantly spreads along the entire string and the note at once ceases. While the tangent is held against the string the point of contact is in effect one end of the string, and little of the energy supplied by the finger goes into string vibration. Hence the soft, intimate tone of a clavichord. On later, larger instruments, with a greater tangent travel, the maximum volume may be felt to approach that of a small square piano, but the clavichord is not for playing to large audiences: 'the harpsichord is used in ensembles, the clavichord alone', wrote Bach's second son, C. P. E. Bach, a great authority on keyboard playing (see BAROQUE, 2; KEYBOARD, 3*b*). In compensation, however, the player commands a sensitivity of

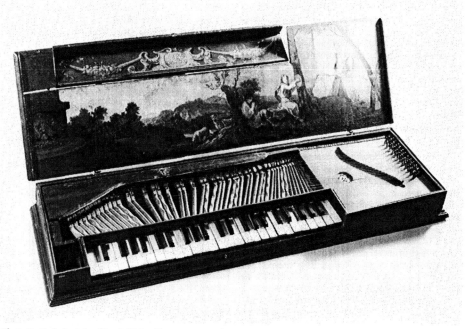

Pl. 1. Fretted clavichord by J. Weiss (Stuttgart, 1702).

Pl. 2. Unfretted clavichord by G. J. Horn (Nickern, 1790), showing the tangents, fixed upright in the keys, and the listing beyond.

control through touch unequalled on any other keyboard instrument before the invention of the piano, and in some ways greater than on this. For one thing, the pitch of a note can be modified through the finger-pressure on the key; by fluctuation of pressure the clavichord can produce a controlled vibrato, known by the old German word *Bebung*, 'trembling'.

2. *Fretted clavichord* (Ger.: *gebunden*). The clavichord as described above marks a late development (below, 3). Co-existent with it but also far earlier is the 'fretted clavichord' (Pl. 1), so-called by an analogy with frets on a lute, etc. Since a tangent determines the sounding string-length at the same time as setting it in vibration, several tangents can be used on the same pair of strings, acting at small distances apart to give different notes a semitone apart. The instrument is believed to have originated somewhat in this way as a means of working a *monochord from a keyboard as a practical musical instrument (instead of shifting bridges along the string with one hand and plucking with the other). Some early portrayals, of the 15th century, show a keyboard joined to the front of a long narrow box with equal-length strings giving between them 28 or 29 notes.

(a) *Earlier fretting systems.* By the 16th century, the bass *short octave has a pair of strings for each note, and above this there are three or four tangents acting on each pair. The strings are tuned each with the first (left-hand) tangent raised, taking little time, while both the tension strain on the frame and the quantity of string wire needed are relatively small. The key levers, set at a skew to bring the tangents in the right places, are as in all clavichords kept in true alignment by pins in the far ends guided by saw-cuts in a fixed wooden 'rack'. Not all immediately adjacent notes are playable at once, nor would the older music ask them to be; but all often-used common chords are available, while thanks to the quick action of the cloth damping as the fingers touch one key after another, restrictions

in playing scales and ornaments amount to remarkably little.

With frettings of this kind the clavichord became the prime instrument for keyboard teaching and practising. Organists used it constantly, and already in the later 15th century it could be provided with pedals, pulling down the keys by rods, or worked as a separate unit.

(b) *Later fretting system.* By degrees the above fretting system was superseded by another, described in Spain in 1555 (Bermudo) and still in use through the 18th century. There may be 23 pairs of strings for the four octaves, each (apart from the bottom octave) giving two or three notes: nowhere is there more than two adjacent semitones on the same string, while each D and A (or sometimes E and B) has a pair to itself. This can bring a safer response in legato or very fast execution, and became almost standard in the main clavichord-playing countries from Portugal and Spain to Germany and Scandinavia; i.e. in neither France, England, nor the Low Countries, where the instrument was almost totally disregarded after the 16th century in favour of the spinet or virginal.

The keyboard compass is four octaves from C, with or without the old short octave in the bass, and is sufficient for the works of J. S. Bach. The fretted clavichord is obtainable today and preferred by many to the unfretted type; whether Bach preferred the one or the other is not known for certain.

3. *Unfretted clavichord* (Ger.: *bundfrei*). This was developed in 18th-century Germany and was often of a large size, nearly 2 m. (6′) long, with five-octave compass and permitting greater dynamic range and sustaining power. Many by the elder and younger Hass of Hamburg brighten the sound in the bass by adding, over the lower part of the compass, 4′ strings (of half-length and tuned an octave higher) each running between the two main ones over a lower bridge (as in a *harpsichord); the tangent

strikes the short string just before the others, pushing it up to their level. It was on such unfretted clavichords that C. P. E. Bach was so highly praised for his expressive playing. The latest-known dated example was built in Stockholm in 1821. Then in 1894, large clavichords built by Arnold Dolmetsch helped to reawaken interest in the instrument.

4. *Repertory.* J. S. Bach, and Froberger and others before him, wrote much for the clavichord, e.g. Bach's '48', *Das Wohltemperierte Klavier* (referring to fully tempered tuning; see TEMPERAMENT), but beyond this the clavichord repertory could be said to amount to all keyboard music written when and where people would normally possess a clavichord. Thus the French 'clavecin' music, written for harpsichord, was well enough known in Germany and as often as not played there on the clavichord. C. P. E. Bach wrote that every keyboard player should possess both instruments and play on them interchangeably, the touch of one being beneficial to the quite different touch of the other.

Kirkpatrick 1981; Neupert 1948, trans. 1965; see also HARPSICHORD; Boalch 1956, rev. 1974; Ripin 1971; Russell 1959, repr. 1979.

Clavicor. Mid-19th-century brass instrument of tenor pitch, tall, with narrow bore and wide bell (sometimes to screw off) and, at first, designed with two valves for the right hand, and the third placed separately, nearer the bell, for the left. First made by Guichard (Paris) from 1838, often in C, the clavicor was the first French valved brass instrument before the *saxhorn for the middle parts in band music. Widely used, it was also made in London (by Pace, for example), the later models with three valves placed normally for the right hand. It can sometimes be seen in old photographs of British brass bands, in which a name for it was 'Alt Horn'.

Clavicytherium. The most frequent name for an upright *harpsichord, known from the 15th to the 18th century, the vertical arrangement saving floor space, and quite frequently made (e.g. by Cristofori, inventor of the piano). Since the jacks, moving horizontally, cannot return under their own weight, some form of lever is needed for each jack to push it rearwards (plucking the string) and return it under the weight of the key or of a weight attached to the lever; or else a spring acting against the end of the jack. The earliest extant stringed keyboard instrument so far known is a clavicytherium, probably south German of *c.*1480 (London, Royal College of Music *collection).

Van der Meer 1978; Wells 1978.

Claviola. Name given to certain minor 19th-century keyboard inventions.

1. With strings moved individually against a resined band (see also GEIGENWERK) or a sliding bow (Libin 1985).

2. With steel bars struck by hammer action (Paris, 1847, later also called *clavi-lame*): not very successful ideas for replacing piano strings by short, thin bars fixed to a long wooden rail at their far ends, so giving deep notes for their size—see PARTIALS, 6*b*; in a similar five-octave instrument following a London patent of 1862 (Edinburgh *Collection) the bar for low A' is *c.*8 cm. (3″) long and under 1 mm. thick. Despite a soundboard and resonator assembly lying beyond the bars the sound (as the instrument stands) seems decidedly unimpressive—though with the advent of the magnetic pickup and amplifier, the struck end-fixed bar has become one basis for an *electric piano.

Claviorgan (organ harpsichord). A combined *harpsichord and *organ, made from the 15th to the 18th century. The organ, with horizontal pipes (e.g. in three ranks) is contained in a large rectangular case with the harpsichord on top of it; it is worked from one of the harpsichord manuals, or has its own manual next to the latter. The oldest known English harpsichord is a claviorgan of 1579 built by Theeuwes, who came to London from Antwerp (London, Victoria and Albert Museum *collection).

Coach horn. English long, straight horn, usually copper, now often seen hanging up in country hotels (for which it is most often a purely decorative replica). Ninety to 120 cm. (3–4′) long, expanding throughout to a funnel-like bell, it came in during the later 19th century to replace the shorter brass *post-horn on mail coaches, and became a favourite with coaching clubs. Bugle-like tunes were published for it, e.g. in Turner's *Complete Tutor* (1898). See especially 'Coaching Calls' by A. G. Shone, *Musical Times*, June 1951, illustrating among other things the adaptations of popular airs to the limited notes of the natural harmonic series (Ex. 1, in this instance 'Auld Lang Syne').

Ex. 1.

Cobza (from Old Turkish *kobuz*). The lute of Romanian folk music: a deep body, very short unfretted neck, and turned-back pegbox. Gut strings, *c.*50 cm. (20″) long, run in four courses tuned variously, sounding e.g. *d a d g*, the first two courses double, having an octave (lower) string on the bass side; the third, two unison strings; the fourth, two unisons plus the octave lower. The cobza is played with a quill plectrum, both in free solo pieces, but especially accompanying the violin in fast, percussive dotted rhythms in accompaniment to the dances *sirba* and *hora*.

Colascione (It., of obscure Turkish origin; Fr.: *colachon*; Ger.: *Calachon, Gallichona*, etc.). A long-necked lute known by a few examples in collections. In its original form, said to have been brought to Naples by Turkish prisoners *c*.1480 and named *tambura* (Tinctoris; see RENAISSANCE INSTRUMENTS), it is a long lute (see LUTE, 7), resembling the old type of *bouzouki; it had two (or three) courses of gut strings and about 21 frets tied round the long thin neck. In Naples it was by degrees italianized and played among the middle classes in styles now best known through some harpsichord music which imitates it even down to a mandolin-like tremolo (Silbiger 1980). During the 19th century it was known as a folk instrument over southern Italy, and was reported as still played by Sicilian minstrels up to *c*.1920 (Sachs 1930).

A later 'colachon' with a larger body and wider neck for six or more strings arose in northern Europe in the 17th century, apparently as a derivative of the *mandora (Gill 1981).

Collections of instruments. A selective list, to assist the newly interested, of public or university collections devoted to musical instruments, or containing an important instrument section, with emphasis on historical (and in many cases, folk) instruments of Western music. Space precludes mention of the greater private collections; all but a few of the ethnological museums (which usually have instruments); and the hundreds of other museums—national, regional, archaeological, folk—which are always to be inspected on the chance of finding musical instruments. Catalogues (but not guides) are given in parentheses, whether or not known to be still in print (dates are of first publication); nor, for that matter, can every collection cited be guaranteed not to have changed its name or location, or been temporarily closed to public view. (Full lists including private collections are by: Lichtenwanger *et al.* 1974; Jenkins 1977; Coover 1981.) For today's instrument-makers, many major collections also issue detailed drawings of important specimens.

1. *British Isles.*
Birmingham, School of Music (Morris and Daw, 1975).
Brighton, Museum, Spencer Collection.
Cardiff, St Fagan's, Welsh Folk Museum (esp. harps).
Dublin, National Museum of Ireland.
Edinburgh, University Collection of Historic Musical Instruments, Reid Concert Hall (catalogue in progress); St Cecilia's Hall, Russell collection of Harpsichords and Clavichords (Newman and Williams, 1968).
Glasgow, Kelvingrove Art Gallery and Museum.
London, British Museum (archaeological: Anderson 1976 (Egyptian)); Fenton House, Hampstead, Benton Fletcher Collection (keyboard; Russell 1975); Horniman Museum and Library, Forest Hill, including the Carse Collection of Historical Wind Instruments (1947), and the Dolmetsch Collection; Royal College of Music (Ridley 1983 (Woodwind)); Victoria and Albert Museum (Keyboard Instruments, Russell 1968, rev. Schott 1985; Non-keyboard, Baines 1968).
Manchester, Royal Northern College of Music, Henry Watson Collection.
Oxford, Ashmolean Museum, Hill Collection (Boyden 1969); Faculty of Music, Bate Collection of Historical Instruments (Baines 1976, checklist Montagu 1988); Pitt Rivers Museum (esp. folk instruments, bagpipes, and ethnological).

2. *Western Europe* (see below for Germany, Austria).
Antwerp, Vleeshuis Museum (Lambrechts-Douillez 1981).
Barcelona, Museo municipal de musica.
Basel, Historisches Museum (Nef 1974).
Bologna, Museo Civico.
Bruges, Gruuthusemuseum (Awouters *et al.* 1985).
Brussels, Musée instrumental, Conservatoire royal (Mahillon, 5 vols., 1880–1912, repr. 1978).
Copenhagen, Musikhistoriska Museet (Hammerich 1909; Skjerne Claudius Collection (part of same), 1931).
Cremona, Museo Civico (Sacconi 1972).
Florence, Conservatorio Cherubini (Gai 1969).
Geneva, Musée des Instruments Anciens.
Gijon, Asturias, Bagpipe Museum (Meré 1970).
Göteborg, Hist. Museum.
Hague, The, Gemeentemuseum (Plenckers 1970 (brass), Von Gleich 1986 (pianos)).
Helsinki, Finnish National Museum (folk).
Lisbon, Conservatorio nacional (Doderer 1971 (clavichords)).
Milan, Museo degli Strumenti musicali (Gallini 1963).
Modena, Museo Civico.
Oslo, Norsk Folkemuseum.
Paris, Musée Instrumental du Conservatoire National (Chouquet 1875–1903); Musée des Arts et Traditions populaires (folk); Musée du Louvre (Ancient Egyptian, Ziegler 1979).
Rome, Museo Nazionale degli Strumenti musicali.
Stockholm, Musikmuseet.
Tervuren, Musée Royal de l'Afrique Centrale.
Trondheim, Ringve Museum (Kjeldsberg 1976).
Verona, Accademia Filarmonica (Van der Meer and Weber 1982).

3. *Germany and Austria.*
Augsburg, Maximilian-Museum.
Berlin, Musical Instruments Museum (Sachs 1922; Irmgard 1975; Krickeberg 1976).
Brunswick, Städtisches Museum (Schröder 1928).
Eisenach, Bachhaus (Heyde 1976).
Frankfurt/Main, Historisches Museum (Epstein 1927).
Göttingen, University, Musikinstrumentensammlung.
Halle, Händelhaus (Sasse 1966, 1972).

Hamburg, Museum für Hamburgische Geschichte (Schröder 1930).

Leipzig, Karl-Marx-Universität, Musikinstrumenten-museum (Kinsky 1913 (Heyer Collection); Heyde 1978, 1980, 1982 (wind); Henkel 1981 (keyboard); Gernhardt *et al.* 1983 (organs)).

Linz, Oberösterreiches Landesmuseum (Wessely 1952).

Lübeck, Museum für Kunst . . . der Hanselstadt Lübeck (Karstädt 1958).

Markneukirchen, Musikinstrumentenmuseum.

Munich, Bayerisches Nationalmuseum (Bierdimpfl 1883); Deutsches Museum (Seifers 1976 (wind)); Städtisches Museum.

Nuremberg, Germanisches Nationalmuseum (Van der Meer 1969 (keyboard), 1979 (brass etc.)).

Salzburg, Museo Carolino-Augusteum (Geiringer 1932; others from 1973).

Vienna, Kunsthistorisches Museum (Schlosser 1920, 1970; Luithlen 1966).

4. Eastern Europe (for Germany, see above).

Belgrade, Ethnographic Museum (folk).

Bratislava, Slovak National Museum (1975).

Budapest, National Museum (Gabry, 1969).

Leningrad, Institute for Theatre, Music, and Cinematography (Blagodatov 1972); Museum of Anthropology and Ethnography (folk).

Moscow, State Central Museum of Musical Culture, M. I. Glinka; State Collection of Bowed Instruments.

Poznań, National Museum.

Prague, Museum of Musical Instruments.

Wrocław, Silesian Museum (Epstein 1932).

5. USA and Canada.

Ann Arbor, Michigan University, Stearns Collection (Stanley 1918; Borders 1988 (wind)).

Berkeley, University of California (Boyden 1972).

Boston, Museum of Fine Arts (Bessaraboff 1941; Lambert 1983).

Cincinnati, Art Museum.

Claremont, Calif, Kenneth G. Fiske Museum.

Dearborn, Mich., Henry Ford Museum (Angelescu 1960).

New Haven, Conn., Yale Collection of Musical Instruments (with Belle Skinner Collection; Marcuse 1958 (keyboard); checklist Rephann 1968).

New York, Metropolitan Museum of Art, André Mertens Galleries for musical instruments (Crosby Brown Collection, 1901–14; Winternitz 1961 (keyboard); see also Libin 1985).

Philadelphia, University of Pennsylvania Museum.

Toronto, Royal Ontario Museum (Cselenyi 1971).

Vancouver, University of British Columbia, Ethnographic Museum (American Indian).

Vermillion, South Dakota, Shrine to Music Museum (Larson, in progress).

Washington, D.C., Library of Congress, Music Division (Gilliam and Lichtenwanger 1961 (Dayton C. Miller Flute Collection)); United States National Museum (Smithsonian Institution);

Museum of American History (Densmore 1927; Hoover, from 1967 (keyboard etc.)).

6. Latin America.

Buenos Aires, Museo . . . del Instituto nacional de musicologia (folk).

Caracas, Museo organológico, Latin American Institute of Musicology.

Mexico City, National Museum of Archaeology.

Quito, Casa de cultura ecuatoriana, Traversari Collection (Rephann 1978).

Rio de Janeiro, Museu Nacional, Federal University.

Col legno (It.). 'With the wood', a direction to string players to strike the strings with the stick of the bow. It was used to imaginative effect by Berlioz in the 'Witch's Sabbath' at the end of *Symphonie Fantastique*, which perhaps suggested to Saint-Saëns its use in his *Danse macabre*, to suggest the rattling of skeletons.

Schoenberg's String Trio, Op. 45, requires a *col legno tratto*, 'bowing' with the wood, not striking with it (cf. BOW, 3).

Componium. See BARREL ORGAN, 4.

Concertina. *Free-reed instrument held in the hands with the bellows between and with finger buttons on both sides giving single notes, the scale divided between the two hands: a difference from an *accordion being that no button by itself gives a chord. The concertina has followed two main courses of development: English, hexagonal, with the notes of the scale given alternately to the two hands; and German, normally square (but 'Anglo-German' models hexagonal) with the bass part of the scale for the left hand, and the treble for the right. The English employs 'double action' (each button giving the same note on both directions of the bellows: see ACCORDION, 1); the German normally employs 'single action' (different notes on the 'press' and the 'draw' of the bellows) and 'Anglo-German' likewise.

1. *English concertina* (see Fig. 1). Developed by Charles Wheatstone (by 1844) from an earlier (1829) small, mouth-blown 'symphonium' and first named 'melophone'; it took the name 'concertina' from the German instrument, and after improvements was established in popularity by 1851. Table 1 shows the basis of the system. Each thumb passes into the small strap and each little finger into the metal bracket opposite. The first and second fingers of each hand work alternately up the scale of C on the middle two rows of buttons; the outer rows supply the accidentals (the sharp and flat signs in the Table referring to the naturals shown immediately to the right or left in the middle rows).

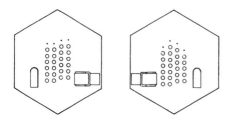

Fig. 1.

TABLE 1.

left hand			right hand		
			c''''		
# g'''	b'''	♭	# f'''	a'''	♭
# c'''	e'''	♭	♭ b''	d'''	#
# f''	a''	♭	♭ e''	g''	#
♭ b'	d''	#	♭ a'	c''	#
♭ e'	g'	#	# d'	f'	#
♭ a	c'	#	# g	b	♭

Table 1 gives the notes of the popular 'treble' concertina (the small dots in Fig. 1 mark the position of eight further buttons that may be provided, to take the C scale up to g''''). The instrument has, however, been made in all sizes from piccolo to bass, and including a Wheatstone 'bass concertina' which sounds on the 'press' only, and down to C with a brass reed over 6 cm. (2¼") long. Other leading makers have been Lachenal, and the extant London firm of Crabb.

2. *Duet concertina.* Patented in 1884 by John H. MacCann, this rearranges the above Wheatstone system (keeping the double action) to provide a continuous scale in the treble for the right hand, for playing the melody with this entirely; and (overlapping this by an octave) a continuous scale in the bass for the other hand for playing the accompaniment independently. There are six rows of buttons for each hand instead of four, the outer rows again giving the sharps and flats (but without D♯). The inner rows respectively give (through all octaves) C and G, E and A, D and D♯, F and B, occupying all four fingers, largely in certain basic sequences. The once-famous Alexander Prince rendered music like the overture to Wagner's *Tannhäuser* on it.

Duet concertinas are now only made to special order. A rather similar duet system used by the Salvation Army and said to be better suited to sacred music has five vertical rows instead of six and is known as the 'Triumph' or 'Crane' system.

3. *German concertina.* The name 'Konzertina' was first used by Carl Friedrich Uhlig of Chemnitz (Saxony) in 1834, for a rectangular-ended instrument—later square—measuring c.12 × 21 cm. (5" × 9"), with five buttons on each side giving a single-action diatonic scale like that of the simple harmonica and melodeon, with the notes of the common chord on the press, the remainder on the draw (Table 2). To this is added a second set of buttons, closer to the hand-straps, for a scale of G a fifth higher, as see Fig. 2, here in the hexagonal format of an Anglo-German concertina; the isolated button for the right hand is the air-release button for the thumb. Further rows of buttons were added, as with the Anglo-German models; but the instrument is not now manufactured, though groups of players still exist.

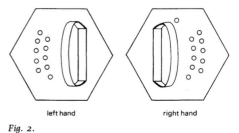

left hand   right hand

Fig. 2.

TABLE 2.

left hand		right hand	
draw/press		press/draw	
a'	g'	c''	b'
f'	e'	e''	d''
d'	c'	g''	f''
b	g	c'''	a''
g	c	e'''	b''

4. *Anglo-German concertina.* Some say this instrument, also single-action, was introduced by a Londoner, Jeffries, who made very fine instruments. It can still be obtained as a 20-key model (as Fig. 2), but the now standard forms have 30 or more buttons. With the popular 30 buttons, a third row, furthest from the hand-straps, makes the instrument almost chromatic and gives some alternative fingerings, e.g. A on the press and G on the draw instead of the opposites.

A further button in each row, and two or three additional buttons placed towards the straps, can bring a total of 39 or 40 buttons, filling in gaps at the ends of the compass, and giving more alternatives. This 'Anglo' concertina is very popular among English folk musicians for its rhythmic capabilities and raucous cheerfulness; it was the instrument of William Kimber of the Headington Morris, from whom Cecil Sharp began to note down the dances.

5. *Bandoneon.* A German square-ended instrument with single action and a fingering system invented in 1846 by Heinrich Band, a music teacher in Krefeld. It continues to have devotees in Germany, and in the USA as the concertina which leads the

polka band among people of German origin. In Argentina it has been for nearly a century the solo instrument of the tango orchestra (usually of two bandoneons, two violins, piano, and double bass). The button management, at first seeming very complicated, is based principally on three rows giving scales of A major (middle row), E major (nearest the straps), and G major (furthest row), each modified to supply all remaining notes, and alternatives for starting scales on either the press or the draw. As developed with up to six rows the range can be five octaves from low C. The square ends are c.25 cm. (10") wide. The bandoneon shares with the German concertinas a characteristic sound from the use of parallel-sided steel reeds, not tapered as in many free-reed instruments; also from having two reeds to each fingered note, tuned in unison or octaves without 'tremolo' tuning. It has also been made in double-action models; but the single action is held to give the best sound. Manufacture in Germany, much diminished by 1945, has been revived by the Arnold firm under the direction of Georg Bauer of Trebgart (near Bayreuth). American instruments are assembled from parts made in Italy and with four reeds to each note (sometimes now tapered to give a more accordion-like sound).

Conch (or shell trumpet). The shell of a large marine mollusc pierced with a hole for sounding with the lips like a trumpet. The *strombus* shell has been sounded in Europe since Antiquity, the blowing hole being made by cutting off the tip. Across the Pacific, the *triton* shell (like a huge whelk) predominates and the blowing hole is generally cut on the side. The *cassis* shell (helmet-shaped) is another that is used.

The shell amounts to an expanding tube of flat-oval cross-section through some four turns of spiral, giving an effective tube-length of c.60 cm. (2'). The fundamental falls usually in the lower regions of the treble clef, and its cooing, far-carrying sound is the sole note of the conch (harmonics being possible but not normally employed) save where a second note is obtained by partially covering the mouth of the shell with the hand—as in the well-known stick dance of Santander (Spain).

Mainly the conch serves for signalling, especially among sea fishermen but also, as in parts of Portugal, to summon the local council or—and formerly in north Wales too—farm-workers from the fields. Central Europe is one of many areas where the conch has been blown to ward off storms. It has been widely sounded in warfare: by the Hawaiians confronting Captain Cook, and for bar-rack calls in India and China up to the present century. Often a bamboo or tubular wooden mouth-piece several inches long is cemented into the pierced hole, and may be handsomely ornamented in brass. In India the shapely *śankh* (from the same root as 'conch'), of a 'chank' shell (*turbinella*)

carved with a lotus flower, is heard in Hindu temple ritual. In certain villages in Peru the conch leads the Sunday procession to mass.

Concussion sticks ('rhythm sticks'). Met over much of the world, two similar wooden sticks are held one in each hand and clashed together. In European stick dances (in India also) they may provide the sole sound-accompaniment to the dance. In Australia, for rhythm accompaniment to songs, boomerangs (or special curved sticks) are seen grasped in the middle, curving towards each other for the ends to clash.

Conga drum (or *tumba*). An African type of drum widely used from Brazil to the West Indies, and thence in the West in Latin-American dance music. The tall, tapering shell (see BONGOS, Fig. 1), up to 80 cm. (32") deep, is open at the bottom and is now either placed in a metal stand or gripped between the knees in the original manner for marking the main beat of the rumba. The membrane, now screw-tensioned, is played with the hands in a great variety of fast quaver rhythms by methods typical of hand-beaten drums generally, e.g. with the heel of the hand alternating with the fingers, or pressing with the ball of the hand (raising the pitch) while striking with the fingers. If using a pair of congas of different widths, they are tuned about a fifth apart. With them may be a larger drum, over a foot wide but of the same shape: the *tumbadora* or *tumba*, placed on a stand next to the others.

Conn-O-Sax. See SAXOPHONE, 4.

Consort. English term (of uncertain derivation) met from c.1570 to 1720 for an ensemble of voices and/or instruments. A relatively late distinction (from c.1660) of a 'whole' and a 'broken' consort, respectively using instruments of like kind (e.g. *viols) and of mixed kinds, is sometimes revived today. For 'Consort Lessons', see BANDORA.

Continuo (abbreviation for It.: *basso continuo*; Ger.: *Generalbass*; in Eng. formerly 'thorough-bass'). Characteristic of the *Baroque period is a bass line under which are numerals that indicate the harmonies above, to be filled in by the keyboardist or lutenist, playing the bass and the harmonies as implied by the figures, while normally one of the deeper bowed instruments (bass viol, cello, or double bass—see VIOLONE) gives weight to the bass line (reading from the same continuo part or from one specially written). Ex. 1 shows some simple, commonly occurring examples, the small notes here showing the chord in its basic position—though the player will distribute the notes upwards over the compass of the instrument as suits its technique and the context. Absence of a figure, as at (*a*), indicates a common chord, major or minor

Ex. 1.

according to the key signature, unless countermanded by an accidental (b). In other cases, the third note up from the bass is understood, as (c), (d), etc., save where its presence would make musical nonsense (for the period), as (e), (f); but resolution to the third (g) is marked in, '3'. Likewise the fifth note is assumed in many cases, but in (h), where it makes a diminished fifth, '5' is put in. A stroke through a number—(d), (j), (k)—indicates a sharp; '2' followed by a vertical stroke also indicates a sharp. *Tasto solo* means: play the bass only, without adding harmonies above it.

The keyboard continuo is essential in things like recitative and trio sonatas. But even where full harmony is supplied by other parts (usually string parts) the continuo is still likely to be necessary at points where these parts may leave off; and while all are playing, the keyboard contribution adds a richness to the textures. Clearly, with the executant's freedom in realization of a figured bass, continuo playing is a subtle art, on which much has been written, past and present; whether and when, for instance, to spread chords, decorate them, or in a slow recitative repeat them. It resolves in the end into a matter of experience, in satisfying the other performers and the listeners. After continuo playing ceased to be everyday practice, editors of baroque music often included written-out realizations, at least as a guide; but it is generally expected today that a continuo player will play direct from the figured bass as his forebears did.

The continuo emerged at the end of the 16th century in Italy, where a practice had already arisen of supporting instrumental or mixed part-music by stringed instruments which could follow the bass part, and fill out the rest from experience and knowledge of the piece. Agazzari (*Del sonare sopra il basso*, 1607) describes in words how each instrument should best contribute—lute, theorbo, *violone*, *arpa doppia* (see HARP, 9b, using its full compass), cittern, or *ceterone* (arch-cittern)—with no more than the figured bass before them, to create, inspired by thoughts of Ancient Greece, a radiance of harmonious sound behind the recitative sung by the actors.

Arnold 1931, 1965; North 1987.

Contrabass clarinet. Pitched below the *bass clarinet by either a fifth (in E♭) or an octave (in B♭). Though not a standard instrument it can bring an unmistakable richness to the low register of a wind orchestra or concert band. As an E♭ contrabass clarinet it is available in the USA built in wood on Selmer's model of c.1930, with metal crook and

bell, resembling a bass clarinet but taller; the lowest note, written e, sounds the lowest G of the piano. The larger size in B♭ was made in France and Germany from the late 19th century, in similar format with the body of wood or metal. Dvořák scored for it in *The Devil and Kate* (1899) where the Devil describes Hell; also Schoenberg, in *Five Orchestral Pieces* (1908).

More widely used today (in Europe, at least) are the all-metal designs introduced in the late 1950s by Leblanc, Paris. These are built in parallel tubes of plated brass, with a bore c.30 mm. and a very small bell at the top: see CLARINET, Pl. 1e for the B♭ size, which descends to the written low c (sounding the bottom Bb of the piano). The E♭ size is sometimes distinguished as 'contra-alto clarinet' (being an octave deeper than the *alto clarinet), and has an advantage in that it is easily played from a tuba part, imagining treble clef instead of bass, and adjusting the key signature and accidentals. Both instruments possess full clarinet compass and flexibility. One or the other may often be heard in music for films, while a large French military band may have one or more of each size. Xenakis scores for the E♭ instrument in *Polytope* (1967), along with the small E♭ clarinet, no other clarinet being employed in the work.

Contrabassoon (in Eng. formerly 'double bassoon'; Fr.: *contrebasson*; Ger.: *Kontrafagott*; It., Sp.: *contrafagotto*). An octave deeper than the *bassoon and written an octave higher than it sounds, like the double bass (though Wagner and Debussy write for it at sounding pitch). Every full symphony orchestra has it available: in Britain, known among musicians as the 'contra'.

1. *Construction*. The standard design is by Heckel, now made also by other makers. It stands on a short steel spike. The conical tube, 550 cm. (18') long or more, is formed in parallel sections, the three main ones of maple-wood, connected by U-bends and kept permanently assembled. A metal bell (or, as in Fig. 1, of wood) curves over at the top (Fig. 1, omitting all keywork). The first section from the crook (bocal) is a narrow conical metal pipe which turns back at the bottom to join a rising wooden section carrying the keywork for the left-hand fingers, in this respect corresponding to the 'wing' joint of the bassoon but, as it were, upside down: the key covering the first hole along the tubing from the crook is the lowest of the three in position but is to be controlled by the first finger, the uppermost; and the hole highest in position is

to be controlled by the third finger, placed lowest. This is arranged for by a simple system of keywork on long axles (such as are employed throughout the instrument for all note-holes to be located at acoustically logical points, six times further apart than on an oboe, corresponding to the pitch of two octaves and a fifth deeper). Next (to the right in Fig. 1) is a descending joint with the keys for the right hand, and (on the extreme left in the figure) the long rising joint with those for the thumbs. In some older models this terminates with an upwards-pointing bell giving lowest note C. The normal curved-over bell takes the compass down to the low B♭' or (as in the figure) to an often supplied but hardly necessary low A', sounding the bottom note of the piano. In many models today the bell curves over at a higher level (less conveniently for players sitting behind).

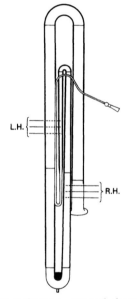

Fig. 1. Contrabassoon, sectional diagram showing positions of the two hands from the thumbs side (the fingers, indicated, lying on the far side).

2. *Reed and sound.* The double reed is larger than for a bassoon, *c.*7 cm. (2¾″) long. For the left thumb there are two 'octave keys' (as on the oboe but not the bassoon) for making the upper register, which can be taken up to the written b♭'. The sound of the contrabasson is quite its own, somewhat suggesting a double bass that is 'blown' instead of bowed. The lower notes are the most telling in the orchestral ensemble, with a full, rumbling sound that can colour the whole orchestra in passages up to the level of a moderate forte. Heckel produced his design by 1877, so it is possible that Brahms knew of it when completing his First Symphony, which makes telling use of these notes. Nearly 30

years later, Richard Strauss gives it its biggest orchestral solo, in *Salome* where John the Baptist descends to his underground prison to the opening theme of the opera, played deep in the bass. Since then, solo pieces have been written from time to time, and there has been effective use in television films, for the instrument records particularly well.

3. *Earlier designs.* First built like a scaled-up bassoon, very tall, *c.*244 cm. (8′): examples of 1714 by Eichentopf, Leipzig (see OBOE D'AMORE), and of 1739 by Stanesby, London (used by Handel in the 'Fireworks Music'). Next, Austrian, through the Classical period (as in Beethoven's *Fidelio*), less tall, though going down only to C or D but otherwise sounding very well; such were still being built up to the 1870s in Germany (by Heckel included). Of new compact designs, with reversed wing-joint, possible through developments in keywork, one of the first is Haseneier's wide-bore 'contrabassophone', of 1847. This became practically the only double bassoon known in Britain through later Victorian times, when it was made by Morton, London. In the USA at least one was made in New York *c.*1860. In France, instead of old-fashioned tall models, the *sarrusophone was often used, until eventually copies were made of Heckel's model.

4. *'Semi-contra' bassoons.* Bassoons built a fourth or fifth below the bassoon instead of an octave, and very rare. There are 18th-century examples (one made in Leipzig by the elder Eichentopf in 1714) and a fine one by Samme, London, 1854 (London, Royal College of Music *collection). Bach's deep bassoon parts in Cantatas nos. 31 and 155 may have been not for such, but for the larger size of bass *dulcian.

See also BASSOON; Langwill 1965.

Contrebasse à anche. See REED CONTRABASS.

Cor anglais (in America 'English horn', after the German, but in Britain always known by the French name. Ger.: *Englisches Horn, Alt-oboe*; It.: *corno inglese*; Ru: *angliískii rozhok*). The most important member of the oboe family of woodwind instruments after the oboe itself. It stands a fifth below the oboe, and its music is written a fifth higher than it sounds.

1. *The instrument.* This is *c.*81 cm. (32″) long, ending in a bell of bulbous form (see OBOE, Pl. 1c). The double reed (see REED, Fig. 3e) is placed on a metal 'crook' or bocal about 7.5 cm. (3″) long and bent at an angle (though it does not appear so in the plate) to enable this relatively long instrument to be held with both hands lying naturally over the keys. Many players support the cor anglais on a sling passed round the neck and hooked to the thumb-rest. The keywork and fingering are practically the same as for the oboe, save that the bottom note is the written *b*, sounding *e*.

2. *Orchestral and solo use.* The rich, dreamy sound of the cor anglais is often heard in the orchestra in long solo melodies, always slow and often of a pastoral character: for example in Rossini's *Guillaume Tell* Overture; Berlioz's *Carnaval Romain* Overture, introduction; and Wagner's *Tristan und Isolde*, in the long off-stage call in Act 2. (The curious way the part is written in *Guillaume Tell*, in the bass clef, must mean that the instrument was here first played by a bassoonist, reading the notes with bassoon fingering). Among other great solos, one thinks of Franck's Symphony, and Dvořák's 'New World' Symphony, and from the same year as this, 1893, Sibelius's *The Swan of Tuonela*, virtually a continuous solo recitative for the cor anglais.

Nearly every oboist possesses a cor anglais, for though only one member of the orchestral oboe section will be regularly playing it, many of the choral works of Bach, including the *St Matthew Passion*, require both of the two oboists to change over to cor anglais for the *Oboe da caccia* parts (below, 4). A player may also need it in chamber music, as Beethoven's Trio, Op. 9, for two oboes and cor anglais, and likewise his Variations on Mozart's 'Là ci darem', for the same. A pleasant concertino with orchestra by Donizetti was recently discovered, but on the whole the cor anglais has appeared more in small combinations, up to Stockhausen's *Zeitmasse* for wind quintet with cor anglais replacing the horn.

3. *Bulb bell and tone character.* This bell (apparently adopted originally from the *oboe d'amore) affects the quality only of the low notes in each register, imparting to them a vowel-like 'aw' quality which contrasts with the open 'eh' sounds from notes emitted higher up the tube to such a degree that, on passing from one register to the next, the cor anglais can seem almost to 'talk'. This apart, one can detect throughout the orchestral double-reed family an adherence to an old empirical premise bearing on the question of balance: that no deeper member of the family shall swamp the soprano. In aid of this, the conical bore of each deeper-pitched instrument is given a more gentle slope. A typical modern oboe may show a slope (to express it simply) of 'one in 42' or near it; the cor anglais, '1 in 51.5'. These figures relate by 1.225, or $\sqrt{1.5}$, the square root of the actual pitch ratio of 1.5 (3 : 2) between the two instruments. In tonal weight they balance, while their very distinctive overall tone-colours arise largely as a consequence of this basic proportioning in the steepness of the conical bore (along with the effect of the larger reed required by the larger instrument in order to sound its lower range).

4. *Oboe da caccia.* See TENOR OBOE, also TAILLE, for the early straight-built instrument used only for playing tenor parts in ensembles. The oboe da caccia, named by Bach (as *hautbois da caccia*) in 20 works of 1723-6, is also a fifth below the oboe but an obbligato instrument as well. Examples include

two made in Leipzig during that time by Eichentopf: curved, with flared brass bell 17 cm. (6½″) wide, not without a visual suggestion of a hunting horn (*corno da caccia*) and in sound quite like a horn heard from a far distance. To make the curve (which is one way of easing the stretch for the hands), the wooden tube, after piercing the bore, is generally found to be sawn almost right across in about 30 places along what is to become the inside of the curve, making cuts which allow the wood to be bent into an arc. The inside of the curve is planed to take a long wooden rib, glued on to secure the curve. The tube is then covered with leather. Reproductions have been made on these lines.

5. *Early cor anglais.* The German name *Englisches Horn* already occurs in a cantata of 1723 by Tobias Volckmar (Dahlqvist 1973). Whether the same instrument as the oboe da caccia, or distinguished perhaps by a bulbous bell, is not known, but this bell, along with the curved shape, is a regular feature of the *corno inglese* from the time when the name appears in Viennese operas from 1749, as well as later when Berlioz and Rossini were writing for the instrument. Less frequently the instrument was built in two straight joints set at an obtuse angle (like the classic *basset horn): both this and the curved form were made up to past the mid-19th century until superseded by the present straight form following that of Brod's *cor anglais moderne* (Paris, by 1840), better suited to mounting keywork on axles and more free in sound.

See also OBOE.

Cor de chasse (or *trompe de chasse*). The large circular French *hunting horn.

Cornamuse. 1. As 'cornemuse', the general name for a bagpipe in France, or in Italy, 'cornamusa' (see BAGPIPE, 3, 4).

2. Renaissance-period double-reed instrument with *wind-cap now reconstructed on evidence from *Praetorius (1619), and resembling a *crumhorn but without the curving tail. Praetorius refers to a plate on which unfortunately no such cornamuse is to be seen. He writes that it was closed at the bottom save for small vents in the side; it had no keys; and the sound was like that of a crumhorn but softer. In pitches it matched the crumhorns, but no specimens have ever been found, nor does any other German source name the word, though in Italy it occurs quite frequently from *c.*1570 as an instrument taking part in concerted music, possibly the instrument that Praetorius describes. For the keys now often provided, see CRUMHORN, 2.

See CRUMHORN; Boydell 1982; Meyer 1983.

Cornet (Fr.: *cornet à pistons*, or simply *piston*; Ger.: *Cornett, Kornett*; It.: *cornetta*; Sp.: *corneta*). Valved brass instrument built to the same B♭ pitch as the ordinary modern trumpet, from which it normally differs visibly in the shorter overall format (see BRASS BAND, Pl. 1, front row). For the soprano cornet, see BRASS BAND, 1a.

1. *The instrument.* The cup mouthpiece is distinctly deeper than a trumpet's, with a shorter and narrower stem. The mouthpipe, with a smaller initial width than in a trumpet, expands for some 35 cm. (14″), bending round to the main tuning-slide, which draws out back towards the player. From this the tube leads forward again, then back through a small subsidiary tuning-slide to enter the third valve. From the first valve the bell section emerges, starting with a wide bend (the fourth bend of the main tube) and thence forwards to the bell mouth. There are also various models different from this classic design, more elongated, or in trumpet format ('trumpet-cornet', a French idea of the early 1900s).

Some instruments retain the separate 'B♭ shank' inserted between mouthpiece and mouthpipe. In former times, when the cornet was used so much in theatre and light orchestras, this shank would be exchanged for a longer 'A shank' for playing parts marked 'Cornet in A' (sounding a third lower than written, the B♭ cornet sounding a tone lower).

2. *Use in bands.* The cornet's main place in Britain continues to be in the brass band, in which (and in France) it has been the lead instrument since before 1840. In military bands, in the USA also, it has been the principal soprano-pitched brass instrument for equally long, but has for some years been yielding the place to the trumpet. From the bands have risen the great past virtuosos, like Isaac Levy, 'the demon cornet player'; and in the USA Herbert Clarke, of Sousa's Band, and indeed Louis Armstrong, who learnt the cornet as a boy in the Colored Waifs' Home Brass Band in New Orleans and like many others (as La Rocca of the Original Dixieland Jazz Band) played it until the fashion in jazz changed to the more penetrating trumpet in the 1920s. The cornet's solo repertory is still mainly of a popular nature, led by fiendishly difficult variations on traditional or operatic tunes like 'Carnival of Venice', but now often supplemented by works from the trumpet repertory like Haydn's Concerto.

3. *Orchestral use.* This has had two chief aspects. First, 19th-century. In France before c.1860, when trumpets in the deeper key of F were still scored for, composers writing for large orchestra would have a pair of cornets in addition to the two trumpets, giving to the cornets the more agile and tuneful passages, e.g. Berlioz, Bizet (as in *Carmen*), Franck (Symphony in D minor), and, outside France, Tchaikovsky (in his ballets). Secondly, in France, Britain, and the USA, as the century went on, cornets became substituted for trumpets in nearly every average orchestra, until in the 20th century, with the more flexible modern trumpet, things have swung the other way: orchestral players tend to perform orchestral cornet parts on the trumpet, save perhaps in works where the composer has called for the cornet to express the more plebeian side of its nature (as Stravinsky in *Petrushka* and *L'histoire du soldat*).

4. *Early history.* The cornet was invented in France c.1828 by Halary (inventor also of the *ophicleide). It was said in Paris (six years later) that his idea had been to apply valves to the circular 'post horn of the Germans'—curiously without mention of the also circular small natural (valveless) *cornet* which had served in French *chasseur* regiments in the capacity of a bugle (see MILITARY BAND, Pl. 2, top row). The short, deep form of early cornets, with two or three Stoelzel valves (see VALVE, 2b), known in England as *'cornopean' (Pl. 1), was retained in cheaper models manufactured in France up to the First World War—though no longer with the full

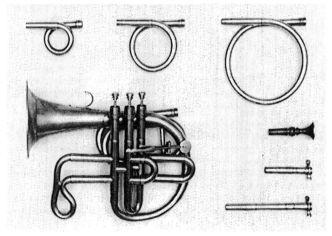

Pl. 1. An early English cornet ('cornopean') by Charles Pace, London (c. 1850), with three Stoelzel valves and 'clapper key' for whole-tone trills. *Above and right, clockwise*: crooks, A♭, G, and F; mouthpiece; B♭ and A shanks.

set of crooks down to F or lower, familiar today only in the scores of Berlioz etc. (see TRANSPOSING INSTRUMENTS, 3). See also ECHO, 1 (echo cornet).
See BRASS INSTRUMENTS; also Webb 1985.

Cornett, cornetto (in older Eng. 'cornet', often with two 't's as much used in modern times to distinguish the instrument in print from the brass instrument, *cornet, though many now prefer the It. form, 'cornetto'; Fr.: *cornet-à-bouquin*; Ger.: *Zink, Cornett*). Wind instrument of the 16th and 17th centuries (in some cases later), usually of wood in curved shape with fingerholes and a small cup-mouthpiece; difficult to play, but a sound of unique charm, highly valued in its day. It has been revived since the 1950s for its parts in works, e.g. by Monteverdi, for which otherwise substitute instruments (often trumpets) have had to be used, with great loss of effect.

1. *Construction*. The normal 'treble cornett' (Pl. 1*a*), length *c*.60 cm. (24"), is made by sawing the wood (pear, plum, maple, etc.) from end to end to carve each half to form a bore expanding from *c*.6 mm. to 24–29 mm. The two pieces are then glued together (as in making *alphorns), planed octagonal, and covered with thin black leather. The narrow end is opened out to receive the stem of the small wooden, horn, or ivory mouthpiece, characteristically shaped rather like an acorn cup.

The holes are six in front and one at the back in the same order as on a recorder; rather wide-spaced, but the curve of the tube helps the fingers in covering them. The lowest fingered note, *a*, can be lowered by the lips to *g*, reckoned the bottom note of the compass in practice. The scale, as given by Speer (1697), runs from *a* in G major, with *c'* ●●●/●○○ and *cross-fingering much the same as for a recorder. For *a'*, all holes open; *b♭'*, all covered except thumb; then as the lower octave to:

a'' ●/○●●/○○○
b♭'' ○/○●●/○○○
b'' ●/●●●/●●○
c''' ●/●●○/○○○

—the highest note he gives, though some parts rise to *d'''*.

Approaching a hundred original cornetts are preserved, including two in England purchased from London by Christ Church, Oxford, in 1605, and preserved in the college library. Among today's instruments, low-priced models in synthetic resin by Christopher Monk (1921–91) in England have proved exceedingly satisfactory.

Most contemporary pictures show the mouthpiece placed to one side of the lips; many successful players today do the same (although they are most frequently trumpet-players in the first place). The

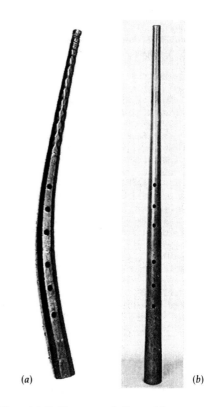

(*a*)   (*b*)

Pl. 1. (*a*) Treble cornet, Italian, 16th century; (*b*) mute cornett.

sound can suggest a gently played small trumpet, but with a liquid articulation of phrase as if a wordless treble voice (see TONGUING). The difficulty in playing is chiefly because the holes do not alone ensure stable notes and in tune: each has to be very carefully focused by the lips and breathing. Once mastered, the technique is very free: during the 16th century the cornett in professional hands, in Italy especially, rose to become the chief wind instrument for executing *divisions upon the soprano part of a madrigal or motet (Monteverdi's *Orfeo* has florid division-like passages for the *cornetti*); players today use much double *tonguing in fast passages and divisions.

2. *Smaller and larger curved cornetts*. The smaller, with a scale a fourth or a fifth higher, is the 'cornettino', named most in German 17th-century choral works. Larger, typically built in an elongated S shape and pitched a fifth below the treble, is the 'tenor cornett', also leather-covered (see PRAETORIUS, Fig. 1, far right). It seems to have been used rather less than the others, yet a fair number

of specimens have survived. A name 'lysarden' ('lizard') met in England between 1575 and 1603 in lists of instruments, especially as owned by city waits, may have denoted it (the dates being rather early for the *serpent in England).

3. *Mute Cornett* (Ger.: *Stille Zink*). Some cornetts were turned in wood in straight form, with no leather covering: originals are comparatively few, but Otto Steinkopf, who led the 1950s revival, made many in this way. More important historically, however, is the 'mute cornett' (Pl. 1*b*), straight but with a conical mouthpiece recess cut in the narrow end of the tube itself. The sound is less bright than with the curved type but sweeter, softer, faintly horn-like. A fair number survive, most in (or from) Italy, where this form was much used in chamber ensembles with viols, lutes, flutes, and recorders. Reconstructions are made.

4. *General history.* The cornett appears to be a sophisticated 15th-century development of the animal horn pierced with fingerholes (see FINGERHOLE HORN), comparable with the roughly contemporary evolution of the recorder from its medieval predecessors. Its prominence begins with the 16th century, through which it was played in instrumental combinations of every kind, and particularly, with trombones (sackbuts) supporting the choir in church music. Much of the cornett's best-known repertory is for this combination (see TROMBONE, 7*a*), English, and in German late 17th-century 'tower music' (*Turmmusik*) played at set hours by the town musicians with one or two cornetts, and trombones, alto, tenor, and bass (Bach's doubling of the voices by these instruments in some cantatas—his only use of cornetts— brought in such players). In Italy right up to the French occupation in 1798 papal processions in Rome were led by the same combination, while perhaps the latest cornetts built in the old tradition are those made in 1805 in Markneukirchen, Saxony, for the Moravians and preserved with some of their trombones in the Moravian Museum at Winston-Salem, North Carolina.

Baines 1957; Monk 1975; Reidermeister 1981.

Cornettino. See CORNETT, 2.

Corno da caccia (lit. 'horn of the chase'). In baroque works, by Bach included, the normal horn of period; see HORN, 5*a*; also HUNTING HORN, 3.

Corno da tirarsi (in It., 'slide horn'—compare 'tromba da tirarsi', *slide trumpet, 3). Named in three of Bach's cantatas (46, 47, and 162); yet there is no trace whatsoever of a slide horn before a German experiment of 1812, nor any other known mention of 'corno da tirarsi', which Bach writes in his own hand. A suggestion, several times put forward, is that it was synonymous with 'tromba da tirarsi', which would leave us then, in two instances where Bach writes 'Tromba o corno da tirarsi', possibly 'whichever you prefer to call it'.

Corno di bassetto. It., *basset horn.

Cornopean. An old name in England for the *cornet, 'horn of praise to Apollo'.

Cornophone. Obsolete French valved brass instrument; see WAGNER TUBA.

Cornu. Ancient Roman horn; see BUCCINA AND CORNU.

Corps of drums. See MILITARY BAND, 3.

Course (Fr.: *choeur*; Ger.: *Chor*). With stringed instruments such as guitars and lutes one is frequently counting the number not of individual strings but of pairs (or more) of strings tuned to the same note and sounded together as one, bringing a stronger, more ringing sound. Each pair is then described as a 'course'. The mandolin, with four pairs of strings, is a four-course instrument, in this case strung with four double courses. Often one of a pair is a thinner string tuned an octave higher, so that every note played on that course sounds in octaves—'an octave course'. Fig. 1 shows some examples schematically, looking at the instrument from the front, the nut along the top; where there is an octave course, the main string is shown thicker than the octave string. Fig. 1*a* shows a modern '12-string' guitar (see GUITAR, 3*b*), which is a 'six-course' guitar with each course double and the three lower of them octave courses. Fig. 1*b* shows a lute with typical 16th-century tuning and 11 actual strings, the first course single, the rest double; Fig. 1*c*, a cittern (old French tuning) with two 'octave triple courses'. The fourth course in the last is tuned higher than the third (as also in the *ukulele, though this is normally single-strung); when such a departure from a straight pitch sequence occurs the term *re-entrant tuning is often used.

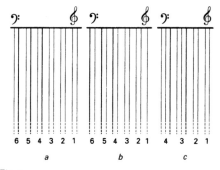

6 5 4 3 2 1   6 5 4 3 2 1   4 3 2 1

a　　　　　*b*　　　　*c*

Fig. 1.

Cowbell (Fr.: *sonnaille*, etc.; Ger.: *Herdenglocke, Viehschelle*, etc.; It., Sp.: *cencerro*). As worn by a leather strap around the necks of cattle, sheep, or goats, cowbells are most often forged bells of various shapes, e.g. rectangular, or widest at the top or at the bottom or in the middle (globular shape). They are mostly made from an iron sheet 1 to 1.5 mm. thick and in length twice the height of the bell. This is bent over, forged to shape, soldered down each side, and pierced with two holes for the suspension ring, to which a rod-like striker is attached on the inside. The bell may then be roasted in a mix of copper powder and loam and tuned by hammering for the bells of a set to sound different notes in the scale, or approximately so, depending on how particular the herd or flock owners may be in this matter. The longest of such bells, made for Alpine calendar festivals, reach a height of 46 cm. (18″) and are worn by white cows. In many countries the bells are alternatively cast in brass in a beehive shape. The striker may itself have the form of a miniature bell.

In Africa there are cowbells carved in wood, with one or two wooden rods as clappers (see AGOGO BELL for an iron version).

In the orchestra, Mahler calls for true cowbells (*Herdenglocken*) in his Sixth and Seventh Symphonies, and Webern in the Five Pieces for Orchestra, Op. 10, the bells to be sounded realistically together (indicated in the score by a long trill sign). Jazz introduced the plated cowbell, square in cross-section, of welded alloy, designed specifically for human operation, and Latin American dance music also adopted this (some say, initially as substitutes for the agogo bell). There is no striker inside, the bell being fixed horizontally to a bracket, to be struck with a drum stick. Usually two bells are provided, of contrasting pitch, but larger sets are demanded by Berio, and sets tuned over several octaves by Messiaen in his later works. These scores sometimes name them 'metal blocks' (by analogy with *wood block), which is reasonable since they are no longer imitating cowbells.

Cowhorn. See HORN, 8; HUNTING HORN, 2; FINGERHOLE HORN.

Crocodile zither. See CHAKHĒ AND CROCODILE ZITHER.

Cromorne. See CRUMHORN, 3; ÉCURIE, 2.

Crook. 1. With many woodwind instruments, the curved metal tube (in America 'bocal', from Fr.) which brings the reed or mouthpiece close to the player's mouth. With saxophone, bass clarinet, etc., it is as often called a 'neck'.

2. With brass instruments, a length of tubing (Fr.: *ton*, Ger.: *Bogen*), usually coiled, which is inserted between instrument and mouthpiece (or sometimes into the main tube at a point further along) to lower the pitch by a given interval, its main importance being with the 'natural' trumpets and horns before *valves arrived in the 19th century,

though even so crooks often continued to be provided. A horn-player might have ten crooks always ready, from 'B♭ alto' (a small coil) to 'C' (three large coils comprising 244 cm. (8′) of tubing). Having inserted the correct crook as marked in the part ('in E♭' etc.), the notes in the part, written in the key of C, tell the player which harmonic (of the natural series of the instrument as it is 'crooked') then to hit: e.g. a written Middle C, the 4th harmonic, the player knowing in his head from experience what the actual pitch of that harmonic will be with that particular crook inserted. While valves led to a gradual disappearance of crooks, composers in general felt that parts for horn or trumpet only 'looked right' if the keynote of the music, whatever it might be, continued to be written in these parts as C. Thus Brahms and Wagner, and the latter's often rapid changes from 'in' one key to 'in' another, impossible instructions for a player to follow literally (he transposes instead), but expressions of the composer's inherited romantic feeling for these instruments.

Cross-fingering. Every recorder player knows that if, while playing a note made by putting down the fingers in order, if the next hole but one (in some cases also the next after that) be covered, thus leaving a hole open in between, the note a semitone lower can be played. Such 'cross-fingering' becomes essential on practically all woodwind instruments that have no keys or only a few, while on many that have a full keywork, cross-fingerings may still be continually needed alternatives. Where the first and third fingers of either hand are put down leaving the hole in between open is sometimes used is 'fork fingering'.

The system depends on the fingerholes being small as compared with the bore diameter (as they usually are to be covered with the fingertips). The small hole impedes communication between the vibrating air-column and the exterior, causing the terminal antinode to overshoot the hole by a little distance towards the next hole. If this next hole is then closed, the impedance is increased and the antinode will travel yet further down the tube, making a longer effective air-column which may suffice to enable the player to make the semitone below; or it may be necessary also to close the hole beyond that, to shift the antinode enough to make the semitone practicable. With some instruments (notably recorders) these methods need entail no more than the slightest loss in strength and stability of sound; with others it becomes a matter of skill and practice to minimize such effects. So expert were 18th-century players in controlling cross-fingered notes that when, later in the century, keys began to be introduced for semitones many players for a long time spurned them, or avoided them as being (in those days of flat leather key-pads over plain seatings) liable to leak air and ruin the instrument's performance.

A less common way of lowering a note by a semitone is to half-cover the following hole with the finger ('half-holing', much used on the tin whistle; see FLAGEOLET, 1).

Distinct from plain cross-fingering is where in the high registers of instruments, with keys or without, the fingers are put down in indirect order to cause harmonics to sound. See OVERBLOWING; also (a post-1950s development) MULTIPHONICS.

Crotales (from Gk.: *krotala*; see CLAPPER, 4). In modern percussionist's terminology, the small cymbals also known as 'antique cymbals'; see CYMBAL, 4.

Crowd (or crouth). See CRWTH.

Crumhorn (Ger.: *Krummhorn*; It.: *storto, cornamuto torto*; Sp.: *orlo*; for Fr., see below, 3). Hook-shaped double-reed wind instrument with *wind-cap, of the period *c.*1480–1650. It has a narrow cylindrical bore, fingerholes as on a recorder, and the reed, placed on a short brass staple, inside a turned wooden cap with a hole in the top. It was revived in the 1950s, first in Germany, by Otto Steinkopf (1904–80) and Hermann Moeck.

1. *Description*. Usually in maple-wood, the end is bent round by steaming after drilling the bore; the bore is between *c.*4.5 mm. for a treble crumhorn and 8 mm. for a bass, and is widened out for the last few inches. The reed is often now of plastic (though cane is usually found preferable). It is placed on a brass staple, of which the only known original example (Vienna) has a slight taper (Meyer, K. T. 1983). The instrument is blown fairly strongly, maintaining constant pressure, while articulating the notes with the tongue against the blowing hole. The strong nasal sound cannot be varied in loudness, making a choir of four or five crumhorns playing in harmony sound quite like that contemporary reed-organ, the *regal*.

Only the fundamental scale is possible, limiting the compass to an octave and a note, so that in choosing or arranging music for playing on crumhorns no part should exceed this range unless a note which does so be omitted or replaced by another that fits the harmony—as players must have frequently done. (Agricola, 1528, with the earliest-known illustration of crumhorns as a family of different sizes, gives for bass crumhorn four extra low notes made by blowing gently: presumably the not unfamiliar 'croak' to the fifth below if breath pressure is relaxed (Meyer 1983: 99).) Some modern crumhorns add a key for the uppermost finger, in some cases also for the thumb, to add one or two notes to the top of the scale. There is no historical evidence for such keys on the crumhorn itself, but there is for some other cylindrical reed instruments of the same period (see DOUÇAINE, 3, 'dolzaina'), so that their addition to the crumhorn could be seen as 'potentially authentic' as well as

rendering the instrument today more generally useful.

2. *Sizes of crumhorn* (Fig. 1 and *Praetorius, Fig. 1). Each is an octave lower than the corresponding recorder:

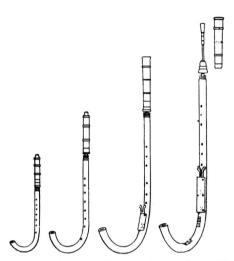

Fig. 1. Crumhorns: treble, tenor, bass, and extended bass (Italy, late 16th century). Brussels, Musée Instrumental.

Descant (or soprano): c' to d″
Treble (or alto): f to g' (in most historical sources a tone higher)
Tenor: c to d'
Bass (with little-finger key): F to g

There is, also from the 16th century, an 'extended bass' going down to low C in a peculiar fashion: a second key, overlapping the little-finger key for F, is for the E; but since further keys would be awkward to fit along the curving tail there are instead two small holes, each covered by a small brass slider which has to be preset before playing for the second key then to give *either* E (both sliders open) *or* D (upper slider closed) *or* C (both closed), whichever of these notes may be the most useful in the bass of the piece being played, for example at cadences.

Great Bass (rare): C to d (with one key, like the ordinary Bass).

Among over 50 original crumhorns, Italian and German, at least 20 are believed to be from the workshop of Jörg Wier (d. *c.*1549) in Memlingen, South Bavaria.

3. *Early history*. The name is first met as an organ register. The instrument is first seen in an Italian painting of 1488, by Costa, but the hooked end perhaps just earlier in some German *bladder-pipes in pictures (and before that in the *Cantigas* manuscript; see MEDIEVAL INSTRUMENTS, 2). The wind-cap may have been the significant new feature, through

allowing articulation, essential for refined music in parts. An early instance with the music preserved is from Florence, 1539, with men disguised as shepherds playing a six-part madrigal on five *storte* (with a *cornett for the top part), all parts fitting the ranges (Minor and Mitchell 1968). Further pieces, from this period up to the early 17th century, marked originally as for—or suitable for—crumhorns, have been published together in the *Pro Musica Antiqua* series edited by Bernard Thomas.

In England, Henry VIII possessed two cases of seven crumhorns each (perhaps made by makers from Venice; see RENAISSANCE INSTRUMENTS, 2). No English music is known that employed the crumhorn. In France, later on, *Mersenne called it 'tournebout' from the shape; later, the word 'cromorne' occurs (see ÉCURIE, 2) but it is not known whether actually referring to the crumhorn.

4. *False 'tournebout'*. In several collections may be seen a nasty instrument looking like a thick black sausage, sometimes labelled 'cromorne': apparently a forgery (see FAKES AND FORGERIES) after a poor illustration in the 18th-century *Encyclopédie* of Diderot.

Boydell 1982; Meyer 1983.

Crwth (Welsh, pron. 'crooth'; the name also formerly met in Eng. as crouth, or crowd). Ancient bowed stringed instrument of Wales, held up like a fiddle, with an overall form of a rectangle, *c*.60 cm. (2') tall with rounded corners. The lower part is an almost square soundbox, the sides of which continue upwards as two arms, joined at the top by a cross-piece to take the tuning pins, the whole betraying the crwth's origin in a lyre of an early medieval European kind (see LYRE, 3). Between the arms, and like these carved in the same piece of wood as the body, is a fiddle-like neck carrying a fingerboard, and acquired as the instrument came to be played with a bow later during the Middle Ages, after which it was still heard played by elderly musicians at the beginning of the 19th century.

The player's left-hand fingers pass through one of the openings between the instrument's arms and the neck, and the thumb through the other. The right foot of the bridge passes through one of two round soundholes to rest against the back of the body like a soundpost. The six strings, horsehair by old accounts, are led through small holes to be wound on the tuning pins at the back, and run in three octave *courses, the deeper string in each course being named the bass or 'vyrdon' (i.e. *'bourdon'). The third course, with its name signifying 'the keynote', lies off the fingerboard, and was mostly plucked with the left thumb 'as a kind of accompaniment'. Otherwise the strings were said to have been bowed all at once or 'more or less all at once', the top of the bridge being flat. Reports differ over the tuning. Some older manuscripts purport to give music for the crwth but it has not yet been deciphered with any certainty.

Medieval instruments somewhat resembling the crwth appear in pictures (first on the Continent) as far back as the 11th century, shortly after bowing was first known in the West. In Wales the crwth long took second place to the harp in the musical hierarchy. Three authentic crwths are preserved at St Fagan's, Cardiff; Aberystwyth; and Warrington. There are also copies.

The English form of the word (see above) is still met in the 18th century in the sense of a 'fiddler' (then playing the violin); the surname Crowther may derive from it (cf. Harper).

Panum 1941; Peate 1947; Remnant 1986; see also BOWED LYRE; Andersson 1930.

Cuatro (Sp., 'four'). Name used in Spain, but especially Latin America from Colombia to Mexico, also in the West Indies, for varieties of small *guitar, similar to the Portuguese *cavaquinho*. The four strings, usually single of metal or nylon, are tuned in many ways, sometimes to a chord (e.g. d'', b', g', d'), or like the *ukulele, and are vigorously strummed. There are also five-stringed varieties, *cinco*, one of them in Venezuela, *cinco y medio*, adding as well a half-length string on the treble side (its peg through the heel of the neck), tuned a fourth above the rest and struck open (Montanaro 1983).

Cuckoo. See WHISTLE, 2.

Cuica. Latin American *friction drum.

Cup cymbal. See CYMBAL, 5; INDIA, 1a.

Cura. Smallest size of the Turkish long lute *saz*.

Curtal. English 17th-century name for the *dulcian and occasionally in the 18th century for the *bassoon.

Cut-up. In an organ flue-pipe, standing upright with the rectangular opening near the bottom, the vertical height of the opening is the 'cut-up'. Sometimes the term is used with the recorder for the distance from the air-slit to the sharp edge.

Cylindrical oboe. A label (though in Western instruments a contradiction in terms) invented by *Sachs for non-Western wind instruments with a large, wide-stemmed double reed and a cylindrical bore, leading to *stopped-pipe behaviour. Chief examples are in Asia: see BALABAN, GUAN, HICHIRIKI; P'IRI; also REED, 5a.

Cymbal (Fr.: *cymballe*; Ger.: *Becken*, sing. and pl.; It.: *cinelli*, or usually *piatti*; Ru.: *tarelki*; Sp.: *platillos*). The circular plate, slightly dished, forged in bronze (sometimes brass), is held in the centre by a leather hand-grip or metal support (Fig. 1a) passing through a hole in the domed 'boss'. Cymbals as a pair clashed together have since at least

Assyrian times complemented the drum in one of the longest-lived partnerships in instrument history, though today for jazz, rock, and much orchestral work, it is the single cymbal struck with stick or beater that is in by far the greater production (below, 3, 'suspended cymbal').

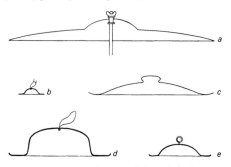

Fig. 1. (*a*) 50 cm. (20″) suspended cymbal; (*b*) Egyptian dancer's cymbal; (*c*) 30 cm (12″) Chinese cymbal; (*d*) Tibetan 'bowler hat' cymbal; (*e*) bronze cymbal, Roman period.

1. *Construction.* Cymbals range in width from 60 cm. (2′) down to 5 cm. (2″), if one includes small types like 'finger cymbals' (Fig. 1*b*), orchestral 'antique cymbals' or crotales, (below, 4), and Asian 'cup cymbals' sounding almost like a little bell. As with other percussion instruments that vibrate through their own stiffness, the frequency given by the lowest mode of vibration ('fundamental') varies with the thickness (the thicker, the higher) and, for a circular plate, inversely as the square of the radius. A finger cymbal with diameter 5.6 cm. ($2\frac{1}{4}$″) will be a good 2 mm. thick (to give more than a brief tinkle) with the note, around g'''', top G on the piano, as its fundamental. An average proper cymbal may be half as thick and at an average width of 45 cm. (18″) have in theory a fundamental some seven octaves lower, near bottom G on the piano, though in practice probably less deep, and distinguishable by ear with a gentle tap on the rim, listening close to. On a normal stroke, higher, inharmonic frequencies (see PARTIALS, 7) take over in dense numbers according to where and with what the cymbal is hit, and time-related in that the energy soon passes to yet higher vibration modes (see Campbell and Greated 1987) to form, after a hard stroke, almost a continuous 'noise spectrum', its peaks undistinguishable to the ear in a brilliant shimmer, enhanced in a cymbal of normal ('Turkish') type through concentric grooves or 'tone rings' turned on the surface. Still the most celebrated cymbal makers are the Istanbul family of Zildjian, now with a main factory near Boston, Massachusetts; also of high repute is the firm of Paiste in Switzerland (see GONG).

Also in use are 'Chinese' cymbals (Fig. 1*c*), of thin metal with turned-up rim and a boss of very characteristic shape. For playing on a stand, a Chinese cymbal is sometimes placed upside down.

2. *Clashed cymbals.* These range between 40 and 55 cm. (15″ and 22″) in diameter, a pair properly being 'married' for one to sound slightly higher than the other in order to minimize any impression of a definite pitch. A leather strap is passed through the central hole in each, the ends slit and plaited in a square 'Turk's' knot on the inside. Above the boss is a felt or leather pad to shield the hand. Clashing is by a glancing movement; then the sound is damped against the player's clothing to match the duration of the note, or the cymbals are raised for them to ring on (*laissez vibrer*). The edges can be lightly touched together for a *pp* note, or agitated together for the 'two-plate roll'—the older kind of roll demanded, for instance, *ff* at the end of Wagner's *Götterdämmerung* where the funeral pyre is ignited. Should a crack appear, the life of a cymbal can often be prolonged by boring a small hole just beyond the crack.

In small orchestras, and bands playing seated, an old custom is to attach one cymbal to the top of the bass drum, to be struck with the other held in the drummer's free hand. Hence the bass drum and cymbals have often been written on the same part, with instructions like *cassa solo* ('drum only') or 'cym.' to show where the two instruments are not to be sounded together. This method, while effective for fast strokes of the cymbals, is inadequate for a full orchestral clash. Thus in older editions of the score of Tchaikovsky's Sixth Symphony, at the great moment in the March appears the composer's caution printed large in Russian: 'The cymbal must *not* be attached to the drum.'

Another old idea, from the theatre, is 'foot cymbals', the pair being attached horizontally to two boards hinged together with a spring, for clashing with one foot.

The 'Hi-Hat', or 'choke' cymbal (see DRUM KIT, Pl. 1, left), was introduced in jazz during the 1920s as the 'Charleston' cymbal, replacing the foot cymbals for marking the off-beats: a pair, *c.* 35 cm. (14″) in diameter, are mounted one above the other on a metal stand with a sprung pedal at the base to move the upper cymbal (higher pitched and usually marked 'high-hat top') down on to the other, with a 'chick' sound.

3. *Suspended cymbal.* This is made in sizes from 20 to 60 cm. (8″ to 24″). In the older method of use, as when Berlioz introduced it, the player suspends a cymbal in one hand to strike it with the kind of beater specified; thus, in the very last bar of the *Symphonie fantastique*, 'one cymbal, struck with sponge-headed stick or bass drum beater'. Today the cymbal is held on a stand between rubber washers (two shown in DRUM KIT, Pl. 1). It can then be damped with the fingers and rolls played with two sticks; the old 'two-plate rolls' (see above) are often performed in this way where appropriate.

Suspended cymbals have become so important partly because two or more of them can be used to give sounds of clearly contrasted 'indefinite' pitches. Also, they can be sounded in all kinds of ways: with a penknife blade (Bartók, Violin Concerto, answering the triangle), scraping with a nail-file, and even bowing with a cello bow (the latter in Schoenberg's Five Pieces, though a later edition changes it to sticks).

In a drum kit several distinct types of suspended cymbal are used, specially designed and selected by the drummer with meticulous care to fulfil their various purposes. A 'ride' or 'top' cymbal is designed for clear execution of repeated notes, e.g.

made with drumstick or wire brush, damping the off-beats with the other hand; a 'crash' cymbal, often rather smaller, is mostly struck on the rim with the heavy end of the drumstick; a third may be a differently pitched double-duty 'crash–ride' cymbal. A 'sizzle' cymbal has brass rivets placed loosely in holes towards the circumference.

4. *Antique cymbals* (or 'crotales'—a departure from the original Greek sense of the word as a *clapper). These go back to Berlioz's reproductions of Roman cymbals from Pompeii (Fig. 1e), approximately 9 cm. ($3\frac{1}{2}''$) wide and used by him in *Roméo et Juliette*, specifying particular notes on the staff; one of the pair is struck lightly against the other. Later composers, chiefly French, continued to specify notes for them (e.g. Debussy at the end of the *Prélude à l'après-midi d'un faune*), but since it was hitherto difficult to find instruments tuned to every note demanded, a substitute has often been found in the *glockenspiel. Latterly, however, small cymbals have become obtainable in chromatically tuned sets, 5 to 13 cm. (2″ to 5″) in diameter, mounted together on a stand and duplicated for playing together. Messiaen wrote with such instruments in mind.

5. *Oriental cymbals*: the following are a few among many kinds. (*a*) *Finger cymbals*. These are of the Egyptian dancer's kind (*sagat*, as Fig. 1b), brass, with gut loops for index and thumb of each hand; such have been manufactured in the West for school music. In North India similar cymbals, *manjīrā*, are joined by a string; one, held in the left hand by the string, is struck with the rim of the other (cf. SOUTH-EAST ASIA, 1a).

(*b*) *Indian 'cup cymbals', talam*, are around 5 cm. wide or less; one, in the palm of one hand, is struck on the edge with the other. These are also manufactured in the West, with names like 'Indian bells'.

(*c*) *'Tong cymbals'*. From Turkey and Greece (*massá*). A flat, springy strip of iron bent round like tongs (or two strips joined at one end) branches at the free ends in two or three curving arms to each of which is riveted a small cymbal; held in one hand, the instrument is slapped against the other in folk dances. Such were made in *Antiquity and the first cymbals shown in medieval Western art are of this type.

(*d*) *Other cymbals*. Among those seen in instrumental ensembles all over Eastern Asia are high-domed 'bowler hat' types (Fig. 1d). These may be held with the rims horizontal, or nearly so, and struck together with up-and-down movements, seen also in European pictures of the 13th to 14th centuries (see MEDIEVAL INSTRUMENTS, Pl. 1), later than the 'tong' cymbals.

Cymbala. In the Middle Ages a word for a row of small bells, sometimes with the notes of the scale marked above them, seen in many 12th-century psalter illustrations. Modern performers of medieval music have assembled sets from old kitchen bells and the like. Yet the question has been raised (La Rue 1982) whether such bells were, through that period, not actual musical instruments but, rather, a symbolic creation by monastic artists illustrating *cymbala* (correctly meaning 'cymbals') of the Old Testament, particularly in the 150th psalm. Their occasional appearance later in a realistic performing context (as in the *Cantigas* manuscript, see MEDIEVAL INSTRUMENTS, 2) may then mark a departure into a practical plane.

Czakan. A Hungarian *flageolet fashionable in the early 19th century. There are examples under this name in many collections.

Moeck 1974.

D

Daira (*dāirā, doira*; from Iranian 'a circle'). A *tambourine, in Balkan countries of Europe similar to the Western tambourine; in the Middle East (Iran), the Caucasus, and Central Asia, with instead of jingle plates, a great number of iron rings sewn round the inside of the hoop. Important in both folk and classical music, it is played by men and in dancing by women. The membrane is said in some areas to be properly of fish-skin from the Caspian.

Damaru. Tibetan 'skull' drum, of two human skulls; see CHINA AND KOREA, 3.

Dan. Vietnam, prefix to stringed-instrument names: see SOUTH-EAST ASIA, I*c*.

Dance band (or dance orchestra). Always will be remembered the orchestra of saxophones, trumpets, trombones, and rhythm section of piano, guitar, bass, and drums, which for the relatively brief span of some 30 years from the late 1920s held absolute sway in the ballroom, night club, and variety theatre, dominating the 12-inch 78s, equally in the song hits of Cole Porter and Ivor Novello as in the jazz compositions of Duke Ellington and Count Basie, and the music of Glenn Miller. The present subject is not the music itself, but how ordinary musicians coped with it; for, unlike the earlier jazz, it is music scored out in written parts (whence the knee-height music desks, suitably draped) with spaces for solos between the ensembles. While of course the leading bands have had their own arrangers, writing for the particular personnel, need arose for the standard printed commercial dance-band orchestrations that enabled musicians everywhere to perform the numbers in correct style (some of these orchestrations being still procurable today).

The standard at first, in the earlier 1930s, was for a 10-piece combination with parts for three saxophones (1st alto, 2nd alto, and tenor, each doubling on clarinet), two trumpets, trombone, and the four rhythm. The two wind groups, reed and brass, are scored for mostly in block harmony, each part often printed on two lines: the upper for a full chorus with trumpet lead; the lower with saxophone lead and brass interjections, often with eight bars lightly scored to accompany a solo. There might also be a violin part, with three optional parts (Violin A, B, and C) condensed on one sheet, and useful especially in big hotel orchestras.

By 1922, Duke Ellington had his famous 14-piece band of four saxophones, three each of trumpet and trombone, and the four rhythm with himself on piano; other big names were using the same or more. Commercial orchestrations then began to include *ad lib*. parts for 2nd tenor and baritone saxophones, 3rd trumpet, and 2nd (and perhaps 3rd) trombone, for a band of up to some 14 players.

After the war came from America the 17-piece combination (Glenn Miller, Count Basie, etc.) of five saxophones with four each of trumpet and trombone, for which commercial orchestrations may even run to a full score. Such are still in some demand, where the 'big band' has retained its enthusiasts through the ensuing period of smaller, varied modern jazz combinations associated with Charlie Parker, Gerry Mulligan, Lionel Hampton, and the many others of those times and since.

Dance gourd (*or ipu hula*). Hawaiian percussion instrument of two gourds joined together: see PACIFIC ISLANDS, 4.

Darabuka (or *derbuka*; Turk.: *dumbelik*). Pot drum of the Near and Middle East, most typically 'goblet'-shaped in earthernware (but also of wood and sometimes brass) with the skin glued or laced over the wide end and the stem hollow throughout (see DRUM, Fig. 1*a*). It is held almost horizontally with the skin facing forwards. Usually it lies on the thigh, under the arm, with the wrist upon the rim, for the fingers to play on the head, rim, or both at once (see MIDDLE EAST, Pl. 1). In some cases it rests on the shoulder, steadied on the palm, again allowing all fingers to play on the head. The right hand moves freely, fingers separated, to execute a great variety of strokes giving sounds deep and drum-like, or hollow-sounding knocks, sometimes high and metallic. Heard on all kinds of popular occasions, the darabuka is also a main drum of classical and theatre music (in Egypt it is also known as *tabla*, and in Iran *zarb*), giving the main beats while another drum, most usually a tambourine, plays higher-sounding, decorative rhythms.

Many earthernware darabukas for domestic music and dancing are narrow with only a slight waist. Modern professional instruments may be manufactured with a plated metal body and screw-tensioned head.

Davul (Turk.; Serbo-Croat.: *tapan*). The large Turkish drum, the biggest of the two-headed drums which are played over the Middle East with a *surna (shawm) on festive outdoor occasions. It varies much in dimensions, the shell (of thin poplar or walnut) being on average some 55 cm. (22") in diameter and 28 to 40 cm. (11" to 16") in depth. The two sheep- or goatskin heads are lapped on to wooden hoops and tensioned with cords. The drum is carried tilted on a strap round the left shoulder. The right-hand head (sometimes with snare) is struck with a stout wooden stick, often with curved end; the left with a light, wand-like stick, filling in between the beats of the other stick (see also BASS DRUM, 5; TURKISH MUSIC). In South Yugoslavia (Macedonia), *tapan* and *zurla* are played by resident gypsies, hired for weddings, etc., the drummer again heightening the occasion with acrobatic antics.

Decibel. A standard measurement of the ratio of two sound intensities P_1 and P_2, expressed in decibels (dB) as $10 \log (P_1/P_2)$. This expression is useful in practice since the ear's response to degrees of loudness is found to be broadly logarithmic. For a reference point in gauging the loudness, P_2 must be taken not as pure silence (when $P = 0$) but as a defined threshold of hearing (found approximately to correspond to an ear-drum amplitude of less than the diameter of an atom). A pianissimo note (on, say, flute or violin) will register from 5 to 10 decibels; an orchestral fortissimo up to 90 dB; the threshold of pain, 130 dB.

Deff (or duff). See TAMBOURINE, 3.

Dessus (Fr.) In early periods, 'treble', 'soprano'.

Deutsche Schalmey. See SHAWM, 1c.

Dhol. A main popular drum of India, two-headed, with cylindrical body (or slightly barrel-shaped) *c.*50 cm. (20") long and 30 cm. (12") wide, carved in wood and played with sticks or the hands. Also called by the diminutive form *dholak*, or in the South *tavil* (see DRUM, Pl. 1), there accompanying the *shawm *nagasvaram*, sometimes also in the classical music. *Dhol* (*dol*) is also the cylindrical tom-tom-shaped drum of the Caucasus region, expertly hand-beaten on the upper head in accompaniment, alone or with other instruments, to dances and ballets.

Di, dizi (*ti, ti-tzü*). Transverse flute of China, of bamboo, typically (not always) wound at intervals with black thread and tipped with ivory or bone at each end. Just over halfway from the mouth-hole (with the stopper close to this inside) to the first fingerhole is a hole over which is gummed a square membrane, usually prepared from the inner skin of bamboo (now sold in packets), or some special tissue paper. This imparts to the sound a reedy, buzzing quality, so indispensable that the *di* may be seen by musicians less as a flute with membrane added than as a membrane that speaks through the flute. The six fingerholes, often oval, are neatly undercut, and further down are two vent-holes at the side, and two at the bottom for attaching a silk tassel if desired. The pitch with all fingers down is on the principal size (*qudi*) around *a'* (near that of a western fife); this and a smaller size (*bangdi*) each have a leading role in particular kinds of opera as well as in folk music.

Transverse flutes have been known in China from about 200 BC, and those with the membrane from the early Middle Ages. For Confucian ceremonies the flute used to have a red and gilt carved wooden dragon's head plugged into one end and the tail into the other. Transverse flutes with membrane are also played in Mongolia and Korea (*taegum*, see CHINA AND KOREA, Pl. 2), while in China there have as well been duct flutes with membrane.

Diapason. 1. The diatonic octave (through 'the notes of the scale'), whence with lutes (see LUTE, 2), and sometimes other plucked instruments, bass strings tuned diatonically over an octave, or part of one, and played 'open', generally with the right thumb.

2. A 'foundation stop' in the organ.

3. In Fr. *diapason* also means 'tuning pitch', and from this the *tuning fork.

Diaphone. An organ pipe patented by R. Hope-Jones (1894) for providing a powerful bass stop, or the bass octave of a loud reed stop. Though used in some cathedral organs, it found its real home in the *cinema organ. In its simplest form, a circular metal valve, faced in leather and felt, is held on the end of a flat spring. When the pallet admits air from the wind-chest, the valve alternately closes and opens the exit to the pipe at a speed set by the natural frequency of the air-column of the pipe. The valve opening and strength of the spring are suitably adjusted for this, the tuning of the note depending on the pipe length and proportions. The device is contained in a wooden box fixed to the base of the pipe.

A more complex diaphone action, patented by Hope-Jones a year later, ensures control by the air-column through incorporating a small bellows (pneumatic motor) which, in conjunction with a spring, opens and closes the valve, here mounted on a rod.

A different diaphone is the long-range foghorn invented by J. P. Northey (1903). The air supply here causes a reciprocating piston, containing the entry ports, to oscillate a small distance to and fro, for the air to issue through fixed ports.

Didjeridu. Australian aboriginal wind instrument, native to northern parts of the continent, and consisting of a branch, up to 180 cm. (6') long, often from a eucalyptus, or gum-tree, with the centre eaten out by termites. The walls of the tube may be thinned at the ends by scraping the inside. The player, seated on the ground, sounds the deep fundamental with loosely vibrating lips, varying its timbre by mouth and tongue, and with these superimposing selective resonance of different harmonics, much as in playing a *jew's-harp. With *circular breathing (through the nose) the sound is sustained uninterruptedly over lengthy periods, varied by accentuations in pitch and volume, and rapid trillings with the tongue. In north-eastern Arnhem Land a blown overtone (around a tenth above the fundamental) is produced in fast alternation with the fundamental in a variety of rhythms. The didjeridu thus functions as a drone below the singer's melody, as a rhythmic accompaniment, and an aural kaleidoscope of timbres. It also imitates bird and animal calls and issues coded instructions to the dancers, who usually perform highly stylized and mimetic movements to the combined music of the songman (who also beats his rhythm sticks) and the didjeridu player. Although similar types of wooden 'trumpets' are used in other parts of the world, the musical functions of the didjeridu and the extremely difficult virtuoso techniques developed by expert performers find no parallel elsewhere. Nor have the aborigines possessed any further instruments, other than sticks or boomerangs rhythmically clashed (see CONCUSSION STICKS) since they first crossed the land bridge into Australia perhaps 40,000 years ago. (For a fuller account see Jones 1983.)

Difference tones. See BEATS, 2.

Dilruba and esraj. Two similar Indian bowed stringed instruments (see INDIA, 2b), both being derivatives of the (plucked) *sitar, with wire strings and played on the lap with the top against the left shoulder. The small, parchment-covered body varies, pear-shaped, or faintly violin-like with inserted shell-like centre bouts as in a *sarangi. The long wide neck is straddled by 16 or so adjustable arching brass frets tied on with gut. Down the near side of the neck (to the player's right) is a wooden ledge holding pegs for some 18 *sympathetic strings which run through tiny holes in the bridge. The four playing strings are stopped with the fingertips. Both instruments are popular, played solo or with other instruments, dilruba over the north, and esraj (or esrar), rather smaller, in Bengal. An old decorative variant of dilruba, with the body carved and painted as a peacock, was the mayuri (or taus, 'peacock'), now seen in many collections.

Diple. From Yugoslavia (Bosnia, etc.), a wind instrument with two narrow parallel bores in one piece of wood, each sounded with a single (*idioglot) reed of elder. It is played either as a bagpipe (also 'mih'; see BAGPIPE, 5c) or by blowing directly into the wide wooden top. If with six holes to each bore the fingers cover the holes on both; if with six for the right hand and only two (or three) for the left, while the right hand is playing on the higher holes,

the left makes a changing drone on the deeper notes from these fewer holes placed low down.

Dital harp. See HARP-LUTE.

Divisions; division viol. 'Divisions' (It., 'diminutions') were in the 16th and 17th centuries a kind of ornamentation by which, in a polyphonic work, a singer or player would fill out the part, especially over the larger musical intervals, with all kinds of improvised runs and figures in short fast notes. A number of instructional works were published showing how to make such divisions over a part (equally on the soprano as in some deeper part) in a written composition. One of the best (1584) is by the Venetian *cornett virtuoso G. Dalla Casa (Il vero modo di diminuir, 'with all kinds of instrument, wind and stringed, and the voice'). 'Division viol' is a bass viol of dimensions suited to playing divisions in a particular English manner (see VIOL, 4).

Dizi. See DI, DIZI.

Dobro. A guitar (or mandolin) of American design containing a metal resonator disc inside the body. See GUITAR, 4.

Dolzaina. See DOUÇAINE, DOLZAINA, 2.

Dombra, domra. Russian and Central Asian types of 'long lute': see BALALAIKA.

Doppione. Renaissance reed instrument mentioned in Italy around 1600 and again by *Praetorius, who says he had never actually seen one, yet giving just enough information for reasonable identification with a unique pair of instruments among those preserved by the Accademia Filarmonica in Verona. Each is a round wooden column (lengths 75 cm. (30″) and 62 cm. (24″)) containing two independent narrow conical bores of different lengths (with fingerholes down each of the two sides) as if the double reed were meant to be placed in one or the other for playing over a different compass. They may have originally been blown through a *wind-cap while blocking one of the bores.
  Weber and Van der Meer 1972.

Double bass (or simply 'bass'; Fr.: contrebasse; Ger.: Kontrabass; It.: contrabasso; Ru.: Kontrabas; Sp.: contrabajo). The 6′-tall contrabass of the violin family, and therefore of the whole orchestra, in which its main function in music from the Classical period onward has been to play the bass line an octave below the cellos; it may be natural while listening to a concert to follow mostly the upper line of the two, but a switch of attention to the lower will instantly bring home the absolutely essential part the double basses play in the orchestral sound. In a *military band the double bass ('string bass') is the only stringed instrument among the body of wind, largely because of the extraordinary property of its *pizzicato* in 'lifting the music off the ground'; and again in jazz, where it is always played without the bow. Its paramount role, however, continues to be in its orchestral capacity, as a bowed instrument.

1. *Construction.* The body length averages 114 cm. (44″), which is only about one-and-a-half times that of a cello; but the sides are nearly twice as deep, close to 23 cm. (9″), lowering the internal air-resonance to support the lower notes. The shape may conform to that of a cello, but usually the shoulders of the body slope in a double curve, which lowers the upper rim and facilitates movement of the left hand far along the string to thumb positions. The back is usually flat to economize on wood and save labour in the making; a flat back is about 5 mm. thick, the upper part sloping inwards towards the neck, and a wide transverse bar inside supports the soundpost. A 'swell back', on the other hand, needs to be carved from thicker pieces and can be as much as 12 mm. thick at the centre. The out-pointed corners of the violin body are often omitted: such points are very vulnerable in an instrument which, through its size and varied uses, often gets rough treatment.

To save cost, basses are also made with front and back of laminated spruce and maple respectively, steam-pressed to shape; and making a very durable construction adequate for many circumstances, though relatively low-priced basses of traditional craftsmanship are available, e.g. exported from Romania and some neighbouring countries.

2. *Strings and bow.* Strings of flexible steel are most often in use now, though those with a nylon core wound with steel ribbon are quite satisfactory. Gut strings have become rare, though the long string-length, an average 106 cm. (42″), arose along with the size of the whole instrument from necessity in order to make 16′ tone from strings all originally of plain gut. With this length the distances up the string for successive notes lie so far apart that the standard tuning of the bass is in fourths, *g d A E* (sounding an octave lower), not in fifths as the rest of the family: the string-length being such that in the lower *positions of the left hand the stretch from first finger to fourth will encompass a whole tone only. Thus on the D string in the first position, the first finger makes E, the second F, and the fourth F♯—the next note, G, being available as the open string above. The third finger is normally put down with the fourth to help in the work of pressing down the string (but in the Italian school the third finger instead of the second makes the F). Higher up the string, from about the 6th position (first finger on *f′*), where the distances become smaller, the third finger can replace the little finger, which is normally too short to lie naturally over the strings when the hand is far up the fingerboard. The left thumb is used for stopping

at the half-way point for fingering higher up, or at the next harmonic point above. Thence one may proceed to the double-octave harmonic at the end of the fingerboard and from there obtain a further octave or more in harmonics alone. The octave harmonic is also much used in playing ordinary passages (and again while tuning the strings).

For solo music the four-string bass is usually tuned a tone higher in order to obtain a brighter sound. Jazz players have sometimes added a fifth string above the others, tuned to *c′*. (For a fifth string added *below* the normal four see 3, below).

Two types of bow are in use: the French, like a cello bow but shorter and stouter; and the German or Simandl bow (named after a former professor at Vienna, his Tutor dating from 1874 still in use). This last bow has a more slender stick and narrower band of hair but a much wider frog, which is held in the hand with the thumb uppermost. The audience can easily detect which is being used from the fact that during pizzicato the French bow is held pointing somewhat upwards but the German downwards. The French bow is the norm in Britain; in the USA either may be used.

3. *Notes below E.* When the basses and cellos are reading from the same part, notes below E are played on the bass in the octave higher (sounding in unison with the cellos). That things have evolved in this way stresses how the main job of the basses in an orchestra is to supply 16′ tone, which they still do if in unison with the cellos. But many composers have written these low notes in the deliberate hope of having them played as they stand. Three solutions are: (*a*) to tune the fourth string down; (*b*) to have a five-string bass, the fifth string tuned to low C or B; or (*c*), today coming much into use, to attach a not very pretty mechanism to the side of the pegbox. Fig. 1 shows a typical form of it—with the four independently moving finger-plates (E to C♯) and their corresponding rubber-covered stopping-levers higher up. The fourth string is led over the extreme top (P), returning behind to the upper tuning-pin on the left (normally the pin for the A string). Close to the top is the C nut, of metal (Q). The E lock (R), for the left thumb, locks down the E lever for playing in the normal way (open fourth string, E); when released the extra string-length makes the lower notes available, so long as the passage is not one of great speed. A retaining rod (S) checks the rise of the stopping levers under their return springs located behind the arms shown projecting to the left.

(Also with a mechanical stopping system was Vuillaume's experimental 'octo-bass', dating from 1848 in Paris: over twice the size of the normal, with three strings tuned *c G C*, stopped by levers from seven pedals, the player standing on a raised platform; the instrument is preserved in the Paris *collection.)

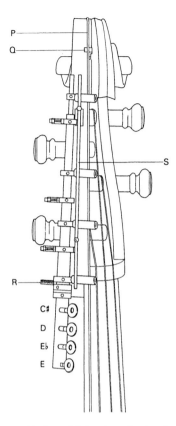

P
Q
S
R
C♯
D
E♭
E

Fig. 1. Double bass: left-hand mechanism for notes below E. The plate (shown as a ring) is pressed down for each note required.

4. *Three-string bass.* Seldom played now (though it may sometimes be seen in folk or other open-air ensembles on the Continent), this was virtually the standard double bass, in Britain and France especially, through most of the 19th century, and still familiar in the early part of the 20th. The tuning is either *g d A* (the first three of the present bass) or *g d G*. This bass was altogether very highly regarded, especially for its powerful sound on the lowest string (in Germany, Richard Strauss recommended some three-string basses amongst the four-stringed). The restricted downward compass (with the *g d A* tuning reaching only two notes in actual pitch below the cello) worried players little: the instrument provided the essential 16′ tone, while giving the strong first beats of the bar so important in the dance and light music which occupied the majority of players.

In Italy, Verdi had to stipulate in *Otello* that the opening of the solo passage before the murder of Desdemona, starting *pp* on the bottom *E*, must be played only by the basses with four strings (lest those with three should ruin the effect by playing

an octave higher). The two most celebrated of past soloists, both from Italy, played on three strings: Dragonetti (1763–1846) and Bottesini (1821–89). The former used a bass by Gasparo and the latter one by Testore of 1694. Dragonetti played during the earlier part of his career with the old out-curved form of bow looking somewhat like a meat-saw, and commonly used with the three-string bass up to its last years. Bottesini (Pl. 1) used his own form of what is now called the French bow; his solo compositions, basically in conventional musical styles of the time, show off his virtuosity with, for example, electrifying arpeggios at full speed up to passages lying well above the treble stave in actual sound, played on the numerous natural harmonics available from the three strings.

5. *Earlier basses: (a) Origins.* Man-high basses played standing already appear in Italian and German pictures of the 1560s; instruments with frets on the neck, four strings (or four as far as one can make out), and altogether looking very capable of bearing the long thick strings needed to give a strong bass to groups of instruments of any kind: in Veronese's *Marriage at Cana* (1563) to violin, cornett, and tenor viols; in a German engraving by Jost Amman to three loud wind instruments playing outdoors.

(b) *Six- and five-string basses.* There are no details of tunings until 1609 (Banchieri), and here for a *violone da gamba* with six strings tuned in the manner of a bass *viol but a fifth deeper, *g d A F C G′*—as if perhaps the instrument already seen in the Munich painting of c.1575 (see RENAISSANCE INSTRUMENTS, Pl. 1), a double bass in shape though with the longer neck characteristic of a viol. Next, *Praetorius (1619) illustrates 'violone' as a true double bass in size and proportion, again fretted and with the six strings here tuned an octave below the bass viol; but (he says) most used were five strings, tuned throughout by fourths from *E′* to *g* (as on the bass today plus a high C string).

Double basses by Gasparo da Salo and Maggini (see VIOLIN, 4) are still being played in orchestras today; but like others of the family have since been given new necks and fittings for the modern four strings. This leaves it difficult to judge how many they may have had originally. From Italy no further particulars have been found until 1677 (Bismantova; see BAROQUE, 2) for a *contrabasso o violone grande* with four strings tuned as today save for the lowest to G since (being of gut) it would otherwise 'be too thick'. Nevertheless, basses, Italian and German, preserved in collections unaltered seem all to have six strings or five (one of the earliest was made in Dresden, 1597, six-stringed, in the Augsburg collection). Many still have the remains of five or so thick frets of twisted gut, for making the notes more accurately and clearly, especially when fingering involved moving the whole fist more than is the practice today. German works up to the mid-18th century also repeatedly

Pl. 1. Giovanni Bottesini, with three-string bass and 'Bottesini bow': photographed aged 67, the year before his death.

give for the *violone* or, in German, *Gross-bass Geige*, six strings tuned a fifth below the bass viol, the lowest G'. The first string is then tuned to the same note, *g*, as that of the cello in its older 'bass violin' form (see CELLO, 4). The purpose of this high open-string range is not described; but in times when such a violone might hold the bass part alone, or alone in conjunction with the keyboard *continuo, the player would have the option of playing either at the written pitch (8' as organists say) or in the lower octave (16', so far as the downward compass allowed) whichever was felt to support the music best—as also, for best clarity of the bass progression of the harmony, the licence to simplify passages written in very fast notes

(e.g. Quantz, see BAROQUE, 2). When it became increasingly usual in orchestras, by Bach's time, and eventually normal, for the bass part to be played on the cello with the double bass at the octave below, it was remarked in mid-18th-century Germany how the instrument sounded stronger and clearer with fewer strings, four (Quantz) or, later in the century, three.

A five-string tuning that lasted longer is *a f♯ d a F♮* (sounding an octave lower), noticed in England (*Talbot, c.1695) when the double bass was a new arrival probably from Germany (for the instrument in Orlando Gibbons's fantasias see VIOLONE), and in Vienna, where the tuning was retained into the early 19th century in solo playing, and the difficult solo part in Mozart's concert aria, K. 612, written for a soloist, seems to require it.

(*c*) *Extra-large and small basses.* Praetorius shows a very large 'Great Contrabass Geig', five-stringed (tuned as today plus a low D), which he says was really meant for playing the bass part in a consort of deep viols with a small bass viol playing the treble—something like which is a group of four viols playing in a French drawing of 1584 (Remnant, 1989, p. 59). Almost exactly matching his illustration is an unaltered Italian example (Brussels collection) standing 228 cm. (7½') tall, with body length 142 cm. (56"; exactly four times that of a violin) and sides 28 cm. (11") deep. Larger still is the giant Italian bass, 288 cm. (9½') tall, body-length 200.5 cm. (78"), once owned by Dragonetti and now, with three strings, in the Victoria and Albert Museum, London; and again larger, Vuillaume's giant mentioned in 3 above.

Also from the Baroque and after are small-sized basses ('chamber bass', Ger.: *Bassett, Bassl*), with body-lengths around 90 cm. (36"). A few are five-stringed. In some of Haydn's early chamber music the viola part goes below the bottom part, as if possibly the latter were performed on such a small bass with the *a* to F tuning mentioned above (*b*), and playing in the lower octave where suitable.

6. *Repertory.* Early solo works include concertos by Dittersdorf, Vanhal, and others, from the 1760s. (Haydn wrote a double bass concerto, but it was evidently lost in the fire at the Eisenstadt Library.) For Mozart's concert aria 'Per questa bella mano', K. 612, see above, 5b. Among the many concertos written by bass soloists after Dragonetti and Bottesini is the concerto in a late Romantic style by Koussevitsky, a fine bass player himself. New works in various advanced styles have latterly been heard at festival competitions. Celebrated player-composers of recent times have been Gary Karr, and also in the USA, Bertram Turetsky (with avant-garde works written in 'analog notation' employing numerous special signs), while Charles Mingus (1922–79), whose astonishing invention and artistry have earned him the title of the first real virtuoso of the jazz bass, notably expanded the repertory in this direction.

Elgar 1960, 1963; Planyavsky 1970.

Double flageolet. 1. *In general*, a pair of duct flutes forming one instrument, the pipes fixed parallel for the two hands to play on them in harmony. Some are in one piece of wood (**dvoinice*, Yugoslavia) and a type made on the Continent from the 17th to the 18th century or later, usually described as *flûte d'accord*. Also pairs of separate pipes held one in each hand in Europe among folk instruments (Italy, *doppio flauto*), and in north India (**algoza*).

2. *English double flageolets* of the earlier part of the 19th century (Pl. 1), well known to collectors, are prettily made in boxwood (usually) with silver keys and small ivory pegs between the lower holes to guide the fingers when they have to cover both pipes. Most are made by Bainbridge (London, the inventor; instruments *c.*1808–35), Hastrick (to 1855, his successor), and Simpson. The pipes are held in a wide head-joint with an ivory or bone mouthpiece and usually 'shut-off' keys to occlude the voicing slit of one pipe or the other for playing on one alone, though this is not the purpose of the instrument. The idea is to play tunes in harmony of thirds and sixths, with one hand on each pipe, the four finger-holes on the right-hand pipe being lower down than the first four on the left. A few keys are provided to extend the scale upwards (partly by overblowing the deeper pipe) and to make semitones; an example of the fingering is in Baines 1957, Fig. 48.

Triple flageolets by the same makers add a fat pipe, attached on the back, which acts as a cavity resonator (see VESSEL FLUTE), with keys worked by the ball of the thumb to make bass notes. Other triple flageolets are ingeniously made of bamboo in the Indonesian archipelago, one pipe a drone; and from Ancient Mexico are triple and quadruple duct whistles from *c.*500 AD, of pottery in one piece, to sound chords (like modern 'three-note' or 'steamer' whistles of plated metal).

3. *Separate flageolets*: one in each hand for playing unison or in harmony. In Italy, folk instruments of cane; see also ALGOZA (India).

Double-pipe. See REEDPIPE, 2.

Double stopping. With string instruments, bowing two strings simultaneously to produce chords. Despite the word 'stopping', one of the strings may be open.

Douçaine, dolzaina. Names of some early wind instruments, so far not positively identified.

1. *Douçaine* (Fr., also *douchaine, doussaine*). Mentioned from the 13th century to the 16th to an extent that indicates that the instrument was of considerable importance, particularly in French and Flemish music. It is listed along with flutes and strings among the *bas* ('soft') instruments (not

Pl. 1. English double flageolet, early 19th century. Photo: Sotheby's.

among the '*haut*': see HAUT AND BAS), but details of it are given in one work alone (Tinctoris, *c.*1487), here under the latinized name *dulciana*: a reed instrument akin to the **shawm* but, as implied in the name, soft in sound, with seven holes in front and one behind as on a recorder, and *imperfecta*, not capable of playing every kind of piece (which at that period could mean limited in compass). With no indication of size or pitch this information is too little for identification. Yet an instrument so frequently named must be among those seen in pictures of the period. (See CRUMHORN—Boydell 1982, and Meyer 1983, ch. 1, for a complete statement of this problem and also of the following).

2. *Dolzaina.* This Italian form of the name becomes very prominent through the 16th century as an instrument played in instrumental ensembles. Practically the only details (Zacconi 1592) are of a reed instrument usually with a limited tenor range of *c* to *d'*, extended on some dolzainas up to *f'* by two keys (see CRUMHORN, 1). No specimen has been found to match this, so again we are left in the dark over an instrument which, could it be identified, might prove very useful in performing early music.

3. *Dulzaina.* The Spanish word has lasted through modern times to denote a folk instrument of Castile, short, conical, with wide double reed on a staple.

It has been manufactured (but now no longer) with simple keywork for semitones. A corresponding Catalan instrument, *gralla*, is very simply made (*c.*33 cm. or 13″ long), played at various festivals.

Drone (Fr.: *bourdon*; Ger.: *Bordun*; It.: *bordone*; Sp.: *bordón, rancón*). On a *bagpipe a drone is a note that 'drones on' below (in some cases, above) the melody in an unbroken stream of sound. The term has also come to be used—as *bourdon* has been since the Middle Ages—with the *hurdy-gurdy, and also where such a note is kept up while playing a fiddle, zither, or suchlike, with a sustained effect although the bow or plectrum continually changes direction: for a few examples, see APPALACHIAN DULCIMER; CHITARRA BATTENTE; FIDDLE, 1C; LANGE-LEIK; LIRA; LUTE, 7; TAMBORITSA. The drone gives to the music of a monophonic (non-chord-playing) instrument, when played on its own, dimensions which fill the room or surroundings and stir people to dance or sing as an unsupported line of melody might do less. Much folk music depends on it, and reconstituted medieval music has also been exploiting it on likely instruments of many kinds.

Instruments with a sole purpose of sounding a drone note (and no melody), e.g. to accompany the voice, are very prominent in India (e.g. *gopi-yantra*, or for a drone compounded of many notes, *tambura*). See also BOURDON.

Drum (Fr.: *tambour, caisse*; Ger.: *Trommel*; It.: *tamburo*; Ru.: *baraban*; Sp.: *tambor, bombo, caja*). For drums of Western music see the following: BASS DRUM; BODHRÁN; BONGOS; BOOBAMS; CONGA DRUM (with tumba); FRICTION DRUM; PIPE AND TABOR (for tabor); RATTLE DRUM ('twirling drum'); ROTOTOM; SIDE DRUM (snare drum); TAMBOUR, TAMBOURINE; TENOR DRUM; TIMBALES; TIMPANI; TOM-TOM (with timp-tom). For drums of other countries, see summary, end of 4 below; also for list of some non-membrane instruments called 'drum'.

1. *Drums in general.* A pliable membrane (the 'head') is stretched over the rim of a hollow structure (the 'shell') strong enough to bear a sufficient tension for the membrane to vibrate effectively when struck by hand, stick, or other beater.

In every inhabited continent, save only Australia, there are rarely native peoples who do not possess a drum, the skin of some animal generally supplying the membrane. For our own drums the skin is of calf vellum, or since the 1950s polyethylene plastic. The latter provides heads of more uniform texture (unlike a calfskin where a thickening over the backbone may have to be evened out) and is also less susceptible to changing atmospheric conditions and wear, though a plastic head too can wear out in time.

The vibration is compounded of numerous nodal patterns (see PARTIALS, 7; TIMPANI, 5) contributing a series of close-packed non-harmonic partials which can to a greater or lesser degree obscure sharp definition of pitch as a 'note'—thus 'drum sound', and its alliance primarily to rhythms. A deep shell, while so frequent among drums, is not a fundamental essential (the modern rototoms, e.g., have a shell of virtually no depth whatever) but it can, owing to the mass of air inside it, have an important bearing on the relative partial pitches aroused in the membrane (see TIMPANI, 5). Meanwhile, every drum is up to some point tuned by the player, whether to a precise pitch (as with timpani, or the Burmese *drum chime) or to relate to another drum by some musical interval, or to secure its 'best pitch', or a variety of pitches when played with different strokes. As well known, the tone quality depends both on the type of beater (see PERCUSSION, 3) and on where and how the drum is struck—as with the immense variety of strokes with the hands for which so much of the drumming in Asia and Africa has long been famous (see e.g. DARABUKA; MRDANGA; TABLA), often momentarily raising the pitch by hand pressure on the head (e.g. pressing with the heel of the hand), or making strokes that exploit the hard resonance of the solid shell.

2. *Tensioning.* In most drums of the West, a head is 'lapped' to a metal or wood hoop termed the 'flesh hoop'. To do this, the vellum (the skin having been de-haired and scraped clean) is cut about 15 cm. (6″) wider than the drum shell. It is placed while wet on a flat surface with the hoop on top; the vellum is then tucked in all round, using a tool shaped rather like the handle of a spoon, and left to dry. (Plastic heads, however, are obtained ready-cemented to a hoop, and supplied in sizes from 15 cm. (6″) diameter for the smallest bongo up to 90 cm. (3′) for the largest bass drum.) The hoop, with its vellum or plastic head, is then placed over the shell and a second hoop, the 'counter-hoop', is placed over it; tension is applied to this by ropes or screwed rods.

The counter-hoop seems to have originated in Europe, by about the 16th century. Without it, as over most of the world still, holes have to be pierced in the membrane, whether for nailing or pegging to the shell, or to pass a tensioning cord through (as Fig. 1c, etc.). To reduce direct wear on the holes, the skin may be lapped on to a hoop of wood or twisted fibres (the original 'flesh hoop'), the tension cords or thongs led round this and through the skin (Pl. 1); or a thick hoop may alone be drawn down, over the skin, while kept in position by a cord threaded through the skin at close intervals.

The tension cord (or 'rope') is led zigzag either to a ring of cords tied fast round the shell (Fig. 1c) or to a second head, making a 'W' pattern. Tension may then be raised by drawing the legs of the 'W' together, in some cases by means of an encircling cord, drawn tight so that each 'W' now appears as two 'Y's; or, better for securing even tension,

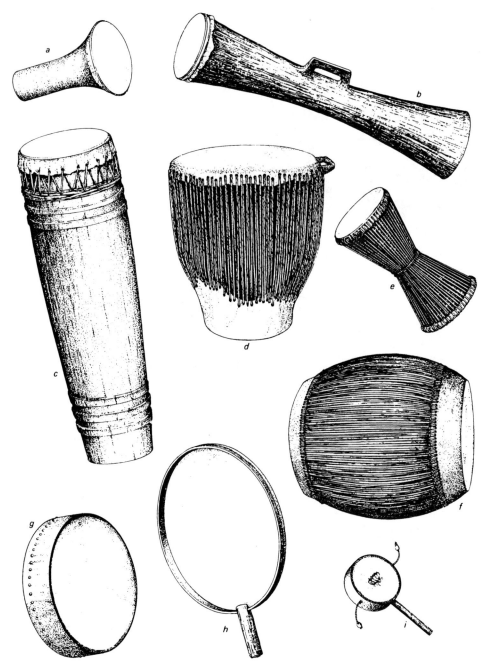

Fig. 1.

Pl. 1. The ṭavil, the double-headed drum which usually accompanies the nāgasvaram in South India.

by a leather tab or 'cuff' on each 'Y' as in the older forms of military drum.

For the circle of black tuning composition applied to the head in India, see MRDANGA; TABLA.

3. *One or two heads.* A single head is the oldest and most widely met over the world, a drum needing no second head unless for a special purpose: for attachment of the lower ends of tensioning cords (Fig. 1d, the part at the bottom shown white being the second skin pulled up round the shell), or in some cases where the drum is held under the arm (notably 'hourglass' drums, 4c below), enabling the pitch of the principal head to be raised by squeezing the cords with the arm; or to carry a snare (side drum)—though there are also single-skin drums that have a snare across the one head, mostly frame drums (4e). Relatively rarely is a second head struck, and its presence may be optional (bass drums, tom-toms). Where striking on both heads forms an essential part of the music, as with classic drums of India and Indonesia (4b (ii)), the shell is often of a length that minimizes disturbance of the vibration of one head by that of the other of different width and pitch.

4. *Classification of drums.* The overall world scheme (see CLASSIFICATION) goes by the shape (of the shell) as being the feature first noticed whether or not the drum be seen in action. 'Upright': shell upright when in use, the head or heads therefore horizontal (e.g. tom-toms of a *drum kit); 'horizontal': shell horizontal, heads in a vertical plane (e.g. bass drum as normally played).

(a) *Kettledrums* ('kettle' in the old sense of a 'bowl'): *timpani, *naqqāra (Middle East, India), 'Uganda drum' (Fig. 1d). In Africa and Oceania especially, carving heavy upright drums from a tree-trunk allows such freedom in design as to render classification by shape hardly possible. Some African bowl drums are carved with feet raising them well above the ground. Also *tabla*, India, especially the left-hand drum of the pair, the other being close to a 'conical drum', *b* (iii), and *drum chime.

(b) *Tubular drums:* (i) *Cylindrical.* Most western drums, *davul, *tabl (Middle East), *ganga (Africa), *dhol (Caucasus, India), *taiko (Japan, the tension cords when tightened here giving a waisted appearance).

(ii) *Barrel* (distinctly wider in the middle). *Gu (China, see also BO, 2); *taiko* (here with nailed heads, Japan); TAPHŌN (Thailand); many in India (as Pl. 1, *tavil*); *mrdanga* (also India), this and the *kendang* (Indonesia, see GAMELAN, 1b), long-shelled for playing with the hands on both heads (above, 3), one smaller than the other and in India characteristically giving the barrel the form of two truncated cones of unequal length meeting base to base, the longer part tapering the most to carry the smaller head (distinguished by *Sachs as 'double conical' drum); Fig. 1f, Ancient Egyptian, only 38 cm. (15″) long, possibly introduced by Nubian soldiery from the south.

(iii) *Conical* (most single-headed, open below): bongos, conga drum (its African ancestor, Fig. 1c).

(c) *Hourglass drums* (dumb-bell shape, of two similar bowls connected bottom-to-bottom, often with a tubular stem between, the whole in one piece): many in West Africa (Fig. 1e and *kalangu): India; *changgo* (Korea); *tsuzumi* drums (Japan); the 'New Guinea drum' *kundu* (with single head, Fig. 1b) is also placed in this category.

(d) *Goblet drums* (with hollow stem): *darabuka* and other 'pot drums' (Near and Middle East), mostly of earthenware, and generally more 'goblet-like' than the small domestic example, Fig. 1a. From Central Europe small neolithic pots have been excavated which have a circle of pointed knobs moulded below the rim; believed by some to be for securing a skin, though such knobs appear on other artefacts as a decorative motif and these 'drums' may only have been pots.

(e) *Frame drums:* (i) The shell is a *hoop* (distinguished from a shallow-model side drum in being light enough to be held in one hand; it is with or without jingles); *bendir (North Africa), bodhrán (Ireland), tambour, tambourine (and see TAMBOUR-INE, 3 for frame drums in general and in antiquity), also *shaman drum, Arctic, Fig. 1h, not always with the handle.

(ii) *Square* frame: adufe (Portugal, North Africa, see TAMBOURINE, 2c).

(iii) *Rattle or twirling drums* (Fig. 1i); see RATTLE DRUM.

5. *Non-membrane instruments called 'drum'.* See BRONZE DRUM; GATO DRUM; LOG DRUM; SLIT DRUM; STEEL DRUM; STRING DRUM; WATER DRUM; WOOD-PLATE DRUM.

Blades 1961, 1970; see also PERCUSSION.

Drum chime. A set of many tuned drums, especially where played by a single performer. Rarely met in the West (in the 1880s a German ladies' ensemble featured a set of 14 drums like shallow single-headed *tom-toms, accompanied by a hammered dulcimer). By far the best-known is the Burmese 'drum circle' (*hsaing-waing* or *pat-waing*; see SOUTH-EAST ASIA, Pl. 1), of up to 24 deep wooden conical hand-played drums of graded size hung in a circle round a balustraded wooden frame, the player sitting in the middle. Each drum is closed at the bottom by a skin of small diameter. The playing heads may have diameters from 5 to 24 cm. (2″ to 10″), tuned by thongs over three pentatonic octaves or more (e.g. G to c‴). Fine tuning is (as with Indian classical drums) with a composition of boiled rice and wood ash, applied during performance as may be necessary. The clear, musical sound was described many years ago by Sir George Scott as 'a beautiful vibrating tone of a piano, incomparable however in its volume and grandeur'. Also in a Burmese ensemble may be a separate set of four to six tuned drums, *chauk ton-bak*, also for one player.

'Drum chime' has also been applied where drums of a tuned set are played by separate performers, as the *entenga* ensemble of Uganda: in one example, 12 deep single-headed drums placed on the ground tilted forward and played by four men with curved sticks over a range of two pentatonic octaves.

Drum kit (or drum set). Essential in jazz or rock music. The basic outfit includes: (*a*) small pattern *bass drum with foot pedal, worked by right foot; (*b*) *tom-tom, one or more mounted on top of the bass drum; (*c*) side drum, with folding stand, sticks, and wire brushes; (*d*) Hi-Hat cymbal (see CYMBAL, 2), worked by left foot (Pl. 1, far left); (*e*) suspended cymbal ('top cymbal', see CYMBAL, 3), one or more mounted on the drum or a separate stand; (*f*) large tom-tom ('floor tom-tom'). The minimum provision is of the bass and side drums and suspended cymbal.

The precursor of the drum set is the 'trap' drummer's equipment of the music hall, then adapted by jazz drummers to their needs in the years before 1920; they used a larger bass drum, on which the foot pedal might also strike a cymbal. Among the traps might be a wood block, *cowbells, 'Chinese' tom-tom, and perhaps a row of three *Temple blocks.

Drum machine, drum pad. Electronic devices. The first is well known, automatically imitating percussion instruments (bass and side drum, tom-toms, and cymbal, especially Hi-Hat) in pre-set rhythms of the kinds required in rock and pop music: a standard feature in electronic portable keyboards and electronic organs, also obtainable in models programmable by the user. A drum pad ranks higher, having a synthetic sensitive surface which is played on with sticks or fingers, again imitating the sounds of the instruments. (See Dobson 1992.)

Duct flute. A general term (now preferred to older expressions such as 'whistle' flute) for all instruments like recorder, tin whistle, ocarina, in which air is artificially led to a voicing aperture in

Pl. 1. A typical modern drum set by Premier, Leicester.

the side; see FLUTE, 7c. The term was introduced by Henry Balfour, first curator of the Pitt Rivers Museum, Oxford, at the end of the 19th century.

Duda, dudy, Dudelsack. Names of *bagpipes, all of Central European types with a cylindrical-bore chanter sounded with a single reed: *duda*, chiefly Slovak, Hungarian, and Ukrainian; *dudy*, Czech; *Dudelsack*, German (properly for the old Slav or Wendish type, but also familiarly, of any bagpipe or '*Sackpfeife*').

Duduk (*düdük*). A wind instrument name widely met from Turkey to the Caucasus, meaning 'pipe', usually a duct flute or the double-reed *balaban.

Dulce melos. Early name for a hammered *dulcimer (and the source of this word). A keyboard version described *c.* 1454 in the manuscript of Arnaut of Zwolle (see HARPSICHORD, 6), but not heard of since, had equal-length strings tuned to the scale and divided by bridges in ratio 4 : 2 : 1; each section being struck by a metal arm thrown up from the keyboard to give the note of the string, undamped, in each of three different octaves.

Dulcian. Fore-runner of the *bassoon, and like this named in Ger. *Fagott* and in It. *fagotto* (presumably through early resemblance to a faggot or torch); in Ger. also *Dulzian*, of which 'dulcian' is a modern anglicization that has been preferred on the whole to 17th-century Eng. 'curtal' (from Fr. *courtaut*, name of a similar instrument, the resemblance here being to some old kind of firearm; Sp. *bajón*).

Dating from the mid-16th century to the start of the 18th, a dulcian has the conical bore of a bassoon but pierced in a single billet of wood (usually maple) by boring up from the bottom for the smaller conical bore with the six fingerholes, the little-finger key, and socket for the brass crook at the top; and downwards from the top (the 'bell') for the larger bore with two thumb-holes and usually one thumb key. Among 50 or more originals (from which copies are now made) the majority are of the bassoon-pitched bass dulcian, in Germany *Chorist-fagott*, about 1 m. (3′) tall, bottom note C. (See SHAWM, Pl. 1, here replacing the unwieldy bass shawm in a marching band, played 'left-handed' and with the bell, with uncharacteristic 'ring' turning, pointing to the right.) It can sound rather like a bassoon with the bell removed (a fingering chart [Speer 1697] is reproduced in Carse 1939). Next, the *Quart-fagott*, a fourth or fifth deeper; and (e.g. Augsburg *collection) an *Octav-fagott*, 215 cm. (7′) tall and of contrabassoon pitch. Also made were smaller sizes, up to an octave above the 'Chorist' and *c.* 45 cm. (18″): Schütz scores for a whole group from *Quart-fagott* to small *Alt-fagott* (up to a′) in his setting of Psalm 24. In Spanish cathedrals such were used up to the 18th century to support the choir, and some of these *bajones* and *bajoncillos* have survived (see PRAETOR-

IUS, Fig. 1, for the whole family in outline). In Bach's Cantata No. 31 (Weimar, 1715) the fine obbligato going down to low G′ is evidently for the Quart-fagott which the town is known to have possessed (Heyde 1987).

In many 17th-century German and Italian works the bass dulcian plays a very active part, elaborating the bass line with fast scale passages and figuration, and is often the only wind instrument among the strings. No English or French specimens are known. The first datable evidence of extension of the compass from C to low B♭′ (matching the lowest string of the French *basse de violon*, the old form of cello) is from France (*Mersenne 1636), from which time construction in two, or three, separate joints, leading to the bassoon, was being followed in at least some instances over Europe (examples in the Vienna collection).

Dulcimer. Generally understood as the 'hammered dulcimer', played with two beaters. See APPALACHIAN DULCIMER for the American plucked instrument (a fretted *zither). Small *glockenspiels made for children have also been called 'dulcimer'.

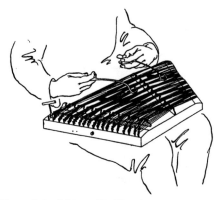

Fig. 1. Swiss dulcimer (Hackbrett)

1. *Hammered dulcimer* (Fr.: *timpanon*; Ger.: *Hackbrett*; It., Sp.: *salterio*; Hung.: *cimbalom*). This has a trapezoidal soundbox (Fig. 1) placed on a table, or on its own four-legged stand, or carried on a strap, with the longest side nearest the player. The hammers are of wood, cane, or wire, about 25 cm. (10″) long, with curved-up ends, and are held with a light grip, usually between the first and second fingers. The soundboard is thick (about 12 mm. (½″), much as in a piano), of pine, cedar, or plywood. The metal strings, tuned on the right, run across it with three or four strings per note (because—again as in the piano—the string must be thin to sound pleasantly with correct overtones, but by itself would give insufficient amplitude effectively to vibrate the soundboard). Fine piano wire may be used, e.g. of gauges 6 to 8 (see STRINGED INSTRUMENTS, 1), thus around half a millimetre thick (20 thousandths of an inch).

Dulcimers are ingeniously arranged to bring the notes within close reach. The strings are raised about 4 cm. ($1\frac{1}{2}''$) above the soundboard by means of two long balustrade-like bridges topped with a thick brass wire (sometimes replaced by individual 'chessmen' bridges). In Fig. 2 they are marked L and R. Bridge R is on the right and the other is at two-thirds of the string-length towards the left. The courses of strings bear, alternately from front to back, on R and on L. Those which rest on R (group R) slope down to the left to pass through openings in bridge L without touching it, to reach the hitch rail (h) on the far left. Of those which bear on bridge L (group L), the longer sections slope down to the right through the openings in bridge R to rail (t), while the shorter sections slope down to rail (h) to give notes a fifth higher than the longer sections owing to the diversion of these strings in the ratio 2 : 3 (perfect fifth). The net result is to provide three striking-zones: where group R rises highest, and where each division of group L rises highest. The figure illustrates schematically a string plan for a simple 17-course diatonic dulcimer for playing folk-tunes in F and C major. On the right, adjacent strings from top to bottom give octaves; over the whole, four notes are duplicated.

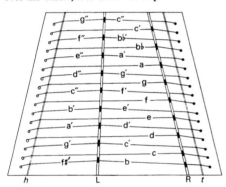

Fig. 2. Strings, shown here as single strings for clarity, rest on bridge L or R at the points indicated in black and pass through the other bridge without touching.

The sound has a characteristic ringing quality since the notes are for the most part undamped (save where there may be time to damp them with the side of the hand). Long notes are sustained by tremolando with the hammers, and with crescendo or diminuendo as desired—something that the pianist can do only by playing octaves. Sometimes a dulcimer is played with the fingers or finger-picks; in England earlier this century when the dulcimer was heard in pubs in several parts of the country, it was sometimes played so, with the nails grown long for the purpose.

In America the dulcimer is mentioned from 1717 in Massachusetts, and was popular in West Virginia, Michigan, and eastwards up to the 1920s. Lyon & Healy manufactured it in Chicago from *c.* 1890 while many that survive in collections were home-made, as they are again, in Britain also, with a revival of folk dulcimer-playing.

2. *Cimbalom.* The greatest area in the West for the dulcimer as a living folk instrument is the eastern part of Europe, from Switzerland (*Hackbrett*) and over the Slav countries and Hungary, where the common name is '*cimbal*' (written in various ways) and the stringing may supply every chromatic note over at least part of the compass. As known internationally, *cimbalom* (short for Hung. *nagy-cimbalom*, 'big dulcimer') is the large concert model on fixed legs, usually with damper pedal and played with yarn-covered beaters, mellowing the sound: the compass is D to e'''. It has been made from about 1874 by the Budapest firm of Schunda: Ex. 1 is taken from a set of studies published by Schunda to advertise the design. While today most often heard in gypsy restaurant orchestras, the cimbalom has also appeared in concert works, e.g.: Stravinsky, *Renard* (1917); Kodály, *Háry János* suite; Bartók, First Rhapsody for violin (with some use of plucking); and so on up to Boulez, *éclats*.

3. *Asian dulcimer and early history.* The hammered dulcimer was known in the Middle East early in the Middle Ages. In Iran and Iraq it is an important classical instrument (*sanṭūr*), trapezoid, with quadruple metal strings and a left-hand bridge that divides in ratio 2 : 1 (the two sections giving notes an octave apart); some late models, played on a table, have the damper pedal. From this area the dulcimer travelled east after the Middle Ages to China (*yangqin*) and Korea, and more recently North India, winning considerable popularity everywhere.

It is quite possible that the European trapezoid dulcimer derives from the same source, for the

Ex. 1.

early instruments played with two hammers, shown in Italian paintings of *c.* 1430, look as if they were evolved up to that point independently—long rectangular soundboxes with few strings, though in one case with a short dividing bridge—to be overtaken shortly afterwards by the trapezoid type. This last came to be made very elegantly through the 17th and 18th centuries, those for instance by Battaglia of Milan being prized collector's pieces. They were much played in Italy in informal ensembles along with other portable instruments. In Germany *c.* 1697 a Leipzig dancing master, Hebenstreit, brought out new elaborate designs called after his first name, Pantaleon (Hanks 1969); from *c.* 1750 the name, for a time, came to be used for the early German *square piano.

Dulcitone. See CELESTA.

Dulzaina. See DOUÇAINE, DOLZAINA, 3.

Dulzian. See DULCIAN.

Dung. Tibetan lama trumpet. See CHINA AND KOREA, 3*c.*

Duo-art. See PLAYER PIANO.

Duplex: 1. *Duplex scaling.* On pianos, the system (patented in the USA by Steinway, 1872) by which the residual ends of the strings by the tuning pins and wrest pins are measured in proportion to the sounding lengths, to contribute harmonic resonance. See PIANO, 4*b.*

2. *Duplex* (or double-bell instruments). Valved brass instruments in which one could change, for example, from *euphonium tone to *trombone tone by turning a valve. One, made in Birmingham, was exhibited at the Great Exhibition of 1851; others followed, by Pelitti, Milan (*c.* 1855), and in the USA Conn was making them by 1887. There were two of them in Sousa's band a few years later. Bell-upwards in form, the tube, having passed from the single mouthpiece through the normal three valves, can be switched to lead either to a wide tube with large bell, or to a narrower with smaller bell, e.g. as advertised *c.* 1870 in Britain, 'E♭ Saxhorn and Trumpet'; 'B♭ Euphonium and Trombone'. See also ECHO, 1.

Dutar (*dutār*, from Persian 'two-stringed'). One of the main lutes of Central Asia, popular among the Uzbek and others in Turkestan: a long lute (see LUTE, 7, and Pl. 5) resembling the Turkish *saz*, up to 120 cm. (4′) in length, with long, narrow neck and some 14 tied frets. (Today it is also made with raised fingerboard, fixed chromatic frets, and tenor and bass sizes for the modern folk ensemble.) The two metal strings are sometimes paired and are thrummed with the fingers, adding extra effects such as by scraping on the wood belly with the nails. In North India, the *dotara* is similar, and is sometimes played with a bow.

Dvoinice (dvojnice). The *double flageolet of Yugoslavia, especially Croatia. Made in one piece of wood, the two pipes diverge a little towards the ends and are sometimes built to sound together in consecutive seconds with an effect recalling that which can be heard in traditional women's folk-singing of the region. The instrument has come to be much manufactured for tourist gift shops, along with such as the *diple and *gusla.

E

Early evolution of instruments. The ways of many of the most primitive peoples when first observed by Western explorers and as yet practically untouched by external influences—as in Tasmania and Fuegia—have indicated that mankind existed for a long time before feeling a need for special instruments for making sound. Man could lure game by mimicking their sounds with the mouth alone, or mouth and hand. In the communal 'ring' dance, the set steps are to a chanted accompaniment—the only singing that may normally be heard in the life of the tribe and its only music. Vigorous rhythmic noises soon heighten the intensity of the dance: slapping the body, clapping, stamping, and the wearing of rattling objects or striking on objects near at hand, or (Fuegia) drumming on a rolled-up piece of hide. Still on Palaeolithic levels, medicine-men bring into their weather- and healing-magic instruments for making 'mysterious sounds' like scrapers of a notched stick or bone, and blowing into a bone or quill, or (again Fuegia) into the windpipe of a freshly killed duck (Gusinde 1937).

Such sound-makers could have been hit upon by mankind at any time wherever materials were to hand. But it is harder to say this of the more complex *bull-roarer, which in all four corners of the earth has served in tribal rites of similar kinds, and so (for there seems no other swung or thrown artefact of a corresponding universality from which it might be thought to derive) lending support to the broad theory of diffusion of culture on which Curt Sachs built his monumental chronology for the appearances of instruments (*Sachs 1928), based mainly on analysis of geographical distribution (e.g. those met furthest from a presupposed source on the Asian continent are likely to be the oldest, those with more confined distributions being more recent). A much condensed summary would run as follows, up to the point where the archaeology of ancient civilizations takes over (see ANTIQUITY):

Upper Palaeolithic: worn rattles, gourd rattle, scraper, bull-roarer, whistles, didjeridu;
Early Neolithic: slit drum, stamping tube, drum, musical bow, flute, panpipe, conch;
Later Neolithic: xylophone, jew's-harp (bamboo), reedpipe;
Early Metal-Age: bell (metal), friction drum, idiochord zither, horn.

Sachs was particularly absorbed by the sociology and symbolism of the instruments. From a musical point of view, one notices the slow succession of instruments that produce melodious sounds: by impact (stamping tubes, early xylophones of two or more split logs); or through skills with the mouth, little with the hands and fingers, as musical bow (mouth bow) and jew's-harp, these for the pleasure of the harmonic sounds selected with the mouth; and, besides panpipes, flutes without holes, giving melody from the blown harmonics (see FLUTE, 8). When a flute has fingerholes they typically number three or four, but played with both hands, using only the first one or two fingers—those which, with the thumb, play the major part in the manual actions of everyday life. Early zithers too, if not simply tapped with a stick, are mostly plucked with thumb or forefinger, rarely with the separate fingers as one plays a harp. The harp, played with all fingers, signals a major change brought about by higher civilization, which has left evidence of systematic tuning to a series of defined modes (see HARP, 10b). The artistic ascendancy of stringed instruments here begins, for, as Aristoxenus recognized (*Harmonics*, trans. Macran, II. 42), it is more difficult to accommodate such changes accurately with simple fingerholes on a wind instrument.

*Sachs 1928, 1940; Schaeffner 1936; Wachsmann in Baines 1961, etc. See also Devale 1988.

Echo. 1. 'Echo cornet', 'echo horn': brass instruments, late 19th century onwards, with built-in mute. A special valve instantly changes the instrument from sounding through the bell to sounding through the mute. For instruments giving tonal contrast by use of two complete bells, see DUPLEX, 2.

2. Echo organ: a department of many church organs, placed in the organ or separately, usually with one of the console keyboards to itself, and containing soft-toned registers, often enclosed by some form of swell shutter.

Écurie (Fr., 'stables'). 'La musique de l'Écurie', a department of the French royal music through the 17th century, is entered here through its bearing on a number of instruments. In precedence it came after the 'Musique de la Chapelle' (singers, with one or two *cornetts and *serpent); and the 'Musique de la Chambre', this with lute players and a small violin group with bass viol and recorder (*fluste*) available; and the big string band of the 24 'grand violons' or 'violons ordinaires' established in 1626 on the basis of the previous dance orchestra (for which several instruments supplied by Andrea Amati still exist; see e.g. VIOLA, 3a).

1. *Players.* The Écurie comprised: the corps of 12 trumpets; nine fifes including the drums; five 'hautbois et musettes de Poitou'; five 'cromornes et trompettes marines'; and the 12 'grand hautbois', the ceremonial wind band for great occasions (see SHAWM, 1b). This last (each man listed as doubling on strings) had, prior to reforms under Lully, two each of *Dessus d'hautbois* (treble shawm), *cornet* (cornett), *haute-contre d'hautbois* (alto shawm), *taille d'hautbois* (tenor shawm), *saque-boute* (trombone), and *basse d'hautbois* (bass shawm). Among the players listed in 1666 are three members of the Hotteterre family who as makers have been associated with the development of the newer baroque woodwind, as the oboes and bassoons which the 12 players eventually changed over to.

2. *Instruments.* Relatively little is known about the two groups of five men, whether they had regular duties at first with the instruments named or, after these were scrapped, violins, flutes, etc.

(a) *Hautbois de Poitou.* As illustrated earlier by *Mersenne, these were a set of cylindrical double-reed instruments with *wind-cap; a bagpipe (the *musette*) played the treble part, and the bass instrument was built in two parallel tubes; no authentic examples of these 'hautbois' are known. They were later abolished, though the appointments endured, some to be held by eminent flute-players.

(b) *Cromornes.* The name (not mentioned by Mersenne, see CRUMHORN, 3) suggests, of course, *crumhorns as, at least, the original instruments. A suite dated 1660, among the Philidor manuscripts at Versailles, is marked for the 'cromornes et trompettes marines' (see TROMBA MARINA) but looks, as it stands, as if written for some different instruments, possibly supporting *trompettes marines* playing the melody (one of the pieces is reproduced in *Grove*, 5th edn., 'Crumhorn'). Dictionaries of the period gave *basse de chromorne* as a name for the bassoon (*basson*). Eventually, as with the 'Poitou' group, players of 'up-to-date' instruments took over the parts.

Benoit 1971.

Edge-tone. The high-pitched vibration that may occur when an air-stream meets a stationary sharp edge. Instruments of the Flute class (see WIND INSTRUMENTS, 1a) have sometimes (less today) been described as 'edge-tone' instruments.

Effects (in traditional, pre-electronic senses). For more than a century it has been the percussionist's lot to be responsible for miscellaneous imitative and joke instruments now and then demanded, like the pop-gun for 19th-century Viennese champagne polkas, steam train imitators for the silent cinema (see SCRAPER), *motor horns, and the mouth-blown

*siren for comedy effects (a wind instrument but entrusted to the theatre drummer since it is not a wind-player's job to watch the stage). Some of the many devices have since acquired the status of a symphonic instrument scored for non-associatively but for the sound-quality in its own right (e.g. *anvil, *whip). Others are still usually termed 'effects', notably those for rendering weather noises by the older methods (now largely supplanted by amplified recordings of the real thing, or synthesized electronically as with the cannon fire in Tchaikovsky's *1812 Overture*). The rain machine is a rotating drum of wire mesh with pellets inside. The wind machine (Fr.: *éoliphone*) is a wide cylinder made of wooden slats, some 75 cm. (30″) in diameter, and rotated under a sheet of light canvas; used by Richard Strauss in *Don Quixote* and Vaughan Williams in *Sinfonia Antartica*. Thunder sheet: a thin metal sheet up to 3 m. (10′) long, hung up and shaken or hit with a gong-mallet; another machine used for thunder is a rotating steel cylinder with stones or metal balls inside. Eric Blom wrote of the wind machine, in *Grove* (5th edn., 'Wind Machine', that 'the objection to it as an element in composition is that it produces by realistic means what music should suggest in its own terms' (such as by vigorous tremolando, or by rise and fall in chromatics, as for example by Wagner in the *Flying Dutchman* overture).

Eight-foot: 1. *Organ, harpsichord, harmonium, etc.* For this and allied terms, '4″' etc., as applied to different registers or stops on these instruments see ORGAN, 2.

2. *Other instruments.* Any instrument that normally sounds its music in a higher or lower octave than it is written can be described (though it is not the custom to do so) as a '4″' instrument (e.g. *xylophone), or '16″' instrument (e.g. *double bass). Equally it may be described as an instrument giving '4′ tone', etc., and much shorter than having to write, or say, 'sounding an octave higher than written'.

Ektar (or *ektār, ektara*, 'one-stringed'). Indian instrument on which a single steel string is plucked with one finger in rhythmic accompaniment to the voice, usually by a religious mendicant. The bamboo stick which holds the string passes into a skin-covered gourd, and is held more or less upright. For other one-stringed instruments used in India for similar purposes, see GOPI-YANTRA, TUILA (the latter sometimes, as in Orissa, also called *ektar*).

Electric guitar. While still basically a stringed instrument, the electric guitar has generally come to be considered along with the electronic, with which it shares so much of a complex electrical technology; even so, it has been too important an instrument for its salient features not to be briefly noticed here. (For a full account, see Dobson 1992.)

1. *Solid-body*. The standard type, having no sound-box. Instead, the six strings (steel or nickel alloy) pass through the magnetic fields of electromagnetic pick-ups mounted on the acoustically functionless wooden body close below the strings to sense the string vibration and convert it into electrical energy: as the frequencies change during playing, so varies the current induced in the coil and the voltage output. This is led, by way of the volume and tone controls, to the amplifier/loudspeaker system normally placed at some distance away. Usually there are two rows of pick-ups, or three, placed at different distances from the bridge, used separately or together for different tone effects, while a number of controls are provided for volume and further tonal effects. There may also be a 'tremolo arm', a lever by which the string tension is varied for *Hawaiian guitar vibrato effects.

2. *Hollow-bodied and Semi-solid Electric Guitar*. The former has a true soundbox made in various shapes (usually arched top with *f*-holes) as well as being provided with pick-ups; the semi-solid adds a solid block down the centre inside. The hollow-bodied was the original type (following earlier use of a contact microphone), introduced in the USA in the 1930s by Les Paul, once of the Gibson Company, and fairly widely used in jazz. The semi-solid, much used in the 1950s and early 1960s and made famous in Britain by the Beatles, was gradually superseded by the solid-body in the 1960s.

3. *Electric Bass Guitar*. This has a solid body and four thick metal-tape-covered strings tuned to the same notes as the double bass and a string-length of some 90 cm. (36"). Created in California by Leo Fender, it was first marketed in 1951. (See Dobson 1992, 'Electric Guitar', 3).

Electric piano. In its various forms, this is an instrument of the electro-acoustic category: vibrations generated in strings or small rods ('tines') struck by light hammers, or aroused by further methods, are sensed by pick-ups corresponding to those of an electric guitar, amplified and heard as sound through a loudspeaker. No soundboard is therefore required. Electric pianos are often considered technologically along with true electronic instruments (see Dobson 1992, 'Electric and Electronic Pianos'), and accordingly can be mentioned here only in brief outline.

1. *String-based*. This, the earlier type, is best known through the 'Neo-Bechstein' (Siemens–Bechstein, 1934) in grand piano form, using magnetic pick-ups and needing one string only for each note. The right-hand pedal raises the dampers as normally. The left-hand pedal is for an independent volume control acting on the amplification system: it allows the tone on held notes not only to be sustained longer than usual but even to be swelled during the sustain.

2. *Non-string-based*. The classic form is here the Fender–Rhodes electric piano invented by Harold Rhodes in the USA during the 1960s. Strings are replaced by small steel tines, one for each note, in length matched to the frequency. Mounted above the tine is a tone-bar, larger in size (much so for the lower notes) and calculated to come close to the tine in resonance pitch. The tine and the tone-bar have often been described as, together, making a kind of tuning fork of unequal lengths. When a tine is struck, its high, inharmonic overtones are prominent, rapidly to decay as the tone-bar vibrates in sympathy, prolonging the sound with enriched quality. The instrument, in form, resembles a mini-piano. It has won much popularity, and is today probably the favourite among electric pianos. Other designs, for example by Hohner, have been based on plucked steel 'reeds', in some cases described as plucked by 'plastic suction pads' to suppress the jarring element in the attack.

Often today the expression 'electric piano' is used in the sense of a fully electronic instrument, with sound generated electronically: in effect, an electronic keyboard (on folding legs) designed especially to imitate a piano.

Embouchure (Fr.). A wind-instrument term with different meanings.

1. In a literal sense of 'mouthing', the manner in which the player's mouth and lips are placed when playing a flute, reed, or brass instrument; the word has been so used in English from the late 18th century.

2. With the flute, often used for the mouth-hole of the instrument itself.

3. In France, also the regular word for the mouthpiece of a brass instrument.

Enanga. In African a trough zither (see ZITHER, 3*b*) of Uganda and the Congo (in some areas *inanga*, *nanga*). In Uganda also a name (or *ennanga*) for an arched harp (see HARP, 10*a*).
   Wachsmann 1953.

English guitar (and allied instruments). 1. *English guitar* (Pl. 1). A favourite drawing-room instrument from the middle of the 18th century, well known especially for ladies (gentlemen played the violin or flute): pear-shaped body (sometimes varied), deep sides (narrowing upwards to the neck from *c*.7 cm. (2¾") at the base), back slightly arched, and metal strings played with the fingers. Generally known in its day as 'guitar' (as distinct from 'Spanish guitar'), and today a familiar antique, it historically marks a transformation of the old *cittern which seems to have commenced in the late 17th century. The strings, in six courses—the first four courses double, of steel or brass, the lowest two single, of overspun wire—are tuned over the chord of C

Pl. 1. English guitar by J. Preston (London, c. 1770)

between frets for bolting on a *capotasto for playing in higher keys. A leading maker is John Preston, London; among others, Liessem, Hintz, and in Dublin, Perry, and Gibson, who also made larger models. A Tutor was published by Bremner, 1758. Devices came often to be fitted by which ladies could avoid risking their fingernails by pressing small piano-like keys; these activate a plucking mechanism contained in an oval wooden box clamped to the foot of the instrument: the 'keyed guitar'. On all these instruments, 'watch-key' tuning (threaded rods turned by separate 'watch-key')—or geared machines—came largely to supersede tuning pegs.

Where in Europe the type originated has proved difficult to establish: see CITTERN, 6 for a German species sometimes retaining features of the old cittern to a more marked degree.

2. *French cistre.* From c.1760 this *cistre* (or '*guitare allemande*', for reasons unclear) was mostly made in Dunkirk and Lille: broadly similar to the English guitar but with seven courses (the lower three tuned *f c G*) and sometimes a lute-like back. The *arcicistre* (i.e. arch-cittern, also known as *théorbe*) has long unstopped bass strings from an upper pegbox and, in many examples made in Paris, a soundbox extended upwards under the bass strings to give these extra resonance.

3. *Portuguese guitar* (or *guitarra*, the guitar itself being in Portugal *viola*). This has resembled the English (from which the earliest Portuguese tutor, of 1796, says it was derived). Today, however, it is best known in the form, with very much enlarged soundbox, which accompanies *fado* singers. Tuning is by screw-rods radiating fanwise, as in many of the later English guitars. There are many different tunings.

Armstrong 1908; Baines 1966.

English horn. See COR ANGLAIS.

Entenga. Ugandan ensemble of tuned drums: see DRUM CHIME.

Épinette. Fr., *spinet. For *épinette des vosges*, the smallest of the European fretted zithers, see ZITHER, 2.

major from *g'* down to *c* (in music written an octave higher), as suited to playing airs especially in this key: Ex. 1 is the start of the finale of a 'Sonata for the Guitar' with violin accompaniment, possibly by J. C. Bach (the 'London Bach'). The string-length is c.42 cm. (17″). Frets, 12 (sometimes more) of metal or ivory. The instruments are handsomely made, with the rose of copper gilt, and a tortoiseshell fingerboard. This last has holes

Ex. 1.

Equal temperament. See TEMPERAMENT, 4.

Erhu. Chinese fiddle, a main variety among the bowed instruments known collectively as *huqin* (*hu-ch'ing*). The small body, usually hexagonal or octagonal in section, of wood, is *c.*13 cm. (5″) long and 8 cm. (3″) wide. A lizard-skin covers the front and the back is open. With the smaller and also important fiddle *jinghu* (*ching-hu*) the body is cylindrical, of bamboo cut from low down the plant near the root. With both types the body, rested on the thigh or lap, is carried on a long bamboo stick (the neck). Above this the two strings (*er*, 'two') pass high, to be stopped by finger pressure in the general Asian manner (see BOW, 3). At a certain distance from the tuning pegs the strings (once silk, now nylon or wire) are drawn towards the neck by a thread loop, beyond which they spread out at the bridge: their effective length from the loop to the bridge on an *erhu* is roughly that of a violin, of which the sound is not unlike. The loop can be moved for quick adjustment to the tuning.

The hair of the long, slender bow (held thumb-upwards) passes between the two strings: the bow cannot be removed without unhitching the hair from one end. The bow is moved low down, close to the body of the instrument, which is held in such a way that the bow touches one string or the other according to whether the hair is moving close to the player's body—when the hair touches the deeper-tuned string—or whether the bow is lifted forwards for the opposite side of the hair to touch the other string. To bring the bow to the requisite angle, the instrument is usually held with the bridge facing well towards the right, as can be observed in CHINA AND KOREA, Pl. I. (This feature of a 'captive' bow, met among similar Mongolian and Siberian fiddles, could have arisen in the distant past to enable horsemen to sling fiddle and bow safely together for transport.) There are also, especially in North China, fiddles with four strings, tuned alternately to (say) E and A below, the bow hair being here divided in two bands, each passing between an E string and an A string: while the bow moves near to the body it sounds both E strings, or away from the body both A strings (the left-hand fingers laid across to make notes on either pair).

In the Beijing (Peking) Opera, the small, brighter-sounding *jinghu* plays the leading role, accompanying the male parts, while the deeper-tuned *erhu* usually accompanies the female parts. They follow the line of the melody with idiomatic inflexions and interpolations. Another fiddle, *banhu* (*pan-hu*) is of a half-coconut with wood belly. For the modern Chinese orchestra complete sets of instruments have been developed in sizes from treble to contrabass, and these are now in general use (as with several other species of fiddle over Asia; see FIDDLE, 2d): the *gehu* and contrabass *digehu* have bodies of a new form, with four strings tuned as the western *cello and *double bass, and therefore played with a free bow.

Erke, erkencho. South American wind instruments, of the Gran Chaco, North Argentina. The *erke* is a straight cane trumpet similar to the *clarín of Bolivia but not reaching such great sizes, and sounded after carnival and during Corpus Christi. The *erkencho* ('small *erke*') or *putoto* (an old Indian word for a *conch) is a cowhorn with a large *idioglot cane reed stuck into the small end: a kind of *reed-horn, sometimes grasped in one hand while the other beats a drum.

Eskimo drum. See SHAMAN DRUM.

Esraj. Indian bowed stringed instrument; see DILRUBA AND ESRAJ.

Estive. Medieval wind instrument; see HORNPIPE.

Eunuch flute. Seventeenth-century term for instruments of *kazoo kinds.

Euphonium (Fr.: *basse en si♭*; Ger.: *Baryton*; It., Sp.: *bombardino*; USA: baritone horn). Valved brass instrument of tenor–bass pitch (built in B♭) looking like a small *tuba (see BRASS BAND, Pl. I). The euphonium is a leading voice in *military and concert bands, and in Britain also in the *brass band (in which the name *baritone denotes a different instrument). The compass (in the brass band written a ninth higher in treble clef) is from b♭′ down to E if provided with three valves: if with four valves, now more used, it will reach almost an octave deeper, and certain notes in the middle of the range (as *c*, B) are easier to play confidently always well in tune. Euphonium solos, without which a brass band concert is rarely complete, include new works as well as traditional settings and borrowings from the repertories of other instruments.

Historically the euphonium is based on the French *saxhorn basse* (see SAXHORN); the present name was apparently adopted by the London maker Henry Distin from a German design of the 1840s by one Sommer, who became a member of Jullien's famous band (Bevan 1978). See also TUBA, 6 (for 'tenor tuba') and VALVE, 3 (for the use of the fourth valve).

F

Fagott, fagotto (Ger., It.). The *bassoon. See also DULCIAN (earliest type of bassoon). For 'alto fagotto', see TENOROON.

Fair organ. See BARREL ORGAN, 5.

Fakes and forgeries. As well known, violins bearing a Stradivarius label are not by Stradivarius save in one instance in a million, yet are not regarded as 'fakes', the imitation being a part of old, recognized, selling practice over what may be good and useful instruments. On the other hand, as the great *collections of old musical instruments were being built up from the late 19th century in Europe and America, collectors were frequently deceived by apparently rare specimens of *lute, *virginal, etc., which had been skilfully constructed with collectors in view from bits and pieces (original or mixed with newly made) or totally new-made following some old or imagined prototype, and perhaps inscribed with a famous name of the past. Most notorious in this trade was Franciolini of Florence (d. 1920), who brought out illustrated catalogues, known from 1890 and now republished (Ripin 1974). A number of his instruments remain on show in museums which may be loath to acknowledge the sad truth should it come to removing from public view what may be the only example they possess of that particular kind of instrument. There are some distinctive types which apparently owe their present existence wholly to this clever craftsman where he followed an unreliable illustration in some earlier book: see BANDORA; CRUMHORN, 4.

Fiddle. Besides a colloquial name for the *violin, used also to cover the numerous bowed instruments—folk, exotic, medieval, etc.—which are not violins.

1. *Medieval Europe: (a) Early history.* After the first known written allusion to use of the bow (in medieval Arabic; see BOW, 3) the most common type of fiddle over Europe was of a type that had spread from the Byzantine empire in the 10th century, there named *lyra*, or *lira* (the classical word for 'lyre' in a new sense). Remains of two actual examples from the Middle Ages have been found in excavations at Novgorod, USSR—no bows with them, but certainly fiddles. One, dated to 1190 (illustrated in *NOCM*, p. 674, Fig. 1), is only 40 cm. (16″) long. Typical are its D-shaped soundholes and provision for three strings, the middle one probably serving as a 'drone' while fingering the others by finger or fingernail pressure alone, downwards or sideways against the string, for there is no fingerboard to press them against: a method (having nothing to do with touching a string at a node to make a *harmonic) which gives the notes as clearly as on a violin and remains normal on fiddles both everywhere in Asia (see BOW, 3) as well as on present folk fiddles of south-east Europe such as the *lira* of the Aegean. Whether this Novgorod fiddle was, like those, held downwards on the knee cannot be known; but it is over Europe in general, alone in the world, that the ancient practice has almost always been for a fiddle to be played standing, holding the instrument up against the chest or shoulder (Pl. 1) with the bow grasped palm-downwards. From the 12th century the strings may be stopped against a short fingerboard (sometimes bearing diatonic frets). Much less commonly, and even up to the Renaissance period, the instrument may be held low (more as a lute is held) and bowed as in Pl. 3, Tuareg one-string fiddle (see below, 2b) or else on the near side as (with rare exceptions) on a *viol.

Pl. 1. Fiddle, three-stringed 'pear-shaped' form, from an English psalter (13th century).

(b) '*Medieval viol*'. By the 13th century such small 'pear-shaped' fiddles (see also REBEC, 2) were largely giving place to more oval-bodied forms, some with a slight waist (below, *c*); but there was also, mainly in the 12th and 13th centuries, a figure-of-eight-shaped fiddle with three strings and held downwards on the knee, usually by a cleric. Whether there was a special name for it is not known. Historians have distinguished it as 'medieval viol' (through being held downwards) though with no connection with the Renaissance viol unless possibly through some obscure link in Spain (see VIOL, 3a).

(c) *Medieval fiddle* (Lat.: *viella*, from Fr.: *vièle*; the northern form of Provençal and It.: *viola*; Eng., Ger.: *Fithele*, *Fiedel*, *Vidill*). The principal fiddle of the 13th and 14th centuries and a leading instrument among the literate classes of society and their minstrels (see MEDIEVAL INSTRUMENTS, 3). A typical form is shown in Pl. 2. The body was, at least as a rule, carved from one piece, with a flat pine belly added. The bridge position in pictures varies greatly (as still in early pictures of the violin). Some tunings and rudiments of technique are in the late 13th-century treatise, written after 1272, by Jerome of Moravia, a Dominican in Paris (Page 1979). First he gives (to list them from the 'bass' side, the left as held: *d G g d' d'*; the notes, however, are almost certainly intended to convey the interval pattern only, not the exact pitch. The first *d* is termed the *bordunus* (see BOURDON); it lay off the fingerboard (as visible in Pl. 2) and a contemporary marginal note informs us that it could be sounded either with the bow or with the thumb (see CRWTH; LIRA DA BRACCIO), but must not make a discord with other strings. The next four strings amount to two pairs: an octave *course, G and g, and a unison top course on *d'*, so that in sum we have basically three strings as on the earlier fiddles, but some of them paired. For a wider compass (only the first position of the left hand is mentioned) the fifth string, *d'*, was tuned up to *g'* and the *bordunus* put over the fingerboard, to provide the notes *d e f*. More often the fiddle is shown with three or four strings only, and from the end of the 14th century in so many different, often decorative shapes that it is difficult for a modern maker of late medieval or early Renaissance instruments to decide which to choose for a model; nor are any representative specimens sufficiently preserved to reveal details of construction and fittings.

Even from after the violin appeared the two fiddles recovered in their wooden cases from the 1545 wreck of the *Mary Rose* have hollowed-out bodies (of about violin length) with flat back and top, C-holes, and a thick neck of almost *guitar width continuing the plane of the belly; nor are they freaks, for practically the same form, with the 'bitten off' corners and wide neck without fingerboard, is seen in Flemish and Italian paintings of the same time, and the actual remains of a fiddle of the same shape and approximate date were not long ago recovered from a well in Poland. (Also in Central Europe, still played in the Jihlava region of Czechoslovakia, are fiddles (*husle*) of another ancient build, though the tradition of their making

Pl. 2. Fiddle (vièle, viella), from the De Lisle Psalter, English (early 14th century); a bourdon string lying off the fingerboard is just visible.

is not known to antedate the 17th century. For some other old forms preserved among folk instruments, see REBEC, 3.)

2. *Asian and African fiddles*. Most have a skin belly. Strings number from one to four, of silk, gut, horsehair, metal. A patch of rosin is often stuck on the body or neck. Nearly always the instrument is held downwards, the player usually seated on the ground, holding the bow palm-upwards and stopping by finger-pressure alone (as see 1 above).

(a) Hollowed in wood, monobloc or the neck of another piece, are: *rabab (Morocco, Algeria—short, boat-shaped); *kemancha ('Pontic fiddle', Middle East, Greece—narrow, parallel-sided body, belly of wood); *kobyz, kyyak (Central Asia—rather shoe-like, the upper part round); *sarangi (India—squarish); *sarinda (India—pointed body); *dilruba and esraj (India—derived from the *sitar).

(b) The body is held on a long pole (the 'neck') somewhat as in older types of *banjo, and either projecting a little way below to hold the lower ends of the strings or prolonged by a cello-like spike, in either case enabling the instrument to be swivelled to change from one string to another while the bow is moved continually in the same plane (see SPIKE FIDDLE, a term often used by Western writers). (i) *Spherical* or bowl-shaped body: derived from a gourd, or still a gourd: *kemancha, 1 (Iran, in Central Asia *ghichak*); *imzad* (Tuareg fiddle, Sahara, with a single horsehair string; see Pl. 3). (ii) *Half a coconut*: *joze* (Iraq and across to China), or as evolved into a 'heart' shape, *rabab, 3 (Thailand to Indonesia). (iii) *Tubular*, bamboo, or wood instead: *erhu (China, sometimes an octagonal or hexagonal tube), others over India and east Asia. (iv) *Frame*, circular, *chuniri (Georgia); or square, trapezoid, built up of wood, most with a second skin over the back; rabab, 2 (Arab countries), also forms in southern India, and *khur (Mongolia).

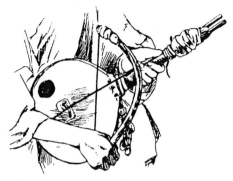

Pl. 3. Tuareg one-string fiddle, imzad.

(c) *Kokyu (Japan, built in the manner of the plucked *shamisen).

(d) In Central Asia, and in China (see ERHU) some of these bowed instruments (and lute types as well) are now made also in 'tenor' and 'bass' sizes for folk orchestras playing arrangements inspired by Western practice (and then apt to sound much as 'arranged' folk music can do anywhere).

Bachmann 1964, trans. 1969; Page 1979; Remnant 1986. See also MEDIEVAL INSTRUMENTS; Crane 1972; Panum 1941.

Fidhla (Old Icelandic stringed instrument). See LANGELEIK, 3.

Fife. The current instrument of a 'drum and fife band' is correctly known as a 'flute', being a 'B♭ flute', a conical flute with up to six keys (see FLUTE BAND). This replaced the true fife as a military instrument in Britain from c.1850 as being playable in different keys and in harmony, though on the Continent the fife continued to serve for routine calls up to the First World War. It is in one piece, cylindrically bored, with a wide metal ferrule at each end, and usually no key; length c.40 cm. (16″) if in B♭ (less if in C). The older 19th-century fifes, in boxwood, are usually slightly spindle-shaped, narrowest at the ends. The scale given by their six holes may sound crudely tuned by concert-hall standards, yet the somewhat over-large semitones can render simple melodies (Ex. 1) all the more instantly recognizable in rough, open-air conditions. There are now revivals of the fife, notably in the USA, as the Old Guard Fife and Drum Corps of the US Army, with dress, drill, and tunes as during the War of Independence; and, in New England, from the Civil War (when many of the fifes were made by W. Crosby, Boston).

See—FLUTE, 5 for the German-Swiss origin of the fife—which in the Tyrol remains a traditional folk instrument, 'Seitenpfeife'.

Ex. 1. (sounds an octave higher)

Fingerboard (Fr.: touche; Ger.: Griffbrett; It.: tastiera). On stringed instruments that have a neck (guitar, violin, etc.) the upper surface of the neck, on which the strings are stopped. For the bowed instruments it is usually of ebony (but not all bowed instruments have a fingerboard; see FIDDLE, 2); with the plucked instruments it usually bears *frets.

Fingerhole horn. Modern term for an animal or wooden horn in which fingerholes are cut in the side for playing tunes. There are signs of such an instrument, of a goat or cow horn, in medieval pictures. In rural Sweden it has survived, with three or four holes, for herding calls, usually played by women. In northern Spain shepherds used it into the 20th century. The Renaissance *cornett is usually held to derive from a medieval type; see also ROZHOK (Russia).

Fingering. See KEYBOARD, 3; OVERBLOWING (woodwind instruments); VALVES (brass instruments).

Fipple flute. Outdated term for instruments of the *recorder and *flageolet kinds.

Fisarmonica. It., *accordion; both button-key and 'piano' types.

Fiscorno (Sp.). See FLUGEL HORN; BARITONE, 4.

Fistula (Lat.). A 'pipe' in any sense, in music a flute or *panpipe. In medieval writings also an organ pipe.

Flageolet (diminutive of Old Fr.: flageol). The name has long been used for manufactured duct flutes (*recorder principle) other than the recorder itself.

1. Tin Whistle. Of tinplate, brass, or, formerly, celluloid, with six fingerholes. It was once called 'penny whistle' (although already at the beginning of the 20th century it was priced 3½d. wholesale). An excellent popular model today is the 'Generation' Flageolet of metal alloy with a head of coloured moulded plastic and a compass of two octaves or more. The holes are of different sizes in order to give the major scale from the bottom note without the complication of *cross-fingering. Thus, the fifth hole from the top is a large one, to emit the major third of the scale (which on a recorder it does not). Accidentals are made mostly by half uncovering a hole. Since the instrument is intended

for playing in only one or two keys, the purchaser is offered a choice of instruments ranging from the flageolet in B♭, 35 cm. (14″) long, to the smallest in G (lowest note g″); a favourite for folk music, and considered the best for playing beside the violin, is the one in D. The tin whistle, through having the fingerholes cut through such thin material, offers the player great freedom of nuance, and folk styles today can demand great expertise, especially in Ireland, with a profusion of grace notes, slides from note to note, and vibrato made by shaking the finger over the next open hole below (all of these features also called for in some styles of baroque flute-playing, and fully described in Portnoi, n.d.).

2. *Wooden flageolet.* These, with six or seven fingerholes, and today best known as folk instruments, were in regular manufacture well into the 20th century, in Britain termed 'English flageolet' to distinguish them from the French flageolet (see below, 3). English flageolets in their prime, up to 1850, were very prettily made in box- or rosewood with silver keys for semitones and an ivory or bone mouthpiece inserted into the top, bringing the hands to a comfortable distance from the face. Among them are *double flageolets.

3. *French flageolet.* The classic flageolet, with four holes in front (see FLUTE, Pl. 2, bottom right) and two on the back, known from the late 16th century though its principle may be far older. Some are exceedingly small, barely 12 cm. (5″) long, very high-pitched, and intended (so it was said) for teaching canaries to sing (*The Bird Fancyer's Delight*, 1717, repr. 1964). Handel alludes to this in *Acis and Galatea* ('Hush, ye pretty warbling quire') in a part marked *flauto piccolo*, perhaps actually played on some small recorder (and in *Rinaldo* also), but Rameau definitely has the flageolet in *Les surprises de l'Amour* (1748). (See also FLAUTO, FLAUTINO, 2.) The curious arrangement of the holes must have originated in connection with a small size of pipe, since six holes in front would be too close together for adult fingers to be able to cover. Hence the fifth hole is transferred to the back, for the lower thumb.

Tune-books for the instrument were published, the first being Thomas Greeting's *Pleasant Companion for the Flagelet* [sic] (1661). This gives popular tunes in a tablature of symbols (cover, uncover) on six lines, one for each hole. Examples of the instrument are largely French, some, from the mid-19th century, made with an adaptation of *Boehm fingering. The flageolet was then much featured in quadrilles, being (according to an instrument dealer's catalogue) 'preferred to the Flute in all dancing rooms on account of its brilliant and pleasing tone'.

Flageolets with the same arrangement of holes are made in Catalonia (Spain) as folk instruments without keys or for the Sardana cobla, with keys, and are named *fluviol* (*flaviol*).

4. *The lip and windway of flageolets.* The old traditional tin whistle is voiced somewhat as a metal organ-pipe: by flattening the tube to form a lip of practically the full width of the pipe (Fig. 1a). A pewter block forms the windway (duct). Fig. 1b shows a flageolet of cane, of the type now commonly imported from Asian countries for sale in charity shops. Home-made 'bamboo pipes' are similar, with cork for the block. The lip, cut through the cane wall, automatically assumes a curvature in two senses where the inside of the tube is reached: as seen from the exterior, and as seen on looking along the bore. To minimize the extent of these curvatures, the width of the lip is kept small, while in compensation (to produce a full sound) the window is given a good height (see CUT-UP), appearing square or even longer than wide—the opposite to Fig. 1a. A simple wooden block, shaved along the top, forms the windway. Fig. 1c illustrates a further stage, employed in flageolets of wood, including most tabor pipes and, in the most mature

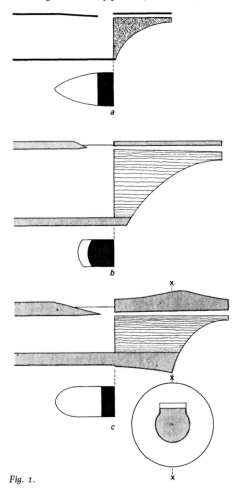

Fig. 1.

form, the recorder. The lip is given a fair width and made straight by centring it higher than the inner line of the bore, then cutting wood away underneath, giving the lip in longitudinal section the form of a wedge. The windway is then centred to match this by means of a block with a raised flat surface as shown by the cross-section in the figure. For some details of the recorder block, see RECORDER, 2.

Flat trumpet. See SLIDE TRUMPET, 2*b*.

Flauto, flautino (It.). 1. '*Flauto*', 'flute', up to the end of the Baroque period (*c.*1750), normally meant the *recorder ('flauto diritto' or 'dolce', the flute itself then being distinguished as 'flauto tranverso'; see TRAVERSO). A problem can then arise where a 'flauto' part descends to *e'* or *d'*, too low for the treble (alto) recorder (the one in general use). This could either have happened accidentally when publishing for recorder a piece originally written for some other instrument; or mean that the part is intended for the flute, especially where it is in a sharp key (favouring the one-key flute; see FLUTE, 4*b*).

2. '*Flautino*': one of the smaller recorders; or a French flageolet (see FLAGEOLET, 3), as e.g. 'fasoletto ò flautino francesco' (Bismantova, see BAROQUE, 2); or else the *piccolo. Monteverdi's *Orfeo* includes a *flautino* 'at the 22nd', which in *organ terminology would signify a 1' rank, lowest pipe sounding *c''* (three octaves above *C*) and in this case a descant (soprano) recorder, playing the music in this same high register.

3. *Flauto di echo*. In Bach's Fourth Brandenburg Concerto the two *recorder parts marked *Flauti* in modern scores are originally marked *Fiauti di echo*, and present some problem. Covering the whole compass of the treble recorder, they make much use of the difficult top F♯, which alone would seem to rule out any blown echo effects. It has been suggested (Higbee 'Bach's *Fiauti d'Echo*' 1986: 133) that the two players were meant to move about in an upper gallery, echoing the violins below. On the other hand, London papers of the period report how an 'Eccho Flute' was featured by James Paisible in his concerts of 1713–18 (Tilmouth 1961). Thurston Dart has argued that this must have been a French flageolet (see FLAGEOLET, 3) and that the instruments in the 4th Brandenburg were of this kind also, adding that Bach's part-writing in the Andante (e.g. bars 7 and 8) shows that they were played an octave higher than written (Dart 1960).

Flexatone. A small percussion instrument waved up and down in one hand (Fig. 1). The flexible steel blade, *c.*18 cm. (7") long, is bolted at the wider end to a wire frame. Waving this sets in motion the two wooden balls (each with an insert of hard rubber) that are attached on opposite sides of the blade by springy wires to strike the blade alternately. The thumb meanwhile presses down on the bent-up part, bringing a rise in pitch of about an octave upwards from *c'''*, due to an effect of increased stiffness in the metal (as one can feel in increased resistance to the thumb). Characteristic sounds are a high glissando or tremolo, not very loud.

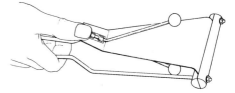

Fig. 1.

The flexatone was introduced in the early 1920s, for light music and variety artists. Among composers to include it are Schoenberg (Variations for Orchestra No. 3, 1929; *Moses und Aron*); Berg (Three Pieces for Orchestra); and Khachaturian (Piano Concerto).

Flicorno (It.). See FLUGEL HORN; BARITONE, 4.

Flügel (Ger.). *Harpsichord; grand *piano.

Flugel horn (or, as Ger., 'flügelhorn'; Fr.: *bugle*, the bugle being *clairon*; It.: *flicorno*; Sp.: *fiscorno*). Valved brass instrument with the same B♭ pitch and compass as the *cornet but with a broader tone because of its considerably more widely expanding tube and bell (Pl. 1; see also BRASS INSTRUMENTS, Fig. 2), derived ultimately from the *bugle. The mouthpiece is deep-cupped and, to interrupt the bore expansion as little as possible, tuning is by an extendable shank immediately next to the mouthpiece and leading at once to the valves.

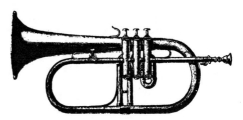

Pl. 1. Flugel horn from Couesnon catalogue (1916).

British *brass bands include a single flugel horn, sitting next to one of the cornet players. In European brass and military bands there may be two or more parts for flugel horn and also, perhaps, one for a small soprano flugel horn in E♭ (Fr.: *petit bugle*, in Ger. usually called simply *Pikkolo*). Jazz trumpeters sometimes take a solo on the flugel horn, and in the orchestra it is scored for in a few works, such as Stravinsky, *Threni*, and Vaughan Williams's Ninth Symphony, in both of which it has an important solo part.

The instrument was introduced first in Germany in the late 1830s to replace the *keyed bugle. In Britain, although the German name is kept, the design follows French models of the mid-19th century.

Flute (Fr.: *flûte*; Ger.: *Flöte*; It.: *flauto*; Ru.: *fleïta*; Sp.: *flauta*). The modern flute, in metal (rarely now wood), is unique among our classical instruments in having been technically redesigned on first principles—the achievement of the Munich inventor and flautist Theobald Boehm (1794–1881) in 1848 (two years after Adolphe Sax patented the *saxophone). Previous flutes, from 'baroque' onwards, were 'conical flutes', tapering to the far end and with simple keys and plain fingerholes (as are today used in *flute bands): for these, see 4 below, also 5 for the earlier 'Renaissance' flute. For other modern flutes, see PICCOLO; ALTO AND BASS FLUTE. Finally, for 'flute' in the widest sense covering all instruments—*flageolets, primitive and non-Western flutes in their great variety—which, like the flute itself (or 'transverse flute') are sounded by projecting air on to some stationary 'edge' (see WIND INSTRUMENTS, 1a); see the typological summary in 7 and 8 below.

1. *Boehm flute* (Pl. 1; centre). The flute, held sideways to the player's right, comprises three parts or 'joints': 'head', with the mouth-hole or 'embouchure hole' across which the breath is aimed through somewhat narrowed lips on to the far edge; the 'body' with the main series of keys; and the short 'foot', which can be rotated for the right little finger to lie comfortably over the lowest three keys. The body and foot form a cylinder with inside diameter 19 mm. ($\frac{3}{4}''$), but the head narrows, with a profile that varies from near-conical to parabolic, to some 2 mm. less where the tube is closed by a metal-faced cork stopper just to the left of the mouth-hole. The material is German silver (nickel silver, silver-plated), or sterling silver, or German silver with the head of silver; there are also satisfactory models in stainless steel. Theoretically, given good design and workmanship, the material should have no bearing on tone and response: yet flutes of the denser metals, 14-carat gold, or platinum alloy, have been claimed capable of particularly full and rich sound and tend to be the choice among great soloists. Wood (cocus, or grenadilla) is now used mainly for piccolos and band flutes: few continue to play on the fine wooden flutes regularly manufactured in Britain up to the 1940s, while in the USA wood was practically abandoned after the First World War, the wooden flute being felt to offer less flexible response than the metal, less expressive tone variation by the player's blowing. A legacy from the

wooden flute is in the form of the mouth-hole, which in a metal flute is raised by a 'chimney' topped by a curved lip-plate, reproducing the depth of a hole through the older wooden tube: with no more than the thickness of the metal wall alone the sound would be poorer, more whistling, and harder to keep in tune.

2. *The keywork.* The normal compass is three octaves from middle c' to c'''', with two higher semitones not often demanded. The holes, covered by padded plates, when closed successively, give the scale of C major through the first two octaves. The plates allow the holes to be as wide (*c.*13 mm.) as the width of the tube makes practicable, enabling them to be located through the octave strictly according to the principles of equal *temperament (like the first 12 frets of a guitar, though the distances from the holes back to the stopper fall short by about 35 mm. (1.4″) owing to the smaller width of the mouth-hole and the partial covering of this by the lips while playing). The plates along the body joint hinge on a long axle, either all of them ('in line'), or with the middle two on their own short axle ('offset'). Interlinkages by small lugs or 'clutches' are required: for example, the three right-hand plates, each to move separately, are mounted on separate sleeves over one long axle, yet each must (for F and F♯) close, via the clutches, the key mounted directly above them on the same axle.

Among specialized flute-makers who have done much to perfect the Boehm flute are Louis Lot (Paris, now Marigaux) and in the USA Haynes, and Powell (Boston, both continuing). In London there is the Guild of Flute-makers, with Albert Cooper a leading craftsman. Among big manufacturers Yamaha has a high reputation.

Some models have 'ring keys', a French preference, five of the main plates having perforated centres. Some small tonal advantages are claimed, and slides can be made from note to note, also quarter-tones (otherwise requiring embouchure movements) and some of the *multiphonics of avant-garde music. A flute can further be supplied with a foot 5 cm. (2″) longer than the ordinary and with an extra little-finger key, to take the compass down to low B♭—important for instance at the end of Mahler's Fourth Symphony (and a reminder that the contemporary conical-bore Austrian flutes usually had this extension).

There have been considerable changes in flute playing styles, especially since the change from the wooden flute: this last was generally played to give the steady sound of the instrument (as the clarinet is normally expected to be heard). The almost continuous vibrato we now hear (made with the breathing as in singing) came in with the French style on the metal flute, from which, especially over Europe (less in America), it has grown into something of an exaggeration with its unending 'wu-wu-wu'.

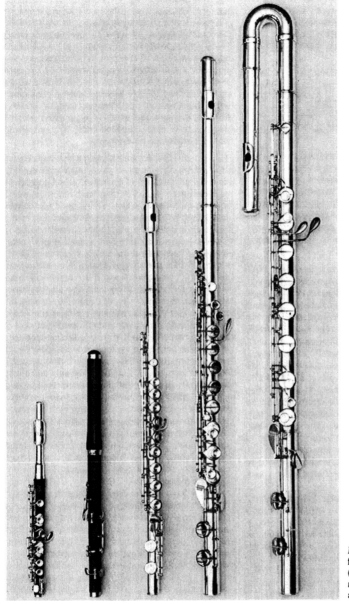

Pl. 1. Group of present-day flutes by Yamaha of Japan (except 2nd from left); *left to right*, piccolo, B♭ flute, flute, alto flute, bass flute.

3. *Higher registers*. The middle register, from *d''*, is fingered as the lower while 'overblowing' to the octave above (2nd harmonics) by slight movement of the lips, jaw, or both, and for the first two semitones raising the first finger. See OVERBLOWING for a table of the higher fingerings up to the top D. The logical layout of the modern flute allows the fingerings largely to follow a regular pattern (Ex. 1): e.g. in 4th harmonics from *e♭'''* to *g'''*, as a hole is uncovered by the right hand, a hole, situated

at (or very close to) three-quarters of the way from the theoretical top end of the flute's air-column, is also uncovered by the left hand as the vent for that note, both hands working chromatically upwards. But a difficulty arises on the note *e'''*. Boehm designed the flute with an open-standing G♯ key, and this gave the correct vent for *e'''*; but with the 'closed G♯ key' which has since replaced it, two holes open on this note instead of the G♯ hole alone, bringing a danger of the E 'breaking' to the

A below when played *pp*. To avoid this many flutes now incorporate the 'split E' device (Paris, 1903), which allows one hole to open, not two, and is recognizable by a thin lever curving between the two plates situated immediately below the G♯ key.

Ex. 1.

4. *Conical flute.* The body is an inverse cone, the bore narrowing to the foot which itself may or may not continue the taper; the head is cylindrical, of about the same internal width as the body of the modern flute. The historically important conical flutes can be put under three headings: (*a*) one-keyed flute; (*b*) those with four or more keys, typically eight; and (*c*) the initial design of Boehm himself.

(*a*) *One-keyed flute.* Now made again after 18th-century models: the type of flute (see also TRAVERSO) for which Bach, Handel, and Mozart wrote, after which one-keyed flutes remained in manufacture well into the 20th century as 'beginner's' instruments. The typical material is boxwood, usually mounted with ivory 'tips'. A flute entirely of ivory however can sound equally well. Pl. 2, centre, shows the typical construction in four joints, the body being in two separate parts, the upper of which (with the left-hand holes) was very often supplied in three or more different lengths for tuning to different playing pitches (in the Plate, the longest is shown inserted, with two others separately below). The earliest conical flutes, as evolved almost certainly in Paris in the late 1670s, had, up to *c*.1720, had the body in one piece as now: original examples are very rare but copies are now made.

The key, usually described as for D♯ (more than for E♭), was through the 18th century normally square. Other semitones, made by *cross-fingering, are in the low register considerably harder to produce with firm sound than corresponding notes on a *recorder and take much practice to develop (for top register fingering, see OVERBLOWING). The sound is less penetrating than the modern can be, due partly to the small mouth-hole (averaging 9 mm. across as against 12.5 mm. today) and also to the other holes being few and small. Yet a recent experimental analysis (Shreffler 1983) demonstrates how its balance in quality through the registers, in terms of partials, may explain the great charm of this flute in music of the period.

Many subtleties in playing are explained in the first known tutor, Jacques Hotteterre's *Principes de la flute traversiere* (1707, etc.). Longer notes would be 'softened' (as it was then said) by shaking with a finger on a hole further down; the next note might begin with a 'beat', striking the note below quickly once or twice. Trills were essential but by no means easy in many cases, e.g. the whole-tone shake on E, 'begun by making F sharp which serves it as a sigh, and ended by stopping the fifth hole and shaking on the fourth which removes the superior Tone further off, and shews the Cadence more, instead of shaking on the 5th which would not be sufficient'. There have recently been made for Irish folk music new versions (some without the key) giving freedom for ornaments just of these kinds, barely possible with the advanced mechanism of the modern flute.

(*b*) *Four- to eight-key flutes.* During the last quarter of the 18th century small closed keys were coming into use in England and Germany as alternatives to cross-fingering on F, G♯, and B♭, and giving correct trills on these notes. This makes four keys altogether (Pl. 2, top—the B♭ key, nearest to the head-joint, is actually on the back, for the thumb). By 1800 every serious player was using them, making six keys on a flute with a foot joint down to low C. Two more keys—a long key on the near side for *c''*, and another on the far side for an alternative *f'* ('long F key', for the slur up from D)—make the total of eight, the most popular number for the 19th-century pre-Boehm flute. Among the English instruments those of Rudall & Rose are now particularly prized, in box, ebony, or cocus with silver keys, square or 'saltspoon' in shape. Many English flutes from that time onwards have the 'large holes', i.e. the 2nd and 5th holes from the top are very visibly larger than the others, correcting the F♯ and adding to the volume over the whole instrument: a feature which greatly impressed Boehm and helped to set him on his path of total reform of the flute. The later eight-key flutes usually have German silver keys, still mounted on pins through raised blocks in the wood (the exceptional cut-glass flutes of Laurent, Paris, are collector's pieces).

The keys led to great extension of technical scope. Schubert's Introduction and Variations (1824), a testing piece still, shows what could be done, and has indeed been successfully performed in modern times on an eight-keyed flute. When Wagner and Verdi were writing most of their operas, the eight-key system was still normal in their orchestras and played by soloists, often adding alternative keys and special trill keys, and a foot joint extended even below B, making up to 15 keys altogether; the head joint of these German instruments is often of ivory. (Flutes, Boehm flutes also, were often from this period built a semitone higher—'in D♭'—for military bands, which play mostly in flat keys: thus in a piece written in A♭, the flute part will be in G, very much easier on the eight-keyed flute, for which the practice arose.)

(*c*) *Boehm.* Boehm began, aged 15, on a one-keyed flute by Proser, London, and in 1832 produced his first revolutionary design, still a conical flute, but

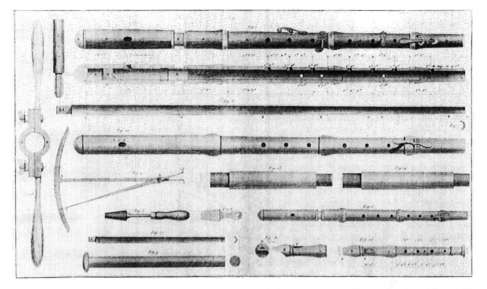

Pl. 2. Flute making, from Bergeron's *Manuel du Tourneur* (2nd edn., 1816). *Top to bottom:* four-keyed flute (with metal slide to head joint); tapered bore-reamer; one-keyed boxwood flute with two alternative joints shown below; *lower right.* one-keyed piccolo; French flageolet. The left-hand joint of the four-keyed flute (*top*) is shown upside-down.

with 'ring keys' giving a fingering essentially as used since, save for his 'open G♯'. This 'conical Boehm' flute was manufactured in Britain and France up to the First World War along with the present 'cylindrical' flute, and there are players now in the USA who have revived it as being a particularly sensitive player's instrument in much 19th-century music. Boehm, however, next felt it rational to substitute a cylindrical tube, at first throughout, then finding a contracting head-joint necessary to prevent the upper registers from sounding too flat. The resulting flute, of 1847, was soon being made in France, where it was speedily altered to have the 'closed G♯' (see 3 above); in the USA, as by Badger, New York; and in England, by Rudall Carte, who also produced cylindrical designs that provide both Boehm and pre-Boehm fingering alternatively on one instrument, the best-known (still played by some up to recently) being their '1867 model', with two small fingerplates close together for the first finger right hand.

5. *Renaissance flute.* The transverse flute was known in 10th-century Byzantium (perhaps from Asia) and by the 12th century in Western Europe, chiefly Germany. During the 15th century it won wide interest as the *Pfeife* ('fife') to which, with the side drum, marched the famed Swiss foot soldiery: a plain cylindrical tube in one piece with six fingerholes. For musical purposes this had come by the beginning of the 16th century to be made in sets of three sizes pitched in fifths apart—treble, alto-tenor, and bass (see PRAETORIUS, Fig. 1)—played from vocal part-books, sounding the music

an octave or so higher (Agricola, 1545, apparently recommending a vibrato). Their bottom notes are respectively *a'*, *d'*, and *g* (though there is evidence that in some cases they were pitched a tone lower (Thomas 1975)). A reference to music specifically played on them is in a collection of French four-part songs from the Paris publisher Attaignant in 1533 (some available in modern edition) where nine items are marked as suitable for flutes (*fleutes d'alleman*, 'German flutes'), two for recorders, and 12 for either, leaving five over. Among the 30 or more original Renaissance flutes, the majority are of the middle or 'tenor-alto' size corresponding with the flute today and now the most available in reproductions; the treble size is rare, as if it had been preferred to play the treble part on the middle size. The bass size, almost 90 cm. (3') long, is less rare (and might be made in two joints, as Praetorius shows). In England, Morley's Consort lessons have a part for 'flute' written down to *g*, but perhaps played an octave higher, to judge from the size of the flute in a well-known painting.

6. *Repertory:* (a) *Baroque.* There are six sonatas for flute by Bach, three of them with a full keyboard accompaniment by the composer. Much flute music was produced by early flautists in France, such as Michel de la Barre. In Italy Vivaldi and Benedetto Marcello, among many others, composed sonatas and concertos, as did Telemann. Quantz, author of the great treatise on flute-playing (Quantz, 1752), proves a rather run-of-the-mill flute composer unless one is very adept in all kinds of free ornamentation.

(b) From the Classical period to the present. Here especially Mozart's two concertos, K. 313 and K. 314; his Andante, K. 315; and the quartets with strings, K. 285 and K. 298. From Haydn, the 'London Trios' (two flutes with cello), and his 'Sonata', which is a fine arrangement of his String Quartet in G by some later hand. Schubert's Introduction and Variations, Op. 160, has been mentioned above (4*b*). Nineteenth-century solo works by flute virtuosos, including Boehm himself, have now fallen out of fashion, though they can be very exciting in performance. The flautist's great regret is that, although he has Bach, unlike the clarinettist he has no Brahms. However, the later French school of flute-playing came to the rescue, inspiring Fauré's *Fantaisie*; Debussy's *Syrinx* for unaccompanied flute and Sonata for flute, viola, and harp; Ravel's chamber music with flute; Ibert's Flute Concerto; and Poulenc's Sonata (a great favourite). And from elsewhere there are sonatas by Hindemith, Prokoviev (Op. 94), Martinů, Henze, and many remarkable avant-garde compositions, including a Solo (1958) by John Cage, in which the player is called upon to produce many strange effects (multiphonics, etc.), as well as to change to alto flute and piccolo in the course of the piece.

7. *Flutes in general sense.* Those below are tubular flutes blown with the mouth: for others, see NOSE FLUTE, and OCARINA for non-tubular or *vessel flutes. Classification runs according to the method of sounding, whether by blowing directly (*a*) across a side hole or (*b*) the open end; or into the flute for the air to be artificially guided to an opening lying beyond reach of direct control from the lips (e.g. recorder)

(*a*) *Transverse* (or 'cross flute'; Ger.: *Querflöte*). Besides the Western flute, classic bamboo flutes of Asia, *bansuri (India), *dizi (China), *fue (Japan), with others in East Africa (Fig. 1*d* of cane), Melanesia, South America. Very rarely (East Asia) the blowing hole is at or near the centre of the pipe, both ends open and fingerholes (if present) to each side, uncovered using fingers of both hands alternately.

(*b*) *End-blown* (blown across the open top end):
   (i) *Plain-cut or* (Fig. 1*a*) bevelled end. Flute usually held somewhat sideways (see KAVAL, Pl. 1): *nay (Middle East), *kaval* (Balkans, Greece, Turkey), others in India, etc.; also (with *stopped pipes) *nanga (South Africa), *panpipe. (ii) *Notched flute.* The breath is directed on to base of a U- or V-shaped notch, Fig. 1*b*), part-covering the open end with the lower lip; the flute is usually held like a recorder: *quena (Andean countries of South America, and see AMERICAN INDIANS, 1), West and Central Africa, Melanesia, unusual varieties in *China and Korea, 1*d*(ii); *shakuhachi (Japan, notch here reduced to a minimum). (iii) 'Double notch'. The blowing side is cut to a 'horseshoe' as also in Fig. 1*c*, opposite side similarly but deeper. Flutes and whistles of antelope horn (Africa), or with opposite side a very deep

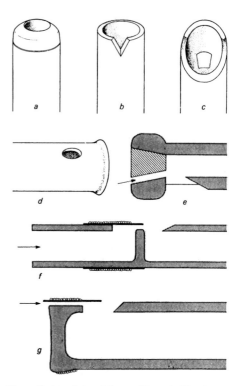

Fig. 1. Various flutes of the world, most of bamboo or other cane, showing the blowing ends.

notch (North Argentina). (iv) '*Tongue-duct*'. Shown in Fig. 1*c* from blowing side, tongue or lower lip guiding breath on to 'window' opposite. Uncommon yet widespread (Central Europe, Russia and Siberia—often a whistle—Spain, Peru). (v) *Giorgi flute.*

(*c*) *Duct flute.* A large and varied class.
   (i) *Block flute.* Inserted wood or clay block, Europe, Asia, the Americas; in Fig. 1*e*, Central Europe, with duct and window on underside, obviating need for beak-shaped top end. *Double flageolet, *flageolet (with tin whistle, French flageolet, flaviol), *fujara, *picco pipe, *pipe and tabor, *recorder, *slide flute, *whistle (European), *anata, and *pincullo (South America). (ii) *Ring flute.* Fig. 1*f*, south-east Asia, blowing end left. The long window half covered by a ring of leaves—or, instead, a piece of wood tied or glued on—and, beneath, an exposed knot in the cane, or lump of wax, which with the ring forms the short duct: India to Indonesia, *Apache flute (North America). (iii) *External duct.* Fig. 1*g*, Indonesia, duct formed by a groove, cut in the knot which here closes top end of the bamboo pipe, and a ring of leaves over it. *Suling* (see GAMELAN), also as double or triple pipe (Indonesia).

8. *Flutes with no fingerholes.* Among these, apart from many whistles and one-note flutes played together in bands (as see NANGA), are flutes on which music is made in various ways on harmonics alone.

(*a*) *Pairs of ritual flutes.* Blown entirely in harmonics, the great size, up to 215 cm. (7′) long, bringing higher harmonics in a melodious range of pitch. Transverse or end-blown (New Guinea *nama* flutes) or duct (Upper Amazon region), the pair usually made a tone apart, the two men blowing alternately (thus leading to a scale), slowly following each other up and down their respective *harmonic series throughout the ceremonies, after which the flutes are hidden away until the next occasion.

(*b*) *Single harmonic flute.* Lower end alternately covered and uncovered by finger or thumb, often very rapidly, to make fast near-diatonic melody: Ex. 2, for a 3′-long flute, the stopped series (see STOPPED PIPE) having a fundamental an octave below that of the open. *Seljefløyte* (Norway, 'willow flute', a duct flute with block as in a willow whistle but the blowing hole in the side for holding sideways, bringing the lower end of a long flute better within arm's reach), *tilinca* (Romania, Hungary, end-blown or duct with block); many elsewhere (as Melanesia, transverse or end-blown, some with lower end permanently stopped but a hole just above it; there may be another hole above that, introducing a mixed technique, partly as above, partly as an ordinary open flute).

Ex. 2.

Bate 1969; Boehm 1871, trans. Miller 1922; Bowers 1977; Meylan (trans.) 1988; Rockstro 1890, repr. 1967; Toff 1979; Vance 1987. See also BAROQUE; Quantz 1752.

Flûte-à-bec (or *flûte douce*). Fr., *recorder.

Flute band and B♭ flute (also G flute). The B♭ flute, often seen in music shops (see FLUTE, Pl. 1, second from left) is a wooden flute, 40 cm. (15″) long, is small but longer than a *piccolo. It keeps the old conical bore, six holes, and from one to six keys. Also known as a 'marching flute', it is the main instrument of a Fife and Drum Band (Corps of Fifes and Drums: see MILITARY BAND). Pitched a minor sixth above the orchestral flute, it is a transposing instrument, written at this interval lower than it sounds. It is described as 'in B♭' because its lowest note, written *d′*, sounds B♭. Marches are printed for the band and are normally played by heart, since with flutes a music card has to be clipped in a

holder strapped to the left forearm, which can feel rather awkward.

Where a band plays in harmony the parts are for first, second, and sometimes third B♭ flutes: E♭ piccolo (a semitone above the piccolo, or formerly an F piccolo, a third above); F flute (a minor third above the orchestral flute); and side drum and bass drum. The F flute acts as a bass and can be strengthened by a B♭ bass flute a fifth deeper (usually built with a metal turned-back head). There are also in Northern Ireland and in some of the Commonwealth countries very much larger bands, with metal Boehm flutes of all sizes down to a large E♭ bass; arrangements of concert overtures, etc. are performed with these after the manner of a brass band.

In Continental and American terminology these band instruments are named, not by lowest note, but in the same way as other transposing wind instruments, i.e. by the actual sound of the note written C in the part. The B♭ flute is then named 'A♭ flute', and so on. There has been a trend in the British Isles to follow this procedure.

The G flute was introduced *c.*1950 for bands and for flute societies who play together using flutes of the orchestral kinds from piccolo downwards. The G flute, a fifth above the flute itself, fills a gap between this and the piccolo: a metal Boehm flute (with foot-joint), *c.*14 mm. bore, and 45 cm. (18″) long. Only certain makers supply it.

Flute clock. See BARREL ORGAN, 5.

Flûte contralto. See ALTO AND BASS FLUTE.

Flûte d'accord. See DOUBLE FLAGEOLET, 1.

Flûte d'amour. A one-keyed flute (see FLUTE, 4*b*) of the period 1730–1800, in length up to 80 cm. (31″, i.e. some 15 cm. longer than the flute of the period), and sounding a minor third deeper ('in A') or a major third ('in A♭'). Frederick the Great owned one among his flutes, and a fair number are preserved. One of the few works specifying it is a Concerto in E♭ by Molter with a part for *Flauto traverso d'amore* (here in A♭, lowest note sounding *b♭*). The bore need be no wider than for the flute, and there exists at least one example of the latter with, among the alternative joints for tuning, one or more longer ones for playing as *d'amour*. In those times, the amateur player played the flute a great deal without accompaniment, and a change to *d'amour* would give the pleasure of the deeper, more sombre quality in flute pieces of suitable character, reading from the flute music and without obliging an accompanist to transpose a line lower.

After 1800 there were made B♭ tenor flutes for use in flute ensembles, resembling the flûte d'amour in length and pitch but with wider bores.

Flute-flageolet. A 19th-century or later piccolo or band flute supplied with alternative head-joint for playing as a *flageolet (see FLUTE, Pl. 2, lower right, the flageolet head shown below the piccolo). Or a flute with an alternative head having a bone mouthpiece in the side for sounding as a flageolet while pretending still to be playing the flute. Wheatstone (see CONCERTINA, I) patented a small mouthpiece that can be clipped over the actual mouth-hole of a flute for the same purpose. Most recent (1983) is a German patent for an alternative recorder-style head to the modern *Boehm flute.

Flutina. See ACCORDION, 7; MUSICAL BOX, I.

Fluviol (or flaviol). See FLAGEOLET, 3.

FoMRHI. Fellowship of Makers and Researchers of Historical Instruments. Founded in Britain in 1975 as an organization of those from anywhere who are actively concerned, its purpose is to communicate in the journal *FoMRHI Quarterly* current work in the history, and authentic reproduction and use of such instruments, and in techniques of repair and conservation. (Hon. Secretary: Jeremy Montagu, Faculty of Music, St Aldate's, Oxford.)

Fontanelle. French term (*Mersenne 1636) revived today for the perforated barrel-shaped removable key-cover (see RECORDER, Pl. 2, and SHAWM, Pl. I) seen on Renaissance wind instruments such as the larger *recorders and shawms. An English term (Talbot) was 'barrel'.

Formant. With many instruments, a particular band of frequencies that is found to reinforce notes or overtones whose frequencies fall in that region. Formants are also largely responsible for the characteristic differences of the vowels in speech.

Fortepiano. Alternative name for the *piano through the Classical period both on the Continent and in England. It is often used today to distinguish pianos of (or modelled after) that period from later ones, and particularly those of the grand form (or 'Grand Forte Piano' as called by the London maker Stodart in the 1790s). The word is still a Russian general name for the piano.

Frame drum. A drum with the membrane stretched over a hoop (and not necessarily with jingles in the hoop). See DRUM, 4d and also BENDIR; BODHRÁN; DAIRA; SHAMAN DRUM; TAMBOUR; TAMBOURINE; TAR, 2; also BIBLICAL INSTRUMENTS, 2.

Free reed. The brass or steel reed used in the *accordion, *concertina, *harmonica, *harmonium, American *reed-organ (and former *'lap organ'); also in toy instruments such as *humming tops, and toy trumpets. The free reed was in use in the Far East (*khaen, *sheng) long before it became known in the West, first as an oriental curiosity (*Mersenne 1636), then in the late 18th century

finding applications in organs about which, however, few original details are preserved beyond various names and dates (see HARMONIUM, 3).

1. *Construction.* The reed (made from sheet brass or high-tempered steel) is riveted or screwed by one end over a close-fitting slot in a stationary metal plate (see ACCORDION, Fig. 1), and is 'free' to move in and out of the slot while vibrating, moving far into the slot if blown hard, scarcely at all if softly—whence the great flexibility of crescendo and diminuendo characteristic of free-reed instruments, in general. A free reed gives its one note only, each note of an instrument requiring a different reed. The periodic motion of the reed, maintained by air-flow from bellows or mouth, sets the air humming in the narrow gap at the natural frequency of the reed. The wave-form radiated through the air is found (and can sometimes be heard) to contain harmonic air-generated *partials, varying according to factors such as the design and shape of the reed (e.g. parallel-sided with square or rounded tip, or tapered almost to a point). Like metal tongues that are plucked (e.g. *musical box) free reeds can be very small for the notes they give—among the smallest vibrators regularly used in acoustic musical instruments (see PARTIALS, 6b). For the deeper notes they are usually loaded at the tip with lead, saving length and ensuring an immediate, steady response.

2. *'Blow' and 'draw'.* In Western instruments the reed is 'sprung up', for the tip to stand just proud of the slot. It will then vibrate only when the air flows in the direction on to the reed then through the slot. It vibrates equally whether the air is blown in this direction, or is drawn through from the other side: an important alternative, (a) as where a harmonium blows air on to the reeds whereas an American reed-organ draws the air past them: and (b) in making possible the compact, portable instruments—harmonica, accordion, etc.—which use both directions in alternation (to avoid quickly running out of wind), with half the total number of reeds sounding on the 'blow', the other half on the 'draw'. See ACCORDION, I, for the distinction between 'single' and 'double' action in many such instruments.

French flageolet. See FLAGEOLET, 3.

French horn. See HORN.

Fretel (or *frestele*, from Lat.: *fistula). Old Fr. name for a pipe of no known particular kind unless sometimes a *panpipe.

Frets (Fr.: *touches* or *frettes*; Ger.: *Bunde*; It.: *tasti*; Sp.: *trastes*). Elevations placed along the fingerboard of a *guitar, *zither, and almost every other instrument on which the left hand stops the strings while the other plucks or strums them, or with some instruments such as *viols bows them.

1. *Purpose and construction.* A fret raises the string clear of the fingerboard, just as the open string is raised by the nut, minimizing frictional damping and allowing the note to ring on clearly after being plucked. There are fixed frets and tied frets. Fixed frets are today normally of metal or of special T-section wire, the stem of the T let into the fingerboard and the top of the T smoothed over. Fixed frets were in use in the 16th century on the *cittern. The guitar and *mandolin adopted them from the late 18th century onwards, having up to then had gut frets, as *lutes and viols have had always. These are of two (usually) turns of gut tied round neck and fingerboard with a special knot by which they can be readjusted (see e.g. Hayes 1930, p. 24). The number of frets varies in Western instruments from seven to about 26, the smallest number being with the gut frets of lute and viol, where the necks are not long enough for more—though with lutes extra frets of hardwood are sometimes glued to the belly.

Some folk and early instruments are fretted for a diatonic scale only (for example, *Appalachian dulcimer). Otherwise they are placed chromatically, the first fret for the semitone above the open string, and the 12th fret for the octave above the open string and coming half-way between nut and bridge to divide the full string into two (the octave ratio being 2:1). Fig. 1 is a diagram of chromatic frets taking the string as tuned to C and showing (on the left) the designation of the frets either by numbers—as is usual today, and in the old 'Italian' tablature (the open string shown by 0)—or else by letters as in 'French' tablature (open string designated 'a'). See also CITTERN, 2.

2. *Placing the frets.* (a) An old way of putting the gut frets on a lute was to place the main diatonic frets by simple fractions of the open string: again considering a string tuned to C, the D fret is put at 1/9 along the string from the nut; the F fret at 1/4, the G at 1/3, and so on as in Fig. 1, far right, reckoning here from the bridge. Intervening semitones are then placed by ear.

(b) Fixed frets (chromatic, as on modern guitars, etc.) are placed according to equal temperament (see TEMPERAMENT, 4): for successive semitones, the vibrating string-length (fret to bridge) will diminish in the proportion 1 to $^{12}\sqrt{2}$ or 1.05946, as shown by approximate percentages in Fig. 1, taking the open string as 100 (that is, multiplying by 50 the figures given in TEMPERAMENT). This proportion is close to 17 to 18 per semitone, or 1 minus 1/18. From this comes the old 'Rule of 18', noticed in 1581 by Galilei and since much used in laying out the frets. The open string is divided by 18 to give the distance of the first fret (the edge which faces the bridge) from the nut. Then divide this result by 18 to place the second fret, and so on. If followed exactly, the twelfth fret (for the octave) will come fractionally more than half-way back from the

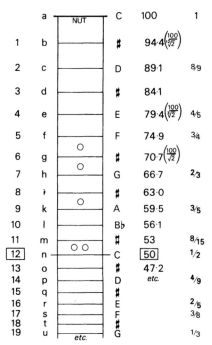

Fig. 1.

bridge (since for strict equal temperament the figure 18 should be 17.817). This may prove advantageous in counteracting the tightening (sharpening) of the string when pressed to a fret, though several other factors also bear on this question.

3. *Action.* The height of the strings above the frets is termed the 'action' and is of crucial importance from the player's point of view (see GUITAR, 1). It may depend on the kind of music for which the instrument is required, as well as on individual preferences, while its adjustment can be a matter for extent attention.

4. *Position dots.* These (or with electric guitars usually square plaques) are inlaid into the fingerboard as a visual guide to the player when changing position of the left hand; they are placed behind certain frets giving main notes of the scale: normally the fifth, seventh, ninth, twelfth (etc.) frets as shown in Fig. 1; but on *banjos, normally the tenth fret instead of the ninth, suiting a basic plagal scale with keynote at the fifth fret (see also CAPOTASTO).

Friction drum. A membrane fastened over a pot or cylinder, made to vibrate by means of longitudinal friction on a stick or cord attached to the centre of the membrane. Friction drums are used in Africa and Asia, and extensively in Europe (there are signs of it in 12th-century pictures), where the sound varies from a deep rhythmic grunting roar heard in festive folk music, to imitation chicken noises from small toys sold at fairs.

The instrument is activated in several ways:

1. *With a friction stick* (see Pl. 1). A thin cane is secured in a hole made (e.g. with a red-hot spike) in a skin membrane. To play, the hand is wetted and rubbed up and down the stick. This is the form common in the Low Countries (*rommelpot*), Italy, and in Spain and Portugal, where the *zambomba* is heard especially at Christmas (and named in many of the Christmas carols). In a Latin-American form, *cuica*, the skin is over the bottom end of the drum-shell, and the player's hand can enter the shell whilst rubbing; modern manufactured *cuicas* may have screw tensioning for the skin.

Pl. 1. A procession in Naples: friction drum, rattle (*triccaballa*), fife, tambourine. *Illustrated London News*

2. *With a friction cord.* Instead of the stick, a hank of resined horsehair is knotted below the skin and pulled through the hand—or both hands if someone else is holding the drum. This form occurs especially in Central and Eastern Europe (called *bukai*, from the bellowing of a bull). With a gut string, it is required in the concert hall by Varèse, and by others since, under the name 'lion roar' or 'tambour à corde'.

3. *Toy version.* (*a*) For chicken noises, a small paper membrane is placed over a cardboard cylinder; the string is either resined or beeswaxed and drawn through by the hand, or through a small piece of folded sandpaper.

(*b*) For noises of crickets, etc., the cylinder and membrane are similar, but the string (or fine gut) is looped round a wooden stick which has a resined groove at one end; the drum is swung round in the air for friction between stick and string to make the membrane vibrate. Under its German name, *Waldteufel*, it was scored for in the 1850s by August Conradi in *A Trip round Europe*. In the Far East, it is made with a paper membrane as little as 1 cm. across.

Frog. See BOW.

Fue. Japanese general name for the transverse *flute (when with a prefix, written '-*bue*', e.g. *komabue*). The flutes of the court music and the theatre are of bamboo with about the length of a European fife. They are bound, except at the holes, with thin cord made from birch or cherry bark, lacquered black. The interior is usually red-lacquered, somewhat tapered, and a piece of brocade (of a particular colour for each type of flute) is tucked into the upper end. The mouth-hole is large, more or less oval without a sharp rim, allowing great flexibility in gliding to the note, varying the attack, and making small intervals assisted by part-covering fingerholes. These are covered by the middle joints of the fingers and (as in India and elsewhere) with the upper thumb held against the flute pointing towards the mouth-hole.

For the different genres of the court music there are corresponding flutes: in order of size, *kagurabue*, 45 cm. long (17"); *ryuteki* (the flute in *Japan, Ex. 1), some 5 cm. shorter but thicker; and *komabue*, 36 cm. (14") and thinner. The *ryuteki* has seven holes, the others six. In the theatre (see JAPAN, 3 and Pl. 1), on the kabuki stage is the seven-hole *shinobue*, which may be of plain bamboo like the various flutes played in folk music (and, with a drum, in *kagura* rituals). The *nōkan*, c.40 cm. long (16")—the sole melody instrument of the *nō* plays—resembles the *ryuteki* but is described as having inside, between mouth-hole and first fingerhole, an inserted tube which constricts the bore and makes the notes of the second octave increasingly flat to the lower octave as the scale is ascended. Especially on this flute, a note is characteristically attacked from well below, strongly and breathily. Malm (1959, see JAPAN) writes of the *nōkan*: 'the indefinite quality of its tone and its music are eminently suitable for supporting the drama without interfering with the declamation of the poetry'.

Fujara (Czechoslovakian). A *duct flute, best known as the two-metre (6') tall 'Detva fujara', a traditional shepherd's instrument of Central Slovakia. The breath is led to the top (where are the block and window) through a 40 cm.- (16") long narrow cane tube placed parallel with the main tube. This is up to 6 cm. (2.4″) wide, and has three fingerholes low down, giving fundamentals as deep as G′. The characteristic motifs descend slowly, with strong, breathy sounds, through a big range of overblown harmonics.

G

Gadulka. Bulgarian fiddle. See FIDDLE, 1; LIRA.

Gaida, gaita, gajda. *Gaita*: Sp., Port., *bagpipe, 3c, or sometimes a tabor pipe (see PIPE AND TABOR). Also, in Colombia, a yard-long *duct flute of Indian origin, played in pairs, one with five holes very low down, the other with two holes and the free hand wielding a gourd rattle. *Gaida, gajda*: bagpipes, the former in Czechoslovakia (Moravia, Slovakia), the latter Bulgaria; see BAGPIPE, 5. *ghaita*, North Africa, *shawm family, see SURNA, also for *alghaita*, Western Sudan. The word may be of European origin, akin to 'waits' in the sense of 'watchman', but other theories derive it from Arabic.

Galoubet. French (Provençal) name of the tabor pipe; see PIPE AND TABOR.

Galpin Society. Founded 1946 in London, for publication of research into the history, construction, and use of musical instruments. Named after Canon Francis Galpin (1858–1945), foremost British historian of instruments during his time. From 1948 it has published once a year the *Galpin Society Journal (GSJ)*, received through membership subscription.

Gamba. Abbreviation of *viola da gamba* in the particular sense of the bass *viol; in Germany, *Gambenchor* is a consort of viols. As an organ stop, see ORGAN, 3c.

Gambang. Indonesian *xylophone. In a Javanese *gamelan the bars, numbering up to 21 and covering four octaves, rest on pads, over a long trough-like stand, and are played with flexible beaters ending in padded discs.

Gamelan. Generic term in Java and Bali for a set of instruments consisting primarily of *gongs, *gong-chimes, and *metallophones, forming ensembles of up to 24 or more executants in music which, itself of long tradition, has in its grand forms made so powerful an impression on the West for a hundred years now.

1. *Java* (Pl. 1). Two mutually exclusive tuning systems (*laras*) are in general use: *slendro*, which divides the octave into five almost equal intervals; and *pelog*, dividing the octave into seven unequal intervals, greater or lesser than a tone, varying in the different gamelans (Ex. 1 shows an approximate transcription of one example). With seven notes to the octave, *pelog* provides for various pentatonic scales (with or without auxiliary notes) according to the 'mode' (*patet*), each mode characterized, among other ways, by its melodic patterns and cadence formulas. In a double gamelan (using both systems) the *slendro* and *pelog* instruments are placed at right angles to each other, enabling the player to turn from one to the other.

The general composition of the gamelan is as follows:

(a) *Idiophones*: Gongs, hanging: *gong ageng, gong suwukan, kempul*. Gongs, resting boss upwards: *kenong, ketuk, kempyang* (pair). Gong chime: *bonang*. Metallophone: *saron*, and (with thinner bars and tube resonators) *gender*. Xylophone: *gambang*.

The gongs have deeply turned-back flanges and pronounced bosses. Their forging, starting from a convex disc of cast bronze, may have preceded the Hindu–Buddhist kingdoms of the 7th century AD, and is a highly respected profession. Those hanging in individual frames are struck with a padded beater: *gong ageng*, the deepest in pitch, up to 1 m. (3') in diameter (sometimes the only gong left unburnished) and in many ways regarded as the most important single instrument of the gamelan; *gong suwukan*, 60–70 cm. (24–27"); and *kempul*, smallest of the hanging gongs, as many as one for each note of the scale. The other gongs rest on crossed cords in box-like stands and are struck with a stick bound with cord; their names onomatopoeically describe their different sounds: *kenong*, very deep-flanged and, in a large gamelan today, one 'kettle' for each note of the scale; *ketuk*, with a shallower flange and more abrupt sound; *kempyang*, a higher-pitched pair of flatter gongs sharing one stand and struck at the same time with a pair of beaters.

(b) *Drums*. Kendang, long two-headed drum (somewhat resembling the Indian *mrdanga*), resting horizontally on a low stand and slightly barrel-shaped, the heads of different widths lapped on to rattan hoops. The hands play on both heads with a great variety of named strokes giving many different sounds. The *kendang* player is usually the leader of the gamelan in that he has the responsibility of guiding the players through tempo changes, and directing when to repeat a section or move on to another. A smaller *kendang ketipung* may be present as well. (A medium-sized *kendang ciblon* is often used for dance accompaniment, while in central Java may be seen the *bedhug*, an ancient barrel

Pl. 1. Gamelan group 'Condong Raos' from Semarang performing in concert fashion on a complete gamelan including both *slendro* and *pelog* instruments, with the famous composer and gamelan-leader, the late Ki Nartosabdho, leading on the drums. *Front:* two gong-chimes *bonang;* horizontally resting *kenongs* and *ketuk.* *Centre:* female singers *pesinden;* male singers *gerong;* bowed lute (fiddle) *rebab;* drums *kendang;* hanging gongs *kempuls* and gong. *Back:* metallophones *slentem, genders, sarons;* zither *siter* and xylophone *gambang.* Photo: E. L. Heins.

drum with nailed heads, struck with a mallet on one head for a powerful booming sound.)

(c) Stringed. Rebab: an elegant downwards-held fiddle of Middle Eastern origin with two strings tuned to a fifth: the player is the melodic leader of the ensemble, seated next to the singer. (See RABAB for instruments of other countries with various forms of this name.) See CELEMPUNG for the large, sloping zither on legs sometimes present, or else the smaller *siter.*

(d) Wind. The only wind instrument is the *suling,* a bamboo flute of the 'external duct' ring flute kind, up to c.50 cm. (2′) long (see FLUTE, 7c (ii)). Unless a four-hole flute is used for *slendro,* a way of using a six-hole *pelog* flute in *slendro* is by keeping the middle-finger hole of each hand always covered, the remainder then supplying five notes to the octave. The *suling, gender, slentem, gambang,* and *rebab* were once regarded as instruments of the 'soft' (indoor) ensemble but since the 17th century

Ex. 1. Lancaran Tropongbang Pelog Patet Nem in contemporary Javanese *kepatihan* notation. ( ) = Gong;) = *Kenong;* Buka = Introduction. A dot beneath a note indicates lower octave.

The *Pelog* scale may be approximately transcribed as follows:

Ex. 2. Transcription into Western notation of part (the second *gongan*) of *Lancaran Tropongbang* as it might be realized by a simple *gamelan soran* in *irama tanggung* (medium 'tempo').

the 'soft', and the 'loud' with the *bonang*, became increasingly combined in one ensemble.

(e) *Performance.* The full gamelan texture includes a *pesinden* (female vocalist) and a *gerongan* (male chorus). The whole ensemble has the hanging gongs to the rear, and before them on one side the *sarons* and *gender*, on the other the *bonangs* and perhaps the *celempung*, with the flute between them behind the drums, and the *rebab* and female vocalist in the middle in front. A piece of gamelan music is known by its form, name, *laras* (tuning system), and *patet* (mode). Each player interprets the fixed melody according to the instrument's technique and function within the whole. Generally speaking, the higher pitched, the more notes an instrument plays (Ex. 2). The various gongs signal ends of phrases, a stroke on a *gong* marking the end of a

gongan (important section), while the *kenong* divides this into two or more, and the others variously provide briefer levels of punctuation according to the form of the piece.

The Sundanese gamelan (West Java) favours smaller ensembles. In the *gamelan degung*, with a tuning akin to *pelog*, a set of small hanging gongs, *jenglong*, plays the slow-moving melody, with the more elaborate variations played on two or three *saron*, *suling*, and *bonang*, with the female singer. The *kachapi, a zither, is also used.

2. *Bali.* The Balinese gamelan has fostered unique developments in gamelan music following the 16th-century collapse of the Hindu–Javanese empire in the face of Islam, upon which a number of Javanese nobles removed their courts to this small island. The gamelans are in great variety and

Ex. 2. (cont.)

are quite among the most enchanting. Most popular today is the *gamelan gong kebyar*. It can accompany every kind of dance, and its instruments include three hanging gongs played by one man, plus two gong chimes of which the *reyong* (in the modern sense) has 12 kettles played by four musicians each with two sticks. The metallophones are used in pairs, one tuned very slightly higher than the other, resulting in *beat tones which, when reproduced throughout the several octaves of a full ensemble, produce the characteristic shimmering sonorities; the metallophones of the *gangsa* group (now called *Kantil*) have thicker bars than the Javanese *gender* and a hardwood mallet gives a harder, more brilliant sound. The drums, *kendang*, direct the performance, and there may also be sets of six or so small cymbals, *cheng-cheng*, mounted on a board boss-downwards, and struck by a pair held one in each hand. (Note: Since the above was written many of the instrument names have been changed or spelled differently.)

3. *Gamelan in the West*. Debussy heard a Javanese gamelan at the Paris World Exhibition of 1889 and became the first in a long line of Western composers to acknowledge its influence: Ravel, Messiaen, Britten, and others. Composers such as Lou Harrison, Ton de Leeuw, and Michael Parsons are now writing works for the gamelan.

In the mid-1950s, performance by Westerners began in the Netherlands, where many museums have gamelan instruments. Enthusiasm for Indonesian music spread to the USA under the influence of Mantle Hood of the University of California at Los Angeles, and many American universities now have performance groups and resident Javanese teachers. Gamelan ensembles are also increasingly to be heard in Australia and, more recently, in other European countries, including Germany, Sweden, and England (as Oxford, Bate *Collection).

Kartomi 1985; Kunst 1949, 3rd Eng. ed. 1973; Lindsay 1979; McPhee 1966.

Ganga. Two-headed cylindrical drum (see DRUM, 4*b*) of West Africa and the Sudan, of about the proportions of the deeper European side drum or larger, up to 45 cm. across (18″), with goatskin heads. With the drum suspended from the left shoulder, the front head is struck, with a hooked stick ending in a flat knob, in many ways to produce different pitches which, in Hausa ensembles with the trumpets *kakaki* (see NAFIR, 2) and shawm *alghaita* (see SURNA), may follow patterns of speech tones. The rearward head is meanwhile played with the left-hand fingers, and can modify the note of the front head, e.g. causing it to rise after a stroke through pressure of the thumb.

Gangsa. In Bali (Indonesia) a metallophone; see GAMELAN, 2. In the northern Philippines, gongs played in ensembles; the gongs are up to *c*.30 cm. (1′) wide with a moderately deep rim and no boss. They are mostly placed flat across the thighs of the kneeling player, or against the ground, and are slapped or tapped with the hands to give a variety of sounds, not tuned to specific pitches. With them may be drums, and iron clappers. (Cf. the more elaborate *kulintang* of the Southern Philippines.)

Gato drum. See LOG DRUM.

Geige. Ger., '*fiddle'*, '*violin'*.

Geigenwerk. Among instruments with strings sounded by friction and played from a complete keyboard (i.e. not as in a *hurdy-gurdy), the earliest known (apart from an idea of Leonardo da Vinci, never carried out) is the *Geigenwerk* of Hans Haiden of Nuremberg, late 16th century. Several metal wheels, with resined parchment or cloth over the rims, were turned by treadle, the strings (of gut, later of metal) being pressed, each to the nearest of the wheels underneath, by the keys. An example made shortly afterwards by a Spaniard, now in the Brussels *collection, has four 18-cm. (7″) diameter wheels, those for the bass notes turning slower than those for the high notes. The idea was taken up again in the 18th century under different names and usually replacing the wheels by an endless band of silk or suchlike, against which the strings are raised by the keys, and will sound softly or louder according to the finger-pressure on the keys. Among such were the *Bogenklavier* (Hohlfeld, Berlin, 1754) for which C. P. E. Bach is said to have written a sonata; and the 'Celestina' (Adams Walker, London, 1772), which was also made as an attachment to a *harpsichord and was ordered as such from the USA, in 1786, with a Kirkman harpsichord, by Thomas Jefferson (who said that it well suited slow movements and accompaniment to the voice).

Other designs pressed the strings to a long resined cylinder turned by a treadle, as the *Harmonichord* (Kaufmann, Dresden, 1809): an instrument in an upright piano shape, for which Weber wrote the Adagio and Rondo in F with orchestra (1811), having, he said, found it devilish work writing for an instrument of such peculiar and strange tone in combination with other instruments. A later invention embodied a violin bow, *claviola*. (See Marcuse 1975, 312ff., for a chronological list of inventions of these types up to 1909.)

Gemshorn (from Ger.: *Gemse*, 'chamoix'). A duct flute (see FLUTE, 7) of horn, e.g. cowhorn, with the apex intact and the wide end covered by a wooden plate with blowing hole in the edge. Close to the hole, a recorder-like window is cut in the horn, with fingerholes further down. As with an *ocarina, the notes depend basically on the sum area of the holes uncovered, though they are now designed to be uncovered in direct sequence. Early illustrations show three holes which, with a larger hole for the thumb, should suffice for an octave scale (Virdung, see RENAISSANCE INSTRUMENTS, 3). Present reconstructions, as first made in quantity by Horace Fitzpatrick in England, have six or more holes and (also like ocarinas) can be obtained as a family of different sizes (Parkinson 1981).

In Italy small versions about 10 cm. (4″) long have been made up to modern times as dove decoy-calls, with a single small fingerhole bored through the tip of the horn.

Fitzpatrick 1972; Parkinson 1981.

Gendang. The long barrel drum of Malaysia, similar in build to the *kendang* (see GAMELAN, 1*b*).

Gender. Indonesia (Java, Bali): instrument of struck bronze bars with tubular resonators below (see GAMELAN, Pl. 1, top left): the softer (more *celesta-like) of the two metallophones of the *gamelan (the other being the *saron, which is without such resonators). The bars, 14 or seven, are strung together over a decorated wooden stand tall enough to give room for the wide resonators of bamboo or, more often, thin metal: these are all of the same height but are tuned to the bars individually by a knot, or by sand or suchlike poured inside. The bars are sometimes very beautifully shaped, each with stiffening ridges along the top from end to end, and most pronounced with the narrower, thicker bars of *genders* of high compass.

A gamelan usually has two 14-bar *genders*, each covering 2½ octaves: the deepest bar of the *gender panerus* being an octave higher than that of the larger *gender barung*. Each *gender* is played with two beaters with wide, padded, disc-like ends; each note is skilfully damped with the hand while holding the beater before playing the next. A third *gender*, the *slentem*, has seven wide, thin bars covering a single octave corresponding (not in all cases exactly) to the bottom octave of the *gender barung*; only one beater is needed, leaving the other hand free to damp (as with a *saron). The music extract, GAMELAN, Ex. 2, shows only the *slentem*.

German flute (from Fr.). In England through the eighteenth century a widely-used name for the flute (transverse flute), arising in distinction from 'flute' in the common contemporary sense of a recorder.

Ghaita, North African *shawm, see SURNA.

Ghatam. Indian *percussion pot, struck with the hands.

Ghichak. Central Asian fiddle; see KEMANCHA.

Giga, gigue. Fiddle names met from the 12th century onwards: respectively German (whence *Geige*) and in Latin texts; and French (with no proved connection with the name of the dance, *gigue*, 'jig'). Whether given to fiddles generally or to any type in particular, is not known.

Giorgi flute. Now of curiosity interest, this is a plain cylindrical end-blown flute designed to be held vertically (like a recorder), invented by C. T. Giorgi, Rome, c.1888. About 52 cm. long (20"), the extreme top has the form of an oval lip-plate with mouth-hole in the centre, like that of a modern flute but leading straight downwards into the flute. Many were made in London by J. Wallis & Sons, usually in ebonite and some with keys. Giorgi and others also devised more complicated flutes with this unusual mouthpiece. Gai 1969. See also ALTO AND BASS FLUTE 2 (albisiphone) mouthpiece. Gai 1969.

Gittern, guiterne. For *gittern* as a medieval name, see CITOLE AND GITTERN. By the 16th century, *guiterne* and *guiterre* were French names for the early *guitar, and 'gittern' came to be used through 17th-century England synonymously with 'guitar'.

Glass harmonica (originally 'armonica'). This was invented in 1761 by Benjamin Franklin while on a visit from America to England. A chromatic set of glass bowls, about half as deep as wide, 37 for a compass of three full octaves, are mounted with the rims closely overlapping on a horizontal square metal axle turned by a treadle aided by a heavy wooden or lead flywheel; the direction is towards the player (like a lathe). The bowls for the sharps have different coloured rims from the naturals and the whole instrument is about 120 cm. (4') long. The bowls are kept moist by a shallow trough of water underneath, partitioned off from the flywheel. All 10 fingers are employed to touch the rims, and since these lie close together the instrument can be played fast and in harmonies. Two celebrated soloists on the instrument were young women, one of them Marianne Kirchgässner, for whom Mozart wrote the Adagio and Rondo, K. 617, for harmonica with flute, oboe, viola, and cello (1791): the harmonica part (compass g–f''') looks on paper almost like a piano part. It is said that Mesmer found the instrument helpful in his hypnosis exper-

iments. It was also said that the friction on the fingertips proved bad for the nerves, and that Kirchgässner retired from playing on that account. Donizetti, in the famous 'Mad scene' from *Lucia di Lammermoor*, wrote an obbligato for glass harmonica, now played on the flute. 'Harmonica' can, of course, name instruments of other kinds, and where it occurs in subsequent scores it is generally likely that some form of *glockenspiel is intended if not the mouth-blown *harmonica.

See also MUSICAL GLASSES. For sounds from friction on glass rods, see SOUND SCULPTURES.

Hyatt-King 1946.

Glass harp. See MUSICAL GLASSES.

Glockenspiel (Ger., lit. 'bell chime', and adopted into Eng., in the USA also 'orchestra bells'; Fr.: *jeu de timbres*; It.: *campanelli*). Tuned metal bars, supported at two points with both ends free, and struck in the centre with beaters. The instrument is not recorded in Europe before the 17th century and was rarely in the orchestra until, with its cheerful sound, so appropriate in various contexts, its use grew after the mid-19th. Modern types include versions made expressly for school music and sometimes termed 'metallophones' (see below, 3), while the *vibraphone is a specialized development.

1. Orchestral glockenspiel (Pl. 1). The steel bars, 8 mm. thick or more, are laid in two rows, naturals and sharps, supported on felted rails or on cords passed through holes in the bars at the two principal nodal points, in theory distant from each end by 22.4 per cent of the total length of the bar, roughly one-quarter (see PARTIALS, 6). There are no resonators. The instrument is often played in its opened case; after use the naturals may be slid under the sharps to close the case. Some recent models can if wished be held on a vertical metal stand. The beaters, held between finger and thumb, have spherical ends of horn, wood, or brass to produce the characteristic bright penetrating sound. Rubber ends give the more *celesta-like sound sometimes required. Compass is written g to c''', sounding two octaves higher, thus reaching to the top note of the piano.

2. Keyboard glockenspiel. This is more scarce, and varies in build from small and portable to the size of a small celesta. The keyboard, actuating small metal up-striking hammers, allows little variation in dynamics, and the volume of sound is anyway not great. Percussionists far prefer the plain glockenspiel (1, above), but there are many works written with the keyboard version in view, e.g. Dukas, *L'apprenti sorcier*; Debussy, *La mer* (the composer writes 'or celesta'); Mahler, Seventh Symphony; Messiaen, *Oiseaux exotiques*. The keyboard glockenspiel is generally understood to sound one octave higher than written, like the celesta. It is also the best instrument for Papageno's music

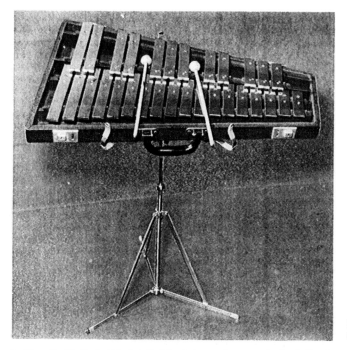

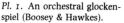

Pl. 1. An orchestral glockenspiel (Boosey & Hawkes).

in Mozart's *Die Zauberflöte* (labelled for 'istrumento d'acciaio', i.e. 'of steel') written with chords of many notes as if it were piano music. It can also be used for the 'carillon' part in Handel's *Saul*; it is very uncertain what instrument Handel actually had, but keyboard metal-bar instruments were used long before in the *carillon countries for bell-tuning and instruction.

Toy pianos are another form. John Cage wrote a suite for toy piano in 1948.

3. *School glockenspiels*. First, simple instruments manufactured for small children, with one row or (chromatic) two, and bars only 1.5–2 mm. thick and therefore quite short for the notes they give (see below, 5). An old name for these was 'harmonica', though some German exporters early in this century already termed them 'metallophones'. (The small household dinner gongs with hollow bun-shaped brass resonators under the bars were also man-ufactured as 'harmonicas'.)

As developed during the 1950s for the *Schulwerk* of Carl Orff (1895–1982) the instruments have bars up to 18 in number, 2–6 mm. thick and often placed over a wooden trough which serves as resonator, an idea borrowed from South-East Asia, where instruments of tuned bars have been in use from the early Middle Ages (see RANAT, RONEAT; XYLOPHONE, 3). The bars can be lifted off, so that with a one-row diatonic instrument an F bar can be quickly replaced by an F♯ bar for playing in G major, and so on. The compass is usually

one-and-a-half octaves and alto and bass instru-ments are also supplied.

For individually mounted bars, each with a horizontal tubular resonator, see CHIME BAR.

4. *Lyra glockenspiel* (or bell lyra or lyra). A glocken-spiel for marching bands, the bars mounted one above another in a lyre-shaped metal frame on top of a staff; the base of the staff is supported in a leather harness like that of a standard-bearer. The bars are nowadays of aluminium, usually in two rows giving two chromatic octaves played with one beater. The sound carries well above the drums, and there are Corps of Drums that use these glockenspiels as their main or only melodic instrument; or else they may use the more recent horizontal models carried on a strap ('marching bells', etc.). The lyra came in in Germany around the 1870s as a musical replace-ment for the old 'jingling johnny' (see BELL TREE), often retaining its pendant horsetails.

5. *The pitch of a bar*. The bar vibrates in a 'bending' manner under the restoring force of its stiffness. The thicker the bar, the greater the stiffness and the higher the frequency. As to length, the under-lying law holds true: frequency varies as wave-velocity divided by the length. But owing to the presence of shear stresses in addition to bending stresses, the wave-velocity itself varies inversely with the length, so that in the result the frequency varies inversely as the length squared. Therefore, for a bar to sound an octave lower than another (of the same material and even thickness), it need

be only 1.4 times as long ($\sqrt{2}$); the widths, if small compared with the length, should in theory hardly affect the pitch, so the basic equation for a freely supported bar is:

$$\text{frequency} \cong \frac{\text{thickness}}{\text{length squared}}$$

or for rough calculation of the note of a steel glockenspiel bar (all dimensions in cm.):

$$\text{frequency (Hz)} \cong \frac{520,000t}{l^2}$$

(For 'overtone-tuning', see XYLOPHONE, 2; for the pitch of metal tubes of similar sizes, see TUBAPHONE.)

To lower the pitch of a bar it is thinned in the central region (e.g. by filing a notch across, or countersinking pits), thus reducing stiffness at the main fundamental antinode (see PARTIALS, 6). To raise the pitch, the bar is filed under the ends, where the sharpening effect of reduced mass outweighs any flattening effect from reduced thickness.
see PERCUSSION.

Gong (Indonesia). See GAMELAN, 1a, e.

Gong and tam-tam. Bronze instruments suspended by the rim and struck at or near the centre with a heavy wool- or felt-covered mallet; some oriental gongs, however, are not suspended but rest face upwards (see, e.g., BONANG).

1. Western orchestral percussion has during the 20th century come to distinguish between: 'tam-tam' (normal orchestral gong) with rim turned back little or not at all, no central boss, and not tuned to a particular note; and 'gong', thicker, with the rim well turned back, usually a central boss, and in some cases tuned to a particular note. Their different sound qualities are up to a point reflected in the sounds of the words themselves ('tam-tam' more metallic; 'gong' more booming). Both words are of East Asian onomatopoeic origin, but it so happened that when gongs were first imported from the East in the 18th century, England adopted 'gong' but the Continent usually 'tam-tam', in neither case then with any distinction of form in mind. An early use is by Gossec in his funeral music for the statesman Mirabeau, 1791, a large tam-tam being carried in the procession.

Diameters vary between about 30 cm. and 95 cm. (12″ and 37″), for the orchestra the larger the better—unless, as in some modern compositions, two or more contrasted pitches are asked for. Thus Boulez has required two or more tam-tams of different (unspecific) pitches—'medium', 'low', etc.—and similarly two or more gongs. A leading gong-maker in the West through modern times has been Paiste in Switzerland, with a reputation on a par with that of Zildjian for *cymbals.

2. Most of the vibration takes place away from the rim with higher *partials persisting longest; but the behaviour of the different kinds of gong does

not prove easy to account for. For example, the higher partials of a tam-tam may surge in a crescendo after the stroke before they decay; and with some gongs the initial pitch may be heard to rise, or fall by up to a whole tone or more, following a stroke. Gong-makers in the Far East may pay great attention to this, knowing by experience how to make a gong that rises in pitch or falls—it is said that a customer will specifically order the one or the other. Only latterly has the phenomenon begun to be researched in the West in scientific terms.

3. For different gongs of the East, see CHINA AND KOREA, 1a, 2a; JAPAN, 1a (*shoko*); GAMELAN, 1a, e; SOUTH-EAST ASIA; also GONG CHIME. Gongs are known to go back to the sixth century AD from China southwards (thus considerably younger, it seems, than the *bronze drum). Individual instruments especially prized for their beauty may be given proper names, have magical powers attributed to them, and receive ritual offerings.

Gong bumbung. See BLOWN GONG.

Gong chime. 1. The set of tuned gongs with one player has its highest importance in music from Burma to Indonesia (see GAMELAN, KULINTANG, SOUTH-EAST ASIA). The gongs, usually bronze, are most typically of the kind also called 'kettle gongs': fairly small, with the rims deeply turned over and a prominent boss on which they are struck. In most cases they are arranged, boss upwards, round a low circular frame of wood or bamboo, held by thongs passed through holes in the gongs. One player sits in the middle of the circle (as see SOUTH-EAST ASIA, Pl. 2, back row, right); or else the kettles are placed in one or two straight rows (see BONANG) also GAMELAN, Pl. 1 (foreground).

The Thai *gong* (*khong*) *wong yai* (SOUTH-EAST ASIA, Pl. 2) has 16 gongs covering just over two octaves in approximately equal intervals (given as from d′ to e‴); the smaller *gong wong lek* is an octave higher, with gongs from 9 cm. (3½″) upwards in diameter; the beaters are hide-covered. (For their participation in the *pi-phat* ensemble, see SOUTH-EAST ASIA, Ex. 1.) Also in Thailand is the gong chime in a large upright crescent frame, *gong mon*, played especially for funeral music. In Burma there are gongs set in rows, *maung zaing*, said to be relatively recent.

2. China, *yunluo* ('cloud gong'): 10 almost flat small gongs hung in a wooden frame held in one hand and hit with a horn hammer on the end of a bamboo stick. All have the same width, being graded in metal thickness from about 0.8 mm. for the deepest note to 2 mm. for the highest. Once used in formal court ensembles, the *yunluo* has been revived for the modern Chinese orchestra with up to 36 gongs; in one type they are graded in diameter.

3. In Western music, sets of tuned gongs first appeared in Italian operas on exotic subjects, notably by Puccini in *Madam Butterfly* (an octave of 'tam-tam giapponesi' *ad libitum*) and *Turandot* (a chromatic octave of '*gong cinesi*'), the written compass in both operas ranging over the bass staff.

Gong drum. See BASS DRUM, 4.

Goofus. *Free-reed instrument; see MELODICA.

Gopi-yantra. Indian one-stringed instrument of an unusual kind with which folk-singers accompany themselves in the north and Bengal. A wood or metal pot, open-topped, has a goatskin stretched over the bottom. Bound to each side are the arms of a bamboo cut to a fork, remaining united at the top to hold a tuning peg for the gut or wire string. This passes down into the pot, to be joined to the skin by a toggle. As the player plucks the string, its vibration is resonated by the skin, giving a soft, clear note. The bamboo arms can be pressed together near the top, which, easing the tension, lowers the note. A southern type, *tuntune*, has a single bamboo stick on the side of the pot, instead of the fork.

The note of the *gopi-yantra* is higher than might be expected from the dimensions and tension involved, apparently because the perpendicular attachment of the string to the soundboard (the skin) results in two tugs upwards on the skin (two cycles of skin motion) for each cycle of string oscillation in the fundamental mode, which therefore becomes largely suppressed in favour of the octave harmonic (Adkins *et al.* 1981).

Gora. South African instrument, at first glance resembling a *musical bow: a 3′-long stick (90 cm.) slightly curved, with one string (traditionally of ox-sinew). But the string is set in vibration by blowing (a rare instance of a blown *chordophone). The lower end of the string is tied to a small piece of flattened quill (vulture, bustard), the other end of which is bound to the stick. Holding the bow with both hands, and with the quill between narrowly parted lips, the player breathes strongly in and out, making the quill vibrate like a reed and setting the string in vibration. Movements of the mouth-cavity select different string harmonics (mostly, it is said, numbers five to nine) to play brisk melodies, while the fundamental may be heard between the notes. The *gora*, originally a Hottentot instrument, was adopted by the Bushmen, and then (19th century) by the Sotho and other Bantu (among whom a name for it is *lesiba*, 'feather'), played especially when cattle-herding.

See AFRICA; Kirby 1934.

Graile (Old Fr., also *graisle*, from Lat.: *gracilis*, 'slender'). A name met in 13th-century romances for some type of small horn, as in the *Chanson de Roland*, where it signals alerts. In castle routine a graile would 'corner l'eau', the summons to wash the hands before dinner.

Gralla. See DOUÇAINE, 3.

Grantang. Tube xylophone of Bali (see CHALUNG).

Gravicembalo (It.). The *harpsichord (corruption of 'clavicembalo').

Grelot (Fr.). See SLEIGH-BELL.

Ground instruments. 'Ground harp' (or 'ground bow') and 'ground zither' are ethnologists' terms for some instruments met in Central Africa, East Asia, and the West Indies, where a string (or rattan rope) is knotted to a soundboard of bark, hide, or tin-plate laid over a pit dug in the ground and weighted down with stones. In a *ground harp*, the string is tied to a flexible pole fixed in the ground and bent over, putting the string under tension; a young African goat-herd 'moved one hand along the bow' (varying the tension) 'while hitting the string with a thin stick, making buzzing and humming tunes'. In Haiti, named 'mosquito drum', it is sounded in certain rites. In a *ground zither* a bamboo is placed upright on the soundboard and the string is led round it and pegged to the ground at each end; one part of the string may be shorter, for a higher sound when hit, as in Vietnam to accompany songs. In the southern Sudan it has been played for certain dances with a second person thumping on the hide.

Whether such primitive devices in any way underlie higher developments in stringed instruments is a moot point; but the ground harp has latterly been experimented with in the West in search of fresh sounds for informal music-making.

Ground drum: a board over a pit and rhythmically struck or stamped on; see PACIFIC ISLANDS (*keho*).

Gu (or *ku*). Chinese generic term for 'drum'. Of the numerous kinds nearly all have the skins fastened by broad-headed nails in one or two rows.

1. *Barrel drums* (see DRUM, 4*b*): (*a*) *Tanggu* (*t'ang-ku*: see CHINA AND KOREA, 1). Vertical (head horizontal), 30 cm. (1 foot) or more wide, with rings for attaching to hooks in a wooden frame composed of four arms curving round the drum. In the theatre the upper head is struck with two wood sticks. The 'flower-pot' drum (*huepen gu* or *kang-gu*), similarly suspended, has a shell which narrows to the base like a large vase.

(*b*) *Ritual barrel drums*. *Jingu* (*ch'in-ku*), the largest, up to 150 cm. (5′) in length and width, is placed upright or horizontally on a stand, played with sticks; *bofu* (*po-fu*), smaller, *c.*40 cm. (16″) long, 20 cm. (8″) wide, and played with the hands; *jiangu* (*ch'ian-ku*) is held horizontally on a pole passing through the shell; for the 'whirling drum', *taogu*, see RATTLE DRUM . Other barrel drums are used in folk ceremonies.

2. *Bangu* (*pan-ku*). Of the theatre and popular orchestras, it is unlike any other drum: small and shallow, it rests (often upon crossed cords) at the top of a slender bamboo tripod (to which may be attached a *wood block). The construction is a flat dome, up to 25 cm. (10″) wide at the bottom, formed of a ring of four to six thick hardwood blocks glued together, leaving a central space which narrows to a small (*c*.6 cm.) opening at the top. The skin is nailed over the whole dome and struck over the central opening of the shell with one or two thin bamboo sticks, for punctuating the declamation or the music with sharp, high sounds. There are also cylindrical, not domed, varieties, constructed similarly.

3. *Zhanggu* (*chung-ku*). An 'hourglass' drum of folk music, resembling the important *changgo* of Korea (see CHINA AND KOREA, 2*b*).

4. *Octagonal frame drum*. See TAMBOURINE, 3.

Guan (or *kuan*; *guanzi*). The Chinese bamboo pipe sounded with a large double reed (in Sachs's terminology, a *'cylindrical oboe'). Varying in length—e.g. 34 cm. (13″) without the reed—it has seven holes in front, thumb-hole behind (between the first two fingerholes), and a compass of fundamentals only. It is played in both folk and theatre music. See CHINA AND KOREA, I, 4*d*; and 2*e* for the equivalent Korean pipe, *p'iri*. See also BALABAN.

Gue. Former instrument of the Shetland Islands. In 1809, A. E. Edmondstone's *A view of the ancient and present state of the Zetland Islands* (Vol. II, p. 59) states that 'Before violins were introduced, the musicians performed on an instrument called a gue, which appears to have had some similarity to a violin, but had only two strings of horsehair, and was played in the same manner as a violoncello.' It was played for dancing. Beyond this (though Walter Scott names the gue in *The Pirate*, Ch. XV) nothing is known about the instrument, which has been plausibly conjectured to have been akin to the *bowed lyre of Baltic Scandinavia.

Guimbarde. Fr., *Jew's-harp.

Guiro (or *guero*, from a name for a gourd). Scraped instrument of Latin-American dance music, made originally of an elongated gourd about 30 cm. (12″) long, dried and cut with transverse notches along the surface. A short stick is swept to and fro over these, typically in eight-quaver rhythms with a stress on every fourth. Commercial models are of hardwood. In concert music the guero makes a brief appearance, also in repeated quavers, in Stravinsky's *Rite of Spring*, named in Fr. *râpe guero* ('gourd scraper', No. 70 in the score); later composers have also called for it. There are also bamboo or wooden tubular types (*reco-reco*), closed at the ends, with a slit cut down the side to emit air resonance.

Guitar (Fr.: *guitare*; Ger.: *Gitarre*; It.: *chitarra*; Ru.: *gitara*; Sp.: *guitarra*, but Port.: *viola*). The Spanish instrument which was already in the 16th century becoming popular in other European countries and has since, besides having its own distinguished concert repertory, virtually become the global instrument of the people—the only existing instrument, someone once said, on which it is 'impossible to make a nasty noise'. Its characteristic figure-of-eight body has for the last 200 years normally carried six strings tuned as Ex. 1. Prior to this it had five strings, each paired (the elegant, narrower 'baroque' guitar); and before that, in the 16th century, four, in smaller-sized guitars such as continue to thrive as folk instruments in Spain, Portugal, and Latin America (below, 5), some of them departing considerably from the historical tuning pattern, others retaining it (Ex. 1 less the lower two strings, often as on the *ukulele with the fourth raised an octave, giving simple accompaniment chords in the most compact form). Among numerous variants of the full-size guitar there have been *bass guitars (in the older, non-electric sense), *lyre-guitars, and a rare experimental bowed adaptation, *arpeggione.

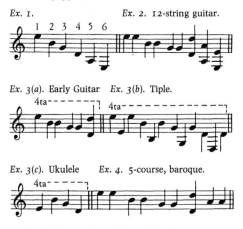

Ex. 1.   *Ex. 2.* 12-string guitar.

Ex. 3(a). Early Guitar *Ex. 3(b).* Tiple.

Ex. 3(c). Ukulele *Ex. 4.* 5-course, baroque.

1. *Classical or Spanish guitar.* The body, on average 48 cm. (19″) long, has back and sides of rosewood, walnut, maple, etc.; the back is flat but may be 'sprung' outwards in the making to give a slight arch. The belly, of thickness up to 2.4 mm., is of close-grained pine, spruce, or cedar ('economy models' often use laminated spruce). Bars are glued to its underside to support the pull of the strings on the glued-on bridge: up to 1800 these ran transversely, but fan-strutting (bars in a fan) became widespread in the 19th century and is now general. The fingerboard is, like the bridge, traditionally of ebony, with metal frets numbering 19, the twelfth fret (the octave of the open string—

see FRETS, 1) being at the junction of neck and body. The standard string-length is c.66 cm. (26″); 'short-scale' models down to 56 cm. (22″) are made to suit small hands. Nylon strings have generally replaced the older strings of gut and overwound silk, and the lower-tuned strings have a core of nylon floss overwound with plated wire. A critical factor, as with other fretted instruments, is the height of the strings above the fingerboard—the 'action' (FRETS, 3). Many mass-produced guitars have poorly adjusted action, a source of much frustration to beginners. Minute attention to the height of the nut will correct a bad action, and an ivory or plastic insert or 'saddle' in the bridge will allow further adjustment; but inexperienced attempts to raise or lower the action can render the instrument unplayable.

2. *Classical guitar-playing.* Guitar music (unless in *tablature) is written an octave higher than the sound, so that the tuning notes are written from e'' down to e (Ex. 1). The 19 frets give a written compass up to the high b'', above which a further octave is possible using *harmonics. The sixth string is often tuned down a note to d.

The waist of the guitar is rested on the left thigh, the foot usually raised a little on a foot-rest. The strings are plucked with the fingernails, though in the 19th century and earlier the flesh of the fingertip was more commonly used, as in lute-playing. The left-hand fingers must stop the strings at the frets with sufficient strength to produce clear notes, remaining arched so that adjacent strings are free to vibrate. A finger can also be laid flat across several strings when several notes are needed at the same fret—known by the French term *barré* and the Spanish *ceja*; a *grand barré* is when the finger is laid across all six. Hand and wrist positions are of utmost importance to the classical guitarist in developing a sound technique; though in folk and pop music the players, often self-taught, have their own idiosyncrasies.

The right-hand fingers are indicated by their initial letters in Spanish and French: p, thumb (Sp.: *pulgar*); i, index (*indice*); m, middle (*médio*); a, ring (*anulár*). There is further Spanish terminology in describing right-hand technique, such as *apoyando*, coming to rest on the adjacent string, giving very clear articulation in scales, etc. (Eng.: 'rest stroke'); *tirando*, 'pulling' ('free stroke'); *rasgueado* (or simpler in Portuguese, *rasgado*), strummed with the fingers and/or thumb. Other effects include *metálico*, playing with the nails close to the bridge; and directions to play a note on a lower string in a high position, making a pronounced change in tone. In the case of harmonics, whether of stopped or open string (see HARMONICS, 2), the required pitch should always be indicated to prevent misunderstanding. For some artificial harmonics the index finger of the *right* hand can touch the string while another finger plucks.

Much of the early music is written in tablature (Sp.: *cifra*); also, Renaissance *lute and *vihuela tablature can be read on the guitar simply by tuning the third string down a semitone to F♯ to match the pattern of lute-tuning (in which the major third comes one place lower down in the scheme).

The *flamenco guitar* is also played with the nails. Typically it is held on the right thigh. It often retains the older wooden tuning-pegs instead of geared 'machines', and has the strings set much closer to the frets to facilitate rapid passage-work. With its lighter construction (e.g. of cypress instead of rosewood) it has a very bright, incisive sound. By contrast, the heavier classical guitar has a more rounded sound and greater sustaining power.

3. *Steel-strung guitars: (a) Six-string.* These guitars, intended for simple self-accompaniment to the voice, are adapted to the purpose through various modifications, including: (i) playing with a *plectrum; (ii) steel strings, standing up to the wear of the plectrum and producing a brighter sound; (iii) a narrower fingerboard and neck (Fig. 1, right), making chords easier to finger, especially in bringing the left thumb round to hold bass notes in certain chord positions (this thumb is not normally used in classical guitar-playing); (iv) the 14th fret (instead of the 12th) lies above the junction of neck and belly, making the neck 4 cm. (1½″) longer (thus, when playing with a *capotasto attached at one of the lower frets, left-hand positions further up the strings are as comfortably reached as when playing on the full string-length).

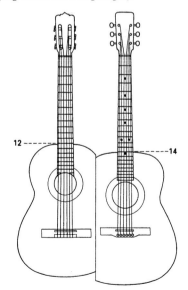

Fig. 1. Guitar: classical and folk models compared.

This '14-fret neck' was introduced in the late 1920s to suit banjo-players when transferring to guitar. It brings the bridge closer to the soundhole (Fig. 1), leaving a relatively large expanse of belly below it. In 'Jumbo' and 'Dreadnought' models (already made in 1931 by the celebrated firm founded by C. F. Martin, who went to New York City from Germany in 1833), the body is increased in width by some 5 cm. (2"), further adding to the resonance in the bass.

Numerous publications show the chief chord positions in every key. Folk-guitarists also sometimes use tunings to a common chord throughout, for this to sound resonantly on the open strings.

Of the steel strings, the lower-tuned are overspun with wire or more often metal tape, to give smoothness under the fingers. Steel strings, needing a higher tension than gut or nylon, demand more support for the bridge and belly, effected by pinning the bridge to a strut beneath the belly (or by attaching the strings to a tailpiece). The neck is usually strengthened by a metal truss-rod inside, and many steel-strung guitars have adjustable bridges by which the height of each string can be individually regulated.

Guitars made for metal strings are nothing new, having existed in various forms from the 17th century (e.g. *chitarra battente*) and with the present six strings certainly from the mid-19th, when they were being made in the USA by Martin.

(b) *Twelve-string guitar*. Ex. 2 shows how the lower three courses (or often the lower two) are here 'octave courses' (see COURSE). The octave string, the thinner, is normally placed to the bass side of the pair (i.e. uppermost on the guitar) so that a downstroke with the right hand will sound the octave before the lower note. The added strings brighten the bass, increase sympathetic resonance, and can extend technical possibilities. The 12-string guitar is also played with 'C tuning', i.e. tuned throughout a third deeper than the normal 'E tuning'; strings of slightly thicker gauge are supplied for this.

4. *Arched top ('cello-style') guitar*. This has a convex top and bottom (carved from thicker wood, as in violin-making), *f*-shaped soundholes, and characteristically a brown and orange 'sun-burst' finish. It was developed in the USA by the Gibson Company from 1923 (along with the mandolin of similar build) and came to the fore as the regular plectrum guitar for jazz, played by famous jazz soloists like Eddie Lang. The steel strings pass over a relatively high bridge to a steel tailpiece, and there are 14 frets on the neck. Many jazz and other guitarists use it still. In a 'dobro' model (the word coined from 'Dopyera brothers', inventors in the USA from 1928 onwards), the bridge bears upon an internal metal resonator disc ('resophonic') invisible beneath a metal coverplate, for producing louder sound.

5. *Small guitars*. These abound over the Hispanic world in immense variety, their names and their stringing differing even within the same region.

Often a small one, about half the size of a guitar, plays the melody, below which a slightly larger one strums the chords and a normal guitar plays the bass—or the melody instrument is one of the *bandurria family (pear-shaped and quite differently tuned). For some examples, see CAVAQUINHO (Portugal); CHARANGO (Andes, traditionally with the body from an armadillo; CUATRO ('four strings', as have many of the others); GUITARILLO; REQUINTO; TIPLE (Ex. 3*b*); VIHUELA, 2. Several in Mexico, have the name *jarana*. The *Terz-gitarre*, as manufactured in Germany for a long time, is tuned a third higher than the guitar.

6. *Early guitars: (a) Origins*. From long before the Christian era, and again in medieval Europe (see CITOLE AND GITTERN), there had been small plectrum instruments with incurving sides. None in pictures looks quite like a guitar; and even though 'guitarra' is named in a 13th-century Spanish treatise it is hardly until the end of the 15th century that we can recognize the characteristic form of instrument. Ex. 3*a* shows a tuning given for the small four-course guitar for which tablature books are known from 1546 in Spain, and from France some ten years later (calling for *guiterre* or *guiterne*). Quite similar instruments exist among the small guitars noted above (5).

(b) *Five-course guitar*. This also existed in the 16th century, but came to the fore around 1600, to remain the normal guitar everywhere up to the end of the 18th century: the 'baroque' guitar, seen in countless paintings and known by numerous preserved examples, many of them having a back of fluted ribs with ivory stringing, and an elaborate 'sunk rose' of vellum in several tiers, partly gilded. A typical tuning of the gut strings is shown in Ex. 4, and a typical body outline in Fig. 2*a* for comparison with later outlines. As with many other stringed instruments the curves of the lower part and of the shoulders are mainly formed by the arcs of two overlapping circles centred at various distances apart on or near the lines marking the greatest lower and upper widths. At the extreme top and bottom, these arcs are linked by short arcs of very wide radius centred somewhere high up the centre line of the body, while further arcs make the waist.

The belly wood is continued a short distance up the neck, joining a fingerboard which is flush with it and has usually nine frets of gut. The sound is on the whole less colourful, drier, more lute-like, than with a modern guitar. A certain William Turner wrote in England in 1697: 'The Fine easie Ghittar, whose Performance is soon gained, at least after the brushing way, has . . . over-topt the nobler Lute. Nor is it to be denied, but that after the pinching way, the Ghittar makes some good work.' These two ways of playing—strumming (*rasgueado*) and plucking (*punteado*)—had been distinguished in the literature from the 16th century and for strumming an unusual chord tablature appeared

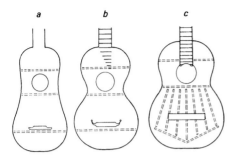

Fig. 2.

in Italy, called 'alfabeto' (Ex. 5). Capital letters denote chords—the letters having no relation to musical notes: thus in the example, 'E' ; means the D minor chord; the others shown are major, 'I', 'B', and 'G' denoting respectively A, C, and F major. The ticks along the line indicate down-and-up strokes of the player's right hand in the *rasgueado*. As is commonly the case with tablatures, the note-values written above continue to apply until a different one is written. (See Murphy 1968.)

Ex. 5. Alfabeto tablature from Sanseverino, 'Pavaniglia sopra l'E' (i.e. in D minor), *Il primo libro per la chitarra alla spagnola* (Milan, 1622).

(c) *Six-string guitar.* The modern arrangement has been traced back to Spain around 1780, first adding a sixth double course, then, during the 1790s, reducing this to the present six single strings, extending the fingerboard on to the belly, and adopting metal frets. The Cádiz maker Pages seems to have been prominent in these developments and also in the change to fan-strutting of the lower part of the belly. One result of adding the low E string and abolishing the old double courses is to lower the overall 'pitch centre' of the instrument, to balance which the lower bulge of the body becomes widened and the bridge is brought higher up. The outline varies a good deal, but Fig. 2b is a typical shape for the early and mid-19th century, though some show an even more exaggerated (narrower) waist, almost the shape of a violin if all the turned-out corners were removed. Others, e.g. by Panormo in London, widened the body to approach modern size. Such were the guitars played by Berlioz and Paganini, and by Fernando Sor and other outstanding guitarist–composers of the period (below, 7).

Then in Spain, from about 1870, Torres (Antonio de Torres Jurado, 1817–92) boldly developed the enlarged models to set the course of future guitar design (Fig. 2c, a modern example). The top and bottom arcs are of increased radius, with their centres further separated, making a vast, round vibrating area in the lower half, fan-barred below and with the bridge at about the centre of it. Torres is said to have received much encouragement from the great soloist Francisco Tárrega (1852–1909), who brought into the repertory transcriptions for guitar of works by the great composers from Bach onwards, while in the native idiom Albéniz is said to have judged the guitar transcriptions of his works superior to the original versions for piano. Tárrega is held as the founder of the modern school of the classical guitar, carried further by Andrés Segovia (1893–1986), who made his international début in Paris in 1924, and by such later celebrities as Oscar Ghiglia (b. 1938) of Italy, and Julian Bream (b. 1933) and John Williams (b. 1941) of Britain, for whom works have been written by many leading composers. The artist usually collaborates with the composer over matters of technical scope and detail (as so often when composers have written virtuoso works for instruments): such was the case, for instance, with works written for Bream by Henze (*Three Tientos*), Britten (*Nocturnal*), and Walton (Five Bagatelles).

7. *Repertory.* The bulk of the music for four-course guitar comes from 16th-century France—Adrien le Roy (c.1520–98), Robert Ballard (c.1575–c.1650), and Guillaume Morlaye (c.1510–after 1558)—while there are also contributions from Spanish and Italian sources. For five-course guitar more than 250 collections of pieces have survived, the most notable composers here including Giovannia Paolo Foscarini (*fl.* before 1621–49), Francesco Corbetta (c.1615–81), Giovanni Battista Branta (d. after 1684), Robert de Visée (guitarist to the Dauphin in the late 17th and early 18th century), Gaspar Sanz (c.1640–c.1710), and Santiago de Murcia (early 18th century).

The 19th century is dominated by the figures of two guitarist–composers, in Italy Mauro Giuliani (1781–1829) and in Spain Fernando Sor, who was styled 'the Beethoven of the guitar'. Lesser contributions are by Matteo Carcassi (1792–1853), Ferdinando Carulli (1770–1841), Dionysio Aguado (1784–1849), and Napoléon Coste (1806–83), whose didactic works are still the basis of much classical guitar instruction today. Nor should it be forgotten that Schubert, Paganini, and Weber all played the guitar and wrote chamber music including it. One of Schubert's friends, Umlauf, records that he used to visit him in the mornings before he got out of bed, and usually found him with a guitar in his hands—'He generally sang to me newly composed songs to his guitar.'

In chamber music the guitar has featured in the 20th century in works from Webern and Schoenberg to Henze and Maxwell Davies. The tradition of guitarist–composer has extended from Tárrega (who has, on his part, been called 'the Chopin of the guitar') to Leo Brouwer (b. 1939).

Important solo works have also been written by Villa-Lobos, Castelnuovo-Tedesco, Turina, Moreno Tórroba (b. 1891), Joaquín Rodrigo (the popular *Concierto de Aranjuez*), Manuel Ponce, Lennox Berkeley, Benjamin Britten, Malcolm Arnold, Stephen Dodgson, André Previn (a Concerto for acoustic and electric guitars), and many other non-guitarists during the present century.

In addition, music for lute, harpsichord, cello, violin, etc., has frequently been published and performed in arrangement for guitar, a tacit acknowledgement of the fact that so relatively few major composers of the past wrote for the instrument.

8. *'Guitars' only in name.* *English guitar (with Portuguese *guitarra*); harp-guitar (see HARP-LUTE); Hawaiian guitar (with *Pedal Steel*).

Bellow 1970; Grunfeld 1969; Heartz 1963; Jahnel 1963; Longworth 1975; Montanaro 1983; Murphy 1970; Sloane 1966; Turnbull 1974; Tyler 1975; Usher 1956.

Guitarra. Sp., 'guitar', but in Portugal the pear-shaped metal-strung 'Portuguese guitar' of the 18th century to the present time, a descendant of the *cittern: see ENGLISH GUITAR, 3.

Guitarillo, guitarró. Names for small guitar used in folk music of Spain and Latin America; see GUITAR, 5; TIPLE.

Guitarrón. A large folk guitar (the sides sometimes 13 cm. or 5″ deep) with from four to 25 strings of gut, metal, or both, made in various forms, especially from Mexico to Chile. Mostly it has eight or so frets. In Mexico, in a *son* (folk ensemble), it has been replacing the harp in the accompaniment to small guitars (vihuela, jarana, etc.). A Chilean type includes to each side of the main courses a pair of short gut strings (*diablitos* or 'trebles') tuned by pegs at the shoulders of the body and contributing high 'drone' notes (cf. the Italian *chitarra battente*). The five main courses are from triple to quintuple, the third including a thick gut string (*bordoncillo*) tuned an octave below the others, which are here metal. The tuning is that of the guitar, but may be set a third or fourth lower.

Gumbang. See BLOWN GONG.

Gunbrī (or *gnībrī*). A simple finger-plucked lute of North Africa, basically a 'long lute' (see LUTE, 7), with the body of wood, a tortoise-shell, gourd, etc., a skin belly, and a pole-like wooden neck (see MIDDLE EAST, Pl. 1, far right), sometimes painted with red or green bands. The tuning pegs are through this neck. The larger instruments (played also South to the Gambia) have usually three strings, the smaller two, tuned to a fifth. There may be a pellet bell on the end of the neck. The instrument has latterly become a familiar object in the tourist shops of Morocco, etc.

Gusla (or *gusle*). Poet's one-stringed *fiddle of southern parts of Yugoslavia, up to 80 cm. (32″) long and held downwards on the knee. Made from a single piece of wood, the shallow oval body is skin-covered and the top of the long neck is traditionally carved with a horse's head. The horse-hair string is bowed with a short arched bow and stopped in the old manner (see FIDDLE, 1) by two or three fingers to make notes roughly a semitone apart, played in constantly changing patterns in vigorous, agitated tempo as a running background to long recitations of heroic epics. Ex. 1 shows (*a*) a characteristic opening phrase, and (*b*) one which may follow later.

Other one-string fiddles accompany narrations and ballads among the Bedouin of Arabia, (see RABAB, 2), in Rajastan in India, and elsewhere.

Gusli (Ru.). Two different stringed folk instruments have this name.

1. 'Wing' or 'bell' gusli, so called from the shape: see KANTELE, the Finnish instrument to which this gusli is akin.

2. 'Helmet' gusli, of Central Russia, a kind of *psaltery, in its older form about a metre (3′) long, held on edge across the knees (or carried on a sling) with the humped side uppermost. The 15 or more gut strings run from side to side (longest string lowermost) over curving bridges on the large pine soundboard which, to the player's left, overhangs a smaller, hollowed-out soundbox attached to it behind. The tuning is diatonic except in the bass, where the traditional music may call for only certain notes of the scale. The right hand plucks the melody and the left, the accompaniment of bass notes and chords.

Known from pictures back to the 14th century, this gusli has been a special favourite among the

Gusla, Ex. 1.

Mari (Cheremiss), said to have been played in every farmhouse by the women. It has since been modernized for concert use, some in 'furniture' models on legs, with 40 strings and levers for raising strings in order to play in different keys, and techniques have become more elaborate, with full chords for both hands, damping with the hand where necessary.

H

Hackbrett. See DULCIMER, 2.

Haegum. Korean fiddle, related to the Chinese *erhu. See CHINA AND KOREA, 2c.

Halbmond. See BUGLE, 3.

Halil. See BIBLICAL INSTRUMENTS, 1f.

Halszither. See CITTERN, 5b.

Hammerclavier (or Hammerklavier). Name for the piano sometimes used in Germany through the early 19th century, notably by Beethoven in several piano sonatas of around the time of the great 'Hammerclavier' (sic), Op. 106 in B♭ (1818).

Hammond organ (drawbar or tone-wheel organ). A type of electric organ (or in modern forms, electronic) that gives the notes of the music in pure tones, to which overtone pitches are added to choice, to imitate a desired tone-colour, or create new ones in endless variety, by setting the drawbars ranged above the keyboards. Introduced by Laurens Hammond in Chicago, 1935, it has been greatly used in churches and halls as well as in home music. The notes and the overtones ('harmonics', but in equal temperament) are obtained magnetically from 91 steel tone-wheels, c.5 cm. (2") wide, geared to a single motor-driven axle, each wheel rotating with the rim close to a permanent magnet wound with a coil. Each rim is profiled with a number of high points equally spaced round it. The number of times per second that a high point passes the magnet, bringing a variation of the magnetic field, gives the frequency of the small alternating current induced in the coil by that particular tone-wheel. From the 91 frequencies made all the time available, the keys select the required fundamentals plus the overtones as pre-set by the drawbars, all superimposed in a complex electrical wave made audible through an amplification and loudspeaker system.

The drawbars are marked in standard organ terminology, e.g. the most needed, the three in the middle, marked 8', 4', 2⅔' (the twelfth), and 2'. The farther a bar is pulled out, the greater the intensity of that overtone (as may be marked by numerals up to 8). Suggested drawbar settings are included in not a few publications of organ music (e.g. 00 8764 021, meaning draw out the 3rd bar to '8', the 4th to '7', and so on (to quote one of many listed for Accompanimental Diapason 8'). Lists of drawbar settings are published (as by Stevens Irwin, *Dictionary of Hammond Organ Stops*, New York, 1939, etc.). The organ will probably also have combination buttons on the left. There are normally two manuals, staggered by an octave, and two octaves of pedals.

Handbells. Sets of small bells with stiff handles of leather or plastic.

1. The bells after casting are turned on a lathe, then burnished. Foundries currently produce a range of five chromatic octaves written C–c″″ (sounding an octave higher): the deepest bell of this set is 30 cm. (12") in diameter and weighs 4½ kg. (10 lbs.), the smallest, just over 5 cm. (2"), weighing 200 g. (7 oz.). The clapper has the form of a solid shaft (Fig. 1, A) pivoted in a yoke (B) so that it is free to swing in one plane only, the bell being struck by a peg (C) fixed in each side of the clapper ball. In the smallest bells these pegs are of nylon, in the middle range of leather bound with felt, but in the largest bells the ball and pegs are replaced by a thick disc of felt. The clapper head is held out of contact with the bell by a felted leaf spring (D) on either side of the shaft. A definite flick is needed to overcome this restraint and make the clapper strike the bell, thus giving the ringer precise control over the timing of the note and its strength.

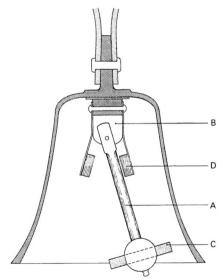

Fig. 1. Section of handbell.

There are two basic methods of playing handbells, 'in hand' and 'off table'. In the former each ringer keeps the same bell, or two bells, in each hand throughout the piece, and the sound of each bell as it is rung is usually allowed to continue. In England this method is generally adopted by the smaller teams ringing one-and-a-half to two octaves, since over this too many ringers would be needed for convenience. The 'bell choirs' of the USA are, however, usually larger than English teams and nearly all ring 'in hand', generally with only two bells per ringer and occasional ones picked up from a table. In the 'off table' style each ringer has before him on a padded table a selection of bells, sometimes as many as 20, from which he may pick them up and play any sequence of notes required of him. After being rung, each bell is returned to the table, thus extinguishing the sound when the correct duration of the note has elapsed— a technique which is here at least as important as the striking of the bell, and enables a wide variety of tonal effects and dynamics to be obtained. Given the necessary dexterity, teams of 10 to 12 ringers can play in this way sets of 140 bells or more.

The larger teams tend to play from staff notation, but the majority of teams in England ring from number and letter systems, some with individual scores, some reading from a large central score directed by the conductor.

2. It seems likely that handbells of definite pitch were originally produced in sets of up to 12 bells for change-ringers (see BELL, 4) to practise on, and that use of these bells to ring carols and simple tunes at Christmas and other church festivals led to the development of tune-ringing on handbells for its own sake. The idea of playing on large sets of bells laid out on mattress-covered tables evolved in Yorkshire and Lancashire in the early 1800s and soon spread throughout the country, and by Victorian times sets of 150–200 bells were used in playing selections from operetta, oratorio, and the popular music of the day. In some parts of the north of England almost every village had a team.

There was a general decline in handbell ringing after the First World War. The last national championship was held in Manchester in 1925, and within a few years there were only a handful of teams left. The art was revived first in the USA, leading to the formation of the American Guild of English Handbell Ringers in 1954. A resurgence of interest in England followed and a national society, the Handbell Ringers of Great Britain, was formed in 1967. In 1978 over 300 teams were registered with it, and 2,000 individual members. A Japanese guild was launched in 1976 and teams have been formed in many other countries. Handbells have also long been played in Europe, as in Spain, the brotherhood of Campanilleros in Murcia playing at religious festivals.

Britten calls for a team of handbells in his church opera *Noye's Fludde*.

3. 'Handbell' can also, of course, mean the single bell, or pair of bells, of heavier build and far-carrying sound, used by town-criers and others since the Middle Ages (see MEDIEVAL INSTRUMENTS, Pl. I), and familiar in Britain up to not long ago with the muffin man on Sundays.

Hand-drum. Popular general term for a *drum played with the fingers, not with sticks.

Hand-horn. A main method of playing the horn through the Classical period. See HORN, 6.

Haotung. Chinese trumpet. See LABA.

Hardanger fiddle (Norwegian: *Hardingfela*). A very distinctive violin of folk music in Norway, usually decorated with much inlay, and carrying four or more metal *sympathetic strings in addition to the four playing strings. The 4th of these is often tuned to A (not G), and the sympathetics to the tonic chord of the music, which consists mainly of dance tunes, played with much double-stopping and 'drone' notes. The fingerboard and bridge are flatter than on a modern violin. The instrument has been known since the 17th century, said to have been first made in Hardanger (near Bergen). Grieg knew it well, and used its tunes for example in Op. 72 ('Norwegian Peasant Dances') for piano. Collections of its music have been published in Norway, as Gurvin 1958–67.

Harmonica (short for mouth-harmonica; also mouth-organ). The small mouth-blown instrument sounded with *free reeds. (For some other uses of the name, sometimes written 'armonica', see GLASS HARMONICA and GLOCKENSPIEL, 3.)

1. *Diatonic harmonica*. The body is a cedar-wood block cut with square openings (Fig. 1*b*). Attached to this above and below are the brass plates with brass reeds riveted on. The typical 10-hole 'vamper' harmonica (*a*) has 10 reeds to each plate: on the underside of the upper plate (*c*) to sound only when air is blown into the holes; and on the underside of the lower plate, to sound only when air is inhaled through the holes (the 'draw'). The instrument is held by the left hand with the lower notes to the left (as on a keyboard). The reeds which sound on the blow give the notes of the common chord of the keynote of the instrument, commonly C (as in Fig. 1); this leaves D, F, A, and B to be sounded on the draw (except that the second hole from the left gives G to make a dominant chord in the bottom register). The alternate blow and draw up the scale prevents running out of breath, since diatonic melodies on the whole require 'blow' and 'draw' notes in equal number.

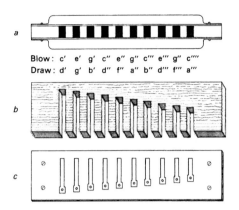

Blow: c' e' g' c" e" g" c''' e''' g''' c''''
Draw: d' g' b' d" f" a" b" d''' f''' a'''

Fig. 1. (a) Diatonic harmonica in C with its notes; (b) body; (c) upper plate with its reeds, placed face-downwards upon (b).

The basic 'vamping' technique is for the tongue to cover three holes where possible to the left of the hole required by the melody. While continuing to sound this note the tongue can be quickly drawn back to add the appropriate accompanying chord, such as on off-beats. The palm of the right hand (fingers pointing upwards) is cupped over the left, and moved to open and close the space between, making a tremolo.

Countless variations have been made on this basic harmonica, principally in duplication of the reeds (two for each note), either in octaves, or for 'tremolo tuning' where one reed is tuned slightly sharper to cause a beat. One can also purchase a wire harmonica holder, placed on the shoulders to hold the instrument for playing it in 'one-man band' fashion, leaving the hands free to strum a guitar or suchlike (or, in the old days, even dance with your partner).

2. *Chromatic harmonica.* The type used by those who adopt the harmonica as a main performing instrument. It embodies, in effect, in a single casing, one harmonica on top of another tuned to a scale a semitone higher, thus the upper in C, the lower in C♯. A spring-loaded button on the right-hand end is fixed to a slide which, when pushed in by the right forefinger, blocks off the C row and opens the other. With 10 holes the scales have the same form as on a diatonic harmonica. Better, and used by soloists, is the 12-hole type, which avoids the different pairing of notes per hole (blow/draw) that occurs between the different octaves of the 10-hole harmonica (Fig. 1) by duplicating the keynote to make four notes of the common chord, C-C-E-G (on the 'blow'), matching in number the four notes D-F-A-B made on the 'draw'. Twelve holes then give a three-octave compass from Middle C with no gaps and giving every note a semitone higher with the slide pushed in (when also C becomes alternatively available on the draw, and F on the blow).

The holes for the melody are selected with the mouth and lips (or two holes if playing in thirds), until the tongue is needed to block off intermediate holes when playing notes at a larger interval apart, up to an octave or more, or following one such interval by another contrapuntally. The artistry attained by soloists like Larry Adler (b. 1914) on this 12-hole chromatic harmonica has inspired works with orchestra by Vaughan Williams, Milhaud, Berger, and Malcolm Arnold. Tommy Reilly is well known among the more recent solo artists. Latterly astonishing effects have been obtained using an attached amplifier while also making all manner of sounds with the voice.

3. *Chord and bass harmonicas.* Harmonicas can be obtained built in almost any key, and also in 'tenor tuning' an octave lower. For harmonica bands there are special instruments designed for giving simple chords, chord and bass, or just bass notes. The small chord instrument gives, from left to right, on the 'blow': C, C chord, G, G chord, F, F chord; on the 'draw', the corresponding dominant sevenths. The bass instrument gives a chromatic scale of 14 notes from c to c♯', all on the 'blow'. Both kinds are available in larger sizes, and some as two instruments hinged together.

4. *History.* Christian Friedrich L. Buschmann (1805–64) is said to have come upon the idea by chance while making an organ-tuning instrument in his father's workshop in Berlin (c.1821). He later took credit for the invention of the harmonica, and the accordion as well. The earliest examples had reeds played only by blowing, set in pipes, rather like *panpipes. From this the familiar instrument was quickly developed. Matthias Hohner, originally a clock-maker, took over making the harmonicas of Christian Messner; his firm, founded in 1857 in Trossingen, Germany, eventually acquired a virtual monopoly in harmonica manufacture, having incorporated many of the smaller firms.

See MELODICA for small mouth-blown instruments differing from a harmonica in being played with piano-style or button keys.

Harmonichord. See GEIGENWERK.

Harmonics. Frequencies that are related as members of a *harmonic series. Harmonics enter constantly in the playing of wind instruments; but in practice, the actual term is most used in connection with stringed instruments, from *violin to *double bass, and also certain others (*guitar, *harp: see below, 2).

1. *Violin, etc.* A harmonic is made by lightly touching a string with a left-hand finger at some nodal point. A harmonic which has a node at that point will then be heard, but not the fundamental nor any harmonic which occurs lower in the series than the one being sought, since all these require the freedom of an antinode at or near that point

(the open loops in Fig. 1). The harmonics are either (a) 'natural', i.e. of the open string; or (b) 'artificial', i.e. of the string when stopped against the fingerboard. In notation of harmonics a diamond-shaped note marks, in terms of ordinary fingering, the place on the string where it is to be touched.

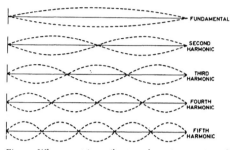

Fig. 1. When a string vibrates, there is a series of harmonic modes tending to generate overtones at 2, 3, 4, 5, etc. times the funamental frequency.

(a) *Natural harmonics* (first met for the violin c.1738, in sonatas by Mondonville, in France). The whole string vibrates at one of its harmonic frequencies, offering a limited number of high notes on each string with a quality which the German term 'flageolet tone' expresses fairly well. The first four harmonics (actually Nos. 2 to 5 in the harmonic series) are shown diagrammatically in Fig. 1. Touching at half-way gives the octave harmonic; one-third of the way from either end for the twelfth above the open string (that towards the bridge being convenient when the hand is in high positions); a quarter from either end for the double-octave harmonic; one-fifth, or equally two-fifths, from either end for two octaves plus a major third above the open string, little used on the violin though on the longer strings of *cello and double bass this and higher harmonics are feasible, the nodal points lying further apart and better for the fingers quickly to distinguish.

Ex. 1 shows two notations, the simplest (a) by writing the actual sound of the harmonic with a small circle over it (originally deriving from the 'open string' sign, i.e. the whole string vibrates); or else (b) to mark by a diamond the place to be touched, with the harmonic above as a small note in brackets.

(b) *Artificial harmonics*. Other notes can be played as a harmonic by stopping the string with one finger and touching it with another. Normally it is the double-octave harmonic, stopping with the first finger (or on the larger instruments the thumb) and touching with the little finger, the distance between being one quarter of the stopped string length—though on the violin, one-third of the length can sometimes be reached, for the next harmonic above. The *stopped* note is written as an ordinary note; a diamond above it marks where the little finger *touches*: e.g. Ex. 1c (violin): finger

d'' (A string) and touch at the place where one would stop the string for the note g'', i.e. a quarter of the way up the string from d'', the harmonic sounding two octaves above this, i.e. d'''' (which is sometimes added in brackets to make sure). Entire scales can in this way be played in harmonics.

Ex. 1.

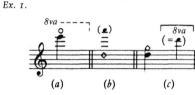

2. *Plucked instruments*. Natural harmonics: touching with the right index finger when the nodal point is from midway onwards towards the bridge; also for artificial harmonics the right index normally does the touching. Notation observes the same principles as for the violin. See also HARP, 4. Among many non-Western stringed instruments, *musical bow, with which the music is based wholly on natural harmonics selected in various ways; *tuila (India), and *qin (China), are among species on which harmonics are essential in the playing.

3. *Flute*. Rarely in flute music, a small circle over a note (or 'flag', for 'flageolet tone'), as illustrated in Stravinsky's *Rite of Spring* (figure 87 in the score) where the three flutes play a high chord of C, each note as a harmonic (the 3rd, 4th, and 5th) of the lowest C, instead of with the ordinary fingerings, resulting in a weird 'disembodied' effect.

Harmonic series. This series, which underlies music in so many vital ways, is set out here for quick reference particularly in connection with *'harmonics' on violin etc., *'overblowing' on the woodwind, and in making the notes on *brass instruments and some of other kinds. See also PARTIALS.

1. *The series*. The mathematical series, $1, \frac{1}{2}, \frac{1}{3}, \frac{1}{4}$, etc., is musically represented in divisions of the length of a string (or, in wind instruments, of an air-column). The corresponding relative frequency-values follow the reciprocal series 1, 2, 3, 4, etc., (twice the wave-length corresponding to half the frequency, and so on). See Ex. 1, which follows the convention of demonstrating the harmonic series on the musical staff with the note C as '1' (the fundamental of the series). As a visual guide, the Cs are shown by minims, each C having twice the frequency of the one before, as matched in the numbering. While most of the practical applications among instruments concern harmonics up to about 8 or 16 only, the series is shown up to 24, which occurs as a note in some 18th-century music for horn and trumpet.

Ex. 1.

2   3   4   5 6 7 8   9 10 11 12

13 14 15 16   17 18 19 20 21 22 23 24   etc.

Every interval in the series is expressible as the ratio of the two numbers involved, e.g. from G, 3 up to E, 5 as 3:5, the natural or 'just' major sixth (and similarly from D up to B, 9:15 = 3:5). Should one or both notes of an interval not be found in this series based on C, the ratio can be gained from a series based on some other note, e.g. F to A, 4 and 5 of the series with fundamental F, 4:5, pure major third just as C to E.

Alternatively intervals may be expressed in *cents (see Table 1) by subtracting the cent values.

TABLE 1.

(1) Harmonic number
(2) Cents above C, to nearest whole number
(3) For comparison, notes of the scale in equal temperament

(1)	(2)		(3)
1, 2, 4, 8	0	C	0
9	204	D	200
5, 10	386	E	400
11	551	(F	500)
3, 6, 12	702	G	700
13	840	(A	900)
7, 14	969	(B♭	1000)
15	1088	B	1100
16	1200	C	1200

Higher harmonics of Ex. 1, omitting octaves of those given above:

17	105	C♯	100
19	298	E♭	300
21	471	(F	500)
23	628	(F♯	600)

2. *The series and the scale.* The ratios between consecutive harmonics are ever-decreasing up the series, which means that intervals occur which do not exist in a scale. We do find an apparent fragment of a scale in 8, 9, 10 of the series (C, D, E) but even here 8:9 signifies a bigger interval than 9:10, bigger by 81:80, in music theory the 'Didymian comma', just over a fifth part of a semitone. In practical music this difference can be

evened out such as by mean-tone or equal-temperament tuning (see TEMPERAMENT). The intervals, however, which involve prime numbers from 7 upwards, or their multiples, are foreign to our conventional harmony. Thus above 5 to 6, minor third (three semitones), comes 6 to 7, close to $2\frac{2}{3}$ semitones, putting harmonic 7 at about a third of a semitone flat to B♭ (indicated in Ex. 1 by the line over the note), and 7 to 8, close to $2\frac{1}{3}$ semitones: two intervals that have sometimes been called 'septimal third' (267 cents) and 'septimal tone' (231 cents). Yet, though a misfit in the diatonic scale, the 7th harmonic is there plain enough in nature and (besides sometimes serving as B♭ on natural brass instruments, as BUGLE, Ex. 1) can make beautiful natural consonances nowhere better heard than (for voices) in Stockhausen's *Stimmung* (1968).

Then the prime numbers 11 and 13: 11 lies close to half-way between F and F♯ in the chromatic scale, and 13 somewhere between G♯ and A (the quarter-tone signs shown against these harmonics in Ex. 1 are those which modern Egyptian musicians have employed for writing their three-quarter tone intervals in Western notation). A number of instruments over the world which can sound only natural harmonics employ 11 and 13 for making scale-like tunes (see JEW'S-HARP; FLUTE, 8) or to serve as F and A in the diatonic scale (see especially TRUMPET, 3c).

Harmonium. A *free-reed organ with foot-bellows: European equivalent to the American *reed-organ with an essential difference in having pressure bellows whereas in the American instrument the bellows draw in air from above by suction. Though harmoniums have not been manufactured since the 1930s, many remain in use, largely in halls and small churches, though the harmonium was intended by its French inventors firstly as an instrument for the household.

1. *Construction.* Inside the case the main components are in four tiers, the upper tiers being removable one by one for inspection. Lowest are the bellows, one for each foot. Above them, the reservoir, an enclosed pressure-equalizer sprung to expand by coil springs underneath. Next above, the wind-chest with, in the top, holes controlled by pallets operated by the stop knobs to admit air to each required register of reeds. Lastly, on top, the 'pan', the kernel of the instrument containing the reeds. The air from the bellows is led directly up to the wind-chest, outside the reservoir, through square wooden ducts or 'wind-trunks' (or 'chimneys') each with a non-return flap valve at the top. The air then passes downwards from the wind-chest into the reservoir below through a wide hole under a palette which rests normally open. The object of thus leading the air from the bellows first to the wind-chest and then to the reservoir below becomes apparent later (below, 'Expression').

2. *The stops.* Inside the pan are four (or more) separate channels running from left to right, one behind the other, one for each of four registers of reeds. Above, their partitions are crossed by the nearly 60 partitions separating the reed chambers for each note of the five-octave compass (C–c′′′). A small instrument may have but a single set of reeds; but four sets provide the normal basis for a harmonium, numbered 1 to 4 as they and their channels lie from front to back. Each set is divided in two halves, bass and treble, by a partition, each half brought into action by its own stop-knob: one for the bass up to the note e′, the other from f′ upwards. This makes eight stops, and to play treble and bass together it is necessary to have drawn at least two stops, one for the bass half, the other over the treble—not necessarily from the same set of reeds.

The standard arrangement is as in Table 1, the stops customarily retaining their names in French. The different tones come from reeds of different widths and thicknesses, but also from the relative sizes of the chambers above the reeds, the more constricted the thinner, more reedy, the tone (higher partials excited in the air as it passes through). Frequent additional stops are two which act over the whole compass: 'G' ('Grand Jeu'), bringing all the above into action; and 'E' ('Expression'). This last closes the hole between wind-chest and reservoir, rendering the latter inoperative, so that variations in pressure from the bellows are passed straight to the reeds, allowing full dynamic modulation whilst playing (though requiring very practised co-ordination of the two feet).

TABLE 1.

Register	Bass	Treble
1. 8′ (*Eight-foot), the main, smooth tone:	Cor anglais	Flute
2. 16′, an octave deeper:	Bourdon	Clarinette
3. 4′, an octave higher:	Clairon	Fifre
4. 8′, more reedy:	Basson	Hautbois

Of further stops (not always named the same), one may be '5': on the treble side 'Musette', a reedy rank at the lower octave; on the bass side 'Sourdine', which plays the 'Cor anglais' with reduced wind. Then, 'O' ('Forte'), combining on each side Nos. 3 and 4; 'C' ('Voix Celeste'), on the treble side, an off-tuned rank combined with the 'Clarinette' to give a 'beat' effect; and 'T' ('Tremolo'), the 'clarinette' sounded with pulsating wind.

3. *History.* An early recorded keyboard application of free reeds was in the *orgue expressif* (Paris, 1810) of G. J. Grenié, who himself said that he had seen an organ built in 1780 with a register of free-reed pipes; 'expressif' alluding to the ability, with free reeds (in contrast to normal organ reeds), to swell the music from total silence, and to keep always in tune. From about the same time in the USA, Ebenezer Goodrich in Boston was making free-reed organs, some apparently dispensing with pipes. The name 'harmonium' appears first in the patent of François Debain (Paris, 1840), to which, two years later, he added extra sets of reeds in divided ranks as now. He then sold the rights to make instruments on his system to Alexandre *père et fils* in 1844 on condition that they did not use the name. They therefore named the instruments 'orgue melodium', and became by far the largest manufacturers; their instruments, with the 'expression stop', were played in concerts by Saint-Saëns, and by Sigismond Thalberg, whose playing moved Berlioz to tears of emotion. Alexandre (who had been making accordions from 1829) further managed to buy the rights for other improvements to the harmonium, including the 'percussion action' invented by L.-P. Martin (Paris, 1842): with this, on pressing a key, a tiny felted hammer strikes the reed of each note of the principal (No. 1) rank, causing it to speak more quickly than it would naturally.

The next leading innovator was Victor Mustel (1815–90; see also CELESTA), a foreman for Alexandre, who set up on his own after having invented the 'double expression', by which the player can control the treble and bass wind pressure separately, by knee levers. The firm was still making instruments in the 1930s. There have been makers in Britain also, for example Hattersley (Sheffield), and Dawes and Rainden, who have invented further additional devices (the 'Vocalion', exhibited in 1885 by J. B. Hamilton and later made in the USA also, has broader reeds, with the stop pallets above them and the note pallets below). Demand for the instruments was increased by small theatre and restaurant orchestras using a harmonium to supply absent missing wind parts; published arrangements for 'salon orchestra' often included a harmonium part for this purpose.

4. *Repertory.* In the harmonium's early days many duets were written for it with piano, for drawing-room performance. Saint-Saëns wrote two sets of pieces; César Franck arranged his own Prelude, Fugue, and Variations and composed many other pieces for the instrument, ending with the 55 pieces in *L'organiste* (completed 1900). Rossini originally scored his *Petite Messe solenelle* (1863) for two pianos and harmonium. The only keyboard music written by Berlioz are three pieces for harmonium (1845). Dvořák's Bagatelles (Op. 47) for harmonium and string quartet were written for a friend who possessed an instrument. Karg-Elert, too, wrote much for the instrument besides his organ works.

5. *Indian harmonium.* The Indian harmonium or 'drone box' is small and portable, about 60 cm. (2′) long. The bellows are on the back for the left hand, while the right can play on the keyboard.

There are stops for drones, and from two to four brass reeds per note.

Ord-Hume 1986.

Harp (Fr.: *harpe*; Ger.: *Harfe*; It., Sp.: *arpa*; Ru.: *arfa*). Harps perpetuate perhaps the most ancient way of harnessing many strings to a soundbox, running from this to a 'neck' at an angle giving them different lengths while standing free to be plucked with the hands from both sides without obstruction. For ancient forms, and those now played in Africa and Asia, see 10 below.

1. General structure and tuning (Western harps). The strings rise from a sloping soundbox (or soundchest) at an angle of about 36 degrees to a curving neck where they are tuned with a key; a straight or out-curving pillar (or column) completes the strong, three-membered construction. The strings are tuned to a diatonic scale, with the small distance between them that suits the fingers with the hands held thumbs upwards (as against thumbs inwards on a keyboard). This poses the question of how, or whether, to provide for accidentals. The ancient tradition of making no such provision continues among many small 'folk' harps, and the fine harps of Latin America (7, 8 below). Designs with additional strings tuned to accidentals have long been tried, as in the Welsh triple harp (6) which some still play. But a major solution is that whereby strings can be shortened while playing to make any desired accidentals, here leading to the pedal harp (2–5), which today in the orchestra stands alone among wholly finger-plucked stringed instruments as that which possesses the volume and power to hold a regular place in symphonic orchestration.

2. Soundchest and neck. The lower ends of the strings are led through holes in a hardwood 'string-bar' which runs down the centre of the soundboard and has a matching bar on the inside. The soundchest has open slots in the back, serving both as soundholes and to enable strings to be knotted or tied to toggles before being drawn tight to the neck, and (in most cases) wedged them in the string-bar by thick pins. The soundboard (or belly) is generally of spruce, usually with the grain (sometimes hidden under a veneer) running from side to side (i.e. at right angles to the string-bar, as in other stringed instruments it runs at right angles to the bridge). It is up to 10 mm. thick, to answer to a total string-tension which in a concert harp may exceed 700 kg. weight (two-thirds of a ton).

Often today the belly bulges out in the lower part (Pl. 1, right), enclosing an air-space underneath, to give added resonance to the bass strings—a feature adopted in the 1920s by the celebrated Chicago harp-makers, Lyon and Healy, and Wurlitzer (who had commenced harp-making in 1889 and 1909 respectively).

The graceful dip, or 'harmonic curve', in the neck is the natural result of the strings rising at a fixed distance apart from a sloping base line, following an underlying principle that their lengths should double for each octave difference (Fig. 1). This, taken literally, would result in the top curve shown in the figure. In fact, as shown by the broken line, the increase across an octave may be nearer 1 : 1.8, since the strings increase in thickness from treble to bass (as in most other stringed instruments) while increasing somewhat in tension as well. Further, the ratio has to be drastically reduced in the bass octave to avoid the deeper strings becoming impracticably long; these are,

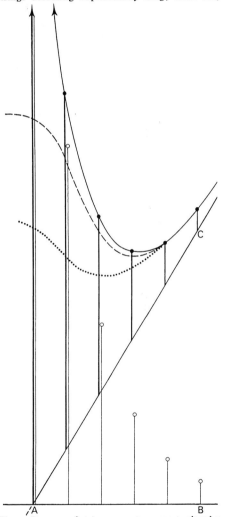

Fig. 1. Diagram of strings an octave apart, placed a certain distance apart and doubling in length for each octave. Shown in fine line: perpendicular to horizontal base AB; in heavy line: the same lengths arising from slope AC, producing a curve with a dip. The modified curves (broken line and dotted line) are also based on AC.

Pl. 1. Modern harps: 'Troubadour' model (*left*), and pedal harp by Lyon and Healy, Chicago (*right*).

therefore, considerably increased in weight (overwound strings replacing gut in the bottom octave), allowing the curve of the neck to flatten out towards the column of the harp and keeping the height of the instrument within bounds. In a harp of small stature, as with Celtic designs, the curve can be still flatter (Fig. 1, dotted line).

3. *The pedal mechanism.* The seven pedals project from the wooden base to which the pillar and soundchest are attached by bolts. The pillar, up to 6' tall, is hollow to contain the seven rods leading up from the pedals to the mechanism of steel links and bell-cranks housed between the broad brass plates of the 'comb' to operate the forks. These are visible on the outside below the bridge-pins against which the strings bear after leaving the tuning pins placed above the comb. There is a pedal for each note of the diatonic scale, acting simultaneously on that note throughout the compass of six and a half octaves upwards from the lowest D (or C) of the piano to the highest G. The strings number 47 (or 48), the gut C strings coloured red and F strings blue. The pedals, from left to right, are for D, C, B (left foot); E, F, G, A (right foot). Each pedal has three positions and a spring to return it to the 'up' position: (i) pedal 'up', giving the note as a flat,

e.g. with the C pedal, C♭, the strings sounding with their full length (thus with all pedals 'up' the harp is tuned to the scale of C♭); (ii) lowered to first notch: the revolving forks in the neck shorten the strings by a semitone to give the natural (with all pedals in first notch the harp stands in C major); (iii) lowered to second notch: the forks now shorten the strings by a whole tone to give the sharp, C♯ etc.

Fig. 2 shows diagrammatically how the forks act, each being a brass plate with two projecting pins between which the string passes. In pedal position (*a*) the string passes clear; in position (*b*) the pedal has turned fork A clockwise, not itself to grip the string but, via the bell-crank B, to make fork C do so; in position (*c*), fork A is rotated further, itself to grip the string, but without imparting appreciable further rotation to fork C, thus minimizing the resistance to the foot.

In ordinary music with a key signature, the scale is pre-set with the pedals, e.g. for E♭ major: the B, E, and A pedals 'up' for the flats and the rest in first notch for the naturals; accidentals and modulations being pedalled as they come. A harpist can make pedal changes extremely quickly, yet there are limits to what can be done in very chromatic or atonal music. Also, a composer may

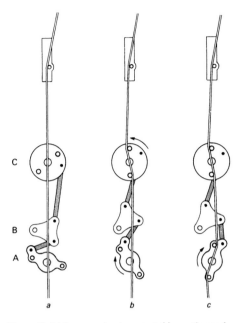

Fig. 2. Pedal harp mechanism as visible on the neck. The bridge pin at the top is shown (*a*) with pedal up; (*b*) in first notch; (*c*) in second notch.

have to think technically while writing for the harp; for example, should he write an A♮ to be played in the same instant as an A♭, then the latter must be made on the G string as G♯, and no G♮ can be played at that same moment. Such enharmonic unisons, often termed by harpists 'homophones', are very important; only three notes in the chromatic scale have no homophone, i.e. cannot be made on another string, namely D, G, and A naturals. A simple illustration of the use of homophones is the chord of the diminished seventh, e.g. from B♭ up to G: A♯/B♭, C♯/D♭, F♭, G. No string is left out, so the chord can be swept glissando over the whole compass. Or, if G is raised to G♯, we have the glissando which follows the flute at the beginning of Debussy's *Prélude à l'après-midi d'un faune.*

4. *Harp-playing.* The harp is tilted back to rest against the right shoulder. The shortest strings then lie most naturally for the outside hand, the right, and the longest for the left. Both hands are used over the whole compass, but the left will normally lead off in the bass and the right in the treble. The strings are plucked near the mid-point, where they can be pulled furthest to the side with the fingertips and the sides of the thumbs. (The little fingers are not used, so five-note chords are not written for one hand.) Numerous intricacies have to be learnt in order to play fast passages and to damp the strings with the fingers or forearms as required. Trills are perfectly possible, and by using homophones (where one exists) a note can be

'trilled' with itself on two adjacent strings. 'Près de la table' signifies plucking low down close to the soundboard, for a more metallic quality as when other stringed instruments are played close to the bridge. 'Sons étouffés' (damped sounds) are made with the thumb and instantly damped with the finger. Harmonics, so much demanded especially by the French composers and indicated by a '○' over the note, are made by touching a string at mid-point with the ball of the thumb and plucking with that same thumb; the string then sounds an octave higher. Solo music for harp has latterly come to demand many novel effects, like strange sounds made by moving the pedals while the strings are still vibrating.

5. *Repertory.* Little has been written by the great composers for harp solo, and its recital repertory rests largely on works by harp virtuosos and on arrangements of keyboard works (for example of the sixth of the first set of Handel's organ concertos, said to have been performed on the Welsh harp in 1741). Setting these aside, there are Mozart's Concerto for Flute and Harp, K. 299 (written in Paris for a Duke and his daughter; a concerto by Haydn for the same instruments is now lost); Eichner's Concerto; concertos by Glière, Reinecke, and Rodrigo; Dussek's six sonatinas; two fantasias and two sets of variations by Spohr (written for his wife); Saint-Saëns's Fantaisie, Op. 95 (with violin); Fauré's Impromptu, Op. 86, and *Une chatelaine en son tour*, Op. 110; Debussy's Sonata for Flute, Viola, and Harp; and Roussel's Impromptu, Op. 21. There is, of course, much further chamber music which includes the harp, mainly 20th-century, for example by Ravel (Introduction and Allegro), Ibert, Goossens, Françaix, and Jolivet; British composers from Bax to Britten; and, among the avant garde, Berio (*Sequenza II*, 1970).

6. *Triple harp.* The Welsh triple harp is without pedals but has an auxiliary row of strings for supplying accidentals. The normal diatonic row is duplicated, with the row of strings for the five accidentals in each octave placed in between. The diatonic scale is thus immediately available to both hands, the accidentals being reached by the fingers of either hand between the strings of the outer rows. This can be done very swiftly, and in fact makes possible chromatic passages that are beyond the powers of the pedal harp—though on the other hand it cannot do all that the pedal instrument can.

The triple harp, known in Italy around 1600 (see below, 9*b*), was adopted by the Welsh harpers in the 17th century, replacing an older single-strung harp (*telyn*) and becoming their normal instrument until it was almost wholly replaced by the pedal harp after the mid-19th century. It is usually very tall, giving great length to the bass strings, and is now made and played again in Wales. The last player in the continuous tradition,

Nanci Richards (1888–1979), played traditional music of Wales and also items from classical composers like Beethoven and Schubert.

Volumes of harp airs were compiled by John Parry of Ruabon (c.1710–82) and Edward Jones (1752–1824) and published in London. Jones's *Musical and Poetical Relics of the Welsh Bards* (1784, 1794) also contains examples of *penillion*, an intricate traditional art of improvising vocal stanzas to a traditional tune played on the harp, and revived at modern *eisteddfodau*.

7. Celtic harp, clàrsach, troubadour or minstrel's harp (Pl. 1, left). Small harps made for folk and early music, with 30 or more strings (over four complete octaves from C) and no pedals. Some can be made from kits. Most designs have, along the neck, hand-turned metal blades, or 'hooks' of metal rod bent in a 'U', by which the strings (or some of them) can be individually raised a semitone (see below, 9c). The harp can then be set in different keys and, up to a point, supply an accidental, especially with the recent 'cam' type blades needing only a push with the finger.

The Celtic harp (sometimes termed Irish harp) derives in size and shape—with the column outcurved in older Irish and medieval style—from the 'portable Irish harp' produced in Dublin about 1819, by the maker John Egan as a drawing-room successor to the old professional Irish harp. It is plucked either with the fingertips or in the older way with the nails.

Versions termed 'bardic' or 'knee harp', or by the Gaelic name *clàrsach* (in Irish, *clàirseach*) are based on older Irish and Scottish models, among them the oldest Irish survivor, the small harp (70 cm. (28″) tall, originally 30 strings) of the 14th century preserved in Trinity College, Dublin—the actual harp from which the national emblem of Ireland is copied. They are without hooks and may be strung with metal, as many historians (though not all) believe to have been an Irish⁴ manner already in the Middle Ages.

The actual harp played up to the beginning of the 19th century in Ireland and to the mid-18th in the Scottish Highlands had 30 to 36 brass strings. Some 12 of these harps are preserved, several of the Irish in the National Museum, Dublin: massive instruments, up to 150 cm. (5′) tall, with the wide soundbox hollowed out from the back (in willow or hornbeam) so that the soundboard is an integral part leaving the back to be covered by a separate board. In Ireland the players, generally blind, travelled the land with a boy to guide and carry the harp, welcomed from household to household. Among the most famous was Carolan (d. 1738), a prolific composer for the harp in both traditional and international styles. The harpers held periodic meetings (as had medieval *jongleurs*) to exchange items and compete together, their last great meeting, in Belfast, 1792, being celebrated through the detailed account by Edward Bunting,

last published in 1840. His manuscripts in Belfast contain a rare example of a folk air as actually performed, copied exactly, 'both Bass & Treble', from blind Denis Hempson, the oldest harper present; the 'bass' has just a few simple chords, otherwise supports the melody with notes here and there in the lower octaves.

8. Latin American harp. A harp of Spanish extraction, typically very large, with a straight column (Pl. 2: the legs supporting the lower end are a local variation). The neck may be of two curved pieces with a space between them crossed by the tuning pins, the strings (gut) being led into this space, instead of to one side as in other harps. Playing is usually with the nails. Over Hispanic America, and particularly in Paraguay, the harp is a leading folk instrument, heard in many kinds of instrumental ensemble, often playing the tune above the accompaniment of guitars.

9. History: (a) Early Western development. The form of the European harp can first be seen dimly in pictures and carvings of the 9th and 10th centuries—Byzantine, Celtic (in Ireland, Scotland), and in France. Where it arose first, no one really knows.

The medieval harp was small, 75 cm. (30″) tall or less, often shown placed on the knee between the player's two arms with its base resting on the bag in which it was carried about. It had about 19 strings (two and a half octaves) normally in England and on the Continent. It is often mentioned as 'merry', and we read of the 'twinkling' of the harp, reminding us of playing with the nails—'toggen with his nayles sharpe' (in an English version of *King Horn*). Machaut mentions 25 strings, also the harp's participation in his compositions, in one case naming it in a *ballade* 'De ce que folz pense'; one can imagine, in delicate polyphony of such kind, how clearly the small harp must have been heard against the voice of the player.

Renaissance harps were a little larger, up to a metre (3′) or more tall with 24 to 26 strings from F to G upwards. They seem often to have been fitted with 'brays'—wooden soundboard-pins shaped in an angle for the string to buzz against the tip, for a more lively sound. Later in Wales (c.1815) it was noted how the brays, cut from hawthorn, were used only in dance music, being otherwise easily turned off by a sideways twist. By the 17th century harps had come to be made about a foot (30 cm.) taller, adding a lower octave to make four complete octaves. A particularly rich literature comes from Spain, where the harp was much used by the clergy for training and accompanying choirs—a factor behind the wide adoption of the harp over Latin America (8 above). From Hinestrosa in 1557 to works like Nasarre's *Escuela nueva* of 1721 much of the music is written in tablature in which the numbers 1 to 7 indicate the strings of the middle octave and the same with added dots or ticks for the other octaves.

Pl. 2. Latin-American harp at Lima, Peru (early 20th century), accompanied by a type of bandurria.

(b) *Double-strung harps.* Many of these works describe how an accidental could be made by pressing the string close to the top with the left thumb or forefinger. However, in Spain as early as 1378 one reads of a 'double harp' (*arpa doble*), and, fifty years later, of an 'arpa gran doble a III tiros'—'of three pulls'—suggesting a triple harp (Lamaña 1969: 34–5). Actual instruments on both systems are preserved in Italy from the years round 1600—a period when 'arpa doppia' (a name which could evidently apply equally to the triple) is named in some dozen musical sources, in most cases as a continuo instrument (e.g. d'India, *Le musiche*, 1609), but also solo, as in *Orfeo*, in an exacting part (for which the Welsh triple harp has been successfully employed) and, with similar runs and accidentals, in works like Trabaci's second book of *ricercari* (1615). On the two-row harp, in order to keep the principal row under the left hand in the bass but the right hand in the treble, the accidentals usually change sides from left to right at mid-point.

(c) *Hook and pedal harp.* The above 'double harp' was also made in Germany up to the mid-18th century, but in that country, where the harp figured prominently in domestic and folk music, greater use was made of the single-row harp with hand-turned 'hooks' of stout iron wire for the semitones—like those of the present Celtic harp (above, 6). Even so, for a quick accidental players had to fall back on the old method of pressing with the thumb, so early in the 18th century several Bavarians, all at about the same time, devised means of turning the hooks by pedals, leaving the hands free. Just before 1750 a German, Gaiffre, showed the idea in Paris, where Naderman adopted a form of pedal-activated hook that moves in and out from the neck to pull the string against a metal

nut placed just below the hook. Next, an improved action due to Cousineau employed pairs of small 'crutches' turning in opposite directions to grip the string without displacing it vertically. Finally, just before the Revolution of 1789, Érard introduced the 'forks' which are in use today, but at first still with 'single action'—only one notch to each pedal. The harp was therefore tuned to the scale of E♭, whence it could be set in all keys round to E♮ (not, for instance, A♭ since D♭ would mean raising C to C♯, thus losing the C).

These chromatic mechanisms rapidly brought harp-playing into the higher orbits of social accomplishments. The music consisted largely of studies by virtuoso harpists like the Bohemian-born Krumpholz (d. 1790; he had received his first lessons from Haydn's father, a wheelwright, who sang to the harp by ear). Next, Bochsa, and Spohr's wife Dorette, both reared on Naderman's single-action harp. The celebrated English soloist Parish-Alvars (d. 1849) began his career on Érard's double-action harp of 1812, and went on to propose a triple (four pedal positions instead of three) which supplied the otherwise missing homophones (see above, 3). Meanwhile in the orchestra the harp had been introduced first mainly in 'historical' roles: biblical in Handel's *Esther*, played in this by a Welsh harper, no doubt on the triple harp (above, 8); or classical, as again Handel, in *Giulio Cesare* (music for the Nine Muses) and Beethoven in the ballet *Die Geschöpfe des Prometheus*; also Scottish, in Boieldieu's *La dame blanche* (1825), in which harp harmonics are said to make their first appearance in an orchestral score.

Up to the 1830s Érard made the 'Grecian' model with a volute at the top of the pillar, before changing to the familiar 'Gothic' form. Many

19th-century pedal harps are still in existence, partly through having been a regular instrument in ballroom orchestras until superseded by piano; but worn-out mechanisms can be difficult to restore. Some instruments have an eighth pedal in the middle of the seven to work shutters over the soundholes in the back for 'swell' effects.

(d) *Harpe chromatique.* A double harp (no pedals) invented in 1894 by M. G. Lyon, made by Pleyel, and for some time in Paris a serious rival to the pedal harp. The two rows of strings (76 in all) rise from two string-bars to cross at mid-point, so making every string available to both hands, above or below the cross (an idea tried earlier, 1845, by Henri Pape, and again later, *c.*1900, by H. Greenway of New York). Debussy wrote *Danse sacrée et danse profane* for it (harp and strings, 1904), but later modified it for the pedal harp. Enesco, too, wrote an *Allegro de concert,* crammed with everything playable on the chromatic but not the pedal harp.

10. *Ancient forms and descendants.* Early harps (see ANTIQUITY) have today been classified as 'arched' and 'angular', both known from Mesopotamia and Egypt.

(a) *'Arched' harps.* These have been seen as developments from the *musical bow; they have a curved wooden neck, joined to a hollowed-out soundbox, and a skin belly through which the strings pass to the wooden string-bar pressing up underneath. Such harps are today played by singers in Central Africa, mainly north of the Equator from the western savannah to Uganda (*enanga*). They have five to 10 deep-sounding strings and are held in every possible kind of way, e.g. as Pl. 3, or upside-down, or horizontally with the neck pointing away. In Ancient Egypt the small ones were held on the shoulder. Among preserved examples, some have fixed wooden pins for four strings only. The soundbox is wrapped in leather, forming the belly and sewn underneath; average total length 120 cm. (4').

India, too, knew arched harps (probably introduced from Mesopotamia) from the 2nd century BC to about the 9th AD, and named *vīnā.* For the classic Burmese arched harp, see SAÙNG; and for an archaic form still played in Afghanistan, WAJI.

(b) *'Angular' harps.* These have a straight pole-like neck jutting from a long soundbox at a right angle or just under.

(i) *'Vertical'* is where the soundbox is held upright close to the chest with the neck pointing forwards from the bottom (somewhat like a European harp held upside down). A splendid 21-stringed example from Ancient Egypt in the Louvre, Paris, along with two arched harps from the same, is 110 cm. (43") tall, again with the string-bar bearing on the skin belly, which is sewn round a wooden body strengthened by ribs from side to side. How Egyptian harps were tuned is not known, though there is

Pl. 3. African arched harp, Chad.

evidence from Babylonian clay tablets of *c.*1500 BC of systematic tuning to a scale which catered for accurate changes from one specific mode to another with minimal retuning (Duchesne-Guillemin 1966, 1969).

Some of the harps in Ancient Greek paintings (see PSALTERIUM) seem to foreshadow the Iranian *chank* played in classical ensembles up to the 19th century; similar harps had been played in China up to the 10th century AD.

(ii) *'Horizontal'* is where the soundbox lies horizontally with the neck rising from the further end. Assyrian art shows it played with a plectrum, the other hand apparently damping (as with the present *waji*). In the Caucasus are angular harps (in Georgia, *changi,* from Persian) held sideways, with six or more strings of twisted horsehair; mostly women have played it, as they did in Ancient Greece.

Morrow 1979; Rensch 1969; Rimmer 1964a, b, 1965–6; 1932.

Harpe chromatique. See HARP, 9d.

Harp-guitar. Several instruments have had this name. 1. See HARP-LUTE, 2.

2. A *guitar with a long narrowing extension to the body reaching to the floor, invented in the USA by E. N. Scherr of Philadelphia, 1831. Examples are in collections; one of them once owned by the celebrated Norwegian violinist Ole Bull (Shrine to Music *collection, South Dakota).

3. A large metal-strung guitar by Gibson, New York, 1896. The neck is offset to the treble side to carry a sideways addition to the peg-head which, further supported by a rod leading up from the soundbox, carries 10 unfingered bass strings. In a later design, instead of the supporting rod, the soundbox itself is extended upwards under the bass strings (as had been done a century previously in the French *arcicistre*; see ENGLISH GUITAR, 2).

Harp-lute. I. English Regency-period instrument for ladies, of individual design invented 1811 by the London organist and teacher Edward Light (b. c.1747). Very many were made, now minor collector's items. Pl. I shows the characteristic body shape, with gilt floral borders over a coloured ground, and nearest the player, the thin harp-like pillar from which a thick neck of complex form undulates downwards. The back is built in staves (as then used in harps). In the harp-lute itself (for this and other varieties see Baines 1966), the neck is less massive than shown, with about nine frets to serve the seven highest strings (of gut). The first four of these are tuned to the chord of E♭ (the notes, however, written in the music a sixth higher, as Ex. 1, from one of Light's publications). The next three, and five open strings beyond, continue downwards diatonically. Three of the latter can be individually raised a semitone by turning a 'ring stop' (a brass oval with a hole through which the string passes) or, one of them more quickly from lower down by rod and thumb-lever. The right hand meanwhile plucks with the fingers, aided by the left thumb. Most instruments were made for Light by A. Barry, London.

Pl. 1. Harp-lute, engraving (*c.* 1816) by Minasi and Stadler after Burney; this particular form was known as the 'British harp-lute'.

Light published a Tutor for harp-lute and also for his next main model, the 19-stringed 'British harp-lute' (1816, later called 'dital harp'; Pl. I). The frets are now reduced to very few, to serve the top string only, or abolished altogether, the instrument becoming more 'harp', less 'lute'. Up to 13 of the strings can be raised a semitone, some by 'ring stops' as above, others by rods moved out from the neck by concealed links and cranks leading from finger-buttons ('ditals', by analogy with

Ex. 1.

'pedal') on the back for the left hand. Later (1828), Light's rival A. B. Ventura, from Italy, replaced these devices by a fork mechanism (with added locking-on catches) as used on Érard's pedal harp; this he called 'harp Ventura'.

2. Prior to the harp-lute, Light had produced (c.1798) his harp-guitar, an *English guitar modified with stave-built body and one or two extra strings; and a harp-lute-guitar, with an archlute-like upper pegbox for further additional strings (see ENGLISH GUITAR—Armstrong 1908).

3. 'Harp-lute' as a modern European name for an instrument of West Africa: see KORA.

Harp-psaltery. See PSALTERY, 2.

Harpsichord (Fr.: *clavecin*; Ger.: *Cembalo, Kielflügel*; It.: *clavicembalo*; Ru.: as Fr.; Sp.: *clavecímbano, clave*. In Eng. 'virginal' originally meant the harpsichord as well as the smaller instrument since known by this name, the word 'harpsichord' appearing during the early 17th century and coming from *arpicordo*, a less common It. name met from c.1690.)

1. *Construction.* Harpsichord, *spinet, and *virginal are all keyboard instruments with wire strings plucked by very small plectra, each held separately in an upright wooden strip or 'jack' (Pl. 1, and see 3, below). For a comparison of their shapes, see SPINET, Fig. 1. The harpsichord ranks as the chief of the three, capable of the fullest sound, through having room for (and usually possessing) two, or three, sets of strings, making up to three strings for every note of the compass, each individual string plucked by its own jack. The jacks for each set of strings form together a row across the instrument from side to side: should less volume of sound be required, a row can be shunted sideways (e.g. by a stop knob) for its jacks not to pluck, leaving the strings of another set (or 'choir') to sound when the keys are pressed. Only quite late in the 18th century were some devices introduced for disengaging or re-engaging a row of jacks without interrupting the playing: indeed, not all early models back to the 16th century had provision for doing so at all, the instruments then sounding at a constant loudness. For the harpsichord player, unlike a pianist or clavichordist, commands no variation of loud and soft by 'touch' alone. Certainly, as the great François Couperin reminds us, writing in 1717, 'it is reasonable to believe that if a finger falls on the key from high, it gives a drier blow than if kept near it, and that the plectrum draws a harsher tone from the string'. Yet however fast or gently a key is pressed the plectrum deflects the string before releasing it always by the same amount dependent on how it is made and fixed in the jack by the maker: the amplitude of the string vibration is virtually unalterable. Yet the skilful player is continually creating illusions of expressive dynamics by other means, for example by contrasts between staccato sound and legato, and between a slowly 'spread' chord and a sharply struck one.

Harpsichord making today generally acknowledges the instrument's true historical nature, rather than following more elaborate modernized models variously influenced by piano construction—with overwound strings in the bass and sometimes a whole row of pedals for changing instantly between numerous stops—which followed upon the resumption of harpsichord manufacture, first in Paris in the 1880s (notably by Pleyel), after the instrument had been very little played for near 80 years. (For 'historical' fingering see KEYBOARD, 3b.)

2. *Layout* (Fig. 1, after Hubbard, a simplified view from above, without the lid, of an early Flemish harpsichord: only certain of the strings, mostly for C over the compass, are shown). The frame comprises: the long straight 'spine' (left); short 'tail'; long, partly curving 'bentside'; and straight 'cheekpiece' (lower right). Round the inside are 'liners' on which rests the soundboard (spruce or pine, averaging 3 mm. ($\frac{1}{8}$") thick) with its front edge on the deep 'belly rail' running across the frame next to the space for the rows of jacks (indicated by 4, 8 in Fig. 1). The frame is strengthened internally by wooden cross-bracing on the bottom level, with wooden ribs above. Underneath, the 'bottom boards' are normally put on last, except in the old Italian practice, where the bottom is laid out first and the sides are built up on this, strengthened by shoe-like 'knees' between sides and bottom, often augmented by struts sloping down from the liners (today there are kits following either principle of construction).

Forwards from the space for the jacks is the heavy 'wrest plank' (D in Fig. 2) bearing the 'wrest pins' (tuning pins) and supported on a stout block on each side. The instrument in Fig. 1 has two sets of strings: the longer '8'' choir which sounds the actual notes of the music (see EIGHT-FOOT); and a '4'' choir of shorter strings tuned an octave higher. The latter are normally sounded only with the 8' choir and seldom by themselves; the octave (4') strings add great brightness to the notes of the 8'—though there are also Renaissance models with no 4' (see below, 7a).

The 8' strings pass from their 'hitchpins' driven into the hitchpin rail, mounted on the soundboard, above the liners of tail and bentside, over their bridge (or 'soundboard bridge', *a*), then forward past the jacks (*j*) and over the 8' nut (or 'wrest-plank bridge', *f*), to the 8 foot wrest pins (*e*) close to the keyboard. The 4' strings are hitched to pins driven through the soundboard into a wide bar underneath, the '4' hitchpin rail' (*b*, shown in broken line), thence over the 4' bridge (*c*) to the 4' nut (*h*)

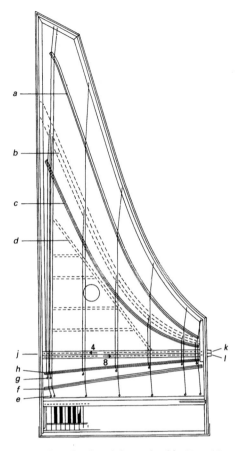

Fig. 1. Plan of a Flemish harpsichord by Hans Moer-mans, 1584: length 211 cm. (83″). The strings for each C and the top and bottom notes are indicated (after Hubbard 1965).

jacks of this row—though still raised when a key is depressed—not to pluck. Below each jack slide, about 2.5 cm. (1 inch) above the keys, is a 'jack guide', similarly slotted but fixed in position. The two actual jacks for each note of the compass are placed between the two strings for that note, one behind the other, their lower ends resting on the key, and their plectra pointing in opposite directions, 4′ jacks usually to the left. (For harp-sichords with three choirs—three strings per note— see below, 4.)

3. *The jack* (Pl. 1). Often of pearwood (or today, synthetics) this is from about 5 to 23 cm. (2 to 9″) long and 3 mm. ($\frac{1}{8}$″) thick. The plectrum was formerly of crow's quill, more rarely and durably of leather; delrin, a modern plastic is usual today. It is fixed in a narrow hardwood (or plastic) 'tongue' mounted in the slot at the top of the jack on a pin pivot. It projects some 3 mm. from the tongue, lying at rest about 1 mm. below the string. As the jack is raised by the key the tongue is kept upright by a chamfer at the base of the slot so that the plectrum plucks the string; the damper, cut in soft felt and wedged in a saw-cut at the top of the jack, is raised at the same time.

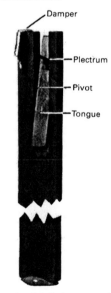

Pl. 1. A harpsichord jack (upper part), showing the parts.

and their wrest pins (*g*). The 4′ hitchpin rail also divides off the 8′ resonating area of the soundboard from that of the 4′ strings, which is in turn delimited by a straight 'cut-off bar' (*d*); the remain-ing triangular area, with the soundhole or 'rose', is traversed by a number of thinner bars likewise glued to the soundboard. For the 8′ strings to pass clear over the 4′ nut and bridge, the 4′ strings must run on a lower level by about 13 mm. ($\frac{1}{2}$″) (all the jacks have the same height but those for the 4′ strings have the plectra on the lower level).

The two projections on the cheekpiece are the extremities of the two 'jack slides' (*k*, *l*) which run across the instrument on the level of the soundboard, each with a slot for every jack of the row. For playing on one set of strings alone the jack slide of the other set can be moved sideways by means of the projection (or in later models by a metal lever leading to a stop-knob above the keyboard) by the 3mm. ($\frac{1}{8}$″) or so required for the

On release of the key the jack descends under its own weight, the plectrum again touching the string (making a slight impact sound, practically inaudible as one note follows after another) but this time to tilt the tongue backwards for the plectrum to pass below. On that instant, just before the damper falls, the tongue is restored to its initial upright position against the chamfer by a spring of a hog's bristle (or today plastic) fixed in the jack to bear on the back of the tongue at a point just above the pivot; the note can then be played again.

Near the top of the jack there may be a wire staple to prevent the tongue swinging back too far—or in cases where the slot is not extended to the top of the jack, a second chamfer fulfils the same purpose. Above the jacks is the padded, easily removable 'jack rail' which prevents risk of a jack jumping too high and failing to return properly.

4. *Three sets of strings*. Since a 4' choir runs at a lower level there is space above it for a second choir of 8' strings, level with the first 8' set, also resting on the 8' bridge, and with its plectra pointing in the same direction as those of the 4'. The three choirs, giving maximum volume when all sounded together, offer a variety of shades when they are not. The three choirs, often specified for short as 2 × 8', 1 × 4', are practically standard from the later 17th century onwards, and for two-manual harpsichords also (below, 5).

English tradition is to place the 4' jacks furthest from the keyboard. The French is to place the 4' jacks between the two 8' rows, whereby the strings of the 'back 8' (jacks furthest from the keyboard,) are plucked farther from the nut and give a very noticeably 'darker' sound (high partials being less prominently aroused).

Two 'extras' are often provided. The 'harp' (or 'buff') stop involves no extra jacks but simply moves felt, or buff leather pads against the strings of one of the 8' choirs immediately next to the 8' nut, muting these strings (without effectively detracting from the sounding length) for a pizzicato effect; it may be found on Flemish instruments back to early in the 17th century.

The 'lute' stop (chiefly on 18th-century English models) is an additional row of jacks (see H in Fig. 3, here a two-manual instrument) placed separate from the others, between the 4' and 8' nuts (requiring a gap to be cut in the wrest plank) to pluck the 'front' 8' fairly close to the nut, for a thinner, nasal tone, somewhat as when a guitarist plucks close to the bridge. While the lute stop is engaged, by its stop knob, the regular jacks of the front 8' (Fig. 3, L) are switched off. (To make room for the 'lute' jacks, most of the 4' strings may have to be led, after the nut (G), through holes in the 8' nut (F) to wrest pins (E) placed nearer the front than those in Fig. 2.)

5. *Two-manual harpsichords* (Pl. 2, p. 158). These magnificent instruments, made chiefly from the 1670s onwards, make it possible, by moving one or both hands from one keyboard to the other, to change back and forth between louder and softer sound without interruption of the playing. There are pieces in the repertory definitely composed for two manuals, as by François Couperin and in Bach's 'Goldberg Variations', where the music is written for the hand on one keyboard to cross over the other hand playing on the other keyboard.

The lower manual is the main one, working the basic 8' and 4' registers, leaving the first 8' to the upper manual. One still needs, however, for maximum sound, to be able to play all three registers from one manual, the lower, and French and English practice provide for this in different ways.

(a) *Coupler*. French, Fig. 2. The upper keyboard with its key-frame (B) is movable backwards (away from the player) by about 1 cm. or less. A gentle push with each hand then slides it to bring the inner ends of its keys above short pegs (R) fixed upright in the lower-manual keys. Then, on pressing a lower-manual key, this raises the end of the corresponding upper-manual key and the front 8' jack (J) with it, so that the front 8' register (when its stop is drawn) becomes playable from either manual until such time as the upper keyboard is pulled forward to its normal (uncoupled) position. A specification may read:

Upper manual: 8'.
Lower manual: 8', with harp; 4'; coupler.

Thus when coupled, all strings are playable together from the lower keyboard (and leaving possible the contrast of one 8' alone on the upper). When uncoupled, the subtle contrast becomes available between the two 8' registers (with their separated plucking points as noted above, 2d) as well as further contrasts between the upper 8' and the various resources of the lower manual.

(b) *Dog-leg*. Chiefly English (though a Flemish invention), Fig. 3. Keyboards fixed, but the front 8' jacks are so shaped in their lower part ('dog-leg') as to be raised from either manual: from the upper alone; or from the lower, if wished along with the other 8' and the 4' for all strings to sound. Typical specification:

Upper manual: lute.
Both manuals: 8' (dog-leg).
Lower manual: 8', with harp; 4'.

Since once the dog-leg stop is put 'on' both manuals play the front 8', the two 8' registers cannot be contrasted on the two manuals in the French way (above, 4); however, the English placement of the two 8' rows of jacks next to each other (L, M) would anyway reduce their tonal contrast, instead of which the lute stop (upper manual, H), having disengaged the front 8', can be contrasted with the back 8' on the lower manual. The typical order of the stop knobs above the keyboards runs: on the left, lute, harp, 4'; right, 8' both manuals, 8' lower manual. (For the 'machine stop' see below, 7d).

6. *Origins*. The first recorded name for a harpsichord, *clavicimbalum*, is from 1397. In representations from the ensuing years (Ripin 1971) the instrument resembles in form the 'half trapeze' kind of *psaltery (that with only one incurving side) and at first little larger, but placed flat and turned round by 90 degrees for adding the keyboard

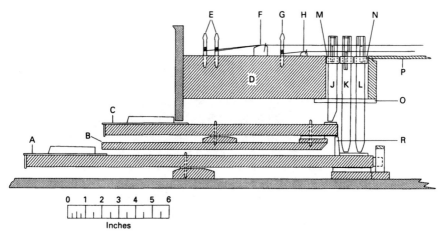

Fig. 2. French harpsichord, by Blanchet (after Russell 1959).

A	Lower keyboard.	J	8' jack, upper manual.	R	Coupler, by means of which the lower manual keys depress those of the upper keyboard. If the upper keyboard and key-frame (B) are drawn towards the player—a movement of only 1 cm (⅓") —the uprights (R) will no longer engage the upper manual keys when the keys of the lower manual are depressed.
B	Upper keyframe.	K	4' jack, lower manual.		
C	Upper keyboard.	L	8' jack, lower manual		
D	Wrestplank.	M	8' slide, upper manual		
E	8' wrestpins.	N	8' slide, lower manual		
F	8' nut.	O	Jack guide.		
G	4' wrestpins.	P	Soundboard		
H	4' nut				

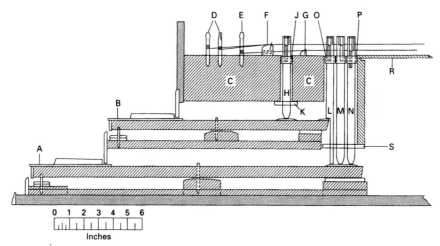

Fig. 3. English harpsichord, by Jacob Kirckman, 1755 (after Russell 1959).

A	Lower manual.	G	4' nut.	N	4' jack, lower manual.
B	Upper manual.	H	Lute stop jack.	O	8' slide, both manuals.
C	Wrest plank.	J	Lute stop slide.	P	4' slide, lower manual.
D	8' wrestpins.	K	Lute stop guide.	R	Soundboard.
E	4' wrestpins.	L	8' jack, both manuals.	S	Guide for both 8' and the 4' jacks.
F	8' nut.	M	8' jack, lower manual.		

plucking action along the original left-hand side, now to become the front, facing the player. The earliest details are from just later, drawn, and described in Latin, in Arnaut 1454, the manuscript in Paris known by the name of Henri Arnaut of Zwolle who, along with others, completed it in Dijon. Besides valuable details of organ and lute construction, it shows three different plucking actions for the 'clavisimbalum', none exactly as used in harpsichords since, and also a type of

Pl. 2. Two-manual harpsichord by Joseph Kirckman (London, 1798): late model with 'Venetian swell', here shown open.

hammer action for the *dulcemelos. (A facsimile of the manuscript appeared in 1932, while many of the drawings are reproduced in Montagu 1976.) For the earliest existing actual instrument of a harpsichord type, see CLAVICYTHERIUM (this of an upright kind).

7. Historic schools of harpsichord making: (a) Italy. The oldest existing harpsichords are Italian, the earliest signed example by Vincentius, of Livignano, near Florence, being dated 1515 (Accademia Chigiana, Siena). Of other makers, the Venetians, Baffo and Celestini, are known by over 20 examples dated from the last quarter of the sixteenth century. All are single-manual and were normally contained in a separate outer case, the whole often seen in pictures laid on a table with other musicians sitting round it. The frame is usually of cedar or cypress (instead of the deal or lime, etc. used in northern Europe). The compass is often from *C* to *f'''* with *short octave in the bass. The Italian instruments in general show a characteristic and endearing warmth of tone, though their original stringing

schemes are now difficult to ascertain since (as with early lutes) almost all have been subsequently altered. Some are judged to have been originally single-strung, others to have had an 8' and a 4', apparently more frequently than the 2 × 8' which became commoner in the next century (as also in Spain at the period of Domenico Scarlatti).

(b) The Flemish school. The celebrated Ruckers family of Antwerp (see also VIRGINAL) are known by harpsichords from 1581 to 1654, over 80 now known, all but in the fewest cases later altered, especially to provide a full five-octave compass (without the short octave), a process known in French as *ravalement*. There were: Hans Ruckers (b. *c.*1540–50, d. 1598); his sons Johannes, known as Jan (1578–1642) and Andreas (1579–post-1645); the latter's son, also Andreas (b. 1607, d. *c.*1655); Jan's nephew, Jan Couchet (1615–55); and his son Jan, still making in 1686. The instruments, with their thoughtful design and meticulous selection of the finest materials, were famous over all Europe north of the Alps, England included. A

characteristic decoration, besides paintings inside the lid by such as Rubens, is by block-printed papers, often in black and white, round the inside of the case. A gilt soundboard 'rose' bears the initials of the Ruckers who made it.

They made single-manual instruments with an 8' and a 4' (and eventually 2 × 8', 1 × 4'), and also a two-manual model which, however, in its intention poses something of a historical problem. Described now as a 'transposing harpsichord', each keyboard moves its own rows of 8' and 4' jacks, plucking the same 8' and 4' strings; but the lower keyboard is aligned to the left of the upper by three notes whereby, while playing on the lower, the music sounds a fourth lower than it is written or played on the upper keyboard—presumably to avoid the need for the player to transpose should voices or other instruments require accompaniment at the deeper pitch.

(c) *France.* From France, England, and Germany very few existing harpsichords predate the 18th century. The two chief French names are of the Blanchet family, working in Paris from the 1680s up to the time when their associate Pascal Taskin (1723–93) succeeded to the business. Such was the destruction during the Revolution that their surviving instruments barely reach double figures. They were equally famous for rebuilds of Flemish harpsichords by Ruckers and Couchet. Their own work is extensively copied today, mostly two-manual (above, 4, 5a). By the 1760s they had introduced 'knee levers', up to six, mounted below the keyboards and pushed upwards and sideways to change the registration during a piece. Taskin also fitted leather plectra of a special soft 'buffalo hide' for the back 8' register, increasing tonal contrast with the quilled front 8'.

(d) *England.* For a surviving instrument of 1579, see CLAVIORGAN. Among early 18th-century harpsichords now surviving are two by the younger Hitchcock, and one of 1721, two-manual, by Hermann Tabel, who came from Flanders. Under him for a time served as apprentices, in London, the founders of the two businesses from which probably more harpsichords have survived than from the rest of European makers put together. Burkat Shudi (1702–73) was from Switzerland; and Jacob Kirckman (1710–92) from Alsace. Shudi was joined in 1761 by John Broadwood (1732–1812) from Scotland, who had married into the family and took over the business on the death of Shudi's son in 1782. Over 50 of their harpsichords are now known, of 1729–93, those from 1770 signed by Shudi and Broadwood. Two-thirds are two-manual and some 15 have Shudi's 'Venetian swell' (patent of 1769): wooden louvres (Pl. 2) hinging above the strings and opened (when the lid is up) by a pedal for the left foot, for a crescendo on the organ swell-box principle. By Kirckman exist probably more than 160, of 1750–1800, half of them two-manual. From 1773 they are signed by

Jacob and his nephew Abraham Kirckman; from 1789 by the latter and his son Joseph, and from 1798–1800 by Joseph alone. Like Shudi's they are usually veneered in walnut or later mahogany (French instruments being painted or japanned and gilded) with five-octave compass from *F'*. A quarter have either a Venetian swell or Kirckman's 'nag's-head' swell, in which the pedal opens a hinged section of the lid over the soundboard. Many harpsichords of both makers have the 'machine stop' (examples by Shudi from 1765) worked by a pedal for the left foot: a knob to the left of the keyboard rests normally pulled forwards. When pushed back (having first put the back 8' 'on') it engages with the pedal and (with the pedal 'up') puts on the front 8' and the 4' as well. On lowering the pedal, these come 'off' and the lute stop comes 'on'; if two manuals, the upper then plays the lute, and the lower can play the back 8'.

Some English harpsichords bear names of music dealers such as Longman and Broderip (from *c.*1780) who sold instruments made by, among others, Culliford, and John Geib, who is noted also for his piano actions. George Washington obtained a two-manual harpsichord from this firm, now preserved at Mount Vernon. Preserved American instruments number, so far as is known, only a few spinets, the makers having switched over early on to pianos.

(e) *Germany.* Among chief 18th-century makers were Hass, father and son, of Hamburg, their instruments dated 1721–64. Some are up to 275cm. (9') long, with a 16' register, sounding an octave lower than the 8' choirs. For the 16' the strings may be found to be, as compared with the 8', from twice as long in the treble to some 38 cm. (15") longer in the bass, and run at a higher level to clear the 8' bridge before reaching their own (which is in some cases placed on an elevated separate soundboard). They are played from the lower manual. (The 16' register excited much attention during the revival of the harpsichord, partly through unauthenticated association with Bach; but whether any of the instruments he possessed had this register is unknown.) A German instrument might also, very rarely, have on the upper manual a 2' register sounding two octaves above the written music, though ranging only up to *c'* or *c''* on the keyboard: for notes above this the strings would be impossibly short for applying jack action. The 2' strings run on the lowest level of all, for the 4' strings to clear them.

8. *Repertory* (a brief list; most of the older German works are equally, or primarily, for playing on the clavichord).

(a) *Early 17th century.* See VIRGINAL for the principal English 'Virginal Books' of 1591–1624, of keyboard music (harpsichord or virginal) by Bull, Byrd, Farnaby, Gibbons, and others of the time. From Italy, Frescobaldi, partitas, toccatas, fantasias (volumes from 1608).

(b) *Later 17th century*. Matthew Locke, preludes etc. in *Melothesia*, 1673. Purcell, *Musick's Handmaid* (Part II, 1689); and *A Choice Collection . . .* (publ. 1696). Chambonnières, founder of the French school of *clavecinistes*, two books 1670. Louis Couperin, passacailles. Kuhnau, sonatas, from 1696 (the 'biblical' sonatas, 1700), Clavier-übung, 1689, 1692.

(c) *Eighteenth century*. François Couperin, four books, 1713–30, with over 200 pieces, most with programmatic titles. Rameau, four collections, 1706–41. Domenico Scarlatti, over 500 sonatas, from 1738. J. S. Bach, concerto in the Italian style; for *Clavier* (harpsichord or clavichord), fantasias; preludes and fugues; six English Suites; six French Suites; *Clavierübung*, two books (with the 'Goldberg Variations'); *Wohltemperierte Clavier*, over 20 suites. Handel, six concertos (organ or harpsichord), over 20 suites; four sonatas and sonatinas. Arne, eight sonatas. Haydn's sonatas up to the 1780s were written for harpsichord, as were some of Mozart's early works.

(d) *Twentieth century*. Works written for Wanda Landowska (1879–1959), the first great modern international harpsichord soloist, playing Pleyel's modernized versions of the instrument, include: Falla, Concerto (1926); Poulenc, *Concert champêtre* (1928); Delius, Dance (1919); Piston, sonatina with violin (1946); Stravinsky, septet, piano (or harpsichord) with other instruments (1952).

Boalch 1956, rev. 1974; Hellwig 1976; Hubbard 1965; Koster 1980; Neupert 1933, trans. 1960; O'Brien 1979; Ripin 1971; Russell 1959, repr. 1979; Schott 1974; Spencer 1981; Thomas and Rhodes 1967; Zuckermann 1969.

Harp-zither. West African instrument; see MVET.

Haut and bas (Fr.). From the later 14th century and through much of the 15th, there was a distinction among the upper classes in France and Burgundy between instruments that were *bas* ('soft': the stringed, the *portative organ, and other softer wind instruments); and the noisier *shawms and *trumpets, which were *haut* ('loud'), still bound to their medieval duties in ceremonial, tournaments, warfare, but now also playing at court dances, where 'they better pleased from the great noise they make' (*Les Eches amoureux*, *c*.1370). When less noise is demanded, this poem recommends 'flageols, flutes, and douchaines (see DOUÇAINE), these very sweet and clear, and other such *bas* instruments'. Still in 1473 the Duke of Burgundy carried in his retinue (besides 12 *trompettes de guerre*) six *haut menestrels*, and four *joueurs de bas instruments*; the 'haut' played shawms and the *trompette saiqueboute* (trombone), and the 'bas' played *fleutes* (recorders), lute, and no doubt many other instruments.

Hautbois. Fr.: 'oboe', or earlier (16th to late 17th century) *shawm. Also the French term for non-Western or folk double-reed instruments. For the use of the word in English before the 19th century see OBOE. For the French 17th-century *hautbois de Poitou* see ÉCURIE, 2.

Hawaiian guitar (or steel guitar). Originally a guitar placed flat across the knees for the left hand to make the notes by pressing the strings with a bar (the 'steel') held straight across them; a main attraction being the limitless scope for vibrato of all kinds and of slides from note to note. Against this, harmonies of two or more strings is confined to such that the tuning intervals between strings allow, since the steel as it is moved along the neck stops them all. The pedal steel guitar (2, below), developed in the USA from the 1940s, has pedals by which individual strings can be instantly changed in tension and quickly back again, having raised (or lowered) the pitch, for their notes to be available in different positions of the steel. Built in long rectangular forms, raised on legs and with magnetic pickups, this later instrument no longer resembles any guitar: players generally know it as a 'pedal steel'.

1. *Hawaiian guitar*. Hawaiians from the late 19th century adopted the method of pressing the strings with the back of a comb or such like. The islanders tuned the guitar to a common chord, the sliding creating a languorous music which in the 1920s caught on in America (often making the slides with a bottleneck). Hawaiian guitars were then manufactured, with the strings running higher over the neck than normally, and by the 1930s mostly replacing the guitar shape by the present rectangular form (e.g. by Gibson, *c*.1935) with extra strings and, in some, pickups.

2. *Pedal steel*. Early models of this are by Gibson ('electraharp', 1940) and by Leo Fender in California. It is not in all respects standardized—it may have one or often two (or more) 'necks' for different tunings, each of eight, 10, or more strings. The steel is a round bar held between thumb and middle fingers, the forefinger resting on top. The right hand wears finger-picks on two fingers and thumb. The sprung pedals are for the left foot (the right operating an electric volume control); the foot is quickly tilted to change from one pedal to the next, or two may be lowered at once. With a single neck there are at least three pedals, each acting on (usually) two of the strings, augmented by a knee lever acting on others; through rods and bell-cranks beneath the strings these give the extra (or reduced) tension required to raise (or lower) such strings by a tone, or in some cases a semitone: the essence of the system, the need for several pedals, being that a given string shall be alterable while others can remain the same. For example, if two adjacent strings are a fourth apart as tuned, a pedal that

raises the lower by a tone brings them a third apart in all positions of the steel, which can be moved in vibrato, etc. just as before. Besides recognized tunings and pedal settings suiting 'country', jazz, or other styles and their appropriate harmonies, players devise their own systems. The instrument at first seems very complicated; but its capabilities in expert hands are quite extraordinary.

Winston and Keith 1975.

Heckelphone. A type of *bass oboe brought out in 1904 by the famous German bassoon-maker Heckel: 120 cm. (4') long, lowest note the written *a*, sounding *A*; a wide conical bore; and played with a double reed that may be as large as some bassoon reeds. The sound is full and fat, like neither bassoon nor the French bass oboe. An unusual mechanical feature (also tried in the USA by Conn on some *clarinets) is use of mobile studs within a ring for the same finger, the stud closing the note-hole some distance away, and the ring performing its normal duty (see WIND INSTRUMENTS, 3). Richard Strauss has the heckelphone in *Salome* (1905) and in *Elektra* (but absent in the reduced score sanctioned by him), and Delius in the First Dance Rhapsody. Hindemith's Op. 47, Trio for viola, heckelphone, and piano (1929), has been rated among the composer's most masterly chamber works. The heckelphone is now only made to order: in 1979 there were said to be only three in Britain. On its first appearance it was noted by some that the great width of bore recalls that of the curious Swiss type of instrument described as *basse de musette*, a copy of which Heckel had constructed for his museum shortly before the heckelphone was announced. Possibly the one at least partly inspired the other.

Helicon. A *tuba made in circular shape for placing over the head, the weight taken on the left shoulder. The first known design was by Stowasser (Vienna, 1849) since which helicons or 'circular basses' were made in most countries. They were much used in British *military bands up to the First World War, and in the USA the *sousaphone was developed from them. Other band instruments, altos, tenors, and valved trombones, have also been made in 'helicon style'.

Helmholtz. Among matters commonly given the name of the great musical scientist Hermann von Helmholtz (1821–94; *On the Sensations of tone*, trans. Ellis, 1875) are: 'Helmholtz notation', his own form of the old German way of specifying which octave is to be understood when mentioning a note by its letter name: thus from the bottom A of the piano, *A'*, to the highest A, *a''''* (Middle C being *c'*; see Introduction); and 'Helmholtz resonator' (see CAVITY RESONATOR).

Hertz (Hz.). Vibration frequency in cycles per second. Named after the German physicist Heinrich

Rudolf Hertz (1857–94), noted for his pioneering work in electromagnetism. 1 kHz. = 1000 Hz. The audible limits of frequency have generally been cited as approximately from 20 Hz. (three tones below the bottom A of the piano) to 20,000 Hz. (more than two octaves above piano range but occurring among high *partials in sounds).

Hibernicon. See BASS HORN, 1.

Hichiriki. The Japanese short bamboo pipe, *c*.18 cm. (7") long (Fig. 1), sounded with a large double reed. A *'cylindrical oboe' akin to the Chinese *guan* and Korean *p'iri*, it is one of the three traditional wind instruments of the court music, along with a transverse flute (see FUE) and the mouth-organ *shō* (see SHENG); see also JAPAN, Ex. 1. The pipe, bound at the ends and between the fingerholes with black-lacquered thread, has seven holes in front and two thumb-holes, the lower of which (located on the back between the fourth and fifth fingerholes) is no longer used but kept closed with the thumb. The bamboo reed is nearly 6 cm. long and 11 mm. wide at the flattened tip, kept in shape by a bamboo collar. The penetrating sound covers a compass of about *g'* to *a''* and is produced with slow inflexions of the pitch, rising to a note in a wailing portamento, matched by the flute player.

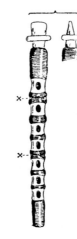

Fig. 1.

Hi-hat. See CYMBAL, 2.

Hnè. Burmese double-reed wind instrument related to the Indian *shahnai* and Chinese *sona* (the name being cognate with these). Typically it has a large brass bell which fits loosely over the instrument, wobbling about during performance; this bell may be held on by a thick red cord wound round the upper end of the instrument, but is sometimes dispensed with altogether. The larger size of two (see SOUTH-EAST ASIA, Pl. 1), heard in grand style open-air ensembles, has a big compass from about

Middle C upwards. For the reed, of palmleaf see
REED, 5.

Hojok. Korean *shawm. See CHINA AND KOREA, 2*d*.

Holztrompete. See ALPHORN.

Hook harp. See HARP, 9*c*.

Horn (Fr.: *cor*, Ger.: *Horn, Waldhorn*; It.: *corno*;
Ru.: *rog, valtorna*; Sp.: *trompa*). Firstly here the
orchestral horn or 'French horn' as it is often called
(having been initially brought to England from
France in the late 17th century, in the time of
James II). See HUNTING HORN for European types of
horn made for this purpose; and for a general view
of blowing horns, past and present, of animal horn,
ivory, or metal in curved shapes, see below, 8.

1. *The modern horn* (Pl. 1*b*, *c*). Formed in a circle,
with the wide bell facing backward, the horn is
held with the right hand normally just inside the
bell mouth, the valves being operated by the left
hand: this is because through the 'hand horn'
period (below, 6) which preceded the invention of
valves (*c*.1815) the right hand took responsibility
for 'stopping' the bell to make notes then not
otherwise obtainable, the left hand grasping the
circle at the top. The right hand remains in the
bell (or, in some schools, holding this by the rim)
largely to be able to 'stop' its mouth for the
frequently demanded effect of 'hand muting' (3*b*).
Some models have a screw-off bell for the horn to
fit into a more compact travelling case.

Main physical characteristics of the horn are
compared with those of other brass in BRASS
INSTRUMENTS, 2*b*: the deep mouthpiece; the tapered
'mouthpipe' of some 75 cm. (2½') of tubing starting
very narrow; at the other end, the 150 cm. (5') of
bell expansion up to the wide flare; and between
these, the loops and coils of cylindrical tubing
through the valves and tuning slides (BRASS INSTRU-
MENTS, Fig. 2. 6). The rotary valves (see VALVE, 2)
are most commonly three plus one for the thumb,
though there may be more (see below, 4). The
horn is built in various different pitches (2, 3); but
the normal custom is to write for 'Horn in F', the
notes sounding a fifth lower, the most used *sounding*
range being from the Bb' below the bass stave to f''
at the top of the treble. Up to the end of the 19th
century (or even later) orchestral and solo music
was also written for horns in other keys than F,
involving different transpositions (listed, along with
the use of the bass clef in certain cases, in
TRANSPOSING INSTRUMENTS, 2).

The presence of four horn players in an orchestra,
occasionally required in the 18th century, really
became established through the next. They form
two pairs: 1st and 2nd horns, originally 'crooked'
in the main key of the movement; the other, 3rd
and 4th, usually in an answering key and, when
writing for 'hand-horn', giving the composer wider
scope for using all four together (see notably
Beethoven's Ninth Symphony).

2. *F and Bb double horn*. The modern horn is usually
a 'double horn': two pitches are combined in one
instrument sharing the mouthpipe and the bell

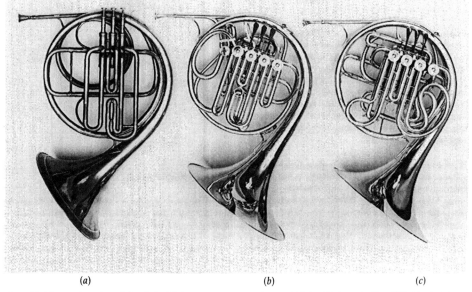

(*a*)   (*b*)   (*c*)

Pl. 1. (*a*) F horn, French model; (*b*) double horn in Bb and F alto; (*c*) full double horn in F and Bb (the last two
by Paxman, London).

but with different windway circuits in between, switched from one to the other by the thumb-valve. The most common two pitches are F (12′, with total tube 374 cm.) and B♭ (9′, 280 cm.). The B♭ pitch makes playing generally easier, the high notes more certain, and carrying through the orchestra in loud passages with less effort; also many of the low notes are firmer and fuller. Many players use the 'B♭' (as it is called) all the time. On the other hand the F pitch, the old tradition for a valved horn, is provided today, not so much for a subtly more traditional horn sound as for greater fluency in certain types of passage (e.g. the fast 'cascading' arpeggios met in classical music) and also in hand muting (below, 3a).

Figs. 1 and 2 illustrate schematically the two main forms of the instrument: heavy lines indicate the circuit (direction marked by arrows) from the thumb-valve S to the exit leading to the bell, B; the three valves for the fingers are shown as circles, each having two valve loops indicated (not to scale) above and below, though on the actual horn they lie one behind the other. Broken line indicates a path or loop that is not in use.

the action can be reversed if preferred, for the horn to stand in B♭ at rest), the path from the mouthpipe (from the left in the figure) proceeds through S directly to the three main valves and out to the bell. When S is released (F horn, Fig. 1b) the valve turns through 90 degrees to divert the path to the compensating loop (F), which adds one-third to the total B♭ tubing (about 1 m. (3′)), and back through the valves by separate passages in the double rotors, these having two passages through the valve, one above the other. When any of the valves are pressed, they communicate with the small increment loops indicated below; then again through S and again through the valves, this time exactly as in Fig. 1a, and so out to the bell. Thus when a valve is pressed, both of its valve-loops are admitted into the circuit, together adding up to the length required for horn in F. There are other possible arrangements of the tubing, for example the B♭ passages through the valves, being common to both circuits, can be led to before, instead of after, the switch valve is passed through.

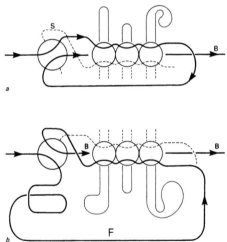

Fig. 2. Schematic representation of valve circuits of full double horn: (a) When playing in B♭ (main B♭ loop marked B); (b) When playing in F (independent main F loop marked F).

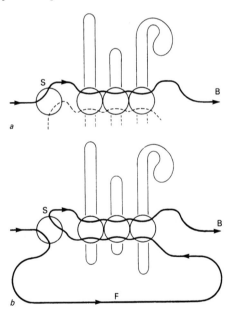

Fig. 1. Schematic representation of valve circuits of compensating double horn: (a) in B♭; (b) in F. (Valve loops are indicated in fine line on smaller scale.

(a) Compensating horn. The earlier form, introduced in Germany in 1897 by the Erfurt maker Kruspe. It works on the same principle as the compensating piston valves earlier invented in Britain for the *tuba, the thumb-valve on the horn (S) being equivalent to the fourth valve of the tuba. When S is turned putting the horn in B♭ (Fig. 1a, though

(b) Full double horn (Pl. 1c). Introduced shortly after the above, perfected by Kruspe and by Alexander (Mainz). The thumb-valve S here requires six exits and rotates clockwise through 60 degrees. Fig. 2a shows the B♭ circuit (valve S pressed) passing through the valves, then again through S to the bell. The F circuit, Fig. 2b, is independent, complete in itself leading from S through a tuning slide (lower left) and through the valves 'backwards' via the other passages in the rotors (communicating with long, F-length loops) to S for the second time and out to the bell.

Nearly all advanced players prefer this 'full double' system, even though it is heavier and rather more expensive, mainly because it is a simple matter to provide each circuit with its own independent tuning-slide.

3. *Single horns, and double horns incorporating higher pitches:* (*a*) *Single F horn* (i.e. in F only). Manufactured for educational purposes should it be considered best to ground pupils on a lower-priced instrument with the traditional 12′ tube-length.

(*b*) *Single Bb horn* (Bb only). This has been in favour off and on among 1st and 3rd horn players, usually however to return to the 'double'. It needs special provision for hand muting—the hissing quality produced by almost entirely blocking the bell with the right hand, as indicated in music by a cross over the note or by 'sons bouchés', 'gestopft', etc. (as opposed to 'con sordino', which normally indicates the use of a separate *mute). On the F horn this action of the hand raises the pitch of the note by a semitone, for which the player compensates by valving a semitone lower. On the Bb horn it raises the note by near a three-quarter tone, so that on the single Bb horn (with no F 'side' to fall back on) an extra valve is needed for the compensation; this may be activated by a second lever for the left thumb. Often it can be tuned in alternative ways, e.g. to help in obtaining low notes that lie in the gap (on Bb horn) between the lowest valved note and the open fundamental; otherwise such notes must be made by special 'loose-lip' embouchure.

(*c*) *Single horn in F alto.* An octave higher than the F horn, first mooted in Leipzig (*c.*1883) to facilitate certain high-lying solo parts of the 18th century (reaching sounding *ab″* in a trio by Haydn). It can be obtained today but the short (6′) tube-length, despite a bell of full width, can hardly avoid imparting a distinct trace of bugle-like quality, so therefore this F alto pitch has proved far more useful if combined with a deeper pitch as a double horn in Bb/F alto (Pl. 1*b*) or F/F alto. Paxman (London) have found how to fit a mouthpipe taper satisfactory for the tone of the F alto side of the horn by means of two separated change-valves linked together for the thumb to move them together. The firm also make a *triple horn* combining F, Bb, and F alto (with two thumb levers) and have latterly even introduced a *Bb soprano* pitch (that of the *cornet) as a double horn in Bb/Bb soprano or a triple horn, e.g. in F/Bb/Bb soprano.

4. *Older models:* (*a*) *French* (*piston-valve*) *horn* (Pl. 1*a*). Normal instrument in Britain before the German double horn arrived after 1930. Orchestral players carried it about in a black velvet bag along with the F crook with which it was normally played. Some fine amateur players remain faithful to it, while in France only recently has this traditional

instrument begun to be deserted in favour of the German (even though Selmer made it also as an F/Bb double horn by using lengthened piston valves). Essentially it is the classic French hand horn with valves added, sometimes detachably. The main bore may be a millimetre less than the normal German bore of 12.1 mm. and the whole bell is markedly narrower, giving the sound a lighter, more transparent quality. Usually in France the third valve, instead of adding a tone and a half when lowered, adds a whole-tone while at rest ('up', termed an 'ascending' valve). To allow for this the instrument is played with a G crook. With the valve down (horn in G), various high notes are produced with greater certainty.

(*b*) *Older German F horn.* In the USA probably the most familiar orchestral horn before the double horn (first introduced there some 30 years earlier than in Britain, it is said by Anton Horner in 1899): the rotary valves are typically sprung with cased clock springs (Ger.: *Trommelwerke*, as used also in (*c*) below). This is the horn on which *The Ring* operas were first performed, when Franz Strauss, father of Richard Strauss, was a principal horn in the Munich orchestra.

(*c*) *Vienna horn*, with double-piston valves (see VALVE, 2). Like the French instrument above, a model with a great tradition (and likewise played with an F crook) but now fast disappearing in favour of the German type. Apart from a wider mouthpiece-socket than elsewhere, the tube keeps a narrow width up to a very full and wide bell section, and the sound has the 'darkest' quality of any.

5. *Natural horn (baroque, classical):* (*a*) *Advent of the circular horn.* There had been small metal hunting horns with a loop in the tube since the 15th century, and a tightly wound multi-coil type from the 16th. By the mid-17th century, fashions were changing on the Continent in favour of the circular horn in an open hoop, bound with buff leather up to the root of the bell. First it was built in a single coil giving a pitch equal to or a little below that of the contemporary trumpet. By the 1670s the French royal hunt was sounding fanfares on such horns around 43 cm. (17″) in diameter with a bell 15 cm. (6″) wide and a pitch of about 8′ C ('C alto'). From the same decade is believed to date the first-known purely musical use of the horn, in an anonymous Czech sonata for strings with *corno da caccia* at this pitch and playing up to the written (and sounding) high *g″*.

(*b*) *F and D horns.* By 1700 in Germany there is already music for the horn in the deeper, 'classic' pitch of 12′ F; in a concerto of that year by Johann Baer the solo part reaches the written *c‴* (16th harmonic), and is interspersed with calls played by the same performer on a post-horn. The F horn at that time is usually two-coiled with about the same hoop diameter as the single-coil horn in high C (the earliest so far known dated example in F is of 1710 by Leichamschneider, Vienna). A 'single-coil' horn may in fact comprise some $1\frac{3}{4}$ circles, because the mouthpipe and bell overlap through a part of the circle as well as projecting from it at the ends; a 'two-coil' will similarly make $2\frac{3}{4}$ circles. The relation between these amounts, not far from the 2 : 3 ratio of the perfect fifth, could be an indication that the 12' F pitch, with its greater melodic possibilities, arose in the first place through giving the 8' C horn the second circle. Next most frequent among deeper pitches is the horn in D, an octave below the contemporary trumpet, and generally in three coils (as the French *cor de chasse* is still; see HUNTING HORN, 3).

Through most of the 18th century, the horn was grasped in one hand with the hoop resting on the uplifted arm (see MILITARY BAND, Pl. 1), or in both hands with the bell aimed backwards above the head. Horns were usually bought in pairs, of which one might be built 'left-handed', for the left of two players standing shoulder to shoulder to point the bell to the left: a left-handed horn has the socket for the mouthpiece or crook to the right of the circle instead of as normally to the left: in each case it is underneath as the horn is held.

(c) *Crooks.* *Crooks, for changing the key of a horn, are mentioned early in the 18th century in Austria and by the 1740s were normal for 'Concert French Horns' (as horns not specifically for hunting music were described in England). Such horns are typically two-coil, c.29 cm. ($11\frac{1}{2}"$) across with 23-cm. (9") bell, allowing a pitch of high A or B♭ with the smallest crook. They continued to be held up in one hand; but they have the wider throat to the bell, much as horns have kept since, and produce the rounder, less 'huntsman-like' sound which in classical works so characteristically and unobtrusively binds the orchestral texture together with sustained notes in the key of the movement, then often to emerge with a motif of their own, all on the natural notes (Ex. 1). The first system of crooks used a tapered 'master crook' to combine with cylindrical 'couplers', each of one or more coils, for the lower keys. These had been superseded after c.1750, first on the Continent, by a set of separate crooks for all keys required, numbering up to nine or more, from high B♭ to low C (and still supplied with many French instruments into the early 20th century). A different system, with crooks inserted into the middle part of the horn (like a tuning-slide) was introduced from c.1755 in Germany better to suit hand-horn soloists (below): in Germany, *Inventionshorn*, and in France, *cor solo*, denoted a horn built on this system. (In 'omnitonic horns', rather rare and little-used designs of the early 19th century, all the crooks are built permanently into the instrument, with various types of device for selecting the one required.)

6. *Hand-horn.* After the mid-18th century it became by degrees usual to hold the instrument downwards

Ex. 1. Excerpt from Mozart, *Sinfonia concertante* for violin and viola, K. 364, last movement (*Presto*).

In E♭

($\begin{smallmatrix}12\\10\end{smallmatrix}$)

as today, with the backs of the right-hand fingers against the inside of the throat of the bell, and the hand slightly flexed (Pl. 2). Then, on bringing the ball of the thumb further round, the bell is partly closed sufficiently to flatten a harmonic by a semitone (or less or more where required) as indicated in Ex. 2 by *a*. Fully stopping, closing the throat of the bell much as in hand muting, raises a harmonic by a semitone (*b*; also given in French Tutors for the upper *f''*, rather than part-stopping the 11th harmonic). Fully opening, straightening out the hand (*c*) is needed for *b♭'*, to sharpen the flat 7th harmonic. This all provides a chromatic scale over the most important part of the compass; with skill the stopped notes can be made to sound not too noticeably different from the natural 'open' notes—the small differences, in fact, often adding a special charm to well-performed hand-horn music.

At first the technique was used only by soloists. Thus Mozart's horn concertos (written for Ignaz Leutgeb, b. c. 1745) with their *a'* and *b'* and chromatic passages, depend on it, while Ex. 1 is from a time when all orchestral players used the hand-horn and bandsmen likewise (see MILITARY BAND, Pl. 2, middle row). The 2nd horn of a pair was customarily schooled to be especially expert in the hand technique, which accounts for Beethoven, for instance, normally giving a solo stopped passage to this player.

The hand-horn left an indelible mark on much subsequent horn writing, particularly in Germany; Brahms's orchestral horn parts, though written at a time when every player had a valved horn in his hands, are nevertheless pure hand-horn music, and Brahms hoped that his Trio, Op. 40 (1865), would be performed this way. Many players were still instructed in the technique as a matter of course in the early part of the 20th century, and it has been extensively revived in recent years for performance of the works originally conceived for it. (The chords which Weber wrote for the horn in the Concertino, Op. 45, are made by playing one note, humming the next, and hoping that the third will become audible as a 'difference tone' (see BEATS, 2)).

After valves first came in a composer might need to be sure that the players used them, as Berlioz in the last movements of the *Symphonie fantastique* (the horn parts, in the original edition of the score, having instructions like 'avec les cylindres [valves], tous les sons ouverts', i.e. no notes to be played hand-horn). Just before this, Schubert's song 'Auf dem Strohm' (1828) has a horn part written for

Pl. 2. Hand-horn player, lithograph (*c.* 1835) by C. Tellier.

Ex. 2. Excerpt from Rossini, *Semiramide* Overture, *Andantino*. Horns in D. a. half stop to lower harmonic; b. fully stop to raise; c. fully open to sharpen.

the early valve-horn advocate J. R. Levy, typical hand-horn music save where the horn doubles the voice in passages impossible without valves. The same player is said to have played 4th horn in the first performance of Beethoven's Ninth Symphony, and there has been much speculation since whether he may have performed the difficult solo in the Adagio with the valves (perfectly possible though it is, and more moving in the *pp* context, without them).

7. Repertory. Concertos include two by Haydn (both in D); four by Mozart (K. 412, K. 417, K. 447, K. 495) plus a Concert Rondo, K. 371; one by Franz Rössler; Weber's Concertino, Op. 45; two by Richard Strauss and one by his father (above, 4*b*).

Some chief works with piano are Beethoven's Sonata, Op. 17; Danzi's Sonata, Op. 28; Schumann's Adagio and Allegro, Op. 70; Glazunov's *Reverie*, Op. 24; Dukas's *Villanelle*; Skryabin's Romance; and Poulenc's *Elegie*. Also, Cherubini's two sonatas (originally with orchestra); and by Saint-Saëns the Romance Op. 36, *Morceau de concert*, Op. 94 (both these with orchestra), and the Romance, Op. 67 (horn and piano). Chamber music includes Brahms's Trio, Op. 40 (with piano and violin); Lennox Berkeley's Trio (for the same instruments); Haydn's Divertimento (with violin and cello); Britten's Serenade for Tenor voice, Horn, and Strings; and Mozart's Quintet, K. 407, also for horn and strings.

There are also many works for two or four horns alone (Rimsky-Korsakov's *Notturno* and Tippett's Sonata are both for four horns); or with strings, including two concertos by Vivaldi, one by Telemann, pieces by Mozart, Beethoven, and (for four horns with orchestra) Schumann (*Konzertstück*, Op. 86).

8. *Horns in general: (a) The prototype.* The horn of domesticated cattle with the tip cut off to leave an orifice for blowing has served from Antiquity and on through the Middle Ages in three main capacities: by herdsmen for calling their herds; for watchmen for alarms and curfews; and by huntsmen (see HUNTING HORN). Their overall importance could be said to follow that same order, with the herdsman's horn first and also the last to survive in the West in regular use, as in Hungary, where Bartók made a thorough study of its wide range of calls on two or three notes (see BAGPIPE;—Bartók 1976).

Horns serve the same purposes in Africa, where they are instantly distinguishable from European horns through having a blowing-hole cut in the side, often oval or lozenge-shaped, the instrument (of an antelope horn, elephant ivory, or gourd) held transversely to the lips. Often the tip is cut off and a small hole made there, uncovered by finger or thumb to produce a note about a tone or a third higher. Horns, with or without this hole, are much played over Africa in ensembles of different-sized horns, to contribute their notes one after another in strange harmonies (compare *'Russian horns'). The hole in the tip can also serve in sending messages by 'speech tone' as with *'talking drums', etc. In Peru and neighbouring Andean countries may be seen a dozen or more lengths of cowhorn, graded in width and joined by strips of cloth or hide to form a circle c.35 cm. (14") across; the *bocina* or *corneta* sounded by herdsmen, and at village church festivals. For European cow or wooden horns with fingerholes for playing tunes, see FINGERHOLE HORN; and for medieval ivory horns, OLIPHANT.

(b) *Metal horns.* (For Roman see BUCCINA AND CORNU, and for the large prehistoric Scandinavian, LUR.) The nearest in shape to these ancient horns today are the brass horns of India, **sringa*. European medieval brass or bronze horns were all of basically ox-horn shape and through the earlier centuries also served in warfare—a usage which afterwards lapsed until the 18th-century introduction of the bugle-horn (see BUGLE). Among the largest instruments are English 'burg-mote horns' (corporation horns, for summoning), of which some nine are preserved, reaching 90 cm. (3') in length: the 13th-century Dover horn was made, according to its cast inscription, by a German, reminding us that many similar civic horns are preserved in Europe, notably in Switzerland.

(c) *Ox-horns in the orchestra.* Wagner has them ('Stierhorn') in the *Ring*: in Act 2 of *Götterdämmerung*, Hagen summons his vassals, three of them successively sounding notes a semitone apart. Ideally an opera house needs special instruments for this, though the notes can be effective if sounded vigorously on a euphonium or the like. A special instrument has also been made for the 'cowhorn' in Britten's *Spring Symphony*.

Fitzpatrick 1970; Gregory 1961; Janetzky and Brüchle 1976, trans. 1988; Morley-Pegge 1960, 1973.

Hornpipe: 1. *Hornpipe, pibgorn.* A **reedpipe formerly played by shepherds, made of cane, elder, or bone, sounded with a single reed (**idioglot), or two such pipes secured parallel together ('double-pipe'). Over the lower end is a horn bell, usually a section of cowhorn. The old Welsh variety, *pibgorn* ('hornpipe') has also a horn at the blowing end, surrounding the reed and pressed to the mouth—single-pipe examples are preserved in the Welsh Folk Museum at St Fagan's. The Basque variety, *alboka* (from Arabic *al-buq*, 'horn') is a double-pipe, also with a horn at each end (Fig. 1). Others, as in Russia, have only the horn at the lower end and are mostly double-pipes and, like Fig. 1, with different numbers of holes in the two pipes for playing partly in harmony. Often again a bag is tied over the blowing end, making a bagpipe (see BAGPIPE, 6): among the Welsh examples is a double hornpipe which must have originally been such.

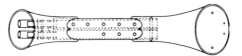

Fig. 1. Basque hornpipe, *alboka*, viewed from above (blowing end, with two reeds, on left).

The English name is met in 1324 when 'Little Alain, hornpiper' was among the instrumentalists of the King's Household (Rastall 1964). After the 15th century the word means the dance, for which, however, the fiddle-like tunes have far wider compass than any actual hornpipe could give.

Balfour 1890; Barrenechea 1976; and see BAGPIPE; Baines 1960.

2. Estives. Chaucer, in his translation of the *Roman de la rose*, puts 'hornepipes of Cornewaile' where the original 13th-century French poem has 'estives de Cornoaille'. 'Estives', a puzzling name, is by itself quite frequent in medieval French, with a less common English equivalent, 'stives' (e.g. 'merry as the blast of the stivour' in a text of *c*.1400), possibly referring to some hornpipe or bagpipe.

Hourglass drum. General term for a drum roughly in the shape of an egg-timer or dumb-bell (see DRUM, 4*c*), e.g. the Korean *changgu* (see CHINA AND KOREA, 2). See also *kalangu*; *tsuzumi*.

Hsaing-waing. Burmese *drum chime.

Hsiao. A Chinese flute; see XIAO.

Huehuetl. The upright drum of the Aztecs of Central America, with jaguar-skin head; a ritual instrument along with the *slit drum *teponatzli. See AMERICAN INDIANS, 1.

Hummel. The former folk zither of Sweden and islands north of the mouth of the Elbe; Danish *hommel*. See ZITHER, 2.

Humming top (or 'pump top'). This attractive toy, manufactured mainly in Germany, is a *free-reed instrument. The rotation of the top draws air out from the interior through specially-shaped louvres cut round the upper circumference, and in at the bottom through the set of free reeds (sometimes now together cut in a disc of synthetic material). The reeds are in three groups tuned respectively to a tonic chord, its dominant, and subdominant. As the top spins, carrying the reeds with it, it activates a train of gears (often enclosed in a cap below the reeds). The gears slowly rotate a slotted plate situated just above the reeds and with a corresponding fixed plate next to it. The slotted plate makes one revolution to about 100 revolutions of the top, and in each revolution the slots allow air to pass through the three groups of reeds in succession so that the chord slowly changes, with a brief silence between them, while the external mingling of the swirling colours holds the eye. The tonic chord is normally in the musical root position, the dominant in first inversion, and the subdominant in second inversion.

Over the world, whistling tops are made by children from dried fruit-shells, etc., spun by a long string. Holes are pierced for the top to sound on the *vessel-flute principle.

Hunting horn. 1. In England for the fox and stag hunt, this is the short, straight instrument, 23 cm. (9″) long, of copper, brass-mounted, with the mouthpiece fixed to it (see POSTHORN Fig. 1*c*). Its high, lively sounds play an important signalling role in the hunt, and for those unable to sound it there are models with a metal reed instead of the proper mouthpiece (see REED, 1). The instrument dates from after the Restoration (1660), when it was about twice as long as it is now; it was reckoned to give a clearer sound than the older curved horns.

Written codes for the more ancient horn made of a cowhorn exist in French manuscripts back to the 14th century, given in long and short notes and mnemonic syllables. From the late 16th century the codes were published and the English code derives partly from them (Halfpenny 1954). A useful modern handbook is by L. C. R. Cameron (*c*.1905, repr. by Swaine Adeney Brigg, London, n.d.); at the end it reproduces the 'Antient Hunting Notes' as published in the *Sportsman's Dictionary* of 1744. Thus, 'Death of a Fox':—òòò—óòò (repeated; ò marks the 'taverne', a kind of whoop).

2. In Germany and Poland the normal hunting horn (*Jagdhorn*) is formed in a small circle like a German *post-horn, and has the pitch and notes of a bugle. It is manufactured under the name Prinz-Pless Horn (*Pless-horn*), after the Silesian nobleman who introduced it in the late 19th century as preferable to older types of semicircular metal horn (see BUGLE, 5).

3. The French hunting horn is the large circular 'trompe (or cor) de chasse', the direct descendant of the baroque horn from which our orchestral horn is also derived (see HORN, 5*b*). It is usually made in three coils, 40 cm. (16″) across, and pitched in D, giving the same notes as the natural orchestral horn in this key. Ex. 1 is the beginning of one of the numerous calls, for which there have been many printed editions.

Some well-known French folk-songs from the 19th century, like 'Le bon roi Dagobert', are based on *trompe* tunes. In 18th-century Germany the same calls as in France were sounded on the same instrument on the grand hunts. Haydn quotes one of them in *The Seasons*, while their 6/8 rhythm is reflected in the rondo finales of Mozart's horn concertos.

The French players form clubs, in Belgium also, and blow the horns very forcefully with much of the idiomatic *tayauté* on the strong beats, a kind of short trill (Ex. 1). The *trompe* is also manufactured

Ex. 1. (sounds a minor 7th lower).

La Vue

etc.

in the key of E♭ for playing with brass bands. This has become very popular in some other European countries, too, where the instruments are now also manufactured.

Huqin (or *hu-ch'ing*). Chinese generic term for fiddles: see ERHU.

Hurdy-gurdy (Fr.: *vielle, vielle à roue*; Ger.: *Leier, Radleier*; It.: *ghironda*; Ru.: *lira*; Sp.: *zanfoña*. An older Eng. name, from the 17th century, is 'cymbal').

1. *General description.* A hurdy-gurdy has strings sounded by a resined wooden wheel instead of a bow (A in Fig. 1). It is held across the lap or, if standing, on a strap. The right hand turns the wheel by a crank-handle (Fig. 1, B). The left hand rests on the lid of a long keybox (Pl. 1) mounted on top of the body of the instrument, with the fingers bent round to push up from below the wooden keys projecting from the lower side of the box. Each key carries an upright wooden blade (Fig. 1, C) which presses against the melody string to make a note of the scale; or two such blades if this string is paired. On release, the key falls clear of the string under gravity aided by rebound from the string. In addition there are from one to four strings that are not stopped by keys but produce a drone.

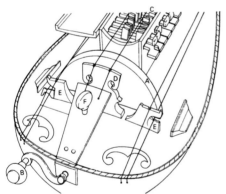

Fig. 1. Hurdy-gurdy (France), general view of right-hand half of instrument.

Once widespread across Europe as a folk instrument, the hurdy-gurdy is now best known as played in France, where it has a strong tradition in the central provinces for folk dances. Many have now taken it up elsewhere, using instruments mostly based on the French model, though not invariably.

2. *French hurdy-gurdy.* This has a body in the shape of a lute (as in Fig. 1) or a guitar. There is no neck, the pegbox being joined directly to the body. The wheel is of pearwood, about 15 cm. (6″) in diameter, and is mounted on an iron shaft. The rim, *c.*12 mm. (½″) wide, has a slightly convex

Pl. 1. ' "Old Sarah", the well-known hurdy-gurdy player', from Henry Mayhew's *London Labour and London Poor* (iii, 1867).

surface, and is highly polished with resin; over it is a curved cover (as in Pl. 1) to keep the rain off. The keys give a chromatic compass of up to two octaves.

The arrangement of the six strings over the wheel is shown in Fig. 1, and their traditional tuning in Ex. 1. In the middle (Fig. 1) are the two melody strings or *chanterelles*, led over the large bridge, D, to the tailpiece and both tuned to *g'*. On the right are the two main drones or *bourdons* (Ex. 1, b and B); and on the left two more drones: the *mouche* (m), aptly named if one recalls the sound of a fly as compared with that of a bumble bee or *bourdon*); and the *trompette* (t), which serves a very special purpose described below. Violin gut D strings may be used, but the two *bourdons* would require the lowest cello strings.

Ex. 1. *a   b*

Only three of the drones are used at a time. When playing in C, as preferred in France, the *grand bourdon* is silenced by sliding it along its bridge away from the wheel. For playing in G the *petit bourdon* is silenced instead, and the *trompette* tuned up to *d'*.

Though the left hand can make a variety of articulations with the keys including a percussive staccato, the main articulation of the music is by interrupting the rotation of the wheel, not actually stopping it, but turning it in measured jerks, which also brings the *trompette* into its special operation. This string bears on a small loose bridge called the *chien*, about 12 mm. ($\frac{1}{2}''$) high and shaped rather like a pointed shoe with the point resting freely in a slot in the foot of the *mouche* bridge (E) which arches over it. When rotation of the wheel is suddenly accelerated the *trompette* vibrates vigorously up and down, causing the *chien* to rock on its 'sole' and strike with the heel upon a plate of ivory or other hard material let into the body at that point. The audible result is a strong buzz, which ceases as the wheel resumes its normal speed, and these brief buzzes of the *trompette* mark the rhythms. The pressure on the *chien* is carefully adjusted with a loop of fine gut leading from the string to a peg placed upright in the tailpiece of the *chanterelles* (Fig. 1, F).

In some parts of France, as in Berry, players today use different tunings, e.g. with *chanterelles* in octaves, *d''*, and *d'*, and the *bourdons* also in octaves, *d* and *D*. The tuning in Ex. 1 is the classic tuning, still much used, which ruled in the 18th century, when playing the *vielle* had become a fashionable accomplishment in society. Many handsome instruments from that period are now restored and in use, and many original Tutors with tunes and duets for *vielle* supply a classical repertory. Some of these suit the bagpipe *musette* (see MUSETTE, 1) equally well; players today have demonstrated how this instrument blends with the hurdy-gurdy very well. In France hurdy-gurdy and bagpipe are still frequently played together for folk dances. Nor has manufacture of the *vielle* in Paris, Mirecourt, and elsewhere ever ceased from those earlier times.

3. *Other European hurdy-gurdies*. Most of these have a body in the shape of a guitar or else of a deep violin (again with no separate neck). Some have diatonic keys only. Mozart scored for the Austrian instrument (*Leier*) in his German Dances K. 602, and this is still played in the south-west of Hungary: the *tekero*, with single melody string, one *bourdon*, and *trompette*, the latter used very expertly to give the rhythm as clearly as a side-drum. Otherwise the hurdy-gurdy has been mainly an instrument of street music, heard well into the 20th century from Portugal (*sanfona*) across to Russia (*lera* or *relya*). The players were often blind, like 'Old Sarah' of London (Pl. 1), described in the 1850s by Henry Mayhew in her old age still playing her 'cymbal' on which, she told him, her favourite tune was 'Haste to the wedding'.

4. *Early history*. The 12th century saw the first of these wheel-operated instruments, named 'organistrum': with the keybox mounted on a separate neck it was a long instrument and manned by two players, of which one, often the younger, turned the handle while the other worked keys of a rotating kind. It was evidently used by the clergy in choir schools, first perhaps in Germany; it is not known to have incorporated a drone. Another name is 'symphonie', becoming in French vernacular 'chifonie' or in English 'synfan'. This, from the 13th century, came particularly to denote a small, secular, one-man portable form: an oblong box with the wheel totally enclosed inside at one end and therefore only 5 to 8 cm. (2" or 3") in diameter. There are no contemporary views of the interior workings, but successful reconstructions have been made, with sprung keys, and some with a drone included; they sound soft and sweet. In the 14th century, after the time of the Black Death, the instrument declined in social status, and the forms closer to the hurdy-gurdies of later times seen in 15th-century pictures are folk or beggars' instruments.

5. *Repertory*. The hurdy-gurdy repertory includes six suites for two *musettes* or *vielles* by Boismortier; six 'sonatilles galantes' and six 'duos galantes' by Esprit Philippe Chédeville (1696–1762); six concertos for *vielles*, etc. by Naudot; and six sonatas for *musette*, *vielle*, etc. in Vivaldi's *Il pastor fido*. There are also French collections of folk music suitable for the *vielle*, such as H. Cochinol: *Chants et dances folklorique du Limousin et du Massif Central* (Paris, 1974).

6. *Organ hurdy-gurdy* (Fr.: *vielle organisée*). This is an 18th-century form which includes inside the body a small pipe organ, sounding simultaneously with the strings, the keys controlling the pipes and the handle working the bellows. The 'lira organizzata', however, for which Haydn wrote nocturnes and a concerto for the King of Naples, was probably of a **geigenwerk* kind, with several wheels and conventional keyboard.

Baines, F. 1975; Bröcker 1973; Muskett 1982; Page 1982a, 1983.

Husle (Czech). See FIDDLE, 1c.

Hydraulis. The first known kind of **organ*. Its invention is attributed to Ktesibios, an engineer in Alexandria, *c*.246 BC, who also devised mechanical singing birds and so on. The organ became named *hydraulis* on account of using the weight of water to maintain air pressure in the wind-chest. Submerged in a tank of water, and resting on the bottom of this, is an inverted bronze dome (the *pnigeus*), round the rim of which are holes for water to be able to pass between tank and dome. Two air-conduits lead upwards from the top of the dome. One of them leads from an external air-pump (or alternating pair of pumps) which will force air into the dome through a non-return valve. By thus lowering the water level in the dome, causing that in the tank to rise, the difference in water levels creates the air pressure which, through the other conduit, feeds the wind-chest and the organ pipes. As air is expended through these it is replenished, and the difference in water level maintained, by pumping further air into the dome. As for the pipes, Vitruvius (d. *c*.AD 26) implies the use of both open and stopped flue-pipes, and sliders for changing registration.

In Rome, Nero acquired an enthusiasm for the instrument, which quickly became a symbol of wealth and flourished as a secular instrument for possibly the next 300 years. The most remarkable survival from this period is the instrument of AD 228 excavated in 1931 at Aquincum in Hungary. This had four rows of pipes, made in bronze; but although inscribed *hydra* this instrument evidently dispensed with the water, the air pressure main-

tained wholly with bellows. The transition from water-power to bellows-blowing cannot be precisely dated, but by the 2nd century AD hand-blown bellows were being advocated for small organs, while the water machine was still thought to be most suitable for larger instruments which had to sound strong (organs were often used in the open air).

Perrot 1971.

Hz. Abbreviation of *Hertz.

I

Idio-. A prefix introduced by Hornbostel and *Sachs (1914) on the basis of the Greek word *idios* in the sense of 'one's own'; see the following entries with this prefix.

Idiochord. 'With integral string'; applied to the many instruments of bamboo, etc., in which strips of the bark are cut free except at the ends, where they are put under tension by inserting small bridges. The strips, plucked or struck, obey much the same physical laws as stretched strings, and these instruments are accordingly classified among chordophones (most of them as 'zithers': see CLAS-SIFICATION; ZITHER).

Idioglot. 'With integral tongue'; applied to wind instruments, many of them folk-instruments, that employ a reed (see REED, 2) made by slitting a vibrating tongue either in a small length of cane inserted into the pipe (as in *bagpipe drones) or in the cane of the pipe itself (see REEDPIPE). Can also be applied to *jew's-harps of Asia and the Pacific where the instrument is of one piece of bamboo.

Idiophone. 'Self-sounder' ('with integral voice'). A class name (see CLASSIFICATION) for hard vibrating instruments of all kinds, whether rigid (as *cymbals) or flexible (as in a *musical box), and especially valuable in a sense of 'percussion instruments less drums', for which no word exists in common English.

Improvised instruments. Objects, naturally occurring or artefact, which, while not existing in the first place for sound producing, become so used, generally to set up or enhance a rhythm. Examples could be endless and from all across the world (see EARLY EVOLUTION). On festive occasions in the West, examples are banging the table-top or, more difficult, rubbing it with a stick held upright for various howling sounds; also *bones, washboard (see SCRAPER), or almost anything that comes to hand.

'Rough music' (Fr.: *charivari*) from the Middle Ages onwards has used household utensils—saucepans, shovels, tongs—along with large handbells and other instruments, all capable of maximum noise and often sounded in public expression of disapproval, the partakers wearing comic masks (e.g. cat, whence Ger.: *Katzenmusik*): a well-known picture is in the early 14th-century *Roman de Fauvel*. Rough music would be laid on outside the dwelling of an unfaithful wife, for example. It may be heard today, in Italy, from a procession of strikers, beating metal dustbin lids and so on, making a terrific noise in which a violent rhythm spontaneously emerges.

Noise-makers may also, of course, be assembled from bits and pieces obtained from other things; but then an instrument is actually being made, crude though it may be (e.g. *lagerphone), though if to imitate some existing instrument, 'improvised' may be appropriate.

Imzad (or *amzad*). Tuareg one-stringed fiddle (Sahara). See FIDDLE, 2*b* and Pl. 3. Similar instruments played over West Africa often have the name *goge*.

India: 1. *Indian classification of instruments*. India has the credit for the earliest-known division of musical instruments into four groups, in the treatise *Nāṭyaśāstra* (c.AD 200), these groups corresponding to those now recognized in Western *classification of instruments: *tata*, 'stringed'; *suṣira*, 'hollow' (wind instruments); *avanaddha*, 'covered' (drums); and *ghana*, 'solid' (idiophones). The following references to individual articles, however, follow Western order, noticing also distinctions between instruments of the North of India and of the South.

2. *Instruments*. Of several hundreds of different varieties found over the subcontinent the following are among the most prominent, or the most interesting in special respects.

(*a*) *Idiophones*. While the principal method of keeping time, other than with a drum, is by clapping or, in classical music, silently gesturing with the hands, small cup cymbals (see CYMBAL, 5) serve this purpose in some dance and religious music, and in the nagasvaram ensemble of the South (see (*d*) below). Also in classical music of South India, the earthenware pot, *ghatam* and the tuned bowls, *jaltarang* may be used.

(*b*) *Drums*. Very highly developed and in great variety. In classical music today, in South India, the long, horizontal two-headed *mṛdanga. In the North, a larger version *pakhāvaj* (or *mrdang*) accompanies the *dhrupad* style of 16th-century court music origin; but most usual in the North is the *tablā, the pair of upright drums (Pl. 1, right). These, and the popular barrel drum *dhol* (or *dholak*), are played exclusively with the hands. Others may be played with sticks: small kettledrums *duggā* (*dukar*) of the Northern *shahnāī* ensemble; barrel

Pl. 1. An ensemble of stringed instruments from north India: (*left to right*) sitạr, sārod, and tambūrā, with tablā (drums) in the foreground.

drums *ṭavil* (for which a stick may be used on the left-hand head, see DRUM, Pl. 1) with the *nāgasvaram*.

Accompaniment on the *tablā*, *mṛdaṅgam*, or other percussion instruments is an indispensable feature of measured music. In the North, the function of the drum is partly to keep time, by means of a repeated ostinato pattern of drum-strokes lasting one bar (*ṭhekā*). In the South, the drum player closely follows the rhythm of the soloist, and must therefore know the vocal repertory intimately. Given the opportunity, however, any drum player will play fast variations, providing a complex rhythmic counterpoint to the soloist's melody.

(*c*) *Stringed*. Plucked instruments have always in India been next in importance and prestige to the voice, whether played solo or in accompaniment to the voice, the flexible and expressive qualities of which are reproduced on the instruments through very special technical adaptations, e.g. in design of frets and bridges, also in the often numerous thin metal *sympathetic strings, contributing a subtle resonance to which the Indian ear is keenly alert: see VINA (*vīṇā*); SITAR; TAMBŪRĀ, serving solely to provide the humming drone accompaniment essential for vocal music; also *sārod*, a smaller plucked instrument of North India (see Pl. 1, centre); also numerous folk-instruments, some one-stringed, like the *gopi-yantra* (with the string led to a drum skin) and *tuila*, these again supplying the essential tonic below the voice.

Bowed instruments: *sārangī*; *dilrubā* and *esrāj*, small bowed relatives of the sitar; *sarinda*, a folk species. In South India, accompaniment to the voice

is generally provided by the *violin, introduced from Europe in the 18th century. To facilitate complete freedom of movement of the left-hand fingers the instrument is held, while the player is seated on the floor, with the body firmly against the chest and the scroll against the foot. It is also played in North India as a solo instrument.

The hammered *dulcimer, related to the Iranian *santir*, is found only in North India, introduced from Kashmir during the Muslim period.

(*d*) *Wind*. Transverse flute, *bānsurī* (in the South, *kural*); folk and pastoral flutes in great variety include end-blown (see NAY) and duct-flutes in the North. Double-reed *shawm relatives: in North India, *shahnāī*; in the South, *nāgasvaram* (see SHAHNĀĪ). Among lesser reed instruments, single-reed gourd pipe, *pungi*. Brass: see TRUMPET, 7*c*; brass horn, *sringa*; also CONCH.

Floyd 1980; Krishnaswami 1971; Grosset, 'Inde', in Lavignac 1913: 339ff.; Popley 1921.

Indonesia. See GAMELAN. Also ANGKLUNG; BLOWN GONG; BONANG; CELEMPUNG; CHALUNG; FLUTE, 7*c* (SULING); GAMBANG; GANGSA; GENDER; GONG AND TAM-TAM, 2; KACHAPI; RABAB, 3; SARON; SHAWM, 4*b*.

Inharmonicity. See PARTIALS, 5; PIANO, 4*c*.

Inventions-horn. See HORN, 5*c*.

Ipu hula (Hawaiian 'dance gourd'). See PACIFIC ISLANDS, 3*a*.

J

Jack. The device that plucks the strings in a harpsichord, spinet, and virginal. See HARPSICHORD, 3.

Jaltarang. Indian porcelain chime of 16 to 18 bowls graded in size, placed in a semicircle on the ground (or on canvas pads) with the largest bowl (with the width of a large pudding-basin) to the player's left. Played as a solo instrument, the bowls are struck on the rim with thin sticks, usually in a fast tempo, and giving very clean notes. Tuning is adjusted with water, which, poured in, lowers the pitch of the sound, at first very gradually (as with *musical glasses).

Japan. The manufacture of Western musical instruments for which Japan is so well known commenced soon after 1868; the firm of Yamaha, making pianos from shortly after 1900, is today said to command near half of the total world production. The traditional Japanese instruments, briefly listed below, for their part reflect an ancient debt to the Asian mainland, most having been introduced at various stages from China or Korea, or thence via the islands. Some have since become considerably modified; others have retained their original structural features almost exactly, as may be judged among the superb instruments of the 8th century AD preserved in the Treasure House Shosoin, at Nara.

1. *Instruments*: (*a*) *Idiophones*. Bells: large temple bells, *ō-gane*, similar to Chinese *zhong* bells, usually housed in bell towers and struck on the outside by a heavy pole swung horizontally like a battering ram; hand-bell with clapper, *rei*; a rattle with pellet-bells, *suzu* (see BELL TREE); *resting bell, *kin*, sounded in Buddhist ceremonies, along with a bronze or iron suspended plate, *kei*, of deeply meandering outline ('fish-mouthed') and the 'wooden fish', *mokugyo* (see TEMPLE BLOCK). Gong: especially the small (15 cm. (6″)), high-sounding *shoko* of court music and Buddhist rites, struck on the inside with a pair of thin, knobbed sticks. Clappers: *shakubyōshi*, two straight pieces of boxwood, *c*.35 cm. (13″) long, clapped together by the choir-leader in courtly genres; *yotsudaki*, bamboo strips played like the *bones. Rattles: include strung wooden plaques, see BIN-SASARA (see also 3, below, Kabuki theatre).

(*b*) *Drums*. As important as everywhere in Asia. Most are two-headed: barrel drums, with nailed or laced heads; *taiko; and 'hourglass' drums, *tsuzumi. See also Pl. 2.

(*c*) *Stringed*. Long zither: *koto (with an older type, *wagon*, see KOTO, 3). Lutes: *biwa, pear-shaped, preserving an older form of the Chinese *pipa*; and the popular long lute *shamisen. Fiddle: *kokyū, in build like a small *shamisen*. See Pl. 1, left to right: KOTO, KOKYU, SHAMISEN.

(*d*) *Wind*. Transverse flute, generically *fue (as a suffix, *-bue*), in many varieties and especially prominent in the theatre (Pl. 2), notably the *nōkan*; end-blown, *shakuhachi, the main flute for solos and chamber music with *koto* and *shamisen*. Double-reed pipe, *hichiriki (court music). Mouth-organ, *shō* (see SHENG, SHŌ). (Conical, double-reed, of Chinese *sona type, used only by street vendors of Chinese noodles.)

Pl. 1. 'The chamber trio' (Piggott 1893).

Ex. 1.   12th century   20th century

Mouth-Organ

Flute

Double-
Reed Pipe

[Sources survive from a later date only]

Metal Gong
Small Drum
Big Drum

Zither

Lute

2. *Court music* (*gagaku*). A survival, almost unique in the world, of a medieval instrumental ensemble. The present repertory (reinstated from 1868) includes music both without dance, using wind, strings, and drums (Ex. 1); and with dance (*bugaku*), this without the strings. In Ex. 1, the bar on the left shows how the piece was performed according to 12th-century sources, i.e. before a massive retardation later ensued (each crotchet of the ancient version being represented by a whole bar

Pl. 2. 'The orchestra of the modern theatre in full dress' (Piggott 1893): front row— *taiko, o-tsuzumi, kotsuzumi, shinobue* (flute); behind— vocalists, *shamisens*.

in the later) along with changes in the instrumental techniques. The result is to render the original *tōgaku* melody no longer perceptible as such: it can just be discerned in the lower notes of the chord-clusters of the mouth organ and in the two wind parts below and the deep *biwa* part; the *koto* plays formalized harp-like figures and the drum pattern has become more elaborate.

3. *Theatre*. The classic *nō* plays have been accompanied on the stage since the 17th century by four musicians playing the transverse flute *nōkan* and the drums *taiko* and (of two different kinds) *tsuzumi*. The *kabuki* theatre adds to these, on the stage (Pl. 2), two or three *shamisen*, while behind the stage, invisible behind a bamboo screen with windows above, are the *geza* musicians playing as required *shamisen*, flutes, and a great variety of percussion instruments: firstly the large barrel drum *ō-daiko*; wood clappers *hyoshigi* (signalling the rise and fall of the curtain); drums of several further kinds, bells, gongs, small cymbals, and a xylophone *mokkin* (of a 'trough' kind; see XYLOPHONE, 3).
  Harich-Schneider 1973; Malm 1959; Piggott 1893, repr. 1971.

Japanese fiddle. A name once given to various types of one-string fiddle manufactured in the West up to the 1930s, first in the USA, for casual music. They may have a skin-covered soundbox (evidently imitating the **kokyu*) or a metal diaphragm and horn as in a **Stroh* violin.

Jarana. Mexican name for various species of small guitar (see GUITAR, 5).

Jawbone. The entire lower jaw of, usually, a donkey, with the teeth kept in if necessary by wire. Holding the pointed end (the incisors) the jaw is hit on one side with the hand to make the teeth rattle, different effects being made by striking at different places along the bone. Now best-known in Latin American music (as *quijada*), it was however played in Europe in the Middle Ages, as well as from the 1840s by Christy minstrel troops in the USA. A modern substitute is the **vibraslap*.

Jaw's harp. See JEW'S HARP.

Jazz. For a brief note on the instrumental constitution of the larger ensembles, see DANCE BAND.

Jenglong. See GAMELAN, 1 (Sundanese).

Jew's harp (Fr.: *guimbarde*; Ger.: *Maultrommel*; It.: *scacciapensieri*; Ru.: *vargan*; Sp.: *trompa*, etc.). Today more usually sold as 'jaws harp'; well known in the popular music of most countries, in Europe from Scandinavia and Scotland to Sicily in the south.

1. *Description*. The frame is forged from an iron rod of diamond cross-section and sometimes thickest in the middle (Fig. 1a). Hammered into the centre of this, to lie closely between the arms of the frame, is the narrow flexible blade or tongue forged in steel and bent into a prong at its free end. The oval part of the frame is held in the left hand, with its two arms against the parted teeth and the lips resting lightly on them. The blade is twanged rhythmically by the other hand. The sound given by this alone, the fundamental of the blade's vibration, is normally a note deep in the bass register. Meanwhile the player moves tongue and cheeks to keep changing the volume of the oral cavity (as in 'oo–ah–ee') and thereby give resonance to one after another of such harmonics of this fundamental pitch as lie within the range of mouth resonance. From the fourth to the thirteenth of the **harmonic series are the most used, giving a scale like that of a natural trumpet. With proper skill and a well-made instrument, the notes sound clearly enough above the reiterated fundamental to be audible to a fair-sized audience. Sometimes, however, the jew's-harp is played simply to supply a buzzing, rhythmic drone, in accompaniment to other instruments.
  The acoustics of the action have been much debated (see e.g. Adkins 1974). The vibrating blade in itself can theoretically produce partials only at non-harmonic 'clamped bar' frequencies high above the fundamental by at least $2\frac{1}{2}$ octaves (see

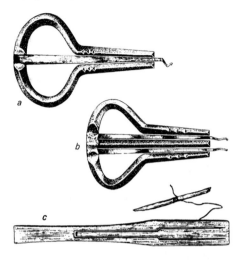

Fig. 1. (a, b) Jew's harp, with one or with two tongues; (c) wooden jew's harp from north-east Siberia.

PARTIALS, 6); but it appears that as the blade passes to and fro through the narrow space between the arms, it disturbs the air to create a wave-form with a regular series of harmonics based on the tongue fundamental (somewhat as occurs also with *free-reed instruments). The jew's harp is classified among idiophones (see CLASSIFICATION), since the vibration of the solid blade is the primary instigator of the sounds.

2. History in the West. The jew's harp, iron or bronze, is known archaeologically by at least 80 examples, some dating back, possibly, to the late Gallo-Roman period; some from Anglo-Saxon times were found buried with their owners, so they were evidently precious possessions. Later, it appears as one of the 14 instruments in the 14th-century carved 'minstrels' gallery' in Exeter Cathedral—though in England up to Tudor times the name was generally not 'harp' but 'trump'; the reason for 'jew's' has never been truly discovered. In the British Isles its greatest popularity, since the 17th century at least, has been in Scotland and Ireland; on the remote Scottish island of St Kilda it was the only instrument known when the last inhabitants were evacuated in the 20th century.

In Austria, a main seat of jew's-harp manufacture from the 17th century has been Molln; the instrument was played especially for serenading. The Tyrol has also been famous for the playing on two jew's harps at once, tuned to tonic and dominant, one method being to hold one in each hand, tongues pointing towards each other and twanging them with the little fingers. Another is to hold two back to back, one tuned a fourth deeper, rapidly flipping them over for an answering phrase in the dominant. A 19th-century virtuoso, Eulenstein, 'joined sixteen together, tuned with sealing wax', a favourite item being his variations on Rossini's aria 'Di tanti palpiti'. J. G. Albrechtsberger is one who wrote concertos for such players and these have been performed again today. The instrument is named in these works 'cremb.' (for *crembalum*) or 'tromb.' (for *trombula*), the latter sometimes since misinterpreted as 'trumpet'. Today, jew's harps can be bought with two blades, the second usually tuned to the dominant of the first (Fig. 1b).

3. Jew's harp in Asia. Iron jew's harps are played as far as Central Asia and Afghanistan, some of them with a narrow two-pronged frame recalling the instruments made wholly in wood or bamboo to the east as far as Polynesia. There are peoples from Siberia to New Guinea who (as on St Kilda) until recently knew no other tuneful instrument. Some in Siberia are of mammoth ivory. The construction generally takes the form of a thin plate of the material with the vibrating blade neatly cut in this and jerked by a string attached near the base of the blade (Fig. 1c). This is believed to represent the earliest form of the instrument. There is indeed an Austrian legend of a girl who made the first *Maultrommel* out of wood.

Jinghu (or *ching-hu*). See erhu.

Jingle. See SISTRUM AND JINGLES. For 'jingle bells' (pellet-bells) see SLEIGH BELLS.

Jingle ring (or Brazilian tambourine). A wooden hoop with pairs of jingle plates in slots as in a *tambourine, but with no membrane (see SISTRUM AND JINGLES, Fig. 1c). The sound, almost all from the jingles, is by waving, or shaking in the wrist, or striking against something. An old traditional dancer's instrument of south Europe (in Sicily called the 'circle') and the Azores, it came into Western manufacture chiefly for school percussion bands, and has been used by rock singers, tapping it gently on the thigh for a soft rhythmic background. Orchestral percussionists have sometimes found this non-membrane instrument useful in delicate passages written for the tambourine.

Jingling Johnny. See BELL TREE.

K

Kachapi (or *kacapi*). 1. A type of zither popular in West Java, a southern relative of the East Asian *long zithers. A long, broad box, raised just off the ground, bears a flat soundboard which may be 150 cm. (5′) long. The ends of the box slope upwards, rather like the prow of a ship. The underside is partly open. Up to 18 wire strings are hitched to pins next to the nut at the right-hand end (the player's right), thence passing over individual movable bridges and through holes in the soundboard to tuning pegs placed in a slanting row in a strengthening strip running along the far side of the box. The bridges, serving for fine tuning, have a triangular shape recalling, for example, those of the Chinese *zheng. The player sits near the right-hand end. The strings are plucked with finger and thumb of both hands (using the nails or finger-picks), the right hand playing the melody, the left hand accompanying, e.g. by a constant repetition of the tonic. The *kachapi* is much played with the flute *suling and the bowed rebab (see RABAB, 3). Through modern times have become popular various forms which combine features of the *siter* (see CELEMPUNG).

2. Over parts of Indonesia, such as the Celebes (now Sulawesi), a lute, with hollowed-out body and one or two strings.

3. *Kachapi vina* is a name from the late 19th century for a type of *sitar popular in India (Bengal).

Kakaki. Long trumpet of the Western Sudan; see NAFIR, 2.

Kakko. Two-headed cylindrical drum of Japanese court music; see TAIKO, 2c.

Kalangu. One of the West African hourglass drums held under the arm, whereby the pitch can be changed by pressing on the tensioning cords passing between one head and the other (see DRUM, Fig. 1e). Usually it is struck on the foremost head with a hooked stick.

Kantele. Traditional stringed instrument of Finland. Corresponding instruments are played by the Baltic peoples (Estonia, *kannel*; Latvia, *kokle*; Lithuania, *kankles*), and in neighbouring parts of Russia (see GUSLI, 1). The strings, now of wire, spread somewhat fanwise over a flat soundbox placed across the knees (or now often on a table). The size and shape, number of strings, and method of playing have in all regions undergone much change over the last hundred years to keep up with the times, bringing replacement of the older folk instruments by the larger and sometimes more complex forms heard today in folk recitals.

1. *Traditional* kantele. The small wing-shaped soundbox (Pl. 1) is hollowed out in pine, the bottom remaining open. It is usually placed with the longest side furthest from the player (tuning pins to the left). The typical five strings are attached on the right, often to a wood or metal cross rod, and are tuned diatonically through a fifth upwards from the keynote. In the principal playing method the left hand is reserved for damping movements. The right hand sounds the strings, mostly with brushing strokes of the fingernails (or sometimes a plectrum), while the left-hand fingers, lying over the strings, press to keep silent those whose notes are not concordant in the phrase being played at that instant. The concordant strings then ring on, contributing volume and richness to the dance or song tunes performed on this little instrument. Thus in a tune recorded *c.*1945, the first phrase lies in the chord of the keynote, F, and the G and B♭ strings are damped; then, in the answering phrase in the dominant, the F and A strings are damped, the required movements of the damping fingers being executed with great deftness.

Pl. 1. Kantele player in eastern Finland (1917).

2. *Later versions.* Since the late 19th century the kantele has been enlarged and remodelled, and in the Baltic states and Russia also, with 30 metal strings or more (compass upwards from *C*). It can be played in the old manner or in alternative ways, both hands plucking. Latterly in Finland the kantele is sometimes turned the other way round, long side nearest. In the USSR since the late 1940s the *gusli* has been developed for use in folk orchestras with a key mechanism for damping with an octave set of piano-like keys (now chromatic). When the keys are not touched, a damper for each note of the scale rests upon all the strings for that note, in every octave of the compass, keeping them silent. On pressing a key, the damper is lifted, for the hand to sound the note in one or as many octaves as wished. This makes possible some effects not possible on other stringed instruments: e.g. any notes or chord, held by one hand on the keys, can be swept, or played in glissandos up and down, by the other, and the notes or chord can be changed while doing so. The increased scope is made use of in solo compositions and arrangements now written for folk orchestra (Tikhomirov 1983).

3. *'Kantele' in the* Kalevala. The word figures in the Finnish saga to the extent that 'harp' figures in *Beowulf*, 'harp' then meaning a form of lyre, an instrument on which the left hand can have a damping function similar to that described above (see LYRE, 3). The medieval *kantele* was perhaps akin to instruments discovered in Russian and Polish sites, wedge-shaped with a large opening for one hand to damp from underneath (see MEDIEVAL INSTRUMENTS—Crane 1972; Panum 1941).

Kantil. See GAMELAN, 2.

Karna. Six-foot long brass trumpet played in Central Asia, North India, and formerly Iran: a medieval Islamic trumpet that can still be heard. A very wide tube (*c*.3.5–5.5 cm., or 1.4–2.2″) leads to a funnel bell bearing an ornamentally wrought pommel. The half of the tube towards the player (the instrument dividing in two for transport) is in fact a casing over a true mouthpipe inside, this tapering to a narrow tip where a sheet-metal mouthpiece is soldered on, its rim held firm by the end of the wide outer casing.

Usually two are sounded together in ensemble with the *surna* (see SHAWM) and small kettledrums (see NAQQARA), now at local festivals, though formerly from palace or town gateways at certain hours or accompanying royalty in warfare (as were corresponding instruments in 13th–14th century Europe). The trumpets give out in some cases long single notes (in Iran likened by former European visitors to the bellowing of a bull) or otherwise vigorous baritone utterances using the 2nd harmonic and the 3rd (which on these instruments sounds about a sixth higher: compare the sounds

of the long *kakaki* trumpets of West Africa, NAFIR, 2).

Kasso. See KORA.

Kaval. End-blown flute (see FLUTE, 7*b*) of shepherds and folk music over south-east Europe, and in Turkey (Pl. 1) where, however, *kaval* (a Turkish word) can also mean a duct flute.

Pl. 1. Kaval, probably south Yugoslavia.

It may be of cane like the **nay* of the Middle East generally, or of wood. The well-known *kaval* of Macedonia (Yugoslavia) and Bulgaria is up to 84 cm. (32″) long, made in three wooden joints fitting together over tapered tenons; the top end is bevelled all round to present a fairly sharp rim to place against the lower lip (or sometimes the teeth, see NAY). In Macedonia two are played together, one sustaining a drone note, and both with a deliberately breathy, 'rushing' tone. A name in modern Greece and the islands is *floyera* (the duct-flute being *souravli*, etc.).

Kayagum (or *kayagŭm*). One of the 'long zithers' of Korea (see CHINA AND KOREA, 2 and Pl. 2, front right, along with the classical *komungo, and the *ajaeng ('bowed' with a stick). The kayagum, by far the most popular musical instrument among Korean amateurs, has 12 strings, pentatonically tuned by the individual movable bridges. They are plucked with the right-hand fingers while the left hand presses down the strings on the other side of the bridges, producing vibrato, portamento, and mordent-like ornaments (compare KOTO, ZHENG). The *sanjo*, a virtuoso 'folk' genre of south-western Korea, is most frequently played on the kayagum, accompanied by the hourglass drum *changgo*. Once no doubt improvised, it is now learnt following the style of the teacher.

Kazoo (Fr.: *mirliton*). Instrument for changing the sound of the voice into something nasal and instrument-like, like that of the traditional comb-and-paper.

1. *Usual form*. This has been in manufacture since before 1900: a cigar-shaped metal tube with a paper or plastic membrane over a hole in the side, held in place, and adjustable for tightness, by a screw-on metal cap with a washer underneath. One hums strongly into the wider end, during which the hand can be flapped over the cup for warbling effects. Other names have been 'zazah', 'zobo-flute', 'vocophone'; while other forms have been in trumpet and horn shapes for 'bazooka' bands, like those in megaphone shape used in some young people's marching bands today.

2. *Older mirlitons*. These are generally of a cardboard tube, *c*.15 cm. (6") long with a membrane of onion-skin, cigarette-paper, etc., gummed over one end (or both), and a hole cut in the side for humming into. Ethnologists have often used the French word for voice-disguisers of these kinds, classified under membranophones. The 'Danse des mirlitons' in Tchaikovsky's *The Nutcracker*, however, seems to refer to *panpipes.

3. *Nyastaranga* (the Indian 'throat trumpet'). This is rather different: a short brass 'trumpet' with a spider's-egg membrane over the base of a mouthpiece-like cup. A pair are held externally to each side of the larynx while humming or singing.

Kemancha (Persian: 'fiddle'). 1. The chief traditional fiddle of the Middle East from Iran (Pl. 1) to Russian Central Asia, in Turkestan named *ghichak*. The spherical body is generally built up in segments of mulberry wood, a shape deriving from a gourd, which is sometimes still used for the body. Let into this just below the level of the small skin belly is the long pole neck with an iron spike driven

into the lower end to support the instrument off the ground (see SPIKE FIDDLE). The belly is traditionally of fish-skin from the Caspian Sea. The three, or four, strings, now metal, are tuned in fourths and stopped, as usual over Asia, by pressure of the fingers against the string alone (see BOW, 3). As a classical instrument it is largely replaced in Iran by the violin, or in the USSR by new versions modernized with fingerboard and tailpiece, a bow with screw tightening, and four strings tuned as the violin.

Pl. 1. A Persian kemancha.

2. Pontic fiddle or 'Black Sea fiddle' of Turkey (*kemençe*) and the Caucasus, also popular in northern Greece (*kementzés* or *lira pontou*). This three-stringed fiddle has a narrow body, *c*.10 cm. (4") wide, hollowed in wood with the sides almost or quite parallel. The belly is of wood, and there is a soundpost. The short neck carries a deep, heart-shaped pegbox open on the back, to which the strings are led through small holes next to the nut (as with the Renaissance Italian *lira da braccio, not to mention some Asian fiddles of quite different shapes). There is a short, thin fingerboard (although by some older accounts the players have not always stopped the strings against it in the European manner). The strings are tuned in fourths: while the melody is fingered on the first and second strings, the next string below will be sounded at the same time as a 'drone'. Typically the first and second are fingered together for the melody to sound in parallel fourths (compare LUTE, Ex. 7). Like the Greek *lira, this fiddle is also played while walking (e.g. leading a procession), supported, still with the body downwards, by the left thumb and first finger, or by a ribbon. There are varieties, as in Armenia, that have wire *sympathetic strings.

3. *Kemençe* in Turkey also denotes a small pear-shaped fiddle similar to the *lira* and played in a similar way.

See MIDDLE EAST; Picken 1975

Kemençe. See KEMANCHA, 2, 3.

Kempul, kempyang, kenong, ketuk. Gongs of the Javanese gamelan (see GAMELAN, 1*a*).

Kendang. The drum of the gamelan and other music of Java and Bali (see GAMELAN, 1*b*).

Kerar. See LYRE, 1.

Kettledrum. See DRUM, 4*a*; NAQQĀRA; TIMPANI.

Key, keywork (woodwind). See WIND INSTRUMENTS, 4.

Keyboard (Fr.: *clavier*; Ger.: *Klaviatur*; It.: *tastiera*; Sp.: *teclado*): 1. *Keyboard layout*. First used in organs, the keyboard was becoming chromatic with raised sharps by the end of the 14th century. To make it, a long panel of wood is marked out and placed upon the key-bed beneath for drilling the holes for the 'balance pins' (the fulcrum for each key) into the 'balance rail' running across the key-bed. The panel is then sawn, the facings of the naturals are glued on (if not already done) and then the sharps. (Reversed colours—dark naturals and light-coloured sharps—were fashionable especially in 18th-century France.) The octave span has varied between about 16 and 16.7 cm.; for pianos today it is 16.5 cm. (6½"). (The German term *Stichmass*, and three-octave span, is often cited for historical instruments.)

It will be noticed on looking at a keyboard that, of the black keys between F and B, G♯ is centred symmetrically between two naturals whereas the other two are set off to the left and right. This brings the centre-lines of the actual key-tails (reaching under the mechanism) at equal distances apart. From C to E things have to be different: five key-tails to fit into the span of three naturals as against seven tails into the space of four naturals from F to B. There is then too much room for all the tails from C to E to have the same width as those from F to B. So (keeping the same width throughout for the black key heads, the raised parts) traditional practice is to make the C and E tails slightly wider than those of F and B, and the D tail more markedly so (in early harpsichords and clavichords often very much so). The key-tails are wide enough to allow for any take-up needed for alignment under the actual mechanism.

2. *Compass*. In the sixteenth century, normally four octaves, C to *c'''* (or up to *f'''*; see also SHORT OCTAVE). By the end of the 17th century F' (FF) to *f'''* was usual for the strung instruments; but for organs, still four octaves from C (later five), the lower range catered for by the pedals or deep manual stops. Larger compass came in with the piano, up to six octaves (*CC–c''''*) by Beethoven's

last days, and seven (*AAA–a'''*) by 1850, the further top notes to *c'''''* added from shortly afterwards.

See SHORT OCTAVE for old means for saving space in bottom octave; and TEMPERAMENT, 3, for 'split keys', e.g. for D♯, E♭.

3. *Fingering*: (*a*) *Numbering*. Thumb represented by a cross or ○, the fingers by 1 to 4: met in early German sources, then, during the 18th century, English, and subsequently described as 'English' system. Thumb numbered 1, the fingers 2 to 5: up to recently termed 'Continental' fingering and now employed exclusively. It goes back to Santa Maria's treatise of 1565 (Spain) and the major publications of the French school, also the earliest English sources, and was adopted in Germany in the 18th century in place of the other system.

(*b*) *Playing*. The major sources of the 16th and 17th centuries consistently recommend that extended scale passages should be played by pairs of fingers, for example by passing the third finger over the fourth when ascending with the right hand, or the third over the second when ascending with the left. This method was facilitated through early keyboards having had a shallower touch and shorter heads to the naturals, bringing the front of the sharps nearer. It would be wrong to assume that earlier musicians had neglected the thumbs completely. In 1565, Santa Maria recommended their use for fast scalic passages, and the fingerings in many anthologies of English virginal music show frequent use of all five fingers.

Bach's son C. P. E. Bach (*Essay on the True Art of Playing Keyboard Instruments*, 1753; see BAROQUE, 2) believed that wherever possible the black keys should be played only by the three longest fingers, and that the thumb and little finger should be restricted to the white keys. Developing precepts suggested to him by his father he defined the thumb as the 'principal' digit and as 'the key to all fingering'. In this way, he established the trend which ultimately led to the scale fingerings taught in present-day Tutors and scale-books for the piano whereby a normal octave scale is divided into two groups, one of three notes, the other of four, representing two distinct hand positions. The main hurdle for the beginner is to connect these as imperceptibly as possible, to this end learning to pass the thumb under the long fingers, or the

Ex. 1.

fingers over the thumb. In scales with sharps or flats, the change of hand position is made most comfortably where a long and short key occur contiguously (Ex. 1). The little finger is generally reserved for the highest note in the right hand or the lowest in the left, and the passing of the thumb under the little finger or the little finger over the thumb is avoided.

4. *Microtonal keyboards.* Used for producing intervals smaller than a semitone, these have been designed from the 16th century onwards in Italy, from Vicentino's *arcicembalo* of 1555, this with the object of reproducing the 'diatonic', 'chromatic', and 'enharmonic' genera of the ancient Greeks. Trasuntino's instrument of 1606 (preserved in Bologna) provides 31 notes per octave, with the aim of making it possible to play with perfect intonation in every key (unlike equal temperament, by which the intonation is in strict musical theory imperfect). Trasuntino's instrument has two banks of 'black' keys, each one divided into two, front and back, and differently coloured; and two small keys inserted between each E and F. If tuned to equal intervals of about 39 *cents, every scale is accurately playable in mean tone. The same arrangement has been embodied since, for instance in an enharmonic grand piano built in Moscow, 1864, designed by V. Odoyevsky (Moscow *collection). A number of quarter-tone pianos and harmoniums have been invented from the 1890s onwards and pieces have been written for them; but works employing quarter-tones have been written more for the string quartet.

Keyed bugle (Fr.: *cor-à-clefs*, Ger.: *Klappenhorn*, It.: *corno segnale a chiavi*). Built in the single-looped, wide-belled older format of the bugle (see BUGLE, 3), this has six or more leather-padded brass keys (Pl. 1) to cover holes in the side of the tubing (raised seatings for the pads being soldered on). Patented in 1810 by the Dublin bandmaster Joseph Haliday (or Halliday, b. 1774 in Yorkshire), it was widely used up to the 1850s in bands in Britain and (from 1815) America, and also to some extent in France and Germany, there often made in brass instead of copper.

The key nearest the bell mouth stands open at rest (as visible in the plate): the instrument then sounds the normal bugle notes from Middle C upwards (all a tone lower on B♭ keyed bugle, this often a C bugle with B♭ crook inserted). Closing this (right little finger) lowers to B♮. Opening the other keys gives C♯ (third finger); D (index; the middle finger rests always on the bridge over this key); E♭ (thumb; often there is also a key tuned for D♯); E, and F, for the left hand on the lower branch and not essentially needed in the compass above *f'*, where all can be done with the right hand. The technique, as evidenced in virtuoso variations of the 1820s on waltzes and opera airs (as in preserved manuscripts by the player McFarlane), could equal that of the cornet, while the emission of most of the notes through the side holes gives the quality an interesting, expressive character quite of its own. However, as valves for brass instruments came in, they were felt to be easier to master and maintain than the keys.

Some keyed bugles have further keys for the left hand on the lower branch of the tube, for making trills, e.g. to sound *f'* in the whole-tone trill on *e♭'*, otherwise hardly possible. In the USA the smaller keyed bugle in E♭ became especially popular; Edward Kendall, founder of the Boston *Brass Band, is one who preferred it, and today enthusiasts have revived it for historical band performances. The name 'Royal Kent Bugle' (in honour of the Duke of Kent, Commander of the Forces in Ireland), dates from 1813, after which the instrument became copied on the Continent, where it is met in some German band scores under the name 'Corno Kent'.

Replacement of the keys on the bugle by valves gave rise to the *flugel horn.

Dudgeon 1983.

Keyed fiddle. See NYCKELHARPA.

Keyed guitar. See ENGLISH GUITAR.

Keyed percussion. An orchestral term covering tuned metal or wooden bar instruments as *glockenspiel, *vibraphone, and *xylophone.

Keyed trumpet. The original instrument of Haydn's trumpet concerto (*c.*1795), rather similar to a

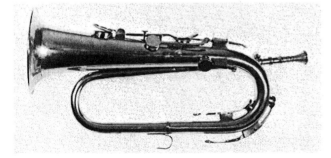

Pl. 1. Keyed bugle by Klemm (Philadelphia, *c.* 1835).

cavalry *trumpet but with four to six brass keys (cf. KEYED BUGLE). Mostly these are mounted across the instrument on struts for playing them with one hand, the trumpet being held flat. Four keys are the essential, opened in turn to raise the lowest natural note, the written low g, by chromatic steps from $g\sharp$ to b to reach the next natural note, Middle C (c').

The keyed trumpet was introduced by the Viennese trumpeter Anton Weidinger, for whom the concerto was written; the prominent alternation (in one place) between low g and $a\flat$ shows how well Haydn had grasped the novel nature of the instrument. Hummel's concerto of 1803 was also written for Weidinger, whose sound in soft passages was said to be as sweet as that of a clarinet. The keyed trumpet then came to be used up to the 1820s in military bands, mainly in Austria and Italy, usually built in a higher key than Eb for use with a wide range of *crooks; but keys cannot be placed to serve more than one tube-length correctly, necessitating much compromise fingering and the aid of one or more further keys.

The term *trompette à clefs* in Parisian opera scores, from Rossini's *Guillaume Tell* (1829) onwards, is generally equated in contemporary French treatises with the keyed bugle (*cor-à-clefs*) rather than keyed trumpet; on the other hand, a valved trumpet is possibly intended, since 'clefs', like the Italian 'chiavi', could refer equally to keys and to valves at that period.

Dahlqvist 1975.

Khaen (or *khen*). *Free-reed mouth organs are played over South-East Asia—Laos, Northern Thailand, Upper Burma, South China, and south to North Borneo. For the reeds and their control by covering a hole in the pipe with a finger, see SHENG. The pipes are of bamboo (or 'elephant grass'), held in a gourd or wooden receptacle, and are generally larger and deeper-sounding than in the *sheng*. The longest one or two pipes are without a fingering hole in order to sound drone notes. The player inhales and exhales through the mouthpiece, the music proceeding without interruption.

The *khaen* of Laos (Fig. 1, left) has up to 18 pipes in two parallel rows, and is normally held obliquely across the face. Each pipe may be open at the bottom as well as at the top, the longest pipe reaching two metres (6') and sounding deep in the baritone register of the voice. The pentatonic music, with changing chords above the drone, and with high and lower pipes sounded often in octaves, has a seductive charm, moving at a leisurely rhythm until accelerating to a fast close. It is heard mainly solo, or in mouth-organ ensembles.

The Dyak instruments of North Borneo have five to eight pipes held in a gourd (Fig. 1, right). The reeds may be cut in palm-wood, as well as in brass. A short bamboo piece with a central hole may be placed across the top of the longest pipe, spreading the sound of the drone. The music has served

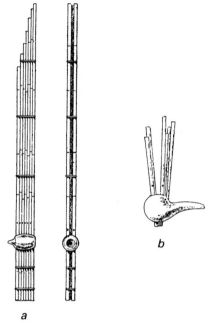

a *b*

Fig. 1. (*a*) Mouth organ (*khaen*), Laos; (*b*) a mouth organ from Sarawak/north Borneo.

particularly in serenading. (For free-reed pipes with the fingerholes of a reedpipe, see REEDPIPE, 3.)

Khlui (or *khloi*). In Thailand, a 'pipe', particularly a bamboo duct flute of the 'ring flute' kind (see FLUTE, 7c (ii)), with seven holes and thumb-hole, and a hole covered by a tissue membrane to impart a nasal quality, as on the Chinese flute *di* or *dizi*. There are several sizes, played solo and in the softer ensembles. The *palwei* corresponds to it in Burma. *Khlui* can also mean a duct flute with block, or a reedpipe.

Khur (or *khur, khil-khuur*). The fiddle of professional minstrels of Mongolia, about one metre (3') long, with the body of a four-sided wooden frame covered on both sides with a skin (see FIDDLE, 2b; also *China and Korea*, Pl. 1, second from right) or today more often with the back of wood. The pole-like neck is surmounted by a carved horse's head (see BOW, 3). The two strings, of horsehair, are usually tuned a fourth apart. The *khur* is played nearly upright, the body downwards, the strings stopped by fingernail pressure as elsewhere in Asia (see FIDDLE, 1).

Kinnari vina. See TUILA.

Kinnor. See BIBLICAL INSTRUMENTS, 1c.

Kissar. See LYRE, 1.

Kit. 1. Dancing master's *fiddle of the mid-16th to the 18th century (Fr.: *pochette*), small enough (*c.*40 cm. (16″)) to be taken about in the pocket of a tail coat, for giving private dancing lessons without having to carry a violin. In the earlier truncheon-shaped form it fits into a tubular leather case along with its short bow. From the late 17th century are also many kits with the body in some small violin shape (and distinguishable from a 'miniature violin' by the longer neck and fingerboard in proportion to the body). Kits were made in all countries, often very beautifully, the narrow type sometimes in ivory. The 'violini piccioli alla francese' that appear briefly in Act 2 of Monteverdi's *Orfeo* are thought by some to have been *pochettes*, though it seems that violins then made in France could be of smaller dimensions than most in Italy by up to some 3 cm. (1.2″) in body length, and suited to playing in a distinctively bright and 'dancing' manner.

Kit. 2. 'Do-it-yourself' kits for early or folk instruments, obtainable since the 1960s, have pre-shaped parts and a step-by-step handbook. Among instruments for which kits may be had are: *bagpipe, *cittern, *clavichord, *dulcimer (*Appalachian and hammered), *harp (Celtic, Gaelic), *harpsichord (probably the most popular kits of all), *hurdy-gurdy, *lute, medieval fiddle, *portative organ, *spinet, *virginal, *viol.

Kithara. In Classical Greek one of the principal forms of lyre (see LYRE, 2*b*); in modern Greek, ''*guitar'. See also *cithara (Lat.).

Kobyz. Fiddle of the Kazakhs of Central Asia; see FIDDLE, 2*a*.

Kokyu. The only native Japanese bowed instrument, not ancient, dating from the 18th century. Structurally it is a bowed version of the long lute *shamisen, smaller than this (*c.*68 cm., *c.* 27″) but likewise with an almost square wooden body with white catskin belly, and open behind (see JAPAN, Pl. 2). Of four silk strings (originally three) the first two are in unison, the other two following downwards in fourths. The long, slender bow is free (i.e. not, as in China, with the hair passed between the strings) and its loose hank of hair is tightened by the two small fingers. To change from one string to the next, the fiddle, held downwards, is turned on a short peg (as with many Asian fiddles: see FIDDLE, 2*b*). The playing is monodic and with much vibrato. Less widely played now than in previous centuries, the kokyu is heard mainly in chamber music with *koto and *shamisen*, and in puppet plays, especially in sad scenes.

Komabue. One of the Japanese transverse flutes; see FUE.

Komungo (or *komun'-go, komunko, 'black zither'). A *long zither of Korea that has been considered the noblest of Korean instruments (see CHINA AND KOREA, Pl. 2, front left). About 150 cm. (5′)) long, ths shallow soundbox carries six silk, deep-tuned strings, of which three in the middle pass over fixed 16 frets increasing in height from the lowest (to the player's right) up to the tallest, which functions as a 'nut'. On these strings the melody is played by the right hand with a pencil-sized bamboo plectrum (held rather like a chopstick) while the left hand presses the strings on the frets. The other strings, 1st, 5th, and 6th, rest on individual bridges to serve as 'drones', but in present-day techniques are not plucked very frequently. A specimen tuning is *E A D B B B′*. Written music, in a special *tablature notation, survives from the 16th century.

Komuz. 'Long lute' of the Kirghiz in Soviet Central Asia. See LUTE, 7*b*, *c* and Ex. 6.

Kooauau. Maori flute. See PACIFIC ISLANDS, 4.

Kora (or *kasso*). Stringed instrument of West Africa (Gambia–Mali region, Fig. 1), often in Western literature described as 'harp-lute' (since the strings

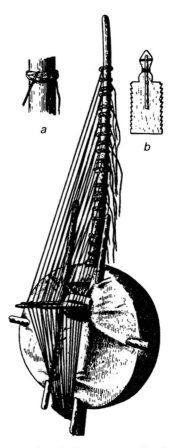

a

b

Fig. 1. kora from the bissagos archepelago (*a*) method of fastening strings; (*b*) bridge.

lie in a plane perpendicular to the belly). The large skin-covered gourd (with crossed sticks under the skin and a pole neck through the gourd) carries the unique feature of a tall bridge, formed of a thin wooden board cut with notches down each side for the strings to rest in: 11 on one side, 10 on the other. The strings of each set are tuned to alternate notes of a diatonic scale of more than $2\frac{1}{2}$ octaves, the deepest-tuned strings being on top. With the neck of the instrument pointed away, the thumbs pluck downwards toward the soundbox and the forefingers upwards, while the arrangement of the strings, right and left dividing the scales, favours stepwise figures played at great speed, sometimes in octaves or with accompanying consonances. The strings, formerly of hide, have their ends tied to raffia leading to the knob at the bottom.

Kortholt, sordun (or *courtaut, sordone*). Two similar and relatively minor double-reed wind instruments known on the Continent *c.*1570–1650. A narrow (*c.*8–10 mm.) cylindrical bore leads down and up again through a round pillar of wood, the bore ending at a hole in the side near the top. A compass of nearly two octaves in fundamentals is obtained since—in addition to the usual seven fingers and thumb—use is made of the other little finger, the other thumb, and the middle joints of both index fingers (each covering a hole offset to the side, which allows the finger to cover its normal hole at the same time).

1. *Kortholt*. Today manufactured for early music (Fig. 1) following an illustration in *Praetorius

Fig. 1.

which shows the instrument *c.*70 cm. (28″) tall with a wind-cap as used with a *crumhorn. Tenor and bass sizes are made, producing the reedy, burbling sound characteristic of Renaissance cylindrical reed instruments, like that of the crumhorn but softer. The name is from an outward appearance which evidently reminded people of a 16th-century short-barrelled piece of artillery, in French *courtault* (or *courtaut*, and whence Eng. *curtal). *Mersenne shows the instrument without a wind-cap.

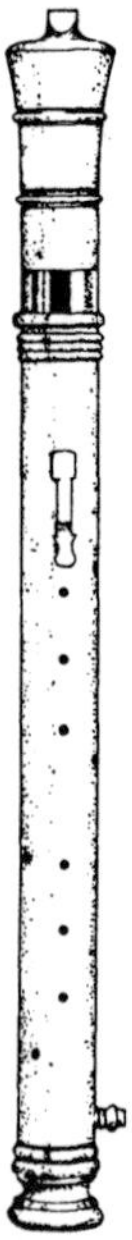

2. *Sordun* (see PRAETORIUS, Fig. 1). Five originals exist including a set of two basses and two 'great basses' in Vienna, the largest *c.*115 cm. (4½′) tall. In these, all but the basic row of holes are covered by elaborately fashioned wooden keys (not shown in the illustration in Praetorius). They are for playing without a reed-cap but with a crook placed in the side. The name is from the Italian, *sordoni*, from the muted sound. In music, a five-part pavan of *c.*1600, from Cassel, names 'sordano', apparently for the part above the bass (range *e–f'*).

See CRUMHORN; Boydell 1982.

Koto. Japanese *long zither, one of the country's great classical stringed instruments, said probably to stem from China early in the 8th century, along with the lute *biwa.

1. *The instrument.* (see JAPAN, Pl. 1). The player sits towards the right-hand end of the six-foot-long (180 cm.) soundbox, 25 cm. (10″) wide, its top slightly convex both from end to end and from side to side (by legend a crouching dragon). Top and sides are together hollowed out in paulownia wood ('foxglove tree'), and the bottom is covered by a thinner board of the same with a soundhole near each end. The 13 silk strings, of equal length and thickness, are stretched at equal tension between two transverse bridges and through small holes in the soundbox, their ends tied together on the underside. Under each string is an individual movable bridge, shaped roughly like an inverted Y. The different placements of the bridges give tunings which vary with the tonal system used but traditionally give five notes to the octave. The strings are plucked with plectra worn on the thumb, index, and middle fingers of the right hand. Modern *gaku-sō* technique is restricted to octave patternings and single notes played by the right hand alone. In *zokusō*, a genre from the Edo Period (and in early *gako-sō*), technique, however, the left hand is used to sharpen notes by pressing the strings to the left of the bridges and to produce vibrato, mordents, and shakes. The left hand plucks the strings in modern *zokusō* compositions only. Innovations of recent years include a *koto* with 17 strings, *jūshichigen*, and raising the *koto* on a wooden stand for playing.

2. *Music.* Literature from the Heian period (782–1184) shows how the 13-stringed *gaku-sō* was not only played by professional musicians in the court

Ex. 1. First section (*dan*) from the *Danmono Rokudan*

First *dan*

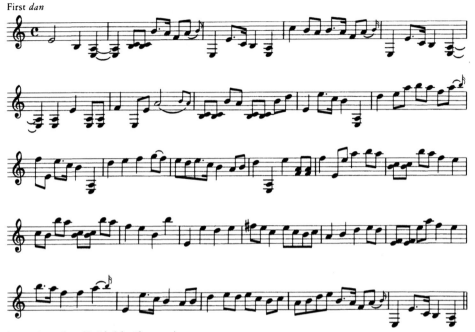

(*transcription from Harich-Schneider 1973*)

orchestra, but also on informal occasions by ladies and courtiers, both as a solo instrument and in chamber ensembles. Solo modal preludes, often demanding virtuoso playing ability, as well as the *koto* parts in court music, survive from the period. However, it was not until the end of the 16th century that a classical solo tradition for *koto*, *sōkyoku*, independent of the court, emerged and flourished. In this, *danmono* is a composition consisting of a variable number of continuous instrumental sections (Ex. 1). A *kumiuta* consists of a number (usually six) of continuous songs (*uta*) self-accompanied on the *koto* in the instrument's idiomatic versions of the same melody; the voice part characteristically anticipates or follows the *koto* by half a beat.

During the latter half of the 17th century, the ascendancy of the *shamisen among the middle class meant that the more refined music of the *koto* waned in popularity, though it has been revived from the 18th century, largely with borrowings from *shamisen* musical forms.

3. *Wagon.* The six-stringed *wagon*, also some 180 cm. (six feet) long, is claimed to be an indigenous Japanese instrument (though Korean origin has been suggested). It is now employed exclusively in the accompaniment of *kagura* and other vocal genres associated with Shinto ritual. The strings are tuned in two three-note groups (e.g. D F A C E G) and technique follows a few standardized patterns combining rapid right-hand plectrum-played arpeggiato and single notes, and left-hand damping and finger-plucking. Another old species related to the *koto*, the *gekusō* (or *sō*), may also be heard today.

Koziol (Poland). See BAGPIPE, 5*a*.

Kru harp (or 'forked harp'). Stringed instrument of unusual kind played in Liberia and nearby parts of West Africa. A widely forked stick is fixed by the stem in the back of a half-gourd. About seven strings (e.g. of plant fibre and 23–30 cm. or 9 to 12″ long) are stretched between the arms of the fork and plucked with both hands, holding the open side of the gourd against the chest. In *classification it is an example not of a harp (since the strings are not directly attached to the resonator, the half-gourd), but of the rare category 'frame zither'.

Krummhorn. See CRUMHORN.

Kuan. See QUAN.

Kuitra (or *kuwītra*). A North African species of lute used in both classical and popular music in

Morocco, etc. (see MIDDLE EAST, Pl. I, second from left), and said to be of Andalusian extraction. The contour of the body recalls European lute-making more than Arab, and the name, a diminutive form of Arabic *kaitara*, may be connected with Old Spanish *guitarra morisca*, 'Moorish guitar'. The instrument is fretless, played with a plectrum, and has a scratch-plate on the belly. The head is turned back at an obtuse angle and carries eight lateral pegs for four double courses of gut strings, for which a usual tuning pattern is given as *d A e G* (embodying intervals of a fourth in irregular order and with octave displacements).

Kulintang. *Gong chime of the southern Philippines; also a percussion ensemble having this as the melodic instrument (see SOUTH-EAST ASIA). The gongs of the chime (one player) rest boss upwards in two rows over wooden supports; in shape they resemble those of the Indonesian *bonang*, though they have no standard tunings. In the ensemble they have with them a drum giving the main rhythm, and many suspended gongs of different size and rim-depth, punctuating the melody in a powerful array of distinctive colours, and providing the music for all kinds of celebration and entertainment over the region.

L

Laba (or *la-pa*). Chinese straight brass trumpet, 60 cm. (2′) or more long, narrowly conical, usually in two or three telescopic joints which are collapsed after use (as with the Tibetan lama trumpet; see CHINA AND KOREA, 3). It has a very shallow mouthpiece with wide rim, and a flared bell which in one older variety is turned back facing the player. Formerly military, and sounded in funeral and wedding processions, it is sometimes now heard in the theatre, in Taiwan as well heralding the acts in calls mostly on two notes a fourth apart. Another funeral trumpet, *haotong* (*hao-tung*), perhaps now extinct, has a curious bell shaped like a long brass flowerpot, giving booming sounds at halts in the procession. In Korea the trumpet is *nabal*. In China, *laba* can also mean the *sona, a reed instrument.

Lagerphone. Australian instrument of 'bush music'. Tin bottle-tops are loosely nailed in pairs to a pole or broomstick which is pounded on the ground; or the pole is notched and scraped, or 'bowed' with a notched stick (compare BUMBASS).

Lambeg drum. See BASS DRUM, 6.

Lamellaphone. A modern term for the African *sansa ('thumb piano') and preferred by many ethnologists since 'sansa' is only one African name among many for this instrument. The term has sometimes been extended to include other instruments that have a tuned set of plucked tongues, as *musical boxes.

Langeleik, langspil: 1. *Langeleik.* The folk zither of Norway, chiefly the southern parts from Telemark to Valdres, west and north-west of Oslo, where the langeleik has been known since the 17th century and is now played again after a period of neglect. The long soundbox, in the form now best known, bulges out slightly along each long side. It is placed on a table with the row of frets nearest, under the melody string, on which the left hand moves fast over the frets, using all three middle fingers together, adding quick trills and other ornaments. The other strings, up to seven, are tuned to the instrument's key-note and the fifth, in several octaves and sometimes also the major third. They are swept with a plectrum along with the melody string, making a resounding 'drone' accompaniment in the rhythm of the tune. If this is a dance in 3/4 time, two beats are struck outwards and the third backwards, for a *springdans*, or one outwards and two back for the quite different rhythm of a *waltz*. The frets are by tradition diatonic, in former times without the rigorous distinction between tones and semitones that pertains in conventional major. See ZITHER, 2, for other European folk zithers.
Ledang 1974.

2. *Langspil.* This, in Norway, is a rarer name for the preceding. But in Iceland it denotes a zither, also fretted, but placed across the thighs for sounding the strings (brass, three or more) altogether with a violin bow. The left thumbnail stops the first string on the frets, the others sounding a drone in octaves. One who heard it played c.1800 said that it sounded rather pleasant from the next room, adding that the player, a woman, often used the fingers alone and not a bow. It afterwards became very rare but has been revived for folk music and in schools.

3. *Fidhla* ('dh' as in Eng. 'this'). Again in Iceland, known up to the early 19th century and played with a bow, this had two horsehair strings running high above an oblong soundbox, with no frets beneath, the melody string being stopped with the fingers from below. Though itself obsolete, a similar instrument is still reported among the Inuit Eskimo of Labrador (*tautirut*).

Laouto (or *lavouto*). Lute-like instrument much used in Greek folk music to accompany other instruments (e.g. violin, clarinet) with chords and lively figures. About one metre (3′) long, it has a large round-backed body of numerous ribs, a belly usually with decorated borders, etc., and an 11-fret neck midway in length between the short neck of a lute (*outi*) and the long neck of a *bouzouki. Four double or triple courses of strings, now metal, are tuned in fifths downwards from (nominally) *a*, some or all of the lower *courses with an octave string. The plectrum is traditionally a folded-over quill of a bird of prey. The instrument comes from Turkey (*lavuta*, from It.: *lauto*) where it was known by the 18th century and is sometimes still played in the towns.
The *laoutokithara* is a recent version with the body-shape of a *guitar (in modern Greek, *kithara*).
Anoyanakis 1979.

Lap organ (or 'rocking melodeon'). A small American *free-reed instrument made from around the second quarter of the 19th century, placed on the lap (or a table). The rectangular case contains the reeds in two rows, naturals and sharps, covered by boards with air-escape holes on top. Above lie the button keys, or in later models a keyboard, played with both hands. Underneath the case are the expandable reservoir and the feeder-bellows, the latter hinging on the right and kept open at rest by metal springs inside, tilting the case up to the left. On pressing the near side of the case down with the left forearm (the fingers still playing the keys) the bellows exhaust, replenishing the reservoir, and the case tilts the other way until the springs expand the bellows and the case 'rocks' back to its first position. Playing was normally confined to the melody with its bass lest the air be at once used up (Libin 1985). A knob on the left moves perforated shutters above the reeds for changing loudness.

The original instrument, by James A. Bazin of Canton, Mass., was known as 'elbow melodeon'. From about 1836, Abraham Prescott, in New Hampshire, was also making the keyboard type.

Latin American percussion. See AGOGO BELL, BONGOS, CABAZA, CHOCOLO, CLAVES, CONGA DRUMS (with tumbadora), COWBELL, CUICA, GUIRO, JAWBONE, MARACAS, TIMBALES, VIBRASLAP.

Laúd (Span.). A *lute; also a relatively modern wire-strung instrument: see BANDURRIA.

Launeddas. The *reedpipe of Sardinia, played mostly for round dances, and very likely a direct survivor of the double-pipe of *Antiquity, like which it is a 'divergent double-pipe' (see REEDPIPE, 3). Two separate cane pipes with fingerholes are held one in each hand. The shorter (*mancosedda*) is for the right hand, the longer (*mancosa manna*, 'left hand') for the left. Also, attached beside the latter, is a long (60–110 cm. (24–44″)) drone pipe (*tumbu*). Each pipe is sounded by an *idioglot single reed and the player, with three reeds in his mouth, makes uninterrupted music by means of *circular breathing (in through the nose). Each of the smaller pipes has a long vent hole, needed for accurate tuning with wax to the correct interval above the drone note: this is very important for the staccato (see BAGPIPE, 1). The two pipes are played polyphonically, using the utmost that the four notes from each makes possible: see Ex. 1, a few bars from a total of some 250 in a transcription by Bentzon (1969), the pipes here tuned a fourth apart.

Leaf-blowing. Many country people know how to play tunes with a leaf, or piece of bark, placed between the lower teeth and lip, or by holding it

against the lower lip with the fingers. The notes are made by varying breath-strength, or the oral cavity, or moving the teeth and lips. Fast folk-tunes have been recorded in Romania, played in these ways on a large fish-scale.

Leier (Ger.). See HURDY-GURDY.

Lesiba. See GORA.

Lion roar. See FRICTION DRUM, 2.

Lira (modern Greek *lyra*, usually transliterated *lira*). Three-stringed fiddle of the Aegean Islands, Crete, also Thrace (corresponding to the Bulgarian *gadulka*), and in Croatia *lirica* (pron. 'liritsa'). Pear-shaped, hollowed and carved in one piece, 40 to 60 cm. (16–24″) long, it is held on the knee (Pl. 1) or (if standing) hanging from the left hand. The pine belly is slightly convex, with D-shaped soundholes (see FIDDLE, 1) and the treble foot of the bridge usually rests directly on a soundpost which passes through a soundhole to the back. The strings, now sometimes metal, run from pegs inserted from the back (though some more recent instruments imitate the violin scroll head). There is neither nut nor fingerboard (though again modern instruments may include these), the first string being stopped with the nails from the side. The middle string, tuned to a deeper note, is bowed at the same time as a 'drone', and equally when playing notes on the third string (the bridge being curved or notched sufficiently to allow this). Usually the third string is tuned a tone below the first to supply the sub-tonic below the open note of the first string. The bow-stick often has pellet-bells (jingle bells) tied along it.

For the straight-sided *lira pontou* or *kementzés* of northern Greece, see KEMANCHA, 2.

Anoyanakis 1979; Downie 1979–80.

Lira da braccio. Italian bowed instrument of the 16th century and part of the 17th, held like a violin, and well known in paintings of the 1490s onwards by Bellini, Raphael, and others. Four or five instruments are preserved in collections. They vary greatly in size, with body length from 38 to 50 cm. (16–20″), the last bigger than the largest *viola.

There are seven strings, two of which lie off the fingerboard, diverging from the rest on the bass

Ex. 1. Triple reedpipe, launeddas, Sardinia.

Pl. 1. Cretan *lira*; note 'soundpost' construction of the near side of the bridge, jingle bells on the bow, and the bow hair tightened with the fingers, also the fingering of the first string (at the side, with fingernails).

side to sound their open notes only (see CRWTH; FIDDLE, 2). The tuning-pegs are in the front of a heart-shaped pegbox which is open at the back for attaching the strings. In the tuning, as it is given in a late 16th-century addition to a lute manuscript in Pesaro (Rubsamen 1968), the first, second, third, and fifth strings are as on the *violin, and the fourth is tuned an octave above the fifth. The sixth and seventh, off the fingerboard, sound octave Ds. The short music examples in the manuscript, perhaps for a beginner, include the beginning of a *romanesca*, written in tablature. The fourth and fifth strings are mostly fingered together in octaves (the higher note thickening the chords) and, at the end, the lateral strings add their octave Ds. The lira was primarily for accompanying the player's voice, recalling Orpheus with his seven-string lyre, to which the name 'lira' here alludes. People would go round the streets singing to it, it was said.

The lira offers illuminating evidence of advances in Renaissance 'fiddle' design prior to the violin family itself. One prominent visual feature is the two-lobed bottom outline, where the arcs of the two intersecting circles of the 'vesica piscis' (often an underlying factor in the geometrical design of stringed instruments) meet in an inward-pointing peak instead of being connected in a continuously rounded outline as in the violin. This lobed shape is present in some other 16th-century Italian instruments, now with four strings but which may have been liras in their original state.

Lira da gamba (*lirone, arciviolata lira*). An instrument larger than the *lira da braccio, and later

(from about the 1570s), held like a *viol, fretted, and with very numerous strings; the finest example claimed as Paduan, is by Wendelin Tieffenbrucker, is now in Vienna. Two bass strings, or two pairs, lie off the fingerboard, nominally tuned to G (as the *cello third string) and the octave above. The main strings, from eight to 13, were tuned in cyclic zigzag ways, e.g. *c′ g d′ a* and so on to *c♯′*, suited to sounding three- or four-note sustained chords in any key, the long bridge being just flat enough to make this possible. Besides solo accompaniment to the voice, the lira da gamba could also be a useful continuo instrument, usually reading from a figured bass part, and it remained in use in Italy through the first half of the 17th century.

Litavry. Ru., 'timpani'.

Lithophone (from Gk. *lithos*, 'stone'). A term for percussion instruments using slabs of stone, marble, etc.

1. Some churches in Ethiopia have a single slab, or a number of them, hanging outside the building to serve as church bells. In Britain, 'rock harmonicas' of basalt slabs from Skiddaw in the Lake District are from the 18th and 19th centuries, the stone bars laid upon straw bundles over a wooden frame and struck with mallets: the largest of those in the museum at Keswick has some 60 bars, from 15 to 93 cm. (6″ to 3′) long, laid in rows to cover six octaves chromatically.

2. 'Sonorous stones' have been most important in Eastern Asia. In *China and Korea they are usually of black limestone (or in very special cases, jade) cut to an inverted L shape and suspended by the corner in a wooden stand (see CHINA AND KOREA, Pl. 2, rear right). Stones used singly are up to 4 cm. (1½″) thick (one example from *c.*1800 BC is preserved in Taiwan) and were used in secular music, in later times, however, often substituted in metal. Sets of stones ('stone chime'), *bianqing*, hung in chromatic sequence in one frame, still have a place in Confucian ritual. As with the *gong chime *yunluo* and bell chime *bianzhong* the stones, originally graded in size, came to be all of the same size (*c.*55 cm. (22″) tall) but of different thickness, the thinner the deeper the note (as in the case of other solid percussion instruments: see GLOCKENSPIEL, 5). In Antiquity, sets of 12 stones were regarded as perfect for preserving the 12 absolute pitches of Chinese music-theory following the series of perfect fifths, with its ties with cosmology and laws of weights and measures.

Lituus and carnyx. 1. An Etrusco-Roman ceremonial trumpet-like instrument of bronze, long and narrow with an upturned hook-shaped bell recalling the crook-like staff of the augurs; a fine example (lacking the mouthpiece) is in the Vatican museum and many reproductions have been made from it. The lituus was sounded in funeral and other civilian rites until, by the first century AD, it had gone out of use and its name became adopted in learned circles for the military oxhorn-shaped *bucina* (Meucci 1989; and see BUCCINA AND CORNU). The Celtic peoples of Europe had a warlike instrument of form akin to that of the old Roman *lituus*, its name recorded in Greek sources as *karnyx* (related to the Latin word *cornu* and Germanic *horn*). This must be the instrument seen wielded by mounted warriors on Gaulish coins and on Trajan's column in Rome, about one metre (3') long, ending in an open-jawed boar's or wolf's head, also in bronze and perhaps totemic.

2. In 18th-century German sources 'Litui' sometimes appears, as in J. S. Bach's Motet BWV 118, composed for an open-air funeral. The little contemporary information equates this 'lituus' either with 'horn', or with 'trumpet or horn' (the parts for it could fit either), with no mention of any visual characteristic. 'Horn' has since been thought the more likely.

Liuto (It.). Lute; for *liuto attiorbato*, see LUTE, 3a.

Livika (or *launut*, rubbing block). An instrument of New Ireland, Melanesia, always cited for its uniqueness: a polished block of wood, c.40 cm. (16") long, cut to form two or three tongue-like surfaces along the top, giving different pitches when rubbed with the hand coated with resin or tree sap, while the instrument is laid on the ground pointing away from the player. It is said to have once been used in funeral rites.

Log drum. A modern addition to Western percussion, developed on the basis of the ancient Central American *teponatzli*. It is a rectangular wooden resonator box with one or more tongues cut in the thick (c.2 cm., ¾") wood of the top, and struck with a heavy mallet to give soft, throbbing sounds. Sets of tuned log drums have been used in school music in the USA and some composers have called for one or more of them, though in some cases apparently having *slit drums in mind.

In a 'gato drum', also from Central America, wooden bars of tuned lengths are screwed by one end to the top of the box, pointing towards the middle and played on with xylophone beaters; being fixed at one end the bars give far deeper notes than in a xylophone (see PARTIALS, 6b). Or the tongues can be cut in the plywood lid of the box with a fret-saw (a 'Crafts-Fair Slit Drum').

Long drum. The earlier, c.1780–1815, English name of the *bass drum, in those times built with the length of the shell greater than the diameter. Sizes vary considerably. The two dimensions next become equal (e.g. 70 cm. (28")) and by the 1830s the diameter is the greater (e.g. in England, 60 × 75 cm.) and the name is 'bass drum'. See BASS DRUM, 5.

Long lute (or long-necked lute). Modern term introduced to cover the many kinds of lute, largely Asian, in which the body appears small in comparison with the long, narrow neck. See LUTE, 7.

Long zither. A term for a series of stringed instruments of the Far East, of kinds quite foreign to the West but high among the most interesting and important in the musical tradition of each region. Chief examples: *qin, *zheng (China); *ajaeng, *kayagum, *komungo (Korea); *koto (Japan). Each consists of a long, shallow soundbox, rectangular or narrowing slightly to one end, with the strings running from end to end, and the player sitting near one end (see CHINA AND KOREA, Pl. 2). There may be an individual movable wooden bridge for each string, shaped like an inverted Y or forked twig (zheng, ajaeng, kayagum, koto) and allowing the tuning to be changed or adjusted without retuning strings at their attachment; or high fixed wooden frets (komungo); or no bridges or frets at all (qin). The strings are plucked in various ways, but the ajaeng is 'bowed' with a wooden stick.

South-East Asian long zithers include the *celemepung (Indonesia) and the *chakhē ('crocodile zither', Burma and Thailand), as well as a species in Vietnam.

All these long zithers are believed to derive anciently from 'half-tube zithers' of a wide bamboo split lengthways, with *idiochord strings raised on the convex surface (bamboo reaching some 10 cm. (4") in diameter in favourable habitats). See ZITHER, 3a (iii).

Lowland pipes. See BAGPIPES, 2c.

Lujon. (from 'Lou' and 'John'). Modern American percussion instrument of six or more thin aluminium plates screwed by the edge over a resonator box, and struck to give booming notes. See PERCUSSION Ex. 1 (Berio).

Lur. 1. Large bronze horns of the Bronze Age, mostly from Denmark and of the period 900–500 BC (the name 'lur' is an old Scandinavian term for a calling horn, given to these instruments after their first discovery in 1797). Found always buried in pairs, their form, in two curves joined at 90 degrees, suggests a mammoth horn, though this beast had long been extinct by the time the lurs were made. Their purpose is not known. They have very good *trombone-like mouthpieces, but it is anyone's guess what kind of sounds they produced in those remote times.

2. The Scandinavian name (see above) also covers wooden horns, the larger of which resembles an *alphorn.
Broholm *et al.* 1949; Lund 1987.

Lute (Fr.: *luth*; Ger.: *Laute*; It.: *liuto*, *leuto*; Ru.: *lyutnya*; Sp.: *laúd*). Peer among plucked instruments from the later Middle Ages to the mid-18th century, with a repertory which, through its earlier or

Renaissance period, far exceeds that of any other instrument of the times in quantity and, many would say, quality. To hear it again (for the lute has no truly adequate substitute) 20th-century revival of lute-making has led to the rise of new expert lutenists (Paul O'Dette in America is one), masters in the most demanding of the old techniques, as intricate, fast, and dashing as on any plucked instrument that has been known since. See THEORBO and CHITARRONE for the large lutes developed principally for *continuo playing; and below, 6, for the parent Arab lute, and 7 for the family of 'long lutes', predominantly Asian.

1. *The instrument.* The swelling body of a lute (Pl. 1), traditionally compared in shape to a sliced pear, is built up over a wooden mould from nine to 37 or more ribs, often less than 0.8 mm. thick and tapering in width to each end. The soundboard or belly may be down to 1.6 mm. thick, often of two pieces joined, and strengthened by transverse barring underneath. The border is sometimes protected by a parchment or cloth strip (the 'lace') and is covered round the lower part by a wooden 'capping strip' usually with ornamental edge. The bridge is glued to the belly, and the soundhole is carved in the soundboard itself in gothic or arabesque patterns to form the rose or 'knot'. The neck bears a flat or slightly arched fingerboard, tied with gut frets, usually eight. The pegbox points backwards at almost a right angle. The strings, of gut (or now nylon); string-length, for an average-size lute, c.60–70 cm. (24–28″). They are generally paired (double *courses) save for the highest-tuned, which is often a single string.

The whole construction is as light as possible, while the strings, thinner than on a *guitar, and the different barring of the belly, give the sound of a lute a character of its own, as compared with a modern guitar: bright (more pronounced upper *partials), more nasal perhaps, and less powerfully colourful. In playing, the right little finger is held always against the soundboard. The techniques for both hands are voluminously set out in tutorial works, particularly of the 17th century.

The number of strings and their tuning have varied through the lute's history. A broad distinction by many makers today is between 'Renaissance lute' for music of the 16th century and 'Golden Age', c.1590–1630; and 'baroque lute', with tunings different from the earlier and including German models played up to Bach's day.

2. *Renaissance lutes:* (a) *Early development.* First mentioned by name in Europe c.1270 in France, the lute as seen in pictures up to the early 15th century is variable in size, with four double courses of strings generally played with a quill plectrum after the Arab manner. Written sources indicate that its tuning up to then had been in fourths, the Arab way. But during the same century the two middle courses came to be tuned a major third apart—giving the same intervals as the top four strings of the guitar. By about the 1470s a string was added on the treble side (Page 1980) tuned a fourth above the others. The actual pitch of the highest string being governed by the length of the instrument, it is likely that the other courses were, in effect, lowered in pitch through the addition.

Towards the end of the 15th century the plectrum was by degrees abandoned in favour of the fingertips, a development leading to the power of playing true polyphony: it was said (Tinctoris c.1484) that an expert lutenist would be able to play all three or four parts of a part-song. From about the same time a sixth course had been added on the bass side, giving the nominal tuning shown in Ex. 1, the 'old tune' (tuning) of the lute. The lowest three courses were octave courses, one of the strings in each being an octave higher to reinforce the upper harmonics in the tone (though in later periods they may be unison courses). The earliest known publications of music for the lute follow by 20 years, in Venice.

(b) *Makers and models.* Our earliest-surviving lutes date from the first half of the 16th century, by makers such as Laux (Luke) Maler (d. 1552) and, a little later, Hans Frei, Germans working in Bologna. Their instruments continued to be highly esteemed up to the 18th century, fitted at one time or another with a wider neck and bridge to take

Pl. 1. Lute by Hans Frei, Bologna, mid-16th century (with neck of later date). Warwickshire Museum.

Ex. 1.

more strings. Possibly five genuine Maler lutes exist and seven by Frei (Pl. 1), all altered since but nevertheless allowing models now to be based on them. With nine or 11 ribs (mainly of maple or fruitwood, or by Maler usually ash), they are of a long, slender shape—though in pictures of the time a more rounded form seems commoner, the survivals of the longer form probably being due to their having been later considered more suitable for conversion.

In the 1580s began a new style of lute-making which was to last some 50 years, leaving some of the most beautiful lutes to have survived, with 13, 17, or 19 ribs of yew. The heartwood of yew is red, while the sapwood is white, and these instruments are so built that each rib is half one and half the other. Examples of such lutes from the 1580s are by Wendelio Venere of Padua (possibly related to the Tieffenbruckers of Venice), while over the next 30 years the number of ribs was increased to 31, 37, and even 53, some made from such exotic woods as ebony and snakewood.

(c) Tunings. The normal stringing for most of the 16th century is six-course, as Ex. 1. The actual notes shown, with top string G, are the most frequently described in English sources (today for brevity often termed the 'G tuning'; otherwise they are most often given a tone higher, 'A tuning'). They are 'nominal' inasmuch as a lute would be tuned in practice as high as it would safely go (nor were all lutes built to the same size).

Ex. 2.

Three excerpts from early lute music illustrate the different kinds of tablature used: German (Ex. 2), from Hans Judenkünig's *Utilis et compendiaria introductio*, c.1519; Italian (Ex. 3), from G. A. Casteliono's *Intabolatura de leuto*, 1536; and French (Ex. 4), from Robert Dowland's *A Varietie of Lute Lessons*, 1610. All are transcribed as for 'G tuning'. The German uses a different symbol for each fret on each string, so needing a great number of them. Italian: treble string, bottom line; frets numbered, with open string 'o'; dot under a note means strike upwards. French, used in England: treble string,

top line; frets lettered, open string 'a'; (often 'c' is written in such a way that many modern transcribers prefer to show it as an 'r' as in Ex. 4); below the stave are seen indications for seventh course tuned D.

From the 1580s it became regular (having been rare before) to add strings on the bass side. John Dowland (b. 1563), one of England's finest composers for the lute (with and without voice), wrote for a seventh course tuned a fourth below the sixth and fingered for the notes in between (Ex. 4). Others put it a tone below the sixth, then added an eighth, but these became difficult to reach for fingering, so that players turned to 'diapasons' (struck open) in diatonic sequence down to C (in the 'G' tuning), also in double courses. This 10-course lute, in use soon after 1600, is made today along with those of six to nine courses.

3. 17th century. From around 1600 the pattern of development exhibits two distinct styles—in Italy, and in France and Northern Europe.

(a) Italy. Italian lutes show a logical continuation of the preceding development with ever more courses in the bass. With the difficulty of obtaining a good sound from these basses with plain gut strings, trials were made at finding ways of increasing their length. The system eventually most widely followed is that where the neck, instead of carrying a bent-back pegbox, is extended upwards to bear a second pegbox at the end of the extension (as on a *theorbo) by which the bass strings can be some half as long again as the stopped strings. These lutes, in Italy termed *liuto attiorbato* ('theorboed' lute), generally had seven stopped and seven long bass courses, many that survive being by Matteo Sellas of Venice (Pl. 2). The *arciliuto* ('archlute'), on the other hand, had longer stopped-string length and generally only six stopped courses, but eight single diapasons of at least twice the length of the stopped strings. There is some debate over when this 'archlute' form was developed, since many of the surviving examples seem to be conversions of earlier lutes, while the historical use of the names *arciliuto* and *liuto attiorbato* is also not precisely clear. What is certain is that the long-necked 'archlute' type was quite common as a continuo instrument by the second half of the 17th century and remained in use through much of the next.

(b) France and Northern Europe. Instead of extending the range downwards while retaining the old tuning, different tunings were tried on the 10-course lute with a view to exploiting to a greater degree the natural resonances of the instrument. One type, 12-course, developed in Northern Europe, sought to overcome the problems of plain gut strings by keeping the bent-back pegbox for the first eight courses, followed by four courses on an extended head, each of them progressively slightly longer (its nut farther along the head from the main nut). We commonly see this 'double-headed' lute in Dutch genre paintings of the mid-century,

Ex. 3.

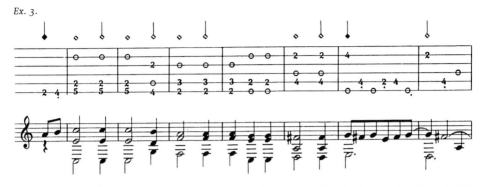

and it is considered at length in Thomas Mace's *Musick's Monument* of 1676, though it is possible that no authentic example has·survived (save perhaps one by Mëst in Linköping, Sweden).

In France this type went out of fashion, to be superseded by a return to 11 courses and a single pegbox; also one of the new experimental tunings came to predominate, the so-called 'D minor' tuning (Ex. 5, the second course often single like the first)

which remained with the lute for the rest of its active life, in England and Germany also. This 11-course lute, with its single, bent-back pegbox, was widely cultivated in France throughout the century, with a foremost exponent in Denis Gaultier ('the younger', d. 1672), and it was the repertory for it which had such a profound influence on the French *clavecinistes* (harpsichordists). It is much to be regretted that we have no surviving 11-course

Ex. 4.

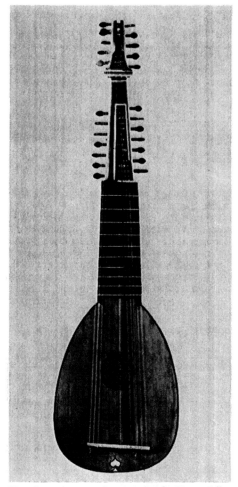

Pl. 2. Fourteen-course *liuto attiorbato* by Matteo Sellas (Venice, 1637).

lute of undoubted French provenance, since this music, perhaps more than any other, exploited the resonances and sonorities of the lute, while seeming to rely heavily upon the qualities of the particular lute for much of its effect.

4. *German baroque lutes.* Under much influence of the French lutenists in the second half of the 17th century the 11-course lute was adopted in Germany, and around or shortly after 1700 given two further courses in the bass. These are led to a small structure added on the bass side of the

pegbox which enabled them to be longer than the other courses by approximately one fret's length. Fine examples of this 13-course lute are by Sebastian Schelle (Nuremberg, working up to c.1745) and J. C. Hoffmann (d. 1750), the chief maker, also of violins and cellos, in Leipzig during Bach's time. One of the first to write for the 13-course lute, S. L. Weiss (d. 1750), ranks as one of the greatest of lutenist–composers.

There is also a German form with extended neck and an upper pegbox on the same principle as in a *liuto attiorbato* (above, 3a) but embodying a short piece that gives a double curve to the head (Pl. 3). There are eight stopped courses and five diapasons, with about one-and-a-half times the length of the stopped strings. This form of the 13-course lute (often in collections mistaken for a small theorbo) represents the last major development of the instrument, which had all but disappeared by the end of the 18th century.

5. *Repertory.* A few chief items from the vast corpus of music in tablature, now often divided into three periods.

(a) *Up to 1590.* Italy (songs with lute, and solo *recercari*, Dalza however including dances): Francesco Spinacino, *Intabulature de Lauto*, 1507 (lost but known by photocopy); Dalza, *Intabulatura.* 1508; Bossinensis, *Tenori e contrabassi . . . col lauto* , 1509; then Francesco da Milano, *Intabulatura*, 1536, etc.; and later works as by V. Galilei (father of the astronomer). France: publications of Attaignant from 1529; Phalèse, 1545, etc.; Adrian Le Roy; works by G. Morlaye and by A. de Rippe from 1552. Germany: Hans Judenkünig, *Utilis . . . Introductio*, ?1519 (elementary in style—see Ex. 2—but interesting as being by a composer born c.1450); Hans Newsidler, *Newgeordnet Lautenbuch*, 1536, etc.; works by Bakfark and Newsidler the younger. From England the early books have not survived, but from Spain the fine collections for *vihuela are playable on the lute.

(b) *The 'Golden Age', 1590–1630.* Italy: Antonio Terzi, for *liuto attiorbato*; Melii, 1614, etc. France, now coming to the fore: Francisque, *Trésor d'Orphée*, 1600, and Besard's huge *Thesaurus harmonicus*, 1603, with pieces by almost every noted European composer including Dowland. Germany: Rude, *Flores musicae*, 1600. England: an extensive solo repertoire exists mainly in manuscript sources; the few printed collections are: William Barley, *A new Booke of Tablature* (one of his 'new books' of 1596, see BANDORA); Robinson's *Schoole of Musick*, 1603; Robert Dowland (son of John Dowland), *Varietie of Lute-lessons*, 1610 (see Ex. 4).

Ex. 5.

over North Africa, it has been to some degree losing its former hold. In Indonesia it is *gambus*. It is at once distinguishable (Pl. 4) from European lutes in general by, usually, two small roses below the main one, scratch plate protecting the belly from the plectrum, narrower neck, a curved end to the pegbox, and no frets. Some instruments are copiously decorated. The silk or now nylon strings are traditionally in five double courses (string-length around 60 cm. or 24″), the first four tuned in fourths, the lowest today written A, with the fifth course a tone below, G. With a plectrum traditionally from an eagle's quill, the playing is largely stepwise, with fast runs, and quick dips to the octave below; chords are limited to an occasional fifth or fourth.

Pl. 3. Thirteen-course German baroque lute by Leopold Widhalm (Nuremberg, 1755).

(c) *Baroque.* France: especially Denis Gaultier 'the younger', *Pièces de luth*, 1664. England: in manuscript tutors, many now published (as the Mary Burwell tutor, etc.), and in Thomas Mace, *Musicks Monument*, 1676. Germany: especially perhaps the numerous compositions (in manuscript, now published) of Weiss (see above, 4), a friend of Bach, of whose own lute pieces seven may be written originally for the instrument.

6. *Arab lute* ('ud). Father of the European lute and star instrument of the *Arabian Nights*, this is today most played from Egypt to Iraq, its country of origin. In Turkey, Armenia, and Greece (*outi*) and

Ex. 6.

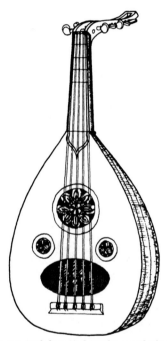

Pl. 4. An Arab lute, '*ud* (Jenkins and Olsen 1976) incorrectly showing frets.

The instrument's deep sounds are heard in most classical ensembles, while solo players range from leading innovatory artists and teachers to the barber resting in the sun outside his shop. Ex. 6 (sounding an octave lower) is a few bars from a

simple study in the Tutor by G. Farah (Beirut, 1956). Observe in the key signature the sign signifying a quarter-tone below E, making in bars 4 and 8 the successive three-quarter-tones required in this particular mode.

7. *Long lute*: (a) *'Short-necked' lute and 'long-necked' or 'long' lute.* In contrast to the foregoing instruments in which the neck is relatively short in length and the general appearance is dominated by the body, there are numerous kinds of lute, important especially over Asia, also south-east Europe (as the *bouzouki), in which the proportions are the opposite: a long neck with a relatively small body (Pl. 5). They are so different, not only to look at but also in the characteristic ways of playing, that musicologists distinguish them by the term 'long-necked lute' or, to save breath, 'long lute'. This is by far the oldest known type of lute, going back in Mesopotamia to *c.*2200 BC and taken thence to Egypt, where actual examples of the XVIIIth dynasty (*c.*1500 BC) and later have been found, even with a wood plectrum still attached by its cord, as seen in the murals. Among its closest survivors are African instruments of the *gunbri kind. 'Short-necked lutes' on the other hand seem first represented by small instruments shown in Greek art from the 4th century BC (see PANDOURA), and later, in the early centuries AD, in Central Asia (Picken 1955) leading eventually to the Arab and European lutes or in the Far East to the *pipa and *biwa. Of long lutes there are only rare signs in

Western Europe before the *colascione, introduced in the 15th century from the Turks and, one could add, the *banjo, originally made in a similar fashion to a *gunbri*.

(*b*) *Present long lutes.* To name but some of a large family: *Round-backed*: bouzouki (Greece), *tamburitsa (and *tambura, Balkans), *saz (Turkey), *chonguri (Georgia), *dutar (Pl. 5; also *setar and *tanbur, Iran, Central Asia), *komuz* (Central Asia), *gunbri* (North Africa, skin belly), *sitar (India, heavily influenced by the *vina), *tambura* (India, giving 'drone' accompaniment); body of a gourd, among them *ektar (India, one-stringed). *Two-lobed*, like a gourd with tightly constricted waist: *tar (Iran, etc., skin belly). *Nearly square*, skin belly: *sanxian (China), *shamisen (Japan). *Triangular*: *balalaika (Russia, also one form of *dombra*, Central Asia).

(*c*) *Tunings and techniques.* The most usual way of playing a long lute (though not in the Far East) is to strum the strings, which most typically comprise three courses, fingering the melody on the first, or else on the first and second together in which case (the second being tuned a fourth or fifth lower— or in some cases higher) the tune will be heard in parallel intervals (compare KEMANCHA, 2). The third course reiterates its open note as a 'drone'. For one single example (for techniques are nowhere always the same) Ex. 7 shows the first few bars of the introduction to a song from the repertory of a famous Kirghiz bard (Central Asia) accompanying

Pl. 5. The Uzbek dutar, played by Usma Zufarov. The elaborate inlay on the neck and fingerboard is typical of old handmade dutars, now largely supplanted by factory-made instruments.

Ex. 7. (after Vinogradov 1961, No. 19)

his long epic on the one-metre (3′) long, fretless *komuz* (three single strings, formerly of sinew), thrumming and plucking with the plectrum, now and then hitting or rubbing the soundboard with the hand to highlight a point in the story; in this instance the second course is tuned highest, the actual melody, on the first course (the middle row of notes) with the 'consecutives' above it fingered at the same time on the second course one or two frets back (Vinogradov 1961).

> Baron 1727; Hellwig 1974, 1981; Lumsden 1953; Mace 1676; Page 1980; Pohlmann 1968; Prynne 1949.

Luthier (Fr.). A maker of stringed instruments, *violins included.

Lyra. Classical Greek, a *lyre; in modern Greek also a folk fiddle, *lira. In medieval and Renaissance Latin also often 'fiddle'.

Lyra viol. In 17th-century England a *viol of smaller dimensions than a bass viol or 'division viol' (see VIOL, 4) suitable for playing 'lyra way'. This refers to solo music written in *tablature, with special tunings and much use of chords, and is referred to already, soon after 1600, as playing the bass viol 'lyra way', or 'leero way', etc. (perhaps an allusion to the chord-playing *lira da gamba). One source (Simpson 1659) mentions a flatter bridge, facilitating chords of more than two notes. Ex. 1 is an example of the music, in tablature of the French kind. The tuning is given below. Early publications are Hume's *Ayres* of 1605 and Ferrabosco's *Lessons*

Ex. 1. Extract from *Narcissus Marsh's Lyra Viol Book* (c. 1660).

of 1609. There were eventually as many as 22 different tunings, mainly to bring open strings on principal notes of the tonality of the music, and also for them to vibrate sympathetically while not bowed (see SYMPATHETIC STRINGS.)

Playford 1652; Traficante 1970.

Lyre. One of the great stringed instruments of Antiquity. The strings run to a crossbar (or 'yoke') supported by two arms lying approximately in the plane of the front surface of the soundbox, on which is a bridge for them to be attached to, or to pass over for their attachment lower down. In most cases they are plucked with a plectrum. The oldest are Sumerian, followed by Egyptian, then those of Greece and Rome. After the early Middle Ages (below, 3) they became extinct in the West (save for a few survivals as a bowed instrument, below, 3), but in Africa lyres are still regularly played, from the Sudan and Ethiopia to Kenya and parts of Zaire where (along with a small importation to Iraq) can be observed ways in which a lyre is handled and may have been handled during the instrument's great epoch in the past.

1. *African lyres.* The main kind (Fig. 1) closely resembles the *lyra* of Ancient Greece: a bowl (wood, gourd, etc.; in Ancient Greece wood or a tortoiseshell) is covered with a skin, soaked and laced down as in making some African drums. The wooden arms are then poked through slits in the skin for their ends to rest underneath on the rim of the bowl. When the skin has dried out the crossbar, with a hole at each end, is fitted on to the tops of the arms. The strings, now usually wire, are attached to a wire loop at the bottom and tuned by fastening the other ends to strips of cloth or hide which are then wrapped round the crossbar. The player accompanies his voice, in some cases plucking with both hands, but more characteristically in a way that seems to be matched in Greek vase paintings. The right hand, with a leather or horn plectrum, strums across the strings near the bridge where they lie close together. On the other side of the strings the left hand, passed through a strap which supports the instrument, extends the fingers fanwise along the strings ready to press (and thereby silence) such strings as are not required to sound during the plectrum stroke (compare KANTELE; also HARP, 10a, *waji*). Rapid figures can be executed as well as two-note chords, and now and then sharp accentuations are made on all strings together. The strings are tuned in the general pentatonic pattern shown in Fig. 1, with string No. 1 tuned the highest and No. 2 the lowest (Plumley 1976).

Among the names are *kerar* (or *krar*, Ethiopia), *kissar*, *tanbur* (Sudan), also *rebaba* (see RABAB, usually a 'fiddle' name). In Ethiopia is also a taller, massive square-bodied lyre *beganna*, with ten strings.

Fig. 1. A player of the lyre *tanbur*, Northern Sudan (after Plumley 1976). The strings are numbered by players as indicated.

2. *Ancient lyres:* (*a*) *Mesopotamia, Egypt.* See ANTIQUITY for chronology back to *c.*2600 BC. The Louvre, Paris, has two Egyptian lyres of the XVIIIth dynasty (*c.*1500 BC), 50 cm. (20″) tall, with square or rectangular wooden soundbox 27 cm. (11″) wide and only *c.*4 cm. (1½″) deep; and curving arms holding a sloping crossbar. The strings may have numbered seven to nine, the lower ends attached to a raised bridge. There seem to be marks on the back where the left wrist was pressed to the wood, as if for damping with the fingers in the manner described (1 above), the instrument again being held slanting forwards.

(*b*) *Greece.* In Homeric times the Greeks had a four-stringed lyre, *phorminx* (or *kitharis*), on which warriors like Achilles, and professional bards like the blind Demodocus (Homer, *Odyssey*, viii) and probably Homer himself, accompanied their songs and epics and led the choral dance. This seems to have been a rudimentary form of the later *kithara*, with a rounded base. From the 7th century BC the Greeks had two main types of lyre. One, the *lyra*, (not unlike Fig. 1 but with arms curving towards each other), was the instrument of musical education and amateur enjoyment; the *barbitos*, a taller, deeper-sounding version prominent in Bacchic scenes of the late 5th century, was the instrument of Anacreon and other lyric poets for accompanying drinking and love songs. The other main type, the wooden *kithara* (Pl. 1), was the instrument of professionals and the contests: no example has survived and the purpose of the thinning of the arms and the strange curls remains unknown but may have been in some way acoustical, not merely ornamental.

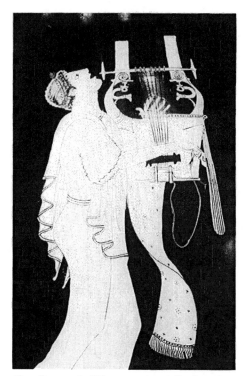

Pl. 1. Singer to the kithara at a contest, Greek amphora (*c.* 490 BC).

The strings were of gut and in number varied from seven to 11. No classical source describes their tuning. The names of the notes of the Greek musical scale were, however, derived from the sequence of the strings of the lyre, so offering clues as to their tuning but leaving much room for argument, while no Classical writer tells us how the lyres were actually played.

(*c*) *Rome.* Lyres were here very variable. No actual remains have been found, but in sculptures they are mostly rather massive in appearance, tall with rectangular outline and the arms bending distinctly forwards over the plane of the soundbox. Some fine examples can be seen in Arles.

3. *Germanic lyres.* A six-stringed wooden lyre, with hollow arms and wooden pegs in the crossbar, was the main stringed instrument of Germanic peoples through the migration period of the 5th to 7th centuries AD, and is almost certainly the 'harp' named in Anglo-Saxon poems, or as Bishop Fortunatus of Poitiers (see ROTE) alludes to it in the same period, their *bombicans harpa* ('buzzing' or 'humming' lyre)—the word 'harp', related to Latin 'carpere', 'to pluck' (through the Germanic soundshift), not yet having acquired the particular sense of a harp. Remains of several of these lyres, varying in shape, have been found in Germany and England, in burials. The 'Sutton Hoo' lyre (British Museum) is an example, incomplete but exhibited along with a reconstruction of the whole. A name for the type in the British Isles may have been *rotta* (or *chrotta*, or in Ireland *cruit*, Wales *crwth*: see ROTE).
Crane 1972; and see ANTIQUITY.

Lyre guitar. 1. One of a large variety of ladies' amateur instruments brought out all over France (and some in England) through the period 1770–1840. At the time, it was usually called a 'lyre'. The inventor, not definitely identified, was presumably inspired by Renaissance depictions of classical subjects. Strung as a six-string guitar, the elegant, lyre-like arms, pointing outwards at the top, are hollow, continuing the space of the soundbox (any small cross-struts at the top being purely ornamental). A flat base is for standing up as a 'furniture instrument' when not being played. A German writer speaks in an article (1801) of the 'Lyre-Guitarre' and its 'feminine admirers who wish to imitate French girls and pose elegantly as Greek kithara-players'. Some said that the sound was dull as compared with a guitar, but great numbers were made and songs were published with accompaniment for 'guitar or lyre'.

2. Other 'lyres', from 1780, are strung more like the *English guitar; their thin, solid, gilded arms support a head from which the fingerboard ends well short of the body (in one form of 'French lyre'); or as in an 'Apollo lyre', reaches it and adds a gilt device (often a crescent) in the soundhole. Some further curiosities of the period or shortly after, mostly French (illustrated Baines 1966), have names compounded of 'harp' and 'guitar' or 'lyre', one of them with the body in the shape of a small harp, another with a round body and three fretted necks all differently strung for purposes no longer clear. More recent, from around 1900 in the USA, have been 'lyre-mandolins', flat-back mandolins with the arms of a lyre-guitar; examples are now rare.

Lysarden. See CORNETT, 2.

M

Machete. See CAVAQUINHO.

Magadis (Ancient Gr.). See PSALTERIUM.

Makers. For a list of instrument makers and inventors cited in the course of this book, naming the articles concerned, see Appendix.

Mandola. Tenor and bass *mandolins for use in ensembles, named by analogy with the violin family: mandola, mandoloncello (or mandocello), and mandolone. Mandolas were already made in the 18th century, and today have considerable popularity for accompanying folk music, for instance in Ireland and France. The entire set, with all sizes, came to be made for 'plectrum orchestras' of the late 19th century, one of the first to attract notice having been in Genoa in 1892, the programme including an arrangement of Hérolde's *Zampa* overture.

Nomenclature has varied over the years. Today one is most likely to find the sizes in Table I available, mostly supplied in a flat-backed or 'Portuguese' format (see MANDOLIN, 2). The tenor mandola is thus a fifth below the mandolin. The mandocello may have nearly the string-length of a cello, with a long neck which brings the 15th fret to the end of the body instead of the 10th or 11th fret. With the octave mandola (a popular size for folk-music) the 12th fret has the octave position, as on a Spanish *guitar. (For *mandola* in an earlier sense see MANDOLIN, 5.)

TABLE I.

Name	Lowest course tuned:	Approx. string-length
Tenor mandola	c	40 cm. (10″)
Octave mandola	G	53 cm. (21″)
Mandocello	C	66 cm. (26″)

Mandolin (often written in the Fr. way, *mandoline*). This lively stringed instrument, played with a plectrum, is made in several different shapes, with a round or flat back, but in all cases mounts four pairs of metal strings tuned as in the *violin (*e″*, *a′*, *d′*, *g*) and of about the same string-length as in this. The mandolin is essentially a melody instrument. It sustains the longer notes by a rapid tremolando with the heart-shaped plectrum, the effect strengthened through the double stringing,

since every plectrum stroke, in each direction, sounds the note twice in quick succession (some electronic organs imitate the mandolin tremolando with ten or so note-repetitions per second). For larger sizes of mandolin see MANDOLA.

1. *Neapolitan mandolin* (round-back or 'bowl' mandolin; Pl. 1). The original form, with a deep rounded body (33 cm. (13″) long) built up in *lute fashion with many ribs, most often of rosewood, though formerly also of maple or satinwood. The belly, very slightly convex, bends inwards at the level of the bridge at an angle of about 10 degrees. The low bridge is normally held in position by down-pressure of the strings, which are fastened at the foot of the body. The fingerboard has 17 frets (the tenth at the end of the body) taking the compass up to *a‴*.

Pl. 1. Neapolitan mandolin, from a catalogue of c. 1900.

2. *Flat-backed mandolin or Portuguese mandolin* (Pl. 2a) with top, back, and sides built up as in guitar-making. The pear-shaped outline is broader than in the preceding, the amount of internal

(a)

(b)

Pl. 2. (a) A Portuguese mandolin; (b) An American mandolin.

air-space remaining much the same. Some of the prettiest models have black-and-white 'barber's pole' inlay around the edge.

3. *American mandolin*. Also basically pear-shaped, sometimes (Pl. 2b) with pointed 'cut away' shoulders (as in many electric guitars). Others follow Gibson's arch-top models of the 1920s, with carved plates, round or *f*-shaped soundholes, and 'sunburst' finish (compare the 'cello-style' guitar; see GUITAR, 4). There are also electric mandolins with pick-ups and tone-controls.

For playing in folk music the flat-backed models are generally preferred, being the easier to hold (especially if standing) and brighter in sound. Most of the prominent solo players of the last 60 years have used an American type, among them Bill Monroe, the 'Father of Bluegrass'.

4. *Symphonic use*. Sufficiently penetrating to be effective in the symphony orchestra, the mandolin has been used chiefly by composers working in Vienna during the first quarter of the 20th century, and not simply for associative effect (Italian serenades, etc.), but as orchestral colour in its own right. Thus Mahler, at the end of *Das Lied von der Erde*,

uses it, for a few notes only, but to express eternal resignation with unforgettable effect. Schoenberg (Serenade, Op. 24, and later *Moses und Aron*) and Webern (Five Pieces for Orchestra, Op. 10) also score for mandolin, while Stravinsky has used it to suggest medieval minstrels (the galliard in *Agon*).

5. *Earlier history*: (a) *Fifteenth to 17th centuries*. Back to the 15th century there had been small instruments with lute-like bodies named in French 'mandore', in Italian 'mandola' or 'pandurina'. They had four or five single gut strings tied to a fixed bridge and usually tuned in fourths and fifths. They became fairly popular in France during the 16th century and some were made with flat backs. *Mersenne (1636) mentioned the vivacity and 'aigu' of the sound, using a quill plectrum, beside which a lute could hardly make itself heard. Tablature books appeared in France from 1578 but have not survived. The earliest extant collection seems to be in a German manuscript of c.1626, containing popular and dance airs with some simple chords, in this case for plucking.

(b) *Eighteenth century*. By the 18th century the mandola, or mandolino, was being made in Italy in numerous regional forms, with five or six pairs of gut strings played with a quill. Today they are usually described collectively as 'Milanese mandolin'. Best-known makers in Milan are the two Presblers, working from c.1730 to the end of the century. The 'mandolino' in Vivaldi's oratorio *Juditha triumphans* (also in a concerto) and in Handel's *Alexander Balus* (with the harp to evoke Apollo's lyre) would have been of this kind. (Also of the 18th century is the 'Roman lute', a type with *theorbo-style upper pegbox for open bass strings; Gasparo Ferrari of Rome made several of those now in museums.)

(c) *Neapolitan and Portuguese models.* The Neapolitan type (1, above) dates from about 1750. Among its early makers the Vinaccia family of Naples made particularly beautiful instruments, strung with either gut or metal, and tuned by plain pegs. The big difference, apart from the violin-tuning, is in the great depth of the body: in the previous types this roughly followed lute proportions, with the greatest depth typically equal to half the greatest width of the belly; but in the Neapolitan mandolin it far exceeds this through the addition of a very high rib (or two ribs) on each side. This increases the air-space inside, strengthening emission of the lower frequencies and giving the instrument its robust sound on the lower strings.

The *Cavatina* in Act 1 of Paisiello's *Il barbiere di Siviglia* and Mozart's famous serenade in *Don Giovanni* (today often played on the harp) are with little doubt for the Neapolitan, and so too are Beethoven's early sonatas with piano. But some concertos, as Hummel's (1799, written for an Italian soloist), have chords of up to six notes, pointing to the 'Milanese' variety.

The Portuguese model, earliest of the 'flat backs', may derive in its shape from the 'Portuguese guitar', i.e. the *English guitar as adopted in Portugal from the late 18th century.

Tyler 1981a, b; Tyler and Sparks 1989.

Mandora, mandore. Medieval, see CITTERN AND GITTERN; Renaissance, see MANDOLIN, 5.

Manicord. An early name for the *clavichord.

Manjira (or *mandora*). Indian cup cymbals (see CYMBAL, 5a.

Maracas. Gourd rattles of Latin American dance music (see Fig. 1a). The original form, as made by South American Indians and others, is of a gourd, with the pulp washed out and the seeds taken out, dried, and put back in the dried shell before affixing a wooden handle. Commercial types, reproducing the 'swishing' sound, are of wood or plastic with lead shot or suchlike inside. A pair of maracas, selected to give sounds of slightly different pitch, are shaken one in each hand in the characteristic eight-quaver rhythms of the rumba and other dances, using quick forward movements of the hands alternately. Many composers have since used maracas in their compositions, Boulez requiring up to three pairs differing in size to give higher and lower sounds. The 'Mexican bean' (e.g. in Berio, *Circles*) is a foot-long (30 cm.) pod, the desiccated seeds rattling inside. In Australia, tribes in Queensland have similarly used pods twice as long as this.

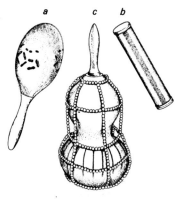

Fig. 1.

Vessel rattles of gourd, or of woven basketry, have played a prominent part in primitive music and ritual. In Europe, much louder kinds of rattle have generally predominated, save for the vessel rattle as a babies' rattle, in Sicily alleged to keep malignant spirits at a safe distance from the child. In the South American homelands of the maracas, too, Indian women will lull infants to sleep with a gourd rattle, strictly provided that it is not one in which the medicine man has put secret magic objects to heighten the instrument's powers.

Marching bells. See GLOCKENSPIEL, 4.

Marimba. Instrument of tuned wooden bars with tube resonators suspended beneath, similar to the *xylophone but an octave deeper in compass (usually *f* to *c''''*). The bars are of similar thickness but wider and longer, giving a mellower sound, less hard and assertive. They are 'overtone-tuned' by removing wood from part of the underside (see XYLOPHONE, 2). The sharps and naturals are on the same level, to suit playing with four beaters when required. For this the wrist is turned inwards, with two beaters crossed under the palm, their angle controlled by fingers and thumb.

The marimba was developed around 1910 in the USA, with antecedents among the folk instruments of this African name in Central America, and became a popular instrument for variety soloists. An early model by Deagan and Leedy, Chicago, was called 'marimbaphone', and this form of the name may be met in modern compositions, in which the marimba often figures as major percussion tone-colour. Milhaud wrote a concerto for it with vibraphone (1947). A remarkable pre-war jazz composer and soloist on marimba was Red Norvo. Deagan also introduced a bass marimba, with a deep but short compass from *f* down to cello *C*, and available in various designs today. The resonators, like the bars, are wide, and the longest have to be turned up at the bottom to avoid raising the bars as high as the player's head. Heavy soft beaters are used.

Martelé, martelleto. See VIOLIN, 5*c*.

'Mary Rose' instruments (from the 1545 wreck of this English warship). See FIDDLE, 2; PIPE AND TABOR; SHAWM, 1*c*; WHISTLE, 2 (boatswain pipe).
Palmer 1983.

Masenqo. Ethiopian one-string fiddle. See RABAB, 2.

Maultrommel (Ger.). See JEW'S-HARP.

Mbira (as a lamellaphone). See SANSA.

Mean-tone. See TEMPERAMENT, 2.

Mechanical instruments. A broad conventional term covering instruments in which music or motifs are played, not by finding the individual notes with the fingers, lips, or feet, but by such means as turning a handle, winding up clockwork, pressing a switch, or (automatic instruments) by arranging for the music to start and stop by itself at prescribed times or hours. See: BARREL ORGAN (with bird organ, 'flute clock', street and fair organ, orchestrion, barrel piano); CARILLON; CHIME, 2, 3; MUSICAL BOX; ORGANETTE; PLAYER-PIANO (pianola).

It has been estimated that, in the 19th century prior to the development of the gramophone, street barrel organs of one kind or another were responsible for more than 85 per cent of the music heard by the average town-dweller, while great numbers of people still living have no childhood recollection of instrumental music other than that provided by a musical box.

The mechanical dissemination of music can be said to have begun with inventors such as Apollonius of Perga (3rd century BC), who was credited with having devised such automatons as singing birds, operated by a water-wheel or windmill which also pumped air into a whistle. But to reproduce actual music mechanically, some form of continuous rotary motion must be accurately converted into the momentary movements needed for sounding each note as required. The classic device for achieving this is the pinned cylinder (BARREL ORGAN; MUSICAL BOX, 1), followed in the 19th century by punched cards or perforated paper roll (BARREL ORGAN, 5), first for pipe and reed organs, then for the pneumatic operation of a piano (PLAYER-PIANO).

For an example of a complicated musical automaton, a piece (by Jaquet-Droz) in the museum at Neuchâtel, Switzerland, has a female figure seated before an organ-harpsichord (see CLAVIORGAN): a powerful clockwork mechanism drives the arms to pre-set positions and operates the fingers in the correct manner. The figure itself moves the eyes and the head, and the breast rises and falls as if in breathing. In James Cox's once-celebrated museum was exhibited in the 1770s a silver swan which preened itself and occasionally stopped to pluck a fish from the water in which it swam. The 'water' was simulated by rotating twisted glass rods, while a carillon driven by clockwork played one of several tunes. Complex musical automatons of this type were very popular from the middle of the 18th century until the early 19th, the music which they played generally comprising popular airs and national songs. (For one of the mechanisms for singing birds, see SLIDE FLUTE).

Bowers 1972; Buchner 1959; Ord-Hume 1973.

Medieval instruments. While seen so profusely in illustrated manuscripts and church sculpture, our understanding of medieval instruments is severely limited through the dearth of actual remains (Crane 1972) where we need them most: that is, of the leading and most representative instruments of the period. Only from the 16th century (or in a few cases from just before) can we know instruments by examining them in the hand, and learn from contemporary literature how to play them. Yet reconstruction of medieval instruments and performance on them offers an irresistible challenge to makers and players wishing to recover their sounds, notwithstanding the further problems in interpreting musical notations which, especially over time and rhythm, often tell us far too little to go on without calling upon intuition.

1. Types of instrument. Up to the age of Charlemagne (d. 814), the old Romanized populations of Europe seem to have continued to play on instruments not greatly changed from Roman times. Letters written in the sixth century AD by Fortunatus of Poitiers (*PL*, 88. III. xiii) tell how in Paris one heard pipes of all descriptions played by the young, trumpets, cymbals, and frame drums by the older, and poems sung to the lyre; and again how the barbarians to the north sung to their own species of that instrument (see LYRE, 3). From the 9th century, as conditions grew safer for long-distance travel, fresh instruments started to appear, largely brought from the Byzantine area and Italy. Craftsmen-priests brought knowledge of organ-building and bell-founding (Theophilus); touring troupes of entertainers brought other instruments (for the instrument names in Latin treatises see Hickmann 1971), and these were further disseminated from place to place as ordinary folk mingled on the long pilgrimages. By the 13th century the most prominent instruments are (apart from church organ and bells) as follows, giving the names generally used for them today: *Stringed*: *harp, 9; *psaltery; *citole and gittern (ancestors of guitar and cittern); *lute, 2; *fiddle (*viele* and others); *rebec, 2; *hurdy-gurdy, 4 (organistrum, symphonie). *Wind*: *flute, 5; *pipe and tabor; *portative organ; *recorder, 5; *bagpipes, 7; *shawm, 2; *horn, 8; *trumpet, 4d. *Drums*: nakers (see NAQQĀRA, small kettledrums); tabor (mainly with pipe, as above); *tambourine, 2 ('timbrel'); *cymbal, 5; *handbells; *jew's-harp. (For the question of a row of small bells arranged in a scale, see CYMBALA.)

Some of the characteristic instruments are seen in Pl. 1, from 'The Romance of Alexander' of 1344, probably Flanders (Oxford, Bodleian Library, also reproduced in facsimile): an array of musicians with, on the left, bagpipe, tabor, nakers, cymbals (clashed up and down), handbells; on the right, fiddle, portative organ, psaltery, and citole (as this name is now interpreted); blowing two trumpets at once is not a unique sight for the period, even if no contemporary written source seems to mention it unless the twin trumpets of Fate.

2. *Problems of identification.* The greatest number of instrument names is Old French. In the romances may be found up to 40 of them, many belonging to instruments of kinds in the above list; yet, out of the total, we do not know for certain the meaning of near half, including for example *rote, and 'estives' (see HORNPIPE, 2), both of frequent occurrence. Turning next to the iconography we run into the opposite, a name being attached to a picture only in rare cases. Among 38 different instruments depicted in one major source, the late 13th-century *Cantigas de Santa Maria* (Escorial Library, j.b.2), made under the direction of Alfonso X ('The Wise'), there are, to point only to a few, four of psaltery kinds, all different, and four of bowed types, similarly; three bagpipes, again all different and unlike any now existing, along with eight or more pipes of unidentifiable kinds, perhaps distinguishing different regions; and among the rest, again the 'double trumpet'. And, of course, no instrument is named; yet to begin to know what an instrument is, one needs to know both what it looks like and what it is called. Many attempts have therefore been made to correlate the

Cantigas pictures, others too, with the long chains of instrument names met in Spanish and French poems, and leading to identifications (in some cases backed by reference to later folk instruments) which though conjectural have sometimes tended to become accepted in modern works as fact.

3. *Use of instruments.* On a rough estimate, about half the literary and poetic references up to the early 14th century are to the single performer, playing alone. The *romances* tell of the dazzling skill of the harper or fiddler (*vieleur*) as he or she gains admittance to a castle to entertain with famous lays; or of the troubadour's minstrel (*jongleur*) possibly accompanying his master's song on the *vièle* or singing the words himself. And so on through to the *Canterbury Tales* (begun 1387), in which every time an instrument is mentioned, it is alone or with the voice, save only with the warlike instruments played together as a sort of band. Apart from these, every major medieval instrument is of some musically self-supporting nature: the hands one above the other plucking the strings, high and low, as if for touches of harmony even if confined to octaves or fifths; or by intermittent 'drone' effects (see FIDDLE, 2), or continuous drone (as bagpipe, and from the snare of the tabor humming beneath the melody of the pipe). Where, in a romance, minstrels with instruments of every kind are assembled for a great wedding, one gains the impression that they performed mostly in turn, 'each pressing forward to be heard', until perhaps at the end they joined forces 'making a great noise such as was never heard before'—repeating verbal formulas of older romancers of the same epoch. Where a manuscript is decorated with very lifelike figures playing many different instruments (apart from David with musicians in a psalter) it is often impossible to discern a meaningful scheme in the artist's assemblage (Pl. 1), if indeed there be one. Now and then, on the other hand, two players in a picture seem to be performing attentively together, or two fiddlers are described as playing together, bringing to mind such as the now often played 13th-century two-part pieces in British Library, MS Harley 978 (Davison and Apel 1947, nos. 41, 42).

Pl. 1. Medieval instruments, from *Le Roman d'Alexandre*, 1344 (Oxford, Bodleian Library, MS Bodl. 264, fo. 188v). For instruments shown, see text.

No less than five major 13th-century Latin tracts on music give special praise to the *vièle*, said by one to be capable of every musical genre. Among textless three-part isorhythmic motets in the Bamberg Code (Aubry 1908) one bears a title 'In saeculum viellatoris', which could mean 'on the plainchant *in saeculum* for (or by) the viella players'. The written compass, *f* to *a'*, is not unusual for such motets, and in no way does it seem 'idiomatic' for instruments unless perhaps in small aspects of notation. But the main further trouble is that these treatises give no explicit information about the execution of textless tenor parts, whether by a voice or whether, regularly or depending on circumstances, on an instrument, and if so on which; the fiddle perhaps, or an organ.

On instrumental participation in the later and more complex polyphony, as in works of Machaut (d. 1377), literary and pictorial evidence puts questions of practical realization today on only slightly firmer ground, specific information being still extremely sparse, although there are textless parts which, to a musician's eye today, may seem to cry out for an instrument along with the voices, and here perhaps especially those of plucked strings (see HARP, 9*c*). See also HAUT AND BAS, and for a continuation, RENAISSANCE INSTRUMENTS.

4. *Sources.* The earliest pictures are of the 9th and 10th centuries, Byzantine (Bachmann 1964) or Byzantine-influenced such as the often reproduced illustrations in the 'Utrecht Psalter' (France, pre-850). A warning should be given against some fantastic figures of allegedly Biblical instruments from the spurious 'Dardanus letter to St Jerome' (Page 1977), copied repeatedly through the Middle Ages and onwards and even cited as lifelike representations in works of quite recent date.

Practically all the finest illustrated manuscripts onwards, up to the 14th century, have been reproduced in facsimile editions to be found in the larger libraries; also of the *Cantigas* (2, above; some of the miniatures are reproduced in *Grove*, 5th edn., vols. III–V). Many standard works on instrument history are well illustrated from the principal medieval sources (e.g. Galpin 1910; Harrison and Rimmer 1964; Kinsky 1930; Panum 1941; Remnant 1986). For examples of music in transcription, among the most useful to start from has been A. T. Davison and W. Apel, *Historical Anthology of Music: Oriental, Medieval and Renaissance* (1947).

Medieval viol. See FIDDLE, 1*b*.

Megaphone. A wide conical tube of metal or cardboard concentrating the energy of the voice in one direction, this was a familiar enough object in the past, mainly for speech, as at sea, though also for singing into, as the 'vamp horns' of English country clergymen, for leading the psalms as well as for giving out notices. Some of those preserved in museums reach 2 m. (6') in length. It has of

course been superseded by the amplified loud-hailer.

Mellophone. Valved brass instrument, American name of the E-flat *tenor cor. In the USA, *c*.1959, C. G. Conn brought out a new version, 'mellophonium', since known as 'mellophone', with wide bell, 26 cm. (10''), projecting straight forwards 30 cm. (1') beyond the main coil of the tube and intended as an improvement (directing the sound forwards) for concert-band use. It has appealed to some jazz trumpeters as an alternative instrument for solos, and has also been manufactured in France and Germany, though its production has now practically ceased.

Melo-. One could write down at least 25 names beginning 'melo-' (or Fr. *mélo-*) for instruments (or components such as the Melodia organ stop), a few of them modern, some electronic, but a good half have been 19th-century varieties of *harmonium and of other *free-reed types, as those that follow below.

Melodeon. 1. The popular small accordion; see ACCORDION.

2. A simple type of American reed organ of the mid-19th century (see REED ORGAN, 2). For the 'rocking melodeon' see LAP ORGAN.

Melodica. A free-reed instrument introduced by Hohner during the 1950s, held like a recorder, with a plastic case, a mouthpiece at one end, and two octaves or more of reeds, sounding only on the 'blow' and controlled by small piano-type keys (those for the sharps given to the left hand). Chords can be played as well as single notes, and larger tenor sizes are available. The Pianica is a corresponding instrument by Yamaha. Instruments in some respects similar have been made in the past with names like 'blow accordion'. Also, long familiar are those of 'toy trumpet' and 'toy saxophone' shape, with finger-buttons controlling the free reeds. Some can optionally be placed on a table and blown through a rubber tube: one such was the 'goofus', a novelty instrument played in some recordings by the American saxophonist Adrian Rollini, and manufactured under this name from the 1920s.

Far earlier than these (1772) was a *Melodika* invented by the famous Vienna piano-maker J. A. Stein, with, laid upon a grand piano, a 3½-octave set of horizontal organ pipes for playing the melody to accompaniment by the other hand on the piano; pressure of the fingers on the organ keys controlled that of the wind fed to the pipes.

Mélophone. *Free-reed instrument seen in many collections; a large, roughly *guitar-shaped body with at one end a handle (like that of a suitcase) pushed in and out with the right hand to work the bellows, while the left hand has buttons for a range of several octaves. Loud and soft, or a tremulant, are made with the handle. Invented in Paris by Leclerc, 1837, and once played by Giulio Regondi, later one of the most famous concertina soloists.

Membranophone. In *classification of instruments, the class that includes mainly drums but also instruments of *kazoo kinds (in which a vibrating membrane can be seen as a primary sound-producer from the purely instrumental aspect).

Mersenne, Marin (1588–1648). French mathematician, a Franciscan friar, and author of the most compendious work on musical instruments along with *Praetorius. This is his *Harmonie universelle* (Paris, 1636), with numerous engraved illustrations. For modern editions see 'Works Cited'.

Metallophone. General term for percussion instruments of tuned metal bars (corresponding to *xylophone for those with wooden bars, and *lithophone for those with stone bars or plaques): see GLOCKENSPIEL; VIBRAPHONE; and (in South-East Asia) RANAT and, for the Javanese *gender* and *saron*, GAMELAN.

The term had already been used in the late 19th century, by German manufacturers, for children's glockenspiels, as today it is used for educational metal-bar instruments.

Metronome. An apparatus for fixing tempos. Simplest is the ball on a calibrated cord, in common use prior to the clockwork type of J. N. Maelzel (1815), for some time the friend of Beethoven, who took much interest in it. This is the pyramidal instrument, having a swinging arm which ticks at each end of the swing, and a movable weight for setting the speed; sometimes also a bell that can be made to strike at every second, third, or fourth beat. From the use of this metronome came the practice of writing the letters 'M.M.', as in 'M.M. [crotchet] = 100', i.e. Maelzel's Metronome set at 100 clicks to a minute, each representing a crotchet. The settings may be from 40 to 208.

About 1945 a pocket metronome, shaped like a watch, was introduced in Switzerland. Metronomes designed to synchronize irregular rhythms (three against five and the like), found in much modern music, have also been devised. Electric battery-operated models are now in common use.

Metronome marks, even when they originate with the composer and not some editor, are not necessarily to be understood as binding. Brahms said in a letter to Henschel: 'As far as my experience goes every composer who has given metronome marks has sooner or later withdrawn them.' Some of Schumann's marks are almost impossibly fast, suggesting that his own metronome was not in good order.

The metronome has been introduced into composition by Ligeti, who wrote a symphonic poem for 100 metronomes (1962), and Gordon Crosse (*Play Ground*, 1977), among others.

Mexican bean. See MARACAS.

Mey (Turk.). See BALABAN.

Middle East: 1. *Overall view of the instruments*. The long chain of predominantly Islamic peoples, Arab, Iranian, and Turkic, from North Africa to Central Asia, can, for the musical instruments, to a large degree be viewed as one entity, even though from Antiquity onwards an outward flow has borne many of the instruments to more distant regions, there usually to assume some different appearance: *lute, *fiddle, *shawm, becoming recognizably 'Chinese', or 'Indian', or for that matter 'European', while on the other hand, within the home area they remain no less unmistakably 'Middle Eastern'. When combined in ensembles, these too display a broadly uniform character, led by stringed instruments—a bowed instrument (now often the violin) together with a deeper-sounding lute and perhaps a psaltery *qanun, or *dulcimer—playing in heterophony (the same tune rendered simultaneously in the different style of each instrument). With this, the essential backing of drums, often of more than one kind, each with its designated function; see Pl. 1, this from North Africa, 1881 (after Norlind 1941): left to right, *req* (tambourine), *kuitra* (replacing lute), *rabab* (shown without the bow), *darabuka* (main drum), *gunbri* (a simple lute). If there is a wind instrument it will most generally be of a *flute kind. Standing apart from such classical and café ensembles is the outdoor combination of shawm (*surna) and drum, leading processions of all kinds (and when heard from a distance often mistaken by Western visitors for Scottish bagpipes). Meanwhile shepherds and boys continue to play on flutes and *reedpipes as they may have done ever since settled communities first grew up in the region eight or nine millennia ago.

2. *Chief instruments:* (a) Idiophones. Not a prominent class. Animal bells of course; cymbals, most of various small types, some in 'clapper' form (see CYMBAL, 5d); jingling instruments; and pellet-bells attached to other instruments.

(b) *Drums.* Small pairs of kettledrums, *naqqāra (Morocco to Central Asia); cylindrical, *davul (Turkish 'bass drum'), *tabl (in some form almost everywhere); goblet, *darabuka (in Iran, zarb); frame drum, *bendir (North Africa), *tambourine, 3, *tar.

(c) *Stringed.* First in importance, and in great variety. *Fiddle, 2; *lute, 7 (long lute). By region: North Africa, lutes: *gunbri, *kuitra, *lute, 6; fiddle, *rabab. Egypt to Iraq, Turkey, lutes: lute, 6 (Arab lute), lute, 7, *saz (Turkey); fiddles: *kemancha, 2, 3, *rabab; Zither: *qanun. Iran, Central Asia, lutes: lute, 7 (with 7c, komuz), *tanbur, *tar; fiddle,

Pl. 1. A North African ensemble: *req* (tambourine), *kuitra, rabab, darabuka, gunbri*.

kemancha, 1 (with *ghichak*); zither, *santur* (see DULCIMER, 3).

(d) *Wind*. Flutes: over the whole area above all the end-blown flute **nay* (with other regional names) until in Central Asia, as in Uzbekistan, a transverse flute may assume first place in classical ensembles. Duct flutes, ubiquitous, mainly as folk instruments. Reed instruments: **surna (ghaita, zamr), balaban* (Black Sea to Caspian areas), these both double-reed; reedpipe, **zummara*; **bagpipe*, or sometimes **hornpipe*, many regional varieties, see BAGPIPE, 6. Trumpets: metal, long, straight, **nafir, *karna*.

Farmer 1957; Lavignac 1913, vol. v; Picken 1975; Vertkov 1963.

Military band (or concert band, wind band). A band of woodwind, brass, and percussion. The military term is 'band'. 'Military band' is a civilian expression, traditional in Britain for such a band whether military or civilian, but now largely supplanted by 'concert' or 'wind band' (or 'wind orchestra') following American practice.

1. *Instrumentation: (a) British and American*. A band broadly amounts to a full orchestral wind department plus saxophones and many additional clarinets and tubas ('basses'). In Britain and the USA published editions usually have parts for:

Flute and piccolo, oboe, E♭ clarinet

B♭ clarinets in three or four parts, mostly played by two or more players to each part: 'Solo', '1st', '2nd', and '3rd' (in USA three parts, '1st', '2nd', and '3rd')

Alto and bass clarinet: often in American editions, but in British seldom except in old editions which have no saxophones

Bassoons: one or two parts

Saxophones: in Britain, alto and tenor; in USA two altos, tenor, and baritone, or sometimes more

Horns (French horns): two to four parts

Cornets (or trumpets): two parts; in USA often three

Trombones: three parts, the third for bass trombone

Euphonium (in USA 'baritone')

Basses: parts for instruments in E♭ and low B♭, the former playing the upper notes where the part is in octaves. Often included is a special part for 'string bass' (double bass), an almost regular addition to a band when playing under cover

Percussion: side-drum; bass drum and cymbals; sometimes a full part for timpani. Xylophone, etc. as required

Conductor: usually a 'short score' in up to four staves

Marches are printed on cards, to be clipped to a card-holder or 'lyre' attached to the instrument. Current tempos for the British army have been stated as 116 paces per minute for a quick march and 65 for a slow.

The well-tried principles of transcribing orchestral music for a band lie basically in adapting the violin parts for clarinets, viola for the same or saxophone, cello for euphonium or tenor saxophone or bassoons, and then distributing the original clarinet and bassoon parts among the other instruments (e.g. cornets, trombones) to reproduce the contrast with the string parts. Harp parts can be a problem: Sousa took a harpist with him.

Compositions written for band have greatly multiplied since the 1940s, notably in the USA, where bands especially flourish as civilian institutions. A high school may maintain a large concert orchestra of wind as well as a wind band and a marching band, with instrument tuition and proficiency tests held within the school curriculum. Extra parts may then be written out for additional instruments (like contrabass clarinet) or players (like second and third flutes), making room for a greater number of musicians and so affording the overflow of competent wind-players, denied through their sheer

Pl. 1. Band of the Foot
Guards (1753): 2 French
horns, 2 bassoons, 4 oboes
('hoboys').

Pl. 2. Bandsmen of the
French Garde Royale, after
1820. Among the instru-
ments note especially: (top
right) cornet ordinaire (see
POST HORN, 2); (2nd row) two
hand-horns (see HORN 6),
*serpent, and *trombone
(this in a form with bell
pointing to the rear; not all
hand positions among the
instruments are correctly
drawn); (bottom row) serpent
Forveille (see SERPENT, 2),
natural trumpet (short
model), and on right, Jingling Johnny (see TURKISH
MUSIC), caisse roulante (see
SIDE DRUM, 4), and bass drum
played with a switch in the
left hand (see BASS DRUM, 5).

numbers a seat in the orchestra itself, an opportunity to play together and feel themselves part of a team.

(b) *Continental bands.* These vary much in size, many of the smaller being virtually brass bands plus clarinets (see BRASS BAND, 2), the music scored in a basically brass-band manner to sound reasonably complete when a number of players may be absent. On the other hand a full *orchestre d'harmonie* in France, or Italian municipal band, may include almost every species of wind instrument existing: saxophones from soprano to bass, flugel horns, bass trumpets, contrabass valved trombones, and even sarrusophones (as Beecham attempted in London with his wind orchestra of 1912). Opera selections are magnificently performed, the leading vocal parts entrusted usually to a solo cornet and a solo trombone.

2. *Festivals.* For organizing civilian band festivals there have been in Britain the National Concert and Military Bands Association, and the Corps of Drums Society; and in the USA the Drum Corps Association and other societies. On the Continent, where interest in bands is very keen, especially from Belgium across to Scandinavia, international festivals are held regularly, usually with American and British bands participating.

3. *Corps of drums.* The basic tradition is for drums with either flutes ('fifes', see FLUTE BAND), bugles, or Highland bagpipes. Some corps today use cavalry trumpets, often with bass trumpets, an octave deeper; or, mainly on the Continent, the large circular French hunting horns (*trompe de chasse*, see HUNTING HORN, 3). With them may be bell lyras (see GLOCKENSPIEL, 4) and other varied percussion. There has also been a trend, especially in the USA, to add more and more instruments, sometimes to include valved brass (so making virtually a kind of brass band) as well as percussion of every available type and drums of all kinds tuned to sound different pitches ('multiple percussion'). In France, expansion has long followed the different course of adding bugles or *trompes de chasse* to an otherwise normal *fanfare* (brass band), the repertory then including published marches and other pieces in which the tunes can be played by, or at least partly by, such 'natural' brass instruments.

A fairly recent development is for a marching band (not strictly a corps of drums) to use accordions, or special glockenspiels, etc., with the drums following behind.

4. *History.* After the medieval shawms and trumpets which, on the Saracen model (see SHAWM, 2), accompanied royalty on campaigns, military music became mainly a matter of drum and fife for foot, or trumpets and kettledrums for horse (as preserved in Britain in the Trumpets and Kettledrums of the Household Cavalry and in France in the Musique à Cheval de la Garde Républicaine). To these, from the late 17th century, began to be added the true military band, playing harmonized music on parades, levees, and at the end of the day for the officer's mess. At first it was small, a four-part combination of oboes with bassoon, instituted in France in the 1660s and becoming normal in Britain and Germany also. A pair of horns were added from the 1720s (Pl. 1) and clarinets in the 1760s (see also Harmoniemusik, under WOODWIND, 3). A late 18th-century British militia band usually had two each of clarinet (by then rarely oboe), horn, bassoon, plus one trumpet and sometimes a *serpent. Numerous marches and small suites survive in print or manuscript; some of the finest slow marches still played are among them.

Following the French Revolution, for the first time bands were seen as a national institution; the Paris Conservatoire was set up largely to foster them. For a great national fête a 100-strong band might be mustered to play marches and national hymns, already nearly a third of the men being clarinettists. Some of the added instruments are seen in Pl. 2, this prior to the arrival of the valved brass instruments which by the 1840s had set the stamp for the future. The earlier British band journals (serial publication of fresh items in band-parts) as Boosé's from 1845 could almost be used today: and when the Royal School of Military Music (as it came to be called) was opened in 1857, the instrumentation taught was hardly different from now. Next, the great American band tradition got into full swing after the Civil War, its first renowned leader being Patrick Sarsfield Gilmore (1829–92), who had been a bandmaster in the US Army during that war and in 1878 toured Europe with a band of 66 players. John Philip Sousa (1854–1932) directed a band of the US Marine Corps from 1880, then resigned in 1892 to form his own band, which gave its first concert in Pittfield, New Jersey, in that year and toured the world in 1910–11.

Adkins 1945; Berger 1957; Dureau 1905; Goldman 1961.

Mirliton (Fr.). See KAZOO. In Tchaikovsky's *The Nutcracker*, an apparent reference to *panpipes.

Mixture. See ORGAN, 2, 3e.

Mock trumpet. See CHALUMEAU.

Modes of vibration. See PARTIALS.

Mokubio. A Western spelling of Japanese *mokugyo*; see TEMPLE BLOCKS.

Monaulos. Ancient Gk.: 'single pipe'; see AULOS, 2.

Monkey drum. See RATTLE DRUM.

Monochord. A string (wire or gut) stretched over a long narrow wooden soundbox with a calibrated rule under the string. Since the time of Pythagoras in the 6th century BC, it has served for comparing the pitch-ratios of musical intervals in terms of proportional string-lengths as a bridge is moved to different positions. In the works of medieval theorists the monochord and its divisions are constantly cited. It was also found useful for tuning organ pipes and bells, remaining so in use for many centuries and serving many other scientific and instrument-making purposes. It is sounded either by plucking the string or by bowing it.

As a quick example, suppose that the rule is calibrated over 100 cm. and, with the movable bridge set at 50 cm., the string is tuned to Middle C (262 Hz). The bridge is then moved to the point where the string sounds in unison with the note being tested, and the point is found to be, say, at 38 cm. (15"). The frequency is 262 times 50 over 38, or 345 (a fraction below f', or by converting the interval above c' into *cents, 475 cents above).

Moon guitar (Chinese). See YUEQIN.

Mosquito drum. See GROUND INSTRUMENTS.

Motor horn (non-electric). 1. The classic 'bulb' variety has a thick brass single reed mounted over a tubular 'shallot', as in a pipe-organ reed (see REED, 1).

2. The klaxon, also used on boats, has a metal diaphragm with a short lug soldered to the centre. This is jerked by a toothed wheel rotating in a plane perpendicular to the diaphragm (the proximity of the teeth to the lug being adjustable by paper shims). An external handle or spring plunger turns the wheel by a chain of gears, giving fast rotation in one direction only, the faster the speed the higher, within certain limits, the sound emitted from the diaphragm.

Mouth-organ. For the familiar mouth-organ see HARMONICA. For the far older series of oriental instruments commonly referred to in the West as 'mouth-organ' (Fr.: *orgue-à-bouche*, etc.), see KHAEN, SHENG.

Mouthpiece, mouth-pipe. The first is that component of a wind instrument that is put to the mouth, as in the case of clarinet, saxophone, also some forms of flageolet, and see BRASS INSTRUMENTS, 1. In the latter, the length of tube into which the mouthpiece is inserted (and forms the first section of the main tube) is the 'mouth-pipe' or, in America, 'leader pipe' or 'leadpipe'.

Mrdanga (or *mṛdaṅga*). The classic drum of Southern India (Pl. 1): a long (about 60 cm. or 2') horizontal drum, widest towards one end, with two heads. The corresponding drum of Northern India, *pakhāwaj*, has been mainly replaced by the *tabla (pair of upright drums), but less so the *khol* of

Eastern India and Bangladesh. The shell of the mrdanga is hollowed in one piece of wood. The heads differ in size, the wider on the left, played on by the left hand, the smaller by the right. They are partly of a double thickness of skin, comprising the main skin (goat, etc.) and over this a thinner skin from which a circle is cut away, leaving a wide ring with the main head exposed in the centre. Each head is lapped and stitched to a hoop of twisted hide. The strap-like tensioning thongs are led round the hoop and through holes in the skins, and may be further tightened by round wooden chocks, wedged under the straps. A black circle of tuning paste, like that used for the *tabla, is applied to each head, and brings the pitch of the left-hand head about an octave below that of the right.

Pl. 1. Mrdanga, North India.

Playing strokes, made with the hands, are in exceedingly intricate variety, using a whole hand, different fingers, the ball of the thumb, and on the rim, or on the head, itself or on the black patch. The strokes, named by a special terminology and taking many years to perfect, are already described in the great treatise of c.AD 200 (see INDIA, beginning).

Mtziltayim. See BIBLICAL INSTRUMENTS, 1g.

Multiphonics. Modern wind-instrument term covering production, in various ways on an ordinary woodwind or brass instrument, of complex sounds composed of two or more different pitches. The year 1967 saw the publication of Bruno Bartolozzi's *New Sounds for Woodwind*, in which are codified all the compound sounds that could be discovered by woodwind members of the orchestra of La Scala, Milan, using trick embouchures and trick fingering, and increasingly demanded in music of advanced kinds. They are seldom chords, even atonal chords, but superposed pitches, some of them impossible to write down in notation. Various signs and symbols may therefore be used to tell the player what to do.

Ex. 1 is from Heinz Holliger's Wind Quintet 'h' of 1969; the holes in the diagrams run downwards from the highest, black signifying 'closed', white 'open' (the standard practice in fingering charts for instruments, as are also the numbers for the keys). There have since been special publications giving fingerings, as by Howell 1974 (flute).

Multiphonics, Ex. 1.

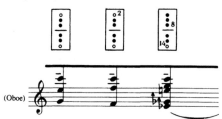

(Oboe)

Musa. See BAGPIPE, 7; *muse-au-sac*, BAGPIPE, 3*a*.

Muselar. See VIRGINAL, 2.

Musette: 1. *Bagpipe.* A French name still commonly used today in Central France for the country bagpipe (see BAGPIPE, 3), but best known as denoting the complex and elegant type, or *musette de cour*, played in wealthy society during the 17th and 18th centuries. This may also have been the first bagpipe regularly to employ arm bellows. Both chanter and drones are cylindrical (the chanter with a bore of about 4 mm.) and both are sounded with double reeds. The chanter has keys for semitones and to reach the high *a''*, a tenth above the lowest note, *f'*. 'Covered fingering' is much used, that is, to close, for each note, all fingerholes save the one through which the note issues. By the 1670s the maker Hotteterre (see OBOE, 4) had added the small extra chanter of flat shape, attached to the main chanter and fed with air through a cross-duct; its purpose is to increase the compass up to *d'''* by six small keys, and it emits no sound until one of these is opened (by little finger or thumb). The drones are in the form of a 'shuttle' drone: a wood or ivory cylinder about 18 cm. (7") × 4 cm. (1½"), drilled with 13 parallel bores connected at their ends to form four separate up-and-down windways, each with its reed inserted into the top. They vent through side slots, regulated by a slider operated from the outside by which a drone can be tuned or silenced. Only three are used at once: if playing in the key of F: *f' c' F*; or in B♭: *f' f B♭*; the low F and B♭ being obtained from the same drone, which has two vents and two sliders.

Rameau several times scores for musettes in sylvan scenes, in *Les Indes galantes* (1735) alone with two piccolos. The drones are not here indicated, and may not always have been used in such works, for there was also in France the alternative of playing the chanter alone, as below or with a *wind-cap.

For *musettes de Poitou*, see ÉCURIE, 2*a*; see also BASSE DE MUSETTE.

2. *Without bag.* A small, simple oboe-like instrument, with or without keys, pitched a fourth higher than the oboe and manufactured by Paris woodwind makers through the 19th century and well into the 20th (in some cases with a slightly bulbous bell) after the above bagpipe form had long gone out of fashion. It is said to have served for the *bal musette* and country dancing in the towns, but later came to number more or less among the musical toys (the *bal musette* having adopted the *accordion). A 19th-century tutor, *Méthode de musette* by Cavaillé, states that the sound of the musette should be 'nasal' and close to that of the 'Breton chalumeau' (see BOMBARDE, 3).

Musical bow (Fr.: *arc musical*; Ger.: *Musikbogen*). The string of a hunting bow is sometimes, by men in New Guinea, loudly twanged or snapped in accompaniment to communal singing; but the term 'musical bow' is applied where the string is played on in gentle ways by which its harmonics are made audible for making a soft music. The instrument may be a hunting bow, but is in the majority of cases made especially as an instrument, and so in every inhabited continent including Europe, where it was formerly played in some eastern parts by peasants. It is probably, as one might readily suppose (though some musicologists have contested this; see GROUND INSTRUMENTS) 'man's earliest stringed instrument'.

1. *Simplest playing method.* Bushmen in the south-west of Africa have had the custom of passing the time humming a 'mood' song while with one foot holding the end of their hunting bow against a resonant surface on the ground, and tapping the string with a thin stick of reed, at the same time touching it with the other hand for one or more harmonics to be distinctly heard above the deep fundamental. By momentarily pressing on the upper end of the bow with the chin the fundamental changes; the harmonics change also, in Ex. 1 from the 3rd and 4th of *c* to the 3rd of *e*.

2. *Mouth bow.* Again rhythmically tapping the string with a light stick, but holding an end of the bow between the lips or teeth and selecting harmonics of the string by moving the tongue inside the mouth much as in playing a *jew's-harp. A deep-pitched string fundamental brings a number of harmonics within resonance range of the oral cavity, to be softly audible above the reiterated fundamental. While tapping, the same hand can bend the bow-stick for two fundamentals to alternate. Main areas: Africa, Melanesia, South and Central America.

See GORA for instances, notably in South Africa, where the string is sounded by blowing.

3. *Gourd bow.* A gourd is lashed to the bow-stick, with a fibre or cloth-pad placed between them. A hole in the back of the gourd faces the player's chest. While tapping the string he may, with the other hand, move the bow to bring the hole nearer or further from the chest, changing the resonance of the air in the gourd and so giving prominence to different harmonics of the string picked up by the air-cavity of the gourd. The method does not lead to the precision of melody obtainable with

Ex. 1. Extract from *Du*, song accompanied by musical bow of the Hukwe Bushmen of the Kalahari desert. Sung by Kafulo while playing his normal hunting bow (4′ 7″ (140 cm.) long). (Recorded in 1959 by Nicholas M. England; transcribed by Mieczyslaw Kolinski; from *Ethnomusicology*, 8 (1964), 24.

mouth resonance (above), but the sound can be heard further, and, moreover, the player can sing to his bow's accompaniment. To obtain two fundamentals, usually about a tone apart, the string is very often tied back by a noose, next to the gourd (as in Pl. 1) for hitting above and below this point.

Pl. 1. Musical bow (gourd bow), Kenya (Hyslop 1975).

Mainly African, the gourd bow is also played in parts of South America, introduced by Africans, in Brazil called *berimbao* (a word which can elsewhere in Latin America, as *birimbao*, mean a jew's-harp).

4. *Other musical bows.* Some bows are sounded by bowing with a short stick or fiddle-like bow, or (Indians of Peru) a mouth-bow is rubbed with a palm fibre. The Araucano (Chile) used to interlock

two bows, the one held to the mouth being rubbed with the other. There are also musical bows in Africa with the bow-stick replaced by a straight rigid branch with a flexible wand inserted in one end or both, and there are many further variations: the unique West African *pluriarc comprises many bows fixed side by side.

As to the antiquity of musical bows, always cited is the Upper Palaeolithic cave painting in Ariège, France ('Les Trois Frères'), in which a man appears to be holding a hunting bow to the mouth; the date is said to be 14,000 BC at the latest, though we cannot be certain that we indeed see here a musical bow.

Balfour 1899; and see AFRICA.

Musical box. The music is from plucking tuned metal tongues arranged as the teeth of a comb. There are two well-known kinds.

1. *Cylinder musical box.* Today, because of its superior manufacture, a highly prized playing antique. A strong clockwork motor on the left turns the brass cylinder. On the right, a train of gears turns at fast speed the fan governor mounted on a thin, delicate, endless screw; also on the right, the tune-change lever moves the cylinder laterally against a spring on the left, to bring, for each tune (there may be from eight to 12), a different set of pins in line with the teeth of the comb (as in a *barrel organ). The cylinder is pinned with fine wire, each pin inserted into its hole by a hollow punch, after which the cylinder is coated on the inside with a layer of special cement, evenly spread centrifugally. (Repinning the cylinder of a valuable old Swiss box for new tunes can still be done by specialist craftsmen.)

The teeth, small tongues of high-carbon steel, are soldered separately to the comb. Each tooth is pointed at the plucked end to make room for the pins of other tunes to pass as the cylinder rotates. In good class movements, the teeth are expertly thinned or tempered to enhance the tone through adjusting the partials (a process akin to 'overtone tuning' in instruments such as the *marimba).

In all but cheap movements each tooth is provided with a damper, a very small curving wire held in a block formed in the underside of the tooth. The barrel pin moves this wire against the tip of the tooth to silence any residual vibration should this note have been played just previously, and releases it to spring back before the new pluck. Thus the note can be repeated with no jarring. Musical boxes made after 1850 may include a drum or a set of eight to 12 bells. There may also be a small reed organ ('flutina' or 'organette') for additional accompaniment to the tunes played on the teeth, and controlled by pins which are usually set in the middle of the cylinder.

The musical box principle was evolved in the latter part of the 18th century in French-speaking Switzerland, first for watches and snuff-boxes. Noted makers of musical boxes in Geneva were Nicole frères (1815–1903) and others later in St Croix (north of Lausanne), though latterly the products have been mainly of 'gift' kinds (musical beer-mugs, toilet rolls, etc.).

Also made since the 1830s are the simple hand-turned children's 'manivelles', of a round case or tin canister with, near the top, a set of brass tongues, plucked in succession by cams branching from the handle, to sound 'tink-tonk' motifs or one or two tunes.

2. *Disc musical box.* Invented in Leipzig by Paul Lochmann in the 1880s, early models were named 'Symphonium' and 'Polyphon'. They were made also in the USA by the Regina Musical Box company, founded in New Jersey in 1892 by Brackhausen, from Germany, and continuing up to 1921. Instead of a cylinder there is a disc of mild steel or tin plate, turned by a sprocket engaging in holes round the periphery of the disc. The disc is punched with bent-over projections on the underside. Each disc plays one tune only, but discs can be reproduced in quantity from a master disc, a great saving in labour compared with the individual pinning required for every cylinder of the Swiss type. Since there is less room for projections towards the centre of a disc, the bass of the music is put there, the pieces being arranged to require low notes economically. It is impracticable for these projections to pluck the comb directly, so plucking is through the intermediary of a set of 'star wheels', one for each tooth, and pivoting freely on an arm placed radially under the disc. Each projection then turns its star wheel which in turn plucks the tooth. Again dampers are required, each having a small brass arm moved by the star wheel to touch the side of the tooth and move away just before plucking occurs. Coupled with the damper there is often another small arm, which acts as a brake to prevent the star wheel accidentally rotating and jamming on a tooth.

A main development of the disc musical box was in large upright coin-in-the-slot models for dance-halls, bars, and the like, and from 1897 made by Regina with mechanism for automatic change of three discs giving different tunes.

Clack 1948; Ord-Hume 1980; Webb, G. 1984.

Musical glasses. Everyone knows that a wine glass will give a note if tapped, or stroked round the rim with a wetted finger; a thin glass gives the same pitch by either means. Such facts have been known for centuries. From 1938, Bruno Hoffmann with his 'glass harp', a set of 47 glasses on a tray and stroked, has performed on them Mozart's *Adagio*, K. 617, written for the *glass harmonica (this with revolving glass bowls): it is said that the glasses could scarcely be distinguished in sound from the accompanying flute and viola in their upper registers.

Most early reports of playing tunes on a set of glasses, up to the mid-18th century, refer to the percussion method, using sticks bound with cloth. Walther (1732) tells of a German who played a concerto on the musical glasses, accompanied by violin and bass.

Musical saw (or 'singing saw'). An ordinary saw played with a fiddle- or special bow. The handle is gripped firmly between the knees, the blade pointing upwards, while the non-bowing hand grasps the tip of the saw between finger and thumb to give the blade a double bend (like an elongated S). While maintaining this double bend, if the blade is given a sharper bend at the handle (while bowing the smooth edge) the pitch goes up for making different notes, while all kinds of vibrato are possible. The French composer Henry Sauguet (b. 1901) produced a piece for *lame musicale* ('musical blade') and piano, appropriately entitled *Plainte*.

Taylor 1976.

Musical tube (or whirling tube). This metre-long (*c*.3′) corrugated plastic tube, whirled in the air while one end is held, came into vogue in the 1970s as an amusing toy. Air is drawn into the tube to rush over the corrugations, forming eddies which establish a vibrating air-column capable of emitting different harmonics up to the 5th or 6th (see HARMONIC SERIES) according to the speed of the air through the tube.

Mustel organ. The harmonium as made, with improvements, by Mustel, Paris, from *c*.1850. See HARMONIUM, 3.

Mute (Fr.: *sourdine*; Ger.: *Dämpfer*; It.: *sordino*; Sp.: *sordina*). A mute acoustically changes the customary sound of an instrument into one which is less resonant, more veiled, distant, or mysterious. Two groups of instruments are the most concerned: the violin family and, among wind, the brass.

1. *Violin mute.* This is three-pronged, of ebony or leather, or in various metal forms, clipped to the bridge for the added mass to raise the impedance difference between strings and bridge, resulting in reduced energy transfer to the soundboard, especially for upper partials. Similar mutes are made for viola, cello, and double bass (and are

especially effective on the viola). The violin mute came in in the 17th century; Purcell uses it in Act 2 of *The Fairy Queen* where Night and Sleep sing, with two recorders accompanying Secrecy between their songs. The instruction to put on the mute, 'con sordino' ('con sord.'), is countermanded in Italian by 'senza sordino' ('without mute'). There are now also types of 'attached' mute (attached to the bridge) used in modern orchestral works where the mute may need to be applied or removed within the short space of a bar's rest.

2. *Mutes for brass instruments.* These are placed in the bell, changing the tonal spectrum in various ways, reducing radiation of lower partials, while resonances within the mute can stress higher frequencies. An ancient form of trumpet mute was in use probably before the violin mute was known. Others came in during the 19th century, since when many further types have been introduced in *dance bands and jazz. Among the chief is the conical or 'straight' mute of cardboard, fibre, or synthetics, closed at the wide end (Fig. 1*a*); corks or ridges on the outside leave a narrow passage between mute and bell. It produces the thin, hissing quality often required from horn, trumpet, and trombone in the orchestra. In orchestral parts 'con sord.' or 'muted' is normally understood to refer to this type. Its predecessor, as known to Richard Strauss and his generation, was similar in principle and effect but generally of wood or aluminium, often with a knob on the end for attaching a string lest the mute should fall out and clatter to the floor.

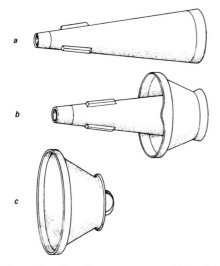

Fig. 1. Three brass instrument mutes: (*a*) 'straight' mute; (*b*) cup mute; (*c*) plunger mute.

The cup mute (Fig. 1*b*) is also conical, but instead of a plain closed end it carries a cup of width matching the bell rim and adjustable by a screw-thread to close the bell to a desired degree, giving different shades of 'blue' sound. The wa-wah or

harmon mute is corked to fit the bell all round. Inside is a tube leading to a small open-ended cup, the air in this case passing through the mute; waving the hand over the cup gives the 'wa-wah' effect. A 'clear-tone' mute likewise fits the bell all round but has two cones, one projecting from the other and again open-ended. The plunger (Fig. 1*c*) is simply a cup (originally from a rubber sink-clearer) with a handle for holding against the bell, to be moved in various ways while playing, e.g. outward and back as made famous on the trombones in Glenn Miller's 'Tuxedo Junction'. Jazz orchestrations have often called for 'in hat': an imitation bowler hat is held in the left hand or fixed to the music stand, for the trumpet or trombone bell to be brought close to it, for a kind of hollow sound.

Tuba mutes remain something of a problem, the very wide bell making it difficult to achieve an acoustically satisfactory result. Once they used to be home-made but are now manufactured in the USA.

The preceding mutes are sometimes termed 'non-transposing' mutes, meaning that they do not alter the pitch of the instrument, whereas mutes which do so are known as 'transposing mutes'. One of these is for the horn, giving the same effect as hand-muting and similarly raising the pitch, for which the player must compensate with the valves (see HORN, 3). Another is the ancient trumpet mute of wood, raising the pitch by a whole tone. When used in the orchestra ('trombe sordinate', etc., in baroque works, some of them funeral cantatas) the players compensated for the rise by inserting a crook, but Monteverdi, in the opening Toccata in *Orfeo*, tells the other instruments to transpose a tone higher if trumpet mutes are to be used.

3. *Other instruments.* In the 18th century the oboe was sometimes muted with a pear-shaped wooden mute or screwed-up paper thrust into the bell (as in the *St Luke Passion* once ascribed to Bach). Berlioz thought of having the clarinet played inside a felt bag (*Lélio*, 1831), anticipating the low-register 'sub-tone' effect of the 1930s, playing inside a large cardboard 'megaphone' with slots for the hands. The low notes of the bassoon can be softened by inserting into the bell an 8 cm.-long (*c.*3″) metal tube of smaller diameter, held in place by a winding of wool. Some early pianos had a 'mute stop' or 'celeste': a leathered strip hinged to fall across the strings, somewhat as with the modern 'practice pedal'.

4. *Further meanings.* 'Mute' also occurs in the name of certain instruments: mute cornett (see CORNETT, 4); mute violin (see VIOLIN, 9). *Sordino* once denoted the dancing-master's fiddle (see KIT), while 'sordone' is both an early organ stop and a Renaissance wind instrument (see KORTHOLT).

Mvet (harp-zither). Instrument unique to equatorial Africa from Gabon northwards. Five or six *idiochord strings, cut in the bark of a 5'-long raffia branch, are raised to rest in notches in an upright stick. On the back of the branch is tied a half-gourd resonator. Holding the instrument slanting upwards, the strings are plucked both above and below the stick using both hands, while the opening of the gourd is moved to and fro against the chest to give best resonance to the sound. Today, metal strings may be used.

N

Nafīr: 1. *Moroccan nafīr.* This is a straight trumpet, some 150 cm. (5′) long, mainly sounded during the month of Ramadan from minarets, in long blasts on one note now likely to be pre-recorded. The copper tube (outside diameter, *c.*16 mm.) is in two lengths, plus the funnel-shaped bell with embossed decoration, reaching *c.*8 cm. (3″) in diameter at the brass-mounted end. The mouthpiece, of sheet metal, traditionally takes the form of a wide cone soldered directly to the main tube, with a flat rim, and no cup. Nowadays the *nafīr* is familiar in often crude versions made for tourist gift shops. The name dates back to the 11th century. See also TRUMPET, 7c.

2. *Kakaki.* A descendant of the above is this straight trumpet, up to 2.5 m. (8′) long, of Hausa and other Moslem rulers of Niger, Northern Nigeria, etc. The construction (often of tin plate) and mouthpiece resemble those of the *nafīr.* Played in pairs in mounted bands, with the double-reed *alghaita* (see SURNA, 2) and cylindrical drum **ganga,* the kakakis utter harsh, chattering sounds on two harmonics a fifth apart in the baritone register, conveying expressions of welcome and homage to the ruler.

Nagasvaram. The South Indian double-reed instrument corresponding to the *shahnai* of the North. See SHAHNAI, 2.

Nail violin, nail harmonica (Ger.: *Nagelgeige*). Iron nails are placed upright round the edge of a round or semicircular wooden soundbox about a foot wide (30 cm.) held in the left hand (grasping with the thumb through a hole in the bottom). The nails are individually set in transverse vibration with a violin bow held in the other hand, bowing them on the outside near their tips. As manufactured from the 18th century up almost to the mid-19th, there may be up to 37 nails graded in thickness and length, giving three chromatic octaves; the nails for the sharps are taller, often bent outwards at the top, for distinction by eye and bow. Another version has instead of nails, iron staples (like croquet hoops). The nail violin reputedly followed an accidental sounding of a nail in a wall by a violinist, Wilde, at the Russian court in 1740 as he hung his bow on it. It became quite well known as an instrument for entertainment, some designs elaborated with sympathetic strings running across the soundbox. It also led in Germany to a 'Nail piano' (*Nagelklavier*) of 1791, in which the keyboard pressed to the nails an endless resined belt moved round by a treadle.

Nakers. Medieval European small kettledrums; see NAQQĀRA.

Nanga. In Africa, a zither (see ENANGA), or a horn; but especially the flutes of the Venda of South Africa, sounded together in harmony in bands of perhaps 24 men, each flute giving one note. They are end-blown flutes of river reed (see FLUTE, 7b) without fingerholes, in length from about 15 cm. (6″) to 140 cm. (54″), each stopped at the lower end with an adjustable fibre plug, and tuned to one note of a scale of four or more notes, for example G A C D, ranging over several octaves: the smallest flute may sound a high *d‴* and the largest a full, strong low *G* (bottom line, bass staff). The flutes of the highest octave (with the leader) begin the music, blowing in turn in a steady tempo, the rest then joining in one after another in the same pattern of notes, accumulating the lower octaves, until the leader's group ceases, followed by the others, leaving the largest flute to finish alone.
Kirby 1934.

Naqqāra (or *naqara*; in medieval Europe, 'nakers', from Fr.: *nacaires*). A pair of small kettledrums lashed together and normally played with two beaters. Of Arab origin, they were introduced into Europe after the later crusades for use in warlike music, though also depicted in the 14th century in non-military scenes and in the next century as well. Over the Islamic world they are today played, from Morocco to Turkestan (USSR) and North-West India, in instrumental ensembles. Usually they have quite small bowls, often of wood or pottery rather than metal, the larger around 22 cm. (9″) in diameter and the other a little smaller. Medieval European pictures may show a similar difference in size between the two nakers (see MEDIEVAL INSTRUMENTS, Pl. 1); Gerson of Paris, soon after 1400, contrasts their sounds (in Latin) as 'dull' and 'penetrating' (Page 1978).

Larger kettledrums have been made in the Middle East for royal bands since the 12th century and came to be used in bands of the Moslem rulers in India up to the 20th century. Such bands were named *naqqāra khana* after the drums; the players were often mounted on horse or camel. From this, in the 15th century, arose the European cavalry kettledrum tradition, in turn leading to the orchestral **timpani.*

Nay (or *nāy, nei,* from Persian, 'reed'). The end-blown flute (see FLUTE, 7b) of the Middle East, from

North Africa to Iran and the Caucasus; other names, used alternatively to *nay*, are *qaṣaba* (North Africa), *shabbāba* (Arab Middle East). For the corresponding instrument of Turkey and the Balkans, see KAVAL. (In Romania, *nai* is the *panpipe.)

Of cane (or sometimes wood or metal), it is in size anything from 23 cm. (9″) long of thin cane to 1 m. (3′) long of wider cane with longer internodes; the fingerholes are from five to eight, usually with a thumb-hole at some distance higher up. The instrument is held slanted well to one side (as KAVAL, Pl. 1) while blown across the top, which is generally (not always) bevelled all round on the outside to make a sharp rim. This is placed in some cases to the side of the lips, in others against the teeth while curling the tongue to direct the breath (to most Europeans the *nay* is the most difficult of flutes to sound, yet in lands where it belongs this comes quite naturally). The compass can reach three octaves, characteristically produced with a breathy tone, to which the player may add a guttural drone, in all giving much scope for 'programme' effects, as when, from Morocco to the Caspian Sea, a shepherd will 'tell stories' on the flute, such as a tale of lost sheep magically recovered; the same is done in north India by shepherds of Rajasthan on the *narh*, a very long *nay*.

The *nay* is often the only wind instrument regularly played in classical ensembles (see MIDDLE EAST), distantly recalling scenes from Ancient Egypt, showing end-blown flutes of reed up to 1 m. (3′) long, as long as the kneeling female player could possibly manage, covering three holes, placed far down, with both hands stretched at arm's length. In a pair of such flutes of *c*.2000 BC from Beni Hasan the measurements (Galpin 1937: 93) point to numerical ratios in the distances from the blowing end to the holes and to the bottom, of 8 : 9, 5 :6, etc., which correspond to musical intervals but perhaps complied with some cosmological system of proportions.

Nebel (or *nevel*). See BIBLICAL INSTRUMENTS, 1*b*.

New violin family. See VIOLA, 6.

Nightingale. See WHISTLE, 2.

Nōkan. Japanese flute; see FUE.

Northumbrian bagpipes: 1. *Small-pipes* (Pl. 1). A bellows-blown *bagpipe retained up to modern times among the working people of Tyneside and today made and played by many further afield. It has a cylindrical chanter (28 cm. or 11″ long, bore 4 mm.) sounded by a double reed and four cylindrical drones each with a single reed. A distinctive feature is the permanently closed bottom end of the chanter: when all the holes are closed

the chanter is therefore silent. Hence the notes (played with 'covered fingering' see BAGPIPE, 1) can be separated by silence, i.e. played staccato. The chanter usually has seven closed keys, opened individually to take the scale of G down to *d′* and up to *b″*, and to supply the middle C♯ and D♯. The drones, with *c*.2.8 to 3.6 mm. bore, are held in a single drone stock. Their reeds, normally of cane or elder, can also be of brass attached over a 'shallot' as in an organ reed (see REED, 1). Each drone sounds through a side hole which can be closed to silence it by a sliding 'bead' on a rod which passes out through the end-cap. As on the French *musette, only three drones are used at a time. If playing in G, the drones are *g′ d′ g*; or if in D, *d′ a d*, in which the *g* drone is reset to *a*, having a second hole higher up controlled by an annular sleeve ('tuning bead').

Pl. 1. Northumbrian small-pipe, being played by William A. Cocks, *c*. 1950.

The repertory is of traditional songs and dances, upon which experts perform complex variations: Tom Clough (1881–1964) was one who surpassed in those', and recordings by him exist. The instrument is made by craftsmen among the players themselves. Cocks and Bryan (1967) give every detail of how to make it, reeds included.

The small pipe began in the 17th century, evidently as an offshoot of the French *musette, and was once played widely over the county. The Duke of Northumberland has appointed a personal piper ever since the mid-18th century. The closed chanter came in during that century and keys were added from 1805. Exceptional chanters have up to 17 keys to be fully chromatic.

2. Half-long pipes. Also bellows-blown, but with an open-ended chanter. See BAGPIPE, 2c.

Nose flute. Flutes blown with the nose are most widely known in South-East Asia and the Pacific Islands, though met in Africa too. Sometimes one nostril is plugged, or closed with the thumb. The sound can be quite strong. Moreover, it has often been reported that in some areas, breath from the nose is believed to contain the spirit, and the music thereby rendered the more meaningful.

Pl. 1. Nose flutes, Semai, Malaya (*The Straits Times*, Annual for 1954).

In Malaya (the Sakai aborigines), Indonesia, and the Philippines, the nose-hole is a small sharp aperture cut in the knot which closes the end of the cane, the instrument being held sideways to

the nostril; or the hole may be in the side close to the knot (Pl. 1). Typically there are four fingerholes, fingered by one hand or both.

Over Polynesia the instrument is of wide bamboo (*c.*3 cm. in diameter), the nose-hole is in the side close to the knot at that end, the flute held somewhat forwards. The fingerholes are arranged quite differently from any other flute. In Tahiti, and in Hawaii (*'ohe hano ihu*), one hand closes a nostril with thumb or index finger while another digit fingers a hole placed not far away. The other hand fingers a hole far towards the other end, which is usually open. The three notes available sound approximately diatonic intervals, and by one old account could be overblown to the octaves. In Tonga and in Fiji, the few remaining players normally finger only the hole nearest to the nose-hole (with the hand which closes the nostril) and the one next to the other end, the rest staying uncovered. This yields four notes a semitone or more apart, in the region around Middle C. As with the Hawaiian type of nose flute the music runs in rapid motifs forming sections repeated in free variation. In Tonga, such a piece, said to have originated in allusion to the call of a certain bird, has been familiar as the radio call-sign: Ex. 1 is a small extract (Moyle 1976–7).

Also in Polynesia are *vessel flutes, small gourds, blown with the nostril (in Hawaii *ipu hokiokio*).

Notch flute. End-blown flute with a notch cut in the top end. See FLUTE, 7*b*.

Nsambi. See PLURIARC.

Nut. 1. (Fr.: *sillet*; Ger.: *Sattel*). With stringed instruments the bar or ridge on which strings bear at the tuning end: see STRINGED INSTRUMENTS, 5.

2. With a bow (violin, etc.), the attachment of the hair at the heel of the bow, i.e. the end held in the hand.

Nyastaranga (India). See KAZOO, 3.

Nyckelharpa (or keyed fiddle). Traditional and unique Swedish folk-instrument, revived today. It has the shape of a long fiddle, made from one piece,

Ex. 1. (after Moyle 1976)

with a key-box fixed on top (the instrument being supported on a strap). The melody strings (one or two) are stopped by wooden blades pushed up by the keys for the left hand, held palm upwards (not palm downwards as on a *hurdy-gurdy). The strings are sounded together by a short bow, the hair tightened by the thumb. There are also six to 11 steel *sympathetic strings tuned to a chord or to part of the scale. There are several varieties of the instrument, distinguished by the number of melody strings and how far the keys are chromatic (Ling 1967). Hundreds of polskas (Scandinavian versions of the mazurka) and waltzes are preserved in *nyckelharpa* tune-books back to 1830 though the instrument is much older, a form of it already existing in the 15th century. It has also appeared in Denmark, and for a time in north Germany (*Schüsselfiedel* in *Praetorius).

O

Oboe (Fr.: *hautbois*; from which Ger.: *Hoboe, Oboe*; It.: *oboè*; Ru.: *goboï*; Sp.: *obóe*; in these pronouncing the final 'e'; the older Eng. 'hautboy' or 'hoboy', deriving from the Fr., was normal until adoption, in the early 19th century, of the It. form pron. as an Eng. word). *Woodwind instrument (Pl. 1*b*), conical in bore and sounded with a double reed: one of the four main orchestral woodwind, the most highly coloured of them all, and historically its senior instrument in that originally and through the greater part of the 18th century the oboe alone was regularly present in the orchestra as soprano woodwind counterpart to the violins.

(a)   (b)   (c)

Pl. 1. Modern oboes: (*a*) oboe d'amore, (*b*) oboe, and (*c*) cor anglais by Howarth of London.

1. *Description*. Just under 60 cm. (2′) long, made in African blackwood ('grenadilla') in three parts—top joint, lower joint, and bell—partly hidden under metal keywork which continually tends to grow more complicated. With the reed inserted, it is as long as a *clarinet, but it looks smaller when being played, partly through the more slender tube and partly because the player's hands come about 5 cm. (2″) closer to the face. The reed, of which the player keeps a selection ready in a small reed-case, is usually made by the players themselves (see REED, 4), or else reeds can be purchased, best in an unfinished state whereby the player can personally undertake the final thinning ('scraping') of the cane.

In playing, the lips are drawn over the teeth with the tip of the reed resting lightly between them. The aperture of the reed being extremely small, little air is actually expended, so that, to relieve the lungs of de-oxygenated air, the oboist will usually quickly breathe out before taking in another breath. The brightly penetrating sound can in an extraordinary way evoke the tender and peaceful emotions, and best when allowed to do so of its own nature. Yet, to cover it with an unending cultivated vibrato is nothing new: Mozart criticized a leading player for it (J. C. Fischer, in London); on the other hand, in the 20th century, Leon Goossens (1896–1988) as he rose to fame captivated British listeners in making the oboe sound (as was said) 'like a violin'.

2. *Compass*. From the $b\flat$ below Middle C, two-and-a-half octaves up to the f''' above the stave, with the g''' above quite often demanded (for details of some of the fingerings, see OVERBLOWING). Some modern pieces rise to a difficult top a'''. Two 'octave keys' are provided. These may be 'simple' (separate keys for left thumb and first finger); 'semi-automatic' (without the need to release the first when using the second, and by and large the favourite arrangement); or 'fully automatic', needing the thumb-key only (as on the saxophone), thanks to an automatic switch-over mechanism controlled by the plate for the third finger, left hand. Fig. 1 illustrates, diagrammatically, the principle of these last two, as an illustration of the 'articulated' type of mechanism which is employed on the oboe in other places also. (There is now often a third octave key, for the thumb, opening a vent located a little below that of the first, for certain advantages in the highest register.)

3. *Systems*: (*a*) 'Conservatoire' and 'thumb-plate'. In Britain there survives a distinction between two fingering systems: the 'Conservatoire system' (named from the Paris Conservatoire) in which the notes $b\flat'$ and c'' and their octaves are made by lowering the right-hand first finger; and the earlier

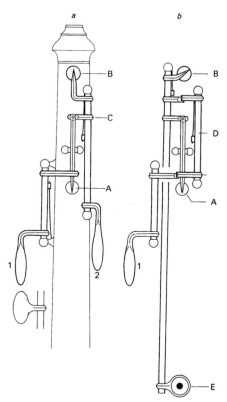

Fig. I. (a) Semi-automatic octaves: pressing the key I (left thumb) allows A to open until key 2 (index finger) is pressed as well, which opens B and then (via the arm C) closes A. *(b)* Full automatic octaves: key I lifts the two arms fixed to the rod D, allowing A to rise while B is held down by the third finger on ring E; on raising this finger (still pressing I) the ring rises to open B and close A.

'thumb-plate system', in which these notes are made by lifting the left thumb from a thumb-plate (indicated in Fig. I, A) which is not present on the other system. British tradition has long favoured the thumb-plate, whereas other countries use only the Conservatoire.

On modern oboes the older ring keys are replaced by padded plates ('plateaux') with, in most cases, a small perforation in the centre (Pl. I). The 'plateau' system provides for improvement of several trills. The delicate intricacy of oboe mechanism makes the instrument rather more expensive to buy than a flute or clarinet of comparable workmanship. Many players continue to obtain their oboes from the specialist makers in Paris (such as Marigaux). One may still come across old oboes with only two rings for the right hand, and a bell giving low B♮ only: these are now quite out of date.

(b) Viennese oboe. Made by Zuleger, and in regular use in the major orchestras of Vienna, this retains many features from the Classical period, as an onion-shaped top end, a different system of keywork, and its own shades of tone particularly suited to the works of Austrian and German composers up to and including Richard Strauss. A contributing factor here is a normal use of 3rd harmonic fingerings (instead of 2nd) on the high notes of the second register up to *c‴*: a classical feature bringing out the power to swell the tone in a region where a phrase tends to reach an expressive climax.

(c) Boehm-system oboes. First designed by Buffet (Paris) and patented along with the Boehm-system clarinet (1844), these have had only limited success, though fresh designs appear from time to time. The 'Boehm system', in these, is usually confined to the right hand, as in the 'sax-fingered oboe' of the 1930s, which it was hoped might interest dance-band musicians as a 'doubling' instrument.

4. *Baroque and classical oboe: (a) From shawm to oboe.* A famous French flautist, Michel de La Barre, recalled in *c.*1730 (Benoit 1971: 455) how after Lully had taken command of the royal music, musicians and makers at the court, the Philidors and Hotteterres, had worked long and hard, consuming mountains of wood, to render the 'old hautbois' (treble *shawm) suitable for 'les concerts' (playing with the violin orchestra). Thus the oboe began. Few traces remain of early stages, from perhaps during the 1660s—some instruments of 'traditional' appearance, e.g. by Haka in Amsterdam, could point to parallel endeavours outside France during the same time—but by the 1680s it was completed and had begun to reach England and Germany, regarded without question as a French innovation.

The old one-piece, keyless shawm was remodelled in three elegantly turned and mounted joints, and the pitch adjusted to give bottom note Middle C, made with a key; the soon following second key, on the side, for E♭, is often duplicated, ostensibly to suit either little finger, making a 'three-keyed' oboe (though the left-hand key may be found to have no hole through the wood under it). The old trumpet-like shawm bell is shortened (giving better balance in the hands), while in the narrow top joint the fingerholes are very small (as they remain today) to complete the second register with fuller control on notes higher than can be reliably made on a shawm. Then, where the two joints meet, there is an abrupt small enlargement of the bore, for the continuing expansion to give freedom to the notes next below. A bigger 'step' of around 3 mm. in the diameter where the bell is put on seems to reproduce a feature of the fashionable bagpipe *musette, of which Jean Hotteterre had already been a noted maker. The steps in the oboe bore persisted until after Beethoven's time, when the Paris makers brought in the present uninterrupted cone and with it the octave keys, not needed before.

From the later 18th century the actual bore widths became reduced in most oboes, giving further fluency on the high notes up to *d'''*, even exceptionally to top *f'''*, as in Mozart's Quartet for oboe and strings (1781).

(b) *Makers.* Among earlier makers whose oboes are now again played on or carefully copied are Denner (Nuremberg; see CHALUMEAU, 2); Stanesby (London); and Bizet (Paris). For the Classical period, Milhouse and Cahusac are two of the favourite makers among present players in Britain. Each made both of the two-keyed models shown in Pl. 2: the earlier and peculiarly English type, the boxwood usually dark-stained with acid, and still a fairly wide bore; and also, from 1770, the handsome, narrower-bore model with the 'onion' bell, originally from Germany and played in England by Fischer, mentioned in 1, above. A leading maker of this last type was Grundmann, Dresden.

(a)   (b)

Pl. 2. Two 2-keyed oboes of the late 18th century: (a) by William Milhouse, Newark (illustrating the English 'straight-topped' design); (b) by Thomas Collier, London (modelled on contemporary German design).

(c) *Reed and fingering.* The reed (with the staple thread-lapped, not corked as in the 20th century) may vary in width so long as the blades are thinned back sufficiently to give the pliancy needed,

especially to tune the *cross-fingerings and blend them into the scale. So well can this be done that the instrument sounds at its most winningly expressive in flat keys, e.g. F major, this requiring cross-fingering for main notes like C and B♭ as well as the tonic itself. The contemporary solo music shows a preference for such keys, which also require less of notes like the lower F♯, a flat note for which a 'twin hole' is often provided (Pl. 2b) in addition to the twin hole anyhow needed for G♯ (Pl. 2a, b); nor is there a low C♯, though its octave is made by overblowing the low C (and 'half-holing' the first hole). For the high notes above *a''*, fingerings (among them those mentioned in 3c above) are almost identical with those of the one-keyed flute (see OVERBLOWING).

Up to the 1820s oboes continued to resemble Pl. 2b but with six to nine more keys—without which the parts in Berlioz's early works would have been hardly possible to render with full observance of the range of dynamics and accentuations demanded.

(d) *Triébert and the modern French oboe.* Already by 1840 the younger Triébert in Paris had produced the model with two right-hand rings that rectify the flatness of F♯; a low B♮; and (anticipated by Brod) the 'half-hole plate' for the first finger by which the hole is opened fully for cross-fingered *c''* (remaining a main fingering although a key gives an alternative) and with reduced opening for 'half-holing' on *d''* (as today). The thumb-plate system (above, 3a) followed by 1849, eliminating the need for left-hand cross-fingering; and in 1870 the Conservatoire system at the hands of his former foreman Lorée, who later (from 1906), in conjunction with the player Gillet, developed the more complicated 'plateau' mechanism.

5. *Repertory.* The chief baroque works include Handel's sonatas in B♭ and G minor and his concertos in G minor and B♭. There are many further concertos and sonatas by Italian composers, including Vivaldi, the Besozzis, and Sammartini; and also by Telemann and others. Bach's Concerto in C minor for two harpsichords is also published for oboe and violin. The highlight of the Classical period is Mozart's Quartet (oboe and strings) K. 370 mentioned above. His Concerto in C, K. 314, is a version of the Flute Concerto in D. Other concertos are by Fischer, Krommer, and (doubtful) Haydn.

Romantic works include a light but charming concerto (with a polonaise) by Bellini, a sonatina by Donizetti, and Schumann's arduous Three Romances for oboe or violin. Then there is rather a gap until Saint-Saëns's Sonata, followed by a rush of concertos, by Richard Strauss, Eugene Goossens, Vaughan Williams, and others; sonatas by Poulenc and Hindemith; and, for unaccompanied oboe, Britten's *Metamorphoses after Ovid* and Berio's *Sequenza VII.* Some ultra-modern works have come from Heinz Holliger (b. 1939) and his

1939) and his school, some requiring *multi-phonics, combination with transistor radio, a supplied tape (as in Holliger's *Cardiophonie*), or, in Globokar's *Atemstudie*, a throat contact-microphone.

Bate 1956; Halfpenny 1949; Haynes 1976; Joppig 1988; Marx 1951; Rothwell 1953.

Oboe da caccia. See COR ANGLAIS, 4.

Oboe d'amore (from It.; Fr.: *hautbois d'amour*; Ger. in the 18th century as Fr., today *Liebesoboe*). A minor third below the *oboe, it has a bulbous bell like that of the *cor anglais (see OBOE, Pl. 1*a*). Bottom note is the written *b*, sounding *g♯*. Length, *c*.63 cm. (25″) plus *c*.6 cm. (2½″) for the metal crook or bocal. The sound is veiled and intimate, much as the name suggests. It is German by origin (in existence by 1719), and is today made chiefly for the works of Bach, who names it first in the *St John Passion* and in some 60 works in all. Of known examples from his time (bottom note *c′*, sounding *a*), nine, with 2 keys or 3 (as OBOE, Pl. 2), were made in Leipzig by the city's chief wind-instrument maker, Eichentopf; reproductions are made today.

Bach appears to have written for oboe d'amore not only for its sound but in some instances when composing in sharp keys, for which the instrument was technically better suited than the contemporary oboe; in several cantatas are parts marked simply 'Hautbois', but in sharp keys and with a low *b* (then a note too low for the oboe), and probably meant for *hautbois d'amour* (Haynes 1985: 53–4). Among his solo works could be put a concerto, BWV 1055, reconstructed from what has been judged to be a later version for harpsichord. Telemann and various minor German composers also wrote for it, but by the 1770s it was obsolete. Then, after 100 years, it was revived in modern form for Bach performances, first by Mahillon (Brussels) with a plain, not bulbous, bell. (Without the oboe d'amore its parts have to be played on oboe or cor anglais.)

Debussy features the revived instrument in the solo melody (*doux et mélancolique*) in the third movement of *Images*. A few other composers have used it, up to Stockhausen in *Punkte*.

Ocarina. A torpedo-shaped duct flute, traditionally of terracotta, with projecting mouthpiece and 10 holes for the fingers and both thumbs. As in other *vessel flutes (see CAVITY RESONATOR) the notes rise in whatever order the holes are uncovered (the pitch depending on the sum area of apertures), but in an ocarina the holes are arranged and tuned to be uncovered in regular sequence as in playing a flute, beginning by raising the right little finger, RH4 (Fig. 1), and so on up to LH1, keeping LH4 and both thumb-holes closed. This gives one octave. To continue a fourth higher, these further holes are uncovered in the order: left thumb, LH4, right thumb. Accidentals are by *cross-fingering. There is no *overblowing to higher notes, the instrument giving practically a pure sine tone with no *partials.

Often a cork plunger is provided in the wider end, for tuning by changing the internal volume.

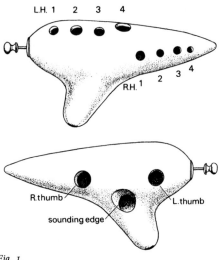

Fig. 1.

Ocarinas are also made in sets for playing in harmony, the largest up to 30 cm. (1 foot) long. Of the common size, those of fine porcelain, as Meissen ware, are much prized.

As to its invention, Christopher Welch (*Six Lectures on the Recorder*, 1911) recalled being told by an Italian, near Bologna, named Mezzetti, how he and a school friend, Donati, had experimented in developing for musical use the pottery bird whistle with a fingerhole in the breast and called *ocarina* (lit. 'little goose', and see WHISTLE) and by *c*.1865 had produced the since familiar form.

The 'tonette' is a fairly recent American instrument on the ocarina principle, made for schoolchildren, also torpedo-shaped (in plastic) but blown at the wider end for holding like a recorder. Interestingly for a 20th-century instrument, the printed instructions distinguish enharmonic fingerings, for such as G♯ and A♭.

Ethnologists often use 'ocarina' as a term for vessel flutes generally, i.e. including those which are not duct flutes but are blown directly across an aperture in the side or top (as when one blows across the neck of a bottle). Such, with or without fingerholes, are carved in wood, or of a dried fruit-shell, or of earthenware like the traditional *xuan of China.

Octavin. Small wind instrument, never more than a curiosity, invented in Markneukirchen, Germany, *c*.1893: like a *bassoon butt-joint, with outwards-turned metal bell and *clarinet-like mouthpiece.

Octo-bass. See DOUBLE BASS, 3.

Ō-daiko (or *ohdaiko*). Japanese, general term for the barrel drums, *taiko.

Oliphant (or olifant, 'elephant'). Medieval carved ivory horn, celebrated in the Chanson de Roland (*c.*1100) where the mortally wounded hero calls to Charlemagne, sounding (*corner*) his olifant with great pain in a blast heard 30 leagues away. In fact, olifants were chiefly kept as tokens of land tenure or in churches as reliquaries. Of some 80 medieval examples known, three-quarters are judged to be the work of Arab craftsmen in southern Italy in or about the 11th century.
Crane 1972.

Ondes Martenot. This is an electronic musical instrument, giving one note at a time, introduced in Paris in 1928.

Open note. With wind instruments, chiefly on valved brass instruments, a note produced without lowering a valve. Also on stringed instruments any note played on an *open string.

Open string. With instruments on which strings are stopped (guitar, violin, etc.), the note given by a string when it is not being stopped.

Ophibaryton. See SERPENT, 2.

Ophicleide. Brass instrument (Pl. 1) of *euphonium pitch and with a similar mouthpiece, but with 11 brass keys along the conical tubing for the fingers and thumbs. Cf. KEYED BUGLE, of which the ophicleide originated as a bass version introduced in Paris, 1817, by the maker Halary. It served through most of the 19th century to supply a bass in brass and military bands and in the brass section of the orchestra, and though from the mid century onwards increasingly replaced by the tuba it was still listed in French manufacturers' catalogues of brass instruments up to the First World War (and at least one personal recollection has survived of its use in the British Army in India during that war). The name, combining the Greek for 'serpent' and for 'key', was coined by the inventor as marking an advance upon the old *serpent.

1. *The keys*. The leather-padded keys, stuffed with swansdown or wool, are all sprung to be normally closed save for the key nearest the bell, this key (termed the first key) standing normally open as on the keyed bugle. With all the keys at rest the instrument has the same pitch as the trombone or euphonium, 9′ B♭ (many, however, are built a tone higher, in C). Closing this first key lowers the harmonic series by a semitone to provide the notes of the harmonic series of A. Progressively opening the other keys shortens the tube-length to provide the higher fundamentals chromatically up to A♭. Then follow 2nd harmonics from A (closing the first key) up to e♭, and so on. From *a* upwards, as harmonics come closer together, only five of the keys are needed, all of them situated on the

Pl. 1. Ophicleide, from Caussinus's *Tutor* (*c.* 1837). Note the open-standing key high on the bell; the player is opening the third key down (C key) with his left thumb.

ascending branch of the tube where the bore becomes widest and the width of the holes for the keys also widest, giving notes best matched in quality to those which issue from or close to the bell. The technique can be as agile as on a euphonium, and the sound has a crisp, 'open', almost vocal quality, though in fortissimo it could, in terms of orchestral dynamics of the period (less powerful than now), become, as orchestration books said, 'savage'. The earlier ophicleides have the keys mounted in brass 'saddles' (as in Pl. 1); but keys on rods and pillars were coming in by *c.*1840, and the coiled crook often replaced by one with a tuning slide (Weston 1983).

2. *Orchestral use*. The ophicleide is best remembered for its parts (now played on the tuba) in the works of Berlioz, as in the *Symphonie fantastique* (with the *Dies irae* in the last movement on two ophicleides), and *Benvenuto Cellini* (a ribald solo). Well known too are the three deep notes in Mendelssohn's *Midsummer Night's Dream* Overture (1826) portraying Bottom asleep in the ass's head—though possibly the part was originally envisaged for some earlier wooden instrument of the serpent or *Russian bassoon kind.

3. *Decline.* A main trouble with the ophicleide lies in the easily damaged keywork and the wearing out of the large key-pads. Also, the player has to master its special fingering, whereas valved instruments have a simpler fingering shared by all, quicker to teach to bandsmen and allowing changes from one instrument to another. However, well-preserved old instruments are by no means rare, and several brass players today have restored the ophicleide to the parts written for it.

Orchestra (from Gk.: the place in the theatre for the chorus; the modern sense of the word dates from the late 17th century in France, followed in Germany by Matheson in Hamburg in 1713 (the orchestra there having primarily an operatic function)). The following sets out only the instrumental composition of a symphony orchestra, with a note on its history. On what actually goes on in an orchestra, and the problems and special situations which daily arise, there are handy works available (as by Del Mar 1987). For full historical accounts see *NOCM* 'Conducting' by Denis Arnold and 'Orchestra' by Michael Hurd.

1. *Composition:* (a) *Strings.* Orchestral music resting absolutely on the united sound of many violins as opposed to one, and equally with the other stringed instruments, a full-sized orchestra will have typically 16 1st violins, 14 2nd violins, 12 violas, 10 cellos, and eight double basses, together adding up to two-thirds of the total personnel (the harp being reckoned separately from the strings). The 1st violins sit on the conductor's left (the top plates of the instruments thus inclined towards the audience). An old custom was for the 2nd violins to sit opposite, on the right, in order that the two violin sections might be clearly heard antiphonally; but today the cellos usually take this place, with the violas behind them and the 2nd violins behind the 1sts. The basses stand behind on the right (though an American method formerly favoured, for one, by Stokowski of the Philadelphia Symphony Orchestra, was to range the basses in a long single row at the back of the orchestra, and this may sometimes still be seen).

The strings are counted by 'desks', two players sharing a single copy (one of the two responsible for turning the pages); the orchestral librarian then counts the number of parts needed as so many desks, and the orchestral attendant the number of stands to put out similarly. Each section has its principal and sub-principal on the first desk, but in the case of the 1st violins, the principal is reckoned to be the player seated beside the violinist who is the 'leader' of the orchestra (in America, the 'concertmaster', from the German term; Fr.: *premier violon*). The leader has the further duty of performing parts or passages marked for 'solo violin', and has an important role in watching over orchestral discipline and in representing the orchestra in discussions that may arise with the conductor.

(b) *Woodwind.* Basically two players (principal or 1st, and 2nd) for each of flute, oboe, clarinet, and bassoon: eight separate parts. To work as a close-knit team they usually prefer to sit in two rows, flutes and oboes in front of the clarinets and bassoons, with in each case the principals close beside each other in the middle. Since much of the repertory requires three players of each of the instruments, a full orchestra will generally have permanently available a 3rd player of each and normally a specialist on, respectively, *piccolo, *cor anglais (English horn), *bass clarinet, and *contrabassoon. For some further particulars, as when a greater number of players is scored for, see WOODWIND.

(c) *Brass.* Horns: four players, the 1st being the principal, though the 3rd (who plays the higher part of the second pair of the four) may also have principal status. Often, a fifth player sits next to the 1st, to take over now and again in what may be a very arduous part. Trumpets: principal and 2nd, often a 3rd, even a 4th (as where there are two *cornet parts to be dealt with). Trombones: three—principal, 2nd, and bass—the last also usually with principal status; they make up with the tuba a four-part team.

(d) *Timpani and percussion.* The timpanist is traditionally distinguished from the *percussion who handle the other instruments, led by their own 'principal percussion' player. Basically these are three, though scores frequently require more than three instruments to be played at the same moment, calling for further players. One player will be specialist on the so-called 'keyed percussion' (glockenspiel, xylophone, etc.).

Parts for piano, celesta, etc., are often entrusted to a member of the orchestra who is also an expert pianist, and since a string player can be spared without leaving a part unplayed, this is who it will be.

2. *Smaller orchestras.* With the numbers above, amounting to around 90 players, the string sound is found to be an optimum in an average programme performed in a large, full hall. Yet many orchestras do well with fewer strings, while in, for example, touring opera or ballet, limited space in the theatre may enforce even large symphonic scores to be played with perhaps barely eight strings in all (the wind reduced less since the numerous individual parts cannot be condensed beyond a certain point without rendering the piece unrecognizable). A 'chamber orchestra' will usually be just large enough to play works by Mozart, for example, with wind up to two horns or as the programme requires.

3. *Women in the orchestra.* In 1931 the London Symphony Orchestra listed 66 players with only one woman among them (2nd harp): in most countries at that time, few professional orchestras would have permitted even this (women players, if not soloists, mostly teaching). But in that same year

the newly established BBC Symphony Orchestra included 19 women (strings and harp), increased by 1949 to a quarter of the whole (and including two oboists and one of the percussion). The great increase since has been in the number of women wind players, and for this, much of the credit is due to the great British oboist, Leon Goossens (see OBOE, 1) as one of the first eminent teachers in Europe to accept women without prejudice as professional pupils, leading the path to their now often dominant share in the most responsible positions on instruments of every kind.

4. *Rise of the orchestra*. During the 1550s, long before the orchestra was so called, the '24 violins' of the king was being established in France (see ÉCURIE), with several players to a part; so it ran up to the time of Lully, who was held to be one of the first to enforce (1656 onwards) the discipline by which all players of a section bowed their instruments in the same way. In Italy meanwhile, the violin family had come to provide the core of the instrumentation of early opera between the recitatives. In this, wind instruments are sparingly used to highlight particular scenes or join in a chorus—recorders, *cornetts, trombones, then trumpets (majestic contexts) and, especially in Germany, *dulcian. Later, from the 1680s, oboes became the first wind instruments to find a regular footing beside the violins (see also RIPIENO), bassoon with them, and following in the 18th century, horns. Flute or recorder, if required for a particular number, were in average orchestras often played by the oboists, in which case a composer would take care not to call for both instruments in the same number unless the personnel were to be augmented for a special reason. The strings varied in strength from violins up to 16 or more to the five or six that served Bach in Leipzig (Carse 1940; Terry 1932).

For each number in a work, any wind instruments involved typically play all or almost all through, then doing nothing until a later number may call for them again. A big change was meanwhile brewing, noticeable already in works of A. Scarlatti and Rameau and maturing in the time of Haydn and Mozart: scoring by *entries*, the players, wind especially, counting bars' rest in between and fully involved in a work from beginning to end. Orchestration had properly begun, shortly to bring with it the responsibilities of a non-playing conductor. In Vienna, Beethoven may have been among the first occasionally to direct the orchestra with the hands alone, from neither violin nor keyboard (Brown 1988). As more different instruments were made normally available to composers—clarinets by the 1790s, trombones rediscovered, the harp, the battery of percussion from the *Turkish music—'Instrumentation' treatises were written to tell the composers how to use them, the best known (Berlioz 1858) by no means the first, then Gevaert (1863), from whom it is said

that most ensuing French composers learnt the tricks of the trade. In Britain a good Victorian account (Prout) is followed in the 20th century by a classic (Forsyth), now however needing to be read in conjunction with more up-to-date literature covering especially the immense expansion of percussion, and the not infrequent incorporation of electronics.

5. *Other uses of the term*. For some of the many other uses of the term 'orchestra', see DANCE BAND (dance and jazz orchestra); MILITARY BAND (wind orchestra). 'Folk orchestras' are based mainly on non-orchestral types of instrument, often in a national or regional setting, while the larger instrumental combinations of the Far East, for example, now often describe themselves in European language as an 'orchestra'.

Orchestra bells. See GLOCKENSPIEL.

Orchestral chimes. See TUBULAR BELLS.

Orchestrelle. Mechanical reed organ. See ORGANETTE, ORGANINO.

Orchestrion. See BARREL ORGAN, 4.

Organ (Fr.: *orgue*; Ger.: *Orgel*; It., Sp.: *organo*). A 'pipe organ' (as also *barrel organ, *chamber organ, *cinema organ, *portative organ), making the sound from 'flue pipes' (*duct flute or 'whistle' principle) of various kinds, and in most organs also 'reeds' (pipes sounded by metal reeds: for organs using reeds without pipes, see HARMONIUM, REED ORGAN, and the older REGAL). See also (electro-mechanical) HAMMOND ORGAN.

1. *Manuals and pedals*. In the course of its history the organ has displayed more variety in matters of size, construction, and national characteristics than any other instrument. To begin with here, an organ may have only one manual (keyboard) but is usually seen to have two or three, with the very largest having up to seven. Each manual directly controls a 'division' of the organ having its own set of stops (ranks of pipes, or 'registers') for the organist to select suitable tone-colours by using stops either singly or in combination, providing contrasts of both volume and tone quality. The pedals form a further division, primarily for playing the bass part (relieving the left hand from having necessarily to perform this duty). When the pedals are involved, organ music is now customarily written on three staves, the lowest reserved for the pedal part.

On a typical British organ with two manuals (Fig. 1), the lower is for the 'Great Organ', the main division; the upper is for the 'Swell Organ', with its pipes enclosed in a box equipped with movable shutters controlled by a pedal at the console, enabling the sound to be 'swelled' or diminished. A third manual, in British practice

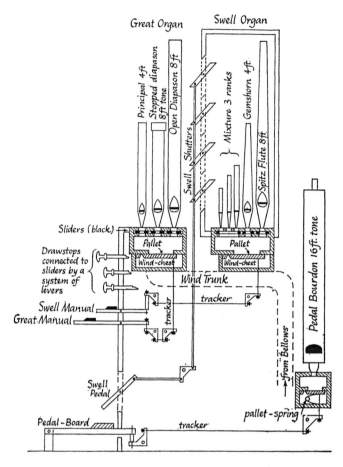

Fig. 1. Generalized cross-section of a fairly conventional small two-manual organ (tracker action), purely diagrammatic, not to scale, and omitting much detail, including coupling mechanism (after Clutton in Baines 1961).

placed lowest, is for a 'Choir Organ', and if a fourth, it is for a 'Solo Organ', and placed above the rest. Both of these may also be enclosed like the Swell Organ. The pipes of all divisions are all, or for the most part, contained within a common organ-case, in which passage boards give the organ-tuner access to the various ranks.

Among the draw-stops on the console are also those for 'couplers', by which a manual division can be played from another manual or from the pedals; for example the draw-stop marked 'Swell to Great' means that while the hands are playing on the lower (Great) manual, those stops which have been drawn on the Swell will sound in addition to those drawn on the Great (but not vice versa). Organ music from the middle of the 19th century onwards may give general instructions or recommendations on registration and on which manuals to play, but earlier composers, with the exception of the French 'classical' school, left very few such indications. From the late 19th century there have also been 'combination' or 'composition'

pedals or brass studs for the feet, and 'thumb-pistons' below the manuals, by which stop combinations may be changed and couplers engaged without the hands having to reach over to the stop-knobs themselves. These combination settings are now usually adjustable by the player, the latest controls employing sophisticated computerized systems.

2. *Example of a church organ.* The list of stops in Table 1 is broadly typical (their number and kind varying considerably) for a medium-sized British two-manual church organ as built (or rebuilt from an older organ) from late Victorian times onward, and still the most familiar, even though the modern trend has been towards a neo-classical instrument more clearly suited to the music of Bach, his predecessors, and his contemporaries. The stops on each division are listed in the conventional order: flue ranks; mixtures (also flue pipes but of several ranks always sounding together, see Fig. 1, Swell Organ); reeds; and finally 'non-speaking' stops, i.e. couplers and tremulants. Apart from these last,

each stop is marked with a name and a figure in feet which shows its pitch. Stops marked 8′ sound the notes at ordinary or 'unison' pitch as when sung or played on the piano (the figure deriving from the nominal length of the longest pipe of the row, sounding C, bottom note of the manual keyboard: see EIGHT-FOOT); a 4′ stop sounds an octave higher, having pipes of half the length; 2′, two octaves higher or 15 notes, counting up the natural keys—hence such stops are often labelled 'Fifteenth'. There may also be a Twelfth, an octave and a fifth above 8′, with pipes of one-third the length, hence a $2\frac{2}{3}'$ stop (8 divided by 3). (A Mixture, however, sounding in high octaves and fifths, and sometimes thirds, is listed with its number of ranks shown by a roman numeral.) Such higher-pitched ranks, at the octaves particularly, have always been indispensable to the organ (and see 7 below, Blockwerk) unless of a small or intimate size: on listening, one can readily distinguish them, adding brilliance and penetration to the full organ sound. Conversely, 16′ stops, sounding an octave lower than 'unison' pitch, add depth and richness to the sound, and are especially important on the pedal division, where they fulfil the same function as double basses in an orchestra when they double the cellos at the lower octave.

TABLE I.

Great	Swell	Pedal
Open Diapason 8	Open Diapason 8	Open Diapason 16
Dulciana 8	Lieblich Gedackt 8	Principal 8
Flute 8	Gamba or Viola 8	Bourdon 16
Principal 4	Voix Celeste 8	Flute 8 (Bass Flute)
Flute 4	Principal or	
Fifteenth 2	Gemshorn 4	
Mixture III	Fifteenth 2	
Trumpet 8	Mixture III	
	Contra Fagotto 16	
	Oboe 8	
	Trumpet or	
	Cornopean 8	

Couplers: Great to Pedal; Swell to Pedal; Swell to Great.

(a) Great Organ (Gt.). Founded on a 'chorus' of diapason stops, those that give an organ its basic tone-quality (for a condensed list of organ stops see 3 and 4 below): Open Diapason, 8′, its pipes generally forming 'case pipes' visible from the front; Principal (or Octave), 4′; Fifteenth, 2′; and a Mixture (often omitted, however, in small organs of some 12–16 stops). The quieter Dulciana and the Flute stops are not part of the basic chorus and serve for special effects. The reed, here Trumpet, though designed to be used mainly with the chorus (a 'chorus reed'), can also serve as a solo stop, accompanied on the Swell Organ.

(b) Swell Organ (Sw.). Complements the Great with tones and combinations on the whole lighter and often more reedy; thus besides a chorus (with stops named as above but of narrower dimensions), a sharply coloured 'string-toned' stop; an optional undulating effect from the Voix Céleste; and reeds of different quality, sometimes including a 16′ reed. The Swell division is frequently coupled to the Great (i.e. both can then be played from the Great manual). If the swell box is then opened, the crescendo of the Swell becomes planted on top of the steady organ-sound of the Great. The swell pedal used to be placed to the right, for the right foot to operate, notches in a vertical bar allowing the pedal to be opened or closed or held at one fixed point between. It is now normally in the middle, and is 'balanced', i.e. it will stay in any position when the foot is lifted. (This swell box enclosing a whole division became fashionable, at first mainly in England, about the mid-18th century; it has no true place in baroque tradition.)

(c) Pedal Organ (Ped.). A manual keyboard has a compass of $4\frac{1}{2}$ to 5 octaves from C to g′′′ or c′′′′ (six spaces above the treble stave, making 61 pipes per rank). The pedal-board, owing to the width of shoes as compared with fingers, covers only the lowest $2\frac{1}{2}$ octaves, from C to f′ or to g′ (32 notes). The pedals used to lie parallel and level, until the present radiating and concave pedal-board became regularly adopted in British and American organs from the late 19th century. Pedal stops are reckoned as sounding an octave deeper than manual stops of the same name: if there is a Principal on the Pedal, it is at 8′, not 4′. The Bourdon, 16′, is of softly booming wooden stopped pipes (stopped pipes require only half the length of open pipes sounding the same notes: see STOPPED PIPE; the Lieblich Gedackt in Table 1 is also a stopped register). Often in small British church organs the Bourdon, situated at the rear of the organ-case (Fig. 1), is the only pedal stop, it being assumed that a pedal coupler will be in use for most or all of the time for the pedals also to sound the higher-pitched manual stops and hence gain power and definition. Sometimes the pedal is called upon to play a solo line at 8′ or 4′ pitch (especially chorale lines in chorale preludes). Such stops can come either from the pedal division's own resources if large enough, or by coupling a suitable stop from a manual not being used by the hands.

(d) Third manual: Choir Organ (Ch.). This, very frequently present, includes distinctively toned stops largely for solo use against quiet stops of another division, among them 'orchestral reeds' such as Clarinet and Orchestral Oboe. It often lacks a proper 'chorus', and where one is present it is frequently a 'flute' rather than a diapason-type chorus. The Choir division is also a likely location for stops of the Mutation class (3d, below). (Its equivalent in France is named Positif; its manual is there next above the Great, with above it that of the Swell, named *Récit* (from an original meaning of the word as a solo voice accompanied by others); German names can vary, the *Schwellwerk* often known by the older name *Oberwerk*, and by no means always enclosed.)

A Solo Organ, if present, may include high-pressure reeds such as Tubas, as well as other stops often designed to imitate orchestral instruments more closely than in other divisions.

(*e*) *Octave couplers.* These may be found especially on the Swell division, actuating mechanism behind the keyboard. Thus when 'Swell Octave' is drawn, the keys also work those an octave higher (as far as keyboard compass permits), or with 'Swell Sub-Octave', an octave lower; the ranks drawn then sound in these octaves as well as the main octave. The stop marked 'Swell Unison Off' cuts out the main octave, so that on playing the keys nothing happens until the 'Octave' is drawn (for only the higher octave to sound) or the 'Sub-Octave' (for only the lower). Octave couplers are best reserved for special effects, although organ builders are sometimes tempted to provide them as a cheap substitute for adequate independent high- and low-pitched stops.

3. Organ stops, flue-work. The metal used is generally of some 30 per cent tin to 70 of lead (or for case pipes the reverse, the cost of tin permitting; some bass pipes may be zinc). The tin and lead alloy can prove the best for sound, being the easiest to work and to adjust for tuning. Wood, such as oak, is also used regularly, particularly for flute-toned stops. Flue stops are commonly described as being of diapason, flute, or string-toned kinds—though there can be much overlap, the individual quality depending on the highly variable factors of materials, scaling, voicing, and wind-pressure.

'Scale' refers to the pipe-widths taken as a whole as they diminish through a stop from bass to treble; thus 'small scale' signifies pipes of distinctively small diameters. 'Voicing' refers (i) to the width of the 'mouth' (shown darkened in Fig. 2) expressed as a proportion of the circumference (in diapasons usually one quarter) and generally the wider the mouth the brighter the tone; (ii) to the height of the mouth or *cut-up, expressed as a fraction of the width of mouth (in diapasons usually one-quarter though not in all stops necessarily the same throughout the rank) and the greater the height the 'duller' the tone.

The following descriptions of stops take British/American practice as a convenient starting-point, at the same time pointing to the main equivalents and variants found in Continental organs:

(*a*) *Diapason quality.* Open Diapasons (see *2a* above): 8′ (Fr.: *montre*, the 'show' pipes; Ger.: *Prinzipal*, i.e. not as Eng. Principal); Principal (*prestant*; *Octav*, 4); Fifteenth (*doublette*; *Octav*, 2). An organ may have two or more Open Diapasons of different scale, a mean value for the diameter of the pipe for Middle C being around 5 cm. (2″). *Dulciana*, small-scale,

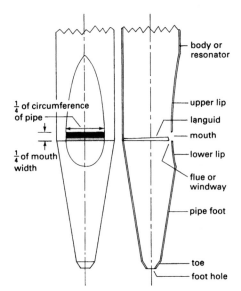

Fig. 2. Flue pipe, from the front and in cross-section.

average diameter at Middle C, *c*.3.3 cm. (1.3″; i.e. less than half the Open Diapason in cross-section area). *Salicional*, a still softer 8′ and like the Dulciana counted in the USA among string-toned stops. *Voix Céleste* (*Celeste*; *Vox Angelica*, similar), a soft 8′ rank always used with another 8′ such as the Dulciana, to which it is tuned slightly sharp to cause an undulation.

'*Acoustic Bass*', 32′: in this, usually a Pedal Open Diapason, 16′, is made to sound together with the Bourdon pipes a fifth higher, to obtain 32′ pitch by difference tones (see BEATS, 2), in order to avoid the expense and encumbrance of a true 32′ rank, although the end result is seldom very convincing.

(*b*) *Flutes.* Flute tone can be produced from either open or 'stopped' pipes. Stopped ranks have the pipes closed at the top by a stopper adjustable for tuning, and the resulting tone is always basically flute-like in quality, even in the case of the *Stopped Diapason*. Many of the names of flute stops are German (sometimes partly anglicized), from foreign organ-builders working in Britain in the 18th century and later.

(i) *Open flutes. Hohl Flute*, 8′, often wood, with wider mouth than Diapason and full flute tone. *Melodia*, similar American stop. *Claribel Flute*, 8′ or 4′, wood, sweet-toned. *Wald Flute*, similar. *Harmonic Flute*, metal pipes usually of 8′ length but sounding at 4′ pitch through having a small hole in the side near half-way up and therefore 'overblowing' to the octave; a full, bright sound (somewhat recalling an actual flute when played in the second register). *Rohr Flute* ('*Chimney Flute*'), 8′, metal, wide-scaled, narrow mouth, and stopped but with a narrow tube (Ger.: *Rohr*), itself open both ends, fixed in the stopped end of the pipe, projecting upwards:

the stopped-pipe pitch is barely changed but the tube adds 'a subtle formant' (Sumner 1952) to the stopped-pipe tone. *Spitzflöte*, 8' (as in Fig. 1), 4', or 2', metal pipes tapering upwards, giving a bright sound with marked upper partials. *Gemshorn*, usually 4' (Fig. 1), with pipes more sharply tapered, low cut-up, and delicate tone part-way between a flute and diapason. *Blockflöte*, 2" wide, named after the recorder; *Nachthorn* (*Cor de nuit*), also wide. *Sifflöte*, from Fr.: *sifflet*, 'whistle', usually a 1' rank of small scale, three octaves above 8'.

(ii) *Stopped Flutes*. *Stopped Diapason*, 8', and *Gedeckt* (or *Gedackt*, as in Fig. 1), 8', quiet clear-toned flutes; the rather differently constructed *Lieblich Gedeckt* ('sweet stopped'), with narrow mouth and high cut-up, has been common since the 1850s. *Nason Flute*, 4' equivalent of the *Stopped Diapason*. *Bourdon*, 16' (cf. 2c above), sometimes found as a manual stop as well as a pedal one. *Bass Flute*, quiet 8' pedal stop of wood, usually stopped but occasionally of open pipes. *Quintadena*, 16', narrow-mouthed and designed for the first stopped-pipe overtone (3rd harmonic) to be prominent.

(c) *String quality and other stops with 'string' names.* *Gamba* (for 'viola da gamba'), 8', etc., small scale, narrow mouth, low cut-up, pipes in many cases tapering (and sometimes ('*Bell Gamba*') with conical flare at top): main 'string' stop, sometimes with a bar in front of the mouth. *Aeoline* (from *Aeolian harp*), a soft string-tone. *Viola* (*Viole*), 8', 4', string tone. *Violoncello*, 8', especially on the Pedal. *Violone* 16' (8'), small scale, soft, on Pedal. *Geigen* (*Geigen Principal*), 8', 4' (16'), louder than the *Gamba*; tone between this and Diapason. *Violin Diapason* (*Horn Diapason*, *Viole d'amore*), 8', a kind of small-scale Diapason. *Keraulophon*, 8', narrow, cylindrical (invented 1843, name from Gk., lit. 'hornpipe').

(d) *Mutations*. These are certain ranks (made to various scales) used only in combination with normal ranks to synthesize fresh tone-colours through sounding at harmonic intervals which mostly contain a fifth or a third. Their names are from French. *Nazard*, $2\frac{2}{3}'$ (an octave and a fifth above, like the Twelfth; see 2); *Tierce*, $1\frac{3}{5}'$ (8 divided by 5, two octaves and a major third above, i.e. a seventeenth, counting the white notes); *Larigot*, $1\frac{1}{3}'$ (an octave above the *Nazard*, the Nineteenth); and more rarely a *Septième* ($1\frac{1}{7}'$) at two octaves and a natural seventh and a *None* ($\frac{8}{9}'$) at three octaves and a natural second above. The pitches of these ranks correspond to the 3rd, 5th, 6th, 7th, and 9th harmonics of the fundamental 8' (see HARMONIC SERIES).

(e) *Mixtures* (see above, 2). In Fig. 3 can be seen on the left the small diapason-type pipes of a Mixture, here of four ranks, receiving wind together from one opening from the wind-chest when that particular note on the keyboard is played and the Mixture stop is drawn. Through the lowest octave of the keyboard the four ranks may sound, respectively, at the Nineteenth (two octaves and a fifth), the Twenty-second (three octaves), the Twenty-sixth, and the Twenty-ninth (four octaves). In the next octave the pattern has dropped, the lowest rank now at the Fifteenth, the next rank above at the Nineteenth, etc., the Mixture 'breaking back', and continuing to do so in each keyboard octave in order that, in the top range, the pipes shall not be of impracticably small size and high pitch. Even so, the smallest pipes may be under 2 cm. ($\frac{3}{4}''$) in speaking length and sound above the top note of the piano. Mixtures are of several types and in a fair-sized organ a division may include more than one of them: *Sharp Mixture* (bright); *Fourniture* (more powerfully brilliant), and *Cymbale* (very high pitched). The *Cornet*, however, is a compound stop used on its own as a solo stop (mainly in the 18th-century French and English repertoire), having 8', 4', $2\frac{2}{3}'$, 2', and $1\frac{3}{5}'$ ranks. It is of powerful flute-type tone and usually made only from Middle C upwards. The *Sesqualtera* is properly a two-rank stop at $2\frac{2}{3}'$ and $1\frac{3}{5}'$, but may be three-rank; on some smaller organs it is found on the Swell in place of a Mixture.

4. *Reed stops.* These vary in tone and power according to the relative length, breadth, and thickness of the metal reeds (see REED, Fig. 1a), the shape of the 'shallot' over which they vibrate, and the form of the pipe or 'resonator'. This is often conical, widening to the top. When of a full length matched to the pitch of the reed, it greatly develops the fundamental frequency (relatively weak in organ reed-tone itself).

(a) *Oboe–Trumpet type.* The pipes are conical, widening upwards. *Oboe* (*Hautboy*), 8', narrow pipes usually with a wider cone added to the top, like a bell. Very common reed stop, especially as a Swell reed (as Table 1). *Fagotto* (*Contra Fagotto*, *Bassoon*), 16', also narrow, found on Swell organ. *Dulzian*, 8', a German soft reed. *Orchestral Oboe*, 8', imitates orchestral oboe (thinner-toned than the *Oboe* stop). *Trumpet*, 8', wide cone, loud to medium. *Cornopean*, rather milder. *Clarion*, 4', version of *Trumpet*. *Tromba*, 8', 16', louder, closer tone than *Trumpet*. *Trombone*, 16', Pedal counterpart to 8' *Trumpet* or *Tromba*. *Bombarde*, 16', 32', powerful Pedal stop; *Posaune* another. *Tuba*, 8', 16', 4', on high pressure, the most powerful organ stop, especially on Solo Organ. *French Horn* (*Horn*), 8', notably as developed in the USA to imitate the orchestral instrument closely.

(b) *Clarinet type.* The pipes are cylindrical, approximately stopped-pipe length. *Clarinet*, 8', imitates the orchestral instrument. *Corno di Bassetto*, 8', fuller tone. *Cremona*, 8', similar (name from Fr.: *cromorne*, Ger.: *Krummhorn*).

(c) *Regal type.* The pipes are not full-sized. *Vox Humana*, 8', very short, wide resonators; often used with the *Tremulant* produced by two different

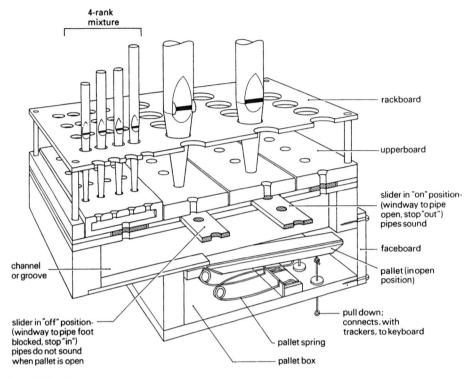

4-rank mixture

rackboard

upperboard

slider in "on" position-
(windway to pipe
open, stop "out")
pipes sound

faceboard

pallet (in open
position)

channel
or groove

slider in "off" position-
(windway to pipe foot
blocked, stop "in")
pipes do not sound
when pallet is open

pull down;
connects, with
trackers, to keyboard

pallet spring

pallet box

Fig. 3. Slider chest.

methods (which causes pulsation in the wind supply).

5. *Organ mechanism:* (*a*) *Wind supply.* Organ wind-pressure is measured in inches (or cm.), calculated as the difference in level of the two columns of water in an open U-shaped glass tube when the air under pressure is applied to one end. Up to the middle of the 19th century the wind was always supplied by hand-pumped bellows, giving an average pressure of some $3\frac{1}{2}''$ (9 cm.) serving the whole instrument. With the arrival of the Industrial Age, and the development of pneumatic action and generally higher wind-pressures, mechanical blowing evolved, using water-, gas-, and finally electrically powered engines. The air thus raised is passed to reservoirs, shaped like rectangular inflatable bellows (usually one for each division or wind-pressure), where it is stored under pressure before passing through wind-trunks to the wind-chests. Various compensating devices such as 'concussion bellows' are often employed to keep the wind-pressure reasonably constant when sudden heavy demands are made on it. Some of the latest neo-classical instruments, however, in addition to using light wind-pressures again, have seen a return to the slightly unsteady wind supply characteristic of earlier organs. Today in large organs using a variety of pressures, electrically driven centrifugal fan-blowers supply differential pressures of up to 50 cm. (20'') and more; some of the air in the first compartment giving the light pressure is passed to the centre of the next for the fan to raise it to a higher pressure, the process being repeated until that needed for the loudest reeds is reached. In such systems conventional large reservoirs are no longer necessary.

(*b*) *Wind-chest.* The pipes of a division stand one rank behind the next upon one or more 'soundboards' (as termed in organ-building) with the pipe-feet over holes leading up from the upper part of the wind-chest—the lower part (the lowest in Fig. 3) containing the pallets and receiving wind from the reservoir (or direct from the bellows) through a wide 'wind-trunk'. This upper part is divided by partitions into channels termed 'grooves', each groove corresponding to one note of the keyboard (one groove appearing in section in Fig. 3) for the wind to be ready to sound all the pipes for that note when the pallet is lowered from the key. Then, for only pipes of the required ranks to sound the note, the oldest method, still much in use, is to provide, immediately below the holes for the pipe-feet, wooden (or plastic) perforated 'sliders', one for each stop and moved by the stop in the direction at right angles to the grooves so that when the holes in the slider align with those under the pipe-feet, pipes of that rank can sound (in Fig. 3 the pipe shown on the right will sound).

This 'slider chest' for selecting stops became used from some time perhaps late in the 15th century, followed early in the next by the 'spring chest'. This, which has had considerable periods of favour in the past, employs instead of sliders a small sprung secondary pallet under each pipe-foot in a rank opened by a long transverse 'stop bar' lowered from the draw-stop. There has also been used since the 19th century, especially in Germany, a 'cone chest', in which grooves and pallets are replaced by long channels, one under each rank of pipes, and crossed at right angles by sets of individual valves, one valve for each note.

(c) Action. The linkage between keyboard and pipes can either be purely mechanical ('tracker' action), carried out by compressed air ('pneumatic' action), by electricity ('electric' action), or by combinations of tracker and pneumatic, or pneumatic and electric. An organ need not employ the same type of action over the whole instrument: one division (or even one soundboard within a division) may use one action, and another a different one.

(i) Tracker action. A 'tracker' is a thin wooden rod, usually pine, that pulls; a 'sticker' is a thicker one that pushes. Each kind has a metal guide-pin at each end, or for a tracker a hook, or threaded wire with leather adjusting nut. Right-angle changes in the direction of pull are made where necessary by small pivoted 'squares' (actually looking nearer to triangular); reversal of pull or push is by 'backfalls' (rocking levers, one visible in Fig. 5). The means of transmitting motion to the pallets controlling pipes not placed directly above the key but at different, often considerable distances to one side or the other, and not placed in keyboard order, is by a 'roller-board' (Fig. 4). On this are mounted close above one another horizontal pinewood or hollow metal 'rollers' of the many different lengths required, each with a projecting arm at one end to receive the tracker from the key and at the other for another tracker up to the pallet. Tracker action was the only method employed up to about 1840, and has never been wholly abandoned; since 1945

it has indeed been returning to favour in the interests of artistic performance. An organ pipe, once the key is pressed, sounds at its constant, unalterable strength up to its silence on release of the key, the timing of these events being thus a crucial factor in phrasing and interpretation and, in the opinion of most, best judged through the direct, sensitive 'touch' afforded by a good tracker action.

A difficulty arises over couplers since these have come to be so extensively used from the 19th century. In an older type of manual coupler, small lugs between the keys of an upper and lower manual were moved, together in a row, for the lower keys directly to move the upper. This was succeeded by trains of trackers and backfalls, these last mounted in frames raised by the coupler draw-stop to engage connections to the coupled manual, still to lower the unfingered keys of this and throwing a great extra load on the fingers. One may still see the organist of a village church, having drawn the manual coupler, leaning over the keys for body-weight to help press them down. Relief from this is one main benefit of pneumatic devices, although modern well-balanced tracker actions place far less strain on the player than earlier ones.

(ii) Pneumatic actions. Pneumatic lever: in this action the heaviness of the touch is relieved by the assistance of a pneumatic lever at some point along the course of otherwise tracker action. The first device was invented in Britain at about the same time by D. Hamilton (Edinburgh, 1835) and by C. S. Barker, who patented it in France (1839), where the great organ-builder Cavaillé-Coll (below, 9) used it in all his organs of any size (sometimes on the Great only). Fig. 5 shows one form of this 'Barker lever'. *Tubular-pneumatic actions*, from rather later, work on either an 'exhaust' or a 'pressure' (or 'supply') system. The key opens a valve which either lets air out of the flexible lead tubing which serves as the connection between console and wind-chest, or admits air under pressure from the main supply; at the other end of the tubing a small motor bellows of soft white leather collapses or inflates in turn to activate a large one, within the lower part of the wind-chest, which opens the pallet

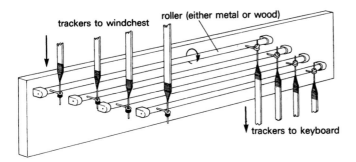

trackers to windchest

roller (either metal or wood)

trackers to keyboard

Fig. 4. Detail of the roller-board.

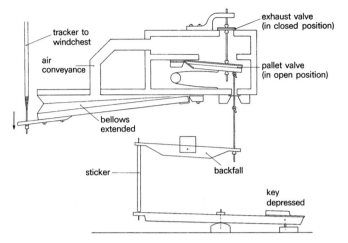

Fig. 5. Pneumatic action: depressing the key opens the pallet valve and closes the exhaust allowing air, under pressure to enter the bellows via the conveyancing. This expands the bellows which pull down the tracker connected to the wind-chest. Releasing the key closes the pallet valve and opens the exhaust valve; the air pressure is balanced and the bellows close.

for that note by means of an attached rod. For coupling, the initial valves of the two keyboards are caused to operate together, through further short lengths of tubing. *Electro-pneumatic action* (from the 1860s) uses electrical relays between the key and the wind-chest, and pneumatics within the chest itself; it is illustrated schematically in Fig. 6.

(iii) *Electric action.* This goes one step further than electro-pneumatic action, by disposing of the pneumatics completely, and having the key-operated electrical contact directly activate an electro-magnet at the other end of the cable to move the pallet. With electro-pneumatic and electric actions, since the connection from keyboard to chest is by cable only, and the action is instantaneous (whereas with tubular actions it can be slow over long distances), a keyboard can be far separated from the organ (a situation, however, which is not necessarily advantageous). In the latest developments signals can now be sent from console to pipes along a single cable, and at the same time can now be put on to a tape cassette which, when replayed, reproduces the signals for the organ to play whatever has been recorded. Pneumatic and electric actions are also used in the stop-knob and combination actions. With electrical systems stop-knobs have sometimes been replaced by tilting stop-tablets, often placed above the highest keyboard.

6. *The 'extension' or 'unit' system.* With the development of electro-pneumatic and electric actions it became possible to make a single pipe serve more than one function (although already in mechanical action instruments a pair of 8′ flue stops might well share the bottom octave of pipes, especially on the Swell in order to save space in the box). By

taking, for example, an 8′ Open Diapason rank of, say, 61-note (five-octave) compass, and adding an extra 12 pipes at the top (making 73 in all), a 4′ Principal rank could be created by electrical switching, the 8′ using pipes 1–61, the 4′ pipes 13–73. By adding a further 12 pipes at the top a 2′ Fifteenth is made possible, and likewise a 16′ Double Open Diapason by adding 12 pipes at the bottom. In this way three or four stops could be created for not much more than the price of one. This 'unit' (as the extended rank is known) principle became the foundation of *cinema organ construction as well as being employed to a greater or lesser extent on many normal organs. Despite its economic attractions, the system has major disadvantages, at least for serious music-making. In the first place it is almost impossible to obtain a correct tonal balance between the various pitches in a 'unit' system. In an independent 8′, 4′, 2′ Diapason chorus the 4′ would be voiced lighter than the 8′, and the 2′ lighter still. The 'unit' system inevitably tends to produce 'top-heavy' effects, although a skilful builder can mask the problem. Another main difficulty arises from 'missing' notes when octaves are played. If, for example, independent 8′ and 4′ stops are drawn and two notes an octave apart are played, then 4 pipes sound. When these stops are part of an extended unit, however, only 3 pipes sound, since the 4′ of the lower note and the 8′ of the upper note have the same pipe. (In the same way if notes two octaves apart are played on an 8′ and 4′ extended rank, and the middle octave added, no change in sound at all will be heard.) The most legitimate and widespread use of the principle in normal organs is in the pedal department, where, for example, an extended 32′, 16′, 8′ flue or reed rank

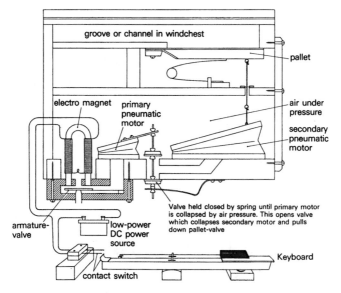

Fig. 6. Electro-pneumatic action: electromagnet is activated when keyboard contact switch completes circuit, causing armature-valve to open and allowing pressurized air in primary pneumatic motor to escape. Air pressure within the chamber (maintained by armature-valve in its activated position) forces the primary motor closed (collapses it), activating the main valve which in turn collapses secondary motor, pulling down pallet-valve.

can save much expense and space in avoiding the duplication of large pipes. Allied to the 'extension' principle is the concept of 'borrowing', whereby stops on one division are also made playable on another (with the stop-knobs duplicated); thus a Great Trumpet may well also be playable on the Choir (enabling it to be used as a solo stop with a firm Great accompaniment) or a 16′ manual stop may be usefully duplicated on the pedals.

7. The organ in the West up to c.1500: (a) The organ and the Church. Following the period of the Roman organ or *hydraulis* and its successors in Byzantium, the organ appeared in western Europe in 757 through a very special present from the Emperor Constantine IV to King Pepin of the Franks. The first organ known to have been produced in the West was then built for the palace of his son, Charlemagne, at Aachen in 826, the work carried out by a priest from Venice. Soon after this the organ became regarded almost entirely as a possession of monastic churches, though there is very little information on how they used it, still less on what was played on it. In Byzantium the organ had been entirely secular, a palace showpiece, paraded before the populace on state occasions. A widely held view among historians is that Western monasteries, for several centuries, rather similarly reserved the organ, capable of the most impressive sound among all the instruments then existing save perhaps the bells in the tower, for splendour on great occasions. It seems that no intrusion was permitted into the sung liturgy of the Church until to a small degree

from about the 13th century, with alternate versets played by the organ and sung by the choir ('Organ Mass'). The term 'organum', known from c.860 for early forms of non-unison church singing, has, in this historical view, no connection with the name of the instrument.

(b) Development of the instrument. Organs were generally not large (the late 11th-century account in verse of a gigantic instrument at Winchester is held to be a fanciful exaggeration). Pipes, all open flue-pipes, reached up to 120 or 150 cm. (four or five feet) tall and were said to be of equal width through a rank. It seems (e.g. from the 11th-century Bern Codex) that further ranks might be present, sounding the unison and the octave, though there is not until late in the 13th century evidence of numerous ranks at the higher octaves, possibly fifths as well, always sounding together—a *Blockwerk*, to use a later German term. The keyboard by that century could cover 2 to 2½ octaves (with keys 6 cm. or 2.4″ wide): the Robertsbridge Manuscript of c.1325 (British Library, Add. 28550) already has pieces, of a secular nature and written mostly in parallel fifths, which demand every semitone within the octave; they are reasonably held to be for the organ (though not necessarily written in England) from their resemblance in the notation to German organ tablatures of the following century (see 11, *Repertory*).

The roller-board was in use before 1400, enabling the pipes to be arranged out of keyboard order and with the longest pipes in 'towers' at the sides, as

Pl. 1. Organ (1735–8) by
Christiaan Müller at St Bavo-
kerk, Haarlem, Netherlands.

seen in the oldest existing playable organ, at Sion
in Switzerland (c.1400), the 'swallow's nest' case
of which is original, though the rest has been much
rebuilt, with pedals added in 1718. Pedals are,
however, mentioned in the Ileborgh Codex of 1448
(from Germany, preserved in the Curtis Institute,
Philadelphia), giving an octave or so for sustaining
bass notes (written down to B♭) and probably acting
on the lower manual keys directly by 'pull-downs',
such as have also been used in various organs
since (as sometimes in England in the 18th century).
Organs were by this period growing larger, and
also made with two manual divisions combined in
the same instrument. This came about through the
organist's wish to have two organs—the main one,
and the small 'positive' for accompanying the
choir—both under his control, the smaller installed
behind his back ('Rückpositiv'), played from a
manual below that of the main organ, the action
passing under the organ bench (see Pl. 1, an
18th-century example; in England this arrangement gained a name 'Chair Organ', which many
believe became 'Choir Organ' when the division
came to be incorporated into the main case). The
slider-chest (5b, above), for silencing at will at least
some of the ranks of the Blockwerk, led to making
varied stops, sometimes including by 1500 reeds
and stopped-flue ranks, and variously combining

them. For example, a list of registrations at Worms,
c.1510, gives among many possible: Principals
4′ + 2′; Höhlflöte 8′ + Principal 4′ or Höhlflöte 4′;
Regal 8′ (a reed stop) + Höhlflöte 8′ + Quint 1⅓′
make an imitation Zink (cornett); Manual and
Pedal mixtures only on the plenum (full chorus).

8. *Renaissance and baroque traditions: (a) Italy.* The
Renaissance organ here remained a one-manual
instrument, a substantial enlargement of the medieval organ employing the spring chest as a means
of separating the ranks of the undivided Blockwerk.
Several 15th- and 16th-century Italian organs still
exist, carefully preserved and restored, among them
the earlier organ at San Petronio, Bologna (da
Prato, 1470–4), and San Guiseppe, Brescia (G.
Antegnati, 1581, with some 12 stops at pitches
including the Quints; three flute stops for solo use;
and pull-down pedals chiefly for sustaining bass
notes). In Italian organ-building no pipe sounds
higher than c′′′′′, top note of the piano, the ranks
where necessary dropping an octave in order not
to do so. Visually the instruments are distinctive,
typically with the front pipes, their tops plainly
exposed, framed under a high Renaissance arch.

(b) The Netherlands. Here too a chief characteristic
is the long-lasting retention of the main *Blockwerk*,
and an upper or *Bovenwerk* (Ger.: *Oberwerk*) for

TABLE 2.

Grand Orgue C–c'''		Positif C–c'''		Récit c'–c'''		Pédale AA–f		Écho c–c'''	
Montre	16	Montre	8	Cornet	V	Flûte	8	Bourdon	8
Bourdon	16	Bourdon	8	Trompette	8	Trompette	8	Flûte	4
Montre	8	Prestant	4					Nasard	$2\frac{2}{3}$
Bourdon	8	Flûte	4					Quarte	2
Prestant	4	Nasard	$2\frac{2}{3}$					Tierce	$1\frac{3}{5}$
Flûte	4	Doublette	2					Cymbale	II
Grosse Tierce	$3\frac{1}{5}$	Tierce	$1\frac{3}{5}$					Cromorne	8
Nasard	$2\frac{2}{3}$	Larigot	$1\frac{1}{3}$						
Doublette	2	Fourniture	III						
Quarte de Nasard	2	Cymbale	II						
Tierce	$1\frac{3}{5}$	Cromorne	8						
Fourniture	V	Voix Humaine	8						
Cymbale	IV								
Cornet	V								
Trompette	8								
Clairon	4								
Voix Humaine	8								

the stops which are to be used separately. All Netherlands builders, particularly the Brabanters who influenced France very decisively, used a large quantity and variety of reeds in their organs, while their pedals are used mainly for cantus firmus parts, as in French organ music. Sweelinck played from 1580 to 1621 on the organ of the Old Church, Amsterdam, built by 1542 and including both an *Oberwerk* (nine stops) and *Rückpositiv* (ten), as well as a partly independent Pedal and the main division, the manual divisions each with one or two different mixtures. Substantial German influence in the north during the 17th century may account for the more international character of the great organs of Groningen, Zwolle, Alkmaar, and Haarlem (Pl. 1).

(*c*) *Spain*. The organ here became fully developed, rather late in the 16th century, by the Netherlanders (e.g. the Escorial organs, by Hans Brebos, *c*.1580). As in Italy, the organs were mainly one-manual, with pedals that sometimes had independent bass pipes for holding-notes. They tended to have more varied and original registers than Italian organs, including a number of reeds of trumpet, cromorne, and regal types, given Spanish names such as *chirimía* and *orlo*. The smaller members of these were sometimes mounted horizontally on the front of the case, as again later in the spectacular big trumpets of the *lengueteria* of the late 17th to 18th century.

A feature of the Spanish organ (also met to some extent elsewhere) is the division of stops into treble and bass halves, so that different registrations can be used in the upper and lower parts of one keyboard (as in a *harmonium). Many historic Spanish organs have fortunately survived unmodernized, even if often in a state of disrepair.

(*d*) *France*. The early 16th-century organs of Bordeaux and Toulouse were one-manual, with specifications of the Italian type; but the famous organ since lost, at Gisors, Normandy (1580), was strikingly Flemish in its constituents, needing little more to form the classic French Grand Organ, the finest examples of which date from the last years of the 17th century, the instruments most fitted to the works of Couperin and De Grigny, and exemplified in the organ for St Louis des Invalides, Paris, built by Robert Clicquot (Table 2). The Pedal is relatively undeveloped, seldom with more than Flûte (= Principal) bass and Trompette 'plain chant'; only with the 19th-century Bach revival, and the demands of Romantic composers, did the Pedal became a generally heavier division.

(*e*) *England*. Of pre-Restoration organs only the cases remain. The Worcester organ, by Thomas Dallam (1613), had on the Great Organ Open Diapasons, 8', 4', and 2', and a Recorder (stopped; ? 4'); the Chair Organ (behind the organist) Diapasons up to 1' and a Flute, 4', of wood. The absence of a Pedal remained an English characteristic to the end of the 18th century or even after. Following the Restoration, builders who were either foreign or had lived abroad during the Commonwealth made organs incorporating some Flemish and French features. Chief among them were 'Father' Smith (from Holland, d. 1708) and Renatus Harris (d. 1724). Smith made instruments for Westminster Abbey and St Paul's Cathedral; Harris was less conventional in some of his features, with more frequent use of reeds. Snetzler (from Switzerland, d. 1785) and Samuel Green (d. 1796) continued the 18th-century tradition, which lasted to the time of Samuel Wesley and Mendelssohn.

(*f*) *Germany*. The North German 15th-century Gothic organ was essentially a one-manual instrument with Pedal pull-downs. It would probably be

TABLE 3.

Hauptwerk		Rückpositiv		Brustwerk		Pedal		Oberwerk	
Principal	16	Principal	8	Principal	8	Gross Principal	32	Principal	8
Quintadena	16	Quintadena	8	Octave	4	Principal	16	Holzflöte	8
Octave	8	Gedackt	8	Hohlflöte	4	Subbass	16	Rohrflöte	8
Spitzflöte	8	Octave	4	Waldflöte	2	Octave	8	Octave	4
Gedackt	8	Flöte	4	Sesquialtera	II	Octave	4	Rohrflöte	4
Octave	4	Querflöte	4	Scharff	V	Nachthorn	2	Spitzflöte	4_2
Rohrflöte	4	Blockflöte	2	Dulcian	8	Rauschpfeife	II	Nasat	$2\frac{1}{3}$
Superoctav	2	Sifflet	$1\frac{1}{3}$	Trichter Regal	8	Mixtur	VI	Octave	2
Blockflöte	2	Sesquialtera	II			Posaune	32	Gemshorn	2
Rauschpfeife	II	Scharff	VI–VIII			Posaune	16	Mixtur	IV–VI
Mixtur	VI	Dulcian	16			Dulcian	16	Zimbel	
Trompete	16	Bärpfeife	8			Trompete	8	Trompete	8
		Schalmey	4			Trompete	4	Krummhorn	8
						Cornett	2	Trompete	4

elevated, on one of the walls of the church, and might be a large instrument with 16′ Principal display pipes as in the Lübeck Jakobikirche. With the later addition of Rückpositiv, Brustwerk (a small enclosed section), and Pedal, the North German baroque organ achieved wide currency, from North Holland to Scandinavia, and also produced a style which prevailed well into the middle of the 18th century. Many famous baroque organs took their ultimate form in stages, an example being the one in the Jakobikirche in Hamburg, built in 1512–16, but rebuilt twice by Dirk Hoyer, and then twice again by Hans Scherer the elder (the last time in 1605–7; Praetorius gives the specification), and finally changed into a late baroque organ by Schnitger in 1688 (Table 3).

This four-manual scheme seems to represent a state of perfection from the point of view of modern concepts of the baroque organ, since:

(i) every division is contained in its own case and so located that it can speak directly out through the front of the organ without any impediments;

(ii) the visual design of the complete organ is heavily influenced by the individual divisions;

(iii) each division is tonally self-sufficient in that it has the stops to produce a chorus which will be approximately as powerful as that of another division, and therefore balance it. Couplers are not intended to be used, and indeed may well not exist in such an instrument;

(iv) in an organ of this type the proportions of the case may be influenced by the length of the Principal pipes, e.g. for the Pedal 32′, Hauptwerk 16′, Rückpositiv 8′, Oberwerk 8′, and Brustwerk 4′. This type of design is sometimes known as 'Werkprinzip';

(v) among other uses the organ would have the following: the Hauptwerk would be used for *pleno* (full organ) and other 'solid' work; the Rückpositiv has the second chorus (not so weighty as that on the Hauptwerk) and is the primary manual for

solos; the Oberwerk is good for accompaniment and echoes; the Brustwerk is almost a second Rückpositiv, but has the freshest and lightest reeds in the organ, and besides is ideal for accompanying singers and instruments; the Pedal, which is very strong and mostly to be played uncoupled, would provide not only matching bass registration for the manuals, but has its own solo stops, e.g. Krummhorn 8′, Trompete 4′, Cornett 2′, Nachthorn 2′, which could be used for playing a chorale in tenor, alto, or soprano registers, accompanied on one or more manuals.

Gottfried Silbermann, from c.1709 to his death in 1753, built some of the most distinguished organs that have ever been made (well over 20 of them still exist, many of them intact, almost all of them in Saxony). Though most celebrated for his big organs in Freiberg and Dresden, his general system can best be seen in his many smaller organs, which followed a remarkably uniform pattern as in the specification from Reinhardtsgrimma given in Table 4 (in which, as often, the figure '3' stands for '$2\frac{2}{3}$').

Silbermann's tendencies were in the 'pre-Romantic' direction, something his contemporaries and friends, Bach among them, were by no means blind to. He virtually eliminated reeds from his organs except in the Pedal; by his scaling methods he thickened the effect of the Principal chorus, causing it to lose incisiveness; and through his system of often placing the second manual division behind the first, rather than above or below it, he weakened the concept of the Werkprinzip design. His instruments are exceptional for their quality, although they scarcely possess all the characteristics demanded by Bach.

9. *The Romantic organ.* The organ did not suit classical and Romantic musicians, who either avoided it or composed rather awkwardly and unresourcefully for it. Nevertheless, harnessing the developments of the Industrial Revolution, the

TABLE 4.

Hauptwerk		Oberwerk		Pedal		
Principal	8	Gedackt	8	Subbass	16	(Manual and Pedal couplers added later)
Rohrflöte	8	Rohrflöte	4	Posaune	16	Tremulant
Quintaden	8	Nasat	3	Principal bass	8	
Octava	4	Octava	2			
Spitzflöte	4	Tertia	$(1\frac{1}{5})$			
Quinta	3	Quinta	$1\frac{1}{2}$			
Octava	2	Sifflot	1			
Mixtur	4 ranks	Cimbeln	2 ranks			
Cornett	3 ranks					

organ responded fully, to become even larger, louder, more complicated, more scientific, less trouble to play, and musically searching to vie with the orchestra with stops of greatly contrasting power, expressive devices like swell-boxes, numerous couplers uniting different divisions, and so on. The builder who gave greatest impetus to 19th-century organ-building was undoubtedly Aristide Cavaillé-Coll (1811–98), who revolutionized the tonal design of the French classical organ to reflect a more orchestral concept, and was the first to apply the Barker lever (see above, 5c (ii)) to the playing mechanism. First demonstrated in the organ for St Denis abbey, completed in 1840, fortunately the concept later proved perfect for the compositions of César Franck, for whose church, Ste Clothilde in Paris, Cavaillé-Coll built the organ in 1859–62 (Table 5).

Cavaillé-Coll's organs have risen above the adverse criticism levelled at many 19th-century builders, partly through the ideas in their design, but chiefly because of the quality of the work. Cavaillé-Coll refused to work with other than slider chests, despite the superficial attraction of other types, and stuck firmly to mechanical action with only the Barker machine added. So, in his structural system, he held very close to his classical forerunners.

German organs, of Ladegast, Walcker, and Sauer, followed a similar path, becoming somewhat Wagnerian, with the manuals diminishing in strength from the Hauptwerk downwards.

In England, perhaps the first outstanding builder of the 19th century was William Henry Hill (1789–1870), who by 1840 had made the English equivalent of an 18th-century German organ, complete with independent Pedal chorus. He exported to Australia and other colonies, which offer some of the best locations for study of English Victorian organs. Hill may later have become overshadowed by the dominating personality of Henry Willis (1821–1901), who, after exhibiting at the Crystal

TABLE 5. Ste Clothilde, Paris (Cavaillé-Coll, 1859)

Compass of the manuals, C–f′″; compass of the Pedal, C–d′. The registers printed in bold face are printed in red on the console. The wind supply is admitted to these registers only when a foot lever ('appel') is operated (one for each division), so that these particular drawstops may be 'prepared' in advance.

Grand Orgue (GO)	Positif	Récit (enclosed)	Pédale
Montre 16	Bourdon 16	Flûte Harmonique 8	Sousbasse 32
Bourdon 16	Montre 8	Bourdon 8	Contrebasse 16
Montre 8	Flûte Harmonique 8	Viole de Gambe 8	Basse 8
Flûte Harmonique 8	Bourdon 8	**Flûte Octaviante 4**	Octave 4
Bourdon 8	Gambe 8	**Octavin 2**	**Basson 16**
Viole de Gambe 8	Unda Maris 8	Voix Humaine 8	**Bombarde 16**
Prestant 4	Prestant 4	Basson-Hautbois 8	**Trompette 8**
Octave 4	**Flûte Octaviante 4**	**Trompette 8**	**Clairon 4**
Quinte 2	**Quinte 2**	**Clairon 4**	
Doublette 2	**Doublette 2**		
Plein Jeu Harmonique VI	**Plein Jeu**		
Bombarde 16	**Cromorne 8**		
Trompette 8	**Trompette 8**		
Clairon 4	**Clairon 4**		

Couplers: GO to Péd., Pos. to Péd., Réc. to Péd., Pos. to GO, Réc. to Pos. (GO: Sub-Octave, Pos.: Sub-Octave, Réc.: Sub-Octave.) Tremolo. (All, together with the four appels, operated by foot levers.)

Palace in 1851, achieved a virtual monopoly of English cathedral organ-building. Willis's work tended in the direction of Cavaillé-Coll, and he even developed the 'Willis' lever, on the lines of Barker, as well as various systems of stop-combination action, eventually leading to the adjustable pistons of Hereford Cathedral in the 1890s. While he was undoubtedly a marvellous organ-builder, he tended to ride roughshod over much of the previous work in organs which he rebuilt, to the extent that pre-Willis characteristics in them are almost impossible to detect. From the end of the 19th century Willis's predominance began to be challenged by Harrison & Harrison, who, with their excellent solid craftsmanship, were responsible for more new and rebuilt cathedral-type organs than any other firm this century, although since the 1970s it has faced increasing competition in this sphere from Noel Mander and others. The Walker firm, active since the early 19th century, created a fine reputation, especially for its diapason choruses and flutes, and has continued to build notable instruments up to the present day.

Console development and control seems to have had a special fascination for English builders, and it is largely from them that the American style of organ console derives. In the United States itself some organs were imported and constructed during the 18th century, the most famous builder being the Moravian, David Tannenberg (d. 1804), living in Pennsylvania. The 19th-century organs of Roosevelt (d. 1886) tended, like their brethren in Europe, to become obsessed with the engineering systems of the time, though redeemed by the determination of builders such as Walter Holtkamp senior (d. 1962) and the Aeolian-Skinner Organ Co. under Donald Harrison (1889–1956) to produce musical instruments.

10. *Organ-reform movement.* Early in the 20th century it began to dawn on musicians that perhaps the works of early composers (e.g. Bach) did not invariably benefit from the use of the full battery of modern inventions. Being largely German-inspired, the movement naturally focused primarily on German music. The Schnitger organ of the Jakobikirche, Hamburg (above, 8*f*), was revealed not as an obsolete relic but as an ideal medium for north European 17th-century organ music; a new '*Praetorius*' organ, modelled on information in *Syntagma musicum*, was built in 1911 by the Walcker firm for the music school in Freiburg. After the Second World War there came a general move in the direction of returning to pre-19th-century principles in the making of organs. France, Britain, and the USA have largely tried to produce an eclectic (or compromise) organ, of which the Royal Festival Hall instrument (Harrison, 1954) is a notable example, while the Germanic countries have stuck to a basically national baroque style, with occasional additions. Important contemporary builders working within classical traditions include

Rieger (Austria), Casavant (Canada), Frobenius, Marcussen (Denmark), Beckerath, Klais, Schuke (Germany), Flentrop (Holland), Tamburini (Italy), and Metzler (Switzerland). The present direction is to concentrate on one particular type of organ, e.g. French mid-18th century, or North German mid-17th century, at Edinburgh University. But it is inconceivable that for the organ, with its long history and susceptibility to fashion, there will not be other solutions to the question.

11. *Repertory:* (*a*) *Renaissance, baroque:* (i) *Germany, Northern Europe.* Ileborgh tablature (1448); *Fundamentum organisandi* (1452) by Conrad Paumann; the *Buxheimer Orgelbuch* (*c.*1460), containing more than 250 pieces, many of them 'coloured', or ornamented, keyboard arrangements of vocal pieces; among South Germans, works by Schlick (1511), Hofhaimer (*c.*1500), Buchner (*c.*1520), Erbach (*c.*1600). In the Netherlands, late 16th–early 17th century, Sweelinck, P. Cornet. Germany, Scheidt (1624); mid-17th century, Tunder, Weckmann, Kindermann, Froberger, and Kerll; late 17th century, Buxtehude (Denmark), Kerckhoven (Netherlands), G. Böhm, Bruhns, V. Lübeck, Muffat, Pachelbel; then J. G. Walther, J. S. Bach.

(ii) *France.* Attaingnant (1531), liturgical organ music and 'coloured' motets; Titelouze (1623 and 1626), hymns and *Magnificats;* Lebègue (1676, etc.); François Couperin (two organ masses, 1690); De Grigny (1699); Clérambault (*c.*1710); J.-F. and Pierre Dandrieu (18th century).

(iii) *Britain.* Compositions by Redford, Tallis, Preston, Blitheman, contained in 16th-century collections; Byrd, Bull, Gibbons, Tomkins (all late 16th–early 17th century); Blow, Purcell; Handel, especially concertos (Op. 4, 7); voluntaries by Stanley, Greene, and Boyce.

(*b*) *Nineteenth century onwards.* (Composers in order of birth date with names of some well-known pieces.) S. Wesley (12 short pieces); Mendelssohn (Sonatas, Op. 65); Schumann (six Fugues on B.A.C.H.); S. S. Wesley; Liszt (Fantasia and Fugue on 'Ad nos, ad salutarem undam'); Franck (Three chorales; *Pièce héroïque*); Brahms (chorale preludes); Reubke (sonata); Saint-Saëns (preludes and fugues, fantasies); Rheinberger (sonatas); Widor (organ symphonies); Stanford (fantasias); Elgar (Vesper voluntaries, sonata); Nielsen ('Commotio'); Vierne (symphonies, pièces de fantaisie); Vaughan Williams (3 preludes on Welsh hymn-tunes); Reger (Introduction and Passacaglia); Karg-Elert (chorale preludes including 'Nun danket alle Gott'); Dupré ('Variations sur un noël'); Howells (psalm-preludes, rhapsodies); Sowerby; Hindemith (sonatas); Duruflé (suite); Flor Peeters (organ chorales); Langlais; Messiaen ('L'Ascension', 'Livre d'orgue', 'La Nativité du Seigneur'); Alain ('Litanies'); Petr Eben ('Faust').

Andersen 1969; Audsley 1905; Clutton and Nyland 1963; Schlick 1511; Sumner 1952; Töpfer 1888; Williams 1966, 1980; Williams and Owen 1988.

Organette, organino. Names for various small *free-reed organs, some hand-tuned, using perforated paper rolls (see BARREL ORGAN, 5), brought out in the late 19th century in France, or especially the USA, and for many years very popular. One type of 'organette' was the size of a musical box, and was manufactured also in Britain. The *Orchestrelle* is larger, up to upright piano size, with suction foot-bellows, made from c.1888 by the Aeolian Co., New York (see PLAYER PIANO) and later by a British subsidiary. Still popular in the 1920s, this had stops for different tone qualities, and a keyboard for optional manual operation.

Organ harpsichord. See CLAVIORGAN.

Organistrum. See HURDY-GURDY, 4.

Organology. A term sometimes used in the 19th century for various biological and anatomical sciences, but in the 20th century seized upon by musical instrument historians desiring to establish their subject as standing on its own beside 'musicology'. First met thus in French (*organologie*, e.g. Schaeffner 1936), it draws on Greek '*organa*' in its general sense of 'instruments', or specifically 'musical instruments' and (though at a risk of misinterpretation as having to do with the organ in particular) has become an internationally accepted term for the study of musical instruments.

Orgue de Barbarie. See BARREL ORGAN, 5.

Orgue expressif. See HARMONIUM, 3.

Orpharion. Elizabethan and Jacobean stringed instrument, invented (it was said) by John Rose of London shortly after he had produced the *bandora. Like this, the orpharion is built with a wavy-sided body (as see BANDORA, Pl. 1, far end of the table), and is strung with wire. It differs in being tuned like a *lute. The player could thus play from lute tablature. There exist pieces written expressly for orpharion, some including notes higher up the string than normally found in lute music, the orpharion having a longer neck in relation to its size. At least two orpharions are preserved: one by Rose himself, dated 1580; the second (also with

slightly convex back) by another London maker, Francis Palmer, 1617, in the Copenhagen *collection. The name is a fusion of 'Orpheus' and 'Arion'.

A name 'penorcon' for a deeper-pitched size is given only by *Praetorius. The 'stump', nowhere described but with one early 17th-century Alman written for it, may have been some special version of this kind of instrument, with lute tutuing plus eight diapasons.

Gill 1960; Wells 1982.

Ottavino. 1. It., piccolo.
2. A small, octave *virginal.

Ottu. See SHAHNAI.

Overblowing. A term constantly used with wind instruments. On woodwind it has the important technical sense of causing notes to rise to harmonics—where this is possible (see WIND INSTRUMENTS, 3)—in order to extend the compass upwards above the fundamentals. The fingerings for the first overblow, to the octave register (or on clarinet to the twelfth) is mostly by straightforward repetition of the low register. The higher fingerings are generally less obvious and differ from one instrument to another. For quick reference (e.g. for a player of one instrument on becoming interested in another, or in an older form of the instrument), the customary high fingerings are tabulated in Table 1 (mostly after Baines 1957, and omitting some alternatives that a complete fingering chart would include). Fingerholes are indicated in a row from the highest on the left; a space divides the two hands. Dot (●): hole closed; circle (○): hole uncovered; stroke through circle (ø): half uncovered; k: open little-finger key for the hand in question (left hand, e.g., G♯ key; right hand, E♭ key), any other key to be pressed being named by the note-letter or occasionally by a special sign.

Scientific explanation how the fingerings produce their results has been greatly advanced through recent times. There are instances (as on modern flute and clarinet) where some specific harmonic of a low-register note appears to be directly involved when a hole is uncovered at a certain distance

TABLE I.

Flute, modern. Left thumb-hole is indicated under the others where open; otherwise closed (b: thumb not on B♭ plate). x, y, the two small trill keys (pressed in the positions indicated).

Note	Left hand	Right hand
d'''	○ ● ●	○ ○ ○ k
e♭'''	● ● ● k	● ● ● k
e'''	● ● ○	● ● ○ k
f'''	● ○ ●	● ○ ○ k
f♯'''	● ○ ●	○ ○ ● k
	(b)	
g'''	● ● ●	○ ○ ○ k
	○	
g♯'''	○ ● ● k	○ ○ ○ k
	○	
a'''	○ ● ○	● ○ ○ k
b♭'''	○ ○ ○	● x ○ ○ k
b'''	● ○ ●	○ ○ y ○ (k)
	(b)	
c''''	● ● ● k	● ○ ○ (k)
	○	
c♯''''	○ ● ○ k	● ○ (●) C♯ key
	○	
d''''	○ ○ ●	● ● ○ C key
	(b)	

TABLE I. (*cont.*)

Flute, one-key. On right, some differences for four- to eight-key flute (among various alternatives).

```
c‴     ○ ● ○    ● ● ● k
c♯‴    ○ ● ○    ● ○ ○ k
d‴     ○ ● ●    ○ ○ ○ k      [NB. Fife:
                              ○ ● ●
                              ● ● ●]
eb‴    ● ● ●    ○ ● ● k      open G♯ key
e‴     ● ● ○    ○ ● ● k
f‴     ● ● ○    ● ○ ○ k      close hole 5,
                              open F key
f♯‴    ● ● ○    ● ○ ○        open thumb
                              Bb key, close
                              hole 4
g‴     ● ○ ●    ○ ○ ○
g♯‴    ○ ○ ●    ○ ○ (● k)    open G♯ key,
                              close hole 6
a‴     ○ ● ●    ● ● ○        open G♯ key,
                              close hole 6
bb‴    (●) ● ○  ● ○ ○        open G♯ key,
                              and F key
```

Recorder, normal baroque (though there are many alternatives suited to different individual instruments). Here as for descant (soprano) recorder; thumb-hole 'half'.

```
bb‴    ● ● ○    ○ ● ●
b″     ● ● ○    ● ● ○
c‴     ● ○ ○    ● ● ○
c♯‴  { ○ ○ ○    ● ● ○
     { ● ○ ●    ● ∅ ●   ●
d‴     ● ○ ●    ● ○ ●
d♯‴    ● ○ ●    ○ ○ ○   ●
e‴     ○ ● ○    ○ ○ ○
```

Clarinet, modern. Speaker key open, thumb-hole closed. b: b/f♯″ key, 3rd finger right hand.

```
c♯‴    ○ ● ●    ● ● ○ k
d‴     ○ ● ●    ● ○ ○ k
eb‴    ○ ● ●    ● ○ b ○ k
e‴     ○ ● ●    ○ ○ ○ k
f‴     ○ ● ● k  ○ ○ ○ k
f♯‴    ○ ● ○    ○ ○ ○ k
g‴   { ● ○ ○    (●) ○ ○ k
     { ○ ● ●    ● ● ○ k
g♯‴    ○ ● ●    ○ ● ○ k
a‴     ○ ● ●    ○ ○ ○ k
bb‴    ● ● ● k  ● ● ● k
b‴     ● ● ○    ● ● ○ k
c‴‴    ● ○ ○    ● ○ ○ k
```

Clarinet, Albert (Simple) System. k as above.

```
c♯‴    ○ ● ●    ● ● ● k
d‴     ○ ● ●    ● ○ ● k
eb‴    ○ ● ●    ● ○ ○ k
e‴     as modern
f‴   { as modern, or
     { ● ● ● k  ● ● ● k
f♯‴    ● ● ○    ● ● ● k
g‴     ● ○ ○    ● ● ● k
(etc.)
```

Clarinet, five–six-key. (For upper register cross-fingerings, see CLARINET, 4b). High register: the following among many fingerings given. E: low E key.

```
c♯‴    ○ ● ● E    ● ● ●
       (or all off)
d‴     ○ ● ● E    ● ○ ●
eb‴    ○ ● ● E    ● ○ ○ k
e‴     ○ ● ● (E)  ○ ○ ○ k
f‴     ● ● ○ (E)  ○ ○ ○
f♯‴    ● ○ ○ (E)  ○ ○ ○
g‴   { ● ○ ○      ● ● ●
     { ○ ● ● E    ● ● ●
```

Oboe, modern. On left, Conservatoire System; right; alternatives for *right hand* on Thumb-plate System (*t*: lift thumb). Right little-finger keys named. *s*: left first finger on 'spatula' attached to small key below. From *e‴* upwards with lower octave key.

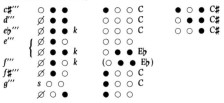

```
c♯‴    ○ ● ●    ● ○ ○ C     ● ○ ○ C♯
d‴     ∅ ● ●    ○ ○ ○ C     ○ ● ● C♯
eb‴    ∅ ● ● k  ○ ○ ○ C     ○ ○ ● C♯
e‴   { ∅ ● ○    ○ ○ ○
     { ∅ ● ● k  ○ ● ● Eb
f‴     ∅ ● ○ k  (○ ● ● Eb)
f♯‴    ∅ ● ○    ● ○ ○ C
g‴     s ○ ○    ● ○ ○ C
       ∅ ○ ●    ● ○ ○
```

Oboe, two-key, classical period. k: Eb key.

```
bb‴    ● ● ○    ● ● ●
b″     ● ○ ●    ● ● ● k
c‴     ○ ● ●    ● ● ○
c♯‴    ○ ● ●    ● ○ ○ k (or C)
d‴     ∅ ● ●    ○ (●) ○ k (C)
eb‴    ● ● ●    ○ ● ● k
e‴     ● ● ∅    (●) ● ● k
f‴     ● ● ∅    ● ○ ○ k (C)
```

Bassoon, modern (German system). c, a, c♯: left-thumb keys on wing joint; Bb, G♯, F: keys on butt.

```
c♯'        ● ● ● C♯   ○ ● ● F
eb'        ● ● ○      ○ ● ●
e'         ● ○ ●      ● ● ●
f'         ○ ● ○      ● ● ○
f♯'        ○ ● ●      ● ○ ○
g'         ○ ● ●      ● ○ ○ F
g♯'        ○ ● ●      ○ ○ ●
a'   a,c♯  ● ● ●      ○ ○ ●
bb'  a,c♯  ● ● ●      ● ○ ○ F
b'   c     ● ● ○      ● ● ○ Bb, F
c″   c     ● ○ ○      ● ● ○ Bb, F
c♯″  c     ● ○ ●      ● ○ ● G♯
d″   c     ○ ○ ○      ○ ○ ● G♯
eb″  c♯    ∅ ● ●      ○ ○ ○
e″   c♯    ∅ ● ●      ● ● ●
```

TABLE I. (cont.)

Bassoon, French System (see BASSOON, 3b for lower register cross-fingering)

```
c♯'       ● ● ○      ● ○ ○
e♭'       ● ● ○      ● ● ●
e'        ● ○ ●      ● ● ●
f'        ○ ● ○      ● ● ● G♯
f♯'     ∅ ● ●        ● ● ○ F
g'      ∅ ● ●        ● ○ ○ F
g♯'     ∅ ● ●        ○ ○ ○ F
a'    a   ● ● ○      ○ ○ ○
b♭'   a   ● ● ●      ● ● ● F
b'    a   ● ● ○      ● ● ○ F
c''   c   ● ○ ●      ● ● ● F
c♯''  c   ● ○ ○      ● ○ ○ F
d''   c   ○ ○ ○      ○ ○ ○
e♭''  c   ○ ○ ○      ○ ○ ○ (G♯)   and trill key
                                    for 2nd finger
e''   c   ○ ● ●      ● ● ○
f''   c♯  ○ ● ●      ● ○ ○ G♯
```

Bassoon, classical, five to eight keys; selected from various alternatives. 1, 2: thumb keys on wing, if present. D, D key, long joint.

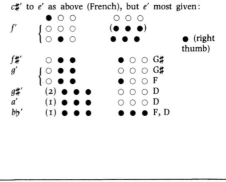

```
c♯' to e' as above (French), but e' most given:
               ● ○ ○        ○ ○ ○
f'    { ○ ○ ○              (● ● ●)
      { ○ ● ○               ● ● ●        ● (right
                                            thumb)
f♯'     ○ ● ●              ● ○ ○ G♯
g'    { ○ ● ●              ○ ○ ○ G♯
      { ○ ● ●              ● ○ ○ F
g♯'   (2) ● ● ●           ○ ○ ○ D
a'    (1) ● ● ●           ○ ○ ○ D
b♭'   (1) ● ● ●           ● ● ● F, D
```

higher up the tube; but with other instruments, especially of older types and bassoons of all types, it can be difficult to link a high fingering with any one particular partial: it is more as if the vibrating air were responding in more complex ways to opening of holes at intermediate points, as by forming a 'regime of oscillation' (Benade 1976) which produces the required high note reliably and in tune.

Overtone tuning. See XYLOPHONE, 2.

P

Pacific Islands. Melanesia, from Papua New Guinea to Fiji; Micronesia, with the Mariana, Caroline, Marshall, and (now Kiribati) Gilbert Islands; Polynesia, with Hawaii, Samoa, Tonga, New Zealand (Maori), and the Marquesas.

The earliest settlers probably travelled from mainland south-east Asia to New Guinea some 20,000 years ago. For the rest of Oceania, no record of settlement exists before the second millennium BC. By tracing the path of Lapitaware pottery, we know that its makers had reached Fiji by 1000 BC, Tonga by 500 BC, and onwards in voyages still recalled in traditional dances and chants. Many instruments of the neolithic cultures met by European navigators of the 16th to 17th centuries have maintained their role in music and dance, save where curtailed by Western intrusion, in some cases even obliterated beyond hope of practical restitution beside ancient arts now encouraged.

1. *Melanesia.* Instruments, apart from those now introduced, include:

(a) *Idiophones.* Rattles (of shells, seed pods, gourd); bamboo *concussion sticks; *slit drums, of bamboo or most commonly hollowed in wood, played during ceremonies and for sending messages, as in Africa and by American Indians; *stamping tubes; bamboo *jew's-harps, especially for courting. See also the unique LIVIKA, of wood.

(b) *Drums.* The long (to c.1 m. or 3'), narrow, single-skin 'kundu' types, hollowed out in elongated 'hourglass' shape, with a handle carved at the waist (see DRUM, Fig. 1b) for holding by one hand while the other hand plays. Some beeswax or resin pellets may be stuck on to the skin to adjust the tone.

(c) *Stringed.* Not common, but include hunting bow twanged, and mouth-bow (see MUSICAL BOW).

(d) *Wind.* Great variety of flutes, large and small, end-blown (plain or notched) and transverse, with three or four holes or without holes (see FLUTE, 7b; panpipes of almost every kind, especially in the Solomon Islands; *conch, side-blown, and substitutes of short, wide bamboo tubes, side- or end-blown. Also *bull-roarer, formerly at initiation rites but largely obsolete.

2. *Micronesia.* The smallest inventory of instruments in the Pacific region, among them concussion sticks; hourglass drums (in eastern Micronesia); nose-flutes; conches.

3. *Polynesia* (for Maori instruments see below, 4).

(a) *Idiophones.* Struck sticks, tubes, pebbles; rattles

(gourd, etc.); split bamboo struck on the arm; spinning rattle (Hawaiian: '*ūlili*: see RATTLE, 3); slit drums; stamping tubes; 'dance gourd' (Hawaiian: *ipūhula*: a large gourd—*Lagenaria* genus, the neck removed—glued to a smaller gourd above, with a hole in the top; thumped on a mat, raised and struck with the fingers, repeating the contrasting deep and brighter sounds).

(b) *Drums.* Polynesian cylindrical drum, *pāhu*, carved from palm wood, stood upright, with single sharkskin head played with fingers and hand. In Hawaii it may be played together with the small 'knee drum', *pūniu*, of coconut, skin-covered, strapped to the knee and struck with a braided thong of vegetable fibre.

(c) *Stringed.* A type of mouth-bow, '*ukeke* (see MUSICAL BOW), with two or more strings over a wide stick: obsolete, formerly used by courting couples. (Among modern instruments Hawaiian by name, the *ukulele and *Hawaiian guitar arose as modifications of European instruments.)

(d) *Wind.* Bamboo *nose-flute, over all Polynesia from Tonga to Hawaii, also Fiji, and in some islands revived after the playing had become almost forgotten; panpipe (obsolete); conch, everywhere, in Tonga sounded by groups at sporting events, etc. *Ipu hokiokio* (Hawaii) is a former vessel flute played by lovers. A reed-horn of rolled leaf is played by children; bull-roarer.

4. *New Zealand.* Maori instruments have included concussion sticks, clappers, and a form of slit drum, *pahuu*. The principal instruments, however, along with the conch, were wind instruments: *kooauau*, a short (c.12 cm., 4¾″) three-holed end-blown flute of wood or bone, now known as blown with the mouth (not the nose); *nguru*, shorter, some of clay or stone, with two holes, playing details no longer known; and, also frequent in collections, the cigar-shaped wooden *puutoorino*, up to 60 cm. (24″), though it is quite forgotten whether it was blown as a flute or (as some old accounts imply) as a trumpet.

Collaer 1965; Fischer 1983; Kunst 1967; Moyle 1976–7; Myers 1983; Roberts 1926.

Pakhawaj. A classic drum of north India, similar to the south Indian *mrdanga*.

Palwei (Burma). See KHLUI.

Pandoura, pandora, pandurina. In Ancient Greek *pandoura* was apparently a name for a small short-necked lute (see LUTE, 7), sometimes three-stringed; or for instruments of lute kinds in general, seen also in the later Roman sculptures and the earliest medieval art in the West. Later, in Renaissance Europe, 'pandora' is the *bandora (spelled either way) and 'pandurina', in the 17th century, a name for a small, slim variant of the early *mandolin or 'mandore' (see MANDOLIN, 5, the 'p' of 'pandoura' here becoming in French and Italian an 'm').

Panharmonicon. See BARREL ORGAN, 4.

Panpipe (pan-flute; or syrinx; from Gk., Pan, the rustic god). A row of tubes of different lengths joined side by side and sounded by blowing across the tops, each tube giving its own note. There may be from three tubes up to more than 40, in most cases made of cane and stopped at the lower ends by a knot in the cane or with wax. Being *stopped pipes, each tube gives a deep note for its length (18 cm. (7") giving approximately a'). Other constructions are of a flat piece of wood with the tubes drilled down into it (from Ancient Rome to present south-west Europe); pottery (Ancient Peru; see 2, below); and, of course, moulded plastic.

1. *Tube arrangements: (a) From longest to shortest.* Almost world-wide. In southern Europe today most likely to be heard as the trade call of travelling tradesmen (e.g. knife-grinders). A notable exception is Romania, where rural gypsy bands have used the instrument, since famous in the hands of Fanica Luca and after him Gheorge Zamfir. The Romanian panpipe (*nai*) characteristically has 20 tubes joined in a curve and giving a diatonic scale from *b'* up to *g''''*; accidentals are made by tilting the instrument towards the upper lip to flatten the note. Brilliant bird-song effects are favourite elements of the performances (Alexandru 1974).

In South America (Amazonia) small panpipes are made in pairs, for two players to blow alternately, one sounding the notes (of a four- or five-note scale) which are omitted on the other instrument.

(b) *Longest tube in the middle.* Such is played in Bavaria and Bohemia; the tubes to one side give the notes of a tonic chord and to the other side the dominant, matching a typical phrase-structure in the folk melodies; also Georgia (USSR), six pipes, tuned for adjacent pipes on each side to sound in thirds when blown simultaneously (as again in *d* below).

(c) *Shortest tube in the middle.* Central America (Panama); and in China, *paixiao*, an ancient pitch-giving and ceremonial instrument, still made (but see below, 3): the pipes (part-enclosed in a red-lacquered case) on one side give a high-pitched whole-tone scale a semitone higher than that given from the other side, making a chromatic scale in all.

(d) *Zigzag.* Alternately long and short up the scale: notably Ecuador, *rondador*, up to 42 tubes, adjacent tubes tuned a third apart: sounding two together, aiming the breath between them, tunes are played in consecutive thirds (presumed a post-Columbian development). Irregular: Melanesia (less frequent than form (a)), as in Solomon Islands, played in quick, short breaths, again sounding two tubes at a time: in one seven-tube example, octaves, a major second, and a fifth (Zemp 1981, and *NOCM* 1378).

(e) *Two-row, one row behind the other.* Peru and Bolivia (Pl. 1), also Melanesia. The further row may be of tubes open at the bottom, or of stopped tubes half the length of the front tubes, in either case adding the interest of fainter, breathy sounds at the octave, or just off the octave for vibrant effect. In the Andean countries are heard large ensembles of panpipes (*siku*) built in different octave registers, the deeper instruments often with tubes up to 60 cm. (2') long, Andean panpipes (*zampoña*, etc.) have come to be widely exported abroad (in some cases very casually made) and are even to be heard, electronically modulated, as a new sound in recorded pop and other music.

(f) *Bundle.* Seven or so tubes tied in a bundle with one tube in the middle: South-East Asia, Melanesia. In Upper Burma, etc., the middle tube, the longest, may be filled with gunpowder for firing off as a musical rocket, for which the top ends of the sounding tubes are suitably bevelled to strike the air at a correct angle.

2. *Panpipes in antiquity.* Though panpipes appear ethnologically among early neolithic cultures of the world, there is little archaeological evidence of them in the West much before the 6th century BC. From a much earlier date (before 2000 BC) some sets of small tubes of bone have been found in excavations near Saratov, in Russia, but these were possibly for distribution individually among a group of performers blowing their notes in turn—a method known up to not long ago, with cane tubes, in rural Lithuania. The well-known Greek legend tells how the nymph Syrinx, to escape the advances of Pan, was transformed into a reed which the frustrated god cut into pieces; he then repented, kissing the pieces and, on hearing the sounds coming from them, devised the panpipe, later celebrated in the Idylls of Theocritus.

The panpipes of red pottery from Ancient Peru (from the Nazca period, c.AD 500; see AMERICAN INDIANS) are mostly with ten tubes made separately and jointed together in the firing, producing at least partly a pentatonic scale; the chief names, still in use, are *antara* (Quechua) and *siku* (Aymara).

3. *Duct panpipe* (on the recorder principle). This, occasionally met in Europe as a folk instrument, appears in a late 14th-century illustrated 'Romance of the Rose' (Valencia Library, MS 387; see *NOCM* 941). The Chinese panpipe (above, 1c) is now also made as a duct panpipe, each tube with its block and window.

Pl. 1. Chipaya Indians from Carangas, western Bolivia, playing *zampoñas* (Andean panpipes).

Pantaleon. See DULCIMER, 3.

Parakapzuk. See BAGPIPE, 6.

Pardessus de viole (Fr., 'the topmost viol'). Small French viol of the 18th century (body length *c.*33 cm. or 13″, total 60 cm. or 2′) made up to the 1750s (notably in Paris by Guersan, and Grosset), often with a striped back of woods of contrasting hue. It was held downwards, gripped between the knees, and initially had six strings tuned as the treble *viol but exchanging the lowest, *d*, for a top string, *g″*. From *c.*1720 a change was made to five strings (Green 1982), replacing the *e′* and *c′* by a string tuned to *d′*, so putting the lower strings in fifths as on the violin and said, in Corette's Tutor, to be better for playing Italian violin sonatas, though retaining the downwards playing position, judged 'more appropriate for ladies'. Most of the music published for it, up to *c.*1770, is for the *pardessus* or alternative instruments.

Quinton appears to have been another name for the five-stringed variety, and not particularly for a model with shallower sides than usual.

Partials. 1. *Partials in general.* Partials are well familiar to the ear as 'overtones' distinguishable in most sounds from instruments, and are in some cases termed 'harmonics'. Most importantly, as subconsciously perceived through the ear they are a chief factor by which we objectively tell the sound of one instrument from that of another, and

recognize it no less amidst extraneous noises of any kind. They are the frequencies given by the various 'modes of vibration' possible in the medium when, after being momentarily 'deformed' (e.g. struck), it vibrates under the restoring force of the tension (strings, membranes), or stiffness (most hard percussion instruments), or air (wind).

2. *Series.* The existence of overtones alone makes clear that almost every method of exciting vibration brings the result that many modes are in progress at once, superposed on one another—somewhat, to take a broad analogy, as over a sheet of water, waves and ripples may proceed at the same time, keeping in their own rhythm but in sum giving to the water at each point along the line a different up-and-down motion from that which it would show if only the main waves were present ('interference'). With instruments, the pitch of the note heard is in most cases (not in all) the frequency of the lowest or 'first' mode of vibration: waves traverse the system directly to the boundaries (e.g. the ends of a stretched string), where they are reflected; this frequency is the fundamental or 'first partial', being the frequency of the first or 'lowest' mode of vibration. In higher modes, the wave divides into a chain of two or many more smaller sections traversed in shorter time, giving to each successive partial a higher frequency than the one before. The series, which the partials together make up, is with ideal strings a *harmonic series, as also with most well-known wind instruments (see STOPPED PIPE for series with odd-numbered partials only); but percussion instruments in general give

rise to one or more series which are non-harmonic, proceeding by their own various mathematical progressions in which none of the intervals ordinarily recognized in our music are present (though our hearing system will often search for the nearest harmonic interval and persuade us that this is what we perceive). The greater the number and prominence of partials aroused, the more ringing or vibrant the sustained tone is likely to be (whence descriptive expressions such as 'with strong upper partials').

3. *Graphic representation and sound spectra.* A wave diagram will show firstly a pure fundamental 'sine wave' (this relating to expression of pendular motion in terms of circular—as when a bob fixed to a rotating turntable is observed sideways on). Then, incorporating partials, each primary undulation takes on peaks and troughs arising from higher modes with faster repetition. Eventually this may lead to waveforms of 'sawtooth' or 'square' kinds, much referred to in, for example, electronic sound synthesis.

Sound spectra ('tone spectra', 'spectrograms'), obtained by laboratory methods (e.g. by 'search tone', or electronic analyser), display as peaks the partials present in a sustained sound as well as indicating their relative strengths. Each spectrum so obtained can of course be only a sample: in practice, with the slightest difference in loudness or expression, on the same or a different note, or sounded by a different player or instrument of the same kind, the spectrum diagram may appear considerably different. Nevertheless such spectra confirm in general terms that aural recognition of tone quality relates to the presence of partials. Thus we may compare the lower notes of an 18th-century flute (few partials, few high peaks, calm, pure sounds) with the same notes demonstrated on a violin or oboe (more numerous partials of significant strength, extending upwards over a far greater band of frequencies).

In some cases we hear the note yet the fundamental may itself barely show in the spectrum; but the ear, taking in a wide range of the partials present, perceives in their superimposed frequencies a 'pattern repeat' at the frequency of the lowest component, the fundamental, which our hearing then recognizes, however weak it be, as the musical pitch of the sound, i.e. the note. Should however the fundamental be artificially eliminated from the pattern (as in making a *harmonic on the violin or in *overblowing on a wind instrument) a fresh pattern takes its place, repeating at the frequency of the next partial above, now to become the note (and containing in its spectrum such of the original higher partials that still fit into the pattern).

4. *Transients and decay.* Of equal importance in sound recognition, these ('quickly passing') are impact or attack sounds excited at the commencement of a note. If notes from violin and trumpet are recorded and then played back with their beginnings shorn off, they can sound almost identical. Transients are of course important not only in instrumental sounds: the primary function of human and animal hearing is identification of noises of any kind however faint and whether the source is visible or not (the eyes can sleep while the ears remain alert). Also, among instruments where vibration is not evenly sustained by bowing or blowing, vibration modes decay at different rates, giving changing character to the tone as it fades away, and so heightened aural effect where notes are allowed to ring on as fresh ones are struck.

5. *Inharmonicity.* Theoretical relative partial frequencies in a series are calculated as for an 'ideal' vibrator, such as a string which is infinitely thin and perfectly flexible. *Inharmonicity* refers to cases where partials which should lie in a harmonic series in practice deviate from it, becoming increasingly sharp as the series is ascended. It occurs with struck and plucked strings to a small degree, and becomes an important factor in tuning pianos, in which, in the extreme octaves, string flexibility is impaired through over-stiffness. The octaves are therefore 'stretched', in effect to match the notes of the high octave to the sharp 2nd partial of the notes an octave below; otherwise the higher note is liable to sound flat, e.g. at the top of an arpeggio.

6. *Bars* (if of round sections, *rods*; if hollow, *tubes*). See GLOCKENSPIEL, 5, for their general manner of transverse vibration; frequencies varying inversely as the square of the length, and directly as the thickness (the thinner, the deeper the note, other things being equal).

(*a*) *Bar freely supported or suspended.* Fig. 1*a* illustrates on exaggerated scale how the bar 'bends' when struck between or beyond the stationary nodes (N), only the first two modes shown. The two supports in actual instruments are placed to favour the first mode, but higher partials may be faintly detected by striking in different places. Briefly, with no attempt to enter into the mathematics of wave mechanics, the relative frequencies from the first partial upwards closely fall in a series of the squares of the odd numbers from 3 onwards: see Ex. 1 for a bar tuned to Middle C (the near octave between partials 2 and 3 arising because 7^2 happens to be near twice 5^2). In practice the intervals may not be exactly as predicted, or may be altered by 'overtone tuning' (see XYLOPHONE, 2), while some frequency due to a torsional ('twisting') mode may intrude. The partials assume a pitch significance mainly where the length of a bar is great as compared with the thickness: e.g. with a triangle (a bent rod, showing partial frequencies variously lowered owing to the bends) the lowest mode is scarcely aroused (and nor, from the non-harmonic intervals above in the series, can the ear readily reconstruct it subjectively); the sound on striking softly will be predominantly from the 3rd or the 5th partial, or in normal playing, from numerous partials high above. See also TUBULAR BELLS, 2.

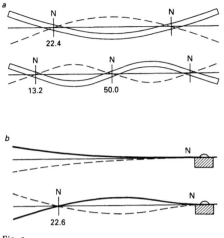

Fig. 1.

Ex. 1. Theoretical pitches of partials of free-ended bar tuned to Middle C; frequency ratios approx. as 9 : 25 : 49 : 81 : 121.

(b) Bar fixed at one end, to a motionless support, the other end free (scientifically a 'clamped/free' bar). This other musically important bar is employed both in rod chimes, etc. and as a flexible tongue. The lowest mode or fundamental (Fig. 1b, upper), giving the note, sounds at a great interval—theoretically some two octaves and a sixth though in practice usually less—below the second mode, which itself (Fig. 1b, lower) would, for bars of similar dimensions, show a frequency near that of the lowest mode where both ends are free. For the fundamental of the clamped bar to give a note in the same musically useful range it will be shorter, and the more so since if it is to be flexible for plucking it will also be thinner (as in the case of a musical box tongue compared with a glockenspiel bar both sounding the same note).

(c) Other forms of vibration. A bar that is clamped at both ends gives the same series of partials as one that is free at both ends. A bar or rod, especially one that is clamped at one end, can also be put in longitudinal vibration, in which vibration is not in a 'bending' sense but takes place in the direction of wave travel as with the air-column of a wind instrument, and also experienced with strings when they accidentally produce a squeak. It is employed in *sound sculptures where metal or glass rods are stroked, giving high sounds (and partials in a harmonic series).

7. Membranes and plates. To consider only circular forms, there are vibration modes in which the nodes are diametric, others in which nodes form one or more circles about the centre, and others in which both are combined. Fig. 2 (after Rayleigh 1877) illustrates the first nine modes of a membrane, with their frequencies relative to the first (the membrane here for theoretical purposes regarded as being of minimal thickness and vibrating in vacuo). Dotted lines show the nodes. During vibration, as the area to one side of a nodal line or circle bends upwards, that to the other bends downwards, then vice versa, and so on. For quick description of a mode a convention is to write the number of nodal diameters first, then the circles, e.g. (Fig. 2, top right) 2/0: two diameters and no circle (that is, excluding the circumference, where the membrane is said to be 'hinged' to the support). Modes with nodal circles (their relative radii given in Fig. 2) have higher frequencies than those without them (with one circle, higher than with one diameter) and at greater intervals apart. With mixed modes, with one or more of both diameters and circles, the frequency series are compounded of the above two kinds.

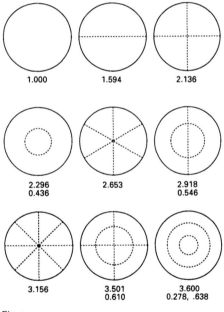

Fig. 2.

Each series of modal frequencies, though it possesses its own mathematical logic, is non-harmonic; yet the diametric frequencies of a membrane upwards from mode 1/0 especially loaded by air, come close to a series running 1.5, 2, 2.5, 3 . . . (numerically half the number of diameters plus 1) which can in practice lead to a series so close to harmonic as to aid the ear in perceiving a definite pitch (see TIMPANI, 5).

With a plate, as compared with a membrane, while the order of nodal patterns is practically the same, the frequencies through each series rise far more rapidly, for with a hard material frequencies are, as with a bar, related to the square of distances. The diametric frequencies, here beginning with 2/0, rise roughly as $1, 1.5^2, 2^2, 2.5^2 \ldots$, and other series show correspondingly wide intervals. Thus the interval between modes 2/0 and 0/2, in theory for a membrane about a major sixth, is for a plate just under three octaves. In practice the intervals may vary considerably from theory, yet the wide separation of the partials enables one to be able to distinguish several of them aurally; for example from a suspended cymbal (though not an ideal flat plate, having a curvature of graded thickness and also a dome in the middle).

If a cymbal be suspended through holes pierced close to the rim, though many partials are scarcely changed in pitch, the sound becomes more like that of a gong, while the principal pitch from a gong is extinguished if the instrument be fixed in the centre like a cymbal. But gongs differ among each other too much in form and thicknesses for general statements on their frequency patterns yet to be possible, and this proves to be no less the case with bells (extreme forms of 'curved plate'). Here there have been found, with the overtones of an average heavy bell, nodal 'meridians', 4, 6, or 8, running to the top from points round the rim and, except with the 'hum-note' and 'tierce' (see BELL, 2), a nodal circle part-way up the bell. But precisely how these overtones may be related in one series or another, if at all, is among the questions still to be fully answered. (See also ACOUSTICS.)

Pat-Waing. Burmese *drum chime.

Pauken (Ger.). *Timpani.

Pedal Steel guitar. See HAWAIIAN GUITAR, 2.

Pellet-bell. The spherical, usually small, shaken bell with a loose pellet inside. See SLEIGH BELL.

Percussion (Fr.: *batterie* or *percussion*; Ger.: *Schlagzeug*; It.: *batteria*). The term used in Western music for instruments employed in the percussion section of an orchestra or band, or in a percussion band, or by the drummer of a jazz or rock group (see also DRUM KIT). Their variety is, of course, enormous, far greater than in any other group of instruments—sounds from metal, wood, membranes (drums)—technically united under the paramount role of the percussionist's principal tool, the stick or beater, except where instruments are struck against each other, or shaken. See individually for the following:

Metal. ANVIL; BELL PLATES; CHAINS; CHIME BAR; COWBELL; crotales (see CYMBALS, 4); CYMBALS; FLEX-ATONE; GLOCKENSPIEL; GONG AND TAM-TAM; LUJON;

SISTRUM AND JINGLES (see also BRAZILIAN TAMBOURINE); SLEIGH BELL (pellet-bells); TRIANGLE; TUBULAR BELLS; VIBRAPHONE. See also STEEL BAND.

Wood. BIN-SASARA; CABAZA; CASTANETS; CHOCALHO; CLAVES; GATO DRUM; GUIRO; LOG DRUM; MARACAS; MARIMBA; RATTLE; SLIT DRUM; TEMPLE BLOCKS; WHIP; WOOD BLOCK; XYLOPHONE.

Drums. Listed at the beginning of DRUM.

1. *Definite and indefinite pitch.* For orchestral composers this has long been a primary consideration. An instrument described as of 'definite pitch' is one that can play specified notes of the musical scale, written as such in the music (unless, of course, this be of a kind which is not written down). Examples include the 'keyed' or 'mallet percussion' (glockenspiel, vibraphone, xylophone, etc.; for a compass chart of these, see XYLOPHONE), tubular bells, and, among drums, the timpani. For instruments of 'indefinite pitch' the sounds cannot be (or cannot easily be) expressed as notes of the scale. This group broadly speaking embraces the rest of the percussion, which before the modern era amounted to a limited number of instruments—e.g. side and bass drum, cymbals, triangle—which are by intention 'indefinite', approaching the point of real 'pitchlessness' as near as can be obtained, whereby they are sounded whatever the harmony of the rest of the orchestra may be, without having to harmonize with it themselves.

The classic division, however, has now often to be qualified in consequence of a parameter that has come much to the fore during the 20th century: relative pitch among instruments of the 'indefinite' category. For example, a pair of temple blocks will give two perfectly distinct contrasting pitches, neither of them tuned to the musical scale (and so by definition 'indefinite') yet capable between them of two-note motifs ('clip-clop', etc.) which can be retained in the mind like melodic themes and be imitated vocally. So too with different-sized tom-toms or suspended cymbals softly struck (or, indeed, with two saucepans, odd pieces of wood, almost anything). One can easily understand how such distinctness of contrasted indefinite sounds among percussion instruments offers excellent material for atonal music. Since the pioneer concert works by Edgard Varèse (notably his *Ionisation* (1931) for percussion only), a composer will score for two, three, or more of such instruments designated as 'low', 'medium', 'high', etc., and combine them with other percussion instruments in such ways that, whereas a theme of traditional kind will run through notes of the scale, an atonal (or rather, 'non-tonal') strand might rise through the 'indefinite' percussion from bass drum through different tom-toms, then temple blocks, to end at the top with the whip, and perhaps with a note on the marimba (an actual note of the scale) thrown in, dissociated from definite-pitch connotation by the overall atonal context.

Ex. 1. Extract from Berio, *Circles.*

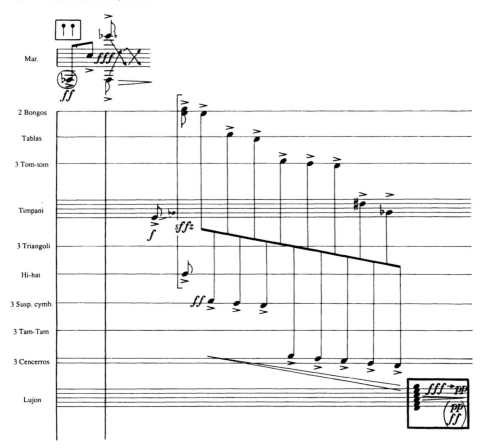

Ex. 2. Extract from Stockhausen, *Kontakte* (⊓ = bongos; ⫾ = log drums; ∆ = cowbells; M▶ = marimba).

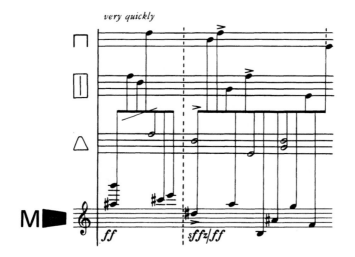

But there arises a complication. Cowbells sound clearly different pitches, and these can be adjusted by the maker to become 'definite', i.e. to give notes of the scale. Tuned sets have been made on these lines, and of sleighbells and the small 'antique' cymbals (which Berlioz anyhow expected to be tuned to notes of the scale), not to mention Puccini's gongs in *Turandot*; all these instruments thus become of definite pitch. But it is not every orchestra that can produce such tuned sets, nor every composer who wants the instruments to be so tuned, indeed most requiring atonal 'indefiniteness' ('low', 'high', etc., as mentioned above). Thus we have to take into account a category of percussion instruments which are hard to define other than as 'usually of indefinite pitch'.

Occasional use is made of struck bottles or mugs (Britten), and imitative noises—thunder, wind, etc. (see *effects*).

2. *Sticks and beaters*. It is quite instructive to tap a table top, first with the fingers (perhaps identifying the main pitch one hears by humming in unison with it); and next with a pencil, when higher pitches stand out and the sound seems much higher. Correspondingly with the percussion, a beater with a large, soft end will make contact with the vibrating surface (solid or membrane) over an appreciable area and for a longer time, and so damp out (smother) the shorter wavelengths of higher modes of vibration, to produce, when used with moderate force, a clear, mellow sound. Conversely, a hard narrow stick produces the opposite effect, eliciting high *partials while the fundamental or the lower modes are weakly aroused, and the result is a more hissing, brittle, or tinkling sound as the case may be.

Through the Classical period we rarely hear of a percussion instrument deliberately sounded in any other than its traditional and expected manner. But from Berlioz onward, composers—and theatre and dance drummers—have increasingly introduced sounds made by using the 'wrong' sticks—as well as by hitting a cymbal ('suspended cymbal') instead of invariably clashing it against another. Any perusal of 'modern' scores, especially from Bartók onwards—though with well-known prior instances in Elgar, Stravinsky, and others—reveals countless novel methods.

3. *Notation*. In light music and band parts it is usual to write for the main percussion instruments together on a single staff (see BRASS BAND, I). Any further instruments are added higher on the staff, usually with the abbreviated form of the name, or, for suspended cymbal, a cross instead of a note head. Orchestral music has for some time preferred to give to each 'indefinite pitch' instrument a separate single line (using no staff). As lines are provided on the page often only for instruments actually required at that moment in the music the player, who will probably have charge of several of them, requires to be told which these are. For

this there are two methods: either to name them, as in Ex. I (a work involving six percussionists), or more recently by graphic symbols, as in Ex. 2. These last are becoming sufficiently well standardized for all players to understand them without the aid of an explanatory list in the part.

Most important in advanced percussion music is careful planning, both by the composer as he distributes the instruments among a stated number of players, and by the individual player so that everything is within reach. Stravinsky's *The Soldier's Tale* (produced in 1918) is still considered a model in both respects, including a diagram in the full score showing how to place the instruments.

Blades 1970; Holland 1978; Peinkofer and Tannigel 1976; Smith Brindle 1970.

Percussion pot. A rather vague term for various means of producing a drum-like sound from the air within an earthenware pot or pitcher without the aid of a membrane. In Spain and Portugal a folk-dance ensemble may be rhythmically backed by a player who deftly flaps a basketry fan against the mouth of the *cantaró*, a large pitcher, giving a sound like that of a bass drum. In Africa a palm-leaf may be used: the 'udo drum' in Nigeria has also an opening in the side of the jar, this and the top being smacked alternately with the hands. In India the opening of the pot (*ghaṭam*) is held against the stomach while the outside is struck on different spots with hands, fingers, and nails, for contrasted sounds like those of real drumming. In *classification these 'air drums' are put under 'plosive aerophones'. Another method is to blow into the vessel, a technique used in American jug bands.

Philomele. See BOWED ZITHER.

Phonofiddle. See STROH VIOLIN.

Phorminx (Ancient Greece). See LYRE, 2*b*.

Physharmonica (or 'bellows harmonica'). At first, the name given by Häckel, Vienna, *c*.1820, to a small *free-reed organ with foot-bellows, to fit beneath the keyboard of a piano for playing sustained melody. Later, the name was given to various predecessors of the *harmonium and *accordion (whence Italian *fisarmonica*, 'accordion').

Piano (or pianoforte; Ger.: *Klavier*. Grand piano, Fr.: *piano à queue*; Ger.: *Flügel*; It.: *piano a coda*; Ru.: *fortepiano, royal*; Sp.: *piano da cola*. Upright piano, Fr.: *piano droit*; Ger.: *Pianino*, etc.; Ru.: *pianino*; Sp.: *piano vertical*). See also SQUARE PIANO for the former oblong varieties; also FORTEPIANO; PLAYER PIANO (pianola, etc.); KEYBOARD (3, fingering).

This instrument which on so many counts has held the central place in our music for near two centuries, and for which more music has been written and published than for any other, is in the first place the invention of Bartolomeo Cristofori (1655–1731), a harpsichord-maker born in Padua and from 1690 onwards working in Florence. Here, already before the end of the century, he had begun to tackle the by no means simple practical problem of sounding strings with hammers actuated from a keyboard and with complete control of softer or louder from the force given to the hammers by the fingers on the keys. A report of his new instruments seen in his workshop in 1709 gives the name *gravicembalo* ('harpsichord') *con piano e forte*—or, speaking the last words quickly, 'pianoforte'. Other designs of the early 18th century for hitting strings with hammers worked from a keyboard, by a French inventor and a German, remained, as far as is known, unexecuted in practice, so no more need be said of them here.

1. *Basis of piano action.* Up to Cristofori's time strings played with hammers had been well known only on the keyboard-less *dulcimer, then made in Italy for homes of the well-to-do (see DULCIMER, 3). Each beater is lightly held between fingers and thumb, to flick it against the strings: that is, having given it speed according to the desired loudness, then to allow it at the last instant to strike and rebound clear. On the piano, an equivalent—but creating a new sound for music—must be effected through a mechanism of levers: pressing down a key propels the hammer at accelerated speed to within a very short distance from the strings for it then to travel free to strike and rebound.

A vital benefit of keyboard action lies in the control over the duration of notes individually through the automatic silencing of each by its damper as the finger releases the key, and the option of holding the key (the hammer remaining poised just below the string) for the sound to continue—facilities without which the ability to play with all ten fingers individually would be musically purposeless. There are very good pianos of the late 18th century, English for example, with actions that embrace little in the way of further complications (see SQUARE PIANO). They require however that the distance of free hammer-travel takes into account the danger of the hammer, when the key is held down (as in legato playing) bouncing up and striking twice. Yet the smaller this distance, which may now be no more than a few millimetres, the greater is the player's control over the loudness and timing of the impact on the strings. The way round the problem is that which Cristofori had discovered in the first place: provision of an 'escapement' which enables the hammer, after striking, to fall a safe distance below (1 cm. or more, on to a padded 'check') while the mechanism that has raised it remains 'up' (the finger being still on the key). Then, when the finger is removed, the whole must drop to the initial

position ready for the next note. For different forms of escapement from Cristofori to the present, see 7 and 8 below.

2. *Early development of the piano.* Three grand pianos survive by Cristofori late in his life, with dates from 1720 to 1726 (in the *collections at New York, Rome, and Leipzig), still outwardly like a harpsichord and with the thin strings (two per note) and small leather-covered hammers making a gentle sound far removed from that since. Cristofori had men working for him, and it is possible on circumstantial evidence (Pollens 1984) that Domenico Scarlatti may already by 1720 have sometimes played and taught at the Portuguese court on a piano brought from Florence. The earliest known pieces expressly for the instrument are sonatas of 1732 for *cimbalo di piano e forte* by L. Giustini of Pistoia, with directions *piano, forte, più forte*, etc., duly marked in (reprinted 1933). In Germany the famous organ-builder Gottfried Silbermann (d. 1753) made grand pianos on Cristofori's system and Bach, on visits to the court at Potsdam, tried them, at first with doubts over the action and a weakness in the high notes, but later, in 1747, expressing fair approval. Bach was afterwards involved in the purchase of a Silbermann *Piano et Forte*, most likely for someone else; he is not known ever to have possessed one or written anything specifically for it. The piano truly entered music with the period of Mozart.

By the 1740s other German instrument-makers were concentrating on square pianos, using more simple actions later developed into the important Viennese action in grands as those played by Mozart (Pl. 1) and often Beethoven (below, 8b). After 'squares' were made also in England (see SQUARE PIANO) there followed the English grand action (8a), upon which advances were made notably by Érard (then working in London) incorporating ideas which largely repeat those of Cristofori. Upright pianos, saving floor space, were first as if the body of a grand were turned upright on a stand (and therefore very tall), with the soundboard to the front and hammers striking from the rear. Such was an 'upright grand piano with the form of a bookcase' by Stodart, London, 1795, and admired by Haydn. Another, the 'giraffe' piano conspicuous in many collections, adds a bulging scroll to the curved side at the top left; it appeared in Vienna c.1800, and was made in Germany for some fifty years. The true upright, with the strings reaching nearly to the floor, tuned at the top and struck from the front, appeared in 1800 in models by Isaac Hawkins, Philadelphia, and by Matthias Müller in Vienna. Then, from 1811, Robert Wornum in London evolved what was often called the 'cottage piano', leading to models of 1829 which became the basis for future development of the upright (which Chopin often liked to play). American makers after Hawkins were mainly occupied

not to have built their first upright until 1862. For an example of modern upright action, see below, 8c.

3. *Main present categories of piano. Grands*: for large halls and up to 275 cm. (9') long, weighing 400 kg. (two-fifths of a ton) or more; 'Grand', around 213 cm. (7'), or 'Boudoir Grand', 180 cm. (6'), and *c*.300 kg.; 'Baby Grand', from 132 cm. (5') down to 122 cm. (4') or less, with simplified action and thicker strings necessitated by the shorter length. *Uprights*, up to 122 cm. (4') tall (the taller 'cabinet' models now being things of the past); 'Mini pianos' (miniature uprights), developed in Britain from 1932, under 90 cm. (3') tall with the strings barely rising above keyboard level (the bass strings running at 45 degrees), and special drop action.

Piano exteriors are usually ebonized (black, either high-gloss or 'satin'), or veneered in walnut or mahogany. It is said that in the year 1980 some 800,000 pianos were manufactured, two-thirds of them in the USA and Japan, where Yamaha has made pianos since 1900.

4. *Frame and strings*: (a) *The frame*. Under the lid of a grand piano one sees the gilt iron frame cast in one piece: a broad curving plate with circular apertures saving weight and the bracing bars reaching forward to the thick wrest-plank of layered wood carrying the tuning pins. The cast-iron frame, the most important of the American contributions to the piano, was first made by Babcock in Boston (1825), for square pianos, to render these, the first widely popular keyboard instruments in the United States, stable in the climate. It was used in grands from 1843 by Chickering (founded in Boston, 1823) and then by Steinway, making possible the heavier hammers, and thicker strings requiring greater tension to reach their pitch, which has led to the characteristic modern sound of the piano: emphasizing the fundamentals, less coloured by partials than previously, and in a concert soloist's fortissimo deafening at three metres away. Of the previous era, a seven-octave grand of 1851 by Érard, up to that time a favourite maker among international soloists, is cited as having borne a total tension of 12 tons (12,200 kg.) weight—the date is two years after the death of Chopin, who had mostly performed on pianos by Érard or especially Pleyel (founded in Paris, 1807). Most instruments then would have had a wooden frame strengthened in the older method (long retained by Broadwood) by iron braces separately bolted on. By contrast, a Steinway grand of 1856 could reach 16 tons, and over 20 tons today.

Pl. 1. Grand piano by Johann Andreas Stein (Augsburg, 1788).

The American technology, along with its advanced industrial methods, was quickly followed by makers that had newly arisen in Germany, notably Bechstein (Berlin) and Blüthner (Leipzig), both founded in the same year, 1856, that Steinway set up in New York, having emigrated from Germany three years before (his original firm, Steinweg, in 1869 becoming Grotrian, later Steinway–Grotrian). Also, among the older firms, Bösendorfer, the great maker in Vienna (founded 1828), began making pianos similarly strengthened, on which Liszt found he could safely play up to as loud as he was able; and the Paris makers too, though managing to preserve that lightness and colourful clarity which still distinguishes the sound of the best French pianos (Pleyel's now manufactured in Brunswick, Germany, by Schimmel).

(b) *The strings.* Pianos have long been 'overstrung': in grands, those of the bottom two octaves or so slant back towards the right on a higher level than the rest slanting to the left—a method due first to Pape in Paris, 1828, for small uprights, and becoming normal for grands by the 1860s. Besides saving overall length, it can develop the sound in the bass through bringing the bridge for the low notes more into the main resonance area of the soundboard. This, of spruce nearly 1 cm. thick and barred underneath, is put on slightly arched, to support the pressure from the strings upon the thick maple bridge; with age the soundboard tends to flatten out, disturbing the balance of pressure over the compass, whereby an old piano may have lost some of its tone.

The strings, of steel, are for the lowest octave single, overwound (except at the two ends) with copper or brass wire (see STRINGED INSTRUMENTS, 1), making them up to 7 mm. ($\frac{1}{4}''$) in visible thickness. The next octave or so, also overwound, is bichord (two strings per note). Upwards from this they are trichord, of plain wire, down to 0.85 mm. in diameter for the highest notes: three strings being used since a thin string gives purer vibration than a thicker and three together give the requisite power—also a slight dis-tuning which, unnoticeable consciously, renders the sound more interesting to the ear. For 'stretched octaves' arrived at in tuning the extreme octaves of the compass, see PARTIALS, 5 (inharmonicity).

The strings are usually led to the tuning pins through holes in a metal block or 'agraffe' (from Fr.: *agrafe*, 'clasp') for each note, to hold them down as a precaution against their lifting under the blow of the hammer, spoiling the tone. Alternatively a long 'capo d'astro' bar (from *capotasto*) may press down on all strings (with an effect anticipated by Cristofori where in some instances he fitted the wrest plank and nut upside down). There have also been various schemes by Steinway (see DUPLEX) and others for proportioning the short lengths of string beyond the bridge to the main sounding length, for any residual vibration in these portions (otherwise damped with a felt strip) to lend support to partials of the note itself. 'Aliquot scaling' (Blüthner) adds in the trichord registers a fourth string to each note, running higher than the others and not touched by the hammer, in order to vibrate sympathetically; through the top of the compass it is tuned in unison with the others, and in the lower regions to the octave higher.

(c) *Hammers.* Originally of leather over wood, these are now of compressed merino wool felt, delicately 'toned' by pricking with a needle. Usually they strike at a little under one-eighth of the string-length to give best suppression of partials such as the 7th and 9th, which do not match the intervals of the common chord.

5. *The Pedals:* (a) *Soft pedal.* In grand pianos, this shifts the keyboard and action, usually to the right, so that where there are two or three strings per note, one of them is missed by the hammer— though it may contribute sympathetic vibration via the bridge. (The term '*una corda*' for use of this pedal dates from times when pianos were bichord throughout.) In uprights the pedal moves the hammers to a position closer to the strings for a 'half throw' giving a softer blow.

(b) *Sustaining pedal* (to pianists 'the pedal'; popularly 'loud pedal'). For the right foot, raising all dampers together. The most important pedal by far. Introduced by Broadwood, 1783, to replace an earlier hand stop, it forms an essential part of the piano's expressive equipment: a trained pianist has the foot over it all the time. Any note played is given longer duration without the finger necessarily remaining on the key, allowing beautiful effects that the hands could not otherwise encompass. Moreover, when notes are played with the pedal down, other strings are free to resonate in sympathy (Debussy exploited the 'washes of colour' from unstruck strings); and especially when playing lower notes (having many notes above them which can vibrate in sympathy) the tone becomes much fuller, though the effect of the pedal is used as much in soft passages as in loud.

In most styles of music it is important, of course, to release the pedal and press it afresh at a change of harmony, normally pressing it immediately *after* a chord is played (impact sounds, as the notes are struck, not then being picked up by other strings). When 'Ped.' is marked in the music and is countermanded by an asterisk or ✱ , it does not always follow that the pedal may not be released between the two signs, the player, through constant and careful listening, using discretion according to the harmony. In the words of the great Anton Rubinstein (1830–94), 'The more I play, the more I am convinced that the pedal is the soul of the piano.'

'Half-pedalling': on the low notes the dampers do not quench vibration as immediately as they do on higher notes, so that if, having played notes in the bass, the pedal is quickly released and pressed again, those strings continue to sound almost as though the damper had not touched them, while notes higher up are separated.

(c) *Sostenuto pedal.* A third pedal, between the other two, regularly present on American pianos since perfected by Steinway in 1874, and now also on most large grands made elsewhere. When pressed, it holds up until it is released any dampers that the fingers have already lifted. Such notes then continue to sound after other notes are struck, so that one can hold, for example, a bass note or chord while both hands play changing harmonies above (and offering far more scope than 'half-pedalling'). It is especially useful in Impressionist and later styles of music (Debussy, however, did not have it) and may also be used in conjunction with the sustaining pedal. An illustration of its effects is Ex. 1, from Berio's *Sequenza IV* for piano. Its first known use was in some French pianos of the mid-19th century.

(d) *Practice pedal.* Often now found as the third pedal in place of the above, on both grands and uprights, this moves a long strip of soft material into a position between the hammers and the strings, muting these while still allowing the main pedal to be used with some effect.

6. *Touch.* This refers (a) to the force of resistance of the keys to the fingers (in better makes of pianos graduated to some 15 per cent less in the treble than in the bass; some pianists prefer a stronger resistance than others); or (b) as where a pianist is said to possess a 'beautiful touch', with the suggestion of more than a great artist's control of shades of loudness (physically dependent upon the velocity given to each key at the lowest point of its travel), but beyond this through some ineffable

power of expressive control experienced but seemingly impossible to explain in purely mechanical terms. Percy Scholes has cited the experiment of repeating a chord many times (with the pedal down) gradually from very soft to very loud, first 'with the utmost rigidity of arms and fingers, and then with the utmost suppleness of all these parts: in the first instance the tone will be found to be hard and harsh, and in the second to be round and pleasant'. If a difference is apparent at these extremes, then other differences in tonal effect, down to the most minute, should be subtly communicable in the pianist's habitual ways of playing. One tentative suggestion has been that the manner of pressing down the keys may exert some direct effect upon the vibration of the soundboard.

7. *Piano actions:* (a) *Cristofori.* Piano actions can be difficult to follow with diagrams (one needs the 'action models' which museums and piano firms often possess, Pl. 2); Fig. 1, however, illustrates the action of Cristofori's 1726 piano (Silbermann's action in pianos at Potsdam being practically the same). The squared top of the upright jack pushes up the corner of the padded block on the underside of an 'intermediate lever', hinged with leather (on the left as shown). This lever accelerates the hammer by throwing it up from the butt end (right). When the key-end is fully 'up' (and the hammer continues the remaining distance free), the corner of the block, moving in an arc centered on the hinge of the lever, has moved away from the tip of the jack which follows an opposite arc centred at the 'balance pin' of the key. The finger remaining on the key, the block then drops, missing the top of the jack and allowing the hammer to fall the requisite distance below the strings (and be

Ex. 1. New resonances from the sustaining pedal: the opening of *Sequenza IV* for piano by Luciano Berio.

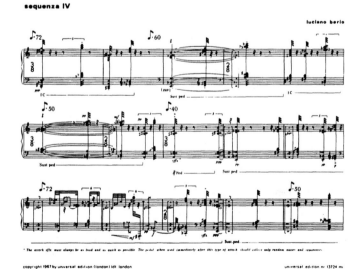

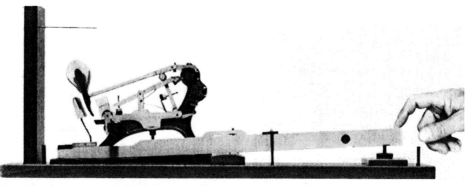

Pl. 2. Grand piano action model (Steinway and Son).

held steady by the check, raised by the key). On lifting the finger from the key, all parts must descend to their rest positions ready for the note to be repeated: but the top of the jack would be obstructed by the corner of the block in its lowered position. The jack is therefore pivoted to tilt (to the right in the figure) to get past, after which it is straightened up again by a spring.

The moment when the two arcs 'miss' is regulated by bending the wire which holds the 'set-off' pad (not marked in Fig. 1).

(b) *Modern.* The grand piano actions derive from Érard's as patented in 1821. Fig. 2 shows one of the several designs. The intermediate lever (again pivoted on the left in the figure and here with a stronger and more complex shape) is raised directly by the key (through a short 'pilot') and the escapement is situated above it. This is the right-angled knee-shaped lever with its shorter leg under the adjustable set-off button. The longer leg, marked 'escapement', is a square wooden rod which pushes against a roller mounted on the underside of the hammer shaft, to raise the hammer up to the point of free travel. The escapement is then jerked aside by the set-off button, so that as the hammer falls the roller drops on to the repetition lever. This is formed of two rails with a space between them in

which the jack can move. If the finger then allows the key to rise by no more than half-way, the top of the escapement springs back beneath the roller so that on then pressing the key right down the hammer strikes again. In this way a note can be repeated without having to press the key the whole distance twice, making possible (especially with the heavier hammers that are used) a faster repetition.

(c) *Upright piano.* Fig. 3 shows a modern upright piano, with the 'tape check' (Wornum, 1842) which corresponds in function in some ways to the repetition action in a grand. Long out of date are the old 'sticker' uprights favourite in Britain up to at least the 1860s: the escapement, with a short intermediate lever, here connects with the hammer high above by means of a tall wooden stick.

8. *Two historic actions: (a) English grand action* (Fig. 4). Developed by Broadwood in collaboration with Backers from Germany and Stodart from Scotland, first for squares and for grands from *c.*1780. The jack or 'hopper' acts directly on a step in the leathered butt of the hammer (there being no intermediate lever between). The hopper is shaped with a projecting slope halfway down, by which, on the rise, it is deflected by the set-off button for

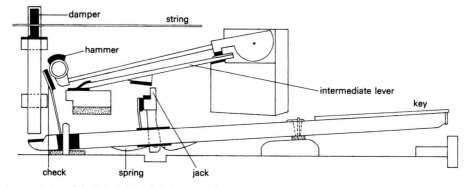

Fig. 1. Action of the Leipzig Cristofori piano, 1726.

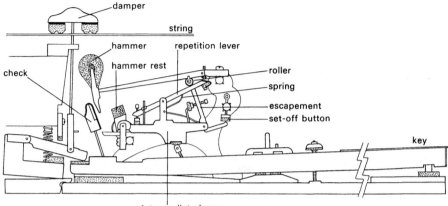

Fig. 2. Action of a modern grand piano.

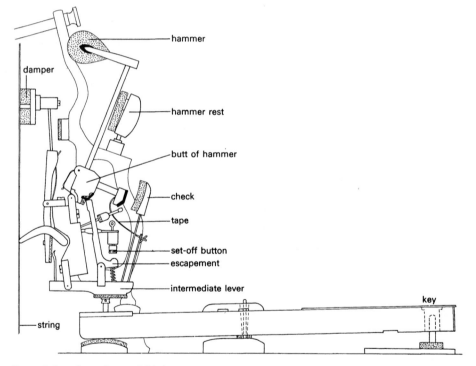

Fig. 3. Action of a modern upright piano.

the hammer, after it has struck and while the key is held by the finger, to fall on the check raised by the key. On release of the key, the check and hammer further descend, along with the hopper which is then, by a spring, brought back to its initial position under the butt of the hammer. A model of efficient simplicity, the action and pianos fitted with it were compared in certain respects favourably, by leading players and composers of the classical period, with the contemporary Viennese pianos. Among later improvements, John Geib was one who embodied an intermediate lever corresponding to Cristofori's.

(*b*) *Viennese action* (Fig. 5). This differs from others in that the hammer is mounted on the end of the key itself and faces towards the player. Developed from the earlier German square piano action by

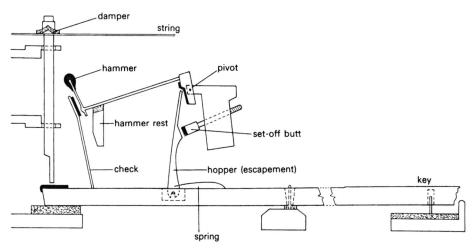

Fig. 4. Action of an English grand piano, *c.* 1790.

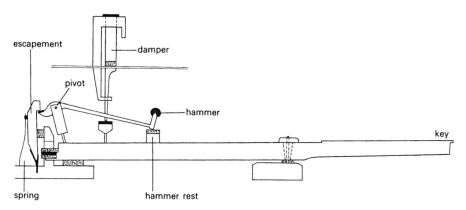

Fig. 5. Action of a south German/Viennese piano, 1780.

(from *c.*1773) adding an escapement, it was employed, with further modifications, in pianos listed by Bösendorfer up to 1909, and is today made again in replicas of instruments by Andreas Stein (d. 1792) and by Walter (d. 1826) and Graf (d. 1851). When the key is pressed, the beak-like hammer butt is caught by the notch in the upright escapement, flinging up the hammer head. Just as this is to continue free to strike, the arc of movement of the beak (the key end having risen) clears the notch for the hammer to fall, while the key is still held, upon the soft-padded rest (there being no other 'check'). When the key is released, lowering the hammer pivot, the beak, in order to retrace its arc and get past the face of the escapement, moves this aside on the leather hinge at the bottom, following which a spring returns it to bring the notch once more above the beak.

Original pianos of both of these types, English and Viennese, may include the amusing 'Janissary

stop' for very effectively rendering the percussion of '*Turkish music'. The pedal, when engaged by the stop, is pressed in march time with the music, operating a mechanism to thump the bottom of the soundboard with a drumstick ('bass drum'), drop metal rods on to the bass strings ('cymbals'), and strike on one or two little fixed bells ('triangle'). (See Mobbs 1984.)

9. *Compass.* The progressive widening of the compass (and thus of the possible range of compositions for the piano) is summarized below, only roughly, however, since increases have been by no means uniform among makers, of the older periods especially:

1720s (Cristofori): 4 octaves, C to *c'''* (in one case to *f'''*)

1760–90: 5 octaves, F' to *f'''* (Mozart)

1790–1820: 5½ octaves, F' to *c''''* (as Beethoven in sonatas prior to 'Hammerclavier' (1818))

1820–50: 6½ octaves, C' to f'''' (Chopin)
1850– : 7 octaves, A'' to a''''; or by 1860 to c'''''

There are instances in Beethoven's earlier works where a high passage reappears in a different key in an altered form as though the composer had run out of notes at the top. Some editors have (as Liszt did) altered the passage accordingly, though discretion is necessary, where for example the composer's reshaping has introduced some fresh effect that should not be sacrificed.

10. *Repertory.* For a brief account of this huge corpus composers are mentioned for the most part in order of birth date. Chamber music and songs with piano are omitted (though containing some of the finest writing for the instrument).

Haydn (1732). Some 14 concertos (for '*clavier*'), 50 sonatas (1760–94).

Mozart (1756). 21 concertos (1773–91), two concert rondos, solo works (from 1762) incl. 22 sonatas (1774–87).

Dussek (1760). Concertos; sonatas, rondos, variations.

Beethoven (1770). *1st period, to c.1802.* Concertos Nos. 1 to 3, sonatas up to Op. 31, among them the 'Pathétique' (*c.*1798) and the so-called 'Moonlight' (1801). *2nd period, to 1812.* Concertos Nos. 4 and 5 ('The Emperor'), sonatas including the 'Waldstein' and 'Appassionata' (1804), 'Les Adieux' (1809). *3rd period.* The 'Hammerclavier', the last five sonatas, the 'Diabelli Viariations' (1823).

Hummel (1778). 5 concertos, some 80 various solo works.

Field (1782). 7 concertos (from 1799), 4 sonatas, and the Nocturnes (publ. 1812–36).

Weber (1786). Conzertstücke with orch. (1821), solos incl. 4 sonatas (from 1812).

Schubert (1797). Sonatas (from 1815; the last three of 1828). Moments musicaux, impromptus. Also duets, as Fantasie in F minor (1828).

Mendelssohn (1809). Songs without words (books 1829–45).

Chopin (1810). 2 concertos (1829–30), polonaises, mazurkas, waltzes, preludes, ballades (the '4 great Ballades', 1832–42), fantasies, studies.

Schumann (1810). Concerto (1845), Carnaval (1835), Fantasiestücke, Novelleten, Études symphoniques (1834), Kinderscenen, etc.

Liszt (1811). 2 concertos (from 1839, later revised), sonata, ballades, polonaises, Hungarian rhapsodies (from 1846), and numerous transcriptions of works by other composers.

Alkan (1813). Études (1848, 1857).

Franck (1822). Variations symphoniques, with orch. (1885), solo works from 1842.

Brahms (1833). 2 concertos (1858, 1881), sonatas (from 1853), ballads, capriccios, intermezzi; variations on themes of older composers, incl. for 2 pianos, on a Theme by Haydn (1873).

Saint-Saëns (1835). 5 concertos (1858–95), solo works incl. Études (up to 1919).

Balakirev (1837). 2 concertos, mazurkas, waltzes.

Grieg (1843). Concerto (1868), lyric pieces, 10 books (1867–1901), Norwegian dances (1902).

Fauré (1845). Fantaisie, with orch. (1918), impromptus (1883–1910, with whole-tone experiment from the 5th, of 1909), nocturnes (esp. the later, 1908–21).

Albéniz (1860). Iberia (4 books, from 1906).

Debussy (1862). Images (1905, 1907), preludes (2 books, 1910–13), etc.

Busoni (1866). Concerto (orch. and male choir, 1904), many solo works incl. Fantasia contrappuntistica (1910–12, on an unfinished fugue of Bach).

Granados (1867). Danzas españolas (from 1892), Goyescas (1911).

Skriabin (1872). Preludes, poems, etc. (from 1892).

Rakhmaninov (1873). 4 concertos (from 1891; in C minor, 1901), Rhapsody on a Theme by Paganini (1934), preludes (Prelude in C♯ minor, 1892, and further sets from 1901).

Ives (1874). 2 sonatas (to 1915).

Schoenberg (1874). Concerto (1942), solo pieces (atonal from 1908) incl. 6 Little Piano Pieces (1911), Piano Suite (serial, 1923).

Ravel (1875). Concerto for the left hand (1921), Le Tombeau de Couperin (1917, later orchestrated), etc.

Falla (1876). 'Nights in the Gardens of Spain', with orch. (1904–15); 4 Spanish pieces (1908).

Ireland (1879). Concerto (1930), preludes, etc.

Medtner (1880). 3 concertos, 5 sonatas, sets of Fairy Tales (1805–20), Forgotten Memories, etc.

Bartók (1881). 3 concertos (1926–45), studies (1918), sonata (1926), Mikrocosmos (graded studies, 6 books, 1926–37).

Turina (1882). Pieces (with Spanish titles, 1909–40).

Szymanowski (1882). Symphonie concertante, with orch. (1932); 3 sonatas (1904–17), Métopes (1915).

Webern (1883). Piano variations (1936), short serial pieces.

Villa-Lobos (1887). Works from 1908.

Prokofiev (1891). 5 concertos (1912–32), 9 sonatas (1909–44), Visions fugitives (1917).

Milhaud (1892). 2 sonatas, several sets of pieces.

Cowell (1897). Concerto, sonatas, 'Banshee' (with the fingers on the strings inside the piano, 1925).

Poulenc (1899). Concerto (1949), movements perpetuels (1918), numerous works up to Intermezzo in A♭ (1944).

Copland (1900). Concerto (1926), Piano Variations (1930), other solo pieces (1920–48).

Shostakovitch (1906). Concertos (1933, 1957), sonatas from 1926.

Messiaen (1908). Réveil des oiseaux, with orch. (1953), Vingt regards sur l'enfant Jésus (1944), Catalogue d'oiseaux (1958).

Cage (1912). Noted especially for inventing, 1938, use of the 'prepared piano', in which screws, rubber pads, etc. are inserted between the strings at specified distances along them, e.g. Bacchanale (1940), Music of Changes (1951).

Boulez (1925). 3 sonatas (1946–57), for 2 pianos, structures (1952, 1961).

Bilson 1980; Colt 1981; Dolge 1911; Ehrlich 1976; Gill 1981; Harding 1933, rev. 1978; Harris 1975; Hoover 1981; Pollens 1984, 1985; Wythe 1984.

Piano accordion. See ACCORDION, 5, 6.

Piatti (It.). *Cymbals.

Pibgorn. See HORNPIPE, 1.

Piccolo (Fr.: *petite flûte*; Ger.: *Kleine Flöte*; It.: *ottavino*; Sp.: *flautín*). Approximately half the length of the *flute and sounding an octave higher than written. The same Boehm mechanism is fitted, save for the absence of a foot-joint: the bottom note is *d′* (sounding *d″*). It is made either in metal with the cylindrical bore of the flute (reduced to *c*.11 mm.), or more usually in wood with conical bore and sometimes a metal head joint (see FLUTE, Pl. 1*a*). In the older orchestral works the piccolo has a primary role of doubling the flute or other instruments in the high octave above. This often leads to its exposure in extremely difficult passages, making piccolo playing a demanding specialized art, normally entrusted to the third member of the orchestral flute section. But there are also works that require two piccolos, like the well-known 'Menuet des Follets' in Berlioz's *La damnation de Faust*, and some works requiring three. Every orchestral flute-player therefore has a piccolo available.

Later orchestration has often used the piccolo for the small, 'innocent' tone-character of its lower and middle compass; extended examples are in Shostakovitch's symphonies such as the Fourth. Nor should one overlook the pleasure so often given by instruments in their lighter vein, as in the popular piccolo duets of the 'Two Little Finches' type, often heard with band accompaniment.

Examples of the 18th-century piccolo with one key are rather scarce. Corette, in 1740, noticed its cheerful effect in dance movements, as in works of Rameau from 1735 onwards. Vivaldi, who wrote concertos for so many instruments, wrote three for *flautino*, which, from the compass employed, was certainly a piccolo, not a small recorder. (For 'flauto piccolo' in Handel, see FLAGEOLET, 3). Among later piccolos with four to six keys, it requires care to distinguish between the orchestral or 'concert' models and the more numerous piccolos made for bands and pitched a semitone or minor third higher, and roughly 29 cm. (11½″) and 27 cm. (10½″) long respectively (see FLUTE BAND).

Piccolo trumpet. See TRUMPET, 2*b*.

Picco pipe. A small *duct flute, now a collectors' piece, usually in boxwood, 9 cm. (3½″) long, with two holes in front and one underneath. It was sold in England from the late 1850s, following recitals by Picco, a blind Sardinian shepherd, on his own form of the instrument. A large compass is obtained, starting in the manner of an ocarina (opening the holes with the end closed by the other hand), and proceeding upwards in normal flute harmonics.

Piffaro (piffero, It.). A shawm, or some similar instrument accompanying a bagpipe (see, e.g., ZAMPOGNA). In the 16th to 17th centuries I *Piffari* were the band composed of shawms, cornetts, and trombones, corresponding to LES GRAND HAUTBOIS in France (see ÉCURIE), or 'Hoboys and Sackbuts' in England.

Pi-nai (*pī*). Double-reed wind instrument of Thailand, differing from all other such instruments (save for a relative in Kampuchea) in its stout body, bulging in the middle, widening a little at each end, but with no bell at all. Around 41 cm. (16″) in length, it is turned in a dark hardwood, with faint rings along the bulge. The six fingerholes are grouped four plus two, yet are fingered with three fingers of each hand. The bore is narrowly conical, and the reed, placed on a staple, is made of palm-leaf (see REED, 5). Its penetrating sound over two octaves or more is heard, along with xylophones (see RANAT), gong chimes, and drums, in the *piphat* ensemble (see SOUTH-EAST ASIA, Ex. 1).

Also in Thailand are instruments also named *pi* but with a bell, and more like shawm-like instruments of elsewhere in southern and eastern Asia.

Pincullo. Cane *duct flute (a 'block flute', recorder principle) of Andean countries of South America, especially northern Chile and Peru, where it approaches the notched flute *quena in popularity. From 30 cm. (12″) upward, it has usually six holes and thumb-hole, and is often played with drums. There are various regional forms, and in Ecuador it can be a tabor pipe (see PIPE AND TABOR).

Piob mhór. Great Highland bagpipe; see BAGPIPE, 2*a*.

Pipa (or *p'i p'a*, pron. 'piba'). Chinese lute: a large 'short-necked' lute (see LUTE, 7*a*) in contrast with the 'long lute' *sanxian*, and one of the most played of Chinese stringed instruments. Very shallow body (Fig. 1) and neck in one piece, with the belly of paulownia wood, today usually with a small soundhole concealed by the bridge.

Four strings, silk, or now nylon overwound with wire, are tuned in the pattern *a e d A*. The frets start with six wooden ridges, each topped with a thin bone or ivory strip; beyond these are tall frets of bamboo, glued on and diminishing in height

Fig. 1.

towards the bridge, typically 25 (taking the first string up to e′′′). The principal frets extend well to the sides of the strings to enable a left-hand finger to pull them sideways to 'bend' the note upwards by as much as a major third. For a special effect the first two strings may be thus pulled together, making a rising glissando chord.

With the *pipa* almost vertical on the knees, the right hand uses, rather than the older axe-shaped plectrum, individual finger-picks, for the thumb included. The music is mainly on the upper two strings, plucked very much (though by no means all the time) in tremolando fashion using all five right-hand fingers in rapid succession, while the hand moves up and down towards the bridge to change the sound from hard and forceful to clear and placid. Meanwhile strong, abrupt sounds from the lower strings are frequently interjected for dramatic effect, music for the *pipa* being chiefly programmatic.

As well as modern compositions, the *pipa* has music written in notations back to the 18th century, some of it preserving pieces which go back centuries earlier. They are 'martial' or 'gentle'. A famous martial piece describes a historic battle of 202 BC, rendering clashing swords, gunfire (striking the lute's belly), drums, and finally the suicide of the defeated warlord. A gentle piece may contain portrayal of the sound of the wind through the reeds, of the sea, or of a distant flute: in all, perpetuating an ancient tradition of providing poetic or narrative entertainment on a musical instrument without dependence on tunes, dance-rhythms, and the like.

The *pipa* came to China during the 2nd century BC from Central Asia, perhaps there originally from Persia. It then for a long time, as seen in pictures, had a turned-back pegbox (rather as the Arab lute), and many features since preserved in the **biwa* of Japan (such as the original four ridges along the neck, few further frets, and a plectrum technique), and in the *dan ti-pa* of Vietnam.

Pipe and tabor. A pipe and a drum played together by one person, the pipe played by the left hand, the drum hanging from the left arm for beating with the right hand. The combination belongs chiefly to western Europe, played for folk dances from southern Spain and neighbouring parts of Portugal, to the Basque regions, the Balearic Islands, Provence in France (Pl. 1), and (up to about 1900) in southern England for the Morris dances in which it is now revived. In the Americas it is popular especially in rural Mexico, introduced by the Spaniards.

1. *The pipe*. This is a **duct flute like a **flageolet but with three holes only, two in front near the lower end and one for the thumb higher up on the back. With these, a high compass of over two octaves is obtainable with one hand only, ignoring the fundamentals (which anyhow would not carry outdoors) and starting the scale on the 2nd harmonics (Ex. 1). The lower end of the pipe can be gripped between the two smallest fingers of this hand. A popular model in Britain today is a 'Generation' metal flageolet in D manufactured with the holes of a tabor pipe.

Ex. 1.

The English Morris pipe (of which reproductions are made) stood in this key: 30.5 cm. (12″) long, in two joints, with bore c.8.5 mm. In some Oxfordshire villages it was considered important for the Morris to be played on pipe and tabor even if country dances were played on violin or concertina. Among the tunes for the Morris were 'Shepherd's Hey', 'Constant Billy' 'Three Meet', and 'Highland Mary'. The Provençal pipe, *galoubet*, resembles the English and is heard especially in the autumn *farandoles* danced through the vineyards (in Pl. 1, however, celebrating an anniversary of the birth of the poet Mistral). Bizet quotes one of the tunes (on piccolo) in his *L'Arlésienne* suite. In Catalonia the leader of the *sardana* bands plays a very small pipe, with a very small drum to match (see COBLA). The Basque tabor pipe (*txistu*, pron. 'chistu') as played in bands of taborers is stoutly built, around 42 cm. (16″) long, with metal mouthpiece and lip, and bound with metal rings. With it goes a bass pipe (*silbote*, 'big whistle'), 63 cm. (25″) long and a fifth deeper, this played without a tabor (the right hand holding the end of the pipe).

Through the Renaissance period pipes of many sizes were in use: the largest of three found in the 1545 wreck of the **Mary Rose* is 80 cm. (31½″) long, as if to sound a scale about an octave and a half lower than Ex. 1, i.e. starting on a′ in the treble voice range (Palmer 1983).

2. *The tabor* (in England pronounced 'tabber'). This traditionally resembles a side-drum in having two heads and a gut snare. Most are fairly small (the English 23 cm. (9″) in diameter), but the Provençal *tambourin* has a shell up to 77 cm. (30″) deep, and the snare lies across the upper drumskin; the player beats on the centre of this snare (Pl. 1), giving to it a strong vibration which sustains the sound between one stroke of the stick and the next, almost as if it were a drone. In medieval pictures, in England and Flanders also, one sees the player

Pl. 1. *Tambourinaires* leading a procession, France, Alpes Maritimes (see text). Photo: *Nice Matin*, 1 Sept. 1980.

striking on the snare in this way (see MEDIEVAL INSTRUMENTS, Pl. 1, here without the pipe).

One notes that, although one might think the pipe is more difficult to play than the drum, it is the latter which occupies the right hand, as if felt to be the primary component in the music, giving the time to the dancers. From the Middle Ages (when the pipe and tabor were heard in all ranks of society) up to today in France the player is named from the drum—'taborer' (Fr.: *tambourinaire*)—while tunes in pipe-and-tabor style by Rameau and others are entitled *tambourins*. The earliest apparent mention, in the late 13th-century treatise of Aegidius of Zamora (Spain), tells how a *tympanum* ('drum') makes sweeter music when joined with a *fistula* ('pipe').

Some of the French Basques use, instead of the drum, the *tambourin à cordes*, *tambourin de Béarn*, or 'string drum' (locally *tun-tun*): a long wooden soundbox with five or six thick gut strings hit with a short thick stick. The strings are tuned to the keynote of the pipe and its dominant (compare the drones of a *hurdy-gurdy and of many *bagpipes).

P'iri. The Korean reed instrument corresponding to the Chinese *guan and the related Japanese *hichiriki*: a cylindrical bamboo pipe 23 to 28 cm. (9″–11″) long with seven holes plus one on the back, and sounded with a large double reed (a *cylindrical oboe). The principal instrument of the court orchestra, it has a loud, brash sound, capable of great subtlety in dynamics and expressive portamento. The standard *p'iri* used is the *hyang-p'iri* ('native p'iri'; see CHINA AND KOREA, Pl. 2, back row, centre). The *T'ang-p'iri* ('Tang' or 'Chinese p'iri'), rather thicker, and used for certain court orchestral pieces, has a compass extended by a few notes produced as flat *overblown twelfths. The *se-p'iri* ('thin p'iri') is like the *hyang-p'iri* but of smaller diameter (hence softer), and is used in court chamber music.

Pirouette (from Fr.). With certain older double-reed wind instruments, as the *shawm, a detachable round wooden component placed into the top of the instrument, surrounding the base of the reed. An English name was 'flue' (*Talbot). See SHAWM, Fig. 1.

Pitch. The pitch of a sound is the number of times that its vibration cycle repeats per second. With a bumblebee, or aircraft overhead, or even on blowing one's nose, the pitch may be identified by humming the note and then finding it on the piano (though a practising musician will often be able to tell it straight off—an ability roughly described as 'perfect pitch'). Music needs a standard reference pitch enabling instruments to be used together: 'concert pitch' or 'playing pitch' (stated in cycles per second or Hz, see HERTZ) of a chosen note, usually the A above Middle C (a', or by the French-American system A4, see Introduction) but with keyboards in some cases the C above this is preferred. The 'A' is carried about by a *tuning-fork or *pitch-pipe; in an orchestra it is given out by the oboe (among wind instruments one of the least affected by temperature change), or, less frequently, by a metal tuning-bar struck with a beater, or by electronic means, though the last is apt to prove irksome and tiring to musicians' ears. Widely used in other circumstances are portable electronic 'chromatic turners' as made by Korg and other Japanese firms. Around 20 cm. long (8″), they are battery- or mains-powered and have an earphone socket. A switch changes between 'meter' and 'sound'. On 'meter' the note from the instrument being tested is received through an incorporated microphone or input lead. The dial is set to the required note of the chromatic scale, in the relevant octave as selected by another switch. The dial shows, both in cents and in frequencies (Hz), deviations up to a semitone each way; if beyond this, the dial is reset to the next semitone. On 'sound', to give out a pitch-signal, the note is set as before; it can be adjusted to other than standard pitch by a tuner button.

1. *Modern pitch*. The present International Standard Pitch is $a' = 440$ Hz, agreed at a conference held in May 1939. Prior to that the general standard was $a' = 435$, a fifth of a semitone lower, except in Britain where it was $a' = 439$, virtually the same as the modern. One might have hoped that, once agreed, $a' = 440$ would remain strictly adhered to, but there has always been a tendency for pitch to rise, due to a number of factors: a soloist may feel that an extra brightness of effect may be gained if the delivery be fractionally sharp to the accompaniment (within, of course, the tolerance of the ear's ability to identify pitch); or the strings of an orchestra may tune on the sharp side in anticipation of the woodwind becoming sharper as the performance proceeds. It is said that in Berlin pianos for concert performance may be tuned as high as $a' = 450$, while some German manufacturers of wind instruments have been obliged to tune their instruments to $a' = 446$ (or above) to keep in step.

2. *Historical pitches*. Over the last five centuries—so far as early values can be estimated from old forks, organs, and other wind instruments—tuning pitch has varied, in the main, over a range of about three semitones, a' varying from as low as our present g' up to the present bb' or even above; this is not a great deal considering the time span. Seldom has any pitch ruled completely for all places and in all circumstances; yet musicians, as they have travelled from country to country, tended to bring some measure of uniformity in ensemble pitch lasting in some cases over fairly long periods between others of instability and change.

The 18th century at first knew especially a French concert pitch up to a whole tone lower than the modern standard, in the region of 392–409 for a'. Thus recorders made in London by Bressan, who had come from France before 1700, can be nearly a whole tone below modern pitch. Largely through French influence on baroque woodwind-making, this pitch became known in Germany as 'low *Cammerton*', or 'French' or 'opera pitch', in some sources by the 1730s, described as about a semitone below *Cammerton. For this last, preserved tuning forks and wind instruments point to the region of 410 to 420 as a general baroque ensemble pitch and on through the period of Mozart (for a full discussion, see Haynes 1985). Modern performances of 18th-century music have widely used a pitch of $a' = 415$, a semitone below modern and enabling keyboard players to make a clean transposition of a semitone downwards should the instrument be tuned to modern pitch. Yet it can often prove too high or too low for original woodwind and many makers now offer alternative pitches.

There were also higher baroque pitches, as among organs in Germany (where J. S. Bach frequently had to write the *continuo part lower than the orchestral parts for the two to agree) and among organs built in England by makers from Germany. Italian performing pitches, too, were said to be high, the Venetian, according to Quantz (writing in 1752), nearly a tone above German *Cammerton*. Such pitches seem to have been inherited from times back to the 16th century, reaching (to judge from original wind instruments) into the 460s or even higher for a', a semitone above modern.

3. *The 19th-century rise in pitch*. By 1820 European concert pitches had begun to shoot rapidly upwards, reaching by 1830, alike in Paris, London, and Vienna, the region of $a' = 440$, with further rises soon to follow. Among possible causes: trends to sharpness among soloists, especially in the larger halls and before the more popular audiences; and certainly the vast expansion of military bands (players from which frequently manned the orchestras) with their tendency, especially out of doors, to play sharp for brilliant effect, in turn bearing influence on the instrument-makers.

Already in 1834 J. H. Scheibler, a leading German scientist on pitch matters, recommended a standard of $a' = 440$ arrived at by averaging out the tunings of grand pianos in Vienna. But further rises up to the 453 region through the 1850s brought directors of theatres and conservatories from all over Europe to co-operate, sending forks and comments to a commission in Paris which in 1859 decided upon $a' = 435$, the famous *diapason normal* ('standard pitch') already mentioned. It came too late, however, for immediate universal acceptance. At Covent Garden in 1879 the organ had to be raised from 441 to 446 since it was impossible to get the woodwind to play any lower and singers too objected to any lowering. The general outcome was a polarization of pitch into 'low' and 'high', the 'low' being the *diapason normal* (confirmed by a conference in Vienna in 1885), the 'high' where circumstances or economics forbade a lowering, and in military bands. In Britain from the 1870s the 'high' or 'sharp' pitch lay at or near $a' = 452$, both for the Philharmonic concerts and for the British Army. The low pitch came only by degrees to replace it, from around 1890, and similarly in the USA. Up to 1930 many provincial British orchestras were still playing at sharp pitch, and a woodwind player taking an engagement outside his habitual orbit would require instruction as to which of his instruments to take, flat pitch or sharp, the wrong one being impossible to use. Many brass bands held to sharp pitch up to well after the Second World War, when eventually the expense of procuring flat-pitch instruments should be faced in order for a band to take part in contests (involving massed bands) along with others which had already made the change.

Ellis 1880; Haynes 1985; Mendel 1968; Thomas and Rhodes 1971.

Pitch-pipe. 1. A small wooden pipe of square section, about 45 cm. (18″) long, with a whistle mouthpiece, much used during the 18th and 19th centuries. It has a leather-covered wooden stopper that can be pushed in and out to give the church choir the note to begin.

2. The reed pitch-pipe was popular in the 19th century as 'Eardsley's Patent Chromatic Pitchpipe'. It consists of a small cylindrical metal case (about 5 cm. (2″) long) enclosing a *free reed, the vibrating length of which is adjustable by means of a cam on which are marked the names of the notes. Such instruments may still be obtainable. Sets of separate small metal free-reed tuners, each tuned to a different note, have also been made. The *tuning-fork is, however, the most reliable pocket indicator of pitch that has yet been made.

Pito (Sp., 'a pipe'). A name for folk flutes, as in Spain for a tabor pipe (see PIPE AND TABOR); in Central America for a duct or a transverse flute; also in Colombia, a *reedpipe of the rare transversely blown kind.

Piva. See BAGPIPE, 4.

Pizzicato (It., 'plucked', abbreviation 'pizz.'). On bowed string instruments, plucking the strings instead of bowing. Its earliest-known specification in violin music is by Monteverdi, in his *Il combattimento di Tancredi e Clorinda* (1624), where he writes 'here the bow is laid aside and the strings are plucked with two fingers'. However, an earlier use of pizzicato, called 'thump', and other special effects occur in music by composers of the English

viol school, for example in Tobias Hume's *The First Part of Ayres* (1605).

Different varieties of pizzicato called for in later music include the left-hand pizzicato (often indicated by a cross), used extensively by Paganini, by which the player bows one string while plucking another; the 'snap' pizzicato, indicated by the sign ↓ and used by Bartók in his string quartets (the string is pulled upwards and then allowed to snap back on to the fingerboard); and the pizzicato slide, also used by Bartók, where the left hand slides up or down the string that has been plucked.

Plagiaulos. See AULOS, 3.

Player-piano (pianola). Pneumatically operated upright piano. 'Pianola', the name commonly used in Britain, appears in the American patent of 1897 by Edwin S. Votey, for instruments marketed by the Aeolian Company. The mechanism was at first pushed up against an ordinary piano, then by 1901 was incorporated in the piano itself, and made so up to 1951.

Each piece of music is set out by punching holes and slots in a paper roll (cf. BARREL ORGAN, 5), which is held on two discs for placing into the opening in the front of the piano. The roll passes over a row of holes (usually 65 or 88) in a fixed brass plate or 'tracker bar' (Fig. 1) and is hooked on to the driving spool below. As a hole in the roll uncovers a hole in the plate, air is drawn through (by the foot bellows) to operate a valve which allows the suction to pass to a 'pneumatic' (a motor bellows). This then collapses (closes) to actuate the hammer mechanism. All the player need do with the hands is to move the tempo and volume

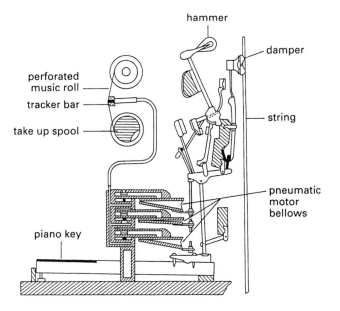

Fig. 1. A player-piano action showing pneumatic operating devices.

Ex. 1. Stravinsky, excerpt from *The Firebird* transcribed for player-piano.

controls, following an indicator line printed on the roll. It was said that in 1920, in America alone, 70 per cent of pianos manufactured were player-pianos. Catalogues of music rolls of classical and light music grew immense, and a roll, in its cardboard box, could often be exchanged for another on a library basis, saving space in the home.

A development from 1904, first by Welte and Sons in Germany, followed *c.*1911 by the Duo-Art system of the Aeolian company, was to record accurately on the roll the live performance of pianists, among them Rakhmaninov, Artur Rubinstein, Debussy, and Gershwin. Exact timing and duration of notes was recorded and, for dynamics, by electrical contacts, the hammer speed on the instant before (or sometimes after) striking, all to be intricately transferred to the paper roll. Only an acute critic might be able to tell, with eyes closed, the reproduced from the live. Many collections of such rolls, signed by the artists themselves, have been preserved in collections and sound archives.

Composition direct for the player-piano, transcending the limitations imposed by the mere ten fingers· of the hands, has been by Stravinsky (including an early version of *Les noces*), Malipiero, Hindemith, Casella, Goossens, Howells, and others. Chords of 30 or more notes can be used, and with all registers sounding at once (Ex. 1).

Recently the digital control of pianos from specially encoded magnetic tape cassettes has made possible further developments. Until· 1978 work had been restricted to the computer laboratory, but it is now possible to play an ordinary piano fitted with the necessary computer and tape interface and then have the piano replay the performance under the control of the tape. The first commercially available instrument operating on this principle is Superscope-Marantz's 'Pianocorder' introduced in the USA in 1978.

Ord-Hume 1984; Reblitz 1988.

Plectrum (or 'pick'). 1. Used with many stringed instruments to pluck the strings in place of the bare fingers. For the *mandolin, and when used on *guitar or *banjo, it is usually heart-shaped of tortoiseshell, plastic, etc. Formerly, from the Middle Ages to the 18th century, it was characteristically of a quill (e.g. from a wing feather of a goose or large bird of prey). Many folk and oriental instruments use plectrums of leather, bark, or wood—including the large axe-shaped wooden plectrum of the Japanese *shamisen*, in size if not in shape recalling the plectrum seen in use with the lyre in Greek vase paintings.

While a plectrum, from its normally hard material and pointed end, brings from the strings a bright and penetrating quality of sound (strong upper partials), it brings a limitation in that, when sounding several strings at the same time, no two strings can be struck without also sounding the string between them.

The finger pick is a slip of hard material attached to, or fitted into, a ring worn on the individual finger or thumb (or a metal point integral with the ring); other fingers can then sound other strings independently (for an example, see ZITHER, 1). Folk-guitarists often use such a pick, for instance to save wear on the thumb playing the bass notes, while beyond Europe there are instruments like the Near-Eastern *qanun* and the *koto* of Japan where one hand or both wear one or more such picks.

2. In a *harpsichord the 'plectra' are the small leather or quill points carried by the jacks to pluck the strings.

Pless-horn. See HUNTING HORN, 2.

Pluriarc. European name ('many bows') devised by the Swiss ethnologist G. Montandon in 1919 for a stringed instrument of Central and West Africa, with regional names *lukombe* (Central Africa), *nsambi* (Gabon to Angola), etc. The soundbox, hollowed in wood, has a flat soundboard nailed or lashed to the top. Up to eight flexible sticks (the 'bows') are tied in a recess under the soundbox, each leading to one end of a string of fibres (or now wire) fastened at the other end to the soundboard at the required tension. The instrument (Pl. 1) is placed across the knees with the bows pointing to the left. The right hand plucks near the soundboard with finger and thumb (armed with finger-stalls or finger-picks); the left hand damps the notes, for the melody to sound clearly. The player, with that keen African sense for sonorities, may move the right knee over the opening of the soundbox to vary the resonance. In some areas the instrument has been played especially at nightfall or on the night before a hunt.

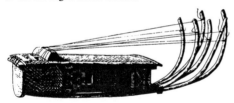

Pl. 1. Pluriarc, Central Africa (Ankermann 1901).

Pochette (Fr.). See KIT.

Polyfant (or poliphant, polyfon). A stringed instrument briefly described in several late 17th-century English sources. No example has been identified (nor any music asking for it) but it seems to have been some complicated kind of lute or *bandora, with, besides stopped strings, numerous unstopped short treble strings passing over the flanks of the body (see BANDURA).

Pommer (Ger.; 14th–15th-century *pumhart*, from Fr.: *bombarde*). The name given in Germany to each size of the *shawm family from the alto downwards (the treble being *Schalmey*).

Ponticello (It.). The bridge of a stringed instrument, especially those of the violin family, whence *sul ponticello*, 'on the bridge', i.e. to bow very close to the bridge. This diminishes the intensity of the

lower partials in favour of the higher, to produce a thin, remote quality, frequently demanded in violin music, in the orchestra included.

Portative organ. A medieval and early Renaissance type of organ (now often referred to simply as a 'portative'), small enough to be carried by a strap for playing while standing or walking (see MEDIEVAL INSTRUMENTS, Pl. 1). Only the right hand can play on the keys since the other has to pump the bellows from the opposite side (or more rarely underneath), the organ being held with the line of pipes pointing away from the body. As seen first in 13th-century pictures, there are two rows of pipes: open flue pipes, usually coloured white or silver and no doubt of tin. Each row has about eight pipes, of sizes that suggest a compass of about two octaves upwards from Middle C (but a wider compass later in the 14th century when the instruments are larger and heavier, and played on the knee or a table). No instrument survives, but reconstructions are now made based on pictures. The notes of the scale were evidently, at least in the earlier truly portable types, given alternately to the front and the back row of pipes, keeping the length of the instrument to a minimum. The keys, sometimes button-shaped, seem to be in two rows matching this, and to be played with two or three fingers of the hand, suggesting a single line of melody only. Problems arise in reconstruction over the wind supply in an organ as small and light as shown in the earlier pictures: how one hand may operate twin bellows, or space be found for an air reservoir.

Sometimes one sees at one end or the other of the rows of pipes a pair of pipes longer than the rest and partly encased in a model castle. One theory is that these could be fed directly from the air supply to sound a drone.

The portative, though obviously complex to make, was in fairly common use, with other instruments or on its own, for private music and dancing among the wealthier classes, and also possibly in church processions. It went out of use during the 15th century.

Portuguese guitar. See ENGLISH GUITAR, 3.

Posaune. Ger. *trombone (but at first, and in the Bible, 'trumpet').

Positions. With stringed instruments such as violin and guitar, on which the left hand is constantly shifted along the neck to make higher notes, the shifts are usually taught as 'positions'. The '1st position' is where the first finger stops the first note of the scale above the note of the open string; '2nd position' is where this same finger is moved up to stop the second note of the scale; and so on (see VIOLIN, 5b). In Tutors and studies, position changes may be marked by Roman numerals or other indications. Practised players, however, are likely to think less in terms of numbered positions than in which particular finger (not necessarily the first) will, when a shift is made, be making the first note so as best to bring the passage under the hand, and in particular cases will perhaps pencil the number of this finger in the music.

For reference, the 3rd position on the top string is where the first finger falls on: violin, *a''* (or viola, *d''*); cello, *d'*; double bass, *c'* (as written). In the 'half position' on these instruments the first finger falls on the semitone above the open string, though not on the cello, where this note is made by back extension of the full 1st position. Intermediate positions also enter, especially on the double bass.

Positive organ. An organ of about *chamber organ size often seen in a cathedral or other large church standing on the floor, usually in another part of the building from the main organ, for use on smaller occasions. 'Positive' is a relatively recent term adopted from German. (For Fr. *positif*, see ORGAN, 2*d*.)

Post horn (Fr.: *cornet de poste*; Ger.: *Posthorn*; It.: *cornetta di postiglione*). A brass instrument sounded originally by postboys riding horseback, then by the guards on mail coaches, to signal arrivals and departures. Music has frequently imitated its calls and post horns are still made in Britain for performing solos in band concerts; also as non-functional decorations for country hotels, in Germany and Switzerland also.

1. *English post horn.* This, of brass, is perfectly straight, *c.*70 cm. (30'') long, and pitched in A♭ (see Fig. 1*a*). A cornet mouthpiece can be used and the harmonics normally sounded are from the 2nd, 3rd, and 4th, *a♭'*, *e♭''*, and *a♭''*, or higher in solo pieces. The favourite band solo, the 'Post Horn Galop' of 1844 by Koenig (cornet soloist in Jullien's orchestra), is based on genuine posting-calls of the day, though the horn used on the mail coaches (the first between London and Bristol, 1784) was a shorter instrument of about the same size as the English *hunting horn. Circular and bugle-shaped models were also used. For the later, larger copper horn, see COACH HORN.

2. *Continental post horns.* These have normally been circular, in one or more coils (today more familiar as an emblem of postal services). They date from the early 17th century, but typically made in a coil hardly more than 7.5 cm. (3'') across, wound with coloured cloth. Held with the bell pointing upwards, they were sounded in rapid calls on two notes an octave apart. Their once-familiar sounds are imitated in many works of the first half of the 18th century, e.g. in Bach's 'Aria di Postiglione' (in *Capriccio sopra la lontananza del suo fratello*, BWV 992); Handel's *Belshazzar* (here taken from Telemann); and Vivaldi's *Il corneto da posta* (RV 363). See also HORN, 5*b*.

Later in the century German and Austrian post horns were made with more coils (see Fig. 1*b*), for

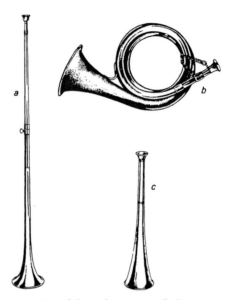

Fig. 1. (*a*) English post-horn in A♭; (*b*) German post-horn in E♭; (*c*) English hunting horn.

a longer tube and deeper pitch allowing higher harmonics to be sounded. In Mozart's 'Sleigh Journey' (K. 605), the two post horns were originally to be played by the orchestra's horn players: one is in B♭, the other in F, this one probably to sound a fourth lower than written. Beethoven (German Dances of 1795) and Schubert ('Die Post', in *Die Winterreise*) both allude to calls of trumpet-like arpeggios, which remained the 19th-century German style. In some 19th-century instruments there is in the coil a small hole which can be uncovered, by a finger of the hand holding the horn, to raise the harmonic series by a fourth, making more different notes available (compare CLARINO, 2). The post horn was also made with valves, to enable it to sound any ordinary tunes, though the *Posthorn* part in Mahler's Third Symphony is in the first edition of the score for the *flugel horn, on which it is now best played (Del Mar 1987). The *cornet was said to have originated, in Paris, late 1820s, as a valved version of the circular post horn.

Hiller 1985.

Praetorius, Michael (*c.*1571–1621). German composer, Kapellmeister at the ducal court of Wolfenbüttel, and author of the most important of all early works on instruments, the *Syntagma Musicum*, Vol. II, *De Organographia* (Wolfenbüttel, 1618). Reprints: Berlin, 1884; Kassel, 1958. English translations: Harold Blumenfeld, 1949; David Z. Crookes, 1986.

The work (well over half of which is devoted to the organ) includes at the end (added by 1620) the 'Theatrum Instrumentorum' or 'Sciagraphia', consisting of 42 plates of engraved illustrations,

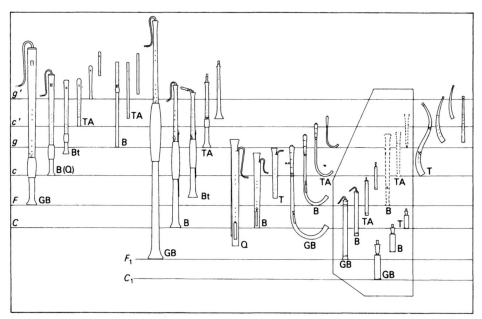

Fig. 1. Families of Renaissance wind instruments, based on Praetorius (1618) and showing all instruments to the same scale, each footed on the level of its bottom note (as named on the left of the figure). GB, great bass; B, bass (Q, quint or quart bass); Bt, basset; T, tenor (TA, tenor-alto). *Left to right:* *recorder, *flute, *shawm, *dulcian, *crumhorn, and (*furthest right*) *cornett. *In box* (rarer families): sordun (see KORTHOLT), *racket, and (*above,* but problematic) *Schreierpfeifen.

most of them to scale (given on each page), and with a full-size ruler of six Brunswick inches (the Brunswick foot: 28.54 cm., approx. 11 English inches) opposite the first plate. (Vol. III, *Termini Musici,* 1619, is occupied with complexities of allocating instruments and voices in performing already-written motets, etc., and the transcriptions appropriate to their various ranges.)

Fig. 1 is based on his illustrations to show the chief families of the wooden wind instruments together, all approximately to the same scale, and rearranged to place the bottom end of each instrument on a horizontal level corresponding to the pitch of its lowest note.

Prepared piano. See PIANO, 10.

Principal, principale. 1. Principal: in an organ a main register of open flue pipes, in Britain at 4' pitch, in Germany, 8' (see ORGAN, 3*a*).

2. Principale: in German baroque trumpet music, a part lying in the register below that of the *clarino* (see TRUMPET, 4*d*).

Psalmodikon. One-stringed bowed zither seen in museums in Sweden, where it served in smaller churches from *c.*1820 to the 1870s as an aid to correct singing of the psalms, the gut string being bowed for preference (it is said) with the short bow

of a *nyckelharpa. The narrow soundbox, with a row of frets down the middle, may be in every shape from a plain rectangle to an imitation of the violin. In England there had been, some 100 years earlier, an instrument called a psalterer, known only by descriptions of the 1720s–30s: apparently a metre-long (3') soundbox, with from one to three strings, frets for two octaves, and held downwards for bowing like a bass viol; psalm tunes were played following letters pasted on (Jeans 1986).

Psalterium (Lat., from Gk.: *psaltērion*). In Ancient Greek a general term for stringed instruments that were plucked (*psallein*) with the fingers, as distinct from lyres, which were normally struck with a plectrum. The chief of such instruments was a harp, of the 'vertical angular' kind (see HARP, 10*b*; BIBLICAL INSTRUMENTS, 1*c*), whence the Church Fathers, from the 4th century AD, saw an allegory, alluded to constantly in their writings, in the *psalterium* with its body (soundbox) upwards and therefore heavenly, as against the *kithara* (lyre) with soundbox lowermost, therefore earthly.

Greek writings mention at least six different names of instruments falling in the *psaltērion* class (e.g. *epigoneion, magadis* or *pektis, sambyke, trigonon*) but what these were, if other than harps, remains unknown. There is no incontestable evidence of Antiquity having anywhere used instruments of psaltery or zither kinds.

Psaltery (from Lat.: **psalterium*; It., sp.: *salterio*; in Medieval Eng. often 'sautrie'). Stringed instrument much used in the Middle Ages and early Renaissance, yet no original example has survived. The strings run from side to side of a flat soundbox made in various shapes, and were plucked with a pair of quills (or one alone) or with the fingers.

1. *Forms of psaltery*. Among the many seen in pictures, the most typical, from the 12th century onwards, has a soundbox with incurving sides (see MEDIEVAL INSTRUMENTS, Pl. 1 second from right), which, like the dip in the neck of a harp, avoids overstretching the middle strings by giving the string-lengths throughout some approach to harmonic proportions (doubling for an octave lower). Thus built, the instrument, though also played across the knees, could be comfortably held up resting on the arms while playing standing (the longest strings uppermost). Italians saw a visual resemblance to a pig's face with eyes and snout: the *strumento di porco*, or as reconstructed today for medieval and Renaissance music, 'pig-snout psaltery' (kits available). In many pictures the top continues above the two curves in a rectangle carrying equal-length bass strings, but, as with much else about the psaltery, the reason for these strings is quite unknown. A 15th-century psaltery might have strings for up to three diatonic octaves, double-strung in metal (silver is mentioned).

Other builds are as if the above form were cut in half down the middle, the oblique side curved or straight ('half-trapeze', like the *qānūn*); or they are completely rectangular. All are seen in the Cantigas miniatures (see MEDIEVAL INSTRUMENTS, 2), and all or most may derive from prototypes introduced (or invented) by Arab musicians in Spain—whence some names met also in Old French: *canon* (from **qānūn*) and *micanon* (half-canon, the halved form).

Fondness for the psaltery played solo or with the voice is reflected in the *Canterbury Tales* ('The Clerk of Oxenford'); or, in delicate ensembles, where Prudenzani's Italian sonnets (*c*.1420) describe, played together, a *menacordo*, *liuto*, *flauto*, and *salterio*: the first gave 'such loud notes that the lute sounded dull [*sordo*] beside it' (so perhaps the poet visualized an early harpsichord, rather than a clavichord); the flute (early recorder no doubt) was 'good', while the psaltery 'as far as I recall, had a finer sound than any that I ever heard'.

From about that time, the hammered **dulcimer* begins to appear in pictures, and by the 16th century the psaltery has almost vanished, save where reported from Mexico and where in southern Europe a dulcimer may occasionally be seen played with the fingers or plectra, like a psaltery.

2. *Harp-psaltery*. Modern term for a medieval instrument first seen in pictures of the 11th century (i.e. about the time when the medieval harp appears and a century earlier than the above 'porco' psaltery). At first glance it is a kind of harp, held edgewise to the body and tuned at the top; but with all straight sides and with 'rose' soundholes indicating the presence of a soundbox behind the strings. These are up to 30 in number, and possibly, in some cases at least, run on both sides of the soundbox (as in the baroque German **Spitzharfe*). It may have been the first actual instrument in the medieval West to have taken over the old Latin name *psalterium*, that is, discounting the numerous medieval drawings which invent (as it seems) forms to match older written interpretations of the word as it occurs in the Old Testament (see MEDIEVAL INSTRUMENTS, 4).

3. *Classification*. In modern general **classification*, all the above are included under the heading 'zither' (in European contexts, however, **zither* covers a distinct family of instruments). The **bowed psaltery* is a wholly modern instrument.

Pungi (or *pūngī*). Indian snake-charmer's pipe (also *magudi*, *tubrī*). Two cane pipes, each cut with an **idioglot single reed*, are stuck parallel together and held with wax in a gourd. The player bellows into the neck of the gourd using **circular breathing* (inhaling through the nose). One pipe has fingerholes, often tuned with wax, and the other has no fingerholes, to sound a drone. The music begins softly, becoming more excited as the cobra (the fangs removed) fills out its hood and sways about. Elsewhere, as in Morocco, snake-charmers use a **bagpipe*, or the end-blown flute **nay*. In India, 'gourd-pipes' such as the above may be met as folk instruments with no connection with snake-charming, played by boys watching over herds.

Puniu. Hawaiian 'knee drum'; see PACIFIC ISLANDS, 3*b*.

Putorino (or *puutoorino*). Maori wind instrument; see PACIFIC ISLANDS, 4.

Q

Qānūn. Plucked stringed instrument of the Middle East, especially Egypt and Syria, Turkey (*kanun*), and Armenia. Related to the *psaltery; it is in modern *classification a zither. The flat soundbox, the left-hand side slanting, may be 90 cm. (35″) long, 10 cm. (4″) deep, and is played on the knees (or carried on a strap round the neck) with the long side nearest and the rows of tuning pins to the left. The bridge on the right rests on four or five square skin membranes. The gut or nylon strings, in some 25 triple courses, are played with a finger-pick worn in a ring on each forefinger; the technique, fast and brilliant, is often in broken octaves between the two hands.

In Egypt the *qānūn* player leads the classical and theatre ensemble (see MIDDLE EAST). During a performance pieces may follow in different modes—major, minor, or with $\frac{3}{4}$-tone intervals (as in tetrachords such as A B♭ C D, with the B♭ here a $\frac{1}{4}$-tone raised)—and therefore the *qānūn* is provided with rows of small metal blades close to the tuning pins for raising strings by a $\frac{1}{4}$, $\frac{1}{2}$, or $\frac{3}{4}$ tone when setting the next scale. Before the present century these blades were absent, so that the player, with no time to retune, had to press on the strings with the left hand near the tuning pins to sharpen them as needed, leaving this hand only partly free to play. Earlier still, to about the 15th century, it appears that the *qānūn* was held up against the body like a European *psaltery. Nothing is known of it before the 10th century, though the name derives in some way from Greek *kanōn* in the sense of a 'measurer of musical intervals' or *monochord.

Qaraqib. See CASTANETS, 4.

Qin (formerly '*ch'in*'). The most revered of the Chinese *'long zithers' (for another see ZHENG). With a history of over 3,000 years, it has a repertory which is the most refined in Chinese music, demanding of the solo performer the highest knowledge, skill, concentration, and musicality.

1. *The instrument.* The black-lacquered soundbox (Pl. 1), c.120 cm. (4′) long, 15 cm. (6″) broad, 5 cm. (2″) deep, is placed usually on a table, with the narrower end to the left and the player seated towards the wider end. Thirteen round studs of mother-of-pearl are set in a row along the far side (the front in Pl. 1), one centrally, six to each side, marking harmonic divisions of the string-length (the same for every string), from each end, $\frac{1}{8}$, $\frac{1}{6}$, $\frac{1}{5}$, $\frac{1}{4}$, $\frac{1}{3}$, $\frac{2}{5}$, up to $\frac{1}{2}$ at midway (the same as in making *harmonics on the violin and cello). Two slots in the underside of the soundbox act as soundholes, the instrument being slightly raised from the table.

The seven strings, of silk traditionally extracted from living silkworms, and graded in thickness—

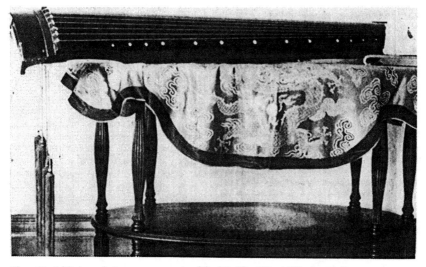

Pl. 1. Qin (ch'in), made in 1705: property of the late Bliss Wiant (Wiant 1965).

Ex. 1. (after Picken 1957).

a)

Molto adagio

b)

Allegretto

etc.

traditionally with numbers of strands matched to the interval ratios of the tuning—are tied underneath in two bunches. At the wider end they are led through holes to the back, where they are wedged to hold the tuning, their remaining loose ends joined to the tassels which hang down. They are tuned pentatonically over a deep range upwards from a pitch as deep or deeper than the lowest string of the cello, e.g. *C D F G A c d*. The deepest or 'first' string is the one next to the studs.

2. *Playing.* The right-hand fingers pluck the strings; the left hand stops them level with the studs, or touches them there for harmonics. In the music, preludes, interludes, and coda sections may be played entirely in harmonics (Ex. 1*b*). Great account is taken of the many alternative strings and positions for making a note with different qualities of sound (in Ex. 1*a*, after Picken 1957, indicated twice by notes with tails up or down). In the Chinese notations the characters tell the player precisely which fingers to use, on which string, at which stud to press or touch: e.g. 'place left middle finger on 2nd string opposite 7th stud, and pull string with right middle finger'. Not infrequent are delicate cascades across the strings, and slides made with a left-hand finger after a note is struck. The music, sometimes with the voice, proceeds mostly at a leisurely pace, unbound by the four-square rhythms of much Chinese music, the pieces being largely programmatic, or indeed in a sense 'literary'. The sum effects are wholly magical, no less so to the untutored ears of a foreigner.

Music for *qin* has suffered attack from recent ideologies, but historical research has continued and young players have come out of Hong Kong, Taiwan, and other Chinese communities outside mainland China. The originally purely intimate performance of *qin* music (at most for a small circle of friends) has found its way into concert halls, and into radio programmes. For such performances, the delicate sound is amplified.

Picken 1957; Wiant 1965; and see CHINA AND KOREA, 1.

Quail. See WHISTLES AND BIRD-CALLS, 2.

Quena (or *kena*). The notched flute (see FLUTE, 7*b* (ii)) of Andean South America, mainly from Chile to Peru; of cane, about 30 to 40 cm. (12"–16") long, with the knot at the bottom perforated by a small hole. The notch is parallel-sided, the base square-cut or rounded. The quena is held like a recorder, the lower lip covering most of the open top end, the breath directed on to the sharp-edged base of the notch. It is not difficult to sound, and readily gives two octaves or more. There are six fingerholes (formerly, sometimes still, five) with a thumb-hole higher up. Semitones are mostly made by half uncovering a hole.

One of the main indigenous, pre-Columbian melodic instruments of the whole region, it goes back to around 900 BC (see AMERICAN INDIANS, 1), and remains a high favourite along with the also indigenous duct flute *pincullo*. It is taught in school classes in folk-tunes, mainly pentatonic (and in published Tutors perhaps ending with some European tunes such as 'La Despedida', alias 'Old Lang Syne'). It is much played with drums outdoors.

Querflöte (Ger.). Transverse *flute.

Quijada (Sp.). See JAWBONE.

Quint, quart, terz. 1. Old prefixes, chiefly German, met from the 16th century to the 19th, distinguishing instruments built or tuned a perfect fifth, fourth, or a third (major or minor) higher or lower than most usual. In the earlier period the terms are mostly applied to wind instruments, as in the *Quint-posaune*, a trombone a fifth below the ordinary. In the later period we find *Quart-geige*, the violino piccolo, tuned a fourth higher than the violin; and *Terz-flöte*, in English the 'F flute', a third above the ordinary (and termed by some collectors 'tierce flute').

2. Quint, or quinta, also often denotes a fifth part in polyphonic music. In the French string orchestras of the 17th century the *quinte* was one of three middle parts (see VIOLA, 4).

3. In organs, a Quint is a rank of pipes which sounds one or more octaves plus a fifth above the basic 8′.

Quinterne, quinton. The first, a 16th-century German name for a mandolin or guitar. For the second ('little five-stringed'), see PARDESSUS DE VIOLE.

R

Rabab (rebab, rubob). The oldest-known Arabic word (*rabāb*) for a bowed instrument (see BOW, 3), today denoting a large number of instruments played from North Africa across Asia to Indonesia. Below, 1 to 3, are fiddles held downwards (pegs uppermost) and bowed thumb-upwards; 4, however, is plucked.

1. *Rabāb* (see MIDDLE EAST, Pl. 1, centre). The small boat-shaped fiddle of classical Moroccan and Algerian music, though from the late 19th century largely replaced by the violin. Hollowed in one piece, with added turned-back pegbox, the lower part is covered by goatskin, often painted green; the upper part is a brass plate perforated with roses. Two thick gut strings are tuned a fifth apart fairly deep in the tenor voice range. For a medieval European descendant (rubebe) see REBEC, 2.

2. *Rabāb, rebab.* The 'poet's fiddle' of the Arab Middle East (e.g. Bedouin). Body of a square or trapeze-shaped wooden frame, skin-covered front and back, fixed upon a wooden pole (the neck). Often it has a single string and is played especially in self-accompaniment to narrations (cf. *imzad*, see FIDDLE, 2*b*; and in Europe, GUSLA). An Ethiopian form, *masenqo*, has the body mounted in a lozenge position on the pole.

3. *Rebab.* Of the Javanese *gamelan, derived from the Middle-Eastern *kemancha. Heart-shaped wooden body (originally coconut), parchment-covered, held on a long spike. Two metal strings, stopped, as with all the above, by finger-pressure alone (there being no fingerboard). Similar fiddles on the Asian mainland are the *sǫs sam sai* (Thailand, see SOUTH-EAST ASIA, Pl. 2) and *tro khmer* (Kampuchea), some beautifully made in ivory.

4. *Rubab, rabab.* A 'short-necked' lute (see LUTE, 7*a*; by no means the only case of a word denoting a bowed instrument in one place and a plucked one in another as here).

(*a*) Afghan and Tajik (Central Asia), north-west India (see also SAROD, a derivative), total length *c*.1 m. (3'). The deep hollowed-out body has small incurved 'centre bouts' suggesting that the instrument was at some time in the past bowed. Skin belly, hollow neck with four frets (or now more). Three (or four) strings, deep-tuned in fifths, and wire sympathetic strings tuned (by some accounts chromatically) along the right edge of the body and clearly heard enriching the sound.

(*b*) Another *rubob*, the Central Asian 'Kashgar' type, is a *long lute with a smaller, rounder hollowed-out body, carved where it joins the neck with a pair of curving horns. The long neck has up to 25 tied-on frets.

Rabel. Old Spanish word, related to *rabab, for a fiddle, and still met, now only rarely, in Castile, also Chile, for a rural fiddle made in various primitive violin shapes with three or four strings.

Racket (Eng., from Ger.; Fr.: *cervelat*, 'sausage'; It. uncertain: *?cortaldo*). Renaissance-period double-reed wind instrument. A small column (Pl. 1, here of ivory) is drilled with nine parallel passages from top to bottom which are connected in series by recesses in the cap at each end of the column. By this means a height of 18 cm. (7″), to take for example a tenor racket, can contain a narrow cylindrical tube amounting to over 150 cm. (5') in all, to sound the bottom C of the cello; or if twice as tall (Great Bass racket) the bottom C of the piano, making it one of the deepest-sounding wind instruments of the period. An upright metal 'staple' with *pirouette takes the bassoon-like reed. The lowest note issues through a hole in the side. Eleven holes at various places round the column are fingered by both hands, thumbs included, the 11th hole being covered by the middle joint of one of the fingers. Rackets are first mentioned in 1576 in Germany (the instrument can just be seen played in *Renaissance instruments, Pl. 1, third from the window on the right), and were made up to *c*.1640. The sound is softly nasal, and was sometimes joined in combination with other instruments, taking one of the lower parts. The three known surviving examples, from Austria, are in the Leipzig and Vienna *collections. There also exist some later rackets built out of historical curiosity by baroque makers including Denner (see CHALUMEAU), with a coiled crook in the top next to a short bell.

The name, according to most German authorities, is more correctly *Rancket*, signifying 'to-and-fro'—though a Stuttgart court inventory of 1589, when the instrument was still fairly recent, has 'Zünd-fleschen, so Rageten' ('tinder flasks or rockets') listed with some other freak or carnival wind instruments.

Tartöld. In the Vienna collection is also a set of five instruments, each having cylindrical brass tubing coiled in a helix (entered at intervals by fingerholes) contained in a brass casing imitating the form of a dragon. A 1596 inventory of whence they came (Schloss Ambras, Innsbruck) lists 'a case of 5 tartöld shaped like dragons', presumably these

Pl. 1. Ivory racket (*?c.* 1580); height, excluding (modern) reed, 18 cm. (7″).

very instruments and giving us their name. Each has its crook for the now-missing double reed.

Rain machine. See EFFECTS.

Ranat (or *ranāt*). *Xylophones and *metallophones of Thailand and Kampuchea (in the latter also written *roneat*). For their place in music, as the *pīphāt* ensembles of Thailand, see SOUTH-EAST ASIA, 3, 4, and Ex. 1.

In each instrument the bars are laid upon a wooden resonance trough, and are tuned over a range of up to three octaves of a scale composed of seven approximately equal intervals per octave. The basically pentatonic music uses five notes per octave, the remainder serving mainly for 'filling in' the faster passages with passing notes. Of both xylophone and metallophone there are two kinds, one (21 bars) with a higher compass than the other (17 or 18 bars), their ranges overlapping by three notes at the bottom. The two beaters sound the bars a great deal in octaves.

1. *Xylophones*. Hardwood or bamboo bars, convex on both sides in cross-section, strung together with twine and played with round-headed beaters. The trough of the higher pitched, in Thai, *ranat* (*ranāt*) *ek* (nominal compass *f–f‴*) has the form of an inverted arch, *c.*120 cm. (4′) long, with central foot; the other, *ranat thum*, is flatter-arched with small feet at each end and compass *d–f″*. See SOUTH-EAST ASIA, Pl. 2, the two instruments in the middle.

2. *Metallophones*. Steel (or sometimes wrought iron) bars on padded rails and played with hide-covered

beaters. The troughs are straight, on a flat base (See the same illustration at each end of the row): higher pitched, *ranat ek lek*; deeper pitched, *ranat thum lek* (or *ranat thong thum*). Compass, same as for the xylophones.

Bars are fine-tuned as needed by applying under one end a composition of lead shavings and beeswax (also used for tuning the *gong chimes, placed under the boss).

Râpe, râpe guero (Fr.). See GUIRO.

Rasgueado (Sp.). On a guitar, 'strummed' (see GUITAR, 2).

Rattle: 1. *Ratchet rattle* (Fr.: *crécelle*; Ger.: *Ratsche*; It.: *raganella*; Sp.: *matraca*; Ru.: TRESHCHOTKA). The common swung rattle, often of beechwood, with a wooden blade fixed by one end for the free end to snap against the teeth of a wooden cogwheel. This is held tight on the handle by which the frame is swung round, to make a succession of strong impact sounds. The teeth are cut to a shape by which the rattle can be swung both ways. Small versions used to be sold everywhere at fairs. Others may have a pair of blades snapping on two cogwheels set to pluck the blades in alternation. The British design which served as official gas warning in the Second World War usually had a panel fixed above the blade to serve as a resonance cavity. For more controllable sound than when swung, the rattle may have a knob on the frame for this to be turned by one hand, the other holding the handle still. And there are orchestral versions in which the frame is held still and the wheel is turned by a handle, sometimes preferred to the swung type should a more evenly continuous sound be required. Richard Strauss used the ratchet in *Till Eulenspiegel* and *Der Rosenkavalier* (Act 3), and before him Beethoven in *Wellington's Victory*, where it represents rifle fire. In history the ratchet rattle goes back to the Middle Ages, for night watchmen and lepers.

Some Spanish and Swiss church towers contain enormous rattles with blades *c.*213 cm. (7′) long and the ratchet wheel turned by ropes; they are for use during Holy Week, when bells are not rung from the Thursday to the Saturday. Corncrakes used to be lured by a small ratchet rattle, the toothed wheel stroked across the thigh.

2. *Shaken rattle*. For rattles that produce sounds of a 'shishing' nature, see for example CABAZA; CHOCALHO; MARACA. Among hundreds of others are the pig's bladder containing dried peas, playfully wielded on a stick by the 'Fool' in May Day and other festivities. Many different types of loud rattles are made in Catholic countries, again for use during Holy Week, sometimes sounded from the steps of the church: (*a*) a pair of wooden mallets pivoted in a frame to knock against a stationary mallet mounted between them (*triccaballa*, see FRICTION

DRUM, Pl. I, second from left; (b) a wooden hammer pivoted above a small board (also made with several small hammers worked by a miniature windmill, for a bird-scarer in fields and gardens); (c) one or two iron loops rather like door-knockers, pivoted over a stout board which is rapidly rotated to and fro in the hand (and formerly used also by Russian policemen and postmen).

Antecedent to these rattles played in the hand are those composed of objects strung together for wearing on the body, as when dancing. In this sense metal pellet bells (see SLEIGH BELLS) could be counted as rattles, and small bells worn on clothing, though such are usually for *classification purposes put under 'bells' (their purpose being to 'jingle', not 'rattle'). For some instruments which, while included in classification under 'shaken idiophones or rattles', 'jingle' rather than 'rattle', again from metal striking metal, see SISTRUM AND JINGLES.

3. *Spinning rattle* (Hawaiian: *'ūlili*). Two small gourds, seeds inside, are fixed on each end of a short stick wound with a string. The end of this is led through a hole in another, smaller gourd placed loose on the stick midway as a hand grip. The other hand pulls the string to spin the two rattling gourds.

Rattle drum (or clapper drum, monkey drum, twirling drum). A small drum on a stick (see DRUM, Fig. 1i) with a membrane, often paper, or a thin metal disc, covering each side. A fine string attached on each side of the drumshell carries a bead or small wooden ball, so that on twirling or twiddling the stick the beads repeatedly strike the membrane (giving the best sound if they strike just away from the centre). Well known especially in Eastern Asia (where street vendors use the instrument widely), the Chinese *taogu* (*t'ao-ku*) is a ritual instrument, as it is in Tibet, here made from a pair of human crania (see CHINA AND KOREA, 3b). In the Middle East and in the West, rattle drums are made chiefly as a toy.

Some ethnologists restrict the term 'rattle drum' to instruments which have, instead of beads on strings, pellets inside, the drum being shaken; those with beads are then termed 'clapper drum'. In parts of Central Europe are ball-and-string rattles all of wood (with no membranes), for signalling meal-times on farms.

Rauschpfeife. See SCHREIERPFEIFE.

Rebec. A kind of fiddle with a 'pear-shaped', round-backed body and normally three strings tuned in fifths, following various Renaissance-period pictures and descriptions. Some modern historians further employ the word as a convenient general term for European pear-shaped fiddles depicted through the Middle Ages, many of them from before we find either 'rebec' or the older word 'rubebe' or 'ribebe' (from Arabic *rabab*): see below, 2.

1. *Rebec, as understood today in early music.* The body (Pl. I, for one example) is hollowed out in one piece with the neck or moulded in plastic. The short neck carries a back-curving pegbox with side pegs for the strings. Original instruments of this pear-shaped form with curved pegbox (and not recent Greek or Balkan folk instruments, see LIRA) have not been found, though there may be seen in collections reconstructions from the 18th century or later when 'rebec', in France, was a name from the past. Modern rebecs take their form chiefly from German works of 1511–45 (Virdung, Agricola, Gerle). The instruments are here named simply 'small fiddles' (*Kleine Geigen*); in Agricola also *Handgeigen*, i.e. held up like a fiddle, not down like a viol. Characteristic is the wide fingerboard surface spreading out above the upper part of the belly at a raised level. The strings could be tuned as the lowest three of the violin. There is no soundpost, and the tone can be rather hollow and echoing compared with that of a violin. The bass of the rebec family has a fourth string, tuned a fifth below the next.

Pl. I. A modern rebec (shown without the bow). Hobgoblin Music, Crawley, W. Sussex.

An Italian poem of c.1420 (see PSALTERY, I) mentions as played together in part-songs *ribecche*, *rubechette*, and a *rubecone*, as if differing in size and pitch, though we cannot be certain what they looked like. The composer Landini (d. 1397) was said to have played, among many instruments, the *ribeba*; but the miniatures, apparently intended to represent these instruments, which surround his portrait in the famous Squarcialupi Codex in Florence and dating from about the time of the poem, show nothing rebec-like among them, but a fiddle of an ordinary early kind with almost violin-like waist. Yet we later have the firm evidence of Tinctoris (c.1484) that the *rebecum* had a swelling back; but only to find that in the 16th century, *ribecchino* is frequent in Italy as a name for the violin itself.

2. *Rubebe*. This word appears first in late 13th-century French romances in the *Romance of the Rose*. At about this same time Jerome of Moravia (see FIDDLE, 2) describes the *rubebe* as having two strings tuned to a fifth (as the Moroccan instrument still has, see RABAB, 1). He does not mention its visual appearance or how it was held, and nor does any subsequent medieval source: we still do not know for certain whether or how far Chaucer's 'small rubible' ('Miller's Tale') resembled what we term a rebec today. (In Northern Italy *ribeba* is locally a name for the *jew's harp, as was formerly Fr. *rebube*).

3. *Polish fiddle*. Agricola (1545) also gives to one kind of his rebecs the name 'Polish fiddle'. Still up to the 20th century in the Carpathian districts of Poland and Czechoslovakia fiddles in rebec shapes were made by shepherds and others for playing at village weddings: hollowed out in one piece with a rebec pegbox for three or four strings tuned in fifths, and a flat fingerboard which in one example from Slovakia spreads out over the belly as noticed above (1). A Polish *mazanki* of this kind, preserved in Poznan, has been tentatively dated to the 16th century.

Hayes 1930; Remnant 1986.

Recorder (Fr.: *flûte à bec*; Ger.: *Blockflöte*; It.: *flauto dolce*; Ru.: *prodolnaya fleŭta*; Sp.: *flauta dulce*. The classic *duct flute of Western music. Among the European names the German reminds us that a wooden block is inserted into the blowing end to form a windway to the 'window' where the tone is generated; the French, that this end is shaped to a beak (or 'fipple') to be placed comfortably in the lips; and the Italian, that the sound is sweet compared with that of many other flutes of the Renaissance. The English name tells us that there was once held to be no better instrument with which to 'record' a tune in the old sense of recalling it to mind and repeating it: thus in Fairfax's *Tasso*, 'to hear the lark record her hymns and chant her carols blest'. One easily forgets that when Arnold Dolmetsch (1858–1940) first turned his attention to it in 1919 the recorder had scarcely been played for 160 years and most people knew the name only as a peculiar term in Act 3 of *Hamlet*, while the recorder (*flauto*) parts in Handel and Bach were played as a matter of course on flutes (often they still are, though less than formerly). NB: The two favourite sizes of recorder known in Britain as 'treble' and 'descant' are in America (also Germany) named 'alto' and 'soprano' respectively.

1. *Construction*. Dolmetsch revived the recorder in its 'baroque' form, initially following originals by

Bressan (1663–1731; see Byrne 1983), who came to London from France (his real name Pierre Jaillard) in 1688 to become England's first known great recorder maker (Pl. 1). This is the well-known form made in three joints, of which the 'head' (with the rectangular 'window') and short 'foot' are turned with handsome mouldings—often now simplified to accord with the more streamlined taste of the 20th century, while low-priced models of the smaller sizes are often made in two joints only. 'Renaissance' models are based on originals of the 16th and early 17th centuries (the outstanding *collection is in Vienna), turned all in one piece without mouldings (Pl. 2); they taper downwards to a less marked degree than the baroque (in which the taper is concentrated in the body joint) and the window is generally wider; they produce a full sound, ideal for playing early music in parts using recorders of all sizes together. The baroque sound, more colourful and expressive, befits especially the concertos and obbligati of the period, almost entirely for the treble recorder.

Pl. 1. Treble (alto) recorder by Peter Bressan, London, early 18th century. Bressan, real name Pierre Jaillard, was born in 1663 in Bourg-en-Bresse, France.

Not, however, that a recorder today need conform strictly to either historic model, having become

or slightly tapered bore of the head except along the top, where it is raised to form the windway. Great skill and experience go into the longitudinal profile of this. The wider from floor to roof, the fuller the sound from the light breath pressure which a recorder requires. On the other hand, if it be narrower, or arched, or sloped to narrow to the slit, it may increase the player's ability to control the rise and fall of pitch which is natural to a duct flute on blowing faster or slower for loud and soft.

3. *Fingering*. A great asset of the recorder is a stability and even quality in the *cross-fingerings almost unmatched in other woodwind. Only for the lowest two accidentals are 'twin holes' practically standard today for the smaller recorders (though quite rare in the past), one of the two small holes being covered for the semitone leaving the other open. Besides the normal fingering (often given on a leaflet accompanying a new instrument) the recorder allows on practically every note a number of alternative fingerings a fraction sharper or flatter than the normal, by which an expert soloist can, especially in slow pieces, further keep the pitch of a note steady in a diminuendo or crescendo. Also, the rise of the fingers above the holes may be varied, or a note 'shaded' by one or more fingers laid against, not wholly covering, holes lower down. The player may thus command many different ways of playing a scale or a passage.

The upper register requires the thumbhole to be slightly uncovered by 'pinching' (bending the thumb for the nail to make a narrow opening). This gives four notes of the scale (a'' to d'' on treble recorder) as overblown octaves, above which further fingerings take the compass up to two octaves plus one note (see OVERBLOWING), save that the semitone below the top ($f\sharp'''$ on treble) is extremely difficult and usually considered as absent.

There has been, initiated $c.1925$ by Peter Harlan, one of the first modern makers on the Continent, a 'German fingering', distinguishable from the normal 'English' or 'baroque' fingering in that the fifth hole in front is smaller than the fourth, for making B♭ (or on descant recorder F) without cross-fingering, though complicating the fingering for B♮.

4. *Sizes of recorder*. Ex. 1 shows the bottom note of each size (a small note indicating where the part is written an octave lower than the sound). Since the pitches have not always been the same through the past, the name of the bottom note is often included in the description, e.g. 'treble in F' (no. 3 in the example). The figures below show approximately the modern lengths, corresponding roughly with the pitch intervals between sizes, e.g. tenor, an octave deeper than the descant and about twice the length. The basses are often blown in the old way through a metal 'crook'.

The sopranino is not often used (the holes lie awkwardly close for most hands). Descants were built during the Baroque in other pitches besides

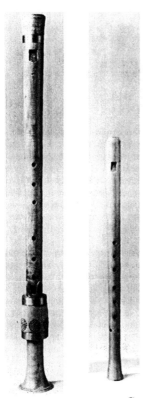

Pl. 2. Renaissance recorders: basset (*left*) and tenor, late 16th century.

established as a wind instrument in its own right, with new compositions, uses in film music and other media, and in arrangements of music of every kind. This has led (largely through the enterprise of the German manufacturers) to general-purpose instruments suited to all demands—even if in a concession to small hands some of the fingerholes may be located far out of line and of widely different size, as would not have been permitted in older times when an instrument was valued for elegance both to the ear and to the eye.

Though normally wood (of very many kinds), the plastic recorder was first designed in London by Edgar Hunt, a descant in bakelite, when outbreak of war in 1939 curtailed the supply from Germany of cheap wooden instruments for school classes.

2. *Block and windway*. These are made in a way traditional among European duct flutes, as see FLAGEOLET, Fig. 1c. In the upper part of the headjoint a channel is carved in the inner wall to form the roof of the windway leading to the narrow slit which aims the breath on to the edge of the 'lip' beyond. The floor of the windway is formed by the 'block', made of pencil cedar (which does not swell when wet) and is $c.2''$ long for a treble recorder. It is shaped by hand exactly to fit the cylindrical

Ex. 1.

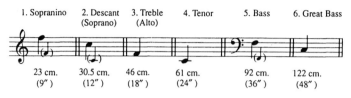

1. Sopranino	2. Descant (Soprano)	3. Treble (Alto)	4. Tenor	5. Bass	6. Great Bass
23 cm. (9")	30.5 cm. (12")	46 cm. (18")	61 cm. (24")	92 cm. (36")	122 cm. (48")

C: in D, known in England as 'sixth flute' (i.e. a recorder six notes above the treble, and often stamped '6'); 'fourth flute' ('4'), in B♭; some contemporary pieces name these. The treble, the great instrument of the Baroque, was in the Renaissance period normally a tone higher, in G (and only rarely so later). Pitched two notes below the F treble is the baroque 'voice flute' in D, known by a fair number of examples: its intention was perhaps to offer a better compass for playing vocal airs at the published pitch (two 'flauti da voce' are named in a work by Loeillet).

The tenor and bass made up, with the treble, the basic Renaissance four-part consort (the tenor taking both middle parts), or, with two trebles, five-part, often playing from the vocal part-books an octave higher. The Renaissance bass is blown through a side opening in the cap at the top; there were also basses in G, in Germany 'basset' (Pl. 2, left, showing the *fontanelle*, protecting the key). Baroque tenors are few but basses remarkably plentiful, as if often played with two trebles in a trio sonata (as the 'Bass Flute' plays in Purcell's last *Ode for Saint Cecilia's Day*). The great bass is a Renaissance size, also made in B♭ (German 'Quintbass', a fifth below the F bass). Though not a baroque size it has been available in baroque format (in C) since Steiber so made it in Germany from c.1950; it is played from the bass recorder part making use of its deeper notes as the opportunity arises. Very rare is the Renaissance great bass ('subbass') in F, 180 cm. (6') tall, an octave deeper than the bass, allowing a group to play the music at written pitch, with tenor or basset on the top part: a beautiful effect that has been demonstrated with the Venetian originals in Vienna, as well as with their modern reproductions. Nor is it less beautiful to hear the two consorts, normal and an octave deeper, combined, the whole music sounding in octaves like a small organ. (For an outline sketch of the whole range see PRAETORIUS, Fig. 1.)

5. Origins and development. The earliest known European duct flute having the recorder's seven holes and thumb-hole was found under a ruined castle in Holland and is believed to date from about the same time that an English court document, of 1388, mentions a *fistula in nomine ricordo*, which could mean 'flute named recorder' and be the first known occurrence of this name (Trowell 1957: 84). The Dordrecht instrument (preserved in the *collection in The Hague) is of descant size (Weber 1976), and resembles many folk flageolets made on the Continent still, in its plain-cut upper end (no 'beak'), cylindrical bore (11 mm.), and narrow, almost square window. Its likeness can be seen in pictures well into the 15th century until, from c.1450, Italian paintings show treble- and tenor-sized instruments, outwardly almost identical with the Renaissance recorders that we know, and being played together. Descriptions of recorder fingerings and technique are available from the 1530s (Agricola, Ganassi, etc.).

The earliest illustration and description of the baroque recorder is Italian, 1677 (Bismantova), closely followed in England by John Hudgebut's *Vade mecum* for the 'Rechorder', 1679, particularly interesting for its information on musical ornamentation. Yet it seems almost certain that the baroque design originated in France along with the oboe and the baroque one-keyed flute (see FLUTE, 4a) in the workshops of the royal instrument makers Hotteterre (see OBOE, 4). Great baroque makers include, besides Bressan, Stanesby, and Denner and Oberlender in Nuremberg.

6. Repertory. Among baroque composers of solo sonatas or of trio sonatas with a second recorder or another instrument are Alessandro Scarlatti, Bononcini, Daniel Purcell, Hotteterre le Romain, Pepusch, Loeillet, Vivaldi (seven concertos), Woodcock (if the works are really his), Schickhardt, Telemann (a great deal, including eight solo sonatas, two solo concertos, and numerous trio sonatas), Handel (Sonatas 2, 4, 7, and 11 of his early set, Op. 1), Babell (concertos for descant recorder), Marcello, and Sammartini. Corelli's Sonata Op. 5 No. 3 exists in an anonymous 18th-century arrangement for recorder.

Among modern works are Hindemith's Trio (ed. Walter Bergmann); Robin Milford, Three Airs (the second was originally an interlude, with harpsichord, in the oratorio *A Prophet in the Land* (1930), one of the first reappearances of a recorder on the orchestral platform); Rubbra, Sonatina (with harpsichord) and *Fantasia on a Theme by Machaut* (with harpsichord and string quartet); Lennox Berkeley, Sonatina; Hovhaness, Sextet (with strings, harpsichord); Francis Baines, Quartet for recorders and Fantasia for six recorders (descants and trebles); Antony Hopkins, Suite; and works by Walter Leigh, Rawsthorne, and Malcolm Arnold. To be added to these are avant-garde compositions written for the leading virtuoso of modern times, Frans Bruggen, among them Berio's *Gesti*.

Hunt 1962; Loretto 1973; Marvin 1972; Rowland-Jones 1959.

Reco-reco. See GUIRO.

Red-hot fountain pen. A 'novelty' wind instrument that came on sale in the 1930s: a miniature *clarinet, of a thin ebonite tube about 25 cm. (10″) long and 11 mm. in bore, with fingerholes and a small single-reed mouthpiece, covered when not in use by the 'pen' cap. The pitch is about an octave above the C clarinet. Said to have been invented in the USA by Adrian Rollini. Jazz soloists occasionally featured its quaint sound in recordings.

Reed (Fr.: *anche*; Ger.: *Rohrblatt*; It.: *ancia*; Ru.: *trostnik*; Sp. *lengüeta*). The flexible vibrating component of reed instruments (see WIND INSTRUMENTS, 1b): a tongue or blade, of cane, wood, metal, plastics, held still at one end. For the reed used in *accordion, *reed organ, etc., see FREE REED. This reed gives only its natural frequency. Other reeds, sometimes grouped as 'beating reeds', may do the same (organ reed, 1, below), or else be associated with a fingerhole pipe. The reed then vibrates at frequencies lower than its natural one according to the changing length of the air-column as the fingers progressively cover the holes. Such reeds may be: *single reeds*, as in folk *reedpipes, and clarinet (1–3 below); or *double reeds*, comprising two facing blades, as with the oboe and its Oriental relatives (4, 5). A bagpipe uses the one or the other, or both.

1. *Organ reed* (pipe organs, Fig. 1a). A brass tongue is fixed by a wedge over the opening of the tubular metal 'shallot', S, and gives its own note, tunable by the tuning wire, T. For such reeds used without pipes, see REGAL. *Reed-horns have a similar reed without the tuning wire (Fig. 1b): 'bulb' motor horn, brass horns as formerly used by Continental railway guards and in hunting (e.g. in France, woodcock); see also HUNTING HORN, I.

2. *Idioglot reed* (Fig. 1c, and see REEDPIPE, Fig. 1a, b). One of the most ancient types of single reed, this is best known in folk instruments: a length of cane closed at the top end by a knot, or often cut from an elder shoot with the pith removed and the end stopped up. The vibrating tongue is cut in the side, downwards as here, Fig. 1a, or often upwards (as REEDPIPE, Fig. 1b). In the *reedpipe, Fig. 1a, the tongue is down-cut in the cane of the pipe itself. In bagpipes, it is almost always used for the drones, and in many cases for the chanter also (see BAGPIPE, 5, 6).

3. *Clarinet, saxophone.* A replaceable tongue, the 'reed' (Fig. 2) is attached over the open slot in a separate mouthpiece (see CLARINET, Fig. 1). It is made from the tall cane (*arundo donax*) seen growing wild in warm temperate climates and cultivated especially for reed-making in certain areas in Europe, notably the South of France around Fréjus

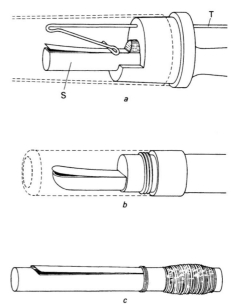

Fig. 1. (a) Organ reed; (b) reed-horn, reed enclosed in cap (dotted); (c) idioglot reed, bagpipe drone. Wind direction from left to right.

(the same cane being used for the double reeds; see below, 4). The single reeds are manufactured by first splitting a stick of cane into three or four strips. Each is shaved flat on the inner side, and thinned on the outside for about half the length to form the vibrating part of the reed, thinnest at the tip. If a reed is too hard, it may be thinned towards the tip with fine sandpaper; if too soft, the extreme tip may be cut off with a reed-cutter, several types of which are marketed. Plastic reeds, also available, are used more on *saxophones than the clarinet, on which other materials have been occasionally mentioned in the past, as wood, bone (it is indeed possible to cut a reed from thin shim brass if musical expectations do not run very high).

4. *Double reed*: oboe and *bassoon, *crumhorn, *cornamuse, *kortholt, *racket, *shawm, *sarrusophone, and many of the bagpipes.
    The reed (Fig. 3) is made from a strip of cane about twice the length of the finished reed. For the oboe reed the initial stick of cane (to be sliced into strips) may have an outside diameter of 11 mm. and for the bassoon 24 mm. The inner surface of the strip is gouged thin, by hand or on a gouging machine. The gouged strip is shaped to narrow towards the ends (Fig. 3a) and, after soaking in water, folded right over at the mid-point, bark side outwards (b). The free ends are tightly bound to a short conical metal tube or 'staple' flattened to an oval at the smaller end (c; when an oboe reed is worn out, the staple is used for a new reed). The cane is then parted at the fold to separate the two

blades of the double reed, which are then thinned down until the reed 'crows' correctly when blown in the mouth by itself. The oboe staple is mounted with cork (*c, d*) for airtight fit into the instrument. With a *cor anglais reed the staple (just visible at the bottom in *e*) fits over the crook (bocal) of the instrument. For a bassoon reed (*f*) the folded cane is bound with thread and wire over a steel mandrel, afterwards removed to leave a hollow rounded stem of cane for placing on to the crook.

Like single reeds, double reeds can also be made from synthetic materials (plastic) for many instruments, such as the crumhorn and other Renaissance types. With skill it is possible to make a reed of practically anything, even a matchbox or yoghurt container. For bagpipes, also *wind-cap reed instruments like the crumhorn, the reed, not being under any pressure from the lips, is flatter, the blades lying closer together (a 'dry' reed). (For alternative use of a single-reed mouthpiece on a normally double-reed instrument, see BASSOON, 4.)

5. *Ancient and Oriental double reeds.* In Antiquity (e.g. *aulos) a double reed was made quite differently, by squashing flat one end of a fresh-cut wild reed from lakes, very much as with a 'whit-horn' (see REED-HORN). The two faces of the flattened part, still joined along the sides, vibrate as a double reed, which is pushed straight into the pipe. Some actual specimens, recovered from a late Egyptian tomb, are in the Brussels *collection, and reeds continue to be made in the same way for Asian instruments of *'cylindrical oboe' kinds.

For instruments of the Asian and North African family related to the shawm, such as *shahnai*, *surna* (for a summary list, see SHAWM, 4), again the material is flattened out, but to a fan shape, tightly constricted by binding over a wood, metal, or bone

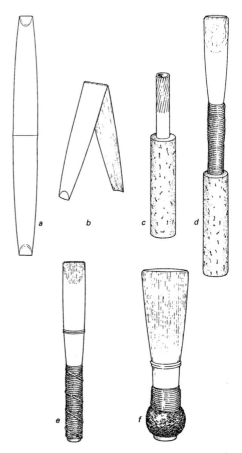

Fig. 3. (*a–d*) Oboe reed; (*e*) cor anglais; (*f*) bassoon.

spike (the mandrel, which often remains hanging from the instrument on a cord or chain). The reed is placed on to a conical metal staple. Typically it is very small to the eye, though the vibrating length can be much the same as the scraped part of an oboe reed. In South-East Asia, however, the reed is generally made from prepared strips of smoked palm leaf, pressed flat, *c.*5 mm, thick. Two or more strips are superimposed, then, after soaking, bent over and bound over a mandrel, each blade consisting of that number of thicknesses of leaf: a very efficient double reed, functioning over two octaves or more (e.g. *hnè*, Burma; *pi-nai*, Thailand; and see also WIND INSTRUMENTS, 3).

6. *Ribbon reed.* Also classed among reeds is the grass blade made to squeak when stretched between the thumbs and blown against edgewise. The sound can be modulated with the tongue to imitate calls of owls. A fowler's lure for duck or crows has a very thin brass tongue 5 cm. (2″) long gripped by one end between two wooden prongs held between the teeth, which then press on them to modulate

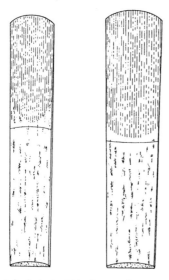

Fig. 2. *Left*, clarinet; *right*, alto saxophone.

the squawk. This might, however, be classed as a variety of beating reed.

Reed-cap. Same as *wind-cap.

Reed contrabass (Fr.: *contrebasse à anche*; It.: *contrabasso ad ancia*). Double-reed wind instrument of brass with keys, made from the late 19th century for military bands by Mahillon (Brussels) and others, and more recently in America by Conn (though the idea goes back to a 'tritonikon' invented in Bohemia in 1839). Made in several coils, it is wide in bore and has a crook for the large double reed. It differs from a *sarrusophone in that the keys (except that which gives the bottom note, *D'*) rest normally closed, one key only being opened for each note. They were originally so arranged that the scale runs upwards from the key for the left little finger to that for the right, in this respect matching the piano, though in later models it may be a little different. In Italy some local bands were using the instrument up to the 1940s.

Reed-horn. General term for calling instruments which have a reed inserted into an animal, wood, or metal horn, for sounding a loud, far-carrying note. See HUNTING HORN; REED, 1*b*. Among ritual reed-horns is the bark horn ('whit-horn' or 'May horn') which children all over Europe used to make of young willow-bark coiled in a cone secured with hawthorn spines, and making the reed from a tube of bark (see REED, 5) that has been slid off a willow shoot after loosening it by tapping with a stick or knife handle (as when making willow May *whistles, these on the *duct flute principle). The sound is a loud squawk, as again in islands of the Pacific where the horn is a cone of rolled leaves.

Among the Indians of British Columbia are carved wooden reed-horns with a large double reed of wood *c.*10 cm (4"). long enclosed inside, or with several such reeds giving different pitches sounding together (Galpin 1937).

Reed instruments. For the different groups see WIND INSTRUMENTS, 1*b*, and for types of reed, see REED.

Reed organ. General term for organs that employ exclusively *free reeds; in particular the American organ, the American instrument corresponding to the European *harmonium, from which it differs in that the bellows draw the air through the reeds (see FREE REED) from below. The reeds are therefore placed above the reed-chambers, with the pallets below and the stop action above the reeds, making for a more compact arrangement than in a harmonium.

The appearance of the instrument is typically ornate, in mahogany often with shelves, mirrors, and ornamental woodwork towering above the keyboard and fretwork below.

1. *Stops.* These move lids above the reeds to regulate the amount of air entering from above, to obtain different sonorities from the same set of reeds by drawing different stops. For example, in the treble half of the compass (the stops dividing at Middle C) the Diapason stop will open the main 8' rank fully and for the Dulciana (or Dulcet) partially; the Principal and the Flute similarly; and a suction-operated fan gives a tremolo for the Vox Humana. The names marked on the stops vary greatly (e.g. for the Principal, 'Bass Forte', 'Treble Forte') and may include such as 'Echo Horn', 'Melodia', 'Viola' (4'), and there may be up to 20 of them. The reeds have round ends and are so fitted that each can be easily pulled out with a hook for attention. The tone is on the whole more stable and less pungent than on a harmonium, some stops coming closer to a pipe organ in quality, though there is no 'expression' stop (since air comes to the reeds before reaching the air-reservoir).

2. *Origins.* It is said that a workman from Alexandre's harmonium business in Paris discovered the suction method of air supply, then emigrated to the USA, where Jeremiah Carhart, in Buffalo, took out a patent in 1846, later annulled. 'Melodeon' was a frequent name for the reed organ in America from about this time. New ways of voicing the reeds for variety of sound were then developed, notably Emmons Hamlin's work on giving a twist to them, e.g. for a special flute-like quality. A great number of makers became well known (some exporting to Europe), as Estey, Kimball, and Mason & Hamlin, up to the 1920s when the numbers built had declined and the makers turned to pianos or pipe organs.

The older models were made in a great variety of sizes for playing hymns from small portable, folding, three-octave instruments used by missionaries, to large pieces of furniture, some with a pedal board and two manuals for organ practice (the air then being drawn by an organ-blower or electric bellows).

Reedpipe. In literary tradition, any rustic pipe made of reed, or of several reeds, (as *panpipes; and '*mirliton*': see KAZOO): but in studies of folk and primitive instruments, a pipe sounded with a reed, whether the pipe be of reed or cane, cornstalk or straw, wood, bone, quill, tinplate, etc.

1. *Single reedpipes.* Shepherds and children almost everywhere in Europe and Asia have made such pipes, cutting in it or adding to it an *idioglot reed (see REED, 2), giving a strong humming sound. In Crete and elsewhere it is a winter occupation to make them of cane in quantity for sale in gift shops through the summer (Fig. 1*a*). They may be *c.*18 cm. long (7"), with the fingerholes burnt out. To play, the reed is put well into the mouth (an expert probably using *circular breathing). There are also strange varieties in northern parts of South America (as Guiana) where the reed is held in the knot of a larger cane, with a small gourd over it or at the other end. A modern practice is to list all these

instruments as 'clarinets', in virtue of the 'single reed'. See also REED-HORN. In Columbia, and in Africa (the Sudan), are 'transverse clarinets', with the reed tongue cut in the side as usual but the pipe held like a flute.

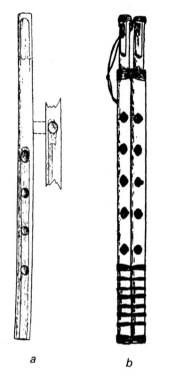

a   *b*

Fig. 1.

2. *Double pipes*. Very often the instrument comprises two pipes sounded together. Following *Sachs they are usually classified as 'parallel' and 'divergent' double pipes.

(*a*) *Parallel*. Two pipes tied or waxed together (Fig. 1*b*, *zummara*, Middle East; the sound is the more vibrant from the slight off-tuning of the two idioglot reeds, occurring naturally or intentionally; or one pipe may be a drone, of the same length as the other or much longer (*arghul*, see ZUMMARA). Addition of a cowhorn bell over the pipes (or in North Africa a small gazelle horn over each) makes a double *hornpipe, or with a bag over the reeds, a bagpipe (see BAGPIPE, 6).

(*b*) *Divergent*. Pipes held one in each hand. Now rare: *launeddas* (Sardinia); but the main wind instrument of Middle-Eastern and Graeco-Roman *Antiquity, *aulos. A pair of such pipes from Ancient Egypt was found (without the reeds) in a tubular case which would have held several different pairs as if for music in different modes.

3. *Free-reed pipes*. Now very rare (Upper Burma: Shan States, Chittagong) is a bamboo pipe held in

a small gourd, with a brass *free reed and seven or so fingerholes. Some are parallel double pipes, the second pipe a drone.

Re-entrant tuning. A term in use from the late 1940s with plucked and bowed stringed instruments where the tuning of the strings departs from regular order from highest to lowest—as for example in many older or small types of guitar (as see GUITAR, Ex. 4) and citterns, where the last string (the one on the bass side of the fingerboard: see STRINGED INSTRUMENTS, 5*c*) is tuned to a higher note than the one before. For some further examples see CHARANGO, COBZA CUATRO, LUTE, 7*c* (long lute), SAZ, UKULELE; and among bowed instruments, LIRA (Greece) and (an extreme case producing a zigzag pattern throughout) LIRA DA GAMBA. See also COURSE.

Regal. A small organ (Pl. 1) employing exclusively reeds (see REED, 1), dating from the mid-15th century to the end of the 17th as a transportable *continuo instrument (the name may be from Fr.: *rigole*, 'shallot'). Usually placed on a table, it has on top a large pair of horizontal bellows worked by a person who stands facing the player seated at the keyboard at the opposite end.

About 30 original regals are known to exist. The reeds are brass (Fig. 1, A), each being wedged in place horizontally over a brass 'shallot' (B), as with organ reeds, and similarly with a tuning-wire; it is possible for three tongues to be cut to the same size and tuned by the wires to successive semitones. Each shallot leads straight into a small brass or tin resonator with air holes in the top (C), to stabilize and mellow the sound. The resonators together communicate into a long transverse space running parallel with the keyboard and covered by a grille (E) or by a sliding panel by which the volume may be adjusted. The bellows (F) feed the wind chest (G) and the keys (H) depress pallets located near the front below the keyboard. The compass is from *E* to *c'''* or thereabouts. The strong, nasal sound can have tremendous effect, as in Monteverdi's *Orfeo* where it suddenly enters to accompany Charon's first recitative in Act 3.

Regals were also made to fold up, bellows and all, to look like a large book: the 'bible regal' is said to have been first made in Nuremberg near the end of the 16th century. 'Double regal' is an old term not really understood.

'Regal' has also been a term for an *organ reed stop.

Mountney 1969.

Renaissance instruments. Generally understood as those in use from the mid-15th century to the early part of the 17th—or even later in cases where an instrument has taken longer to assume the character of *baroque. Relatively few have survived from the 15th century. Then, with the 16th, follows a wonderful legacy of near 800 examples of all

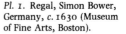

Pl. 1. Regal, Simon Bower, Germany, c.1630 (Museum of Fine Arts, Boston).

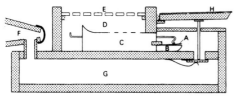

Fig. 1. Section of a regal.

major types, stringed and wind, very largely Italian or German, even if by no means all of them are preserved wholly in their original state. There are organs, harpsichords, and virginals; viols, violins, lutes, citterns, harps, flutes, recorders, shawms, dulcians, crumhorns, cornetts, trombones, trumpets; and rare or unique examples of less common types.

1. *Instruments and music.* Firstly, the great corpus of music for *lute and other fretted instruments (as *cittern, *bandora), all written in *tablature; and that for organ and *harpsichord, in England and France written in staff notation (for the well-known English collections of 1591–1624 see VIRGINAL, 4)—'virginal' then denoting equally the harpsichord). Secondly, many people today would see the 16th century, apart from the solo lute and keyboard music, especially as an 'Age of Consorts': small groups of musicians playing instruments of like or mixed kind, of different sizes matched to the various ranges of the parts in vocal polyphony from treble to bass. There are signs of different sizes of

an instrument already early in the 15th century (see, e.g. REBEC, 1; RECORDER, 5); but, for example, the learned Flemish composer Tinctoris, (c.1484), while giving valuable information on instruments severally, has nothing to offer on 'sets' of like instruments on which such music might be performed instrumentally. The first known work to do so is not until 1511, by Virdung, the earliest printed book covering instruments and illustrating sets of recorders and crumhorns. Next, Agricola (1528) adds to these flutes, shawms, viols, and fiddles (*Geigen*) which can reasonably be matched to the early violins and the rebecs described by Gerle, Ganassi, and Lanfranco, or at the mid-century in France by Jambe-de-Fer shortly preceding the first extant violins by Amati.

Then, especially with deeper basses added and fresh types of wind instrument appearing, wealthy patrons of music amassed instruments in sometimes vast numbers (often listed in surviving inventories (Baines 1957)). A well-known picture of c.1565 (Pl. 1) shows the composer Orlando Lassus (d. 1594) presiding at the virginal surrounded by Italian musicians of the Munich court posed with a selection of the instruments, from violin to *racket. Mostly such musicians played in groups of five or so, stringed, wind, or mixed, reading (or having memorized) from vocal part-books (the leading players probably filling out their parts in turn with *divisions). For a state occasion further players would be brought in, at Munich in 1568 to perform a 40-part motet by Lassus's contemporary, Striggio, on a Sunday with eight trombones, eight viols,

Pl. 1. Lassus with his musicians of the Bavarian court chapel, miniature by Hans Mielich from the Mielen Codex, 16th century. Around Lassus at the *virginals is (*left*) the *viola da braccio consort supported by *violone, and (*right*) *lute; behind the boy trebles stand the wind players, with (*left to right*) ?*crumhorn, or *cornamuse (only top visible), bass *recorder, *flute, *trombone (sackbut), mute *cornett, *racket, cornett.

eight recorders of the large sizes, the rest supplied by voices, all supported by a harpsichord and a bass lute (Trojano 1569).

For lighter instrumental music there were books (mostly from after *c.*1550) of *ricercari*, dances (as Claude Gervaise's four-part collections of *danseries*), and pieces in dance forms. Ever popular among them are, in England, Anthony Holborne's five-part *Pavans, Galliards, . . . for Viols, Violins, or other Musical Wind Instruments*, 1599 (British Library). For a complete list of printed instrumental music before 1660, see H. Mayer Brown (1967).

By the time *Praetorius described the instruments (1618–19), composers were already specifying particular instruments for the various parts in a work (from the Gabrielis in Venice, then in Germany, Schütz) or for successive numbers in a work (Monteverdi). Music was entering the Baroque but the instruments were still 'Renaissance': see PRAETORIUS (1618), and MERSENNE (1636).

2. *Makers.* Some of the greater makers of stringed and brass instruments are mentioned in entries on these. The wind instruments of wood (or ivory) rarely bear names of makers but are often branded with a mark or initial. Most frequent, on over 100 of the finest examples (half of them from the old Italian ducal collections and the Philharmonic Academy of Verona) the mark has the enigmatic form somewhat like a pair of exclamation marks (see RECORDER, Pl. 2 for an example). Recent research has been able to link this mark with the Bassano family of musicians and makers, of Venice

with a large branch established in London at the instigation of Henry VIII (Lasocki 1986).

As demand continues to grow for replicas of early instruments, stringed and wind alike, that for playing can stand comparison with the best extant originals, much has come to depend on accurate drawings published by museums and specialized journals. These also help to save the precious objects from the risks and wear of being measured over and over again, while the measurements themselves can be valuable in evidence of schemes of mathematical proportion observed by makers in the development and execution of the beautiful models which we see in every important kind of instrument of the Renaissance, of the Baroque too, and onwards still to please the eye notwithstanding modifications needed to accommodate technical advances of later times. The proportions in such models may derive from simple multiples or fractions, or an additive series of the 'Fibonaci' type, much cited in this connection ($1 + 2 = 3$, $2 + 3 = 5$, and so on making 8, 13, etc.) and having a link with the Golden Section, in that the ratio between any two consecutive terms of such a series quickly approaches (never exactly to equal) the chief ratio of that acme of geometrical proportion itself (see VIOLIN, 1*b*).

For separate references to Renaissance instruments see (stringed): BANDORA; BASS LUTE; CELLO, 4; CETERONE (arch-cittern); CHITARRONE; CITTERN; CLAVICHORD, 2; COLASCIONE; DOUBLE BASS, 5; FIDDLE, 1*c*; GUITAR; HARP, 9; HARPSICHORD; LIRA DA BRACCIO; LIRA DA GAMBA; LUTE, 2; MANDOLIN, 5;

ORPHARION; PSALTERY; REBEC; THEORBO; TROMBA MARINA; VIHUELA; VIOL; VIOLA, 3; VIOLIN, 6; VIOLONE; VIRGINAL. (Wind): BASSANELLI; BOMBARDE, 1; CORNAMUSE, 2; CORNETT; CRUMHORN; DOPPIONE; DOUÇAINE, DOLZAINA; DULCIAN (curtal); FLUTE, 5; KORTHOLT; PIPE AND TABOR; POMMER; RACKET; REGAL; SCHREIERPFEIFE; SHAWM; SLIDE TRUMPET, 3; TROMBONE, 4; TRUMPET, 3, 5 (see also FONTANELLE; PIROUETTE; WIND-CAP).

Agricola 1528, 1545, repr. 1969; Arnaut of Zwolle, n.d. (ed. Le Cerf and Labande 1932; see also HARPSICHORD, 5); Banchieri 1609; Ganassi 1535, repr. 1970 (recorder); Ganassi 1542, repr. 1970 (principally viols); Gerle 1532, 1546, repr. 1977; Jambe-de-Fer 1556, repr. 1958–63; Lanfranco 1533 (esp. viols, violins); Tinctoris c.1484 (ed. Weinmann 1917; partial edn. Baines 1950); Virdung 1511, repr. 1970; Virgiliano c.1600 (ed. Castellani 1979; gives fingerings on many instruments); Zacconi 1592.

Requinto (Sp.). 1. In Spain and Latin America a small, bright-sounding guitar, varying, like most small guitars, from one country to another in size, strings, and tuning (see GUITAR 5). In Colombia, for example, it may be a little smaller than a *tiple, and strung with four triple courses of steel, tuned as the first four of the guitar (in Venezuela it may be called a *cuatro). Accompanied by the guitar, it is played with a plectrum, *punteado* (plucking), though now often replaced by the *bandola. In Mexico, also in Argentina and the other southern countries, it is a little smaller than a guitar, with six courses (single or double) tuned a fourth or fifth above the guitar and played either with a plectrum or *rasgueado* with the fingers, for dancing or to accompany the voice.

2. The name, signifying 'higher-sounding than the ordinary', denotes in Spanish military bands the small E♭ clarinet (see CLARINET, 4c).

Resin. See ROSIN.

Resting bell. A general term for a cup or bowl held mouth upwards in the hand or placed on a cushion, and struck on the rim with a wood beater. In Japan (*kin*), of brass or bronze, it belongs to Buddhist ceremonies and domestic shrines, and is of any width from c.4 mm. up to a metre (3¼″–3′); Western percussionists know it as 'Japanese Temple Bell' or 'dobachi'; Henze has scored for it. For an Indian ceramic resting bell, played in sets, see JALTARANG.

Restoration of instruments. The subject has come much to the fore in recent years, relating not only to workshop techniques (not entered on here) but to policy over certain aspects involved. A very important distinction is between 'restoration' and 'conservation'. To take for example a rare old lute or keyboard instrument that a collection has acquired, perhaps long ago, in some clearly altered

state: a majority of curators would now insist that it is, as it stands, a historical document; whatever its state, it may give evidence of the past which on no account should be recklessly obliterated by irreversible replacement of parts, and still less by the only too familiar process, widely favoured through the post-war decades, of 'restoration to original condition'. This last, dependent on informed guesswork on the part of whoever is in charge, may lead to a beautiful object for exhibition to the public, for whom it may serve well to illustrate history; but to a serious researcher (probably also a maker and reconstructor of early instruments) its value may be irretrievably lost.

Reyong (Bali). See GAMELAN, 2.

Rgya-gling (Tibetan). See CHINA AND KOREA, 3c.

Ribible (or 'rubible'). See REBEC, 2.

Ring flute. See FLUTE, 7c (ii).

Ripieno (It., 'filling up'). Baroque works with orchestra often distinguish between the *concertino*, of solo players (or front desk of violins), and *ripieno*, all together. Handel in his oratorios, performed with perhaps 12 violins and four oboes, often begins an aria 'senza ripieni' (in the violin or oboe parts or both) followed by 'con ripieni' or 'con ripieni per tutto'; or he may mark a number 'senza ripieni la prima volta', or 'ripieni per seconda volta' ('second time only'). The term has survived as 'repiano' with a particular meaning in the British *brass band.

Rock harmonica, rock gong. See LITHOPHONE.

Rocking melodeon. See LAP ORGAN.

Roman lute. See MANDOLIN, 5b.

Rommelpot. See FRICTION DRUM, 1.

Rondador. See PANPIPE, 1d.

Roneat. See RANAT.

Rose. On stringed instruments, the decorative disc frequently incised in or inserted into the soundhole of a *lute, baroque *guitar, or *harpsichord; cut in wood, in Gothic or arabesque patterns, or built up in paper or parchment, and often gilded.

Rosin (resin, colophonium; Fr.: *colophane*; Ger.: *Harz*). Clarified hard rosin sold in blocks for the bows of stringed instruments, for the bow-hair to 'bite' on the strings, prepared from residues left on distillation of turpentine. There are special types, e.g. for metal strings, and for double bass.

Rote (Fr., Eng.; Ger.: *rotta*; Sp.: *rota*). Stringed-instrument name met from the 6th century AD to the 14th, yet it is not absolutely certain what instrument it referred to in any place at any time.

1. *Early period.* First, Bishop Fortunatus of Poitiers in the 6th century alludes in a poem to praises sung by the Roman to the *lyra*, the Briton to the *rotta* (in one version *chrotta*), the barbarian (i.e. Germanic) to the *harpa*. The last fairly certainly then generally meant a species of lyre (see LYRE, 3) and perhaps 'rotta' did so also, the plucked ancestor of the Welsh bowed *crwth. Makers today of early instruments have been using 'rotta' for reproduction of the early Germanic and Anglo-Saxon lyres, of which actual remains exist.

2. *Middle ages.* A 12th-century Swiss manuscript (at St Gallen) says that the old *psalterium* in the shape of the letter 'delta' had become altered by musicians for comfort, given more strings, and called by them *rotta*. This could relate to the tall triangular instrument, then relatively new, termed by modern historians 'harp psaltery' (see PSALTERY, 2). Such an instrument, as far as can be made out in its eroded state, is carved on a capital of *c.*1100 at Moissac (France, on the Tarn) beside the words 'Eman (Heman) cum Rota' (Steger 1961). For two centuries to the 13th 'rote' occurs continually in literature, typically in Old French romances, nearly always to rhyme with 'note'. A later instance is in the *Canterbury Tales*, where the Friar could play upon the rote, in a manner referred to later in the poem as 'harping'—so a plucked instrument of some kind; but no 'harp psaltery' is to be seen in England, leaving 'rote', among the 13 different kinds of instruments referred to in the *Tales*, one which eludes a true identification.

Rothphone. A rare metal double-reed wind instrument, made in different sizes: virtually *sarrusophones remodelled in the shape of *saxophones, from soprano to bass. Invented by Ferdinand Roth in Milan, patented (1906) by the maker Bottali, they look like thin saxophones. Intended for military bands, they were still listed in 1937 by Maino & Orsi (Milan) under the name *saxorusofoni.* See Joppig 1988 for a photograph of the family.

Rototom. A remarkable tunable drum invented in the USA in the 1960s by the percussionist–composer Michael Colgrass, and now well known. It has no shell and is tuned on the mechanical principle of rotary timpani (see TIMPANI, 3). The flesh hoop, with plastic head (Fig. 1, A), is borne on a star-shaped metal frame (B), which turns freely on a vertical central stem. The counterhoop (C) is joined by the tension rods to a lower frame (D) which engages a screw-thread in the stem. The stem is square at the base, to be held stationary in the stand or drum bracket below. On turning the drum with one hand both of the hoops rotate together but D moves up or down on the thread fcto change the tension on the head. When played

with soft-ended beaters the rototom can give absolutely clear musical notes of a range of up to an octave: if of the smallest, 15 cm. (6″) in size, upwards from around *d′*. Larger sizes are up to 45 cm. in diameter (18″), tunable upwards from about G. First used in television music and the like, the rototom has since spread to rock music and other fields. There are now also pedal-tuned models, leaving both hands free while changing the pitch.

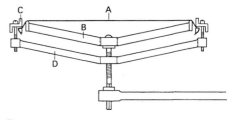

Fig. 1.

Rozhok (diminutive of *rog*, 'horn'). Russian folk wind instrument of wood (the older ones wound with birchbark) with fingerholes (five and one on the back) for playing in much the same way as the Renaissance *cornett. The small wooden mouthpiece (or cavity cut in the top of the pipe) is similarly placed towards the side of the lips. The chief areas are around Vladimir and Kalinin (formerly Tver) where *rozhki* of different sizes are played as a group, from a treble *c.*40 cm. (15″) long to a bass an octave lower *c.*80 cm. (30″), this often with a large brass bell. They are heard in spirited polyphony, made up by the players on the lines of folk choral harmony, in which they sometimes join; they are said to have been played thus from about the middle of the 19th century.

Smirnov 1959.

Ruan. See YUEQIN.

Rubebe. See REBEC, 2.

Rührtrommel (Ger.). See SIDE DRUM, 4.

Russian bassoon. See SERPENT, 2 and Pl. 2.

Russian horns. Sets of metal horns with which music was once performed by a squad of men each with a horn of different length and sounding one note. The first horn band was organized in St Petersburg for the Empress by the horn-player Maresch in 1757, and became widely imitated elsewhere, even up to the 1830s. Sets of horns are preserved, each usually a widely conical straight tube bent sharply round at the mouthpiece end. Music of all kinds was performed in full harmony, the fast passages perfected by rigorous training (Ricks 1969).

Russian theorbo (or *torban*). An 18th- to 19th-century instrument related to the *bandura.

Rute (or ruthe). A switch of twigs or cane, used with the bass drum during the classical period. See BASS DRUM, 5.

Ryuteki. Japanese flute; see FUE.

S

Sachs, Curt. Musicologist (b. 1881, Berlin; d. 1959, New York). Towering figure in the history and ethnology of musical instruments. Co-author (with E. von Hornbostel) of the classification that has become regarded as standard (see CLASSIFICATION). From 1919 to 1933 director of the great Berlin *Collection, then in Paris, and from 1939 to his death professor at Columbia University of New York. Among his many works, apart from collection catalogues: *Geist und Werden der Musikinstrumenten* (1928, repr. 1965); *Handbuch der Musikinstrumentenkunde* (1930); *History of Musical Instruments* (1940); *Rise of Music in the Ancient World* (1943); *Vergleichende Musikwissenschaft* (1959, esp. pp. 73–5).

Sackbut (from Fr., *saqueboute*, a word roughly signifying 'draw out the end'). *Trombone; its name in England (and France) from the late 15th century until replaced by Italian *trombone* in the course of the 18th century. For 'sackbut' in the Book of Daniel, see BIBLICAL INSTRUMENTS, 2.

Salpinx. Ancient Greek, a calling instrument, especially a long straight trumpet of which no certain example has yet come to light. While nothing like as important in Greece as the *tuba* was in Rome (see TRUMPET, 7), there was, nevertheless for a period, a prize at the Pythic games for whoever could sound it over the greatest distance.

Samisen. See SHAMISEN.

San hsien. See SANXIAN.

Sansa (or *mbira*, etc.). African instrument of iron (or wooden) tongues attached side by side to a wooden base for plucking with the thumbs (Pl. 1); widely known in Western countries as 'thumb piano', and among musicologists as *'lamellaphone'.

The base may be a thick piece of hardwood 18 cm. (7") long, but more frequently forms a top of some kind of box which acts as a resonator. The tongues may number from three to 16 or more, and when, as most commonly, of wrought iron, are about 1 mm. thick, hammered thinner towards the free end. They are held in place by iron rods, one to hold them down, the other to act as a bridge. These also allow a tongue to be tuned by pushing it further inwards or outwards. Jingles of shell, or loose metal collars, may be placed round the base of the tongues.

Pl. 1. Sansa player, Cameroons.

The instrument is held in the two hands with the tongues pointing towards the player; the longest tongues are generally in the middle, as suits the arc through which the thumbs move from one tongue to the next. In a quick figure a forefinger may help, plucking a tongue from below. Tuning is mostly of a pentatonic kind, the player improvising lively motifs, often in two parts, with great agility and a sound somewhat recalling that of a large *musical box (which likewise has metal tongues).

Some instruments have a second row of tongues placed above the first. Modernized versions now manufactured and sold in the West usually have tab-like tongues in diatonic sequence, with a shorter row placed higher for the sharps.

The *sansa* seems to be wholly an original product of African iron technology. Its age is unknown; it has been reported by European travellers since 1586. Its main range is from Nigeria, through the Congo, south as far as Zimbabwe and Mozambique.

Santur. See DULCIMER, 3.

Sanxian (or *san hsien*). Chinese long lute (see LUTE, 7), three-stringed, played with a plectrum. Like its descendant, the Japanese *shamisen, it has a long, square, unfretted wooden neck which dips downward where it meets the small body, traditionally to continue through this (but now more likely to be detachable). The body, *c.*15 cm. (6") wide, is carved out, basically square but with the corners much rounded off. The front and back are then covered with snakeskin (whereas those of a *shamisen* are covered with white catskin). The total length varies up to *c*.90 cm. (3'). It is seen played in *China and Korea, Pl. 1, second from left.

Originally developed in China during the Middle Ages (apparently from a Central Asian prototype of the Iranian *setar* kind, the name also meaning 'three-stringed'), the *sanxian* is a popular instrument today, played in various ensembles and to accompany the voice. There are several regional varieties.

Sarangi (or *sārangī*). A major traditional bowed instrument of India (Fig. 1). Varying in size, around 60 cm. (2') overall, the body is carved from one piece of wood, joined to a short, broad neck which is open on the back and communicates with the interior of the body through a wide hole. The 'pinched in' shape, giving the bow access to the outer strings, is covered by goatskin. The three gut strings (sometimes with a fourth of brass) lead from a brass nut to a 'comb' at the base of the body; an ogee-shaped opening above the nut is characteristic, at least with the older instruments. The usual tuning follows the pattern *c′ g c*.

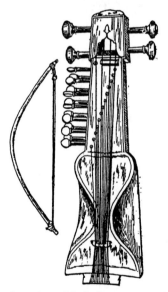

Fig. 1. Sarangi, north India (Lavignac 1913).

Two rows of pegs down the right-hand side (the bowing side) tune the wire sympathetic strings, led from the interior of the neck through a diagonal series of small perforated ivory bushes (as in a *sitar) through holes in the bridge under the playing strings; they formerly numbered around 11 but today may be some 24. The melody strings are stopped with the nails from the side, giving great facility of glissando, sliding the nail, by which the

sarangi is especially valued in accompaniment to the voice, though it is a solo instrument also.

In South India it has been superseded by the *violin.

See INDIA.

Sarinda (or *sārindā*). A fiddle of North India and Afghanistan, mainly a folk instrument, with three strings. In the extraordinary skull-like shape, the two concave lower pieces are each formed of a carved wooden shell, glued in place (a similar construction as used for the middle bouts of the *sarangi, *sarod, and various other Indian instruments). Below these concavities is the small parchment belly. The part above is usually open but may also be skin-covered.

Sarod (or *sārod*). North Indian lute of classical music (see INDIA, Pl. 1), derived from the Afghan plucked *rabab* (see RABAB, 4), with the depth of the body similarly extending some way upwards to meet the short neck terminating in the peg-head. The wide parchment belly gives the *sarod* a characteristic mellow timbre. The fingerboard, broadening towards the belly, was originally wooden and fretted. It is now of metal and fretless, to enable the fingers to glide smoothly along the strings, facilitating (cf. SARANGI) a quasi-vocal style. The four melody strings and six drone strings are plucked with a triangular plectrum, e.g. of coconut-shell. There are also about 15 sympathetic strings with their pegs close together along the near side of the neck (like those of the *sarangi*). Some varieties have a small gourd attached on the back, at the top, and some more recent designs of *sarod* show other variations.

Saron. Javanese instrument of struck bars, prominent in the *gamelan. Seven polished bronze bars, covering a five- or seven-note octave (*slendro* or *pelog*; see GAMELAN), are laid on pads over a trough-like wooden stand, each bar positioned by two upright metal pins passing through holes in the bar. Bars of a high-pitched *saron* are highly domed in cross-section, reaching over 2 cm. ($\frac{3}{4}$″) thick along the centre, but for deeper notes they are wider and almost flat. The single beater has a hammer-shaped end, of horn or wood; the other hand damps each note immediately following the stroke.

Of three sizes of saron (see GAMELAN, Ex. 2, for a music excerpt), the *saron panerus* ascends over an octave above the treble staff, full and penetrating in sound. An octave deeper is the *saron barung*, and an octave below this is the *saron demung*, sounding down to about Middle C. A village gamelan may have one saron only, and with bars of iron.

For the other, softer-sounding *metallophone of the gamelan, see GENDER (this with tubular resonators).

Sarrusophone. Double-reed wind instrument of metal, now little used. Shortly after Sax patented the *saxophones, another wind-instrument maker in Paris, Gautrot (later Couesnon), put into production a corresponding family of double-reed instruments, with similar keywork and fingering and the same notation and transpositions. He generously named them after Bandmaster Sarrus of the 13th Infantry regiment, who, he said, had first suggested the idea. The invention is said to date from 1856; but in October of 1851 Queen Victoria noted having heard at the Great Exhibition 'an organ accompanied by a fine and powerful instrument called the sarrusophone'. The soprano looks like a brass oboe; from alto to contrabass the tube is doubled back from one to five times, and is normally silver-plated. The tenor (in B♭) is 70 cm. (28") tall; bass (B♭, Fig. 1), 90 cm. (36"); E♭ contrabass, 130 cm. (51"). For the deepest, B♭ contrabass, the reed is c.8 cm. (3") long, 2.5 cm. (1") across the tip.

Fig. 1. Bass sarrusophone, Bb (Soyer 1927).

Over the years a fair number of bands in France, Italy, and Spain came to employ them, chiefly as outdoor substitutes for oboe and bassoon; they were made in France up to c.1930. In Italy the baritone and the bass may still be seen in the largest municipal bands. Their sound is not as full as a saxophone's, partly since with a double reed the conical bore must start narrower and then continue narrower all through.

Some orchestral works include a part for contrabass sarrusophone (Stravinsky's *Threni* is a late example). This, from the days of Saint-Saëns, was often used in France and Spain for contrabassoon parts and has also been manufactured in the USA (for bands, by Conn from 1921) while in literature it is immortalized in Sir Thomas Beecham's account, in *A Mingled Chime*, of his 1908 production of Holbrooke's *Apollo and the Seaman*. In jazz, Sidney Bechet played a solo (on either tenor or baritone)

in 'The Sheik of Araby', in a recording made during his time in Paris.

The *reed contrabass is an instrument sometimes confused with the sarrusophone, but its key system is quite different.

Sasara. See BIN-SASARA; JAPAN, 1a.

Saùng (or *saùng-gauk*). The Burmese harp, one of the country's most beautiful solo instruments, and today honoured as its 'national instrument'.

Pl. 1. Burmese saùng-gauk (classical arched harp).

Typologically an 'arched harp' (see HARP, 10a), it is held sideways across the knees or on a stand, the curving neck, from the curving root of an acacia species, to the left. The neck continues along the long hollowed-out wooden soundbox beneath the belly of deerskin (often red-lacquered), bearing upwards against this as a string bar, the strings tied to it through holes in the skin: a construction that recalls the arched harps of Ancient Egypt from which the *saùng* may ultimately derive. The 13 to 16 silk (or nylon) strings, mostly played with the right hand, are tuned over a range of about *c* to *f"* in various basically pentatonic schemes (one of the main tunings begins *c e f g b*). Intermediate notes, also high notes on the shortest string, are made by pressing with the left thumb or thumbnail close to the curving neck (much as formerly in some harps in Europe).

The student of the modern *saùng* must master complex theories of modes and tunings, as well as intricate playing techniques. Various types of finger-strokes are used: upwards strokes of the index finger, outwards and upwards with a hooked finger, or with hooked index finger and thumb together. The basic repertory comprises 13 *kyò* ('string') songs which date from the 18th and 19th centuries. They are composed in the oldest of four harp tunings (*hnyìn-lòn*), and are usually accompanied by finger cymbals (*sì*) and clappers (*wà*).

The *saùng*, serving Buddhist royalty, is depicted from the 7th century AD, when similar harps were played in India.

Simonson 1987.

Saxhorn. Family of valved brass instruments patented by Adolphe Sax (see SAXOPHONE) in Paris, 1845. They are the parents of most of the deeper valved instruments of the present *brass band (other than German). Still in France the alto instrument, in Britain *tenor horn, is known in full as *saxhorn-alto*.

1. *Shapes and sizes.* The saxhorns (illustrated in Kastner 1848) were, but for the smallest, built bell-upwards, and pitched alternately through the family in E♭ (sometimes F) and B♭ as follows, naming the modern descendant in parentheses:

E♭ soprano (today the soprano cornet)
B♭ contralto (this later disappeared, players preferring the cornet)
E♭ alto, also called tenor (as in Britain, tenor horn)
E♭ baryton (baritone)
B♭ basse (euphonium)
E♭ contrebasse (E♭ bass)
B♭ contrebasse (BB♭ bass), added to the family by 1851.

The original dimensions were mostly narrower than they have since become. For valves, Sax first used the sturdy, relatively cheap to make, piston valves of the Berlin type (see VALVE). Two afterthoughts were: B♭ *suraigu* ('very high'), with the pitch of the present piccolo trumpet and included by Berlioz in the March in Act I of *Les Troyens*; and an E♭ *bourdon* (sub-bass) which remained little more than experimental, though several examples by Sax and later makers have been preserved as curiosities in Europe and the USA. Also in *Les Troyens* is the fine solo for alto saxhorn, in 'The Royal Hunt and Storm', which however the composer later transferred to the horn.

2. *The spread of saxhorns.* By the time of the invention, makers in most countries were producing new valved band instruments in various pitches, but Sax was the first seriously to conceive them as the single family unified in technique and musical effect. They were immediately imported into Britain and later made by the firm of Henry Distin (later absorbed by Boosey). In the USA, after the saxhorns first arrived, makers began to show a characteristic independence, especially in making models in which the bell points back over the shoulder. These were very popular through the time of the Civil War. In Germany, it seems from Wagner's own reported words that it was Sax's instruments which at least partly inspired the quartet of tubas for the *Ring* (see WAGNER TUBA).

3. *Saxo-tromba.* A very slightly different family, now forgotten, produced by Sax at the same time as the saxhorns, with narrower bell section for a hint of trumpet quality intended to suit mounted bands.

Saxophone. The wide conical tube of plated or gold-lacquered brass is sounded with a single-reed mouthpiece akin to that of a *clarinet. It was invented nearly 150 years ago by Adolphe Sax (patented in Paris, 1846) and its regular place thenceforth was for long in the *military band, in which it is as essential today as then. In orchestral music its impact has been small compared with its towering success in jazz, won first in America in the late 1920s and partly due to the volume of which it is effortlessly capable of producing, the tube expanding at an angle around three times as great as in our other conical reed instruments: the mass of vibrating air inside a saxophone is very large indeed, while the holes for the notes are of proportionate width. These are covered by keywork which makes the saxophone look more complicated than it really is, the fingering being quite straightforward, save on extreme high notes.

1. *The family.* All the saxophones (the four main ones in Pl. 1) have the same standard written compass (Ex. 1, top), plus in many cases nowadays a key for an extra note (small note in Ex. 1); the sounding ranges are given below. The fundamental scale is repeated from the written *d'* (the six main holes closed) at the octave, on pressing the thumb-key. This controls two small octave keys which change over automatically from *a''* upwards (compare OBOE, Fig. 1b). The high notes from *d'''* to *f'''* are obtained by also opening four keys (including a bunch of three placed high up on the left of the instrument) to give these notes as 2nd harmonics of fundamentals which play no part as such. An extra plate for the first finger is lowered to give an alternative top F, lowering the second finger also. Above this a further octave is obtainable, used mainly by jazz and rock soloists, by means of fingerings which are not standard but are chosen from a multitude of possible alternatives as a player finds best on the particular instrument; various publications list such fingerings.

(a) E♭ *sopranino.* Length *c.*48 cm. (19″), rare but manufactured; used in some wind groups playing special arrangements. (The part in Ravel's *Bolero* arose from the composer's uncertainty over the upward range of the soprano, on which Marcel Mule (b. 1901) played the part at the first performance, 1928, as others have done since.)

(b) B♭ *soprano* (occasionally made in the shape of the alto—a 'bent soprano saxophone'). Not a regular instrument in a saxophone section, though Duke Ellington's lead saxophonist, for one, plays it in some of the earlier recordings, while always cited is Sidney Bechet, who in the 1920s adopted it as his main alternative to the clarinet. Otherwise, the very charming sound of the soprano is best heard as the top voice of a saxophone quartet (with

Pl. 1. Saxophones, soprano, alto, tenor, and baritone (descending to low A) by Yamaha of Japan.

Ex. 1.

alto, tenor, and baritone), the Paris quartet founded and led on soprano by Mule being one of the most famous up to recently.

(c) *Eb alto*. The first in general demand; in jazz and dance orchestras for long the leader of the saxophone section (see DANCE BAND). Among the great soloists, Charlie Parker evolved his breathtaking 'bop' style on the alto. The best-known solo concert works are also for alto, two of the finest, Glazunov's Concerto and Ibert's *Concertino da camera* (1934), both dedicated to the famous soloist Sigurd Rascher (b. 1907), who went to the USA from Germany. The alto was the first saxophone to be given a part in the symphony orchestra, from a virtuoso obbligato of 1868 in Ambroise Thomas's *Hamlet*, and the well-known solo in Bizet's *L'Arlésienne*, up to numerous later works such as Walton's *Belshazzar's Feast* (1929), and Honegger's *Saint Joan at the Stake* (1936, in which three alto saxophones replace horns in the orchestra).

(d) *Bb tenor*. Second in popularity only to the alto, and usually regarded as the most exciting solo saxophone in jazz from Coleman Hawkins, from the 1930s, and such as John Coltrane in the 1950s. Chiefly on the tenor has been developed the 'growl' made from the throat while blowing, and (besides the extra high notes) notes below the normal compass obtained by one of the several 'distortions' of embouchure now used in obtaining special effects. In the symphony orchestra the tenor came to the fore later than the alto, as in Vaughan Williams's Fourth Symphony and Prokofiev's *Romeo and Juliet* (especially the second suite), both works of 1935. A tenor in C or 'C Melody Saxophone' used to be popular for playing from song copies without need for transposition, and was also adopted by several soloists in the USA; it is about 8 cm. (3″) less in height than the tenor.

(e) *Eb baritone*. A superb instrument, now always made with a long bell (Pl. 1) giving a written low A, sounding the bottom C of the *cello. Its throbbing sound will be well remembered in the solos of such as Duke Ellington's Harry Carney, and as played by Gerry Mulligan in the 1950s. Several concert composers have written for solo baritone, and Stockhausen, with alto, and tenor, in *Carré*, 1960.

(f) *Bb bass*. Over 120 cm. (4′) tall, technically as flexible as the others and in regular manufacture. It has been featured by a few early jazz players, as Adrian Rollini, and again by recent soloists, as with great effect by Harry Gould. It is also heard in full saxophone ensembles using all from soprano downwards.

(g) *Eb contrabass*. Two metres (6′) tall, very rare, made to special order.

2. *Reed and mouthpiece*. The reed (see REED, Fig. 2), of cane, though plastic reeds are available for some of the saxophones, has average length: soprano, 58 mm. (2.3″); alto, 71 (2.8″); tenor, 81 (3.2″); baritone, 90 (3.6″)—figures which (save for the last) roughly match the square roots of the pitch ratios between the instruments. The reed is placed on the lower lip, the sides of the mouth tightened round the mouthpiece. Vibrato made with the jaw was regular among the older jazz and dance-band players but has since the 1940s rather dropped from fashion, allowing more free scope for other tonal effects. The mouthpiece itself has undergone a change from about the same time: from the original wide interior giving a suave sound to blend with the brass and woodwind in a band or orchestra, to a more constricted interior favouring a more ringing, 'exciting' quality. Several types of mouthpiece attachment are available for connecting to an amplifier–loudspeaker system, e.g. a transducer with sensor inserted through a hole drilled in the tip of the mouthpiece, and output socket clamped to the saxophone neck.

3. *The invention*. Adolphe (Antoine Joseph) Sax (b. Dinant, near Brussels, 1814; d. Paris, 1894) first worked with his father, Charles Sax, a leading wind-instrument maker in Brussels. He studied clarinet at the Conservatoire there and produced designs for improving this and particularly (his first patent, 1838) the *bass clarinet. He left no account of how the idea of the saxophone first came to him; but in 1842, a few months before he left Brussels for Paris, Berlioz reported it in the *Journal des débats* thus: 'a brass instrument . . . rather like an ophicleide in shape but with a mouthpiece like that of the bass clarinet', adding 'there is not a bass instrument to compare with it'. In the 1846 patent one of the drawings is of an upright design, a largish instrument with flared bell pointing upwards and a saxophone-type mouthpiece, as if, as many now believe likely, Sax had commenced by experimenting with his bass clarinet mouthpiece on the *ophicleide—a regular product of his father's workshops—resulting in a saxophone initially of bass or baritone size (McBride 1982).

The saxophone family was officially adopted by the French army by 1854, from which time a number of examples are preserved in collections. They are hardly different from those still manufactured up to the 1920s: plain, brass- or nickel-plated; the bell, shorter than now, gives Bb only; there are neither 'pearl tips' for the main keys nor rollers for the little fingers; the thumb works two independent octave keys; the gap in the keywork about half-way down shows the absence of the now standard 'articulated G♯' for the whole-tone trill on F♯ (by trilling on F♯ while holding down the G♯ key). Rather smaller widths for the tube in conjunction with the old form of mouthpiece give the 'historical saxophone' the velvety sound which is to be imagined when thinking of Bizet, or Sousa's band, or Tom Brown's Saxophone Sextet in the American music-hall around 1915.

4. *Saxophone variants*. In the late 1920s, C. G. Conn, Elkhart, Indiana, celebrated manufacturers of wind

instruments, added to their list an 'English-horn-saxophone' or 'Conn-O-Sax' in F, shaped in imitation of the *cor anglais. Also in F (one of Sax's original tonalities for alto saxophone), Conn offered a 'mezzo-soprano saxophone', shaped like the alto but smaller. For 'Jetel-Sax', see TAROGATO. See also SLIDE SAXOPHONE.

Horwood 1980; Kool 1931.

Saxo-tromba. See SAXHORN, 3.

Sax-tuba. See BUCCINA AND CORNU.

Saz. The *long lute of Turkey, a favourite instrument played also to the east up to Azerbaijan (USSR) on the Caspian, and in Europe in local varieties across to Albania on the Adriatic. The Greek *bouzouki is a descendant.

The pear-shaped body (Pl. 1) has, from the side, a characteristic appearance of a deep scoop, deepest at the level of the bridge. The more expensive instruments may be hollowed out, to thicknesses down to 4 mm. or less; but most are built up of ribs, like a lute. The belly, slightly convex, may incorporate on each flank an oblique gusset of darker wood. There may be no soundholes of any kind. The frets, of fine gut or nylon tied round the long, narrow neck, vary in number and positioning. There is a great deal of historical theory behind it, but a typical urban *saz* as sold in Istanbul will be fretted for a Pythagorean scale plus two further frets in the first octave, required in certain modes. Thus in the tetrachord beginning with the open string, one of the extra frets comes between the semitone fret and the whole-tone fret, thereby bisecting the minor third to give two successive three-quarter-tones; the pattern then repeats in the tetrachord which starts a perfect fourth above the open string.

The metal strings run in three double *courses, the deepest-tuned being in the middle (e.g. d', g, a), and are played with a hide plectrum. Sizes range from the small *cura* ($c.75$ cm. (30'') overall length) to the *meydan saz*, of twice the size (Picken, 1975).

Schalmei (Ger.). See SHAWM.

Schelle (Ger.). *Sleigh bell (pellet-bell); *Schellembaum*, *bell tree.

Schreierpfeife (or *Rauschpfeife*). German names for a Renaissance double-reed instrument played with a wind-cap over the reed (like a *crumhorn), mentioned in many court and town inventories, and evidently found useful in music where the *shawm would be too assertive. Some 12 examples of various pitches are known, most in the Berlin and Prague *collections. The bore is conical but at a smaller gradient than in a shawm, and the bell is scarcely flared. The name *Rauschpfeife* occurs early in the 16th century after which, up to the mid-17th century, it is with one exception always

Pl. 1. Saz (Bate Collection, Oxford).

Schreierpfeife or some other form of this word, such as *Schryari*, e.g. in Praetorius (whose illustration of them, PRAETORIUS, Fig. 1, is however rather puzzling in showing tapered exteriors). The Berlin instruments came from a church at Naumburg, Saxony, which has preserved old inventories in which these same instruments are clearly included under the name 'Schreiarien', while the Prague examples are listed in an inventory as 'Srayffaiff'. Reproductions made today may be offered under either name (Boydell 1982).

Schwirrholz (Ger.). *Bull-roarer; Schwirrscheibe, *buzz disc.

Scordatura (It.). Some music for stringed instruments, chiefly in the Baroque period and for those that are bowed, requires one or more of the strings to be tuned differently ('*scordato*') from the normal, e.g. to allow greater use of open strings in a piece, or render feasible certain kinds of passages in double stopping. The music may then be written in a way that allows for this, as in the best-known instance of Bach's Fifth Suite for unaccompanied cello. The A string is here tuned down to G: a diagram of the tuning notes (the 'Accord') is given at the beginning, and every note to be played on this string is written as it would be fingered if the string were still tuned to A, i.e. a tone higher than it is going to sound.

Scraper. Any instrument with a notched or corrugated surface for scraping to produce a fast succession of impacts. See GUIRO; LAGERPHONE, this from Australia, where also aborigines of the north-west may accompany songs on a notched stick. Among archaeological finds in Europe are animal jawbones cut with notches, possibly for making a scraping sound. Still in parts of Europe scrapers may add to carnival noise, or be used for rousing labourers at dawn. See CHINA AND KOREA, 1a (iii), where, in ritual, sound by scraping answers sound by knocking, both on wood.

Jazz, from its early days, has sometimes used as a scraper the domestic washboard (corrugated galvanized plate in a wooden frame); it is played rhythmically with the fingernails, or with thimbles on the fingers.

The ratchet *rattle has been classified among scrapers, to which one could add the klaxon horn (see MOTOR HORN), and, from silent cinema days, a loud and most effective steam locomotive imitator composed of a foot-square wooden box (30 × 30 cm.) with a pair of strong spiral springs stretched across the inside to be scraped by a stout metal blade moved swiftly from side to side.

Rather different—more like running a stick along railings—are instruments such as the Spanish 'bone-ladder', in Catalan, *ossets* ('bones'): a number of bones tied at intervals horizontally to a string loop hanging from the neck, to be rasped with a metal ring at local festival dances.

Seljefløte (Norway). See FLUTE, 8b.

Semanterion (or *semantron*, Gk.). Instrument used instead of a bell in Greek Orthodox monasteries over south-east Europe: a long narrow board of resonant wood (e.g. maple) or an iron plate of various shapes, struck with a mallet. The board may be 2 m. (7′) long or more, carried on the shoulder balanced by one hand while the mallet strikes in fast rhythms, in some cases on two pitches by striking in two places, e.g. ♩ ♪ (etc.); or the board or iron plate is hung up permanently. The use is said to go back to the 6th century AD (or in some instances to prohibition of bell-ringing under Turkish rule).

Seraphine. Name given in the USA and England from the 1830s to various small *free-reed organs standing on legs: first apparently by Lewis Zwahlen, New York, 1832 to his 'harmonicon organ' (Libin 1985), then a year later by John Green, London, in his 'Royal Seraphine'. This had the size of a small *harmonium, with foot-pedals connected by cords to bellows inside the casing of the instrument above; some described its sound as hard and rasping, and it became superseded from c.1850 by the harmonium. Later the name was used now and then for *reed organs of American types.

Serinette, bird-organ. See BARREL ORGAN, 2.

Serpent (It.: *serpentone*). A deep wind instrument played from the 17th century to the 19th (reproductions are now made). Besides the characteristic instrument in serpentine form (Pl. 1) there have been others more like short, thick *bassoons; see below, 2, upright serpent.

Pl. 1. 'Le serpent du village', picture postcard, Paris, Musée National des Arts et Traditions Populaires.

1. **Serpent** (*true form*). The wide, undulating, conically expanding wooden tube, covered in black leather, has six fingerholes and a brass crook to take a cup mouthpiece (of brass, or often ivory), with which the serpent is sounded like a brass instrument. The wood—walnut was recommended—is hollowed and shaped in two halves (or in some cases, shorter, overlapping sections) glued together and bound with canvas before applying the leather. The compass ranges from the C below the bass stave (with lower notes possible by 'looselipping') to two-and-a-half octaves above (French works sometimes write the notes a tone higher, as see a fingering chart, c.1816, reproduced in Carse 1939). Great skill with ear and lips is needed to produce the notes in tune and even in quality. The sound lies somewhere between that of a soft *tuba and a strong bassoon.

Reputedly invented in France late in the 16th century by a canon of Auxerre, the serpent, without any keys, for long served in French churches (and the royal chapel; see ÉCURIE) to support the plainchant ('*serpent d'église*', Pl. 1, from an old picture postcard, possibly retrospectively posed). There are 19th-century accounts of how some players would improvise a bass to the chant, or insert scale-like cadenzas between the verses (Hillsman 1980). In Italy it was played in Bologna Cathedral along with trombones up to 1700; in England, Handel adds it to the bass part in the 'Fireworks Music' (1749).

Towards the end of the 18th century it began to enter military bands, strengthening the bass part played by bassoons. This led to the serpent well known in English collections: usually with brass keys, two or more, following the example of other wind instruments of the time. The open end is brass-mounted, the overall height reduced by some 75 mm. (3″) by narrowing the bends, and the instrument held more slanted. The holes are bushed with ivory and are set out for holding the instrument, not with both hands over the tube (i.e. palm downwards) as more usual previously, but with the right hand underneath (palm upwards as Plate 1): more secure, but the index finger of this hand then covers the lowest hole of three instead of the highest—the reverse from normal wind-instrument practice. The most necessary key is for the left index finger, giving B♮, the note with all holes open being B♭. Such serpents were built up to c.1850, some (e.g. by Thos. Key) with 13 keys, leaving no plain holes for the fingers. Sometimes the left thumb works keys on the front of the tube, the arm then placed right over the first bend, while holding the instrument well sideways. There are a few Tutors for the serpent. One player (André of the Prince Regent's Private Band) had a Corelli violin concerto arranged for him. Perhaps the last player before the current renewed interest is one photographed in a Bohemian village near Vyškov in 1950, with a keyless serpent of the old form in his hands (Kunz).

In the Tolson Museum at Huddersfield, Yorkshire, is a perhaps unique serpent of twice the ordinary size and pitched an octave lower. Built c.1840 by two local weavers, it has latterly appeared in programmes under the name 'Anaconda', coined for it by R. Morley-Pegge (1959).

2. *Upright serpent* (Fr.: *serpent droit, serpent basson, basson russe* ('Russian bassoon')). Continental 'reformed' serpents were made from 1790 to c.1830, mostly built like a bassoon, with two straight wooden joints connected at the bottom by a bassoon-like 'butt joint'. A coiled or looped crook takes the mouthpiece. There are three or four keys, and a flaring bell which in most 'Russian bassoons' is of brass in the form of an open-jawed dragon's head (Pl. 2), 'realistically' coloured. 'Serpent' in Wagner's *Rienzi* Overture would signify some instrument of such kind (see also CIMBASSO). Other types retain the old serpent construction but with

the tube running up and down instead of undulating (*serpent militaire*, etc.). The *serpent Forveille*, named after its Parisian inventor (c.1823), is also of leather-covered wood but has a brass left-hand joint with chimney-like fingerholes (not visible in the poor likeness in *military band, Pl. 2, bottom line), possibly borrowed from the all-metal *bass horn then used in England, it is an efficient design, of which there are numerous examples in collections, in contrast to rare variants of a similar nature called serpentcleide, ophibaryton, etc.

Pl. 2. Upright serpent, or 'Russian bassoon'.

Sese (or *zeze*). The 'stick zither' (see ZITHER, 3c) of East and Central Africa, for accompanying songs and dancing. A flat wooden bar held on edge has three or so high projections cut in one end to serve like frets under the plucked string. The open mouth of a gourd attached below the other end is moved to and fro against the chest as a variable resonator (as in a 'gourd bow'), see MUSICAL BOW, 3, and the Indian *tuila*. On one side of the bar, or on both, is a further string, for the thumbs to pluck in accompaniment.

Setar. A classical long lute (see LUTE, 7) of Iran, resembling the *tanbur*, usually, though the word means 'three-stringed', with four strings.

Shahnai (or *shahnāī, sahnāī, senai*). The leading reed instrument of northern India, one of the Asian *shawm family, with its counterpart in the south, *nagasvaram* (see below, 2). The player is accompanied (Pl. 1) by another who sustains a drone on a similar instrument (*shruti*, *ottu*), which has holes only towards the bottom, for tuning the drone note with wax.

1. *Shahnai*. In popular use, processions, etc., the *shahnai* may resemble the short *surna* played over all western Asia. But for playing in classical styles (as made famous by Ustad Bismillah Khan) it is up to 60 cm. (2') long, conically bored in a thick, expanding tube of a close-grained wood, with seven fingerholes (no thumb-hole) and a short, flared brass bell. The double reed (see REED, 5) is of specially cultivated 'pala' grass, and is placed on a conical metal staple from which hang spare reeds, etc. Some place a lip disc on the staple, but most do not, obtaining a range of two octaves or more, using lips and tongue, and shading the holes with the fingers, to reproduce the constant pitch-inflexions, slides, and other expressions essential also to Indian solo playing of stringed instruments.

2. *Nagasvaram*. Typically a slender-built instrument which can exceed 80 cm. (32") in length, with a bell of metal or wood; there exist examples wholly encased in silver. It is heard in temples, accompanied by the drone (*ottu*), barrel-drum *tavil* (played on the right head with the fingers, on the left with a stick) and perhaps the small cup-shaped bronze cymbals, *talam*. It has been used for classical styles longer than the northern *shahnai*, a great master having been T. Rajaratnam Pillai. There are also small versions, *mukhavina*.

Shakubyoshi. Clapper; see JAPAN, 1*a*.

Shakuhachi. The end-blown flute of Japan, one of the most important instruments of the solo and chamber music. A stout instrument (Fig. 1), it is traditionally made from the root end of bamboo, where the knots show as ridges on the outside and the end curves a little forwards. The usual length is *c*.55 cm. (22"), but there are other sizes, e.g. to match the ranges of different singers and other instruments. The interior, generally lacquered red, narrows from *c*.22 mm. (7/8") at the top, where the rim is cut to a slope leading down to a sharp-edged piece of horn or ivory on to which the breath is directed (revealing the *shakuhachi* as a development from an original notched flute; see FLUTE, 7*b*). The four large fingerholes and a thumb-hole higher up give a pentatonic series of the pattern *d' f' g' a' c'' d''* over two-and-a-half octaves or more, semitones being made by half-covering, while the manner of blowing commands all the nuances in timbre, pitch, and sliding up to a note, characteristic of Japanese playing of many other traditional instruments. The *shakuhachi*, originally an instrument of Zen Buddhism, attained its present form in the 17th century. Later it came to be said that it was carried by wandering priests who, not allowed swords, relied on the instrument as a weapon in defence against robbers.

The classical *shakuhachi* repertory distinguishes *honkyoku* ('original pieces' composed for one or more *shakuhachi*) from *gaikyoku* ('outside pieces',

Pl. 1. Shahnai players, north India.

Fig. 1.

items played in combination with the *koto* and *shamisen* or borrowed from their repertories).

The instrument is nowadays also turned in wood, sometimes in two joints; and there have been trials with European-style chromatic keywork, first *c*.1922 in Japan and latterly by enthusiasts in Western countries, though, as with our recorder, the traditional form continues to prevail.

See also JAPAN.

Shaman drum. Frame drum of the Eskimo, Lapps, and other Arctic peoples: the membrane, often of a walrus stomach, is lashed with sinews to the thin wooden hoop. In one type the drum is grasped by crossed cords beneath the membrane, the other hand wielding the thin stick with skin-covered end. In another, a handle (DRUM, Fig. 1*h*) is attached to the hoop (as in most *rattle drums), and the stick may be held in the middle, for hitting the membrane from underneath, alternately with each end. Among such peoples of the far north the drum was formerly said to have been the most important possession along with the fire-tools and family charms, and been played at every feast. The shaman, singing while vigorously beating it, might bring it close to his mouth to modify the tone of his voice. The Chukchi of the far north-east of Siberia had, as reported in 1909 (Bogoras), no other instruments save a *buzz disc of walrus ivory, and whalebone whistles or calls (some with a

whalebone tongue between pieces of wood, see REED, 6) for imitating the cry of the eider duck at ceremonies.

Shamisen (or *samisen*). Japanese *long lute, corresponding to (and derived from) the Chinese *sanxian*, and one of the most widely played of the country's traditional instruments. (See JAPAN Pls. 1, 2).

The small, almost square body is constructed from four pieces of wood (e.g. quince) and is covered on top and bottom with catskin or dogskin. The long, thin neck, square in section and without frets, dips down to pass through the body and protrude slightly at the other end. The three strings of twisted silk are fastened below the bridge by a silk cord, and are struck with a large axe-like wooden plectrum. The nut is so constructed that the lowest-tuned string can vibrate against the wood beneath, to contribute a jarring quality. A characteristic drum-like 'snap' is produced when the plectrum hits both string and skin. Tunings vary according to the genre or the vocal range of a singer, the standard patterns being a fifth plus a fourth, or the reverse, or all in fourths. Instruments vary in size for different purposes, the largest being the *gidayū shamisen*, used mainly in *bunraku* (puppet drama), accompanying the narrator.

The *shamisen* rose to be the most popular instrument of the Edo period (1615–1868), when large repertories of narrative and lyrical music for voice with *shamisen* were composed, and chamber music with *koto* and the flute *shakuhachi. In the popular *kabuki* theatre *shamisen* players sit behind the transverse flute (*shinobue*; see FUE) and drums (*tsuzumi*; *taiko*).

The *shamisen* tablature most used today puts arabic numbers 1 to 7 (representing the notes of the diatonic scale) horizontally, on three lines for the three strings. Fingering are shown by roman numerals for the strings and by Japanese numerals for the fingers, while special techniques are indicated by signs.

See also JAPAN.

Shawm (formerly in Eng. more usually 'shalme', 'hautboy', 'hoboy'; Fr.: *hautbois* or, before 1500, *chalemie*; Ger.: *Schalmei*, *Pommer*; It.: *pifaro*, *piffero*; Sp.: *chirimía*). Wind instrument, predecessor of the oboe, with conical bore and a double reed generally placed on a 'pirouette' (see below, 1*a*), and more powerful sound. Through its main period, from the 14th century to the 17th, its duties lay in professional music for ceremonial or festive occasions performed outdoors or in large buildings. For a summary of the numerous relatives of the shawm in Asia and North Africa, see below, 4.

1. *Renaissance shawm*. The old European shawm has been revived for early music, in its main sizes from treble to bass (see outlines in PRAETORIUS, Fig.

1), modelled on original 16th- and 17th-century examples preserved notably in the *collections in Berlin and Brussels.

(a) *Sizes.* The lowest notes for each are given in Ex. 1. The note given with seven fingers down is shown as a minim, above which the compass extends upwards by about an octave and a sixth (sometimes more). There is no thumb-hole. Shown as crotchets are notes made with additional keys, for the lower little finger and thumb.

Ex. 1.

Treble shawm (Fr.: *dessus de hautbois*; Ger.: *Diskant-Schalmey*): a plain thick-walled pipe, 64 cm. (24″) long, externally almost cylindrical, with spreading bell, turned in one piece, usually of box or maple. Below the fingerholes are a number of permanently open 'vent holes'. Fig. 1 shows (a) the brass staple, its lower part wound with thread, and (b) the wooden pirouette, recessed on top to make room for the base of the reed (c). The lips are pressed to the flat top of the pirouette, allowing the reed to vibrate fairly freely inside the mouth while being tongued as on an oboe.

Fig. 1.

Alto shawm (in Eng. originally 'tenor'; Ger.: *Altpommer*): *c.*75 cm. (30″), the lowest note made with a brass key acting inside a removable wooden protecting 'barrel' or from Fr. *fontanelle*, with small holes to let the sound out (as in RECORDER, Pl. 2). The pirouette is as above but longer.

Tenor shawm (Ger.: *Tenorpommer*), *c.*110 cm. (43″): the reed, and pirouette if used, are placed on an angled brass crook. The *basset shawm* is similar but with the three additional keys.

Bass shawm (*Basspommer*), known in Germany by 1535: *c.*2m. (6′) tall, played standing with the bell resting on the ground by one foot, and a somewhat bassoon-like tone. A Venetian engraving of the Doge's procession in 1610 shows, however, the lower end of the bass shawm supported by a boy walking ahead of the player, who is therefore somehow dispensing with the normal crook (Ongaro 1985).

Great-bass shawm (*Grossbasspommer*): *c.*270 cm. (over 9′) tall, and capable of satisfactory notes through makers' skill (as with the above, also large recorders and bassoons) in the matter of bunching the fingerholes in two far-separated groups, each group of three within the span of the hand—though in at least one example the fourth hole is provided with a key.

(b) *The shawm band.* The principal formal role of shawms through much of the 16th century and up to the middle of the next was in a group, playing stately music in up to six parts, generally, in some cases regularly, enriched by a *cornett playing the 2nd treble part and a trombone for the part above the bass. On the bass, the bass shawm might be replaced in a procession by the handier *dulcian, as in Pl. 1, detail from a large painting by van Alsloot of a religious procession in Brussels, 1616, well known even if it is not easy to identify from their proportions precisely which middle-sized shawms are taking part (and the leader, next to the cornett, holds his hands impossibly far down on his unusually slender treble shawm). For the similar French royal band up to the 1650s (see ÉCURIE) six-part *pavanes pour les hautbois* are preserved in the Philidor manuscripts at Paris (for one of the pieces, see Baines 1957, Fig. 64). As was usual for much ensemble music of the period they are written in the key of F or C; but one gathers from Praetorius that a shawm ensemble played the parts to sound a tone higher than written: this because the written keynote *f′* is almost impossible on the normal treble shawm with lowest note *d′*. Praetorius recommended that it should be built a tone lower, and that is how this instrument is often reconstructed today.

In later music, some of the Leipzig cantatas of Knüpfer include 'bombardi' in three parts, presumably shawms of the town musicians. But their main duties were outdoors, and in England, treble and tenor shawms, with trombone for the bass, were played by town waits up to the end of the 17th century when oboes replaced them, the instruments being exactly the same as in Germany, etc.

(c) *Variants of shawm.* There was also made in Germany and the Low Countries during these later times, and mentioned under the name *Deutsche Schalmey*, a slender-built type of treble and tenor shawm, with wide but elegant flared bell and smaller fingerholes more like those of the oboe. This type was primarily for military music, with dulcian for the bass. There are examples by Denner (see CHALUMEAU).

Pl. 1. Denis van Alsloot, detail from 'Procession of the Religious Orders of Antwerp' (1616), showing band of dulcian, three shawms, curved cornett, and sackbut (trombone).

See SCHREIERPFEIFE for shawm-like Renaissance instruments played with a *wind-cap.

In England, from the time of the coronation of Henry VIII (1509), is a mention of 'still shalmes' or 'still pipes', as if more quiet instruments: a Bristol apprentice in 1549 gained the reward of 'a viall, a Rebuke [*rebec], a still shalme, and a lowd shalme'. It has been suggested that the 'shawm' from the wreck of the *Mary Rose, cylindrical in bore, with two brass keys and original length of *c.*110 cm. (43″), may have been 'still'.

2. *Early rise of the shawm.* The source of the shawm, as a double-reed instrument of wood with expanding bell, remains largely a mystery, but the general view is that it derived from the Middle-Eastern *surna* towards the end of the Crusades, and was like this usually a small instrument with about the pitch of a Highland bagpipe and played particularly with trumpets and drum (*nakers, or tabor). During the 14th century it reached the treble size, and the alto, named *bombarde* (whence '*Pommer*') appeared. Through the 15th century both played for the courtly *basse danse*, the evidence here being that the bombarde played the tenor part (*a cantus firmus*); the shawm improvised floridly above this; and a trumpet (see SLIDE TRUMPET, 3*b*), or later in the century a trombone, played a contratenor part. One can see in this combination the germ of the 16th-century shawm band (1*b* above).

3. *Traditional shawms today: (a) Keyless types.* A few derivatives of the old shawms are, or have been till recently, to be heard in folk music, as in Central America, *chirimía*, of Spanish extraction; and on the Yugoslav island of Krk at the head of the Adriatic, *sopel* (*sopila*), made in two sizes tuned a fourth apart (each with pirouette) and played together largely in approximate sixths and sevenths (rather as the Croatian double flageolet *dvoinice* sounds in consecutive seconds). (For the Yugoslav *zurla*, see below, 4*a*.)

(*b*) *Tiple and tenora* (Catalonia, Spain, also Roussillon across the border in France). These splendid instruments (Pl. 2) of the *cobla* ensembles have long dropped the Catalan shawm name *xeremia* (Sp.: *chirimía*), being known simply as the *tiple* ('treble') and the *tenora*. They keep the pirouette and the old wide bore while adding keywork of 19th-century type. Both are transposing instruments: the *tiple* is pitched in F (a fourth above the oboe); and the *tenora* is a fifth lower, in B♭, and has a long metal bell for the second *tenora* player to be able to reach notes down to *f♯* (sounding *e*). Seated beside them is the pipe and tabor (*fluviol*), the leader; behind stand two trumpets, valved trombone, two bell-front baritones, and a double bass. (For the Castillian *dulzaina*, see DOUÇAINE, DOLZAINA, 3).

4. *Oriental shawms* (usually now termed by Western writers 'oboes', following *Sachs). Seen everywhere (see MIDDLE EAST, 1). The metal staple usually

Pl. 2. Tiple and tenora players, Barcelona.

carries a loose 'lip disc' of metal, bone, etc., on which the player presses the lips to leave the reed free inside the mouth, while replenishing the breath by *circular breathing.

(a) *Wooden in one piece.* Cylindrical down to the bell: *surna*, with *ghaita*, *alghaita* (North Africa), *karamouza* (Greece), *zurla* (Yugoslavia).

(b) *Brass bell* Conical bore: **shahnai*, with *nagasvaram* (India), **hnè* (Burma), **sona* (China), *ngyagling* Tibet, see CHINA AND KOREA, 3), *sarunai* or *selompret* ('trumpet', Indonesia), very variable.

(c) *No bell at all.* **Pi-nai* (Thailand).

(d) *Of cane.* Cane *reedpipes sometimes in Africa, etc., imitate the *surna*, etc. by adding a conical bell of metal or spirally rolled leaves.

Sheng, sho (or *shō*). Free-reed mouth-organ of China (Pl. 1) and Japan respectively, the *sheng* (in Korea, *saeng*) dating back to at least the 11th century BC; the *sho* from Tang China in the Middle Ages. For other mouth-organs of the Far East south to Borneo, see KHAEN. The *sheng* in the 18th century aroused the European interest in the free reed which led to the invention of the Western free-reed instruments (*accordion, *harmonium, etc.), though none of these have adopted the Oriental method of combining reeds with pipes and means of sounding the different notes.

1. *Pipes and reeds.* The upright slender dark-stained bamboo pipes, closed at the bottom, are held in a circle, in an order of height to please the eye, round a wind-chest of lacquered wood (or today in China, plated metal) recalling in shape a small gourd. Through the projecting mouthpiece the player both blows and 'sucks'.

   Each reed-tongue is cut, often pointed towards the tip, in a thin oblong brass or copper plate, lying

perfectly flat in the plate to vibrate equally in whichever direction the air is made to flow. The plate is cemented over an opening near the closed lower end of its pipe. The small, light reed will then vibrate provided that the pipe resonance is not too far removed from the pitch of the reed. In each pipe, invisible in the back, is an open slot which allows this resonance. But on the outside, just above the windchest, is a small hole which if left uncovered annuls the resonance, and the pipe is silent until the hole is stopped with a finger. In this the fingers of both hands are used, for any chosen pipe to sound, or number of pipes for a chord. A gap is left in the circle of pipes for a finger to reach two pipes which have the small hole on the inside.

2. *Sheng.* In China four of the 17 pipes used to be dummy (with no reed) and in Japan two are dummy; but now in China all pipes are functional. Today they give a chromatic octave, commonly *a'* to *a''*, plus four diatonic notes above. They are not arranged throughout in regular sequence, the pipes for the tonic, D, and fifth, A, being together on the right (modern instruments may be sold with a fingering diagram). The reeds are tuned with blobs of wax. The *sheng* is popular as a solo instrument, and in orchestral performance sounds chords from

Pl. 1. Sheng, China (Oxford, Pitt Rivers Museum).

simple intervals to complex note clusters often, as in Japan, with many notes lying a tone or semitone apart.

3. *Sho.* The notes and arrangement of the pipes are basically as in China (discounting the modern changes in the latter) giving *a'* to *f♯'''* in (to use Western terms) D major plus G♯ and C♮. In the *gagaku* and *bugaku* court music, the *sho* is one of three wind instruments (along with the transverse flute and the double-reed pipe **hichiriki*). The player has beside him a small brazier over which he will now and then warm the instrument, to dispel condensed moisture. The *sho* plays a series of slow six-note chords (see JAPAN, Ex. 1) in which the notes enter successively with a crescendo from the lowest note upwards. The chords are linked by standardized progressions, the player again both inhaling and exhaling, the lowest note in a chord being held until the next chord is begun.

Sho. See SHENG, SHO, 3.

Shofar. The traditional ramshorn of the Jewish synagogue, sounded on certain feasts of the year. It is ritually made, the horn being straightened, the wider end then bent upwards, and the whole partly flattened. Two notes are sounded, often a fifth apart and sometimes more. For 'shofar' in the Old Testament, and its translation in Latin and English, see BIBLICAL INSTRUMENTS, 1a. In Elgar's *The Apostles* (1903) the shofar is represented by an extra trumpet, 'preferably a straight trumpet' (says the score), sounding *e♭'* and *c''* in upward slurs, and rapid tonguings on the lower note.

Shoko (gong). See JAPAN, 1a.

Short octave. Often in keyboard instruments, up to the 17th century included, space is saved at the bass end of the keyboard by omitting four of the sharps in the bottom octave (keyboard music written before *c.*1700 hardly ever needing them) and using two of their black keys for naturals.

1. *Compass from C/E.* The commonest arrangement is with a compass down to C (see Fig. 1): C is given by what looks on the keyboard like E; D and E by the lower two black keys. The compass is then described as being from C/E. On a *harpsichord the bottom strings themselves will follow the order C F D G E A. On an *organ, the system avoids the

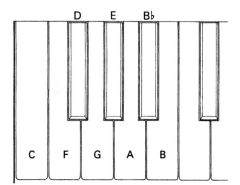

Fig. 1. Diagram of bass 'short octave'.

cost of large metal pipes for notes rarely used. It takes but little time to get used to, and allows the hand to span some wider intervals than otherwise (Koster 1980), as illustrated in Ex. 1, from the left-hand part in Peter Philips, *Pavana Dolorosa* (Fitzwilliam Virginal Book, LXXX).

2. *Compass from GG/BB.* The other common arrangement is where the lowest note is the G below (GG), this given by the apparent low B (BB) while the lower two black keys give the AA and actual BB, the strings running thus: GG C AA D BB E F, then as with an ordinary keyboard. The compass is here described as from GG/BB.

Side drum, snare drum (the latter name in America; Fr.: *caisse claire*; Ger.: *Kleine* or *Militärtrommel*; It.: *tamburo piccolo* or *militare*; Ru.: *baraban malyi*; Sp.: *tambór, caja*). The familiar drum beaten with two sticks on the upper or 'batter' head (from Fr.: *peau de batterie*), while the lower or 'snare' head is crossed by the snare which vibrates against the head when the drum is struck.

1. *Orchestral side drum.* Thirty-six cm. (14″) long, but the depth of the metal shell can vary from barely 8 cm. (3″) up to 40 cm. (16″) in a deep military model. In the USA 16.5 cm. (6½″) is cited as most suitable for general purposes.

The snare head is normally slightly thinner than the other. The snare is of gut, wire-wound silk, or (especially from the 1930s) spiralled wire, and in

Ex. 1. Peter Philips, *Pavana Dolorosa* (*Fitzwilliam Virginal Book*, No. LXXX), (from Koster 1980).

most cases can be released by a catch to become silent for a deeper, tom-tom sound or a 'muffled drum' effect (obtained in the 18th century by draping the drum with a cloth). The tensioning rods have grooved tops for turning with a coin. 'Double tensioning' is where the rods are divided, anchored to the shell in the middle; the snare head can then be given a little less tension than the other. The drum is clamped on an adjustable stand, usually at a slant.

2. *Marching side drums.* These often retain the older rope tensioning. This requires some 10 metres of hemp cord, led zigzag from one counterhoop (see DRUM, 2) to the other, passing through buff leather 'cuffs' which are pushed down for tightening. The drum is hooked to a leather 'carriage' passed round the neck and rests against the thigh. The top counterhoop has brass knobs for resting the drum upside down on the ground. Tied round the lower hoop and falling in a loop below is the plaited 'drag rope' by which the instrument was in former days carried on the back when not being played. In shallower models a wire frame on the side, when raised, supports the drum against the thigh.

3. *Playing.* The sticks are of hardwood, often hickory, which is very tough. The left hand is held palm upwards, the stick lying in the web of the hand under the thumb and resting on the middle finger; the right hand is held palm downwards, the stick gripped between thumb and forefinger, all four fingers above. Rotation of the wrists effects the actual beating, which is mostly by the hands alternately ('hand-to-hand') or often in the pattern L–R–L–L R–L–R–R, the 'paradiddle'. There are old traditional grace notes, single, double, and triple, in use from the 17th century, perhaps earlier: the 'flam' (from Fr.: *fla*), the 'drag' (Fr.: *ra*), and the 'ruff', all executed hand-to-hand except for the small notes of the 'drag' which are made by one hand. The roll is made with a double stroke for one hand followed by the same for the other, and first learnt in slow motion, eventually becoming a sort of controlled rebound. In jazz and rock music, however, the sticks are both held like timpani sticks (between thumb and forefinger, the thumb on top) and the roll is by alternate single strokes. Jazz brought in the explosive 'rim shot' on head and rim together, and the use of wire brushes, or more recently brushes made with metal strips for a stronger sound.

4. *Older side drums.* The side drum probably arose from the two-headed portable drum played widely over the *Middle East; early signs in Byzantine art of the 11th century show it struck on both heads. Whether it then had a snare is not possible to see. See PIPE AND TABOR for the medieval tabor, a small snare drum which, from the 14th century, is seen also played with two sticks as now and, by German and Swiss soldiers, with the fife. By the 16th

century it was larger, by 1600 very much so (as in Rembrandt's 'The Night Watch'), up to 80 cm. (32″) in width and depth, with heads of sheep- or donkey-skin. Counterhoops had, by 1500, replaced the older way of pulling down the flesh hoops directly (which involves perforating the skins for the cords to pass through; see DRUM, 2). The snare, of gut or twisted thongs, is still across the struck head. This large drum ('tabor' in England up to Henry VIII's time, then 'drome', from German or Dutch) gave the pace to foot-soldiers on the march and military commands.

By the time of Marlborough's campaigns (1704–12) the side drum was growing smaller again, becoming in the course of the 18th century hardly bigger than the present deep marching models, and such may be visualized where Handel writes 'with the Side Drums' at 'La Rejouissance' in the score of the *Fireworks Music.*

Around 1800 the shallower drum with brass shell (instead of wood) had come into use as well, and was through the 19th century distinguished on the Continent from the older, deeper pattern in name and also in function when both were used together. The deeper was the *caisse roulante* (see MILITARY BAND, Pl. 2, bottom line), in German *Wirbeltrommel* or in scores usually *tamburo rullante*, all meaning 'roll drum'; the snare was by degrees abandoned on this and the name became changed in Germany to *Rührtrommel*, in the sense of 'beating drum' (that which gave the beat on the march). The shallow drum was the *caisse claire* (in the same Plate, top line), in Germany *Kleine* or *Militärtrommel*, more tightly tensioned to serve for crisp rhythms and short rolls—the long rolls being the preserve of the other, deeper drum. The contrast is well shown in Richard Strauss's *Ein Heldenleben*, after No. 49 in the score (Ex. 1). The Rührtrommel is made in Germany today with a shell up to 50 cm. (20″) deep (and a different instrument from the *tenor drum, on which its parts are usually played in Britain and America). Later composers wishing to contrast the sound of two different side drums have generally specified them simply as 'small' and 'large', or 'high' and 'deep'. In France the very shallow type is also called *tarole.*

Ex. 1.

kleine Militärtrommel   *ff*

grosse Rührtrommel   *ff*

As a folk instrument the side drum is very important over much of the west of Europe, played expertly at dances and calendar festivals, sometimes providing the music on its own, as in some tarantellas in southern Italy and sword dances in Piedmont and Belgium.

Siku. See PANPIPE, 1*e*, 2.

Siren. A disc with holes drilled through it near the edge at equal intervals is rotated above a fixed disc with similar holes. Air blown at the fixed disc escapes in puffs through the other disc each time the holes align, causing periodic motion in the air beyond. The rotating disc may be turned by machinery: or, as with the mouthblown siren long familiar for comedy effects ('wheep!'), the holes are at opposite slants in the two discs for the outer to be driven round by the blown air (an invention ascribed to Charles de la Tour, d. 1859). A popular siren today (by 'Acme') has six holes per disc (here, plastic), so one revolution per second would give a frequency of 6 Hz (inaudible); blowing harder, 100 r.p.s., say, gives 600 Hz (about d''); 800 r.p.s. sounds above the top note of the piano. The waveform may contain harmonics, since the effective width of passage through the holes varies with time (the holes as they align forming a crescent opening, then a circle, etc.). Among composers who have required the siren are Varèse, Milhaud, Xenakis.

A siren can have two concentric rings of holes, differently spaced to produce simultaneous pitches at some constant interval apart, e.g. with five holes in the outer ring to four in the inner, a major third (as with some factory sirens); or with three rings, a three-note chord.

The older siren, used for scientific purposes, had a single disc which rotated over a fixed tube through which the air was blown.

Sistrum and jingles: 1. *Sistrum proper* (Gk.: *seistron*, from *seio*, 'shake'). Originally a cult instrument of Ancient Egypt sacred to the goddess Hathor, later taking part in other rites, and in Rome associated with the Isis cult. Most commonly (Fig. 1*a*) a bronze strip bent in a loop with a handle. Through holes in the strip two or three thin rods pass loosely from side to side, their ends bent to stop them falling out, and giving a soft jingle when waved. Some later examples have metal rings or discs on the rods to add to the jingle, and such are still used by the Ethiopian church and have occasionally entered the modern orchestral percussion.

2. Other uses of the name. 'Sistrum' has also denoted in the Renaissance period the *triangle, *xylophone, and even the *cittern (through confusion with the French *cistre*); and from the 19th century to today, a *bell tree (Fig. 1*b*). 'Sistro' in Rossini's *Barber of Seville* is so far unidentified (the part is often played on the triangle); an account of a local festival in the Nice area, 1847, speaks of a 'sistro ou battoir formé de 6 clochettes'. See also TRIANGLE.

3. Folk sistrum. Common among folk instruments, especially in Europe, is the type exemplified in Fig.

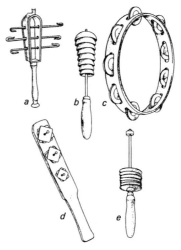

Fig. 1.

1*d*, with squares or discs cut from tin plate, strung on a twisted wire holder, or loosely nailed in pairs or threes along a piece of wood, or strung on short wires held in slots along the wood. For bottle-caps nailed to a long stick, see LAGERPHONE (Australia).

4. Spurs. The jingle of spurs as a horseman enters the scene on foot has been imitated in operetta (as in Johann Strauss's *Die Fledermaus*) by some device such as that shown in Fig. 1*e*, often found in old theatre-drummer's kits: the steel discs, slightly dished and strung loose on the rod, clink together as the instrument is moved vigorously up and down. A felt washer prevents them from flying off.

Sitar (or *sitār*). Indian lute, one of the major instruments of Indian classical music (see INDIA, 2 and Pl. 1, left).

1. The instrument. The large body, now of wood but originally a gourd, up to 40 cm. (16") wide, is cut with openings for securing a wooden neck-block (to hold the neck) and the slightly convex wooden belly (without soundhole). The broad neck, 7½ cm. (3") wide, is of a hollow construction. Often a smaller gourd is bolted to it below the region of the main tuning-pegs. Some 21 brass frets are tied to the neck, arching above it to leave room below for *sympathetic strings, and movable for the intervals required by different scales.

The metal strings run over the neck towards the near side and form three groups. (i) Four principal playing strings usually tuned (taking the tonic of the music as C) $f\ c\ G\ C$. (ii) Three thin strings to the player's right, $g\ c'\ c''$, the last two of these with their pegs in the side of the neck (Fig. 1, A, B) and with upright nuts further down (indicated by the black dots at C, D); these are the *chikari* strings, not stopped but struck together as a kind of rhythmic drone. (iii) Eleven or more sympathetic strings (*tarab*) with their pegs also on the side of the neck, emerge (not shown in Fig. 1) from small bone bushes and are tuned to the scale of the *rāga* in which the player is to perform. The bridge of the sitar (as of the **vīnā*, from which this bridge is derived) is of a unique kind, being a broad plate of bone or horn (E): the top surface is very carefully sloped down in the direction of the frets, with the effect of filling the sound with high **partials, giving a nasal ringing. The sympathetic strings have a smaller, lower bridge placed just above.

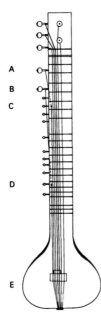

Fig. 1.

2. *Playing.* The sitar is played with a finger-pick made of a loop of fine wire and worn on the right index finger. The fingering of the strings is with the left middle and index fingers, pressing behind the frets and frequently using the expressive device by which a string is pulled sideways by the left hand after plucking with the right, to 'bend' the note, raising the pitch by up to a fifth. It is for this reason that the strings lie to one side of the neck, allowing room for this sideways deflection over a fret.

In performance the repeated tonic (or 'drone') essential to Indian music is generally supplied by the lute **tambura*, while equally essential is the drummer, with the paired drums **tabla*. It would exceed the present scope to try to summarize the form and subtlety of their combined, improvised performance.

The sitar was developed through the Muslim period from one of the Iranian 'long lutes' (see LUTE, 7), the name from Persian *setar*, by degrees absorbing technical features of the *vīnā* as demanded by the nature of Indian music.

3. *Sūrbahār.* This, invented in the early 19th century, is an enlarged sitar, *c.*150 cm. (5') long, with deeper tuning and wider frets. It became popular in Bengal until superseded by the sitar itself as developed in techniques by artists like the world-famous Ravi Shankar (b. 1920).

There have now been, from 1965, electric (transistorized) sitars and *tamburas*, to aid performance in public concert halls.

Siter (Indonesia). See CELEMPUNG.

Sleigh bell (Fr.: *grelot*; Ger.: *Schelle*; It.: *sonaglio*; Sp.: *cascavel*). The usual orchestral and trade term for the well-known spherical and shaken 'jingle bell' or, as preferred by musicologists, 'pellet bell', with a slit-like mouth and a metal or clay pellet inside. Such bells were once cast in bronze, the pellet embedded in the core prior to casting. Now they are forged or pressed, and sewn in a row on a leather strap or a long handle. Since the Middle Ages they have hung from the collars of horses and dogs or been worn on dancers' legs or wrists, or sewn to jesters' caps; also attached to instruments such as tambourines (along with or in place of jingle discs) or to the bow of a fiddle (often see LIRA).

The term 'sleigh bells' derives from light music. In Mozart's German Dances, K. 605 (see also POST HORN) they are written to sound chords, needing tuned sets. There have since been in Britain and America amateur groups playing tunes on such sets, the bells for each note sewn to an individual leather strap. Orchestrally the size, irrespective of tuning, can be important. The old carriage and harness bells were often large, 10 cm. (4") or more across, and of thicker metal than the bells commonly sold nowadays; they produced a more powerful and deeper sound—the largest were known as 'rumblers'. Bells approaching these in size are needed in works like Elgar's *Cockaigne* Overture (1902), where they are shaken *fff* (marked by a long *tremolo* sign) supported by the triangle.

Slentem. See GENDER.

Slide flute (Swanee whistle, lotus flute, etc.; Fr.: *flûte-à-coulisse*; Ger.: *Stempelflöte*). A duct flute blown like a **flageolet but with, instead of fingerholes, a plunger (with leather or plastic washer) pushed in and out from the lower end. As manufactured, now usually in synthetic resin, a length of about 30 cm. (one foot) allows a plunger movement of *c.*18 cm. (7"), giving a **stopped-pipe range of nearly two octaves upwards from about middle D. Suited especially to glissandos, Ravel uses it so in *L'enfant et les sortilèges* (1925) for sounds of the night. Others have introduced it since, Berio's *Passagio* (1963) using five.

Small wood or metal slide flutes were made in the 19th century as bird-calls and for toy symphonies, the Swanee whistle following in the

1920s. Before these, some mechanical singing birds used a miniature slide flute: air enters through a cam-operated valve to give a succession of 'cheeps' while another cam-wheel moves the slide to keep varying the pitch.

In India and the Far East bamboo slide flutes are made as toys; or in New Guinea, as a large end-blown slide flute, formerly to render the howling of a demon in puberty rites.

Slide guitar. See HAWAIIAN GUITAR.

Slide saxophone (Swanee-sax). There have been different varieties of this novelty instrument, first manufactured c.1927, on which, while blowing a small saxophone mouthpiece, tunes are played, sliding from note to note, by moving a hand-knob to uncover a long slot in the internal air-channel. In a British design the plated casing conceals a square-section metal channel of constant width and open along the top to form the slot. In this runs a flat steel strip, moved by the knob; but as the notes go higher, the strip issues from the end of the channel, so in order to clear it, the mouthpiece leads to the channel from the outside at an angle. A French design allows the mouthpiece to be placed in the normal way, at the blowing end itself, and the slot is opened and closed by a flexible rubber strip pressed to it or raised from it as required by a roller device moved by the hand-knob.

In the name (see also SLIDE FLUTE), no connection has yet been found between 'Swanee' and Stephen Foster's 'Old Folks at Home'.

Slide trumpet. A slide has been used on trumpets in several ways: 1, slide moving outwards as on a *trombone; 2, slide moving backwards; 3, the whole trumpet moved outwards along a single tube.

1. Slide moving outwards: (a) Slide trumpet (modern). Trade name for a B♭ trumpet built like a small trombone, made in the 1930s to interest dance-band players but little used.

(b) Trompette à coulisse (Fr., 'slide trumpet'): 1820–50, with a short, 25 cm. (10″) slide located under the bell. Made in fair quantity by Courtois and others, though there is little record of their use. (For soprano trombone, see TROMBONE, 5a.)

2. Slide moving backwards: (a) Slide trumpet, English (Pl. 1). Made c.1798–c.1860, played in orchestra and band, in the former by some leading players almost to the end of the 19th century. Built in the classic form of the natural trumpet, the rear bow contains a slide which draws backward a little way towards the player's face; a bent shank for the mouthpiece prevents the slide from hitting the chin. Two fingers move it by lugs fixed to a hollow rod concealing a spiral return spring or length of elastic rubber; or, in the earlier designs (as Pl. 1) a cord from a clock-spring contained in a casing mounted on a cross-stay (usually with a second casing for a spare spring). The instrument was claimed by the trumpeter John Hyde as his invention. Many examples are still to be found, some of the finest by Pace or Köhler, both of London (the words 'Harper's Improved' often seen on the bell do not seem to have anything to do with the type of spring). The instrument is built in 6′ F with crooks for lower keys. The primary intention of the slide was to correct the F and A of the natural scale; but with the higher crooks it will lower by a whole tone, making possible almost a full diatonic two-octave compass, which the earlier soloists would exploit with practically the fluency of a valved instrument. The slide trumpet was played especially in Handel's obbligati in preference to the widely used *cornet. The last Handelian soloist on the instrument, John Solomon (d. 1953), was especially famed for his performances with the contralto Dame Clara Butt (d. 1936) of the aria 'Let the Bright Seraphim' from *Samson*.

(b) Flat trumpet. Written for by Purcell in his music for Queen Mary's funeral (1694), this is known from a description (*Talbot) also to have had a slide that is drawn backwards; 'flat' referring to its

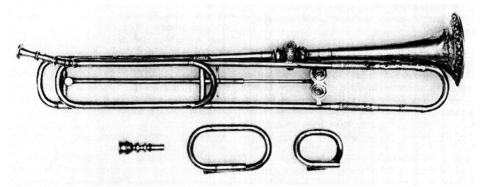

Pl. 1. Slide trumpet, showing bent mouthpiece shank and, below, correct mouthpiece, and D and E♭ crooks (C crook on the instrument).

capability of being played in minor keys, as Purcell writes for it. No example is preserved, but possibly it may be seen in engravings of James II's coronation (Halfpenny 1951).

3. *Sliding mouthpipe*: (a) *Zugtrompete* (Ger., 'slide trumpet'). Mentioned in Germany from the 16th century to the 18th: a natural trumpet with a telescopic first branch (carrying the mouthpiece), the trumpet being moved bodily along this with one hand, the other steadying the mouthpiece against the lips. The shift for a whole tone is therefore twice that required by the instruments above (1, 2). Only one example is preserved (of 1651; Berlin *collection), yet the *Zugtrompete* was evidently much used by town musicians, playing chorale melodies from the tower, also to some extent in church music. Bach includes it, as '*Tromba da tirarsi*' (from It.: *tiro*, 'slide'), in four cantatas, in one, No. 77, with a difficult and high-ranging obbligato (see also CORNO DA TIRARSI).

(b) *Renaissance slide trumpet* ('minstrel's trumpet'). The above *Zugtrompete* can reasonably be identified in pictures through players' attitudes, holding the trumpet somewhat downwards in both hands (see TROMBONE, Pl. 2, the two further figures), not raised in one hand in the usual trumpet manner of the times; and a trombone is most unlikely to be seen in close association with ordinary trumpets through the period concerned. During the 15th century a trumpet is often seen played in similar attitudes, again suggesting a sliding mouthpipe (Sachs 1950), while Burgundian court records from the 1420s onward name a player of the *trompette des menestrels*, listed with players of the shawm in distinction from those of the *trompette de guerre*. One might see the sliding mouthpipe as a likely step towards the invention of the trombone (around the 1450s), though some historians deny that the evidence is sufficient to warrant the view that a slide trumpet existed already in such early times.

Slit drum (Fr.: *tambour-à-fente*; Ger.: *Holz-* or *Schlitztrommel*). Wooden percussion instrument of many tropical peoples, used in ceremonies, to accompany songs and dances, and for sending messages.

1. *With a single slit*. A length of tree-trunk, from c.50 cm. (20″) to well over 2 m. (6′), is hollowed out through a long slit down one side, leaving both ends solid. The sides of the slit are struck with wooden beaters. (Since not properly a drum, having no membrane, some writers prefer 'slit gong'; but then, neither is it a gong.) Main areas are across Central Africa; South-East Asia and the Philippines; New Guinea to Tonga; Central America and the Upper Amazon. To hollow a log, after marking the line of the slit, the maker usually proceeds straight downwards, using a long, slightly curved iron chisel, or knife or spear, and then working to the sides; in the Solomon Islands (Melanesia), where

hollowing was once done with clamshell tools, two men with iron tools can complete an average-sized slit drum in three weeks, though in Africa, by one account, one man can take a year. A South American method is to introduce heated stone balls to char the wood while hollowing, formerly with a stone axe. Fig. 1 shows a frequent African form with a short, narrow central slit between the wide openings and providing two thick lips for striking upon.

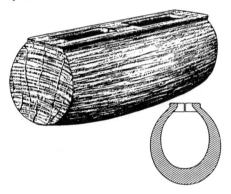

Fig. 1. Slit drum from the Cameroons; length 45 cm, (18″).

In Africa and South America the two sides of the slit are generally made to differ in thickness, the thinner side giving a deeper sound than the thicker, chiefly for sending long-distance messages in drum language based on speech. In Melanesia, however, only one side may be struck on (sometimes by two men) and messages sent by 'long-and-short', e.g. in the old days: /..// /..// /..//..// (etc.) announcing the killing of a prisoner (to be eaten).

2. *With several slits*. In West Africa there may be three or more parallel slits, 3 to 4 mm. wide and of different lengths, made by hollowing from the ends of the log, then plugging one end of this. Each length of intervening wood will give, when struck, different pitches which can be tuned by inserting wedges at the ends of slits. The sound has been described as almost xylophone-like, to which other players may add by striking the log in other places. Bamboo can be used instead of wood.

3. *Log drums*. Instruments different from both the preceding in forming the slits as thick 'tongues' with their free ends facing towards the middle. See TEPONATZLI (Ancient Mexico); LOG DRUM.

4. *Use in Western music*. Some modern compositions have incorporated slit drums: Stockhausen in *Gruppen* calls for six giving contrasted pitches, having borrowed them from an ethnological museum for the first performance. Some more easily made substitutes for the real thing have become available from percussion manufacturers.

Pl. 1. Some of the brothers Baschets' instruments (*The Telegraph*).

Snare. The gut or metal cord which in many drums over the world is stretched across the head to vibrate against the membrane when the drum is struck. With two-headed drums struck on one head, the snare may be across this (e.g. Fr. *tambourin*, see PIPE AND TABOR) or across the other (as *side drum). It goes back in Europe at least to the Middle Ages.

Snare drum. The American name of the *side drum.

Sona (*so-na, suona*; from Persian *surna*). Chinese member of the Asian shawm family (see SHAWM, 4). Of wood, widening outwards from the narrow top usually in a 'scalloped' profile, with a flared brass bell on the end. Length, 30–45 cm. (12–18″). Seven fingerholes and thumbhole. The small triangular double reed (see REED, 4) is placed on a conical metal staple on which is a lip-disc (in some instruments with one or two small brass bulbs below it). A popular instrument, loud and piercing, heard especially in the theatre. Some recent models follow Western manufacturing technology and have simple chromatic keywork. The *sona* is of Moslem extraction, and dates in China from around the 14th century. The Korean equivalent is *hojok*, and the Tibetan, *rgya-gling*: see CHINA AND KOREA, 2e, 3).

Sopel (or *sopila*). See SHAWM, 3a.

Sordino, sourdine (It., Fr.). *Mute.

Sordun. See KORTHOLT.

Soundpost. The upright stick of pine that in many bowed instruments is wedged between back and belly at a point close to the treble side of the bridge; see VIOLIN, 3.

Sound sculpture. Combinations of the sonorous and the visual, conceived from the 1930s in America and Europe, and well exemplified in the *structures sonores* of the brothers Bernard and François Baschet (b. France, 1917 and 1920), who have exhibited from 1955 in many countries, attracting visitors through their strange sounds and arresting visual design (Pl. 1). The sounds are here generated by rubbing glass rods, or by striking metal rods, discs, or wires or combinations of these, and are amplified by wide, shallow cones or 'horns' of light metal folded into fantastic shapes. In one of the glass instruments, giving a chromatic octave, the rods, 6 mm. thick ($\frac{1}{4}''$) are stroked with wetted fingers for their longitudinal vibration to excite transverse vibration in brass rods, thence to a thick bar for the vibrations finally to be radiated by the large cone. The sound can be almost like a trombone played fortissimo.

Music by friction upon glass rods had been tried by the German physicist Chladni in his *Euphon* of 1790, but with small volume of sound: part of the originality of the *structures sonores* as sound-producers lies in the purely mechanical (i.e. non-electrical) amplification by the cones.

Sousaphone. An American form of *tuba built to rest upon the player's left shoulder with a very wide, forward-pointing, detachable bell (Pl. 1) up to 60 cm. (2′) wide; named in honour of the great bandmaster John Philip Sousa (1854–1932) at whose suggestion the instrument was first made. Like other band tubas it is built in both E♭ and BB♭ pitches. Often now the bell is of fibreglass or suchlike, less heavy and better for marching routines where the sousaphones (in the USA in the rear rank) nod their bells this way and that: the vast bell being spectacular in intent, having no special acoustic value. The sousaphone was first made apparently by J. W. Pepper, Philadelphia,

Pl. 1. Sousaphone by Boosey & Hawkes, London.

then by C. G. Conn. Early photographs of Sousa's band show an original pattern with the bell pointing straight upwards like a huge flower vase.

South-East Asia. The countries from Burma, through Thailand, Kampuchea (Cambodia), and Vietnam to the Philippines, North Borneo, and Indonesia, are sometimes grouped musically as 'gong-chime' cultures, from the variety of gongs and *gong chimes so important in ensembles with other instruments over most of the area. Such ensembles range in size from the largest Javanese *gamelan, in which the players may have perhaps 75 instruments before them, to village groups with only a few. Prominent on the mainland are the louder ensembles with gongs, xylophones, cymbals, drums, and a loud wind instrument usually of a double-reed kind, and playing for theatre events, shadow plays, entertainments, and for religious celebrations: in Burma, *hsaing-waing* (Pl. 1, taking its name from the unique *drum chime that leads it); Thailand, *pi-phat*, the name from the wind instrument which is here the leader; Kampuchea, a similar combination; Vietnam, ensembles differing in not having the gong chime but only the single gongs. Softer groups (Pl. 2), e.g. for weddings or folk ceremonies, bring in the stringed instruments, dispensing with the loud wind instrument. For corresponding ensembles of the southern Philippines, see KULINTANG. (For fuller description of the instrumental ensembles in the various countries see *NOCM*, 'South-East Asia', by Helen Myers.)

1. *Instruments* (see also GAMELAN). To mention a few:

(*a*) *Idiophones.* Gongs, hung singly or in sets, punctuate the music; gong chimes are usually in a circle round a low frame. For xylophones and

Pl. 1. Burmese hsaìng-waìng ensemble, with hsaìng-waìng (tuned drum chime, *centre*), hnè (conical shawm with flared metal bell, *centre right*), kwì-waìng (bossed gong-chime, *right*), poat-má (large barrel drum suspended from a pole frame, *centre left*), yagwin (cymbals, *left*), accompanying a marionette play (*above*).

Ex. *1*.

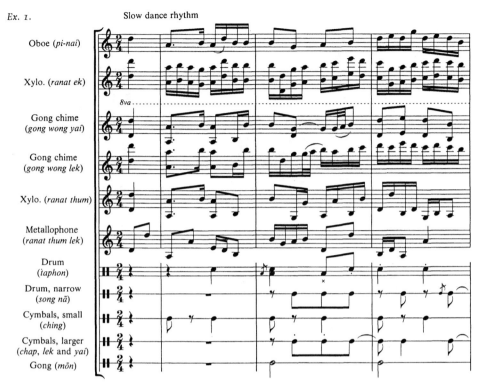

Pl. 2. Mahōrī ensemble of Thailand: front row (*left to right*), small hand cymbals, sǒ sām saī (spike fiddle); centre row, jakhē (zither), ranāt ēk lek (metallophone), ranāt ēk, ranāt thum (xylophones), ranāt thum lek (metallophone); back row, khlui (flute), khǒng wong yai, khǒng wong lek (gong-chimes), rammanā (frame drum), thōn (goblet drum).

*metallophones, with the bars over a 'trough' stand, see RANĀT (Thailand, etc.). Cymbals vary from *c*.12 cm. (5″) in diameter up to 59 cm. (2′) in Vietnam; also in Thailand and Kampuchea are small thick cymbals, as see CYMBAL, 5*b*. A small slit drum (Burma, *byauk*; Vietnam, *mo*) marks the time along with, in Burma, a long clapper of split bamboo. Among Indonesian bamboo folk idiophones: *angklung (swinging bamboos), *chalung (tube xylophone).

(*b*) *Drums.* Apart from the Burmese *drum chime, mainly a horizontal barrel drum, as Thailand *taphon, and Kampuchea *sambhor* (here leading the loud ensemble); also 'goblet' and frame drums, often in the ensemble, and (Vietnam) an hourglass drum.

(*c*) *Stringed.* Lute, Vietnam *dan ti-pa* (resembling the Chinese *pipa); long lute (see LUTE, 7), Vietnam *dan tam* (Chinese *sanxian). Fiddle, resting on the ground by a spike (cf. RABAB, 3), Thai *sǒ sām sā* (Pl. 2), Kampuchea *tro khmer*, Vietnam *dan nhi*. Long zither, see CHAKHĒ, Thailand (with 'crocodile zither', Burma); Vietnam, *dan tranh* (*dan thap luc*), Indonesia, *celempung, *kachapi, 1. Harp, Burma, *saung-gauk.

(*d*) *Wind.* Flutes (bamboo): transverse, Vietnam and sometimes Kampuchea; duct, 'ring flute' (see FLUTE, 7*c*), Burma, *palwei*, Thailand and Kampuchea, *khlui (khloi); all these usually with a membrane hole as with the Chinese flute *di (dizi). Double-reed (see SHAWM, 4: Burma, *hnè (with drooping bell); Thailand, *pi-nai (bell-less). See KHAEN for free-reed mouth organs; also BLOWN GONG (Indonesia).

2. *Music Example.* Ex. 1 is a fragment of the music of a Thai *pi-phat*, from a suite used in ballet performances (transcribed in Western notation by

Phra Chen Duriyanga, 1948; for the tuning of the scale see RANAT). The piece gives an illustration of Far-Eastern 'heterophony' (as distinct from 'harmony' in the Western sense based on chords). While the plain melody is stated on the 'oboe' *pi-nai*, the other instruments render it differently, each in its own particular laid-down style, together to create a sonorous texture of an intricacy that goes far beyond any mere unison of notes and figuration. Below the tuned percussion instruments (lines 2 to 6) is the main drum *taphon* (line 7): the lower notes (bottom space) with the right hand on the wider head commanding many strokes, among them (marked by a cross) a short damped sound made with open fingers and palm; with the left hand (upper notes, top space) a dot marks a light stroke on the rim with straight fingers and damped, while a line marks a similar stroke but a long sound (undamped); double notes indicate both hands.

Among the rest, the small thick cymbals *ching*, *c*.6 cm. (2½″) wide and joined by a cord, give the main beat throughout. The other cymbals may have widths of 14 cm. (5½″) and 25 cm. (10″) respectively. The hanging gong *mōn* is *c*.35 cm. (14″) in diameter, with a boss. Pl. 2, also from Thailand, shows a large ensemble of the quieter kind, with many of the instruments listed above.

Spiccato. See VIOLIN, 5*c*.

Spike fiddle. Term used by many Western writers for fiddles, chiefly Asian, in which the body of the instrument (spherical, tubular, etc.) is borne on a stick or pole that transfixes the body, with or without an added iron or wooden spike sticking out from the bottom (see FIDDLE, 2*b*, SOUTH-EAST ASIA, Pl. 2). Curt *Sachs, writing first in German, used the term *Spiessgeigen*, later translating it

(1940) into English 'pierced fiddle', perhaps a better term than 'spike fiddle' in not suggesting a distinct protruding spike, which not all these instruments possess: there may be only a short stump to which the ends of the strings are tied, or nothing visible at all. The term 'spike lute' may also be encountered, here never with a 'spike'.

Spinet (Fr.: *épinette*; Ger.: *Spinett*; It.: *spinetta*). Keyboard instrument with plucking action as in a *harpsichord but a different and more compact shape (Pl. 1). The name is originally Italian, in which it covered instruments of *virginal types. It came in England during the 17th century to denote those of the type illustrated. Since this ceased to be made the *square piano has often been popularly called a 'spinet', as has also, sometimes in America, a miniature upright piano.

1. *The instrument.* It can be seen in Fig. 1b how the spinet derives from the harpsichord (a) by slewing this round to the right, making a smaller instrument with room for one string per note only. The harpsichord's curving 'bentside' is reproduced on a smaller scale (b): a name 'bentside spinet' is now sometimes preferred, to confirm the distinction from 'spinet' in its early sense of a 'virginal' (c): as was also a contemporary English expression, 'leg-of-mutton spinet'. As in a harpsichord the longest strings are along the main straight side or 'spine' but now lying furthest from the keyboard (the opposite to a virginal, Fig. 1c); and the tuning pins and nut (N) are immediately beyond the keyboard on a strong beam with the soundboard beyond that—and rather restricted in functional area especially for the lower end of the five-octave compass (typically from GG). The jacks are fitted in between the strings as in a virginal, in twos plucking in opposite directions for adjacent semitones. The case is usually veneered in walnut.

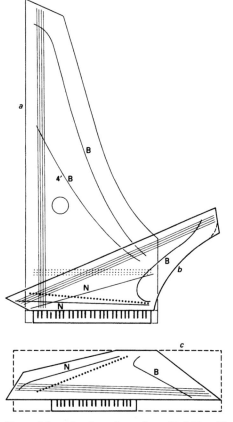

Fig. 1. Schematic views from above (B, bridge; N, nut; rows of jacks indicated by lines of dots). (a) Harpsichord (including 4′ bridge); (b) spinet; (c) virginal, rectangular and polygonal forms.

Pl. 1. Spinet.

2. *Makers*. The earliest known dated spinet is of 1637 (Brussels *collection) by Zenti of Viterbo, Italy, who may have been the first to find this way of making a harpsichord as a smaller instrument (he later for two years worked in England at the court of Charles II). The design became popular in France (less so in Germany) and very much so in England, where makers turned to producing it as a domestic instrument instead of the virginal. Among makers of the most numerous preserved spinets are: last third, 17th century, Stephen Keene, Charles Hayward; 18th century, Thomas and John Hitchcock, Baker Harris, and John Harris, who went to Boston, Massachusetts, in 1768. The oldest known American-made spinet is of 1739 by Clemm, Philadelphia (New York, Metropolitan Museum).

Spinets are made today though perhaps not as popular as virginals, partly because these are suitable for music of the Renaissance, and partly because they may be felt on the whole to produce a richer sound than a spinet (though generally over a four-octave compass only).

Spinning rattle (Hawaii). See RATTLE, 3.

Spitzharfe (It.: *arpanetta*). A German domestic instrument of the period 1650–1750, up to *c*.90 cm. (3') tall, rising to a peak (*Spitz*) on one side, and placed on a table: a type of upright *psaltery, with wire strings on both sides of the vertical soundbox, tuned at the bottom and played with the nails or finger-picks. It is often seen in museum collections.

Split idiophone. A bamboo, sliced part of the way down to form two long prongs which will slap or rattle against each other when the cane, held in one hand, is struck on the other arm. The prongs may be carefully shaped for the points almost to touch before being wedged apart at the base. Chiefly East Asia, but may be met in various forms as a folk instrument westwards to Southern Europe.

Split keys (keyboard). See TEMPERAMENT, 3.

Spoons. Two spoons—wooden or metal—are held back to back. The most common way of playing is to place the first finger between them and strike them on the knee, either directly or with the other hand, or these methods alternately. They are used almost everywhere at domestic feasts, to accompany dance music. In Eastern Europe special wooden spoons have sometimes been made (i.e. real, not improvised, musical instruments), some with pellet bells strung along the handles.

Spurs. See SISTRUM AND JINGLES, 4.

Square piano (Fr.: *piano carré*; Ger.: *Tafelklavier*; It.: *piano a tavola*; Sp.: *piano de mesa*). Actually rectangular, on four legs, keyboard towards the left (Pl. 1): the first popular form of *piano. In England it was made from the 1760s and gradually superseded by uprights *c*.1820–50. In the USA however it long remained the favourite over this whole period, developing into a massive instrument (Pl. 2) rivalling in tone and power the grand piano itself, and only ceasing to be made by Steinway in 1888. Great numbers survive: elegant models of the late 18th century are familiar as converted into sideboard tables, the working parts removed; but if in good original or restored condition are again enjoyed by many for playing music of the Classical period in the home, sounding unmistakably like a piano, light, delicate, and not essentially different save in expressive range from a grand piano of the same era—both having thin strings at not great tension and small leathered hammers striking with correspondingly small force. Chopin himself is said to have often played on a square; and before him the first public recital recorded in history on any piano was by J. C. Bach, in London, 1768, playing his own square piano by Johannes Zumpe, and doing much to popularize the instrument.

1. *Early square pianos: (a) Origins*. To make a piano in this rectangular shape with the strings running from side to side was the idea of German makers accustomed to building the *clavichord, likewise rectangular. The earliest known square piano is of 1742, by a Bavarian, Johann Socher, in the Nuremberg *collection; and from Germany Zumpe introduced the instrument into England, making it in quantity in London (examples exist from 1766) and exporting to France and America. His normal square, little over 150 cm. (5') long and some 47 cm. (18½") from front to back, has five-octave compass with two strings per note, the lowest strings overspun.

(b) Early action. Later known as 'English single action' (and retained in some squares after 1800), this consists simply of a wire fixed more or less upright in the key-lever with a leathered knob on top. This directly throws up the hammer, hinged with leather to the hammer-rail which lies across the instrument under the strings. Thus there is no escapement (see PIANO, 1): if the key be held down the hammer falls on to the knob, not always wholly to eliminate the chance of it bouncing back following a hard blow.

Zumpe's dampers are on horizontal levers above the strings, and are held down with small whalebone springs until lifted by vertical 'stickers' (often also of whalebone) raised by the keys (more compact damper systems came into use from the 1780s). In place of a sustaining pedal there are two hand-levers on the left, one for each half of the compass, to tilt the damper-rail upwards, taking the dampers with it. The place of a soft pedal is taken by a 'buff stop', which raises a soft-padded strip under the strings close to the nut to mute them, and this was retained

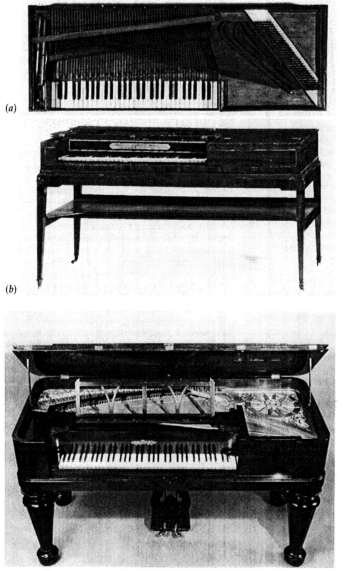

Pl. 1. Plan and general views of a square piano by Johannes Zumpe and Gabriel Buntebart (London, 1770).

Pl. 2. Square piano by Jonas Chickering (The Metropolitan Museum of Art, Rogers Fund, 1975).

on most square pianos thenceforth. A wooden dust cover, loose or hinged, may be provided, also reducing noise from the action: the lid of the piano was however usually kept shut (having house ornaments displayed on top), so a 'lid swell' is often found, a pedal which raises a hinged part of the lid on the right, above the soundboard (cf. the 'nag's head' swell; see also HARPSICHORD, 7d).

(c) *Improvements.* Among improvements of the 1780s, the tuning pins were moved by Broadwood from the right-hand end (the clavichord position) to along the back at the other end of the strings,

where, among other things, there is better room for them. There may then be a compass extension above f''' to c'''', fitting in the extra keys without diminishing the soundboard area, by having the hammers rise through a gap or slot at the rear (and acting without dampers). Also escapements: the neat 'English double action' by Broadwood and co-workers; that of 1794 by Geib (later building fine squares in New York) incorporating an 'intermediate lever' (see PIANO, 7); and in Germany, actions of 'Viennese' type (see PIANO, 7b) being given escapements by 1780. In external style, the plainer 'Georgian' and 'Sheridan' styles, with a separate stand on square tapered legs, are on the whole visually preferred today to 'Regency' with rounded corners, lattice work, and thick screw-on legs; or larger 'Victorian' models.

2. *Square pianos in the USA*. Early extant examples are by makers in Philadelphia, as Charles Albrecht, from 1789, and in New York, Dodds & Claus, from 1791; and in New England, Benjamin Crehore, of Milton, Massachusetts, under whom worked as apprentices two of the greatest figures in the development of the piano, both starting by making squares. These were Alphaeus Babcock (1785–1842), by whom the now universal one-piece cast iron frame was invented first for squares (1825); and Jonas Chickering (1798–1853), with squares from 1822 and by the 1840s developed into the big American 'Grand Square Piano'. This (Pl. 2) is nearly 213 cm. (7') long and half this from front to back, too heavy to be moved about. It has triple stringing (single in the bass, some instruments with cross-stringing), full repetition action (see PIANO, 7), seven-octave compass, and a rich 'plummy' tone, just distinguishable from that of the contemporary American grand perhaps by a crispness of touch in the bass owing to the relative shortness of the bass key-levers imposed by the layout of a square piano.

Sringa (*śṛnga*, Indian: a 'horn', cognate with European 'cornu', 'horn'). Best known as the large brass or copper instrument (in South India *kombu*) of two widely conical half circles joined to form a tall S held high in both hands (or sometimes to form a circle), and usually with painted designs in red. The bell rim is often hollow, containing seeds to jingle as the horn is waved about. The typical Asian shallow-cup mouthpiece is of sheet metal, soldered to the horn, which is sounded, often in pairs, on festive and religious occasions, sometimes on very high notes. How ancient this horn is, is not certain; nor whether the resemblance in form to the prehistoric *lur of Europe is no more than fortuitous.

Stamping tube (Fr.: *tuyau pilonnante*; Ger.: *Stampfrohr*; whence Eng.). Percussion instrument generally of wide bamboo, used especially over South-East Asia, the Pacific Islands, South America, and the West Indies. The tube, from 30 to 180 cm. (1–6') long, is closed at one end by a knot (any intervening knots being cut out) and, held vertically, closed end downwards, pounded or smartly dropped against the ground or other hard surface. Besides the knocking sound one hears the clear note from the *stopped-pipe air-column inside. Two or more tubes of different lengths may rhythmically accompany songs and dances, in some cases as substitute for the music of gongs or drums. In the Solomon Islands of Melanesia a player may hold a set of ten different-length tubes between the fingers of both hands and the toes of both feet, striking them on stones and making pentatonic music. In South America the bottom end of a tube may be closed with a skin; or the knot may be perforated for the player alternately to pound the tube and smack the open end with the palm of the hand.

Staple. A short metal tube upon which is made, or placed, a double reed in many wind instruments. See REED, 4, 5.

Steel band. A band of instruments termed 'pans', traditionally fashioned from large oil drums. To make a pan, first the top of the drum is beaten into a concave shape (sinking) and marked off into sections, each of which is hammered so that it corresponds to a specific pitch (grooving). The top is then usually cut off the drum at a depth which will define the instrument's overall pitch: 'tenor' pans are about 20 cm. (8") deep; 'guitar' pans (Fig. 1, after Bartholomew 1980) about 45 cm. (18"); and the entire drum is used for 'bass' pans. Burning and then cooling in water help give the pan a good tone, and it is ultimately fine-tuned with a small hammer. Pans are played with pairs of rubber-tipped sticks, long notes sustained by a fast tremolo. There may be 10 or more pans in a steel band, with tenor instruments playing the melody, guitars the harmony, etc. The rhythm section of a band includes such as *conga drums, *maracas, and *tambourines. Repertory includes both dance and classical music, and the art of arranging for steel band is a skilled one.

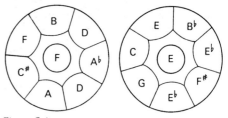

Fig. 1. Guitar pans.

The home of the steel band is Trinidad and Tobago, its origin lying in the Trinidad *tamboo bamboo* bands which were formed to circumvent the banning of African drums under the Peace Preservation Act of 1884. Members of such bands took bamboo tubes of various lengths and banged them together, struck them with other objects, or beat them on the ground (see STAMPING TUBE). With the 20th century the bands grew larger, adding dustbin lids, bottles, and pieces of scrap metal, until during the 1940s bandsmen discovered the oil drum's possibilities as a tuned instrument and the steel band was born. The early steel bands in Port of Spain gained notoriety through street fighting between supporters of rival bands, and subsequently membership of a band often coincided with anti-establishment political views. Since then, however, the steel band movement has been officially recognized: bands are sponsored by local businesses and given government support, and participate in the festivals and competitions held regularly, while steel bands have become familiar elsewhere in the Caribbean, the USA, and Britain, and been introduced into the curriculum of some schools.

Steel guitar. See HAWAIIAN GUITAR.

Stone chime, sonorous stones. See LITHOPHONE.

Stopped pipe. A pipe that is closed at one end and sounded from the other, as in *panpipes and stopped registers of the *organ.

1. *Open and stopped pipes.* Oscillation of air particles to and fro within the pipe, generated at the blowing end, is passed from one layer to the next and so transmitted (the 'wave') to the other end. *Open pipe.* At this other end, where the wave again meets the air outside, reflection takes place: the wave returns in reversed phase to the first end. Reflection here brings it in phase with the following pulse. Down the pipe and back then represents one full wavelength, performed in the time of one complete cycle of vibration. The actual length of the pipe thus corresponds to a half-wavelength. *Stopped pipe* (far end closed). The stopped end checks motion of particles (a displacement node), returning the wave without change of phase. Change occurs as the wave returns to the open end, and only after another journey to the stopped end and back again is a full cycle completed, i.e. after four traverses of the pipe in all. The actual pipe-length now corresponds to a quarter-wavelength.

The stopped pipe will therefore be of half the length of an open pipe that sounds the same fundamental: or if they are equal in length, the stopped pipe sounds an octave lower. A simple experiment is with a cardboard tube. Blowing across one end (covering it as little as possible with the lips), the other end open, one can detect a soft 'ghost' note. Repeating but with the far end covered with the hand, the note (stopped pipe) is an octave lower—actually not quite, since the antinode at an open end overshoots the pipe by a small distance ('end correction', variously estimated at around one-third of the diameter), so that the note is as if from a pipe longer than in fact it is, and more so with an open pipe, having an end correction at each end. A limitation of the stopped pipe as a musical instrument is of course that fingerholes cannot be used without unstopping the pipe. Hence the panpipe, and also the possibility of the *slide flute.

2. *Partials.* With an open pipe, the standing wave will divide through formation of intermediate nodes (N) into two, three, etc. equal smaller lengths bounded by antinodes (A):

A   N   A
A N A N A
A N A N A N A

giving frequences two, three, etc. times that of the fundamental (see HARMONIC SERIES). In a stopped pipe there is always an antinode at one end and a node at the other: so it cannot be nodally divided in two equal sections, nor in four or any other even number, but only in three, five, etc.:

A   N
A N A N

The absence of even-numbered partials characteristically gives stopped-pipe sound a distinctive quality, not necessarily less powerful, but smoother and less vibrant.

3. *Reed instruments.* Those, e.g. *clarinet, which have a cylindrical tube continuing so (or almost so) up to the blowing end, behave as a stopped pipe: the end with the reed, sealed from the external air by the player's mouth, effectively corresponds to the closed end of a stopped pipe, but now allowing fingerholes anywhere up to the open end. A clarinet is about as long as a flute but the fundamentals sound approximately an octave deeper. An experiment here is to smack the fingers down on the holes of the clarinet without putting the instrument in the mouth: the 'ghost' notes (open pipe) are an octave higher than those when the clarinet is actually played (stopped pipe). The clarinet is not, however, a stopped pipe perfectly, as faint traces of even-numbered partials in the tone-spectrum may reveal.

For 'conical' reed instruments (e.g. oboe), giving the partials of an open pipe, see WIND INSTRUMENTS, 3.

Stopped trumpet. See TRUMPET, 4.

Streichmelodeon. See BOWED ZITHER.

String drum. 1. See PIPE AND TABOR, 2.

2. A name used by some modern composers for the 'lion roar': see FRICTION DRUM, 2.

Stringed instruments (Fr.: *instruments à cordes*; Ger.: *Saiteninstrumente*; It.: *cordi*; Ru.: *Strunnye instrumenty*; Sp.: *cuerdas*). A clear fact of music history is that, from Antiquity to today in every major civilization, it is almost invariably stringed instruments that have held the highest place among instruments: mainly because the vibrating stretched string uniquely combines a clear fundamental pitch with rapid and accurate tunability and re-tunability (repeated tightening, slackening, and re-tightening). Not that the string is capable of music by itself, being too thin to communicate appreciable periodic vibration to the air directly; it must, via a bridge, pass the vibration to the larger surface of a soundboard—a wooden plate or a skin diaphragm, alone or covering a soundbox—from which are radiated the soundwaves that reach the air.

1. *The strings.* Among materials, vegetable matter has figured little apart from many tropical instruments with strings of twisted fibres of rattan-palm, etc. Animal materials have always predominated (that is, before metal): sinew; horsehair, silk (the classic string material in the Far East); and above all gut, normally sheep-gut ('catgut' living on as a joke term). Fragments of strings judged to be of sheep-gut and 1 mm. thick have been found with an Egyptian lute of 1500 BC.

A chief European centre for manufacture of gut strings has long been Italy, particularly Rome. The small intestines of sheep under a year old are taken warm from the slaughter-house immediately to commence the long and repeated processes of scouring, washing, slicing into strips for twisting into threads on a frame, and bleaching and polishing. The former violin E string (now replaced by steel) was spun from some five to seven threads and the double bass D from up to 85. Though now so extensively superseded by nylon, plain gut strings remain normal for the harp and are obtainable for most other instruments, for at least some of the strings. There are also now firms specializing in gut strings made according to older methods of the Renaissance onwards.

Nylon, dating from 1938, provides filament strings having much the same density and thickness as gut without inequalities of the kind that could make the selection of gut strings a trying business in older days; it is, of course, also less prone to break or become rough to the fingers with wear.

Metal strings go back historically to the 13th century in the Arab countries for certain instruments of the lute kind, but were rare in the West before advances in commercial wire-drawing in Germany from the late 14th century. Thicknesses of metal strings are specified in millimetres or thousandths of an inch; or usually for keyboard instruments in 'Music Wire Gauge' numbers. These run from No. 1 (0.2 mm. in diameter) up to No. 32 (2.2 mm.); a grand *piano may use Nos. 14 (0.81 mm.) to 32.

A problem arose in the 16th century over deep tunings from gut strings of restricted length, as when adding extra bass strings to the lute. These would have to be thick enough to deliver the low frequencies and even then, despite special methods of twisting, would tend to be too stiff to sound

really well. The solution of loading a gut string with an overwinding of fine wire, preserving full flexibility, has been so far traced to the mid-17th century, since which the deeper-tuned strings in all instruments, gut or metal, have come to be overwound ('covered'); thus, for instance, an Austrian *zither will sound the low A below the bass staff (*A'*) with an overwound metal string a mere 45 cm. (18″) in length, albeit at modest tension. Today the overwinding is often with metal 'ribbon' (or 'tape'), an American innovation of the late 1930s and giving a very smooth surface.

2. *Vibration and 'string equation'.* Though one might think that a string vibrates simply from side to side, in fact the deflection caused by sounding it travels along the string in both directions from that point to be reflected at the ends as two waves travelling in opposite directions: their resultant interference is responsible for the visual appearance of a long loop. The motions involved prove to be exceedingly complex and are not the same if the string is plucked, hit, or bowed (see BOW, 1). The 'string equation' interrelates length, tension, thickness, and material to the note produced. The fundamental frequency (*f*) follows from the general law: $f = c/\lambda$, where *c* is the wave-velocity, given by the square root of: tension (*T*) divided by mass per unit length or $\pi r^2 \tau$ (radius *r*, density τ); λ is the wavelength, of which the vibrating length of the string (*l*) represents half. Using the units *f* (Hz), *l* (cm.), *T* (kg., in the equation qualified by 981, gravity, since tension is being expressed as a weight), *r*, or more conveniently *d* (diameter; this time in mm.), and τ (at water = 1)—the equation can be reduced to:

$$f = \frac{5588}{l \times d} \sqrt{\frac{T}{\rho}}.$$

The average density of steel (7.8) being about six times that of gut or nylon, a steel string will be thinner than a gut string of the same length and at the same tension by $1 : \sqrt{6}$ (or approximately $1 : 2\frac{1}{2}$). But strings are generally tensioned to near breaking-point to sound their best, and this involves a rather higher tension for the steel string. Average tension per string is quoted at around $6\frac{1}{2}$–7 kg. for classical guitar (increasing slightly towards the sixth string); much the same for the violin (but lessening towards the lowest string); about twice for cello; three times for double bass; and 10 times or more for piano. Steel strings tend to give a brighter sound than gut owing to slower damping of high harmonics. Yet the replacing of gut with steel is obviously not of critical musical consequence or it would hardly have been possible for the musician to accept the change (see also VIOLIN, 5*a*).

The tension at which a string will break is proportional to the tensile strength of the material divided by the diameter of the string. The frequency at which it breaks is the same, however, for a thick string as for a thin, the thicker requiring (to reach the frequency) a tension greater to exactly the same degree that it is thicker. (For all these matters see Abbott and Segerman 1974.)

3. *The soundboard* ('top', 'belly', or, after the Fr., 'table'). The classic material is low-density wood from the conifers, chiefly the pine family, such as silver fir or more particularly close-grained spruce. Thicknesses vary from under 2 mm. in a lute to 1 cm. in a grand piano, balanced to the thickness and tension of the individual strings. Were the wood either too thick or too thin—or, to use the useful expression introduced by American acousticians, were its 'wave impedance' too different from that of the strings—then most of the available string energy would be reflected back, little of it passing to the soundboard; or if too near that of the string, this would discharge energy so quickly that vibration would immediately come to a stop.

The wooden soundboard, though it must respond to every note fed into it, with its partials, and whether a single note or several in a chord, is (unlike a simple diaphragm) non-isotropic owing to the grain: vibrations travel some four times faster in the direction of the grain than across it. Usually a soundboard is 'barred' in some way, with one or several softwood bars glued to the underside, often in positions crosswise or askew to the grain so that, besides offering structural support, their stiffness accelerates wave transmission along the 'slower' direction. Plywood may be mentioned in this connection, having a middle layer with the grain at right angles to the rest; as it is also strong it has latterly won some successes with keyboard instruments and harps, though wood has remained always preferred.

The soundboard will have its own natural resonances, which a violin-maker will often test by ear, tapping the plate or bowing it on the edge, to gain an idea of how evenly it will respond over the range required of it in the completed instrument. Where it forms the top of a soundbox the lower notes gain support from the air contained (the 'air resonance'). This is normally well below the main wood resonance, even though raised very considerably by the soundhole or soundholes, in which air oscillates in and out under the pumping action of the table (see CAVITY RESONATOR). Some soundboxes perform their duty without any such hole at all (e.g. *saz, *sitar); but soundholes further divide up a soundboard into distinct areas, influencing the vibration patterns, and some hold that this is one of their major functions. It may be noted in passing that the shape of the instrument can in many cases be drastically changed without very noticeably, if at all, impairing musical quality. There have been guitars and violins in every conceivable shape (waistless, three-cornered, etc.; see VIOLIN, 9a) produced during the 19th century with apparently most satisfactory results by some of the finest luthiers in Paris and Vienna; but musicians do not feel happy playing on an unconventional-looking instrument, nor are audiences happy to see them do so.

4. *Striking-point.* Naturally, strings are normally excited (plucked, hit, bowed) at the point along their vibrating length where they give the best sound in the judgement of the player, or with keyboard instruments, the builder, the striking points being a critical concern (see HARPSICHORD, 4; PIANO, 4c).

On the fingerboard instruments, the normal point is frequently departed from for different tonal effects obtained by subduing the intensity of upper harmonics (sombre tone) or exciting them more while weakening the lower (metallic tone). A late 18th-century French mandolin Tutor puts it thus: further from the bridge (over the end of the fingerboard) for *son flûté*; close to the bridge for *argentin* ('silvery'). One hears the contrast a great deal in guitar recitals. See also violin, 5b.

5. *Terminology:* (a) Nut. With non-keyboard instruments this bar upon which the strings bear leaving the tuning pins or pegs is traditionally of ivory, or of ebony, the grain running at right angles to the strings. The term is used equally with keyboard instruments, though 'wrest-plank bridge' is often preferred (it carrying the 'wrest' or tuning pins), the actual bridge being then the 'soundboard bridge'. See COURSE for the term much used where strings are duplicated, triplicated, etc. (but with keyboard instruments, usually 'bichord', etc.).

(b) *String-length and scale.* The vibrating length of a string, with fingerboard instrument, that of the open string. Sometimes with these it is termed the 'scale', more generally in a comparative sense, e.g. 'long scale' where a fretted instrument, such as a guitar, is given a relatively long string-length for that type of instrument. Most important, in keyboard instruments 'scale' relates to the lengths and proportionate lengths of the strings from treble to bass as chosen in the maker's plan.

(c) *'Left' and 'right'.* A small point with fingerboard instruments and others in which the left hand fingers the strings over the neck is: which side is the left and which the right in description of the instrument. The 'first' string is that which runs closest under the fingertips of the left hand, basically the principal melody string and (with exceptions, see FIDDLE) the highest tuned. On the violin it is to the player's right and to an observer the left; on cello and guitar it is the other way round. So it can be with other particulars of the instrument also. To avoid confusion, descriptions often prefer 'the treble side' (that on which lies the first string) and the 'bass side' (the other).

See also SYMPATHETIC STRINGS.

String length. The vibrating length of a string. See STRINGED INSTRUMENTS, 5*b*.

Strohfiedel (Ger.). See XYLOPHONE, 5.

Stroh violin. A *violin with a metal diaphragm and horn, named after its inventor, Augustus Stroh (1828–1914), an acoustician and electrical engineer from Frankfurt who became a colleague of Sir Charles Wheatstone (see CONCERTINA). Patented in London in 1899, the violin body is replaced by a shallow, circular wood soundbox, the top of which is formed by a corrugated aluminium diaphragm. The motion of the bridge is communicated to this by a rocking lever. From the bottom of the soundbox issues a metal horn, to direct the sound forwards; often a smaller horn points backwards for the player to hear the notes better. *The Strad* magazine in 1902 described it as sounding 'as loud as four ordinary violins. The G string is a dream. It possesses the deep rich quality of a fine cello A'. It was used for recording purposes by violinists as celebrated as Jan Kubelik, and also in dance orchestras and by street musicians. Today there are fiddlers who prefer it for playing folk dances.

Stroh also designed one-string fiddles with diaphragm and horn, later copied by others as 'phonofiddle'. (The instruments are not to be confused with *Strohfiedel* ('straw fiddle'), an ancient German name for a *xylophone.)

Pilling 1975.

Structures sonores. See SOUND SCULPTURES.

Stump. See ORPHARION.

Stviri. See BAGPIPE, 6.

Suling. Javanese 'ring flute' (see FLUTE, 7*c* (iii), the sole wind instrument of a Javanese *gamelan.

Surbahar. See SITAR, 3.

Surna. Middle-Eastern representative of the shawm family (see SHAWM, 4): in Turkey, *zurna*; Yugoslavia: *zurla*; Northern Greece: *zournas* or *karamouza*, Egypt: *zamr* (Pl. 1); North Africa: *ghaita*. It is turned in wood (often plum or walnut) in one piece including the bell. Length varies, from 20 to 60 cm. (8″–2′). It has seven fingerholes; thumbhole on a level between the first two fingerholes; and 'vent holes' lower down (typically three, then one, then below this another three). The wood is cylindrically bored as far as the bell, but into the top is inserted a two-pronged, narrowly bored tube, *c*.10 cm. (4″) long and often of boxwood, which in effect narrows the bore up to the first two holes (leaving these clear between the prongs); it is not really certain what its acoustic function may be. Into the top of it goes the conical metal staple

carrying a loose lip disc and small double reed (see REED, 5, also for the 'spare parts' that often hang from the staple). Compass, from little over an octave up to a good two octaves, with the pitch of a 'conical pipe' owing to the conical staple, the pronged tube perhaps in some way helping.

Pl. 1. Players of the *zamr* (*surna*), small and large, with a drum *tabl*, Cairo.

The player, using *circular breathing and little or no tonguing, is frequently accompanied by another who sustains a drone on a similar instrument, and almost always by a drummer. It is chiefly in Egypt that a small size and a larger, an octave deeper, may be combined (as Pl. 1), and in Yugoslavia (Macedonia), where the larger *zurla* changes the drone note to agree with changing modes in the melody (Rice 1982).

The *alghaita* is the type used in the royal mounted bands of Muslim emirates in West Africa (northern Nigeria, the Cameroons): with three or four holes only, and sometimes oversewn with leather, played beside the long trumpets *kakaki* (see NAFIR, 2) and the drum *ganga*.

Susu. See BELL TREE.

Swanee whistle. See SLIDE FLUTE, *Swanee-sax*, see SLIDE SAXOPHONE.

Sympathetic (or resonance) strings. Additional strings, always of wire, included in a number of stringed instruments to provide special background resonance. The oldest instruments known to possess them seem to be Indian and Central Asian (e.g. the Indian fiddle *sarangī). In Europe they appear in the 17th century, mostly in bowed instruments: *viola d'amore; *baryton; the Harding fiddle of Norway; and sometimes *tromba marina. See also LYRA VIOL. Sympathetic strings are usually tuned to a scale in the key in which the instrument is going to be played.

With ordinary stringed instruments (lacking sympathetic strings) the sympathetic resonance of strings which are not being played at a particular moment can take up vibration, via the bridge, to be an important ingredient in the sound, notably with the piano.

Symphonie (medieval). See HURDY-GURDY.

Syrinx. Ancient Greek, a pipe, usually a *'panpipe'.

T

Tabl (or *ṭabl*). General Arabic word for a drum; in particular the two-headed cylindrical drum seen over North Africa and the Middle East accompanying the reed instrument *surna* in outdoor music (see SURNA, Pl. 1, Egypt). Carried on a strap, it is struck on both heads with thin sticks (or a stick in one hand and knotted thongs in the other). In shape it can recall small medieval drums of Europe (see SIDE DRUM, 4).

Tabla (or *tablā*). The paired drums of North India, with an indispensable role in most forms of classical and concert music, instrumental or with the voice.

1. *The instruments* (Pl. 1). The two drums are set upright, resting on padded cloth rings, close together before the player sitting cross-legged. Both are single-headed but differ in shape, pitch, and methods of playing. To his right, the *tabla*, or *daya* ('right'), with a thick wooden shell, cylindrical or narrowing upwards; to his left, the *baya* ('left'), a

Pl. 1. Tabla player.

deep earthenware or copper bowl and with a head about one-and-a-half times wider, and tuned about a half-octave or more deeper. To each head is glued a ring cut from a second skin, leaving the middle of the head exposed. In the centre of this the circle of turning composition (of flour and black ashes, see MRDANGA) is applied in layers: on the *baya* this circle is a little smaller and centred a little to the side (giving this drum a rather duller sound). Each head is lapped and sewn on to a thick hoop of twisted leather. This is drawn down by wide hide straps passed round the hoop through holes in the two thicknesses of the head, and led down to a second hoop round the base of the shell. On the *daya* the straps are further tightened by cylindrical wooden chocks pushed under the straps about half-way down the shell.

Even among the multitude of subtle drum techniques over Asia, that of the *tabla* stands out for intricacy and variety of sound, and the knowledge and skill expected in their production: on the *daya*, with the palm, fingers, or fingertips on the different areas; and on the *baya*, for example, on striking, pressing near the edge with the heel of the hand, then sliding it forwards with a rise in pitch (Pl. 1, left hand).

2. *Origin*. The tabla seems to have risen to the fore in the 18th century, then starting to replace the classic long, horizontal *pakhawaj* (two-headed, 'double conical', like the *mrdanga*), as if it had been found that the contrasting right- and left-hand contributions to the music were executed most clearly on two small separate drums (as perhaps suggested by the Muslim small kettledrums, *naqqara*) rather than on the two ends of a single long drum.

See INDIA; also Fox Strangways 1914, ch. 9.

Tablature. Instrumental notation in terms not of notes on a stave but of the fingering of the instrument, using letters or numerals and signs for the note values. Keyboard tablatures are known for organ from *c.*1420 in Italy, and thereafter follow various systems, many of which now seem excessively complicated and of historical interest only, the important repertory being available in transcription. An earlier example, written partly in tablature and possibly for an organ, is in the 14th-century Robertsbridge manuscript (British Library). Tablatures for the fretted instruments, known from the late 15th century onwards (for examples see CITTERN, LUTE), maintain practical importance: players today often prefer to play the music directly from the tablature rather than from transcriptions in staff notation. For one thing, tablature is not concerned with the actual (absolute) overall pitch at which an instrument may be tuned, whereas in staff notation the tuning note of the top string of the lute for example (see LUTE, 2) is generally transcribed as G, but may elsewhere be transcribed as A, obliging the player to make a transposition, whether or not the instrument be itself retuned.

Instructions for tuning may be given in a chart at the beginning, indicating for each string the fret which gives the unison with the open note (signified in French tablature by 'a') of the string above, having already tuned this. Thus Ex. 1, to the right of the double bar, shows how to set the 'old tune' of the lute (see LUTE, 2a): having tuned the top string as required, the next is tuned to give the same note at the 5th fret ('f'), whence its own open note ('a') will sound a perfect fourth lower; and so on. To the left of the double bar, below the six lines, are given the tunings for four open diapasons (their notes indicated by ///a, //a, and so on) each to be tuned to a higher string by octaves; e.g. string //a to the octave below the note of the fifth string at the 2nd fret ('c'). (The notes here added along the bottom show the result, in actual sounds in the 'G tuning': see LUTE, 2c.)

Ex. 1.

///a //a /a a

(*C D E F   G c f a d' g'*)

Today tablature is sometimes used for the guitar in rock music, as where strumming may change to arpeggiato chords or a solo riff; and also in Flamenco (called *cifra*) and some folk styles.

Tabor. See PIPE AND TABOR.

Taegum. Korean flute. See CHINA AND KOREA, 2d.

Taiko (after a prefix, '-daiko'). A main Japanese name for drums other than the 'hourglass' drums **tsuzumi*. Two-headed, the shell is hollowed out (usually in *zelkova* wood, of the elm family), and the drum is played with two sticks on one head or both. *Ōdaiko* can cover all barrel drums with the heads (often cowhide) nailed on with rows of brass tacks. *Shimedaiko* covers those with a relatively shallow shell, slightly bulging, and the visually arresting feature of heads of much greater width than the shell supporting it, each head being sewn on to a wide iron hoop (as with **tsuzumi* drums also). (The skins for the heads, sometimes horsehide, are, after dehairing, said to be left for a year covered with salt, which is then washed out.)

1. *Nailed heads: ōdaiko* (in particular sense), the large barrel drum, *c*.85 cm. (*c.*34″) long, with an iron ring for lifting and carrying in festivals. In the kabuki theatre behind the scene (see JAPAN, 3) it is placed horizontally on a wooden stand, the player seated by one end, striking on one head with thick sticks; it announces performances, marks the time of the music, and has special strokes to portray (rather than imitate) wind, rain, etc. In some religious ceremonies it is placed across the body for striking on both heads. The *tsuridaiko* (or *taiko*) is the 'hanging drum' of the court music, with shallow shell suspended in a tall, ornate circular frame in front of the other musicians, and is struck on one head by the two hands alternately, the sticks with leathered ends. The *gakutaiko*, 'music drum', smaller, resembling a 'Chinese *tom-tom', is played with sticks rather like those of a *side drum.

2. *Roped heads. Da-daiko*: gigantic, perhaps the largest drum in the world. Suspended with the heads vertical, the shell up to a metre (3′) in depth, with heads up to 2 m. (6′) wide, requiring added leather round the main skin. In the full court music one *da-daiko* stands on each side at the rear of the ensemble, suspended in a tall circular frame rising to a peak decorated with fabulous beasts and birds, bordered by flames, in all some 4 m. (15′) high and surmounted by a 215 cm. (7′) pole bearing a golden sun and rays. The player, or pair of players, stands on a platform before this splendid structure, to strike at long intervals with round-ended beaters, giving a deep, heavy sound. *Daibyoshi*: used in Shinto ceremonies, also kabuki; horizontal shell, *c*.48 cm. (19″) long, 20 cm. (11″) in diameter, and played on both heads with plain wooden sticks. *Kakko*: leads the tempo of the court music. Smaller than *daibyoshi* (the shell is *c*.30 cm. (12″) long and half this in width midway along), it has deerskin heads 25 cm. (10″) wide. Placed horizontally on a stand to one side of the *tsuridaiko* (1) and opposite the small gong *shoko* (see JAPAN, 1a), it is played on both heads with slightly knobbed sticks. *Nōdaiko* (or *taiko* in the ordinary use of the word): folk festivals; and one of the three drums of the Nō theatre along with the two *tsuzumi*: shallower shell, with diameter 26 cm. (10″); heads *c*.30 cm. (12″). Tilted on a stand (JAPAN, Pl. 2) and played on the uppermost head with two thick sticks, the arms held straight and held high before each first stroke. *Okedo*: folk music, also behind the stage in kabuki; upright, and with heads here not overlapping shell; two sticks on one head.

3. *'Fan drum'*. Differs from the preceding in being small, held in one hand, with a single head over an iron ring joined to a wooden handle (height 25 cm. (10″) or more, including the handle): played with one stick along with flutes in Buddhist folk festivals, also an off-stage instrument in kabuki.

Taille. French, from the 16th century to the 18th, for the choral part, or member of an instrument family, which other languages call 'tenor'; thus *taille de violon*, a name for the *viola. The term was taken over in Germany in certain cases, as where Bach in his cantatas heads a part '*Taille*', here short for *taille d'hautbois* (see TENOR OBOE; also ÉCURIE, 1).

Talam. Indian 'cup cymbals'; see CYMBAL, 5*b*.

Talbot, James (1664–1708). Regius Professor of Hebrew at Cambridge University and of major importance in musical instrument history for his recording of the particulars (notably measurements) of instruments of all kinds as used by musicians in London during his time. They are contained in his manuscript preserved in Christ Church Library, Oxford, Music MS 1187 (written between 1692 and 1695; Unwin). For many instruments Talbot's are the first known detailed particulars since Mersenne (1636), and they have continually been cited since their publication in the *Galpin Society Journal*, 1948–68: Wind Instruments, *GSS* 1 (1948); Bowed Instruments, 3 (1950); Bagpipes, 5 (1952); Lutes, 14 (1961); Other Fretted Instruments, 15 (1962); Harps, 16 (1963); Harpsichords, 21 (1968).

Talking drum. Originating among Europeans in West Africa, this name refers to the sending of messages over great distances ('bush telegraph') by means of a pair of drums, or a *slit drum, or sometimes a horn, etc., giving two pitches that convey the effect of the higher and lower vowel-sounds of the 'speech-tone' languages.

Tambour. 1. French, 'drum'; *tambour à corde*, see FRICTION DRUM.

2. As adopted in English in recent times, a *frame drum, chiefly for school music, with a skin or plastic membrane glued or nailed over a hoop as with a tambourine but without jingle plates. Sizes range from c.20 to 40 cm. (8 to 16″) in diameter.

Tambourin (Fr.). See PIPE AND TABOR, 2 (where also for *Tambourin de Béarn*).

Tambourine (Fr.: *tambour de Basque*; Ger.: *Tamburin, Schellentrommel*; It.: *tamburino* or, in popular language, *cembalo*; Ru.: *buben*; Sp.: *pandero, pandereta*). The frame drum (see DRUM, 4*e*) with the membrane stretched over a wooden hoop with slots for the pairs of metal jingle discs carried on wires, sometimes two rows of them.

1. *Orchestral tambourine*. Hoop diameters are c.15 cm. (6″) and upwards, a normal preference being c.25 cm. (10″). The membrane (head), vellum or plastic, is nailed or glued to the hoop: tambourines have also been made with screw-tensioning but the screws and their brackets can get in the way of some techniques, besides adding to the weight of an instrument which is essentially one to be raised in one hand. If the head is too slack it may be wetted, then left to dry.

A natural 'folk' way of playing in European countries is to mark the tempo of a dance with strokes on the head with the free hand (or against the knee), setting the jingles ringing, and to prolong the jingle between the main beats by shaking. Beyond this are the many techniques with the fingers of one or both hands, on membrane or rim, with the jingles playing a varying part in the sound (as in Middle East, see below, 3). For soft, delicate orchestral rhythms with the fingers the tambourine may be held horizontally, the jingles gently colouring the sound. A roll in which the jingles contribute most of the sound, other than by shaking, is that by which the moistened thumb is rubbed round the edge of the membrane, the friction producing a hissing sound from the jingles, though, since the thumb must soon come to a stop, a roll cannot last for more than perhaps eight seconds even in pianissimo, when the thumb moves at slowest speed. Among many unusual effects, perhaps best known is Stravinsky's where Petrushka expires to the tambourine dropped from a small height on to the floor (or a cushion).

2. *Tambourines in history*. Ancient frame drums (Lat.: *tympanum*; see ANTIQUITY and BIBLICAL INSTRUMENTS) were, as far as can be seen, without jingles; these appear in the Middle Ages first in the Middle East and by c.1300 in Europe. There might also be (as sometimes still) gut snares under the membrane and, later, little bells hung on cross-wires. The earliest known medieval name is French, *timbre* (Fr., from *tympanum*, and the original meaning of this French word); in Eng. it became 'timbrel' during the early Renaissance period; see BIBLICAL INSTRUMENTS, 1*d*). Though much associated in history and folklore with women, tambourines have always been played no less by men, in the Middle East also. In southern Italy today, large, heavy tambourines, with jingle plates roughly cut from tin plate, vigorously accompany the tarantella, requiring a strong man for the purpose, marking the 6/8 rhythm with great expertise by blows on the skin and shaking between. In England, men played the tambourine for folk dances in parts of Sussex up to the 20th century, in some cases striking it with a cow's tail.

For women, some very beautiful French tambourines are preserved from the 18th century, often large; a London supplier in 1839 (Poole 1982) offered sizes from 30 to 40 cm. (12–16″), 'common', 'ladies' best', and 'military'; these last, the most expensive, for military bands, made with iron tensioning screws.

3. *Some other frame drums*. Over the Middle East and North Africa tambourines are played less in the common European manner (striking and shaking) than with subtle use of both hands on the membrane, the fingers of the holding hand participating. There are, besides jingle-less frame drums (*bendir*), tambourines (*deff* or *duff, req,* *tar*) very much like the European, and essential to

much classical music (see e.g., MIDDLE EAST, Pl. 1). From Iran to the north and east instead of jingle discs, numerous iron rings are strung round the inside of the hoop, see DAIRA. Though the frame is normally circular (often sold by sieve-makers) it can be hexagonal (examples from Chile) or octagonal (China, in folk ceremonies). A rectangular frame drum without jingles has been discovered from Ancient Egypt, as well as a small circular one which seems to have once had a second head now missing (Paris, Louvre). See also SHAMAN DRUM, this beaten with a stick (as a frame drum is beaten with a wooden spoon in winter 'bear dances' in Romania).

Commonly described as the 'square tambourine' is a species well known in Spain, Portugal (adufe, from Arab.: deff), and North Africa: of wooden slats forming a square frame, held together by cross-wires inside and by sewing a skin tightly over both sides, making two heads. Inside are rattling beans (there being no metal jingles). Country women in Iberia play deft rhythms with the fingers of both hands, in North African manner.

Tambura (or *tamburā*). The Indian large lute with the body of a gourd, or of wood in gourd shape, which supplies the tonic accompaniment essential to refined music of stringed instruments or voice. In this it sounds the four metal strings one after the other in regular time, in constant order throughout, gently sweeping them with two fingers of the right hand, always on open strings. The instrument, held upright (see INDIA, Pl. 1) or horizontally, is typically c.130 cm. long (over 4'); the gourd is up to 45 cm. (18") wide; the wooden belly is slightly convex with ornamental border; and the surface of the neck is flat. The tuning-pegs of the 1st and 2nd strings lie sideways in the pegbox; those of the 3rd and 4th stand upright. The 1st string is tuned to the fifth (sometimes the fourth) of the tonic; the middle two to the upper tonic; the 4th (of brass, the rest steel) to the tonic below. The bridge resembles that of the *sitar and *vina in being a broad plate with curved surface. To enhance overtones, which in India both performers and listeners consciously hear, a silk or wool thread is put under each string at the bridge, while threaded on each is a small bone bead for shifting over the surface of the bridge when fine-tuning.

Tamburitsa (or *tamburica*). Popular long lute (see LUTE, 7) of Yugoslavia. The name is a diminutive of *tambura*, a general term for a long lute over the Balkans, and coming from Turkish (in which it denotes one type of *saz). The instrument is pear-shaped, as in a *bouzouki, with long, thin fretted neck and two, or three, *courses of metal strings played with a plectrum, traditionally of cherry bark or goose-quill. On its own it is heard in brisk 2/4 tunes played on the first course with the second course, tuned a fourth lower, reiterating its note in the same rhythm (a so-called *drone);

or there may be three courses, the third course here enriching the 'drone' at another fourth below; or the first two courses of three may be tuned in unison.

In a Croatian *tamburitsa* orchestra it plays the melody under the name *bisernica*, with chords below played on the larger *bugariya* (or *brač*, from Ger.: *Bratsche*, 'viola') and the bass on the *berda* (It.: *bordone*, 'bourdon') or *bas*. This last is sometimes a large three-stringed contrabass rested on the ground by a spike. In Bosnia the names may be *bugariya* for the melody instrument and *shargi* for the larger playing the chords.

Tam-tam. The usual orchestral gong. See GONG AND TAM-TAM.

Tanbur (or *tanbūr*). 1. A very early name for a long lute (see LUTE, 7) today denoting many varieties over the Middle East from Syria and Iraq to Turkestan in Central Asia. Reaching over 1 m. (3') long, with pear-shaped body, it has a long neck carrying sometimes 30 frets, and two, or three, *courses of metal strings tuned to the same kinds of patterns as those of a *tamburitsa, and again sounding the lower string or strings in the same strokes of the plectrum, as a 'drone'.

2. See LYRE, 1.

Tangent. 1. The upright metal blade that strikes the strings of a *clavichord.

2. 'Tangent Piano': an instrument (Ger.: *Tangentenflugel*) made for some years from c.1770 in Germany (most examples are by Späth and Schmahl of Regensburg from 1790). Like a grand piano to look at, the strings are struck by thin vertical wooden rods with leathered ends, thrown upwards from the keyboard to strike and then fall back (i.e. not, as in the clavichord, remaining against the string until the key is released). In the perfected designs each tangent was given extra speed by an 'intermediate lever' as in most piano actions (see PIANO, 7), and there may be an *una corda* device (soft pedal). The sound is said to be very beautiful.

Taogu. See RATTLE DRUM.

Tapan (or *tupan*; Yugoslavia). See DAVUL.

Taphōn. Principal drum of instrumental ensembles in Thailand: a barrel drum (see DRUM, 4b (ii)), hollowed in teak, with length c.48 cm. (19"), greatest width c.34 cm. (13½"), and played resting on a stand. The two heads are each dressed with a round black patch of tuning paste (as with the *tablas of India) made from boiled rice and palm ashes, and serving to regulate the depth of the sound. For a few of the many special hand strokes for each hand see SOUTH-EAST ASIA, 2. Along with the *taphōn*, the ensemble may include the *song-nā*, a longer and narrower drum, c.56 cm. (22") long, rested on the lap; unlike the *taphōn*, it is here the left hand that plays on the slightly wider head.

Tar: 1. *Tār*. A Middle Eastern *lute played in popular and classical music from Iran to Georgia, distinguished by a hollowed-out wooden body carved in figure-of-eight form, i.e. in two bulges, the lower one the larger, and the opening of each part of the '8' covered with skin. The long, fretted neck carries a pegbox with side pegs for three or more *courses of metal strings played with a plectrum. Tunings vary from place to place (e.g. *a e d*, sometimes with octave courses). Little seems to be known of its origin.

2. *Ṭār* (thus beginning with the 16th letter of the Arabic alphabet, not with the 3rd as above). Tambourine of many Arab countries, in most cases with jingle-plates as in Europe. See TAMBOURINE, 3.

Tarogato (or *tarogató*; Hungarian). A wind instrument looking rather like (and sounding like) a soprano *saxophone but made in wood, with plain fingerholes and keywork based on that of the *clarinet. It was invented in Budapest *c*.1890 by the maker Schunda (who had seen the soprano saxophone), to restore in modern guise an old *shawm said to be of Turkish origin called tarogato, formerly played by some town watchmen; examples are preserved in the National Museum, Budapest. (In the same spirit of nationalism Schunda produced the big cimbalom: see DULCIMER, 2). The tarogato is still made, especially in Romania where it is a favourite in folk music.

During the 1930s copies of the tarogato were made by the French firm Jerome Thibouville Lamy, stamped 'Jetel-sax' (i.e. 'J-T-L-sax') but were mainly regarded as curiosities.

Tarole (Fr.). See SIDE DRUM, 4.

Tartöld. See RACKET.

Tasto (It.). 1. The 'key' of a keyboard instrument. In music with a figured bass accompaniment, *tasto solo* means that the bass notes should be played without harmonies above.

2. The 'fingerboard' of a bowed instrument: *sul tasto*, 'on the fingerboard', i.e. with the bow well away from the bridge. Sometimes called '*flautado*'.

3. *Frets of a stringed instrument.

Tavil (or *ṭavil*). Barrel drum of South India: see DRUM, Pl. 1.

Tea-chest bass. See BUMBASS.

Telyn. Welsh, 'harp'. See HARP, 6.

Temperament. Term covering the various systems that have been used for fixing the intervals of the notes within an octave, and needed particularly with keyboard and other instruments on which notes cannot be adjusted in tuning by the player during playing.

1. '*Equal temperament*' (E.T.). This, normal today, divides the octave into 12 equal semitones by giving to each a frequency ratio equal to the 12th root of 2 (1.05946) which, multiplied by itself 12 times, leads to the octave ratio 2:1 (see CENTS). The theoretical ratios in relation to the bottom note of the octave are as in Table 1 (mostly here to four figures) for the chromatic scale on C (see Table 2 left column, for the intervals in cents). Tuning in practice is mainly by octaves and fifths, slightly by ear, narrowing each fifth from its natural value of 1.5 (3:2), then to *beat at just below one per second in the middle octave. For every scale the intervals are exactly the same, so that music can modulate freely from one key to any other, as from the Classical period onwards it constantly does. The theory of equal temperament, propounded already by *Mersenne (1636), became largely accepted by the late 18th century (though in England not in organ tuning before the 1850s). Recently, however, with the movement to restore authentic sounds in music of the 18th century and earlier, older tuning principles have regained practical significance in instrument-making and particularly keyboard tuning, such systems being founded, in one way or another, in pure, natural musical intervals, existing also in the *harmonic series, but none exactly matched in E.T. save for the octave (2:1).

2. *Pythagorean system*. The ancient method of constructing the diatonic scale on the basis of the pure perfect fifth, ratio 3:2. The pitch ratios of the notes to the lower keynote (see Table 2 for the scale of C) are given by powers of 3:2 transposed into a single octave by means of powers of 2. The note E is found as four perfect fifths above C, giving (3/2)⁴ or 81/16, lowered into the basic octave by

TABLE 1

C	2	F♯	1.414
B	1.888	F	1.335
B♭	1.782	E	1.260
A	1.682	E♭	1.1892
A♭	1.5874	D	1.1225
G	1.4983	C♯	1.0595

dividing by 4 (that is, by 2 for each octave above) making 81/64. This is a wide major third (408 cents) which, unless severely 'tempered', is hardly usable in polyphony and harmony as developed through the Renaissance, centred on the intervals of the common chord. Whether sung, or on the organ, this, for musical comfort and satisfaction, calls for the pure major third, ratio 5:4 (386 cents), differing from the Pythagorean by 81/64 divided by 5/4, or 81/80—a ratio famous throughout the history of music theory as the Didymian comma (after the Greek, Didymus, b. 63 BC) amounting to more than a fifth of a semitone (21.5 cents) and very obvious to the ear. Similarly the chord of F needs the pure third to A, a comma lower however than the A arrived at by perfect fifths from F or C which should be heard in a chord of D; and a plain keyboard cannot provide both.

3. *Mean-tone temperament.* By c.1500 theorists and organ-builders had worked out this system which resolves problems of the above kind by favouring the pure major third while reducing the fifth by a quarter of a comma, i.e. by 3:2 divided by the fourth root of 81/80 (which, 80 being 2^4 times 5, works out at $\sqrt[4]{5}$). This, approximately 697 cents, flattens the fifth by an amount which the ear will comfortably tolerate (the tuner setting it by experience). In Table 2 under 'mean-tone $\frac{1}{4}$-comma', and subtracting cents, all major thirds are of 386 cents or so and all fifths 697 or so (these being rounded-off figures). Moreover a consequence is—to express it most concisely in cents rather than by ratios—that two of these fifths add up to 1,394 which, subtracting 1,200 for the octave, leaves 193 for the whole tone, exactly half of the major third 386 and eliminating the natural distinction (see again HARMONIC SERIES) between C–D (9:8) and the smaller D–E (10:9). With this, which gives the system its name, the scales of C and D, and the others too, all start with the same whole-tone interval.

But a trouble arises among the pure thirds themselves when it comes to sharps and flats in the scale. G♯, for the chord of E, will be two pure major thirds above C, ratio 25:16. Yet as A♭ a third below the upper C it should stand above the low C as 2 divided by 5:4, or 8:5. The enharmonic difference amounts to some 41 cents, getting on for a quarter tone, and where G♯ is provided the chord of F minor is virtually unusable. Other 'black' keys can similarly be used either for a sharp or for a flat, not both: the most usual choice among them being C♯, E♭, F♯, G♯, and, of course, B♭. A complicated way out met in some keyboards was by divided or 'split' black keys of which, for example, the front half gives D♯ and the rear half E♭, each acting on separate strings (or pipes) for the sharp and for the flat. But the main developments were the following.

4. *Modifications of mean-tone.* Before the end of the 16th century it had begun to be recognized that, while many musicians and organ-builders would prefer the above system, the ear would tolerate, or even perhaps react favourably to, small departures from the strict major third such as could be made with the object of bringing each enharmonic sharp and flat closer together, thus offering wider scope in tonality and modulation. The simplest method was to reduce the perfect fifth not by a quarter of a comma but by one-sixth, i.e. by the sixth root of 81:80, making (in theory) a fifth of some 698 cents. This stretches the major third to 394 cents, but it reduces the enharmonic discrepancy on G♯ to 19 cents—less than half what it had been. Again, it yields a 'mean-tone', now half of 394 cents.

Other important methods through the 17th and particularly the 18th centuries were to modify the above 'regular' mean-tone systems by 'irregular' systems, in which (e.g. to make A♭ and G♯ the same note) some of the fifths are reduced by less than others in order to tamper less with the most important thirds. J. S. Bach was probably most familiar with tunings of such kinds (rather than with equal temperament), allowing free modulation from key to key with good effect, as in his 48 Preludes and Fugues (*Das wohltemperierte Klavier*— 'The Well-tempered Keyboard'). A name often associated with this development is that of the German organist Andreas Werckmeister (1645–1706), though in fact he was a prominent advocate and exponent rather than a discoverer. In fact, one of the earliest accounts of mean-tone tuning (in Pietro Aron: *Toscanello in musica*, Venice 1523) could already be called 'irregular' in that after first tuning C–E pure and the fifths C–G, G–D 'a little flat', the A is made so that D–A and A–E sound equal (and thus smaller fifths than C–G).

TABLE 2. Intervals in cents above C according to Equal, Pythagorean, and Mean-tone temperaments.

	E.T.	Pythag.	Mean-tone ($\frac{1}{4}$-comma)	Mean-tone ($\frac{1}{6}$-comma)
C	1200			
B	1100	1110 (243/128)	1083	1092
B♭	1000	996 (16/9)	1007	1003
A	900	906 (27/16)	890	895
G♯	800	A♭ 816	A♭ 814	806
			G♯ 773	787
G	700	702 (3/2)	697	698
F♯	600	612 (729/512)	580	590
F	500	498 (4/3)	504	502
E	400	408 (81/64)	386	394
E♭	300	294 (32/27)	E♭ 311	305
			D♯ 269	
D	200	204 (9/8)	193	197
C♯	100	114 (256/243)	D♭ 112	108
			C♯ 76	89
C	0			

5. *Expressive intonation*. It should perhaps be noticed that temperament has nothing to do with the flexibilities in melodic intonation that often occur naturally and, with non-keyboard instruments and in singing, are often taught, such as those known in French as *notes sensibles*—sharpened leading-notes—and their complement, the flattened semitone above the tonic. In each case the direct opposite to the tuning of mean-tone temperament applies, in that the sharp is higher than the flat, and (as Berlioz put it, perhaps unnecessarily strongly, in his treatise on instrumentation under 'Concertina') mark 'the practice of musicians' as opposed to 'the doctrine of acousticians' (i.e., of course, those up to his time).

Barbour 1951; Barnes 1979; Campbell and Greated 1987; McGeary 1989.

Temple blocks (Chinese or Korean). Hollow wooden percussion instruments carved in a skull-like shape, properly of camphor-wood, with wide slit-like mouth. Their traditional carving and lacquering in red and gold imitate their Chinese prototype, named 'wooden fish' (*muyu*). The carving of this, resembling a fish with no eyelids, represents the wakeful attention required at prayers. As Western instruments, two to five of different sizes, up to c.20 cm. (8″) across, sounding from high to low (not tuned to specific notes), are clamped in a row to a stand and struck with a soft or hard stick. Their clear, musical pitches are due to the air vibrating in the hollow interior: a form of struck *cavity resonator (if the mouth be partially closed the pitch falls accordingly). Temple blocks became added to dance drummers' kits by the 1920s and orchestral percussion sections have them available for the parts that Walton (three blocks in *Façade*), Britten, and others have written for them, sometimes (as Copland) under the name 'Chinese blocks'.

The term 'temple' comes from their former use in Confucian ceremonies (see CHINA AND KOREA, 1*a* (iii)). The temple block is said to derive originally from an instrument of the *slit drum kind: there are in fact, in China, rarer versions in the shape of a complete fish, with a long slit down the back.

The *mokubio* is a Japanese version (*mokugyo*) that has become known among percussionists since the 1960s and may be cylindrical in shape.

Tenora (Catalonia). See SHAWM, 3*b*.

Tenor cor (Amer.: *mellophone; Fr.: *cor alto*; Ger.: *Altkorno*; It.: *genis corno*). A more easily played substitute for the *French horn in military bands, and quite often seen in amateur bands. It is circular like the horn, a little smaller, and held in the same way except that some models have the valves arranged for the right hand. The pitch is F (6′, as the horn in F alto), with an alternative slide provided for E♭. The mouthpiece is horn-like but wider, and as compared with the horn itself the sound is less lyrical. The tenor cor was introduced

in the 1860s by either Besson in Paris or Distin in London, and then by Distin in New York under the name 'Melody Horn' (see MELLOPHONE). During the 1920s it was quite often played in the jazz bands.

Tenor drum. A British and American drum, two-headed like the *side drum but wider (up to nearly 75 cm. or 30″), without snare, and played with sticks which have ends of hard felt. In a marching Corps of Drums the sticks are wielded in a spectacular manner, always twirling—though in the USA the tenor drum has been partly replaced by the set of 'timp-toms' (see TOM-TOM). Composers have scored for it, sometimes to be played with wooden sticks, while it also serves for the *Rührtrommel* parts in German works (see SIDE DRUM, 4).

An early appearance of the name is in the 1839 price list of D'Almaine of London (Poole 1982), but with nothing to show whether a drum of the same size and character as later.

Tenor horn (Amer.: alto horn; Fr.: *saxhorn alto, alto*; Ger.: *Althorn*; It.: usually *genis*). Valved brass instrument, in Britain pitched in E♭, a fifth below the *cornet, with the bell pointing upwards. A standard component of the *brass band in Britain, and used also in France.

For 'tenor horn' in America, and *Tenorhorn* in Germany, see BARITONE, 2, 3.

Tenor oboe. An 18th-century instrument with the same pitch as the *cor anglais (English horn), first made in France in around 1670 for playing the tenor part in four-part music of *oboes with *bassoon (see MILITARY BAND, 4). Built straight, like a large oboe, it has an angled brass crook for the reed, and two keys. The bell may be pear-shaped, or flared with an ovoid cavity inside; or in England there is usually no true bell, merely an almost straight end (the instrument c.75 cm. (30″) long). Where Bach names a part below the oboes *taille (French equivalent to 'tenor'), it would nominally have been played on this, though the contemporary *oboe da caccia* (see COR ANGLAIS, 2) if more readily available, would have sounded much the same in the harmony. In England the tenor oboe was made throughout the 18th century and bought by church bands, often named 'vauxhumane' (i.e. *vox humana*, also an organ stop). Many have been preserved in country churches along with other wind instruments, and perhaps first brought into use here by veterans from infantry bands of Marlborough's time.

Tenoroon. A small-sized *bassoon. Several such sizes have been made in the past: octave bassoon or *fagottino*, c.63 cm. (25″) tall and sounding an octave above the bassoon; and tenoroon (*basson quinte*), 80 to 96 cm. (32–38″) tall, pitched either a fourth or a fifth above the bassoon. Many are preserved from the 18th century onwards, though very little was said about their uses. Almenraeder (see BASSOON, 4) was one who recommended them for child beginners. Some 18th-century English parishes bought a tenoroon for the church, though for what particular purpose is not recorded. Later London makers up to recently occasionally made one to put in the shop window. Among the very few compositions that include a small bassoon (apart from the earlier *dulcian) two are German: a Parthia by Trost with 2 Fagotti octavo and 2 Fagotti quarto (Hedlund 1958) and a solo sonata by Kirnberger for *Quartfagott* in F, apparently a fourth above the bassoon. From America is a march of 1807 by Uriah K. Hill with a part for tenoroon (Eliason 1982), this from a period when tenoroons are listed by the Hartford maker Catlin. The rather unsatisfactory sound of small bassoons can be gauged by playing a bassoon recording at appropriately faster speed.

An 'Alto Fagotte' (or 'Caledonica') made by Geo. Wood, London, in the 1830s was a freak design intended for a single-reed mouthpiece: a few examples survive in collections.

Tenor tuba. Where a score has a part with this name—as in Richard Strauss's *Don Quixote* and *Ein Heldenleben*, Stravinsky's *The Rite of Spring*, and Holst's *The Planets*—it is normally played on the *euphonium (Amer.: baritone), though it seems possible that Strauss may have had, at least at first, the tenor *Wagner tuba in mind (Bevan 1978).

Teponatzli. Ancient Mexican instrument sometimes seen as related to the *slit drum. A log is hollowed out from the underside to leave (along the top) two tongues, pointing towards the middle between narrow and accurately cut slits along the sides. They are thinned at the free ends, where they are hit with mallets to give two different deep pitches said to have been heard several miles away. The teponatzli and the upright cylindrical hand-beaten drum *huehuetl* were sounded together in Aztec festivals and in funerals. The instrument is still played in parts of Central America, and has given rise to modern orchestral and educational wooden instruments known as *log drum.

Theorbo (Fr.: *théorbe*; It.: *tiorba*, a name of very uncertain origin). A lute known from the end of the 16th century to the mid-18th, normally of a large size and intended for *continuo playing or alone in accompaniment to the voice. Long, unstopped bass strings (diapasons) run from a pegbox lying above that of the fingerboard strings. See CHITARRONE, I for the question of distinction between 'chitarrone' and 'theorbo'.

I. *Description.* In Italian examples up to c.1650, this upper pegbox appears much as shown in CHITARRONE, Pl. I, with a general difference that whereas on that very tall instrument the diapasons may be up to twice the length of the stopped *courses, on a theorbo they do not exceed one-

and-a-half times. For reasons outlined under CHI-TARRONE the top or top two courses of a theorbo are tuned an octave lower than they would be on a lute or archlute and this can give accompanying harmonies a very rich sound. The tuning generally followed the 'A tuning' of the lute (see LUTE, 2b) with diapasons, e.g. from G down to low A'.

Some puzzle arises over the identity of numerous instruments met in collections, mainly from the first half of the 18th century and many of them German, in which the upper pegbox is carried above the lower by a jinked piece (see LUTE, Pl. 3). Such specimens, though with bodies about lute-size, have long been exhibited as theorboes, but are now considered more likely to be examples of baroque 13-course lute (with no octave lowering of the top courses): see LUTE, 4.

2. *Music.* Many instructions for accompanying on the theorbo are French, c.1660–1730. In England it was the most regular plucked instrument for accompanying the voice: Playford's song publications from 1639 onwards name it 'Theorboe-lute', e.g. 'with a thorough-bass (figured continuo) for the Theorbo-lute, Bass viol, Harpsichord or Organ' (*Banquet of Music*, 1688, an early mention of the *harpsichord in this connection in England). Mace (1676) shows how the bass line might be realized on the theorbo—great leaps back and forth between the deep diapasons, and chords and fast running decorations above—in an idiomatic style quite different from keyboard styles (Huws-Jones 1972), and as different again from the older, pre-baroque, ways of accompanying the voice on the lute itself.

Thumb piano. See SANSA.

Thunder sheet. See EFFECTS.

Ti. Chinese flute; see DIZI.

Tibet. See CHINA AND KOREA, 3.

Tibia. I. (Lat.). Ancient Roman name for a *reed-pipe, corresponding to Greek *aulos.

2. Organ reed stop (esp. see CINEMA ORGAN).

Tilinca (Romania). See FLUTE, 8b.

Timbales (in full, *timbales creoles* or *cubaines*—not to be confused with the French name for *timpani). One of the drums of Latin American dance music, forming a pair, differing from *bongos and *conga drums in being intended for playing with drumsticks: the counterhoops project above the heads whereas with hand drums they are drawn lower down to give freedom to the hands. Cylindrical, with diameters up to 35 cm. (14"), the two drums are held on a common stand. The main quaver rhythms are played on the larger drum, the smaller 'filling in'. Frequently a pair of *cowbells (modern form) are mounted above the timbales, for the right hand to play with the stick while the left hand continues on the larger drum.

Timbrel. See TAMBOURINE, 2.

Timpani (or kettledrums; Fr.: *timbales*; Ger.: *Pauken*; It.: *timpani*—a sing. '*timpano*' exists; Ru.: *litavry*; Sp.: *timbales*). The large cauldron-like instruments tunable to different notes, and, though not historically the oldest drums of the West, the oldest in the orchestra and without question the classic drums of symphonic music. Normally of copper, two, three, or more timpani of differing sizes are played by one performer, each drum tunable over the range of a fifth by changing the tension of the head (calfskin, or nowadays of plastic, which can give very clear notes).

1. *Hand-screw timpani.* The traditional timpani are tuned by six or eight T-handled screws which draw down the metal counterhoop (in Fig. 1*a*, shown in section, the superior type with projecting lugs with holes for the screws). Such remained in professional use in British orchestras up to the 1950s, and many amateur societies rely on them still. Otherwise they have been almost entirely replaced by the more expensive pedal timpani or other 'machine' drums (see below, 2, 3) which enable the player to retune instantly to different notes.

Most music up to the mid-19th century and much since is scored for two timpani, normally tuned to the tonic and dominant of the movement. The central notes of their respective tuning-ranges lie a fourth apart, *d* and *A*. This makes the compass B♭ to *f* for the smaller and low *F* to *c* for the larger, allowing eight tonalities, from *F* down to B♭, to have the tonic on the small drum, the ancient

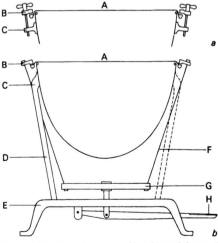

Fig. 1. (*a*) Section of top part of hand-tuned drum; (*b*) section of a pedal drum, showing the basic principle.

choice (in many old scores the two notes are written C and G whatever their actual sound, matching the notation of the classical *trumpet with which the timpani were intimately allied). Changes in tuning are mostly demanded between movements or, if during a movement, allowing sufficient bars' rest for retuning with the handles. Average diameters for a set of two drums are 63.5 cm. and 71 cm. (25″ and 28″). A hole in the bottom of each drum takes up temperature changes in the air.

Works of the Romantic period increasingly call for three drums, as Brahms in some of his major works and Tchaikovsky in most. With the third drum of an intermediate size, the other two became more separated in size to add a whole tone at each end of the tonal compass, the lowest useful note of each drum now usually considered to be, from the smallest downwards, *e*, *A*, and *D*; typical diameters then are 61, 66, and 75 cm. (24″, 26″, and 29½″).

2. *Pedal timpani* (Pl. 1). The general principle of these is illustrated diagrammatically in Fig. 1*b*. The head (A) is to be tightened from below by the pedal while the main stress on the shell remains within the top region (B–C) as on a plain hand-tuned drum. The shell is supported on four metal struts (D) rising from the heavy base (E). The tension rods, one of them shown (F), lead down to a disc- or star-shaped frame (G) which is moved up or down by the pedal (H). The classic system is that designed in Dresden by Pittrich, from 1872. Later designs include lighter-weight models, as by the leading American timpani maker, Ludwig, some with fibreglass shell, and with the tension rods passing inside the shell, emerging near the top to engage the counterhoop.

Pedal actions are very sophisticated, with balanced movement that can be held in any position and an adjustable pitch indicator placed up beside the rim. On one single pedal drum different notes can be played quickly one after another, though never to the point of dispensing with the need for two or more separate timpani.

There are also 'single handle' machine drums, with one large handle instead of the pedal, allowing a drum to be quickly retuned with one hand, leaving the other hand free to strike. These appeared in Germany *c.*1850 and are the kind that Wagner wrote for in the *Ring*. In Act 1, Scene 3, of *Götterdämmerung*, the second of two timpanists plays seven different notes on two drums within the space of 28 bars, including Hunding's sinister rhythm, dead solo.

The first attempt at a 'machine drum' tunable by a single movement is, needless to say, credited to Leonardo da Vinci. Little more was done before a spate of inventions in every country, from a rotary drum (below, 3) by Stumpff, a German living in Amsterdam, in 1821, to the 'Dresden' pedal drum noticed already. Some pedal drums built to earlier specifications back to the 1840s are said still to have been in use in the Munich opera house in the 1960s (Tobischek 1977).

Pl. 1. Pair of pedal timpani (model by Premier, Leicester).

3. *Rotary timpani.* These are mounted on a central column which rises from a base and for one part of its length has a screw-thread. The tension-rods lead down to a frame which engages the thread, while another frame, supporting the shell, turns freely on the column. Hence, when the player rotates the drum one way or the other by one hand, both frames rotate together but the tensioning frame moves up or down the screw-thread. The mechanism is usually concealed inside the shell, but in older models may lie outside it. Also, the action is in some cases reversed, the shell engaging the screw and the tensioning turning free, so that in this instance the shell is moved up against the head to increase the tension. These drums do not, of course, leave both hands free from tuning as the pedal does, and the rotation can move the player's favourite striking spot out of reach. But a timpanist has only two feet, and if he must quickly change the note of a third drum, then a rotary drum or one of the old hand-tuned drums can be the solution. A similar rotary principle is used in *rototoms.

4. *Timpani playing.* The two sticks are of cane or wood with ends of felt over a harder felt or cork core, and of various degrees of softness to suit the music or follow a composer's instruction. Each stick is held between thumb and index finger, the wrist held low. The drums are struck fairly near the rim, the sound being if necessary damped with the fingers while holding the stick. The two hands are used as far as possible alternately ('hand to hand'), reserving 'double beats' with the same hand for where necessary in fast passages. This frequently leads to crossing one hand over the other from drum to drum. Ex. 1 is a timpani flourish in Purcell's *The Fairy Queen* (Symphony to Act 4), one of the earliest written solo passages for timpani and lying naturally for alternate hands starting with the left—as one can test for oneself in dumb-show, the small drum tuned to D being placed on the right (though on the Continent it may be on the left). Ex. 2 on the other hand shows a simple group of notes calling for cross-beating in either of the two ways indicated (cross-beats shown bracketed) and executed with a rhythmic swing and a fine visual effect recalling the timpanist's historical parent, the cavalry kettledrummer with the drums slung on either side of the drum horse and the reins attached to the drummer's stirrups. In complete contrast, Ex. 3 is from one of the first major composers to write for pedal drums, Richard Strauss, in *Till Eulenspiegel*: the part is simply headed 'Pauken', without stating initial tunings in the old manner. After a few pages in the score the drums give out five notes of the principal theme (which is indicated in Ex. 3 by small notes): the first two notes on the middle drum of three and the last two on the large drum, ending with a roll.

Ex. 3.

Ex. 1.   *Ex. 2.*

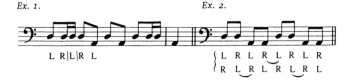

The timpani roll is also made with hand-to-hand strokes. Among special effects, the glissando with the pedal, upwards or downwards, first became familiar to audiences in works by Bartók, most wonderfully in the Adagio of the *Music for Strings, Percussion, and Celesta* (1935). Rarer is *con sordini* or *coperti* (covered with a cloth), originally done with cavalry kettledrums at funerals (with trumpets likewise muted) and later, e.g., demanded by Mozart in some operas.

5. *Pitch and size.* The sound of a drum is composed of non-harmonic partials with, from timpani, a predominance of those arising from vibration modes having diametrical nodes only (see PARTIALS, 7). The relative frequencies of these partials, although non-harmonic, come in theory not far away from harmonic, and it has been further shown by trials in the USA with actual timpani that these frequencies are considerably lowered by the mass of air inside the drum and then make a series very close to 2, 3, 4, 5, . . . If then taking, for example, G as the pitch of the first of these partials (the one generally regarded as the heard pitch of the drum), the series runs practically G d g b d', etc., thus including the intervals of the fifth, which timpanists often listen for while tuning. One might ask why the diameters for a pair of drums quoted above (1) lie closer than would match tuning ranges a fourth apart: it may be bound up with the lowering of partial frequencies by the enclosed air, of which the larger drum holds the greater mass. There are in fact, made in Germany for school music, some timpani with cylindrical shells wide open at the bottom, with listed diameters and tuning ranges which agree quite closely with the direct theoretical relation between diameter and pitch.

6. *Early kettledrums.* See NAQQARA for medieval small kettledrums or 'nakers', often carried on a belt round the waist—or by a boy walking in front (see MEDIEVAL INSTRUMENTS, Pl. I). The large drums which had reached the West during the 15th century were brought to England from the Netherlands by Henry VII and were primarily horse-drums. As these began to appear in the orchestra during the 17th century, they were played with heavy sticks, or often in later periods with sticks with disc-shaped wooden ends about 5 cm. (2") across and giving a very crisp sound. Such are still illustrated in 1845 (Kastner, *Méthode complète et raisonée de timbales*), though by then Berlioz had been insisting on the choice of soft-ended sticks ('sponge sticks' he terms them) for orchestral use. The 18th-century kettledrums, sometimes placed together on an iron stand, were usually smaller in diameter than later (often around 50 cm. or 20"), with the two of a pair different by only about 2 or 3 cm., which may point to a very considerable difference in tension, giving a markedly crisper sound from the smaller drum whose duty it was to sound the tonic. Cavalry kettledrums in Europe today will often be seen to preserve such small dimensions.

Unusual tunings are demanded in a number of lesser-known works by 18th-century composers, also use of more than two drums, as where Christoph Graupner in a Sinfonia of 1747 gives six timpani a melody on the notes from low F up to d—very much like Holst in *The Planets*. But the major orchestral breakaways from the old tonic-and-dominant tradition are in the works of Beethoven: timpani entrusted on their own to principal themes, as in the first bars of the Violin Concerto, and in the Scherzo of the Ninth Symphony, in the latter exploiting the full tuning-range of octave Fs—this only one of his several very unusual tunings for the two drums.

7. *Solo repertory.* From the Baroque, pieces of 1685 by Philidor have sometimes been revived including a march for two pairs of drums tuned respectively to g and e, and c and G (Titcomb 1956). Later, Kastner (1845) tells how a Berlin timpanist had recently performed a concerto on six drums, running from one to another on a sort of gallery, throwing the sticks in the air and going through the most extraordinary motions without his execution suffering in the least, all accompanied by eight trumpets and full orchestra. There are timpani concertos by P. Pieranzorina, a timpanist born in 1814, and Julius Tausch, c.1878. A sonatina for two timpanists is by Tcherepnin (1940); six pieces, *Recitative and improvisation*, by Elliott Carter (1966); and a few other works, not that most timpanists feel any great need for concertos.

Timp-tom. See TOM-TOM, 3.

Tin whistle. See FLAGEOLET, 1.

Tiple (Sp., 'treble'). 1. Small *guitar with four or five *courses of strings (now metal), made in numerous forms in Spain, and in Latin America especially Colombia (where it has been rated as the 'national instrument'), Venezuela, and up to Mexico. It may be about half the size of a guitar or somewhat more, and be tuned like the upper strings of the guitar, to a higher pitch or with the lowest course raised an octave as on a *ukulele; but there are many different local tunings also. Besides accompanying songs, the tiple in ensembles may strum harmonies above the guitar playing the bass (and a *bandola playing the melody). There are also both folk commercial makes of the tiple, with the outer courses double and the inner two courses triple with an octave (lower) string in the middle (also GUITAR, Ex. 3b, Colombia): in the USA, Martin was making this from c.1920.

2. Tiple, as a wind instrument of Catalonia (Spain): see SHAWM, 3b.

Tof (drum). See BIBLICAL INSTRUMENTS, 1d.

Tom-tom. A drum adopted by jazz drummers of the 1920s, subsequently to become one of the most important of drums both in rock music (see DRUM KIT) and in the modern percussion section. The name apparently comes from the Caribbean as an English word for the native drums.

1. *Chinese tom-tom.* In early jazz the tom-tom was after a Chinese type, fairly shallow, with somewhat bulging shell painted with dragons and flowers, and two heads secured with wide brass nails in Chinese fashion. This, now known as a 'Chinese tom-tom', has become little used.

2. *Modern tom-tom.* This has a deeper cylindrical shell (laminated or acrylic) and usually two screw-tensioned heads. Diameters are from 25 to 45 cm. (10–18″), and depths about the same; there may be an internal felt damper to reduce 'thud'. A drum kit will include from one tom-tom to three or more of different sizes to sound higher or lower, perhaps about a third apart. They have brackets for attachment to the bass drum or to a separate metal stand. A 'floor tom-tom' is a large one standing on its own three legs. Among modern composers who have included tom-toms, Stravinsky has three in *Agon* and suggested their use in *The Soldier's Tale* in place of his original side-drums with the snares silenced.

There are also single-headed tom-toms, and these can be tuned fairly well to specific notes (like *timpani) by turning the tuning-screws with a coin. They can be obtained as a set of eight named 'Concert-toms', from 15 to 40 cm. (6–16″) in diameter.

3. *Timp-tom.* From the late 1960s there have also been 'timp-toms' (or 'multi-toms'), single-headed and tunable, for school music (sometimes listed as 'timpani'), and for marching bands, in which three (or more) are carried by one player on a frame, the smallest (c.35 cm. (14″) or less in diameter) in the middle. They are mostly played with beaters. Each timp-tom can be tuned over about a fourth, and the three may be tuned to a common chord.

Tong cymbals. See CYMBAL, 5.

Tonguing. The principal means of articulation on wind instruments. In written music it is normally assumed that every note will be tongued unless joined to the preceding note by a slur. On the flute and on brass instruments this is by a flick of the tongue against the teeth, and on reed instruments against the tip of the reed. Where the music has dots under a slur, the notes are lightly separated by tonguing, matching the effect produced on the *violin when this sign appears.

In very fast passages 'double tonguing' is often used: the player moves the tongue as in 'tu ku', possible also on reed instruments. Other ways of tonguing were in use from the 16th century to the mid-18th; notably, when playing runs of quick notes, that which was generally described as 'te re' or 'di ri'. The 're' was apparently something like a very soft 'de', usually falling on the second quaver of a pair, giving a stylish lilt to the music. Great importance was attached to it. In Ex. 1, an Italian elementary example of its period (Bismantova, 1677), the author recommends practising it, on *recorder or *cornett, by speaking the syllables aloud while fingering the notes silently on the instrument. Tonguing such as in Ex. 1 is still in use on the *txistu* of the Basques (see PIPE AND TABOR 1). French players of the Baroque period came to change the consonants round, placing the 're' (or 'ru') on the first of the pair, save for the initial note of the passage: a group of six quavers would then be tongued 'tu tu, ru tu, ru tu', possibly lengthening the first of each pair. Many players of early music have studied such methods very thoroughly in the quest to do full justice to the period.

Flutter-tonguing is by trilling 'r', making a whirring effect. It belongs almost entirely to the 20th century. In Richard Strauss's *Don Quixote* all the wind instruments do it (clarinets and brass in Variation 2, for the sheep). Schoenberg and Webern demand it mainly from the brass, but Britten has all the wind flutter-tonguing in the second movement of his *Sinfonia da Requiem*. In French military-band transcriptions it has been used on the clarinets to render the violin orchestral *tremolo*.

Tonkori. A rare, somewhat zither-like wooden instrument of the Ainu people of Hokkaido in the north of Japan, long and narrow, c.130 cm. (51″) by 8 cm. (3″), and partly hollowed out. Held at a slant, it has side pegs for up to five fibre strings resting at each end on a thin bridge and attached to a leather tailpiece at the pointed lower end. They are tuned to various intervals, not necessarily in order of pitch, and are played with both hands, accompanying songs and in solos that may include suggestions of bird and animal sounds. Even a century ago the instrument was uncommon (Savage Landor, *Alone with the Hairy Ainu*, 1893), the bamboo *jew's-harp being played far more. No connection of the *tonkori* with any instrument of neighbouring peoples has yet been proved.

Torban (Russian). See BANDURA.

Ex. 1. Baroque double tonguing (after Bismantova 1677, as for recorder or cornett)

te   te re; te;   te re te;   te;   re le re, te re le re; te   re; te.

Toy piano. See GLOCKENSPIEL, 2.

Toy trumpet. See MELODICA.

Transposing instruments. Instruments for which the music is written higher or lower than it sounds by some given interval. (Should the interval always be an octave—as an octave higher with guitar and double bass—then the instrument need not be considered a transposing one).

Stringed instruments are rarely transposing (an exception is the *violino piccolo). Practically all the regular transposers are wind instruments. With these the operative interval is in most cases stated in the instrument's designation, e.g. 'B♭ clarinet' or 'clarinet in B♭'. The rule is that the named note is that which the instrument will sound when the player reads the note C.

These transpositions are for the benefit of the performer, in that they enable a player to change to differently pitched instruments of the same family while continuing to use the same fingerings for the written notes, or, with brass instruments, the same harmonics, etc. The composer or arranger arranges for this with the appropriate transposition, to which he is so accustomed that when writing a part for

TABLE 1. Woodwind Transpositions

Parts as written	Actual sound
Alto flute (in G)	Fourth lower
Oboe d'amore (in A)	Minor third lower
Cor anglais (in F)	Fifth lower
Bass oboe or Heckel-phone (in C)	Octave lower
Clarinet in E♭	Minor third higher
Clarinet in D	Tone higher
Clarinet in C	As written
Clarinet in B♭	Tone lower
Clarinet in A	Minor third lower
Basset horn (in F)	Fifth lower (see Note below for notes written in bass clef)
Alto clarinet in E♭	Major sixth lower
Bass clarinet (normally assumed to be in B♭)	Here two notations: (i) normal, in treble clef: a ninth lower; (ii) Wagner and some others: a tone lower, using bass clef freely. The part then looks more 'bass' but infringes the purpose of transposing since it makes the player 'rethink' while fingering
Bass clarinet in A	Similarly two notations: (i) tenth lower; (ii) minor third lower
Saxophone, B♭ soprano	Tone lower
Saxophone, E♭ alto	Major sixth lower
Saxophone, B♭ tenor	Ninth lower
Saxophone, E♭ baritone	Octave and a sixth lower (so that by imagining bass clef instead of treble, one can read the actual sounds, but remembering to add three flats to the key signature)

cor anglais or for horn in F, and wanting the sound of F, he writes the C above without having to stop to think. A conductor or other experienced score-reader then does the opposite, seeing (in this example) C but mentally 'hearing' the F below, with no conscious effort. Only in more complex instances might he have to pause for an instant on a first reading of the score, to see what the harmony of the wind instruments actually amounts to. Schoenberg held that these transpositions should be abolished, in full scores at least, but they are so ingrained that to write all wind parts at sounding pitch has been found to make things harder, not easier.

TABLE 2. Brass Transpositions

Designation	Sounds above/below the written notes	
	horn	trumpet
In B♭	'B♭ alto': tone lower 'B♭ basso': ninth lower (see Note 1)	Tone lower
In A	Minor third lower	Minor third lower
In A♭	Major third lower	Minor sixth higher (see Note 3)
In G	Fourth lower	Fifth higher
In F	Fifth lower	Fourth higher (see Note 4)
In E or E♭	Sixth lower (minor or major)	Third higher (major or minor)
In D or D♭	Seventh lower (similarly)	Tone or semitone higher
In C	Octave lower (see Note 2)	As written

Notes to Table 2

1. Horn in B♭. Parts in older music frequently fail to specify 'alto' or 'basso', in which case the matter has to be decided as best one can by context (if with many high notes, 'basso'). 'Horn in A', or 'A♭', is occasionally 'basso' in later music, e.g. Verdi, then sounding a tenth lower.

2. 'In C'. Occasionally in the earlier Viennese classics this is 'C alto', sounding as written.

3. The octave difference between 'in A' and 'in A♭': in early 19th-century music, usually 'in A' means trumpets crooked down to A; 'in A♭', crooked up to A♭. Should in either case the transposition listed above make nonsense of the music, then try the other! In the same period 'in B♭' occasionally reads a seventh higher.

4. 'Tromba contralta' in F in Russian works, e.g. Rimsky-Korsakov, sounds a fifth lower than written.

Tables 1 and 2 are laid out from the score-reading point of view. In Table 1, wherever the key is stated in parentheses, it is, or can be, omitted from the designation of the instrument. A part 'in C' (sounding as written or an octave lower) needs to be specified as such in cases where (as with clarinet, trumpet, etc.) the instrument can be in other keys also. With the brass in Table 2, in older times a horn or trumpet was put in different keys by inserting *crooks and the heading tells which crook to insert; players today, no longer using crooks, make at sight such transpositions as are then often necessary; but this is of no concern to the score-reader.

Note also: bass clef when used for low notes of horn and occasionally trumpet; the older practice is to write the notes an octave lower than they would be if in the treble clef (Ex. 1a). The preferred modern practice is to continue into the bass clef logically (Ex. 1b). The context usually makes it clear which method is adopted.

Ex. 1.

(a)

Sounds on Horn in F

(b)

Cornet transpositions: as horn from 'in Bb' (alto) downwards; but 'in C' sounds as written.

Bass trumpet: as horn in Eb, D, C, and Bb 'basso'.

Wagner tubas: Wagner himself changed his method for these in the full scores of the *Ring*.

(i) In the Prelude to *Götterdämmerung*: tenor tubas in Bb, sounding a ninth lower; bass tubas in F, sounding an octave lower. Bruckner follows this method in his Seventh Symphony, but in the Eighth partly the next (ii).

(ii) *Das Rheingold*: sounding respectively a tone and a fifth lower than written.

(iii) For the rest of the cycle the scores have (tenor) 'in Eb' sounding a sixth lower (but in bass clef a third higher); and (bass) 'in Bb' sounding a ninth lower (but when in bass clef, a tone lower).

Band instruments: see BRASS BAND.

Transverse flute. The ordinary flute, and others that are also held sideways: see FLUTE, 7a.

Traverso. Short for It.: *flauto traverso*, *"transverse flute', sometimes, as in Bach, *traversa*. Today, the name 'traverso' is frequently used for the baroque flute, to avoid confusion with 'flute' (or *flauto*) in the old sense when, unqualified, it usually means the *recorder. The term had already been used in 1932 by Terry (*Bach's Orchestra*, 131).

Triangle. Percussion instrument made of a steel rod, usually around a centimetre thick and long enough to be bent into a triangle measuring from 10 to 25 cm. (4″ to 10″) along each side and open at one corner. It is best suspended by a fine gut,

held in the hand or by a clip attached to the music stand. The beater is a steel rod, thinner than that of the triangle and up to 15 cm. (6″) long. For single strokes the triangle is struck on the outside, choosing the place where the sound will best suit the music, normally the most high and silvery that the instrument will give. The trill is made on the inside from side to side: for a crescendo one begins near the top corner, gradually coming downwards where more force can be given with the beater. Some special effects include use of a wooden or soft-ended beater, giving a more bell-like sound with lower partials more prominently excited.

The triangle shape suggests that the instrument was evolved primarily for trills or quick rhythms (the same rod if quite straight would give much the same sound if suspended but would halve the speed of trilling). In folk music the triangle is used chiefly in those southern parts of Europe where the castanets are played, and in similar quick rhythms. Its widest non-orchestral use has, however, been in large sizes as a far-carrying calling instrument, e.g. as a fire alarm, giving a loud, clanging trill.

Many old forms (the triangle is seen from the 14th century) have five or six loose iron rings on the lowest side, apparently to jingle in fast rhythms; some village-bands in Bohemia are said still to have had such rings on their triangle at the beginning of the 20th century. In the Renaissance period the instrument was also made in a trapeze-shape with a holding-ring at the top and called, from its appearance, a 'stirrup'; this had no open corner and must have sounded more like a little bell.

An early orchestral use of the triangle is said to be in a Hamburg opera of 1710, in a 'folk' scene. Grétry, and Gluck (*Iphigénie en Tauride*, 1779), used it for exotic colour, and it became added to the military *Turkish music. Berlioz, in Act 1 of *The Trojans*, calls for a whole *jeu de triangles* to accompany a group of antique *sistrums shaken on the stage, and modern works may call for four or so different triangles, contrasting in sound from high to low.

Triple harp. See HARP, 6, 9b.

Tromba contralta. Valved trumpet envisaged by Rimsky-Korsakov, pitched in F a fourth below the Bb trumpet and scored for, as a 3rd trumpet, in several works by him (first in the opera *Mlada*, 1889) and by other Russian composers. The parts sound a fifth lower than written, but are now played on an ordinary trumpet.

Tromba da caccia (or *di caccia*). Named in some German baroque works, such as Telemann's Violin Concerto in F, with high parts up to the 18th harmonic (written *d‴* above the stave). Argument continues over whether some trumpet is meant (possibly a coiled one), or, as more believe, the horn (from Fr.: *trompe*). The parts have often been played on horns, an octave lower than on trumpets, as also those for *Tromba selvatica* (Telemann, *Musique de Table*, 1733, here in E♭ and again with this high compass).

Tromba da tirarsi. See SLIDE TRUMPET, 3a.

Tromba marina (from It., or 'trumpet marine', from Fr.; Ger.: *Trumscheit*): 1. *Baroque type*. A tall stringed instrument of the 17th and early 18th centuries, standing up to 212 cm. (7′) (Pl. 1), the soundbox, open at the bottom, resting on the floor. The single gut string is bowed high up near the top with a short thick bow, while the other hand touches the string *below* the bow at points where it will sound in harmonics, mostly from the 8th to the 13th, making a scale like that of a natural trumpet and at about the same pitch (see TRUMPET, Ex. 1): hence 'tromba'; but 'marina' remains a puzzle (Adkins and Dickinson 1982). By most accounts all the notes were made with one finger or the thumb of the non-bowing hand.

The bridge is shaped with one foot acting as a fulcrum for the other which extends to the side, to rattle against an ivory or metal plate fixed to the soundboard, heightening the 'trumpet' effect (as with the 'trompette' string of a *hurdy-gurdy). The example shown adds wire *sympathetic strings concealed inside the soundbox. Many of the museum specimens were obtained from monasteries and convents ('Nonnengeige') in and around Germany, the harmonic positions often marked by paper slips glued on, though in some cases these appear to be positioned as if the string had come to be stopped as on a *double bass, bowing low towards the bridge.

Original pieces or parts for tromba marina are from *c.*1660–1740. Lully wrote for it in a 'Divertissement pour les matelots' (for Cavalli's *Serse*, 1660), though whether because he and others thought that 'marina' alluded to use by sailors, or because it actually did so, one cannot say (cf. 3, below). Others are in A. Scarlatti, *Mitridate Eupatore* (Venice, 1707), and sonatas and duets by minor composers in Germany, Switzerland, Italy; see also ÉCURIE, 2. Occasionally some non-harmonic notes are written, obtained by some method not clearly described.

2. *Earlier form*. In the 15th to 16th centuries, known only by paintings and descriptions: a tapered soundbox 120–150 cm. long (4 to 5′), triangular in section, with a similar jarring bridge, and generally held up against the chest. Glareanus, in Switzerland (1547), names it *tympani schiza* ('drum' plus Late Latin 'stick'), saying that it was played in the streets, making the harmonics mostly with the thumb and, one gathers from him, in the range from the 4th to the 8th (and so sounding like trumpet calls of the time). His and many other illustrations show an additional string, half or two-thirds the length of the main one, and bowed at the same time as a 'drone'. By the 17th century

Pl. 1. Tromba marina by Renault, Paris, 2nd half of 18th century (London, Royal College of Music).

the tromba marina, rested on the ground (above, 1), is still shown with the three-sided soundbox without separate neck and with 'drone' strings up to three; a Stuttgart court inventory of 1589 (see RACKET) lists the *Trumscheit* as a carnival instrument.

3. *Survivals in folk music*. These were reported in Bohemia from the end of the 19th century, the instrument, 'trumerina', played either like a double bass or (a photograph of *c.*1890 (Kunz 1974)) in the correct way by a street musician accompanied by hurdy-gurdy and triangle. More recently in Poland (*Grove*, v, 'Folk Music'), the *maryna* seems to have looked rather like a home-made three-stringed double bass with jingles on top for banging the instrument on the ground to mark the rhythm: the name was here said to derive from an earlier two-stringed 'tuba marina' widely used by raftsmen, apparently for signals, which seems very strange.

Trombone (Eng. and Fr. formerly sackbut, *sacqueboute*, also Sp. *sacabuche*, before these languages adopted It. *trombone* in the late 18th century; Ger.: *Posaune*; Ru.: *trombon*). The brass instrument with the forwards-pointing 'slide', some 60 cm. (2') long at rest. The slide (Fr.: *coulisse*; Ger.: *Zug*; It.: *tiro*) corresponds in function to the valves of other brass instruments though, going back to the 15th century, it is historically the older device by nearly four centuries, making the trombone the first, by a long way, of our brass instruments to possess a regular chromatic compass. There are also trombones with valves replacing the slide, though their uses have become relatively few today: see VALVED TROMBONE.

1. *The slide.* A trombone takes to pieces in two parts, the 'slide' and the 'bell'. These are put together with their cross-stays (or 'braces') at 90 degrees for grasping in the left hand, leaving the other free to move the slide, while the part of the bell reaching behind over the left shoulder provides some counterbalance to the weight of the slide. This comprises an 'inner slide' of two parallel fixed tubes, on which run the two legs of the 'outer slide' (with a U-bend or 'bow' at the bottom) moved mainly from the elbow, the cross-stay held lightly between thumb and finger.

The trombone is built in '9" Bb, giving the *harmonic series of this with the slide closed (1st position). To go down the scale the slide is extended by semitone 'positions' until it is drawn back again to continue the scale downwards from the next 1st position note below: see Table I, the notes to the left of the zigzag line, and here shown only from the F above the bass staff (f'). Seven slide positions are needed, in order to reach the note Bh, this followed by 1st position Bb, and from this downwards again to 7th position E. This E is the lowest note apart from the fundamentals or 'pedals', reached after a gap in the compass (arrowed in Table I) and seldom used below the pedal G (4th position). Above the notes shown, the normal compass is up to bb', or c''; higher notes, up to f'', are reached mostly in solos.

Each semitone shift is a little greater than the one before, increasing in proportion to the total tube-length of the instrument as this is made progressively longer: for the semitone from 1st to 2nd position some 8.4 cm. ($3\frac{1}{3}''$), but from 6th to 7th, 11.3 cm. ($4\frac{1}{2}''$). Thus the correct positions of the slide give every note perfectly in tune (which is not automatically the case with valved instruments). A necessary allowance, however, is called for, above the notes in Table I, where the 7th harmonic is by nature too flat for normal use as ab' in 1st position (the 3rd being therefore used), and the g' next to it requires a 'raised' 2nd position.

Alternative positions (Table I, to the right of the zigzag line) are used a great deal (those most commonly used are shown ringed). This may be to avoid big shifts in fast passages, e.g. using the f in 6th position where next to the c below; and especially in legato playing, in making a slur, for instance from c' (Middle C) or b to d', taking this last note in 4th position, with small or no slide movement but 'with the lip' (being to a different harmonic) instead of some 7 to 10 inches up the slide to d' in 1st position (on the same harmonic—a note anyhow by nature tending to be a fraction flat—and with a faint suspicion of portamento unless lightly tongued). The two methods give the slur entirely different musical expressions, in some ways analogous to the choices of fingerings available to the cellist.

A by-product of the slide is of course the glissando, for which the alternative positions are very often essential (and are sometimes specified by a composer to ensure maximum effect, as by Stravinsky in *The Firebird*, 'Danse infernale').

2. *Modern trombones.* The generally large width proportions of tubing and bell today were developed mainly in America from the 1930s in response to the new scope for the trombone opened up by the large jazz, dance, and show bands (see DANCE BAND), in which players came to seek a rounder tone, less rasping in forte than was possible from the older, basically French models generally familiar up to that time—save in those American symphony orchestras in which wide dimensions long traditional in Germany might be found. Bore widths (of the inner slide) range from general purpose 'medium' (c.12.5 mm.) or 'medium large', to 'large' (up to 14 mm.), this last principally for orchestras calling for the weightiest sound from the trombones. Often one sees a coil of tubing in the bell, brought into play by a valve for the thumb: for this see 3, below.

The top of the slide used always to be slightly tapered to fit securely into the bell, but now there is usually instead a screw-threaded collar, with a lug ('slide lock') rotated to engage with the outer slide while the instrument is not in use, preventing risk of this dropping off should the instrument be picked up by unaccustomed hands. The inner slide has at the bottom of each leg a sleeve ('stocking')

TABLE I.

Harmonic	1st	2nd	3rd	4th	5th	6th	7th
6	f'	e'	eb'	(d')	db'	c'	b
5	d'	c#'	c'	b	(bb)	a	g#
4	bb	a	ab	g	gb	(f)	e
3	f	e	eb	d	db	c	B
2	Bb	A	Ab	G	Gb	F	E
1 (pedals)	Bb'	A'	Ab'	G'	Gb'	(F')	E'

or thickening in a dissimilar metal as the bearing surface for the outer slide. Naturally, lubrication is essential. For this, special preparations are obtainable in spray form, replacing such as cold cream diluted with water condensed from the breath (otherwise expelled through the 'water key' mounted on the slide bow).

3. *Thumb valve.* The 'F attachment', the additional tubing in the bell, with the sprung rotary valve for the left thumb, is credited to the Leipzig maker Sattler as long ago as 1839. It lowers the instrument instantly by a perfect fourth into F—a 'B♭/F trombone'—primarily for producing the low notes indicated in Table I as missing; but it also provides a valuable means of avoiding many long shifts of the slide in fast passages. For example, B♭ (valve at rest) and *c* (valve tuned) come both in the 1st position, the latter note as a 3rd harmonic of the F trombone. When playing with the valve turned, the player has to remember to make every shift longer than it would otherwise be by one-third (the ratio for the fourth deeper in pitch being 4 : 3).

4. *Bass trombone.* Up to the end of the 18th century trombones were made in three different sizes, alto, tenor, and bass, corresponding to these voices in choral music. Their parts were written in alto, tenor, and bass clef respectively (many remaining so printed today). This established the traditional trombone section of three players, though now all playing the B♭ trombone (nominally 'tenor') or, especially for the two lower parts, the B♭/F instrument. Of this, there are special large-bore models, the modern 'bass trombone' (Pl. 1), for the third player, responsible for the bass trombone part. A problem here is that the standard slide-length is insufficient for a 7th position with the valve turned (bottom B) or even for a true 6th position (C). Hence usually now a second thumb-valve, first introduced in America, which in combination with the other, lowers the instrument to E, E♭, or D (according to the design) to give correct 6th and 7th positions. Rollers are provided for the thumb to move rapidly on to the second valve, and the instrument can also be used on contrabass trombone parts as in Wagner's *Ring*, descending to the bottom E of the piano, the notes below B being produced as pedals.

In Britain up to the 1950s bass trombone parts were invariably played on the G bass trombone, a large instrument with a handle on the slide for reaching the lowest positions, and for the orchestra a thumb-valve attachment (Boosey & Hawkes) lowering the pitch to D. Some amateur brassbandsmen may still be using it: (collectors have become interested in it too).

5. *Other pitches and older models:* (*a*) *Soprano*, an octave above the trombone itself: see SLIDE TRUMPET, 1*a*; also occasionally mentioned in the 18th century in Germany (*Diskantposaune*; an example is 58 cm. (23″) in length).

(*b*) *Alto*, in E♭ (sometimes F): still available in Germany and the USA, about 30 cm. (1 foot) shorter than the ordinary trombone on which its parts are normally played—though some first trombonists have used the alto for better tonal balance with the rest in classical works in which the part lies continuously very high. Berg scores for it in *Three Orchestral Pieces*, and Britten in *The Burning Fiery Furnace.*

(*c*) *Tenor* (B♭, in France sometimes in C). The older French and British models, often silver-plated, have an average bore of 11 mm. and bell 15 cm. (6″) wide. The light, vocal sound (quickly nasal when blown hard), now almost forgotten, can be heard in old recordings of works of Elgar, whose own trombone (by Boosey) is displayed beside Holst's (by Hawkes) in the Royal College of Music *collection, London.

(*d*) *Bass.* See 4 above for the British G trombone. In France all three parts were regularly played on the narrow-bore tenor (Courtois, Paris, a favourite maker) before the arrival of American models. In Germany, an F bass trombone, with handle on the slide and a plain coil in the bell to reduce length, was made for bands up to the First World War.

(*e*) *Contrabass*, in B♭ or C. Many types have been made of this relatively rare size. Most have a 'double slide', requiring no greater slide shifts than the ordinary trombone. This has four legs (instead of two) to form a double inner slide and again for the outer; the second and third legs of the inner slide being connected through a stationary bow at the

Pl. *1*. Bass trombone by Conn, Elkhart, Indiana.

top (an invention also used on some English and German bass trombones of the early 19th century).

6. *Early trombone, or sackbut.* First seen in pictures from *c.*1460, the trombone was evolved probably in Italy or Flanders, whether from an earlier instrument with more elementary slide is disputed (see SLIDE TRUMPET, 3*b*). It rose to become through the 16th century and up to the mid-17th by far the most important wind instrument for the lower parts in music of all kinds. Some fifty dated examples are preserved from pre-1650 (the earliest of unquestioned date by Schnitzer, 1579, Verona *collection), all but perhaps two by the makers in Nuremberg (see TRUMPET, 4*c*), tenors predominating, basses next, altos rather fewer.

The bores are narrow, for a tenor *c.*10 mm. (about that of a contemporary trumpet) and continuing so until past the bend in the bell, which is at first, somewhat funnel-like, later more flared but still a bare 10 cm. (4″) wide at the rim (where the brass 'garland' is engraved with the maker's name and date). The joints were mostly left unsoldered, taken apart for transport, cleaning, and storage. The stays are of flat brass with hinged, leather-lined clasps, or else composed of two tubular sections that fit together telescopically, to ease the slide (and were generally retained thenceforth until slide stocking came in around 1850). In 16th-century pictures the right hand often grasps, thumb upwards, the slide itself (Pl. 2), not the stay. Yet technique could be very agile: *Mersenne tells us that *divisions were played as fast as on *cornett or bass viol. Original mouthpieces have hemispherical cups like those for the trumpet. The unforced sound of the instruments when played in parts, less resonant than that of trombones today, has the quality of blending easily and naturally with the voices, cornett, or other instruments when combined with them in the polyphony of the time.

In their pitches, the tenor, on German and Italian evidence from the 17th century, gave A in the 1st position—but a very high A, even above the modern B♭ (the present B♭ pitch seems to have been decided upon first in 18th-century Vienna). The slide was reckoned to give four diatonic positions, A, G, F, and E. This put the lower B♭ almost off the slide, but tenor parts go down only to *c*; should a tenor trombone be required for playing bass parts, a crook was inserted between slide and bell. The old Nuremberg bass trombones (*Quartposaune*, in E, or *Quint-*, in D: see QUINT, QUART) often have an extra slide in the bell, extendible backwards by a long rod (not while actually playing): this would make possible the low G′, met in works by Schütz.

Well known today are pieces written for the three trombones with cornetts for the treble parts (see below, 7*a*). This combination, already mentioned by 1500 for supporting church choirs, survived locally in Germany and Italy through the 18th century (see CORNETT, 4), a period from which

Pl. 2. German trombone (sackbut) player, engraving (1538) by H. Aldegrever; note the small bell, and the trombonist's old-style grasp of the slide (the other two instruments are probably slide trumpets, *Zugtrompeten*).

comparatively little is heard of trombones, for the main wind-instrument fashions then were French, and the trombone, with the cornett, had no place among them after Lully abolished them both from the royal music in the 1660s. Exceptions for the trombone are in Austria, in music for the Imperial Chapel in Vienna, by Fux, Caldara, and others, with obbligato sections for trombone, often the alto; and in opera, as Mozart's, where they appear in solemn scenes continuing a tradition going back to Monteverdi's *Orfeo* (while in the Tuba Mirum of the *Requiem*, Mozart imaginatively interprets *Posaune* of the German Bible, (see *Posaune*)). In England, Handel's majestic parts in *Saul* may have been performed by Germans from the king's band. In France, however, the trombone was rediscovered in the revolutionary period, e.g. by Gossec, as a bass strengthener for the orchestra in music for public ceremonies, and became so adopted everywhere in the fast-growing military bands. From this point the modern era of the trombone could be said to have begun.

It produced after 1800 some quaint models (see BUCCIN) and later with the bell pointing back over the shoulder (made in London by F. Pace, and see MILITARY BAND, Pl. 2). But the significant development, in France, and by the 1810s Austria, lay in the trend towards playing all three parts on one instrument, in B♭, and in Austria preferably with a wide-bore instrument for the bass part (and to the great annoyance of critics deprived of the notes below E in the *Freischütz Overture* until the thumb-valve came in). Alto and bass trombones continued to be made (above, 5); but Brahms's orchestral works would have been first performed with basically the same three instruments that are used today.

7. *Repertory:* (a) *Early part-music naming trombones.* Giovanni Gabrieli (1557–1612), *Sonata pian'e forte*, for two four-part groups, all parts for trombones (evidently from alto downwards) excepting the two top parts, marked for *cornetto* and *violino* (from the compass, viola); *Canzon*, 15-part, in three five-part choirs with the top parts similarly. Other works of the period are now published in editions for playing on trombones or brass group. Heinrich Schütz, trombones in many works for the church, especially the poignant *sinfonia* for four trombones alone to the motet 'Fili mi, Absalon' (1629). Secular music for three trombones with one or two cornetts: John Adson, *Courtly Masquing Ayres* (1621); and especially Matthew Locke, *Music for His Majesty's Sagbutts and Cornets* (1661), also found along with pieces by Charles Coleman and Nicholas Lanier in a collection entitled '5 part things for the Cornetts' (c.1670). German (music for the Leipzig town musicians): J. Pezel, *Fünff-stimmige blasender Musik* (1685); and J. G. Reiche (the trumpeter who for some years played for Bach), *Neue Quatricinia* (1696).

(b) *Later works.* Among the older concertos are those by Albrechtsberger (for alto), Wagenseil, Reicha, and the player F. A. Belcke (1832). David's Concertino, Op. 4, has long been a favourite, along with Rimsky-Korsakov's Concerto (originally for trombone with military band). In the later repertory are works by several composers known for solo works for practically every orchestral instrument: Saint-Saëns (Cavatina), Hindemith (Sonata), Tcherepnin (Andante), Gordon Jacob (Concerto), Milhaud (*Concerto d'hiver*), Frank Martin (Ballade); also Bernstein, 'Elegy for Mippy II', and Bloch, *Symphony for Trombone and Orchestra*.

The modern school is of special interest and promise, the trombone being capable of the most varied novel sound-effects, as in Berio's *Sequenza V*, and above all in works from 1962 by Vinko Globokar, himself a remarkable trombonist, combining the instrument with the voice (spoken into it) and electronics, e.g. *Discours II* (with tape).

Bate 1966; Gregory 1973; Wick 1971.

Trompa, trompe, trump. Trompa (Sp.), 'horn' (French horn). Trompe (Old Fr., also medieval Eng.), 'trumpet' (or sometimes in Eng., 'trump'); or (later Fr.) 'horn', as *trompe de chasse*, *hunting horn, 3. All three forms of the word have also meant the *Jew's-harp (on which tunes are played in natural harmonics as on the old trumpets).

Trumpet (Fr.: *trompette*; Ger.: *Trompete*; It.: *tromba*; Ru.: *truba*; Sp.: *trombeta*). Originally the instrument of command in battle, herald of authority, proclaimer of the destiny of man ('The Trumpet Shall Sound'); the great trumpet music of the Baroque harks back constantly to these themes, uttered within the restricted scope of the old 'natural' instrument before *valves existed. With these, first coming into use on trumpets in the 1820s and rendering the instrument fully chromatic, capable of the same melody as other instruments, the history of the trumpet took a new turn, leading by degrees (and much helped in the 20th century by jazz) to the popular instrument we know so well today. For general points distinguishing a trumpet from the other brass, see BRASS INSTRUMENTS, 2. For special historical forms, see KEYED TRUMPET; SLIDE TRUMPET; also BASS TRUMPET. For a short account of trumpets or trumpet-like instruments of non-Western cultures, not all of metal, see 7, below.

1. *B♭ trumpet.* The most usual modern trumpet in orchestras, bands, and in jazz, seen in every music store (Fig. 1b) and that on which a student normally begins. Its music is written a tone above the actual sound. See VALVE for a summary of the fingering. First made, in Germany in the late 1820s (below, 3b), the B♭ trumpet has borne the brunt of the work for over 100 years. The familiar format, with the mouthpipe leading directly to the tuning slide in the front bow, whence the tube returns to enter the 3rd valve, originated in Paris, in Besson's models of the 1880s. Since then the mouthpipe has normally been given a gentle taper (see BRASS INSTRUMENTS, Fig. 2) and the design has been brought to perfection by Besson (later also in London) and notably in the USA by Vincent Bach and others. For the valves to give true intonation on notes like the written low D and C♯, the 3rd valve slide can be extended by the attached ring, and in many models also that of the 1st valve by a hook or lever ('trigger') for the thumb. Popular bore-widths (of the cylindrical parts) are 'medium', 11 mm. or just over, up to 'large', near 12 mm. for heavy orchestral duty. The most usual written compass is up to the C or D above the staff; but higher notes are frequently played (and in jazz, topping Louis Armstrong's once famous high F by a tone or more).

In orchestras, many players follow a traditional French preference for the C trumpet, higher in pitch by a whole tone and affording an extra brilliance in the high register. It is usually built with a bell of the same length as in a B♭ trumpet, the main loop carrying the valves being therefore distinctly shorter.

2. *Smaller trumpets, above C.* First introduced in 1885, bicentenary of Bach's birth, for players of the valved trumpet to cope with the high-lying solo and obbligato parts that appear in so many of his greatest works. With the higher-pitched *harmonic series brought by the shorter tube-length, the

harmonics required by the music are mostly more widely separated and therefore more easy for the lips to distinguish securely. There are various sizes, most of them known from that year or soon afterwards.

(a) *From D to G.* D trumpet, in the principal key of the baroque trumpet but with half the tube-length of this. It is built in normal trumpet format, now often as a D/E♭ trumpet, i.e. in E♭ with alternative tuning slide and valve slides for lowering into D. Up to the 1930s a straight-built model, 1 m. (3′) long, was a great favourite in oratorio performances, known to audiences as 'Bach Trumpet'. Among recent composers, Stravinsky, and Britten (in *Peter Grimes*), have scored for the D trumpet. The F trumpet was originally made (again first in straight form) for Bach's Second Brandenburg Concerto, in which the trumpet rises to the (sounding) *g‴*. It has since been made, in normal format, often with alternative slides, as an F/E trumpet. Also available from some makers is a G trumpet, and this may be convertible to F. All have, however, been largely superseded by the following.

(b) *Piccolo trumpet*, an octave above the ordinary B♭ trumpet. This remarkable little instrument, already offered by Mahillon (Brussels) from 1908, has been in wide use only from the 1950s, and not only in baroque works but also in concertos such as Haydn's (see KEYED TRUMPET) and in music of many other kinds. With tubing no longer than for an English *post horn, it is mostly built in a normal trumpet format (Pl. 1) though there are longer models without the bends. It may have alternative slides for A. Bores are up to 'medium' as above (1); bell width *c.*9.5 cm. (3¾″, as against *c.*12.7 cm. or 5″ for a B♭ trumpet). For orchestral purposes it requires the 4th valve (Pl. 1) for notes below

(sounding) *e′* down to the often demanded fundamental *a*.

Of course, the available choice of all these trumpets, ordinary and small, for a symphonic work or whole programme means reading the music with different fingerings and transpositions: but being anyhow constantly confronted in the standard repertory with parts for 'trumpet in D', 'in E', etc. (see TRANSPOSING INSTRUMENTS, Table 2), such transpositions at sight are part of the orchestral trumpeter's way of life.

3. *Other and older valved trumpets: (a) In F and other pitches below the B♭ trumpet.* As valves came into use on trumpets, first in Germany, they were naturally applied to instruments built in the chief tonalities of the existing natural trumpet as E♭ and F, and retaining the set of crooks for lower keys, so that the player could, in music in these keys, continue to sound the tonic and other main notes with full open-note quality (a less cogent consideration as valves improved). For various valve systems (up to the mid-century often with two valves only) see VALVE, 2.

The instruments are mostly built in the traditional 'long' format (otherwise in various 'short' models with an extra loop) and the mouthpipe leads directly to the 1st valve. Though by 1900 almost superseded by the B♭ trumpet, most military band music continued to include E♭ trumpet parts, reduced however to mainly non-essential background harmony and often omitted. Well known among British collectors is the F trumpet of Mahillon (Brussels) which many orchestral players adopted from the 1890s in a move to thwart the prevalent custom of playing trumpet parts on the cornet (see also SLIDE TRUMPET, 2a).

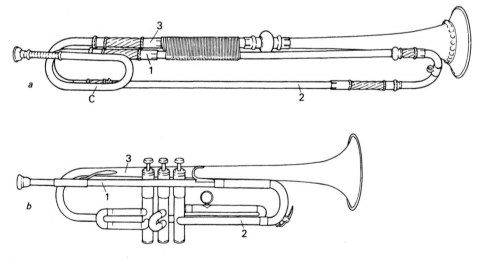

Fig. 1.

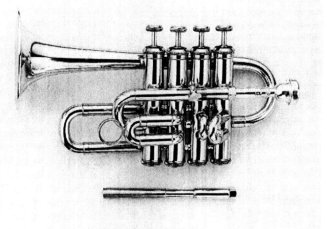

Pl. 1. Piccolo trumpet (Vincent Bach) with four valves and (*below*) shank to lower the instrument from B♭ to A.

(*b*) *B♭ trumpet.* This followed the preceding very quickly in Germany from the late 1820s as an adjunct to the E♭ trumpet in cavalry band music. By the time of Wagner's later operas it is already mentioned as the most used orchestral trumpet, and so in France also, even though composers everywhere continued to *write* for trumpets mainly in the older, deeper keys (see CROOK). Again the mouthpipe leads straight to the 1st valve, and so well into the 20th century where not superseded by the modern format (above, 1). In the German B♭ trumpet it does so still; having rotary valves, the instrument is held flat (all three branches of the tube parallel with the ground).

(*c*) *Straight valved trumpets.* For the straight high D trumpet, see above, 2*a*. Likewise following the heraldic image of Antiquity and the Middle Ages are those familiarized in Britain by the trumpets of the Royal Military School of Music—three-valved and accompanied by valved trombones built also straight, to match. Fanfares composed for them are by, among others, Bliss and Walton. A straight two-valved trumpet in A was among the first of those built for Bach performances. 'Aïda trumpets', to be played on the stage in Act II of Verdi's opera, are correctly pitched half of them in A♭ and the others in B♮, each requiring only one valve for the famous tune.

4. *Natural trumpets:* (*a*) *Format.* Fig. 1*a* is after a trumpet of the classical period (German, late 18th century); the long main loop gives the tube-length for 6′ F, here shown with a crook inserted for 7′ D. The bows (each with an eye for tying on a banner) are normally not soldered but are kept airtight with beeswax, under the ornamented ferrules ('garnishes'). The bell branch, with a small

pommel or 'ball', is in old German practice firmly held to the mouthpipe branch by tasselled cordage over a wooden spacer block (in England they lie at a slight angle, usually with the mouthpipe let into the side of the ball). Original mouthpieces have a hemispherical cup meeting both rim and throat sharply. With the small bore (average for the 18th century 10.6 mm.) and the long tubing, the sound is at once recognized: of a celestial purity on the upper notes, while gaining a menacing, almost hissing quality on the lower—as heard today from State Trumpets and those of the Household Cavalry. These are pitched in E♭. Ordinary duty trumpets, or as often called, 'cavalry trumpets', are also in this key but are solidly built of thicker brass in two loops, making only some 40 cm. (16″) in length overall and giving a sound of perhaps rather less brilliance.

(*b*) *Notes of the natural trumpet.* Ex. 1 (harmonics numbered) shows these up to the written high A. A difference from modern valved trumpets is that Middle C represents the 4th harmonic, not the 2nd harmonic as with the valved. Military calls use up to the 8th harmonic (for publication of British calls see BUGLE, 1); classical orchestral parts to the 12th or 13th, well into the register where the harmonics have begun to make a scale which baroque music takes up to the 16th (high *c'''*), while Bach was by no means alone in writing up to the 18th (*d'''*, sounding *e'''* on his trumpets in D).

Ex. 1.

2 3   4 5 6 (7) 8   9 10 11 12 13 etc.

A difficulty with this scale is that it requires the 11th harmonic for F (f''), for which it is by nature a quarter-tone too sharp (or for F♯ a quarter too flat); likewise the 13th is by nearly the same amount too flat for A (see HARMONIC SERIES). Where these are quick passing notes such departures are hardly noticeable; but it is not at all certain on contemporary evidence how far players as a whole managed to correct them with the lip on held notes: there are players today who show it to be fully possible with the original instruments and mouthpieces; also to lower a harmonic by a semitone to produce notes such as b' (middle line), occasionally met, e.g. in Bach's works. (See CLARINO, 2, for the harmonic vents uncovered by the finger, often provided in replicas used by today's players.)

(c) *Makers.* Some hundred of the trumpets made by the celebrated makers of Nuremberg are preserved (the earliest of 1581, by Schnitzer, in the Vienna *collection), most by members of the Hainlein, Ehe, and Haas families (Pl. 2), working through the 17th century up to the mid-18th; their instruments were in demand in Italy as well and, it would seem, France. By the classical period, trumpets were made for orchestral use in F (as in Vienna by Kerner) with crooks for keys down to low B♭, as required in the off-stage calls in Beethoven's *Leonora Overture* No. 3. Fine English trumpets are by William Bull (d. *c.*1707), many of silver, followed by such as Rodenbostel, and late in the century, William Shaw, and through the next, Henry Keat.

(d) *Earlier history:* (i) *Medieval.* The trumpets, all straight and from 1 to 2 m. (3–6') long, bear at least one pommel (at the base of the bell) and were sounded in pairs in signals of the kind of which the first two notes of the 'Last Post' (first known as a trumpet call) are a distant memory. In later times straight trumpets continued sometimes to be made for special purposes (as the silver trumpets of the Doge in Venice, carried in processions up to the 17th century). Not all of those seen in collections can be accepted as genuinely of an early date. A straight trumpet recently discovered beneath Billingsgate, London (1984), now in the Museum of London, is however judged to be of the late 14th century. Probably the most complete relic of its kind and date, it is in four sections, cylindrical, save for the bell expansion, and adding up to *c.*160 cm. (63″) in all, with bore *c.*12.5 mm. and one pommel. The bell flare (to *c.*8 cm. or 3″ at the rim) is neatly fashioned in the method still traditional up to not long ago: one edge of the flat sheet is cut with teeth which are then bent alternately up and down in order to receive, after bending to form the tube, the other (feathered) edge of the sheet for the two to be soldered together. The mouthpiece is simply a widening of the tube (no cup, as see also NAFIR) terminated with a narrow ring serving as a rim.

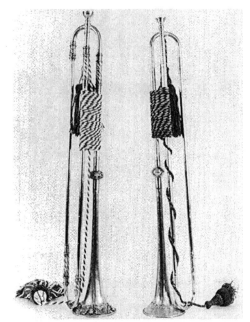

Pl. 2. Pair of baroque trumpets by J. W. Haas, Nuremberg, *c.* 1700.

(ii) *Renaissance.* Shortly before 1400 the makers were forming U-bends, at first with one bow turned upwards to carry the bell, and the other downwards for the mouthpipe, lowermost, giving the whole an elongated 'S' appearance. Very soon it became more usual to bring the mouthpipe up beside the bell as since, a more stable construction and better for a mounted trumpeter to grasp in one hand. Dufay quotes from actual military calls in his Gloria 'ad modum tubae' (first half, 15th century (Baines 1976: 85)), such calls rising to the 6th harmonic with flourishes up to the 8th. Ex. 2 is the opening of a trumpet toccata ('tucket') from Bendinelli (1614), who goes on to describe how a corps of trumpeters would improvise (or learn) the peculiar kind of polyphony illustrated by the Toccata which opens Monteverdi's *Orfeo* (1607): one trumpet, perhaps the leader, plays in the style of a toccata, the next above at the same time in that of a sonata ('sennet', or quinta). Below these, two trumpets drone on the two lowest harmonics, and the whole is crowned by a free *clarino* in the diatonic region above. The *clarino* then, by the mid-17th century, came to be developed on its own, musically, in concertos with strings and organ, leading to baroque trumpet music as now generally known, while a lower part may be named

Ex. 2. Bendinelli, Toccata.

principale, occupying the primary register of the trumpet as heard in day-to-day court ceremonial and again on the battlefield.

5. *Coiled and curved trumpets:* (*a*) *Coiled*. Rare examples exist of a baroque trumpet, in the usual key of D, but formed in a spiral *c*.20 cm. (8″) across. What they were made for is very uncertain (see CLARINO, 2; TROMBA DA CACCIA). Often seen in collections is a trumpet, usually German, with the tube coiled in a helix inside a brass case resembling a quart pot, and sometimes called a 'box trumpet' (from Ger.: *Büchse*).

(*b*) *Curved* (Fr.: *trompette demilune*). In 1774 in Carlsruhe a player, Woeggel, introduced a trumpet curved downwards in an arc to bring the bell into a good position for hand-stopping (see HORN, 6). The main object was to produce a complete scale in the lower register (from *c″* downwards) by part-closing the bell. Such instruments, with the crooks inserted midway along, were then made up to the 1840s for military bands, in France especially, and are not uncommon in collections. In Germany, hand-stopping came to be done mostly on trumpets of normal 'short' format (two loops), and especially in cavalry bands for accidentals. There are hints that such stopping may have been used at times in the orchestra also, for example in Mendelssohn's *Ruy Blas* Overture for the important *b* in a part otherwise for natural notes only.

6. *Repertory*. The solo repertory begins with the sonatas with *basso continuo* in Fantini's *Modo per imparare . . . di tromba* of 1638. It continues with sonatas with solo trumpet written for Bologna Cathedral by Cazzati, Corelli (one sonata), Torelli (very many, and a *Concerto con tromba*), and D. Gabrielli (a composer also remembered in connection with the *cello). Then, among the better-known composers, we have Purcell (sonata), Vivaldi (concerto for two trumpets), Telemann (six concertos), Reutter the younger (two concertos), Molter (five), Mudge (one), Leopold Mozart (one, 1762), Hertel (four), and Michael Haydn (a concerto and part of a serenade). Next come the concertos for keyed trumpet by Joseph Haydn and Hummel, but for a long time very little of note for the valved trumpet. Among some more recent works are Hindemith's Sonata; Poulenc's Sonata with horn and trombone; and several works for trumpet, piano, and strings, from Saint-Saëns (Septet, Op. 65) to Jolivet (Introduction) and Shostakovich (Concerto, Op. 35).

7. *Ancient and non-Western metal trumpets:* (*a*) *Egypt*. The two trumpets from the tomb of King Tutankhamun, *c*.1350 BC, are the earliest known: one silver, 58 cm. (23″, about the later Roman cubit), the other brass and gold, *c*.50 cm. (19½″), each with slightly expanding tube, a short conical bell, and no mouthpiece save for an external ring round the blowing end (it seems clear from wall paintings that nothing is missing). With each is

a wooden protective core which the Egyptian trumpeter, often depicted at the head of troops, carried with him tucked under the arm. The Israelites adopted such trumpets (see BIBLICAL INSTRUMENTS, 1*a*), and may have sounded calls on two pitches, not unlike those of a *shofar (Wulstan 1973).

(*b*) *Roman tuba*. From about 90–120 cm. long (3′ to 4′), and tapering gently outwards to a narrow bell, the tuba was to the Roman people the first in prestige among their cup-mouthpiece instruments of hammered bronze (see BUCCINA AND CORNU; LITUUS AND CARNYX) in civilian life as well as military: yet no really representative example has been discovered, nor do we know what sounds (apart from 'taratantara' in the poet Ennius) were produced on it, either in Rome, or in Byzantium, where armies employed the tuba also.

(*ç*) *Islamic and other Asian trumpets*. The Roman tuba may have in turn led in some way to the medieval trumpets of the 11th century onwards, Islamic as well as European. For present examples of the former, see KARNA (Central Asia, India); NAFIR (North Africa, with *kakaki*, Sudan); many more in India (*turi* is but one of many names, the instrument here made also in various other shapes, some folded like the European trumpet). Further east (and sometimes in India) are continuously conical trumpets, often telescopic for compact storage after use: *dung* (Tibetan lama, see CHINA AND KOREA, 3), *laba and others (China). In the main, the Asian long trumpets are sounded on the lower two or three harmonics only, but in India may be heard fast playing up to the 12th—not unlike that from long trumpets which have been preserved by religious brotherhoods in southern Spain.

8. *Trumpets of wood, cane, etc.* (also see ALPHORN): (*a*) *Plain hollow branch*. *Didjeridu (Australia); *vaccine (West Indies).

(*b*) *Bark or leaves*. These, rolled into a long cone with a cane tube inserted for blowing into, are ritual trumpets (Amazon region) used in pairs sounding deep, gruff notes. In these, and the *vaccine*, the instrument is sounded without *embouchure in a brass-player's sense but simply by strong puffs to disturb the air in the tube in a way which by itself sets the lips fluttering in a loose vibration: *Sachs, writing in German, distinguished this primitive method by a term 'Längstuba', which though difficult to translate, expresses the matter fairly well.

(*c*) *Upright trumpets*. Hollowed from a tree trunk, these include: *ludi* (Africa, Lower Congo, 90 cm. (3′) tall, blowing hole in the side); *mabu* (Melanesia, Solomon Islands, about the same size, blowing hole in the top, again for one deep note, but different-sized instruments may be played together).

(*d*) *Cane, bamboo, wood, with bell of cowhorn, gourdneck, pottery, etc.* End-blown, this end often cut obliquely, presenting an elliptical aperture, the trumpet held to one side: *trutruca* (Chile), others in Assam and West Africa. Side-blown (round or square hole next to closed end): numerous in Africa; *clarìn* (Andes, also *erke*, North Argentina; the *bajones*, Bolivia, etc., of several long tubes tied in a row like panpipes, end-blown and sounded in groups at church feasts, may now have mostly disappeared).

(*e*) *Gourd*. Especially Central and East Africa, gourds are grown to make 'tubes' up to 2 m. (6') long, side-blown, often played in ensembles, each trumpet contributing its own note as with ivory and gourd horns also, see HORN, 8a.

Altenburg 1795; Bate 1966; Smithers 1973; Tarr 1988.

Trumpet marine, Trumscheit. See TROMBA MARINA.

Trutruca. Long bamboo trumpet, 1.5 to 4 m. (5' upwards), of the Araucano Indians in Chile and nearby. The cane is cut in half lengthwise to smooth the interior, then rejoined and sealed with horse intestine. A cowhorn bell is tied to one end, and a smaller cane in the other end, cut across obliquely, forms the mouthpiece. A cult instrument, protective against drought or epidemics, it is sounded in ritual dances, in fast, vigorous figures ending with a swoop up to the highest harmonic possible. It is reported back to the 17th century along with other remarkable instruments such as the crossed musical bows.

Tsabouna. See BAGPIPE, 6.

Tsuzumi. Japanese small hourglass drum (see DRUM, 4c) played with the fingers. Each of the two heads well overlaps the shell, the rim of the skin being lapped and stitched to an iron ring, from 20 cm. (8") wide. The tension rope (traditionally silk) is led to and fro from one ring to the other, passing through six holes in each skin. Midway along the drum this rope is drawn inwards by another which encircles them (giving a visual impression of a waist). The lacquered shell is hollowed and carved in wood. Between its two cup-shaped ends is a straight, slightly spindle-shaped middle section about 9 cm. (3½") in diameter, the whole shell forming a single hollow, *c*.25 cm. (10") long in the case of the *ko-tsuzumi*, the most familiar type and one of the two (below) required in *nō* plays along with the stick-beaten *taiko*.

1. *Ko-tsuzumi*, the 'shoulder drum', held on the right shoulder (see JAPAN, Pl. 2, front row, second from right), with painted decoration on the heads. These are here built up on the back with clay to fit over the shell. Pieces of wetted paper are stuck on the rear head before playing to adjust the tone. The right fingers play on the front head using many different strokes, all named, while the left hand grasps the drum by the ropes; e.g. for the

pon stroke this hand squeezes the ropes at the same instant, for a special wavering sound.

2. *O-tsuzumi*. A little longer (length 29 cm. or 11½"), rested across the left thigh (same plate, second from left). It has thicker skins (with neither clay nor papers applied, but the heads are warmed before performance), and is more tightly tensioned and struck harder, for some strokes moving the whole arm.

3. *San-no-tsuzumi*. Larger again, and leader of the Korean genre of the court music (instead of the *kakko*).

See JAPAN.

Tuba (in bands usually termed 'bass'). The largest of the valved brass instruments. In the orchestra the player sits with the three trombones, making a fourth member of the team and extending its compass down to the bottom D of the piano. (For *tuba* in the original Latin sense of a trumpet see *trumpet*, 7b.)

1. *Sizes*. Bands use two sizes of tuba (see BRASS BAND), the smaller in E♭, comprising some 400 cm. (13') of tubing excluding the valves; the larger in BB♭ ('double B flat') with 550 cm. (18') of tubing. Orchestras in Britain mostly use the E♭ instrument. This has been made from the 1950s (for bands also) with a bell of BB♭ proportions, 38 cm. (*c*.15") wide for a fuller sound, and is commonly described as a 'double E flat' tuba. American orchestras use the larger types, usually built in low C ('double C') and German often now also rather than in E♭ (or in older tradition F, the original pitch of the tuba). For the quite different French orchestral tuba, see below, 2d. The tuba part, in orchestra and in military or concert bands, is written in the bass clef at sounding pitch; but in brass bands in treble clef and transposed for the fingering to match that of the cornet.

As well as the normal build—or often in the USA with the bell turned forwards (see below, 3)—basses in both E♭ and BB♭ have long been made also in circular form, placed over the head (see HELICON), less seen today than formerly except as the *sousaphone*, with huge bell pointing forwards above the player's head.

2. *Valves: (a) General arrangement*. The British and French piston valves are mounted parallel with the main tubing (Pl. 1), the right hand passing under the upper large U-bend and the bell pointing to the right. In America the piston valves are most usually set at an angle, the right hand reaching over the instrument and the bell therefore pointing to the left—as also in German tubas, on which rotary valves are used (see VALVE, 2).

For bands, basses are obtainable with three valves. The E♭ bass, especially, is however also made with four, making deeper notes available and also certain other notes more securely in tune. Even so,

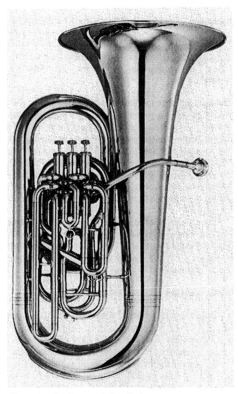

Pl. 1. E♭ tuba (Boosey & Hawkes).

increment loops join the circuit, automatically supplying the extra length needed now that the instrument is lowered a perfect fourth by the fourth valve. But the deepest of the valved notes still have to be watched against sharpness. With a three-valved instrument, also made, increments to the first and second valves come into play when the third valve is lowered to make the valve combinations 2 and 3, and 1 and 3, automatically in tune. The system is also frequently provided on the *euphonium, this also with three valves or four.

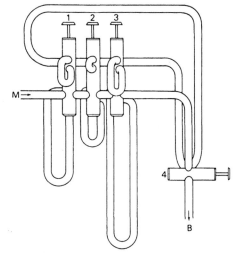

Fig. 1. Schematic illustration of Blaikley's compensating fourth valve (employed in most British tubas): M, lead from mouthpipe; B, exit to bell.

a consequence of defects inherent in all normal valve systems is a player's concern against sharpness on many of the notes made with two or more valves together, for example on the deeper notes when a strong attack is demanded; also in very exposed passages as for example in the *Ring*, where Wagner gives the tuba ('contrabass tuba') the boldest, deepest, and most memorable solo passages in its regular repertory (notably at the beginning of *Siegfried* where it represents the dragon).

(b) *Compensating pistons.* In Britain the problem is largely overcome through 'compensating valves' (Blaikley's compensating piston of 1874), long fitted by Boosey & Hawkes to their high-quality basses, whether with three valves or with four. Fig. 1 illustrates schematically how this works with four valves (the principle being very similar to that of a 'compensating' double horn, see HORN, 2). The valve-loop of the fourth valve (shown lying horizontally on the right) is led through the tops of the other three valves, which are made tall enough to contain it. Each of these three valves carries a small 'increment' loop situated above the main loop. While the fourth valve is not in use these small loops are out of the circuit, nothing passing through them. If the fourth valve is lowered and one or more of the other valves are lowered too, their

(c) *Five- and six-valved tubas.* Neither the Continent nor America have adopted the above system with its manufacturing complications and extra bends and angles in the tubing. Instead, for orchestral uses especially, a fifth valve may be included, lowering by amounts that vary. It may, for example, lower the open pitch by approximately a three-quarter tone or just over. This provides on the CC tuba a perfect low F with valves 4, 2, and 5, these adding to the open tube respectively $\frac{1}{3}$, $\frac{1}{15}$ (by traditional fractions), and, say, $\frac{1}{10}$ (fifth valve), together adding up to $\frac{1}{2}$ as required by the 3:2 ratio for a perfect fifth. A sixth valve may also be provided to offer useful alternative fingerings (both five- and six-valve tubas now made in the USA usually with rotary valves). No system is, however, perfect, and in very exposed deep passages, the player may rapidly adjust some valve slide even while actually blowing.

(d) *French tuba.* In France the orchestral tuba has up to recently always been pitched in C, a tone above the euphonium. It reaches the lowest notes with the aid of six pistons (three for each hand), while of course it can easily reach notes well above the normal range of other tubas, the most quoted example being 'Bydlo' in Ravel's orchestration (1929) of Mussorgsky's *Pictures from an Exhibition*, rising to $g\sharp'$. Players elsewhere may prefer to change to a smaller instrument than their normal to perform the part (see also TENOR TUBA).

3. *Early tubas*. The first valved basses were made in Germany and Austria in the late 1830s, mostly with the name 'bombardon'. In general they follow the shape of the then 10-year-old *ophicleide, and are built in F in order to reach the low notes of that instrument with the aid of three valves (often of the double-piston or 'Vienna' type; see VALVE, 2). With their fairly narrow dimensions the sound is warm and pleasant but without the power and resonance of the later tubas.

The instrument from which the present term 'tuba' derives is the *Bass-tuba* introduced by the famous bandmaster Wilhelm Wieprecht in Berlin, 1835, and made there by Moritz. Again in F, it was given the almost conical bell, virtually without a flare, typical of Prussian brass instruments of the time. It had five valves of the 'Berlin' piston type, divided between the two hands: the first two, for the left hand, are the whole-tone and semitone valves for the tuba as it stands in F; the next two (right hand) are longer whole-tone and semitone valves tuned for the low C which the instrument becomes when lowered a perfect fourth by the fifth valve (also right hand). From the point of view of intonation of low notes this system has certain gains over any that has been devised since; but later instruments were made to conform with general practice (three or four normal valves only) and so remained in use in the German army up to the First World War.

While British basses derive chiefly from the French *saxhorn, the typical German models, with wide bell and rotary valves, stem most from those, from the same period, by such as Červený in Bohemia (then in Austria). This maker in the 1880s introduced the *Kaiserbass* ('Emperor bass') of widest possible dimensions (in Bavaria familiar as that cherished idol the 'Bierbass').

Both French and German basses were exported to the USA from the 1840s (for bell-over-the-shoulder instruments, see SAXHORN, 2). Much later in America, in the early days of the phonograph, came the 'Recording Bass', in normal tuba format but the bell pointing forwards to face the recording horn: it can be very audible in some old orchestral recordings, boosting the double bass part. The model has since been regularly manufactured as an alternative form of tuba for concert hall and band (see also BARITONE, 2).

4. *Solo repertory*. Well known is Vaughan Williams's Tuba Concerto written for the F tuba at a time (1955) when some leading players in London, including Philip Catelinet (by whom the work was first performed), were still using this instrument,

following the older British tradition. With piano, there is a Sonata by Hindemith and a Suite by Gordon Jacob, and among concertos with band accompaniment, those by Edward Gregson (b. 1945), Derek Bourgeois, and others.

Bevan 1978.

Tubaphone. Instrument of struck metal tubes of no great size, laid out like the bars of a *glockenspiel, resting on wooden supports lined with felt, or suspended on cords knotted between the tubes. No resonators are needed. It is made chiefly for children, but there have also been concert models, arranged in the manner of a four-row xylophone (see XYLOPHONE, 4) and sometimes heard as a solo instrument in band concerts. Khatchaturian has it in *Gayaneh*.

As compared with a glockenspiel, for the same note, a tube is a little longer than a solid rod, since the thickness factor in the frequency equation becomes $\sqrt{(D^2 + d^2)}$ where D and d are the outer and inner diameters of the tube.

Tube xylophone. See CHALUNG.

Tubular bells (or orchestral chimes; Fr.: *cloches tubulaires*; Ger.: *Röhrenglocken*; It.: *campanelli, campanelli tubolari*). 1. *Description*. Tall, plated brass tubes, closed at the upper ends, hung by cords from a tall frame and struck against the top with a rawhide or plastic mallet. There are 18 tubes in a normal chromatic set, graded in length but of the same diameter (usually 2.5–3.8 cm.; or $1''$–$1\frac{1}{2}''$). The sharps are hung behind the naturals, with their upper ends at a higher level so that they can be reached by the mallet. The normal range is written c'–f'', sounding these notes in effect (see below, 2). A horizontal felted damper is worked by a cord or, more usually, a pedal. Some works best require special extra-large tubes unless some other bell-substitute is to be used (see BELL PLATES; CHIME, 2, 3). Among such works are Berlioz's *Symphonie fantastique* (last movement) and Puccini's *Tosca* (the opening of Act 3, which the composer took from the actual bells as heard all over Rome on a Sunday morning, and are still heard today).

An early mention of tubular bells is in Paris, c.1867; then in England, in a patent by John Harrington of Coventry, first in bronze. Sullivan is said to have tried them out in *The Golden Legend* (1886). As substitutes for church bells, they became for a long time familiar in small orchestras and bands in diatonic sets, usually in the key of E♭. They have also been incorporated into organs and, from the 1920s, electrically amplified in carillons (see CHIME, 2). In modern writing for percussion, however, the tubular bells have gained an important place in their own right (not as church bells), even playing chords, tremolos, and glissandos.

2. *Pitch of tubular bells*. Whereas a short metal tube gives out mainly its fundamental pitch (see TUBAPHONE), the sound of a much longer tube is a

mingling of higher *partials, making the sound at once closer to that of a large bell. The dominating partial is from the 4th mode of vibration, which from the smallest tube of the normal compass, c.95 cm. (37″) long, gives f‴ (accompanied by a hum from the 2nd mode far below). Makers and players, however, consider the tube to sound an octave lower, f″, which although not among the partials generated from tube, seems clearly present. This is apparently because the 4th, 5th, and 6th mode frequencies are (in theory) related as 9^2, 11^2, 13^2 (see PARTIALS, 6), which in practice can come close enough to 2 : 3 : 4 for the ear to relate them so and mentally supply '1' at half the frequency of '2', i.e. an octave below the 4th mode frequency, or for this 95 cm. tube f″: an aurally created 'strike tone', analogous to that said to be heard from actual bells.

Tuila (or ṭuila, toila). One-stringed folk instrument of central and eastern India, used for accompanying the voice, playing at dances, etc.: a form of 'stick zither' (see ZITHER, 4c), historically interesting as an early predecessor of the north Indian *vina, and prominent in medieval sculptures of gods and goddesses. A ½″-thick bamboo pole, as long as can be managed in the vertical playing position, has the string (cotton, etc.) tied near the top, where a small open-mouthed gourd is fastened on the back. The gourd rests on the left thumb, which moves it about against the chest to control the resonance (as with *musical bow, 3).

The lower end of the string is fastened to a beak-shaped wooden tailpiece which raises the string above the stick. The chief way of playing is for a middle finger of the right hand to pluck while the index finger touches the string just above for harmonics (the octave and the twelfth) of the four notes which are stopped at the higher end of the string by the left hand. In this way a whole scale can be played softly in harmonics, the fundamentals sounding all the time below.

There are corresponding instruments over South-East Asia, while other types of 'stick zither' in India (as the popular kinnarī vina) have a fretted second string and further gourds on the back (representing a later stage toward the development of the vina itself).

Tulum (Turk.). See BAGPIPE, 6.

Tumba, tumbadora. See CONGA DRUM.

Tuning-fork (Fr.: diapason; Ger.: Stimmgabel; It.: corista). The two-pronged device, of tempered steel, obtainable from music dealers and in a wide selection of pitches from suppliers of scientific instruments. The note and pitch (in vibrations per second; see HERTZ) are stamped on the fork, the most used being the fork for the tuning A(a′) at the standard *pitch (a′ = 440), or for the C above this. Metals used are such that there is virtually no variation of pitch with temperature. One prong is struck, e.g. on the knee, and the stem is usually pressed to a resonant surface. If held to the ear, the plane of the two prongs must not be at 45 degrees to the ear lest the air waves from them interfere and no sound is heard. When pressed to a table the sound, though louder, dies away sooner, through drain of energy to the table-top. Adjustable forks are obtainable. The fork also can be bowed with a violin bow or kept in vibration electro-magnetically.

Tuning-forks from the past are naturally of immense value as evidence of former playing pitches, the great study in English from this aspect being by A. J. Ellis (see PITCH), who lists some 150 forks from the 18th century onwards and from all over Europe. One fork (a′ = 409) was owned by Taskin, the great harpsichord-maker in Paris; another (a′ = 421.6) by Stein of Vienna, whose pianos Mozart played; others are official forks for the standard pitches like the French diapason normal of 1859 (a′ = 435). One of the most celebrated forks in this list (a′ = 422.5, measured by Ellis) was preserved in its box inscribed 'This Pitchfork was the property of the immortal Handel, and left by him at the Foundling Hospital, when the Messiah was Performed in 1751: . . . Invented by M. [John] Shore, Serj. Trumpeter, time of Purcell.' Shore was also lutenist to the Chapel Royal, and an old fork in the list (a′ = 419.9) was thought to have possibly been made by him; he is said to have invented it in 1711. The old forks were made by welding a stem to the centre of a metal bar bent round in a long horseshoe shape; the present form, milled from a steel plate, was developed in the 19th century, notably by Rudolf Koenig in Germany.

Turkish music (Fr.: bande turque; Ger.: Janitscharmusik; It.: musica alla turca). Music involving additional percussion instruments—mainly bass drum, cymbals, triangle—now and again featured through the classical period, e.g. in Mozart (Die Entführung aus dem Serail), and Haydn ('Military' Symphony). Through 'Turkish music' these instruments first gained a place in the European orchestra and *military band.

The first signs are from the 1720s, when the Turks had been pushed back beyond Hungary and Western powers were able to procure genuine sets of instruments of the famous military bands of the Janissaries, crack troops of the Turkish forces, and since the 14th century recruited as boys from Christian subjects. Visitors to modern Istanbul may have witnessed the music in progress as now revived in 17th-century costume (the Janissaries having been disbanded in 1826) and based as far as possible on original sources. One sees bass drums played with stick and cane (see BASS DRUM, 4), pairs of small kettledrums held on the left arm (see NAQQARA), cymbals, and *surnas for the melodies, doubled by ordinary Western valved trumpets (since no record survives as to what the original natural trumpets did). In front are singers, each with a

Ex. 1.

'Turkish crescent'—a staff surmounted by a brass crescent and hung with horsetails—raised up and down in time with the music.

The 18th-century West rejected the small kettledrums and the wind instruments while picturesquely adding the triangle, played in bands by a boy. Gluck has it in the Turkish music for the Scythian storm in *Iphigénie en Tauride*. Next was added a tambourine, played in a spectacular manner by a black man. In Ex. 1, from the manuscript of a late 18th-century opera *La constanza alla fine premiata*, by the obscure composer Orodaet, 'tamburo ord.' may mean the tambourine. With the bass drum ('tamburo grosso') the lower Cs are struck with the heavy stick (right hand) and the upper Cs with the cane (or a switch) on the other head of the drum. A marching band might include the Turkish crescent in the form of the *bell tree or 'Jingling Johnny'. See PIANO, 8b, for 'Turkish music' effects once built into this.

Twirling drum. See RATTLE DRUM.

Txistu. See PIPE AND TABOR, 1.

Tympanum. Lat., 'drum' (see BIBLICAL INSTRUMENTS, 1d; TAMBOURINE, 2).

Typophone. See CELESTA.

U

'Ud (Arab lute). See LUTE, 6.

'Ugab. See BIBLICAL INSTRUMENTS, 1*f*.

Uilleann pipes (pron. 'ill-yin'). The main Irish
*bagpipe, best known before the 20th century as
the 'Union pipe'. Whichever may be historically
correct, the Gaelic name (signifying 'elbow pipe'
after the right elbow, which works the bellows) is
now the accepted one. The chanter is gently conical,
with double reed and lowest note usually *d'*. The
three drones have narrow cylindrical bores (the
deepest with a metal upturned end) and are tuned
to D in three octaves (*d' d D*). The instrument is
unique among bagpipes in two respects: the chanter
can be made to sound a complete upper octave;
and accompanying chords can be made on three
additional pipes called 'regulators', provided with
brass keys. These are opened with the lower edge
of the right hand without interrupting the music
of the chanter, in which a vibrato is often made
by shaking a finger over one of the open fingerholes.

The player, seated (Pl. 1), ties a leather 'popping
pad' above the right knee. Against this he can
momentarily close the end of the chanter, so that
when all holes are also closed there is no sound.
Thus notes can be detached, as with the *Northumbrian pipe. A rapid closure, at the end accompanied by a smart increase in arm pressure on the
bag, causes the chanter to jump to the higher
octave, in which it will continue to sound, while
fingerholes are uncovered, until the pressure is
relaxed.

The three regulators are held along with the
three drones in one large stock, all resting in a
bunch across the thigh. Each regulator is a conical
pipe with a double reed, and is stopped at the lower
end in order to be silent until a key is opened.
There are four keys to each (the small regulator
may have five) arranged so that when three keys
which lie level on the three pipes are struck together
the result is one of four possible three-note chords.
The chords are usually played staccato in the tempo
of the tune, but not always continuously: when
suddenly introduced in the middle of a jig, reel, or
hornpipe, that they give the most exhilarating lift
to the music. In slow tunes it is possible in a limited
way to make regulator chords with the fingers
during the moments when the melody occupies
one hand only. But most players now, especially
in slow airs, rarely touch the regulators, if at all,
allowing the poetry of this most expressive of
chanters to be heard unencumbered above the
gentle humming of the drones.

Pl. 1. 'Sporting' Capt. Wm. Kelly playing the Uilleann
Pipes; note the bellows (right arm), the 'popping pad'
(above right knee), and the bunch of regulators and
drones lying across the body (the white disc, lower
left, is the end of the bass drone).

The instrument was developed mainly during the
18th century, the small regulator introduced after
1750; a Scottish version too is known from a Tutor
by Geoghegan and by surviving examples. Three
regulators were present by the early 19th century,
and a complicated 'double bass' regulator was also
incorporated in some later instruments.

Ukulele (*ukelele*). Popular four-stringed small relative of the *guitar, half this in size, with rear
tuning pegs and 12 frets, and strummed with the
nails and fingertips. Tunings follow the pattern of
the first four strings of the guitar but with the
fourth string raised by an octave, the whole being
set at a higher pitch, commonly by a fifth, *b'*, *f♯'*,
d', *a'* (or a tone below or a semitone higher than
this). Failing special strings, violin A and E strings
can be used. The ukulele derives from the *cavaquinho type of small guitar introduced in the late
19th century, by Portuguese immigrants, into the
Hawaiian Islands, where it gained its name, lit.

'little flea' (said to have been the nickname of an officer who was a keen performer on it). It became popular in the USA from *c.*1916, after which it was normal practice for song editions to show ukulele chord fingerings by small square diagrams ('chord boxes', in popular music often used also for guitar and other fretted instruments): the line across the top represents the nut (open strings) and the lines running downwards the strings (the 4th on the left), while the spots show where to stop the frets. Always the tuning is stated, e.g. 'Tune uke G C E A' (naming the 4th string first).

The *baritone ukulele* is nearly one-and-a-half times the size of the above (string-length 50 cm. or 20″), usually with 15 frets and tuned as the first four strings of the guitar at actual guitar pitch. It succeeded a 'tenor ukulele' in the 1960s.

Ukulele banjo (banjo ukelele, banjolele). A *banjo-type body adapted to ukulele stringing, and giving room for 16 frets: once famous in Britain as the instrument of the Lancashire singer and comedian George Formby, it is also in manufacture today.

Union pipe. See UILLEANN PIPES.

Utricularius (Lat., 'bagpiper'). See BAGPIPES, 7.

V

Vaccine (boom-pipe, canuto). West Indian, originally from Haiti and Jamaica: a large bamboo tube, 1 m. (3') or more in length and around 6 cm. (2½") wide. It is blown into with strong, energetic puffs, which make the lips vibrate and the tube give forth a deep, booming sound (see TRUMPET, 10). Tubes of different lengths are sounded together.

Valiha. A main traditional instrument of the Malagasy Republic (Madagascar): an idiochord tube zither (see ZITHER, 3*a* (ii)), having 14 or more 'strings' raised from the bark of a bamboo tube 80 cm. (*c.*30") long or more and 7.5 cm. (3") or more wide. The strings are tuned by small movable bridges and, with the instrument held at a slant, are plucked with the nails cut to points (or with finger-picks for the little fingers). It is believed to have been introduced from South-East Asia 500 years ago. Valiha music has long fallen under European influence, the tunes harmonized in thirds and so on. Also, during the 20th century, metal strings have been used, lashed to the tube at each end, and the tube itself may be made in other ways, e.g. of wood, halved for hollowing and rejoined.

Valved trombone. With valves replacing the slide, valved trombones have been, since their introduction in the late 1830s, manufactured in most countries and much used instead of slide trombones, e.g. in the Latin countries of Europe and America, especially in theatres (taking up less room in the pit) and in bands.

1. Normal models. A valved trombone can be built in any shape, including circular (see HELICON), but usually it retains a recognizable *trombone format (Pl. 1). Valves bring a great agility to the technique even if the more subtle qualities of the slide trombone are lost. Verdi, with valved trombones in mind, wrote passages as in Ex. 1 that are virtually impossible on an ordinary slide instrument. It was the American-style dance orchestra of the 1930s that began to weaken the hold of the valved trombone in its former strongholds: as an Italian bandsman said, pointing to his valved instrument, 'this for *banda*; for orchestra, *a tiro* ['slide']'.

Ex. 1.

(ff)

2. With independent pistons. In Belgium up to the 1950s orchestras were largely using instruments on Sax's system of six independent valves (1852), which eliminate valve combinations and the intonation troubles arising from them. The pistons, three for each hand (those for the left hand placed horizontally), individually admit tubing to correspond with each position of a slide from the 1st to the 6th (the 7th with all pistons 'up'). The technique is fluent since valves below the one required for a note can be equally held down or released as most convenient in the passage being played. The system was also tried on other brass instruments, examples being preserved in collections.

Valves (Fr.: *pistons*; Ger.: *Ventile*; It.: *chiavi, cilindri*, etc.). The means by which the majority of present *brass instruments gain their chromatic compass, the basic provision being three valves.

1. The principle. Fig. 1 is a diagram of an ordinary piston-valve, seen removed from its fixed casing: a brass or nickel-silver cylinder inside which short passages of thin brass pass across in different directions one above the other. Each valve, when lowered against a spring, admits an external loop of tubing (broken line in Fig. 1) to add this amount to the main tube of the instrument (the pistons being kept in alignment each by a lug fixed in the casing). When the valve is 'up' (at rest), the windway entering from 1 crosses through the valve by means of the passage marked 2 to emerge at 3 on its way to the next valve (or the bell, as the case may be). When 'down' (right), 2 becomes inoperative: the windway enters now at 4, and so through the valve loop to 5 and again to emerge at 3. The lengths of the loops can be calculated in the traditional way by simple fractions, or by proportions in equal temperament (see TEMPERA-

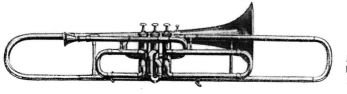

Pl. 1. Tenor valved trombone, Couesnon, Paris, 1915.

MENT, 4). The fractions are the easier to consider. The first valve (first finger) adds one-eighth to the instrument's tube-length to lower the harmonic series by a whole tone—see Ex. 1, the notes marked 1. The second valve adds one-fifteenth, to lower by a semitone (notes marked 2), and the two together (marked 1/2) lower by a minor third. To complete the chromatic scale several notes require the third valve. This again lowers by a minor third (adding one-fifth to the total), but is normally reserved for making these further notes by combination with the others as shown. Note that the seventh harmonic is omitted, being skipped over by the player since its pitch lies a third of a semitone below B♭, disqualifying it from normal musical use. The written compass shown, up to 'top C', is usually regarded as the safe range for general purposes, although players often go considerably higher.

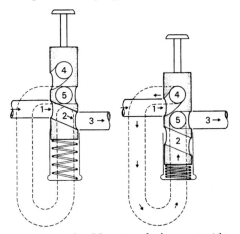

Fig. 1. Piston valve: *left*, section of valve at rest; *right*, valve lowered.

To take the compass below the lowest note in Ex. 1, as often necessary especially with bass instruments like the *tuba, there is a gap to be filled down to the fundamental C a diminished fifth below. The simple method is to provide a fourth valve which lowers the instrument by a perfect fourth (see TUBA, 2a), and so on below this according to which other valves are brought into use as well.

2. *Types of valve.* Valves are first publicly reported in 1815 (in the Leipzig *Allgemeine musikalische Zeitung*) as the invention of Heinrich Stoelzel (1772–1844), a Silesian horn-player; a patent followed in

Berlin, 1818, signed by him together with another player, Friedrich Blühmel, of whom less is known. The original form of valve seems to have been that which later came to be known by Stoelzel's name (below, 2b, and see Heyde 1987a).

(a) *Present systems.* The piston-valves now in widest use (Fig. 1) basically follow the design of 1839 by Périnet, Paris. The horn, however, normally uses *rotary valves*, possibly first thought of by Blühmel and in Germany used on all valved brass instruments. Each valve here contains a rotating cylinder (rotor) which is turned through 90 degrees to divert the tube circuit through the valve loop (Fig. 2); horn valves are turned either by metal linkages, or by a looped string ('string action'). Special spray lubricants are commercially obtainable for piston-valves; rotary valves are self-lubricated by condensed moisture, save for sparing application of a special oil to the rotor bearings.

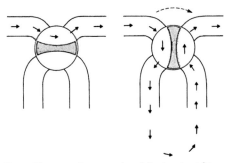

Fig. 2. Diagram of rotary valve: *left*, at rest; *right*, valve pressed (i.e. rotor turned through 90°).

In Vienna some leading horn-players remain true to *double piston* or *Vienna* valves. These have for each valve two short parallel pistons connected at the bottom by a bar moved by a long rod reaching up to the finger-plate and spring. With the valve 'up' the windway passes straight through both pistons, down one and up the other; when the valve is lowered, it is diverted through the valve loop. One of the oldest valve systems (invented by Sattler, Leipzig, 1821), this valve was among the commonest in Germany up to the 1850s on all valved instruments, trumpets included.

(b) *Other piston systems up to the early 20th century.* Commonest in France and England are *Stoelzel valves*. In each of the narrow pistons the windway

Ex. 1.

leads down to the bottom, thence to pass to the next valve through a U (or else to lead to the bell); see CORNET, Pl. 1. Lowering a valve admits its valve loop as in the common piston-valve. The spring is above inside the casing (as it is also in many designs of ordinary piston-valve). These valves were still provided in France up to the First World War on lower-priced cornets. So too, in Germany for band instruments, were *Berlin pistons* (*Berliner-pumpen*), a neatly simple type due to Wieprecht, 1833.

(*c*) *Further early systems.* The numerous other inventions of the 19th century in all countries, and exemplified by instruments in collections, would make a long list. America enters very early, from 1825 (Eliason 1970) with those of Nathan Adams, of Lowell, Massachusetts: a 'permutation trumpet' in F with the valve loops admitted by internal vanes, rotated by a lever. From the same year Adams made one of the earliest known rotary valves, possibly the first. Later are *Allen valves* (J. Lathrop Allen, Boston, *c.*1850). In these, the entry and exit tubes for each rotary valve are flattened where they join the valve casing for the circular section to become a tall, narrow ellipse of the same area, and the passages in the rotor similarly, so enabling the tubes to be set closer together and the rotor to be reduced in width. Allen valves (made also by others) are to be seen in many preserved instruments made in the USA up to the 1870s, by which time makers were turning to the French Périnet pistons.

Quite common on early English instruments are '*disc valves*', deriving from a patent of 1838 by John Shaw, soon improved by Köhler, London, who used them on brass instruments of every description: a brass disc is rotated against a stationary disc to divert the windway through the valve loop, the two discs kept in contact by a light spring.

3. *Problems.* With valves of any normal sort a problem arises when two or more valves are lowered together. Thus the low D (Ex. 1) theoretically needs four-thirds the tube-length of the G a fourth above, an addition of 33.3 per cent. But the first valve adds 12.5 per cent (one-eighth) and the third adds 20 per cent (one-fifth), together making 32.5 per cent only. The shortfall amounts on the B♭ trumpet to approximately 1 cm. or, on a large tuba, 4 cm. (1.6″): the note comes too sharp and the player must drag it down with the lips, though accustomed to doing this almost unconsciously. However, the problem is often mitigated by pulling out the tuning-slide of the third valve a little, to make up the difference (each valve loop incorporates its own tuning-slide). Among several remedies, see TUBA, 2*b* for the compensating pistons much used on British *euphoniums and tubas. Also TUBA, 2*c* for up to five or six plain valves; and VALVED TROMBONE, 2 for Sax's system of six independent pistons, which removes the problems entirely.

Vessel flute. *Classification term for instruments of the Flute class which are not tubular but *cavity resonators. Examples are *ocarina, *gemshorn, and many *whistles.

Vibraphone (or vibraharp). Instrument of tuned metal bars (Pl. 1), built in the same shape as a *marimba. The bars, of aluminium alloy and about 12 mm. ($\frac{1}{2}$″) thick, are suspended on spring-tensioned cords. The two rows, for the naturals and the sharps, are placed on the same level. This makes it possible to use two beaters (soft-ended) in each hand for playing four-note chords, very characteristic with this instrument (as with the *marimba also).

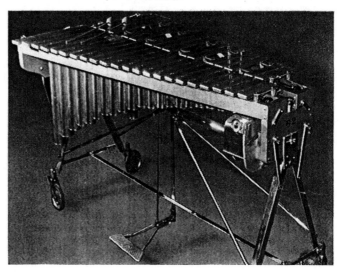

Pl. 1. Vibraphone (Boosey & Hawkes).

The special feature of the vibraphone is the long axle running beneath each row of bars along the top of the tubular resonators and bearing circular metal or plastic vanes, one for each tube and rotated together by an electric motor. The opening and closing of the tubes causes an alternation of resonated and non-resonated sound, making the vibrato from which the instrument gets its name. The motor may have certain set speeds, or be variable-speed to make from about three to eight pulsations per second. Very important is the damper: a long felted strip for each row of bars, moved against them by a pedal. Its use demands much skill, as in half-damping for fast notes to be sounded yet without losing vibraphone quality. Damping with the fingers may also be needed, for instance where certain notes are to have shorter duration than the others in a chord played with the dampers lifted. The normal compass is f to f''' (see XYLOPHONE for a comparative compass chart).

In the early design by the Leedy Drum Co. in the USA, 1916, the vibrato was obtained by moving the resonators up and down. The rotating fans followed about 1921, after which variety soloists made the instrument well known, as again later in the advanced jazz of Lionel Hampton. In the orchestra, Berg has it in *Lulu* (1934) and Milhaud wrote a Concerto (1947) for vibraphone and marimba. Two British works of around 1950— Britten's *Spring Symphony* and Vaughan Williams's *Sinfonia antartica*—link vibraphone chords with frost and freezing (as also in Walt Disney's famous cartoons). But mainly the instrument has become an essential member of orchestral percussion for 'abstract' colour in its own right.

More recent from the USA is the 'electravibe', in which the resonators and fans are replaced by a pick-up under each bar, to convert the acoustic vibration into electrical for amplification, and with vibrato control by a pulsator and optional 'fuzz' and 'wah' units as used with electric guitars.

Vibraslap. Modern American substitute for the *jawbone of Latin American dance music. A bent-over thin, springy metal rod, shaped for grasping in one hand, carries on one end a small wooden box with loose metal rods (or rivets) imprisoned inside and with air-holes in the end. The other end carries a wooden ball which is hit by the other hand or smacked on the fist to shake the rod so that components of the box vibrate like the teeth of the jawbone.

Vièle. (Old Fr. form of the Romance word *viola*). The principal type of medieval fiddle; see FIDDLE, 1C; MEDIEVAL INSTRUMENTS, 3.

Vielle (Fr., from *vièle*). *Hurdy-gurdy.

Vihuela. 1. Spanish stringed instrument of the Renaissance period. The name is the Spanish equivalent of 'viola', but whereas this in most countries has denoted a bowed instrument, 'vihuela' has the principal meaning of one that is plucked. The Renaissance vihuela is shaped much like a contemporary *guitar, but has six *courses of strings tuned in the manner of a *lute, i.e. with the major third between the third and fourth courses, not between the second and third as on a guitar. There are 10 frets. The instrument held a place in Spanish courtly music through the 16th century corresponding to that of the lute in Italy and elsewhere, and has similarly left a large musical repertory written in *tablature. Early collections include those by Luis Milán (1536) and the blind Miguel de Fuenllana (1554). A technical description is in Bermudo (1555). Guitarists today play this repertory from the tablature, tuning the third string a semitone lower.

The appearance of the vihuela is known from pictures, and matching these, a presumed example preserved in Paris (Musée Jacquemart-André, said to bear the mark of a Spanish monastery and to date from c.1500). Its photograph has often been reproduced: a large example (like the lute, the vihuela varied in size), with a body some 10 cm. (4") longer than the present Spanish guitar, shallower sides, and five small roses placed in a quincunx instead of one large rose.

The vihuela was also termed 'vihuela de mano', ('sounded with the hand'), to distinguish it from the 'vihuela de arco' ('bowed'), i.e. the *viol.

2. In Latin America, *vihuela* is a quite different instrument, a smallish five-course metal-strung guitar which in Mexico plays the harmony in a *son* (folk ensemble). The deep, swell-backed body joins a rather short neck on which may be tied three or so nylon frets. The strings, single or double, are usually tuned as the first five of the guitar with the lower two (or three) to the octave higher.

Vina (or *vīṇā*, *bīn*). Classic instrument of Indian music, existing in two chief forms, one in the north, the other in the south, the first being the older.

1. *Northern vina* (*rudrā vīṇā*, the 'vina of Shiva', or *bīn*), Pl. 1. A wide wooden tube (originally bamboo) up to more than 1 m. (3') long, to which two large gourds, c.40 cm. (16") in diameter and open below, are attached one at each end by bolts which are hollow, for the cavities of gourd and tube to connect. The gourd near the tuning pegs is usually (not always) rested above the player's left shoulder, the other on the right knee or hip. Along the tube are 22 to 24 chromatic frets of metal over wood, nearly 2.5 cm. (1 inch) tall and waxed in position. Over these run the four main playing strings of metal, the first of them, the highest-tuned and chief melody string, being to the player's right (the opposite to most stringed instruments). The tension is low and the tuning pattern deep, e.g. $f \, c \, G \, c$ if taking C as the tonic, though it may be deeper.

Pl. 1. Vina, north India, from an old lithograph.

An important feature (and adopted from the vina by the *sitar and many other Indian stringed instruments) is the table-like bridge, often ivory, mounted at the extreme lower end; its surface is skilfully rounded for the strings to buzz slightly while the right thumb and index finger sound them with wire fingerpicks. Another important feature (also adopted on the sitar) is the expressive left-hand bending of notes, pulling a string sideways along the fret after plucking, tightening it and raising its pitch in a portamento even up to a fifth.

Three further metal strings, not stopped, are sounded softly in accompaniment: on the left side is the highest-tuned, struck with the left little finger in a reiterated drone; on the other side, with the pegs further from the main nut, are the two *chikari* strings, tuned to high octaves above the keynote (e.g. *c', c''*) and struck upwards with the nails of the little fingers to maintain the underlying rhythm. There may also be nine or so *sympathetic strings passing under the frets and tuned by more pegs along the side. As with other main stringed instruments a performance begins with the slow, free *ālāp* in the character of the chosen raga, which is developed and accelerated to end with the fast *jhālā*. In classical playing in *dhrupad* style the vina is traditionally accompanied on the long barrel drum *pakhawaj*.

In Western *classification the northern vina is seen as a highly developed form of 'stick zither' (see ZITHER, 3*c*), in that it has neither the separate neck nor the integral (non-detachable) soundbox of a *lute. It reached its present form by the 16th century, developed from single-string instruments of kinds such as are now preserved in the mendicant's *tuila*; the name vina had anciently denoted an arched harp (see HARP, 10*a*) which vanished from India by *c.*1000 AD.

2. *Southern vina* (*sarasvatī vīṇā*, relating to the Hindu goddess of this name). Unlike the above, this can be seen as a species of 'long lute' (see LUTE, 7). The large rounded body is carved in wood and the belly is of wood (usually with a pair of rose soundholes). The hollow neck (either integral with the body or made separately) curves back at the top and the 24 brass frets arch across it. A small gourd is usually attached below the end of the neck, probably (in the sitar also) a symbolic allusion to the older northern vina. The instrument is played in a low, slanting position, with the body resting on the ground to the player's right.

The metal strings are again seven, but all three of the auxiliary strings are on the right-hand side. The four main strings are tuned to a similar pattern as in the north save that the first is here the tonic and the third is an octave below this; the side strings run *c g c'* (for tonic C). The accompanying drum is the *mrdanga.

See INDIA.

Viol (rhymes with 'dial'; Fr.: *viole*; Ger., as It., or *Gamba*, plural *Gamben*; It.: *viola da gamba* (also in Ru.); Sp.: *vihuela de arco*). Bowed instrument of the Renaissance and Baroque periods, normally with six strings and seven gut *frets tied round the neck (Pl. 1). It has a large and varied solo repertory, while its special pride is the music composed for the family of viols, treble, tenor, and bass, in England from the reign of Elizabeth I up to the Restoration (below, 3*c*), and constituting without question the most distinguished corpus of purely instrumental chamber music written prior to the 18th century. Few instruments are more perfectly suited to domestic music-making than the viols, for with the frets they should be easy to play in tune; and if able to play one viol it becomes a simple matter to play the others, all being held downwards between the knees, and all being fingered and bowed in the same way—unlike, say, the violin and the cello, which are fingered quite differently from each other.

1. *Description.* Viols differ in many ways from the instruments of the violin family, the two having been evolved for different musical purposes. Among distinguishing features one notices the wider neck of the viol to take the six strings and the proportionately greater length of the neck, giving good room for tying on the seventh fret (one-third of the distance from nut to bridge). The shoulders of the body slope up to the neck; the back is flat, bent inwards towards the neck; and the sides are deep, in a treble viol quite twice as deep as in a violin. In viols of the 17th and early 18th centuries, the most copied today, the body construction is generally kept rather light; belly and back are flush with the sides instead of overlapping them as in the violin family, and outward points at the centre bouts are lacking, making a plainer outline. The purfling or inlay can, however, be very ornate, often with interlaced trellis designs on sides and back and a floral design on the belly. The internal reinforcement of the body is normally kept light, matched by strings that are fairly thin and low-tensioned. Through all these things the sound of a

Pl. 1 Viol, from Christopher Simpson, *The Division Violist* (1659).

viol is less strong and the tone more nasal than in the violin family, while the frets (now often of nylon) impart the ring of an open string to every note. But it is the peculiar ability of a set of viols to integrate their sounds that gives so especially pleasing an effect when the instruments are played together.

Among further details, the tailpiece is hooked to a wooden post at the base of the body; the soundholes are usually C-shaped; and at the top of the long pegbox a human or animal head is often carved instead of a scroll, or the scroll may take the very beautiful form of an 'open scroll', carved through from side to side.

2. *Tuning, bowing; sizes of viols.* Normal viol tunings (Ex. 1) follow the scheme of the Renaissance lute. Though the smaller viols rarely need to play on the lower strings, these can add sympathetic resonance when not bowed. The strings were once normally gut, the lowest three eventually overwound, but nowadays nylon (perlon) or steel-core strings also serve quite well. The bow is slightly outcurved and held palm-upwards, inclined with

the bow stick nearer to the bridge. The second finger is placed between stick and hair with the third finger below the hair, to produce subtle differences in hair tension as the wrist is flexed with each stroke. The stronger stroke is the 'push' stroke (Fr.: *pousser*), the opposite to the down-bow of the violin.

An English 'chest of viols' would consist of two each of treble, tenor ('mean'), and bass. The sizes of the viols vary considerably. Today a treble viol has an average body length of around 40 cm. (15''). The bass viol may have double this, around 80 cm. (30''). The tenor varies more (and in former times might be tuned a tone higher than shown in Ex. 1), but it averages some 53 cm. (21'') in the body. (Sometimes in Germany today the bass viol with bottom string D is termed a 'Tenor', the next above being 'Alt', following a chart in *Praetorius in which 'Bass' is for a tuning a fifth deeper.) Most of the old viols played today have survived through having at some later time been converted into violas or cellos. By being so kept in use, they have been saved from the ravages of woodworm, and have now been converted back.

Among the great former makers in London are John Rose, up to 1600; Henry Jaye, who worked up to past 1660; and Richard Meares, of the 1670s. The bellies of these English viols are generally made from three separate lengths of wood moulded to the arching, plus the four smaller pieces required to complete the upper and lower bouts at the side. It also seems (Kessler 1982) that in some cases this plate is not carved to the arch, but is of thinner wood then bent.

One of the surviving viols by Rose, a full-sized 'consort bass', has the festooned (scalloped) outline which became favoured by some makers in Germany, and could be compared with the scalloped outlines of the contemporary *bandora and *orpharion, of which Rose is said to have been the inventor.

The London viol-making tradition came near its end with Barak Norman (d. 1740), who also made violins and cellos. His handsome viols, and those in Europe from the same period, show a certain stylized perfection which new-made viols now often tend to follow rather than the more free and vigorous models of Rose and Jaye.

For the 'division viol', see below, 4b.

3. *History:* (a) *Origins.* It has long been held that the viol arose in late 15th-century Spain as a bowed modification of the plucked *vihuela, guitar-like in shape and tuned like a lute. The viol, with this same tuning and the frets, was distinguished as the *vihuela de arco.* Recent research (Woodfield 1984) places this development in Aragon: pictures of the 1470s in Valencia show in the hands of angels, six-stringed bowed instruments of roughly guitar size though with short, deep middle bouts (suited to bowing) and C-shaped soundholes in addition to the 'rose'. The bridge appears to remain

Ex. 1

Treble　　　　　　　　Tenor　　　　　　Bass

flat-topped, in which case the middle strings could have been bowed only in chords of two or more notes. This early viol might, on the other hand, have been developed from far older bowed instruments of various shapes, held downwards and pictured in Aragon up to the 15th century. Woodfield goes on to show that the viol reached Italy following the election of a Valencian, Rodrigo Borgia, to the papacy in 1492. The arched bridge then appears, the arched belly no doubt also, and in 1502 six viols were heard played together at the Ferrara court. By 1520, viols had reached Germany, and soon, under the patronage of Henry VIII, England, the players (of 'Vialles greate and small') brought by him from Italy.

(b) *Early Italian viols.* Preserved examples from the 16th century are of all shapes; even past 1700 Cremona violin-makers were making bass viols in practically the shape of a cello. In the fine Venetian viols by the Linarol and Ciciliano families, with steeply sloping shoulders, the front is smaller at the top than the back, brought about by sloping the neck-block upwards towards the rear (Edmunds 1980). The signs are that they originally had neither bass-bar nor sound-post (both in most cases added to the instruments since). It was written in Venice in 1543 (Ganassi) that should the tenor and treble viols be on the large size, requiring a lower tuning pitch, it might be necessary to match the bass viol to them by moving the bridge downwards, or else to choose for it thicker strings; or if the treble were too small, to reverse the process. Ganassi (like Gerle in Germany, 1532) says that players might use five strings, not six, omitting the bottom string. Ganassi, also referring to playing from part-books, stresses how the players should convey the sense of the words through strength of bowing emphasized by appropriate movements of the head and expressions of the eyes.

(c) *English consort music.* The first important works composed for viols, from the 1560s, are of the *In nomine* type built always upon an old cantus firmus which Taverner set with this title in a mass. Tye and Byrd are among the chief *In nomine* composers of pre-1600, after which others continue to use the form up to Purcell. By 1600 were added the magnificent fantasies and pavans in anything from three to even seven parts by Byrd, Tomkins, Coprario, Ferrabosco the younger, Gibbons, Jenkins, William Lawes, and Locke. Most has come down to us in manuscript collections (many of the pieces now available in modern editions). Some of the collections have a part for organ, played on *chamber organ (or other keyboard) and ranging from a fully written part to an outline of the whole. English compositions were well known on the Continent, many being preserved in Germany.

4. *Music for bass viol.* The viol consort apart, the musical history of the viol is virtually that of the bass viol or (in the most familiar meaning of the family name) viola da gamba.

(a) *With other instruments.* From the 16th century always an important choice for the bass part in mixed ensembles, and so through the Baroque on the *continuo save where displaced by the cello. In Philip Rosseter's *Book of Ayres . . . to be song to the lute, Orpharion, and Base Violl* (1601) the viol part is printed upside down at the top of each page for the player sitting at the opposite side of the table. For violin with bass viol (or two of either or both) are fantasias and suites with organ or harpsichord by Ferrabosco, Corprario, and Gibbons, and again, much later, for these instruments by Buxtehude.

(b) *Division viol.* A special province of the bass viol lay in the art of playing *'divisions'—variations improvised (or learnt) over a given bass or 'ground', and already given great attention in early works on the viol, like Ortiz's *Tratado de glosas* (Rome, 1553). Rather than the full-sized bass viol of the 'chest', a smaller instrument was preferred for this and became termed in 17th-century England a 'division viol'—for example, in the title of Christopher Simpson's important work in this field *The Division Violist* (1659). The player might begin by 'breaking the ground' with increasingly fast and elaborate runs and figures, and then 'descant' upon it on the higher strings, and finally proceed to do both virtually at once, with wide leaps, while yet aiming for artistic unity over the whole performance.

(c) *Lyra viol.* For this and for playing the bass viol 'lyra way', from *tablature, see LYRA VIOL.

(d) *French works.* From c.1675, by composers and soloists of a great school that bore wide influence over Europe. Marin Marais (1656–1728), a pupil of Lully, rose to be one of the greatest of solo viol players. Among his countless 'pièces de viole' for one, two, or three bass viols with continuo is one solo piece which amusingly expresses the apprehensions and agonies of undergoing an operation for the stone, with running commentary written beneath the music (see *NOCM*, 1920 for excerpts). For the repertory a seventh string was frequently included on the Continent, tuned to low A, this and the two above being overwound strings. Louis and François Couperin also wrote pieces for viols. In Germany, two at least of the sonatas by

Bach for viola da gamba are arrangements from other works; but outstanding is the obbligato in the St Matthew Passion ('O joy to share'), with chords of many notes, one characteristic of the instrument's baroque solo style.

5. *The last phase.* The bass viol continued after this to retain a certain popularity. The famous player and composer of sonatas Carl Abel gave his last concert in London just before he died (1787), his viol buried with him. Through the 19th century there were still here and there (as in England) devotees of the viola da gamba, even if not always to play music originally written for it. Wider revival was in progress by 1890, in France, and in England with performances of viol consort music by Arnold Dolmetsch (1858–1940), on restored instruments before he was soon making his own. It was through no fault of his that later on, around the 1920s, a cellist might win public admiration for playing Bach's obbligati for viola da gamba on a massively restored bass viol with no frets and a bow held and moved as on a cello, nevertheless in its way helping to bring the very existence of the viol to wider notice.

See also PARDESSUS DE VIOLE; VIOLA BASTARDA; VIOLONE (with Great Double Base); also BASS VIOL (USA, early 19th century).

Edmunds 1980; Ganassi 1542; Harwood 1974; Harwood and Edmunds 1978; Hayes 1930; Kessler 1982; Playford 1654; Pringle 1978; Woodfield 1977, 1978, 1984.

Viola (in Eng. formerly 'tenor'; Fr., Sp.: *alto*; Ger.: *Bratsche*, deriving from the older It.: *viola da braccio*; It.: *viola*, the Eng. normally pronounced as the Italian; Ru.: *alt*). Held like the violin but a little larger in size, the viola is the essential middle member of the violin family, in the *orchestra and equally in chamber music, here most notably in its crowning genre, the string quartet. The viola is made in the same way as a violin but is tuned a fifth lower, *a' d' g c*, thus having no high E string but instead a low C string. Matching this deeper range the notation is in the alto clef (Ex. 1), though where a part rises high a change is usually made to the treble clef.

Ex. 1.

1. *Viola size.* The difference from a violin is not very great: a body length greater by about 6.5 cm. (2½″)—that is, on average, for the viola is not completely standardized in size and can vary by 2.5 cm (1 inch) either way. To the ear, on the other hand, the viola is at once distinguished. This is because it is not of a size that would give it an overall tone-character strictly intermediate between that of a violin and a cello. For this it would need the body of a size which, though made in the early days (below, 3), since became discarded as

unmanageable, particularly as the music came to demand a technique equal to that of the violin. The viola is on this account small for the tuning to which it is committed, with a result that it speaks not simply as an alto species of violin but in most ways with a voice of its own—as in a relatively 'distant' quality on the top string, warm and bold on the lower—bringing, alike to the orchestral strings and to the quartet, a scope for variety in texture which, so largely thanks to the viola, never palls.

2. *Strings and playing.* Viola strings are usually of gut overwound with silver or aluminium (the former plain gut A string being now much less used); steel strings too are occasionally employed. The bow is if anything shorter than a violin bow and about 10 per cent heavier, with a distinctly wider band of hair. The fingering is like that of the violin save where differences arise due to the larger size. Violinists have seldom experienced any difficulty in playing the viola also, and many great musicians, past and present, have liked especially to play the viola in a quartet; Mozart did so, and also Bach (as recalled by his son C. P. E. Bach) in his instrumental ensembles, both of them players of the violin also. Violin teachers often teach the viola as well, until at advanced stages it forms a specialized subject (the earliest Tutors that are both specifically for viola and are still in use are French, of the years 1805–15, by Bruni, and by Martinn).

3. *Historical development: (a) Early period.* The viola was one of the violin family from its beginnings when, by the 1530s, the family (see VIOLA DA BRACCIO; VIOLETTA) had been created in northern Italy for playing music, dances especially, written in four parts with the viola to play the two middle parts. The earliest viola existing is of the large 'tenor' size, dated 1574 if the label is truly genuine (Hill *collection, Oxford) built by Andrea Amati for the French royal violin band: its body is nearly 48 cm. long (18¾″), a dimension equalled or approached by other makers up to around 1700, Stradivari included. These tenors were, however, usually given a proportionately short neck—a tenor of perhaps 20 years later than the Amati is preserved in the same collection with its original neck, which reduces the string-length, rendering the simple parts then written playable without calling for an excessive stretch of the arm.

Also made—some believe from not as early as the large tenors—are the 'contralto' (alto) violas, with bodies around 42 cm. (16½″) about the average today; fine early examples are by the Brothers Amati, by Gasparo, and Maggini (for the dates of the makers see VIOLIN, 4). Among Stradivari's moulds and drawings preserved in Cremona some marked by him 'T V' ('tenore viola') and 'C V' (contralto viola): these names, for instruments with the same viola tuning but differently sized, referring to the five-part writing for strings common through the 17th century, with the lower viola part needing the C string, the upper often hardly at all though going higher. Modern groups of players have tested the use of such instruments with fine effect, notably in works of Lully's period for the French royal band. Here there are *three* middle parts for viola-tuned instruments, known as 'les parties' ('de remplissage', 'filling in'), said to have often been written by the composer's assistants. If *Mersenne is correct, they were supposed to be played on violas of three sizes, four men to each part.

The magnificent tenors, able to sound full and bright on all strings, have—like the large cellos ('bass violins') of the same period—almost all been 'cut down' since (see CELLO, 4a). One might wonder how the first Amati came to select dimensions which in both cases have proved too big for posterity. With the meticulous attention given by the early master to every detail of geometric proportion commencing with the body-length (Coates 1985) it is hard not to believe that some proportional scheme also governed this dimension through the family. From the actual dimensions it looks as if he may have scaled down the proportion of twice for an octave difference in pitch to something like $1\frac{2}{3}$ (5 : 3) for an octave difference in size, and so the perfect fifth (arithmetic mean of the octave) from $1\frac{1}{2}$ to $1\frac{1}{3}$ (4 : 3) as a proportion for a tenor viola to a violin, then providing strings at suitable thickness and tension.

(b) *From the 18th century onwards.* With the four-part string writing that afterwards became normal, players continued with violas of the more manageable smaller range, with the overwound C string helping to compensate for the small size. A viola once owned by Mozart was said to have a 40 cm. ($15\frac{3}{4}''$) body, which would now be considered rather small (though many such are in use) and tend to sound weak on the lower strings. An average through the 19th century was a 42 cm. ($16\frac{1}{2}''$), since which the trend, largely initiated, from 1937, by the British soloist Lionel Tertis (1876–1975), has been for violas of around 42.5 cm. ($16\frac{3}{4}''$), for orchestral use also.

Some notable earlier works in the solo repertory had already been associated with large violas. First, Paganini asked Berlioz for a work to play on a large Stradivari viola he had recently acquired (now preserved in Washington, DC), though the result, *Harold in Italy* (1834), failed to please him, having too many bars' rest for the soloist, and the work was first performed in Paris by Urhan (see VIOLA D'AMORE). Nearly a century later, Tertis, though for a quite different reason (finding the work too strange), declined the first performance of Walton's Concerto, which many would place among the finest written for the instruments of the violin family. The soloist on that occasion (in 1929) was, in fact, Hindemith, in his day no less celebrated as a viola virtuoso than he became as a composer;

he too played on a large viola. The next international celebrity, Scottish-born William Primrose (1904–82), expressed less interest in dimensions than in quality of sound, preferring this to be 'mezzo', rather than 'contralto'; among the many famous violas he had possessed he prized especially the Andrea Guarneri of 1697, with 41.3 cm. ($16\frac{1}{4}''$) body (Riley 1980).

4. *Repertory.* From the 18th century come Telemann's Viola Concerto, concerto for two violas, and many trio sonatas for viola with violin or other instrument; J. G. Graun's sonatas and a concerto; Georg Benda's four concertos; Dittendorf's Viola Concerto and a concerto for viola and double bass; Vanhal's Concerto; Carl Stamitz's at least three concertos and four *sinfonie concertante* with viola solo; Anton Stamitz's four concertos; and Mozart's *Sinfonia concertante*, K. 364 (in which the viola is tuned up a semitone to sound more penetrating—as again among the works by Vanhal and Stamitz), the Trio K. 498 (with clarinet), and duets with violin, K. 423.

The 19th-century repertory includes: Beethoven's Notturno, Op. 42 (arr. from Trio, Op. 8); Hummel's Sonata; Spohr's Duo with violin, Op. 3; Weber's Andante and Hungarian Rondo (for his brother, subsequently published by Weber for bassoon); Berlioz's *Harold in Italy* (3c, above); Mendelssohn's youthful Sonata; Schumann's *Märchenbilder*, Op. 131 (viola and piano); Anton Rubinstein's Sonata, Op. 49; Brahms's two clarinet sonatas adapted for the viola by the composer, and two *Lieder* for contralto voice, viola, and piano, Op. 91 (intended for Joachim and his wife); and Max Bruch's *Romance* and some works with clarinet.

Among later works are Hindemith's sonatas Op. 11 and Op. 25, his *Trauermusik*, and *Der Schwanendreher*, both for viola and orchestra; Walton's Concerto (above, 4); and numerous works by British composers written for Lionel Tertis (see above, 4), including Holst's Lyric Movement and Vaughan Williams's Suite for Viola (with orchestra). A performance of the Walton in the USA by Primrose decided Bartók to go ahead with his own concerto for the viola. He left it, on his death, far from completed, but as afterwards assembled from the composer's sketches, by Tibór Sérly, it now has its place in the standard repertory. Further works include Britten's *Lachrymae* (with piano or string orchestra) and Stockhausen's *Kurzwellen*, with, among six players, viola with contact microphone. Berio's Sequenza VI also has a solo viola.

5. *Instruments with four strings tuned a fifth or a fourth below the viola.* From the years round 1600 are hints of such: e.g. Banchieri (1609), a 'violino per il basso', a fifth below the viola, listed as the lowest of the family; a singing manual by Hizler (1628) names a *Tenorgeige*, similarly tuned (along with an *Altgeige* with viola tuning) and 15 years before, in a Cassel court inventory, a 'large 4-stringed *Tenorgeige* tuned upwards from G or F' (Baines

1951: 33). No surviving instrument of the period has been positively identified as likely to have had such tuning—though among possibilities in pictures, see RENAISSANCE INSTRUMENTS, Pl. I, partly obscured by the standing *violone player, the rather large instrument apparently held slanting across the thigh like a guitar.

Much later, in the 19th century after various proposals for enlarging the viola to match the sound to the violin (as a 'contra-alto' by Vuillaume, 1851, with greatly widened bouts lowering the air-resonance pitch), several makers and musicians became intrigued by the notion of 'filling the gap' between violin and cello with an instrument tuned an octave below the violin (so bottom string G), even if there were no music written for it. Best remembered is the German viola-player Hermann Ritter (1849–1926). Having first produced (1870) a 'viola alta' with 48 cm. (18¾") body, the biggest he could manage (and later criticized for sounding no longer like a viola (Riley 1980)), on this, at Wagner's own request, he led the violas in the first full performance of *The Ring*. By 1905 he followed it with a 'viola tenore' an octave below the violin and literally twice its size, held between the knees; and also a 'viola bassa', cello-tuned and twice the size of his 'viola alta'. In Italy, a 'contraviolino' by V. De Zorzi (1902) also tuned an octave below the violin, had a body one-and-a-half times violin length (54 cm. (21.6")) and sides 5.8 cm. (2.3") deep (Gai 1969).

6. *New violin family.* In the USA, from the 1920s, F. L. Dautrich resumed such experiments with a 50 cm. (20") viola played downwards like a viol, a 'tenor' a fourth deeper and looking like a small cello, and a small bass an octave lower, also tuned in fifths. And now, starting from around 1960, again in the USA, a most interesting redesigning of the entire violin family has been by the Catgut Society under the leadership of Carleen M. Hutchins. Her main precept, more scientific than simple proportional measurement, rests on accurate confirmation by electronic methods of the known fact that with fine violins the main wood resonance-frequency (of the belly) and the main air-frequency (of the contained air) come, respectively, near to the open A and D of the strings. With a viola and often with the cello they come higher than the corresponding open strings, reinforcing the view that these two instruments are 'too small' for their pitch. Very briefly, Mrs Hutchins accordingly set about enlarging and adjusting them to bring the resonances down to the second and third open strings as in a good violin, which the instruments should then fully match in richness and quality of sound. So promising were the results that she proceeded to augment the family with other instruments designed on the same principle, keeping the violin as the focal point: thus (naming the bottom string) the enlarged viola ('vertical viola', body 51 cm., 20", normally to be played downwards, c);

tenor (body 66 cm., 29", G); baritone (body 86 cm. (34"), 10 cm. (4") bigger than a cello, C); and two basses tuned in fourths (A' and E'). And above the violin, a soprano (c') and a treble (body under 28.5 cm. (11"), like a quarter-size violin but tuned an octave above the violin, g'). The actual string-lengths of the instruments are not necessarily in strict proportion to body-length but are adjusted to playing demands. Their total effect in music arranged for them is said to be stupendous, offering immense possibilities for string music of the future— and perhaps even of the past: a cellist is reported to have said, after testing the new baritone, that here at last was something which he could pit against the modern piano in a trio, provided that he could manage so large an instrument. (The enterprise was first described by Mrs Hutchins in the *Scientific American*, Nov. 1962.)

Nelson 1972; Riley 1980.

Viola bastarda. A name first met in Italy near the end of the 16th century, apparently for a bass *viol of less than full size and tuned in various ways for specializing in playing *divisions. *Praetorius shows some tunings, using fourths and fifths, bringing octave intervals between many strings. He further identifies the term with English *lyra viol, perhaps a mistake through hearsay.

Viola da braccio (It., 'on the arm'). Renaissance period term for a member of the *violin family or *viole da braccio* in distinction from the *viol family or *viole da gamba; the bass of the violins (later the *cello) was thus '*basso di viole da braccio*' although of course necessarily held 'on the legs'. During the 17th century in Italy 'da braccio' was dropped leaving 'viola' in its present sense of the middle instrument of the family. Germany took the opposite course, dropping 'viola' and adopting 'da braccio', familiarly '*Bratsche*', likewise specifically for the *viola.

Viola da gamba (It., 'viol held on the legs'). The bass viol; or in the plural, *viole da gamba*, the *viol family as a whole, as see above.

Viola d'amore. Eighteenth-century bowed instrument, now numerous in collections. Held like a *viola and of roughly similar size, it often has a wavy ('festooned') outline and wavy ('flame') soundholes (Pl. I), and no frets. The six or seven gut strings are generally tuned to a common chord such as D major (or in one of six concertos by Vivaldi, D minor) to make special use of chord-playing in the key of the piece. Beneath these strings run the same or twice that number of wire *sympathetic strings, passing under the fingerboard and tuned to choice, for instance to the scale of the music. Many wrote for it, especially through the first third of the century in Italy and Germany, e.g. Bach in the St John Passion and cantatas nos. 36c, 152, 205 (see Terry 1932, ch. 6). Later concertos and sonatas are by Carl Stamitz and others, well after which some were still playing it: Meyerbeer includes it in *Les Huguenots* (1836), the part played by Crétien Urhan (see VIOLA, 4*b*), and even much later Charpentier in *Louise* (1900), followed in four years by Puccini in *Madame Butterfly* (offstage at the end of Act 2 in unison with the hidden voices). Such parts are usually now played on the viola; but a modern school of players, chiefly in Germany, has led to further use of the viola d'amore by Janáček (*Katyá Kabanová*, 1921), Hindemith (solo works), Prokofiev (*ad libitum* in *Romeo and Juliet*, 1938), and others. In Britain, its chief exponent and historian has been Harry Danks.

Pl. 1. Viola d'amore by Johann Paul Schorn (Salzburg, 1712), the type with 14 sympathetic strings.

Mozart's father, Leopold, names it along with an 'Englisches Violett'. This, with up to 16 sympathetic strings, has since often been identified with some rather large instruments usually with festooned body. Why 'English' is not known, though England seems to have been connected with the appearance of a slightly earlier five-stringed bowed instrument

tuned to a common chord; compare CITHER VIOL, a later 18th-century instrument.

Danks 1976.

Viola da spalla. Early name sometimes given to the *cello in Italy and Germany up to the mid-18th century, apparently referring to a band passed over the right shoulder to support the instrument instead of grasping it between the knees, or for playing standing. An early mention in Italy, as *violoncello da spalla moderna* (Bismantova 1677), gives for it an old, awkward diatonic cello fingering (1, 2, and 3, making a tone followed by a semitone. ('Primo Violino di spalla', on the other hand, means today in Italian opera houses the leader of the orchestra, often raised above the rest on a small dais beside the conductor.)

Viola de arame (Port., 'wire-strung guitar'). In the Azores the popular metal-strung *guitar, made in several forms.

Viola di bordoni. See BARYTON.

Viola pomposa. An early 18th-century name met in Germany and apparently borne by two kinds of instruments, both with five strings. One (the larger) was like a large viola with deep sides (a good 6 cm. (12½'') deep in an example of 1720 by Hoffman of Leipzig) and, with the aid of overspun strings, tuned like a cello plus a high *e'* string. It was once mistakenly said to have been 'invented by Bach' (compare the violoncello piccolo, see CELLO, 6*c*). The other (smaller) was like a smallish viola, tuned as a viola plus a high *e''* string (thus an octave above the other kind) and known equally as *violino pomposo*. It has a part in two works by Telemann and one by J. C. Graun, in each case beside a flute. No actual example answering to this latter type seems to be known.

Violetta. In the 18th century a name for the *viola (for 'Englisches Violett' see viola d'amore). Earlier, *violette* was in Italy a name for the violin family (see *viola da braccio*), as in 'violette senza tasti', 'without frets', i.e. not *viols (Lanfranco 1533).

Violin (Fr.: *violon*; Ger.: *Violine, Geige*; It.: *violino*; Ru.: *skripka*; Sp.: *violín*; the familiar name 'fiddle' being frequently used even by violinists and connoisseurs when speaking of the violin). The violin has for four centuries excelled in practically everything, from solo and chamber music at its greatest heights to folk dances. And beside its supreme qualities as a solo instrument, it has the rare capacity to be combined in large numbers to produce sounds equally captivating, without which the orchestra would never have come into being. Yet, familiar as it is, and despite ceaseless investigation, the violin remains to a great degree acoustically inexplicable: it may well continue forever to hold its mystery as a marvel of the wood-carver's art.

1. *The body.* The essence of the violin is the bulging soundbox, on average 35.6 cm. (14″) long, which converts the bowed string vibration into violin sound via the bridge.

(a) *Construction.* As with many other stringed instruments, the front, or 'belly', is made from two pieces of spruce joined together, and for the violin these are from a single thick wedge hewn from the tree in such a way that the grain will match identically on either side. After carving and planing the arching, the thickness of the belly will be some 3 mm. in the middle area, diminishing towards the sides. The back is carved from maple, joined in the same fashion, or sometimes from one piece (which can be handsome but does not in itself necessarily add to the value). The thin sides or ribs, of maple bent by heat, are shaped round a wooden mould (a number of such moulds for assembling violins, violas, and cellos are preserved from workshops of the old Italian makers including Stradivari). Strength is gained from the top and bottom blocks inside the body (Pl. 1, and see STRINGED INSTRU-MENTS, 3) and from a small block at each of the four corners, and by lining the ribs with narrow strips (side linings) for the belly and back to be glued to them.

The purfling round the edges of the violin is usually of black-dyed pear with white poplar between (or in cheaper instruments it is inked). The suggestion has been offered that where tone improves with age, one cause is that the glue in the purfling has disintegrated through desiccation to a degree that brings added flexibility of the belly towards the edges. The effect of the varnish upon tone is, however, usually very much overrated. Oil varnish gains in becoming integrated with the wood, while it dries very slowly, whereas spirit varnish dries immediately but has the defect that it shows up every scratch.

(b) *Body outline.* Varying though the shape may be even among instruments by the same master, it is at once clear to the eye that none of the major curves of the outline are simple arcs from start to finish. Each is generally composed of three arcs of different radius and centred at different points inside and outside the outline. Altogether, including those that form the out-pointing corners, there may be some 12 different arcs (on each side). See Fig. 1, a Stradivari of 1703, taken from a recent two-dimensional analysis (Coates 1985) of selected violins (and of viols and other instruments) by great makers from Andrea Amati (the violin with 1564 on the label, Hill *collection, Oxford) to Nicolò, Amati, and Stradivari. Arrows mark where a curve meets another of different radius.

2. *Neck and fittings.* The neck and the scroll, this last a form of Ionic volute, are carved from maple, the neck being mortised (or in older days nailed) to the top block. The little semicircle at the root of the neck, visible from the back, is the 'button'. Fingerboard, tailpiece, and pegs are now usually of ebony. The tailpiece is held to the tailpin at the base of the instrument by a loop of gut. The bridge, of maple, is placed between the nicks of the soundholes, or *f*-holes, and presents a sloping face, slightly curved on the fingerboard side but

Pl. 1. Violin, belly detached to show interior: *left*, the belly showing the bass-bar; *right*, back and sides, showing top block, bottom block, corner blocks, and side linings.

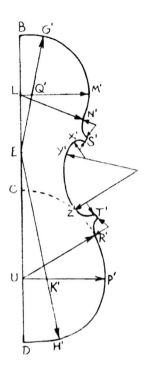

Fig. 1.

damping effect which eradicates any hollow 'echo-ing' sound when the strings are bowed—though at the same time reducing the sound when they are plucked to the dry snap of the *pizzicato. Second, for the vibration from the bowed strings to be distributed in an optimum manner, also to increase strength under the string pressure, the bass-bar (Pl. 1, left), also of pine, is glued lengthwise beneath the other (G-string side) foot of the bridge.

4. *Violin-makers*. Table 1 lists some of the major Italian makers through the greatest period, in order of the year, or approximate year, of their deaths. The cities where they worked were favourable in climate for seasoning wood and not distant from the southern slopes of the alps whence came the slow-growing spruce so essential to the craft; and they had good access to the trade with the East, whence came the gums for making varnish. Cremona figures the most prominently, beginning with Andrea Amati (born before 1511, d. 1570-1), whom many believe to have first achieved the basic form of the violin; and his sons, the 'Brothers Amati', Antonio and Girolamo (d. 1630), father of Nicolò. From Nicolò Amati's workshop came Andrea Guarneri, great-uncle of the celebrated Guiseppe Guarneri 'del Gesu', rated by many the equal of Stradivari. In Brescia, born some 30 years after the first Amati, was Gasparo da Salò (d. 1607), and his pupil Paolo Maggini (d. 1632).

perpendicular on the tailpiece side. Fingerboard and bridge are often referred to in playing instruments ('sur la touche', etc.; see below, 5c), so violinists are familiar with their names in other languages: fingerboard—Fr.: *touche*, Ger.: *Griffbrett*, It.: *tastiera* or *tasto*; bridge—Fr.: *chevalet*, Ger.: *Steg*, It.: *ponticello*.

The actual forms of the neck and fittings date from late in the 18th century when makers in Paris found how to 'modernize' the violin to keep up with the demands of advancing techniques (below, 7). Every older violin of value then became, or has been since, refitted in these respects—save where the original pegbox and scroll have been skilfully grafted on to the new neck, a quite different neck from that originally provided by the Amatis, Stradivari, and their contemporaries.

3. *Soundpost, bass-bar*. Two vital internal components (again, neither of them now exactly as they originally were on the older instruments). The bridge of a violin bears on the soundboard in an asymmetric manner. First is the soundpost, a round stick of pine wedged between belly and back just to the tailpiece side of the treble (E-string side) foot of the bridge, its exact position and tightness being very critical. The belly at this point, partially deprived of vibration by the soundpost, then forms a kind of fulcrum for the bridge to rock upon, making the other foot of the bridge do most of the work in communicating vibration. It also exerts a

TABLE I.

Death date		Place of work
1684	Nicolò Amati	Cremona
c. 1695	Francesco Rugeri	Cremona
1698	Andrea Guarneri	Cremona
c. 1705	Giovanni-Battista Rogeri	Brescia
1710	Giovanni-Battista Grancino (i)	Milan
1720	Pietro Giovanni Guarneri	Cremona
c. 1720	Carlo Giuseppe Testore	Milan
c. 1730	Giacinto and Vincenzo Ruggeri (Rugeri)	Cremona
1735	Giovanni-Battista Grancino (ii)	Milan
c. 1735	Alessandro Gagliano	Naples
1737	Antonio Stradivari	Cremona
c. 1739	Giuseppe Giovanni Guarneri (son of Andrea)	Cremona
1742	Matteo Goffriller	Venice
1744	Giuseppe Guarneri ('del Gesù')	Cremona
1747	Carlo Bergonzi	Cremona
1748	Lorenzo Guadagnini	Piacenza
1750	Domenico Montagnana	Venice
c. 1758	Santo Serafin	Venice
1762	Pietro Guarneri	Venice
c. 1775	Carlo Ferdinando Landolfi	Milan
c. 1780	Gennaro Gagliano	Naples
c. 1780	Nicolò Gagliano	Naples
1786	Giovanni-Battista Guadagnini	mainly Turin
c. 1800	Lorenzo Storioni	Cremona
c. 1818	Giovanni-Battista Ceruti	Cremona

Antonio Stradivari (b. ?1644, d. 1737) first worked, up to the mid-1660s, with Nicolò Amati (1596–1684). On this account he is often named as one of Amati's celebrated pupils. Some 650 instruments have been ascribed to him and are believed to exist today—mainly violins, with perhaps 16 violas and 50 cellos, and a few instruments of other kinds such as two guitars. He developed his designs through stages recognizable to the connoisseur, achieving his classic violin form by c.1700. Many of his instruments are known by the names of past owners, for example, among the violins, the 'Hellier' (1679), the 'Betts' (1704), the 'Alard' (1715), and the 'Sarasate' (1724).

Why do his violins so excel? Modern wave-analyses of his and of other fine old Italian violins have certainly exhibited optimum characteristics for tone and response. Age is not a major factor: Stradivari's reputation was of international stature in his lifetime. His selection of materials is not exceptional. A craftsman's genius, self-critically applied through the years, can best account for his pre-eminence. It has, however, been proposed that historical fortune has been on his side, inasmuch as he arched the violin body less than was common at the time, and that when the instruments later came to be altered (new necks etc.: see below, 7a) the 'Strads' answered to the process particularly well. Among his children, two sons, Francesco and Omobono, continued together in the craft to their deaths six or so years after their father's.

The outstanding master outside Italy up to those times is the Austrian, Jakob Stainer (d. 1683), of Absam in the Tyrol. The great Italian school was led into the 19th century by Pressenda and Rocca, both of Turin; but by that time the market was coming to be dominated by the French makers, Nicolas Lupot (d. 1824), F.-L. Pique (d. 1822), C. F. Gand (d. 1845), all famous today. Among the older English makers were especially Benjamin Banks (of Salisbury, d. 1795), and John Betts (d. 1823), followed by J. F. Lott (d. 1871).

Instruments by such makers, above all Stradivari and Giuseppe Guarneri del Gesù, have been copiously copied in violins advertised as 'copy of' or 'after' while sent out with a label inside bearing the name of the master with no such qualification. No old violin seriously suspected of being a genuine original can pass without certification by a firm of recognized experts. The finest examples, as they come on the market, often continue like other great works of art to fall into the hands of collectors, and at a price; one famous 'Strad' sold for £25 in 1794, went for £12,000 in 1954, and might fetch 40 times that today (and a cello no less, or even more). The great demand for Italian violins of the 18th century as playing instruments has no doubt been because they proved to be best adaptable for use in large halls. The earlier instruments tend to sound softer and sweeter, which is why, at the beginning of the 19th century, the high-arched models of Nicolò Amati fetched the highest prices of all.

To meet the huge demand for violins, cheaper instruments have long been produced on the lines of cottage industry—'outworkers' each specializing in some particular component—as in Mirecourt in the Vosges, Mittenwald in Bavaria, and Mark-neukirchen in Saxony; also (from about the 1860s) in factories inferior violins numbering up to tens of thousands a year are assembled with the front and back pressed out by machine (not the same as arching the front first by bending the two pieces of wood, hints of which have been observed among violins by the greatest old masters (Lolov 1984, and see VIOL, 2).

Yet violin-making on the highest plane is far from being in decline: a violinist or connoisseur would continue the above summary Table through the 19th century and into the 20th with names that are now very highly thought of. Modern makers will spend three years at one of the violin-making schools that exist in many countries, Britain and the USA included, and become capable of producing exact and worthy copies of the old masters. Violins are also made in smaller sizes for children, down to 'quarter size' (with body-length up to 30 cm. or 1'), and even smaller for the Japanese Suzuki method of teaching (after Shinichi Suzuki, 1948–81), in which children are taught from the age of two, with fiddles down to 'sixteenth' size and bows to match.

5. *Violin-playing: (a) Strings.* The four strings are tuned in fifths: *e''* (first string), *a'*, *d'*, and *g* (fourth string). In Stradivari's day, and up to the end of the 19th century, they were of gut, with a metal-overwound G string. Today one is most likely to find a steel E string, and the A and D of gut wound with aluminium and the G overwound with silver wire. But strings with a roped steel or nylon core covered with steel ribbon are also in use. Steel strings, higher tensioned than gut, are not successfully tuned by the pegs alone, so require screw attachments ('fine tuners' or 'adjusters') on the tailpiece (see also MUTE). On the relative merits of gut and steel opinions vary. Gut can be ideal when playing the earlier music, especially using the older types of bow, whereas in later music, requiring the most movement of the left hand, gut can become rough on the fingers and, with the modern bow, give less carrying power.

The violin is placed against the collarbone or shoulder and gripped there by the chin against the chin rest (a device which much surprised French audiences when Spohr introduced it—then a very small one—in 1819). The instrument is supported from below by anything from a small pad to a large wooden frame (shoulder rest). This is to prevent the fiddle drooping towards the floor and to leave the left hand free from supporting it.

(b) Fingering (see separately for *harmonics). The fingering is basically diatonic, e.g. on the G string,

index finger for A and the little finger D, the same note as the next open string above. For semitones the appropriate finger is shifted up or down the fingerboard. For notes higher than *b''* (little finger on the E string in first position) the whole hand must be shifted to a higher position, such as the third (index finger on A), and so on. This, and the return shifts, make one reason for securing the instrument with the chin for the hand to move freely. Needless to say, since the distances between fingers diminish as the string is shortened, the difficulties of learning to play in tune are formidable, the violin, unlike most other kinds of musical instrument, offering no ready-made guide to the fingers. Higher positions concern the lower strings too, whether to bring a passage better under the fingers, or for the sake of the different sounds produced by the different strings: hence, for example, the instruction 'sul G' or 'sulla 4ᵃ', meaning the whole passage should be played on this string, not proceeding to the next as might be the normal thing to do. Vibrato too is easier if the hand is free—a movement of the left hand or forearm, causing the stopping finger to roll without moving from its place, but causing a fluctuation in pitch which may amount to an eighth of a tone each way. Double-stopping is possible in intervals up to a tenth, or more if the lower note be an open string. In chords played across more than two strings no more than two of the notes can be properly sustained with the bow, and this applies with the polyphonic lines implied in Bach's sonatas for solo violin (Ex. 1). Chords on three or four strings can also be held by the left-hand fingers while the notes are sounded one after another in broken chords (arpeggiando), detached or slurred.

Ex. 1. Bach, Partita II, Chaconne, bars 88–9.

(c) *Bowing.* It is in no sense derogatory to the violin's musical powers to recall how in times before recording and broadcasting the audience at a solo performance was held perpetually alert through eyes riveted upon the movements of the violinist's bow. In sound, the immense variety in tone and effect comes through combination of bow speed and interruption of the speed through the pressure of the right first finger on the stick, and the distance of the bow from the bridge.

The *bow is drawn across the strings with the stick leaning slightly away from the bridge (i.e. further from the bridge than the hair). Where there is reason to indicate the direction of the bow, ⊓ marks a 'down bow' (to the player's right) and V an 'up bow'. 'In the same bow' means that the notes are played in the same stroke; 'separate bows' means that they are played up and down (or vice versa). 'On the string' means that the bow

is not lifted between notes; 'off the string' means that it is. The following are among the principal bowings.

legato (It.): slurred notes, played smoothly, on the string (and including the most difficult of all strokes to perfect, where a note is to be continued through a change of bow).

detaché (Fr.): non-legato 'on the string'.

martelé (Fr.; It.: *martellato,* the 'hammered' stroke): for staccato (in separate bows or, if the music has dots under a slur, in one bow); made by pressure and quick release of the first finger on the stick at the beginning of each stroke, and done in the upper half of the bow.

sautillé (Fr.; It.: *saltato, saltellato*): a very fast staccato that comes when playing on the string at the middle of the bow, at a point where the spring of the stick causes the bow to bounce without being lifted by the hand.

spiccato (It.): a bouncing staccato 'off the string', nearer to the nut and lifting the bow between notes.

portato (It.; used especially where there are lines under a slur over the notes): a light articulation by pressure and release of the first finger without halting the bow; also used for notes repeated in one bow, and occasionally in scale passages (Ex. 2).

Ex. 2.

All the violin music up to the Classical period can be played with above uses of the bow, and within a compass of somewhat over four octaves. Then, in the 19th century, virtuoso performers from Paganini onwards brought in a number of tricks.

'Flying staccato' (Fr.: *jeté*): notes played many to a bow using its natural bounce (therefore not at the heel).

Ricochet bowings: the bow dropped on to the string and allowed to rebound slowly or fast—often used in arpeggiando figures or up and down arpeggios.

Left-hand pizzicato in descending passages: plucking with the finger next above the stopping one (marked if necessary by +).

Combination of pizzicato and glissando where the left-hand finger slides up or down from the stopped note to rest on another note before the sound dies away (marked by *pizz.* under a slur, and since used with great effect by Bartók).

Tremolo (tremolando): a very fast shaking at the point of the bow, effected in several ways.

Sul ponticello (It.): played close to the bridge, for a thinner quality of sound. *Sul tasto* (It.; Fr.: *sur la touche*) over the fingerboard, for a dulled quality.

6. *Earlier violin history:* (a) *Early violins.* (For a note on violin predecessors, see FIDDLE.) One of the earliest pictures—before the instrument assumed the classic form of an Amati—is in a wall-painting at Ferrara dated as early as 1505–8 (illustrated in Remnant 1989), about the time when Andrea Amati was born. The corners do not yet stick out far, the bridge is placed far below the *f*-holes (as if not yet a soundpost), and there are probably three strings; the great Italian collector Count Salabue (d. 1840) left a rather vague account of an Amati dated 1546 still with three strings. Four strings are described 10 years later than this, in France (Jambe-de-Fer 1556), with particular reference to the violin band of the French court (see ORCHESTRA, 4), playing for dances and ballets. The English court also had one, first manned by Italians. At Munich a smaller team of seven **viole da braccio* (violin family) played during dinner, their leader performing on the violin florid **divisions* 'with such sweetness and clarity that all who hear give pride of place to that instrument' (Trojano 1569).

A humble illustration of the popularity quickly won by the violin as an instrument for day-to-day music, especially for dancing, is a manuscript of *c*.1600, at Nuremberg, a collection of cheerful well-known tunes written out in four-line **tablature*, with numbers for the left-hand fingers. The Tudor 'country dances', whatever their origins may have been, by the time of Playford's collection *The English Dancing Master* in the mid-17th century, are purely violin music, not at all comfortable for any other non-keyboard instrument to play. The tunes travelled round the country, and correspondingly (some the same tunes) in the Low Countries and Scandinavia until every community across northern Europe had its fiddler (in France, 'violonneux') playing at feasts and weddings, eventually to leave a corpus of violin-inspired folk music almost comparable in bulk to that of the concert hall, along with memories of renowned players like Neil Gow (1729–97) of Scotland.

(b) *Violinist–composers of the Baroque.* Nearly all from Italy, a few of the early names are of 'stunt' men, Farina, and Biagio Marini, both also performing in Germany, and (with published works from 1617 onwards) entertaining audiences with successions of double-stops, hitting the strings with the bow-stick **'col legno'*, and 'programme' effects like bird and animal imitations (ever since a stock-in-trade encore of popular fiddlers everywhere—trivial no doubt, yet what other musical instrument has the capacity to do it?).

On the serious level, the great Italian school of composing for the violin rose after the mid-century

with Corelli to become its most renowned and in his day successful figure. He and his compatriots played with a bow (see BOW, Fig. 1c) suited to *cantabile* expression as the contemporary French bow, up to several inches shorter and held differently (thumb under the hair), was suited to music in dance forms. The English too had been playing in the French way until the Italian, Matteis, taught them 'to hold the bow by the wood only and not to touch the hair which was no small reformation' (North *c*.1728). Some 'folk' fiddling, however, has escaped this reform; a player may still be seen playing with the violin held low against the chest in the early manner and the bow perhaps held in this old way.

A great bonus for performance study are some ornamented versions of slow movements from Corelli's sonatas Op. 5, published by Estienne Roger in Amsterdam near the end of the composer's life: not personally by Corelli, but 'as he played them', with very fast slurred runs of many notes, decorating the plain melody of the original. Two well-known Corelli pupils are Geminiani, who settled in London where he wrote *The Art of Playing on the Violin* (1751, five years before Leopold Mozart's even more informative *Versuch*); and Locatelli, who settled in Amsterdam and is noted for the extreme technical fireworks in his music published as *L'arte del violino* (1733). Tartini in Padua left another notable contribution from this period in his *Arte dell'arco* (1758).

7. *The modern violin:* (a) *The new neck and fittings.* In Paris by the 1780s François Tourte had finally created the modern violin bow (see BOW, 2), making possible stronger attacks and strokes that depend on elasticity of the stick in a different way from previously (e.g. *martelé*; see above, 5c). For stronger string resistance to bow pressure, the bridge height was increased by some 5 mm., and the angle of the strings over it by up to eight degrees. With the original form of the neck with its upper surface lying in a straight line with the soundbox (Pl. 2a), the fingerboard was canted up by an inserted wedge. To avoid need for a thicker wedge to match a higher bridge (which would make the neck-plus-fingerboard awkwardly thick, hampering fingering, especially on the lower strings) the new form of neck—not entirely new, since one meets it on some older bass viols—slopes backwards, needing no wedge for the fingerboard, and brings the level of the nut just below that of the belly (Pl. 2b). The neck is also a little longer. Then, to support the greater down-bearing, and the more so when playing-pitches had started to rise, the old bass-bar was by degrees replaced by a longer and deeper one.

Who instigated the change, which practically every old instrument has undergone (including, as far as is known, every violin by Stradivari), has proved very difficult to establish, save that it began in Paris. In 1794 Nicolas Lupot had come there

(a)

(b)

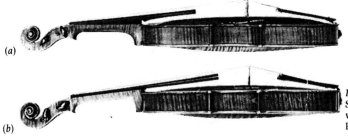

Pl. 2. (a) violin by Jacob Stainer, 1668; (b) modern violin by J. B. Vuillaume, Paris, 1867.

(from Orléans) to work at first with Pique, and these two, probably in conjunction with other leading luthiers of the city at that time, were very likely the first to refit and to build violins with the new neck and fittings. Both makers had, unusually for their time, shown a particular interest in the models of Stradivari with relatively flat (low-arched) plates, and these were found (Skeaping 1955) to respond best to the alterations and do justice to the recent technical advances due to Viotti (below, who himself had left Paris for London two years previously); the modern special fame of Stradivari could be said to date from this time.

(b) *Viotti and after.* Jean-Baptiste Viotti (1752–1824), born in Italy, came to Paris in 1782. 'The father of modern violin-playing', he had advanced teaching principles which met increasingly difficult expectations without losing the best in the old Italian tradition. He occupies a place of extra-ordinary importance in the master–pupil chains of great soloists up to the present time. Himself a great-grand-pupil (as it were) of Corelli, via Pugnani, he taught, to name but one, Pierre Rode (d. 1830) of France, acclaimed in every Continental capital, and from whom the line continues to no less than Joachim (for whom Brahms wrote his Violin Concerto), Auer (founder of the great Russian school), Heifetz, and Menuhin, each of whom has in turn unfolded fresh aspects of style, technique, and repertory. A recording by Joachim, perhaps the oldest in existence of past great players, of a Brahms Hungarian dance strikes one not only with its small use of vibrato but with its considerable amount of portamento, common enough until (it has been said) soloists developed a distaste for it as they increasingly heard themselves on records. But this is also partly fashion: connoisseurs of solo violin-playing say that there have been at least five recognizable changes in style during the 20th century.

As always, difficult things that a great player can do are likely to appear in a contemporary concerto. Beethoven's Violin Concerto abounds with passages that can be found in solo pieces by Viotti, Rode, and their contemporary, Kreutzer—for example the very opening two bars of the solo part. The concerto was, in fact, first performed by Franz Clement, who had been a child prodigy and gave Beethoven advice on the part. It is touching—

and in a way in keeping with violin's demon powers—that having given his fine performance of one of the greatest musical works of all time, and with improvised cadenzas included, he should have entertained the audience in the second half of the concert by playing a piece with the violin held upside down.

(c) *Baroque revival.* Modern reconstruction on original lines commenced around 1930 in Germany, and now and then an unaltered violin comes to light—though its value for performance will naturally depend on whether it is anyhow a good instrument or not. Some feel today that when the instrument is restored to its original lightness of stringing and played with a bow equally light of the older kind, then learning the violin becomes a pleasure from the very beginning, a harsh sound well-nigh impossible.

8. *Repertory:* (a) *Baroque.* From Italy come four sets of trio sonatas and one set with cello by Corelli; some sonatas and the famous but doubtfully attributed Chaconne of T. A. Vitali; numerous solo violin concertos from Vivaldi, of which Op. 8, *Il cimento dell'armonia*, contains the *Four Seasons*, and also concertos for two, three, and four violins and sonatas for one or two. Other sonatas include those by Geminiani, F. M. Veracini, and, especially, Locatelli and Tartini (two books, including the 'Devil's Trill' Sonata).

From other countries, notably Purcell's Sonata in G minor and his two sets of sonatas with two violins (including No. 9 in F, the 'Golden Sonata'); Bach's two concertos for solo violin, in A minor and E major respectively, and his Double Violin Concerto in D minor, six solo sonatas (partitas), two with continuo, and six sonatas with harpsichord (*Klavier*); some sets of sonatas for one or two violins (or other instruments) by Handel; Telemann's sonatas and sonatinas; and Leclair's sonatas.

(b) *Classical.* Haydn wrote perhaps three violin concertos and a sonata in G; Mozart six concertos, the Rondo K. 373, the *Sinfonia concertante* in E♭ (see VIOLA, 4), and 34 sonatas; Beethoven the Violin Concerto, Op. 61, two Romances, Op. 40 and Op. 50, the Triple Concerto, and sonatas including Op. 23 in A minor, Op. 24 in F (the 'Spring' Sonata), the three sonatas of Op. 30, Op. 47 in A (the 'Kreutzer' Sonata), and Op. 96 in G. Paganini's 24

Caprices are well known for their display of violin technique. Schubert wrote four sonatas and the *Rondo brillante*, Mendelssohn the Violin Concerto in E minor and four sonatas, and De Bériot some 10 violin concertos.

(c) *Romantic and 20th-century.* The following are some of the best-known works over this period, proceeding in order of composers' births. Vieuxtemps, concertos, etc.; Franck, Violin Sonata in A; Lalo, *Concerto russe* and *Symphonie espagnole*; Brahms, Violin Concerto, Double Concerto, three sonatas, Op. 78, Op. 100, Op. 108; Saint-Saëns, concertos and sonatas; H. Wieniawski, Violin Concerto in D minor, fantasies, etc.; Bruch, three concertos, including the well-known one in G minor; Tchaikovsky, Violin Concerto in D; Dvořák, Violin Concerto in A minor, Sonata in F; Grieg, three sonatas; Fauré, Violin Sonata in E minor, Op. 108; Janáček, sonatas; Chausson, *Poème*; Elgar, Violin Concerto in B minor, Sonata in E minor; Debussy, Violin Sonata in G minor; Delius, sonatas; Glazunov, two concertos; Sibelius, Violin Concerto in D minor; Vaughan Williams, *The Lark Ascending*; Schoenberg, Phantasy, Op. 47; Kreisler, many works; Ireland, two sonatas; Bartók, Violin Sonata for unaccompanied violin, several duos, two sonatas with piano; Enesco, sonatas; Stravinsky, Violin Concerto in D; Szymanowski, two concertos, sonatas; Webern, Four Pieces, Op. 7; Berg, Violin Concerto; Prokofiev, two concertos, two sonatas; Hindemith, Violin Concerto, sonatas; Walton, Violin Concerto; Messiaen, Theme and Variations, *Fantaisie*. In other solo genres, the jazz violin of Stephane Grappelli (b. 1908) is as fresh as ever.

9. *Some violin variants* (see also HARDANGER FIDDLE; KIT; STROH VIOLIN; VIOLINO PICCOLO).

(a) *Experimental models.* From early in the 19th century, at first mainly in Paris, there have been experimental designs of violin quite different in shape from the normal, yet claimed to produce good violin sound. Among them a more or less triangular design by Chanot and the acoustician Savart (1791–1841) is not forgotten inasmuch as models of this type have had a limited revival for the making of fiddles by school children.

For the 'New Violin Family' recently brought out in America, see VIOLA, 6.

(b) *Mute violin.* Made up to the 19th century for practising the violin without disturbing people in the house: usually like a violin but without the back, and with no sides save for a small portion to support the neck.

Boyden 1965, 1980; Campbell 1980; Coates 1985; Heron-Allen 1885; Hill 1902; Mozart 1756; Nelson 1972; Skeaping 1955; Walls 1984; Witten 1982. *Dictionaries of Violin Makers*: Jalovec 1968; Lütgendorff 1958; Stainer 1896; Vannes 1951.

Violino piccolo. Occasionally named in German baroque works. A cantata by J. Michael Bach, an older cousin of J. S. Bach, names a 'Quart Violino, non di grosso grande' ('not of big size') tuned, as the transposition of the part shows, a fourth above the violin. Bach himself writes for violino piccolo in the First Brandenburg Concerto, here tuned a minor third above the violin. Nowadays a three-quarter size violin is sometimes used. For the problem of Monteverdi's use of the term, see KIT, 1.

Violoncello. See CELLO, and for 'violoncello piccolo', CELLO, 6b.

Violone. Originally in 16th-century Italy a general name for a *viol, or by the end of that century a bass viol, particularly one of larger size and deeper tuning. A fine original instrument (Vienna *collection) of 1585, by the Venetian maker Ventura Linarol, in shape broadly resembles other Venetian viols of the period; height 173 cm. (68", some 10 cm. less than an average double bass), body 100 cm. (40"). It is one of the instruments that have been much copied as a violone for *continuo playing, serving also for the parts for 'Great Dooble Base' in nine of Orlando Gibbons's fantasias for viols, here written down to low A'.

Through the Baroque period in Germany, 'Violone' signified a double bass, of whatever the model or size it might be (see DOUBLE BASS, 5b). These features primarily distinguish 'violone', in today's usage, from the ordinary four-stringed double bass, except in so far as the violone might be a conversion from an older bass of some smaller size.

In Italian music of the Baroque, 'Violone' generally means the early form of cello (Bonta 1977; see CELLO, 4b). In large-scale performance with many instruments the part would be played also on the deeper instrument, in Italy *Contrabasso* or *Violone grande* (double bass), or there is a separate part for each (as in Germany there may be separate parts correspondingly for *Violoncello* and *Violone*).

Virginal. Keyboard instrument with the same plucking action as a harpsichord and spinet, by small plectra mounted in jacks (see HARPSICHORD, 2); and in shape either rectangular, c.150 cm. long (about 5', Pl. 1) or polygonal (Pl. 2). The strings, one for each note, run parallel with the keyboard with the longest strings nearest (see SPINET, Fig. 1, for comparison of the layouts of virginal and spinet: the latter also singly strung but distinctively different in most other respects, and with the longest strings farthest from the keyboard). A virginal has proved again today, as it did through the 16th century and much of the 17th, a valuable domestic instrument, taking up little room, and strong in sound, partly because the soundboard can lie across practically the whole instrument, allowing the nut (N in SPINET, Fig. 1c) as well as the bridge to be placed on a resonant area.

Pl. 1. Virginal by Stephen Keene (London, 1668).

The name 'virginal', still unexplained, has not to do with the 'Virgin Queen': it is the oldest known name on the Continent, already met in a treatise of c.1460 by Paulirinus, a native of Prague. Before the modern revival of the instrument the name was familiar to most through the important late 16th- to early 17th-century collections of English music known as 'Virginal Books' (below, 4), in which connection it must be remembered that 'virginal' in that period equally meant a harpsichord.

1. *Polygonal forms*. Known from the 1510s, these are characteristically Italian, made in cypress wood ('Queen Elizabeth's Virginal', in the Victoria and Albert Museum, London, is polygonal, judged to be Venetian of c.1570). The outline, eliminating the two rear corners of the basic rectangle, has five or six sides with the keyboard projecting in front; older examples have an outer case, which, rectangular, leaves space at the rear corners for boxes (for tuning implements, spare wire, etc.), the whole placed on a stand or on a table for playing (RENAISSANCE INSTRUMENTS, Pl. 1). The oldest exist-

ing Flemish example is of 1548, by Karest (Brussels *collection). Today, kits are available, equally for rectangular models.

2. *Rectangular forms*. The most typical product of the Flemish makers (for the celebrated Ruckers family see HARPSICHORD, 7b) and then of the English (surviving instruments dated 1641–71, e.g. by John Player, and Stephen Keene, who both afterwards turned to spinets). The front of the case reaches forward on each side of the keyboard, making a continuous straight line along the front (a 'recessed' keyboard) with room on the left for a box, and on the right more space for the bass end of the bridge. Flemish compass is four octaves, C–c′′′, with (originally) bass *short octave (whereas Italian may reach up to f′′′); English: a complete bass octave, or else the deeper short octave starting on low G′ (Pl. 1).

Frequent among the Ruckers virginals is the type later called in Flemish *muselar* (examples from 1581). The keyboard, instead of being placed almost

Pl. 2. Virginal ('polygonal spinet') by Antegnati (Brescia, 1537) (jack rail removed to show the line of jacks).

centrally or somewhat to the left, is over to the right: the strings of the lower part of the compass are then plucked at a very considerable distance from the nut (around 33 per cent for the longest string) for the instrument to give an evenly mellow quality throughout, with strong fundamentals. Less frequent are the *spinett* models with the keyboard well to the left, to pluck the lower strings very much closer to the nut, giving the whole effect a more brittle, sparkling quality.

3. *Small virginals*. Both Italian and Flemish makers (virginals from France and Germany are very few) have also left half-size or 'ottavino' virginals sounding at 4' pitch, an octave above the normal: popular especially in Italy, as domestic instruments perhaps chiefly for accompanying the voice alone. The Flemish went further, in the 'mother and child' virginal, made from *c*.1580 onwards: the small virginal, the 'child' (marked by Ruckers, 'k', for *kind*), is housed in a compartment to the left (or right) of the main keyboard and can be played there; or it can be taken out and placed on top of the 'mother' for the jacks of this (the jack rail having been removed) to push up from below the inner ends of the key-levers of the child, for both to sound at once (in octaves), while still allowing the child to be played on its own.

4. *Virginal Books*. The following are the most important Virginal Books.

(a) *Fitzwilliam Virginal Book* (compiled 1609–19 by Francis Tregian, left to Cambridge University in 1816 by Viscount Fitzwilliam; once called 'Queen Elizabeth's Virginal Book' though she never owned it). Near 300 pieces, Bull, Byrd, and Farnaby predominating.

(b) *My Ladye Nevell's Booke* (1591, presented to Queen Elizabeth, and since in private ownership). Forty-two pieces, most by Byrd.

(c) *Will Forster's Virginal Book* (compiled by 1624). Seventy-eight pieces, again most by Byrd.

(d) *Benjamin Cosyn's Virginal Book* (no indication of date). Ninety-eight pieces, largely by Bull, Gibbons.

(e) *Parthenia* (1612). Printed (unlike the collections above). With 21 pieces by Bull, Byrd, and Gibbons.
See also HARPSICHORD.

Vocalion. See HARMONIUM, 3.

Voice flute. A recorder pitched in D below the treble: see RECORDER, 4.

Volynka (Ru.). See BAGPIPE, 5b.

Vox humana. 1. An organ *8' reed stop with short, wide resonators; or a tremulant stop in *American organs.

2. An 18th-century English name of the *tenor oboe.

W

Wagner tuba (in Ger. also *Ring-Tuba*). This is principally made for performance of the *Ring*, in which four are required: two *Tenortuben* in B♭ (with the pitch of the *baritone or B♭ horn) and two *Basstuben* in F (with the pitch of an F tuba or F horn). For their notation, see TRANSPOSING INSTRUMENTS.

The four instruments are built in the oval format (Pl. 1) common among German band instruments, with fairly wide bores and rotary valves. The mouth-pipe tapers to a narrow dimension in order to receive a horn mouthpiece, for the instruments are to be played, in the 'Ring', by four of the eight horn players, who change between horn and tuba as the parts instruct (the valves accordingly being given to the left hand). After Wagner, Bruckner uses the instruments in a similar manner in his last three symphonies; Richard Strauss, e.g. in *Elektra*; and Schoenberg, *Gurrelieder*.

Pl. 1. Wagner tuba (tenor in B♭) by Demusa, Markneukirchen.

It appears that soon after starting work on *Das Rheingold* in 1853 Wagner was shown the instruments (*saxhorns, presumably) recently produced in Paris by Sax and that these suggested to the composer (Westernhagen 1973) this masterly addition to his orchestral palette, with their effect which arrests the listener from their first entry (the opening of Scene 2 of *Das Rheingold*), where they solemnly announce no less than the 'Valhalla' theme itself.

It was hardly until the 1930s that most large opera houses outside Germany first procured genuine Wagner tubas (many from Alexander Bros., Mainz). Prior to this, in Britain the nearest equivalents among brass band instruments were employed; or in Paris (and the choice of Lamoureux) *cornophones*. These, introduced by Besson, 1880, were virtually saxhorns with the bell turned forwards, and are occasionally to be found in Britain as antiques, having once had a small fashion in *brass bands.

Wagon. See KOTO, 3.

Waji. Harp of the Kafir people of Nuristan in north-east Afghanistan; its name is from a very early Arabic word for a harp. It has attracted special attention from its ancient construction and method of playing. Four strings are tied between the two ends of a thick arched stick, which passes through two holes near the centre of the skin covering the roughly rectangular wooden sound-box. The older men pass it round to accompany their intoned narrations, one hand, with a plectrum, strumming all the strings (tuned over a cluster of deep notes about a tone apart) in a short, continually repeated rhythm, while the other hand damps one or two strings for these not to sound at that moment: a damping technique also characteristic among *lyres.

Waldhorn (Ger.). The orchestral *horn.

Waldteufel (Ger.). See FRICTION DRUM, 3.

Waldzither (or *Halszither*). See CITTERN, 5*b*.

Walking-stick instruments. Made in the 19th century for casual amusement and now antiques, the favourites were flutes or piccolos, with a single key made in wood to resemble a knot in the stick (and occasionally as a sword-stick). Others include clarinets, and violins (tubular, with the bow stored inside).

Washboard. See SCRAPER.

Water drum. Chiefly West African, a pail-sized receptacle containing water on which a smaller bowl (usually of a gourd) is floated upside-down and hit with a beater (e.g. a spoon) to make a knock and a drum-like boom as the water conducts away the vibrations of the trapped air. Somewhat different are American Indian membrane drums (e.g. 'Peyote drum') which are part-filled with water when played, to adjust the pitch and quality; these have also been described as 'water drum'. There is also, again in Africa, 'improvised' water-drumming: girls deftly smack on the river at night, making sounds like drumming (Central African Republic); or make in the ground small pits holding water, for smacking individually (Sudan).

Water organ. See HYDRAULIS.

West Indies. Drums proliferate in West Indian music, frequently played in pairs: while one instrument (the Jamaican *kbandu*, and the *boolay* of Trinidad and Tobago) sustains a basic rhythmic pattern, complex, syncopated rhythms are improvised on the other (the Jamaican 'playing cast' and the 'cutter' of Trinidad and Tobago). Many different sizes and shapes of drum are in use, ranging from the large bass drum associated with Rastafarian ritual to the East Indian *tassa* drum, a goatskin-covered clay or metal bowl. The drums are played with fingers, palms, and sticks of all kinds.

Among many other instruments: gourd and other rattles; the *steel band from Trinidad; bamboo instruments such as the *idiochord 'bamboo violin'; flutes, and the blowing tube *vaccine; improvised banjos and guitars (with the small *cuatro guitar); and the cowhorn *abeng* (Jamaica) played by the Maroons, descendants of slaves who escaped from the Spanish in the 17th century.

Whip. Percussion instrument, a type of *clapper, formerly the slapstick of the theatre drummer. It is made of two flat pieces of hardwood: one is generally longer, to form a handle; the other is hinged upon this at one end with a strong spring. A deft shake makes it strike on the other with a sound like the crack of a whip. An older form is of two identical boards hinged together, each with a grip for the fingers, but with a disadvantage in needing both hands. The whip appears in Mahler's Sixth Symphony and in many works since. It was probably first introduced in Vienna for comedy polkas (in which a real whip could be dangerous). Actual whip-cracking takes place in rural festivals in Central Europe, chiefly around the New Year, 'to drive winter away' with whips up to 6 m. (18′) long. See CLASSIFICATION, 4a.

Whistles and bird-calls. The familiar metal whistles in Fig. 1, *a* to *d*, each with an eye for the lanyard, all have antecedents over the world made in plant material or pottery.

1. *Disc whistles* (*a*). The once well-known Christmas cracker whistle, used also in singing kettles (those not with a *siren), is of two metal plates, each with

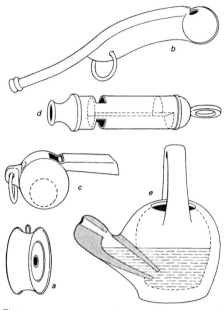

Fig. 1.

a hole in the centre, and separated by a space. Held between the lips, either blowing or sucking generates an 'edge-tone' at the hole opposite, rising in a 'wheep' with increasing air-speed. Like so many whistles, it has principally in the past served bird-catchers to lure wild birds by imitating their calls, such as larks, linnets, and widgeon. Another form is a plum stone with a hole bored in each face.

2. *Duct whistles* (most of them are manufactured in Britain by the Acme firm). Boatswain's pipe (*b*) 10 cm. or 4″ long (also recently still made in Italy as a fowler's call): varied signals are conveyed by cupping the hand over the hole in the spherical cavity; several were found in the *Mary Rose. Referee's whistle (*c*), with a cork pellet which is blown about inside for a 'chirrup', again once a bird lure. Scout or police whistle (*d*), divided down the centre by a metal plate to make two half-round *stopped pipes, one shorter than the other to make a powerful *beat. Some South American Indians make such whistles of clay. The three-tone railroad horn in America (usually sounding an inverted major triad) gains its power from the huge air-pressure available from the braking system. 'Silent Dog Whistle': a very small stopped duct whistle with bore *c*.3 mm. in diameter, and the length adjustable by a screw plunger from *c*.2 cm. ($\frac{3}{4}$″ sounding in the octave above the piano) to less than 1 cm. and to humans inaudible save as a faint hiss, but heard by a dog, it is said, a mile or more away over even ground.

Willow or May whistle, which no doubt some country children still know how to make: the bark of a piece from a young branch is cut circumferentially half-way along and tapped with the back of the knife (correctly while singing a special little song) until it will slide off; a 'window' is then cut in it 4 mm. ($\frac{1}{2}''$) from the top. The wood underneath is pared down to shape the windway, the slit, and the tube (leaving the far end solid, as a stopped pipe) before replacing the bark. Cuckoo, most simply a short duct flute with a hole in the stopped end: Bulliard's *Aviceptologie françoise* (1778) identifies the notes as $f\sharp''$ and d'', adding that with the hole left open the turtle-dove can be imitated.

Clay whistles, widely sold as toys and gifts, are of two main types, both having a small duct-flute component of clay forming the tail of a bird or the spout of a little jug. The bird has a fingerhole in the breast for making a second note (a parent of the *ocarina). The jug, on the other hand, is partly filled with water, enough to cover the inside end of the inserted spout (Fig. 1e). Blowing speed produces a variable chirrup as the air escaping through the water opens and stops the short tube of the spout: for the nightingale of the Toy Symphony, it is also manufactured with a metal canister. The quail, on the other hand, is a short, narrow pipe to which air is fed from a soft purse-like skin bag (or as manufactured, a rubber bulb) lightly tapped with the fingers while held in the palm of the hand, to reproduce the 'wet-my-lips' call of the male bird at night, the female's answer being very accurately imitated by Beethoven in the 'Pastoral Symphony', on the oboe.

3. *End-blown (ductless) whistles*. Carved in wood in very numerous shapes and often with one or two fingering holes in the side: notably over Africa for hunting, but also played musically together in bands.

Wind-cap (from Ger.: *Windkapsel*; also 'reed cap'). With certain double-reed wind instruments of the Renaissance period (see CORNAMUSE; CRUMHORN; SCHREIERPFEIFE), also bagpipe practice chanters (see BAGPIPE, 2a), a wooden cap with a hole in the top is placed over the reed (see REED, 4).

Wind instruments (Fr.: *instruments à vent*; Ger.: *Blasinstrumente*; It.: *strumenti a fiato*; Ru.: *dukhovye instrumenty*). Below are considered some general aspects of wind instruments in the ordinary sense of those which are blown from the mouth; and here particularly those played with fingerholes or keys—in the orchestra, *woodwind—as distinct from *brass instruments, which with few exceptions are not. Articulation of the notes is generally by *tonguing.

1. *The main families*. All depend on some arrangement by which the airflow of the breath is interrupted to form a succession of pulses which, in tubular instruments, initiates and maintains a 'standing wave' longitudinal oscillation of the air in the tube. The arrangement takes three main forms. (For full accounts see works cited under ACOUSTICS.)

(*a*) *Flutes* (including those of 'duct flute' type like the recorder: for a typological survey see FLUTE, 7). When a jet of air meets a solid, fixed edge (as that of the mouth-hole of a flute, the top of a *panpipe, or the 'lip' of a recorder) it will, if the direction, distance, and speed be correctly adjusted, divide in a regular succession of eddies, spiralling alternately inwards to the flute and outwards from it. This brings a fast alternation of motion at the head of the air-column, at frequencies controlled by feedback from the standing wave which is formed by repeated passage of the motion down the tube and reflected from the other end. Also among flutes, not tubular but *cavity resonators, are OCARINA (and GEMSHORN), and see WHISTLES AND BIRD-CALLS.

(*b*) *Reed instruments* (those with fingerholes or keys). The flexible *reed is sealed from the outer air by the player's mouth, to vibrate as a kind of valve as the breath escapes past it, causing, in this case, an alternation of air-pressure, at frequencies again controlled by the resulting standing wave in the pipe as the holes are opened and closed. The reed may be double (e.g. oboe, crumhorn) or single (clarinet, saxophone), but also, cutting across this division, is the important distinction between conical bore and cylindrical, as illustrated by taking as examples the four instruments just named, and in that order (Table 1).

TABLE I.

	double reed	single reed
conical	1. Oboe	4. Saxophone
cylindrical	2. Crumhorn	3. Clarinet

Thus arranged, articles include:

1. BASSOON; BOMBARDE; COR ANGLAIS (English horn); DULCIAN; OBOE; SARRUSOPHONE; SHANAI; SHAWM.
2. AULOS; BALABAN; CORNAMUSE; CRUMHORN; HICHI-RIKI; KORTHOLT (sordun); RACKET.
3. CHALUMEAU; CLARINET; HORNPIPE; LAUNEDDAS; REEDPIPE.
4. SAXOPHONE; TAROGATO.

In *bagpipes, two of the above categories are often combined in one instrument. See FREE REED for the rather different class of reed instruments that includes (mouth-blown) harmonica and *sheng*.

(*c*) *Brass instruments*. In these, also certain non-brass instruments like *alphorns and the Renaissance *cornett, the player's lips, placed against a cup-like mouthpiece, vibrate in a manner in some ways analogous to that of a double reed, but under muscular control. For a list of articles see BRASS INSTRUMENTS, 5. Most of what follows here concerns only woodwind.

2. *Fingerholes.* These are numbered (as when describing instruments and their fingerings) starting with the hole nearest to the blowing end as '1'. In a 'fingering chart' the convention is for a black circle to denote a hole covered by the finger and an open (white) circle one that is uncovered, showing these either in a vertical column or a horizontal row: for printing in a book, the black circle can be conveniently represented by a point (full stop) and the white by the letter 'o', with the first hole on the left (as in a number of fingerings given in the present work). A thumb-hole, and the keys, if any, are indicated in various ways. Often there are, lower down than the last fingerhole (or key), one or more permanently open 'vent-holes'.

Fingerhole instruments have a natural basis in that the speed of soundwaves in air is such that pipes of the most convenient lengths to handle will sound fundamental pitches lying in a range musically agreeable to the ear; and a row of holes placed to suit the natural span of the fingers and successively uncovered is almost bound to produce a melodious series of notes, whether or not of an 'official' scale. Among flutes of all kinds over the world the average full sounding-length comes to about 40 cm. (15"), corresponding to a fundamental wavelength twice this, 0.8 m., which divided into 340 m. per second as the speed of sound in air at 'average' temperature gives 425 *Hz, just below the note a'. The flute will in fact sound lower by up to a semitone or even more owing to the small size of the apertures (mouth-hole, 'window', fingerholes) compared with that of the bore of the tube, and in many flutes to partial covering of the blowing aperture by the player's lips—both factors of great importance, whether in making intervening semitones (e.g. by *cross-fingering), or in tuning the notes or modulating their pitch for expressive reasons. (See also STOPPED PIPE, 1c, for 'end correction'.)

Seldom can more than nine digits cover holes (since usually one thumb must support the pipe). Through times prior to key mechanisms this would restrict the fundamental scale to nine notes plus one (this with all holes uncovered). In practice, on this keyless level, the little finger of the uppermost hand plays no part. The fingering then assumes a scalar symmetry matched to the structure so frequent in melody: e.g. with the three fingers of the upper hand giving the principal keynote, then addition of the same three fingers of the lower hand gives the answering dominant at the fourth below, in a movement as 'natural' as the musical interval itself; and still, with the most sophisticated key mechanisms, this same applies.

3. *Overblowing.* Practically all flutes can continue the fundamental scale upwards by overblowing to the octave (2nd harmonics) often followed by use of 3rd, 4th, etc. harmonics (see HARMONIC SERIES). Reed instruments vary. Those with a cylindrical tube can theoretically overblow only to odd-numbered harmonics (see STOPPED PIPE), from the 3rd harmonics at the interval of a twelfth above the fundamentals. On simple fingerhole examples like crumhorn or reedpipe, whichever the type of reed, this cannot readily be done, if at all; nor would it serve much purpose, leaving a gap in the scale above the basic nine or ten fundamentals. Only on the clarinet, with its keywork, the accurate overblown twelfths and above not only augment the compass but supply the musically most important part of it. See OVERBLOWING for high-register fingerings of the main woodwind instruments (see also MULTIPHONICS).

The hardest behaviour to understand is that of the conical bore reed instruments, which overblow to both even- and odd-numbered harmonics as the flute does. This has nothing to do with the kind of reed (a double reed can be exchanged for single; see BASSOON, 4). Physics explains it on the basis of a 'spherical' wave-front, emanating in theory from the apex of a complete cone, which is in practice non-existent (with the oboe it would lie over 7 cm. (3") beyond the reed). But to express it in simple graphic terms is not so easy. Here Charles Taylor (1975: 69) may be helpful: a wave returning to the narrow end of a conical pipe loses velocity and no real reflection takes place there; the wave is damped out, so that one need consider only one wave-journey outwards and back, and equally so whether the narrow end be open or (as on oboe) in effect closed, the possible harmonics being the same in either case. Nor does the pipe have to be conical all through; among double-reed instruments, distantly related to the oboe, played in other parts of the world, some (see SHAWM, 4; SURNA) are cylindrically bored, but the reed is carried on a long metal *staple which supplies the theoretical, though absent, apex by which the instrument may be capable of a useful octave overblow.

4. *Keywork.* Keys are of two principal kinds. An 'open key' is sprung to keep open when at rest. Usually it is named after the note given when it is closed. The key for the little finger on large recorders is a typical open key, and is the earliest known type of key. A 'closed key' keeps normally closed by its spring (a stronger spring than for an open key since there is no finger-pressure to ensure airtightness). It is named after the note it gives when opened. The single key of the baroque flute is a typical closed key. A ring, as seen on clarinet and most oboes encircling a fingerhole, is connected to a key placed somewhere else along the instrument; when the finger is lowered it lowers the ring also (see also BOEHM SYSTEM). On the modern flute and the saxophone, where the holes, being exceptionally wide, are covered by padded plates, these may also where necessary perform the function of rings. Many other mechanical interconnections are used in keywork. For example, see OBOE, Fig. 1, an 'articulated' mechanism by which

two different fingers control the same key, one to open it, the other to close it.

5. *Breathing.* With wind instruments, the blowing is always referred to as the 'breathing'. Tuition nowadays gives it meticulous attention, with every instrument from flute to tuba, to ensure that breath is taken in deeply in the natural manner (swelling the abdomen, not contracting it) followed by fully controlled outflow (contracting the abdomen). See also CIRCULAR BREATHING (involving inhaling through the nose).

6. *Manufacture.* The materials most used before the 18th century were the yellow boxwood (native or imported from the Near East) and maple, with ivory a luxury alternative for the smaller instruments, or ebony. Then, in the course of the 18th century, these came to be rivalled, and in the next century generally superseded, by imported tropical woods of the family *Leguminosae*, first rosewood and cocuswood and finally, today standard for oboes and clarinets, African blackwood (or grenadilla). Ebonite was once highly thought of for clarinets and various synthetics have proved satisfactory since. The making of the instruments is primarily lathe work, turning the wood roughly to shape, boring it with augers and reamers (see FLUTE, Pl. 2, lower left), then finishing the exterior. Next, the fingerholes, which in many instruments with small holes are 'undercut', i.e. to be wider where they meet the bore, for freer emission of the notes. This is done with a kind of inverted countersink, introduced inside and turned from the outside. Keys, which often used to be made by specialist key-makers, are forged or finished from castings. The steel springs, needle or flat, are mounted and the pads (skin-covered or synthetic tissue, over card) are cemented in the key-cups (replacement springs and pads of graded widths are obtainable from instrument suppliers). The instrument is finally checked for tuning, minute corrections being made if necessary to the holes and the bore. (For repairs and maintenance, see Brand 1942; Springer 1976.)

On coming into possession of an old or early instrument of the 18th or 19th century the first thing is to look for a maker's name on it and then, unless already an expert, consult Langwill, *Index of Wind-Instrument Makers* (1960, several times updated) to get a closer idea as to the date. (For a list of early Tutors, Warner 1967.)

Wind machine. See EFFECTS.

Wood block. Percussion instrument of a rectangular hardwood block, typically about 18 cm. (7") long, hollowed out below the slightly domed top to leave a deep slot, *c.*7 mm. wide and reaching almost to the back of the block. Often a second slot is cut in the bottom of the block, its opening facing the other way. Holes are usually drilled through the solid ends for a metal attachment to a *drum kit. The block is struck with a drumstick or some other

beater, to give a high, abrupt sound compounded of the pitches given by the wood and (often about two tones deeper) by the air inside the slot. It came in with jazz, since when many composers have used it, as Walton in *Belshazzar's Feast*, where the God of Wood follows the God of Iron (*anvil) and the God of Stone (*whip). It is also made in different sizes up to a foot long (30 cm.) to give contrasted sounds, high and low, rather like those of *temple blocks. Stockhausen and Berio have so used it.

There is also a 'tubular' type double-ended, each cylindrical end slotted, one with a deeper slot (and deeper sound) than the other. This type, less penetrating, is much used in school percussion groups.

The normal rectangular type derives from the Chinese *ban* (*pan*) used by food pedlars, night-watchmen, and sometimes in the theatre, where it may be attached to a drum (see GU, 2). The tubular type reproduces a West African form which, however, has wooden-rod clappers loosely tied inside for shaking the instrument like a wooden bell.

Wood drum (or wood-plate drum). This minor addition to the percussion is virtually a *tom-tom with wood replacing the drum-skin. 'Wood-plate' drum is the recommended term since 'wood drum' can be muddled with German *Holztrommel*, which normally means a *slit drum.

Woodwind. Fr.: *bois*; Ger.: *Holzblasinstrumente*; It.: *legni*; Sp.: *madera*. 1. Collective orchestral term for *flute, *oboe, *clarinet, *bassoon, and their subspecies (*piccolo, etc.) (see ORCHESTRA, 1*b*). Many works of the early 20th century, when composers were writing for very large orchestras, demand more woodwind players than usual. Richard Strauss's *Elektra* includes no fewer than eight clarinet parts (E♭ clarinet, four ordinary and two basset horns, and bass clarinet). Stravinsky's *Rite of Spring* needs five of each woodwind (the equals sign '=' in the list at the beginning of the score denotes 'changing to'):

piccolo; 3 flutes (3rd = piccolo 2), alto flute
2 oboes, 2 cors anglais (2nd = oboe 4)
E♭ clarinet, 2 clarinets, 2 bass clarinets
  (2nd = clarinet 4)
3 bassoons, 2 contrabassoons (2nd = bassoon 4)

The saxophone, when used in the orchestra, is also counted among the woodwind (even though, like the modern flute, not made of wood), being a reed instrument and played by one who normally also plays the clarinet.

'Woodwind' is a term with strong overtones of the Romantic period. The older expression was simply 'wind instruments' or 'the wind', whether or not including the brass. This is now often preferred by groups specializing in baroque music, in which the 'wind' may include a pre-Romantic instrument like the recorder; and still more so with earlier music which may call for shawms, etc., and particularly the cornett, which cannot be properly described as either woodwind or brass.

2. 'Woodwind Quintet' is the American term for the chamber-music combination of flute, oboe, clarinet, horn, and bassoon, known in Europe as 'Wind Quintet'. Its repertory really starts in the early 19th century, with works by Danzi and Reicha, and leads on to numerous works from later in the century up to the present time.

X

Xiao (*hsiao*). End-blown flute of China. Of smooth bamboo, in fine examples incised with Chinese characters, it measures up to 75 cm. (30″), with five fingerholes, a thumb-hole above them, and a pair of vent holes below the lowest fingerhole. The *xiao* is a notched flute; some varieties have a plain U-shaped notch (as in a **quena*) but in the normal type a knot in the bamboo covers the blowing end but for a small half-round perforation next to the notch. The *xiao* is one of China's most ancient flutes, forms of it being known back to *c*.1000 BC. The **shakuhachi* of Japan is one of its descendants and the Korean *tanso* is another (see CHINA AND KOREA, 2*d*).

Xirimía. See BAGPIPE, 3*d*.

Xuan (*hsüan*). Chinese vessel flute of clay, shaped like an egg (*c*.7 cm. (3″) tall) with flattened base (for standing upright when not in use), a hole at the top for blowing across, and a varying number of fingering holes, e.g. one for each thumb plus three for the fingers. Formerly a ritual instrument (older even than the **xiao*) carried in processions, rather than played, it is now manufactured as a collector's piece. (Western writers have sometimes referred to it as an **ocarina*, from which the *xuan* differs in not being a form of **duct flute*.)

Xylophone. Percussion instrument of tuned wooden bars. Widespread over parts of Africa (below, 4), Central America, and South-East Asia (**ranat*, **gamelan*), as well as familiar in Western music in two main types distinguished as xylophone and **marimba*. Fig. 1 shows for quick reference the customary ranges of these last along with those of three chief instruments with metal bars. Xylophone parts are *written* an octave lower than the (sounding) compass shown, as are **celesta* parts, but for **glockenspiel* two octaves lower. For those instruments which are played with beaters held in the hands (the celesta, with keyboard, the chief exception in this respect) a universally recognized collective term can hardly be said to exist: they have been called 'tuned percussion', or 'keyed' (each bar a 'key'), or as in America, 'mallet percussion'.

1. *Xylophone bars*. These are *c*.4 cm. (1½″) wide, 2.5 cm. (1″) thick, of rosewood, supported on cords or pads at the two main nodal points as in all these instruments (see GLOCKENSPIEL, 1). Beaters have spherical ends of wood, hard rubber, or plastic; they normally strike in the middle of the bar, where

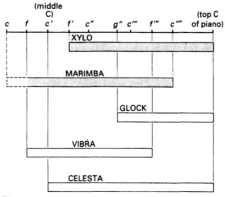

Fig. 1.

the fundamental mode of vibration has an antinode (a point where greatest vibration-motion can be excited other than close to the two ends). The row of sharps is placed on a higher level than the naturals for their ends to overlap a little, which brings the striking points closer together. There are, however, models with the rows level, as on a marimba (which also has wider bars). Tubular resonators (metal or synthetic) are suspended beneath the bars, each tuned to its bar in the manner of a **stopped pipe*. For this each resonator is closed at or towards its lower end. Externally, however, the tubes can be of any length required for visual effect, e.g. for their bottom ends to form an arch.

The basic playing technique is to strike with the two beaters alternately (if playing a scale, moving the hands together along the bars). 'Double' beats (consecutive notes with the same beater) and 'cross over' beats are, however, frequently needed (as with **timpani*) for fluent rendering of a passage. A player will often work out beforehand how to beat a passage of any difficulty, and at least partly memorize it in order not to have to look at the music as well as at the instrument and the conductor.

2. *Design of bars; overtone-tuning*. The simple rule governing the relative lengths of bars (e.g. for an octave lower increase the length by √2: see GLOCKENSPIEL, 5) is applicable to a bar of even thickness. Those of most xylophones however are like those of a marimba, thinned on the underside in the middle part, giving the side view an appearance of a short or long arch. Credit for this tone-improving process goes first to xylophone

makers of Africa, from whom, with little question, the instrument passed to Central America as the marimba, known there from the 17th century, to become a leading folk instrument and, in Guatemala, the 'national instrument'. From this marimba, the thinning method was taken over in the modern instruments developed in the 20th century in the USA. It mellows the tone, lowering the pitch of a bar, even very considerably, while reducing the relative strength of the dissonant overtones from the partials (see PARTIALS, 6) which otherwise, especially in the lower octaves, can almost overpower the notes themselves. Moreover, the thinning leaves the partials practically unchanged in pitch, thus widening their intervals above the note. The main partial (from the 2nd mode of vibration) can then be expertly brought, on a xylophone, from the sharp eleventh above (natural to the vibration of a free-ended bar) to a harmonious twelfth, and on a marimba, it is stated, even to two octaves above.

3. *Trough xylophones*. Well known in school music, these have the bars laid over an open-topped box or 'trough' with a sloping floor to make it deeper towards the bass end, and thus to act as a resonator for the whole compass. This follows ancient practice for xylophones in South-East Asia and Indonesia, borrowed by Carl Orff for his educational music (*Schulwerk*) and put into production from the 1930s in Germany by Maendler. As on the school metallophones also (see GLOCKENSPIEL, 3) the bars are quickly removable and different sizes (alto, bass, etc.) are available.

4. *African xylophones*. In many African languages known by names ('marimba' being one) which are similar to, or the same as, those of the **sansa* kind, with plucked tongues. The xylophones vary greatly in size, tuning, and construction. The number of bars ranges from one to two to 25 or more. Small, light instruments may be suspended from the player's neck. Larger, still simple types have wooden bars that are laid across boxes (as in Tanzania), across clay pots (Nigeria), or even across a pit in the ground (West Africa, the Central African Republic, Kenya). The bars of the more sophisticated 'frame' xylophones are mounted on a rigid wooden structure, and often have attached gourd resonators over which may be gummed buzzing membranes, in some cases said to be from the cocoons of a large spider, or nowadays it is said, cigarette paper. Xylophones are often played in groups: those of the Chopi people of south-eastern Africa comprise some half a dozen instruments of various sizes. Many of the East African types show equidistant tunings of five or seven notes to an octave, which has led many Western scholars to conclude that such instruments bear influence of Indonesia, where equidistant xylophone tunings are also common.

Over Africa generally tunings vary considerably, different tunings being used even in xylophones of the same community.

5. *Four-row xylophone* (Fig. 2). The older European xylophone, normal for orchestras and concert soloists before adoption of the present form. It is the instrument for which Saint-Saëns wrote the well-known part in *Danse macabre* ('the white skeletons race and leap . . .'), and in Russian symphony orchestras it has been customary up to quite recent years. The bars lie crosswise to the player's body, the shortest furthest away, like the strings of a **dulcimer*; the wooden beaters, too, have a resemblance to dulcimer hammers in their shape. There are no resonators. The bars, threaded on cords, are laid upon long tied bundles of straw about three-quarters of an inch (2 cm.) thick, whence in Germany the old name *Strohfiedel* ('straw fiddle'). Later instruments may have solid rails instead, as in Fig. 2. The main scale zigzags up through the two middle rows and the outer rows provide the sharps in duplicate, making these available to either hand. When not in use the instrument can be rolled up, with the straw bundles inside, and transported in a compact box.

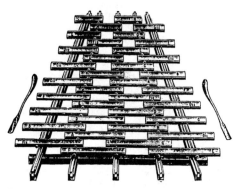

Fig. 2.

This instrument was developed in the early 19th century by popular soloists in Central and Eastern Europe, who added extra rows of bars to the previously existing folk instrument with one or two rows only, known back to the 15th century. (Xylophones with bars laid out in the normal modern fashion have also been known in the past in Western Europe: an 18th-century English drawing shows a street busker 'playing the sticks'; and in the USA small xylophones in the present format were manufactured from the 1890s, prior to the improved, resonated designs since in use.)

Xylorimba (or marimba-xylophone). A form of xylophone with the compass extended downwards to include the lower notes of a **marimba*.

Y

Yueqin (or *yüeh-ch'in*). Chinese 'moon guitar' (*yue*, 'moon'), with bright, silvery tone, used in ensembles and to accompany the voice (as in Peking operas) and played usually with a small plectrum. The distinctive circular body, with wooden belly, is about 35 cm. (14") wide and only 3.5 cm. ($1\frac{1}{2}$") in depth. There are traditionally two pairs of silk strings tuned a fifth apart, and on the very short neck two frets, plus a further eight or so glued to the belly, giving a scale of seven roughly equal intervals to the octave. There have also been varieties with hexagonal bodies instead of round. Modern instruments may have three strings, the second and third strings tuned a fifth and an octave below the first (this around *b'*), and 19 to 24 chromatic frets, four of them on the neck.

The *ruan* is a far older form with circular body and is also played today. The neck is much longer, carrying the frets up to about the 12th (as on a guitar), and the frets on the belly are more numerous. There are four strings tuned in fifths (in the medium-sized *ruan* upwards from about *G*); for the modern orchestra there are even four different sizes, the largest tuned like a cello and the smallest like a violin.

Yunluo. See GONG CHIME, 2.

Z

Zambomba. Sp., *"friction drum'.

Zampogna. The principal bagpipe of Italy, met in several forms native to the southern half of the country including Sicily (here *cornamusa*, etc.), though frequently heard far to the north in the hands of itinerant musicians. Tied in the sheepskin bag is a single large wooden stock holding four pipes (see BAGPIPE, Fig. 1d): two drones, usually fairly short; and two chanters, one for each hand, played together in two-part harmony, the left hand playing on fingerholes placed lower down its pipe than those played with the right hand on the other pipe. The instruments are locally made, normally with separate bells which are sometimes made to screw off.

1. *Chanters of equal length: zampogna a paro* ('equal'), South Calabria, Sicily. Chanters, 35 to 40 cm. (14–16") long, the bore cylindrical for most of the length, and all four pipes with a single reed (see REED, 2) though they may be sometimes double reeds without perceptible difference to the sound. The right-hand chanter has four fingerholes and a thumb-hole higher up; they give a scale of five notes starting on the leading note, in Ex. 1 (top)

f'♯. The left-hand chanter, with four fingerholes only, takes the scale down to the lower dominant (*d'*). Below (Ex. 1) is the start of a *pastorale* from Sicily on this bagpipe, showing the characteristic counterpoint based on thirds (compare the *lau-neddas of Sardinia) leading to a pendulating tonic-and-dominant in 6/8 rhythm by the left hand below the melody played by the right. Fingerholes may be tuned with wax: in Ex. 1, the C serving equally as C♯ (as one would sing it) in the opening, and as C♮ in the following 12/8. Among rarer types also with equal-length chanters and single reeds, a *surdulina* of Italo-Albanian communities of northern Calabria has very short pipes—the small drone as little as 6 cm. or 2½" long—and the fingerholes level on the two chanters (compare DIPLE).

2. *Unequal chanters, the left-hand the longer.* Chanters with gently expanding bore (drones cylindrical) and all pipes with double reeds (bound with thread to an unsoldered metal staple; see REED, 4). By far the best-known Italian bagpipe, this is almost always heard in duet with a small, bagless pipe (*ciaramella* or *piffero*), *c*.30 cm. (12") long with double reed, on which the tunes are played by a second man to a simple two-part accompaniment on the

Ex. 1.

bagpipe. In the commonest size the chanters are about 40 and 65 cm. long (16 and 26") with holes as 1 above, save that the fourth hole of the longer pipe is covered by a key (*zampogna a chiave*) usually acting inside a protective barrel (see FONTANELLE). Also, this chanter gives notes an octave lower than those of the shorter. The drones, *c*.35 and 15 cm. (14 and 6"), sound in octaves. Some instruments are exceedingly big (Pl. 1), with the left-hand chanter approaching 150 cm. (5') and giving lowest note G or F; in parts of Sicily this largest size is also played as a solo instrument. The zampogna with equal-length chanters is, on pictorial evidence, the older, seen from the 16th century. Unequal chanters follow soon after, without the key, and known as *zampogna zoppa* ('lame'), but since almost wholly superseded by the type with a key. This type is said to have spread from Naples during the 18th century, during which the *ciaramella* became its regular companion.

Pl. 1. Zampogna, Sicily, from picture postcard, Maurice Byrne, 'Palermo—Lo Zampognaro'.

Traditionally these *zampognari* have come to the towns for the *novena* days before Christmas, playing before roadside shrines and so on. They first play together, then the *ciaramella* breaks off to sing the nativity song to the accompaniment of the bagpipe alone. Many composers have alluded to such Christmas music, once heard far and wide as players, or a *zampogna* player by himself, took to the road: Handel in *Messiah* (Pastoral Symphony, entitled 'pifa' from the north Italian word for 'bagpipe'), and Bach in the Christmas Oratorio (Sinfonia to Part II).

Guizzi and R. Leydi 1985.

Zamr. See SURNA.

Zarb (Iran). See DARABUKA.

Zeze. See SESE.

Zheng (*cheng*). The main Chinese ***'long zither' apart from the rare and venerable **qin*.

The long (*c*.130 cm. (4') or more) rectangular or slightly tapered soundbox is placed usually on a table, the player seated towards the right-hand end (see CHINA AND KOREA, Pl. 1, on right). The soundboard, of a special softwood, arches from front to back, in some cases also from end to end. The strings, 13 to 23 (most often 16 or 18, of twisted silk or now often metal) are led, on the right, through holes to toggles under the soundboard; and, on the left, either similarly, or to wooden pegs placed in a row across the soundboard. Openings in the bottom of the soundbox are needed when attaching strings, and also serve as soundholes, the instrument being slightly raised on small feet.

The strings are tuned by individual movable forked wooden bridges (like those of the related **kayagum* of Korea and **koto* of Japan). Their positions (adjusted by hand) form a long curve across the soundboard, the parts of the strings to the right of the bridges giving a pentatonic scale of three octaves or more—e.g. with 18 strings, G A c d e . . . g'' a'' c'''—with the highest note nearest the player, the lowest furthest. The right hand plucks with the first two fingers and thumb in both directions, using the bare fingertips or sometimes finger-picks; often octaves are struck (Ex. 1) and harp-like glissandos over all strings or some. The left hand is meanwhile poised over the strings to the left of the bridges, ready for two things especially: a gentle pitch-vibrato by rhythmic pressure on a string with three fingers together; and to 'bend' a string, raising it by up to a third in order to slur or glide between two notes made on that same string (Ex. 1, arrows); the glide is either upwards by pressure after plucking, or downwards by pressure before plucking followed by release. Less often a string is pressed down to make a single note with different quality from the same note plucked on the adjacent free string. The playing can sound sweet and melodious in a small chamber, or more loud and twangy before a large audience.

The *zheng* is extensively manufactured, also now exported to the West, while continuing experiments with modernization have led to models with pedal mechanisms for altering the pitch of notes and generally extending the instrument's technical possibilities. In early forms the *zheng* was known back at least to the 4th century BC. By the 8th century AD it was used in ensembles of the court music,

Ex. 1. Gaoshan liushiu 'High mountains, flowing streams' for *zheng* solo, first section.

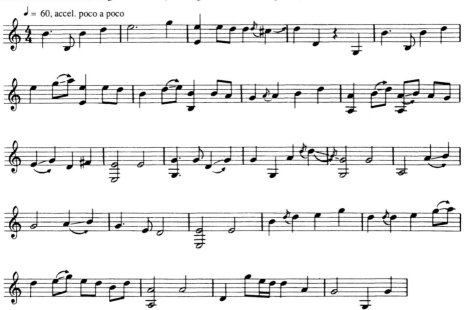

♩ = 60, accel. poco a poco

but more recently especially as a solo instrument. Ancient melodies are preserved, while large collections have been transcribed from live performances, mainly in the south and Taiwan.

Zhong (*Chung*). China, bell, struck on the outside (see JAPAN 1(*a*)).

Zieh-harmonika (Ger.). See ACCORDION.

Zil (Arab., Turk.). See CYMBALS.

Zimbelstern. See BELL WHEEL.

Zink (Ger.). See CORNETT.

Zither (Fr.: *cithare*; Ger.: *Zither*, whence Eng.; It., Sp.: *citara*; Ru.: *tsitra*). A stringed instrument native to Austria and Bavaria, developed during the 19th century from earlier and simpler forms (see below, 2), akin to many others in northern and central Europe, many of them also played today. The *Appalachian dulcimer of America is yet another. For 'zither' as a general ethnological term, see below, 3.

1. *Austrian zither.* The zither has a shallow soundbox around 60 cm. (2') long (Pl. 1), typically of pine veneered with rosewood. It bulges on the far side, and has spiked ball-feet to keep it still while placed on a table for playing (the table-top often giving extra resonance to the sound). Along the near side

runs a series of some 29 metal frets. There may be in all 34 strings, the highest-tuned of steel, the others overwound on metal or silk. They run from hitch-pins on the right to tuning pins or machines (geared pins) on the left.

Five strings pass over the frets. These are melody strings, stopped with the left thumb and first three fingers, and plucked by a metal pick or 'zither ring' (see PLECTRUM, 1) worn on the right thumb. Strings one, two, four, and five are nominally tuned to the same notes as the *viola, namely *a' d' g c*. String three is tuned to *g'* and is mostly reserved for playing in thirds with notes on the *d'* string, stopping with the first two fingers.

The remaining strings form two groups. First, 13 chord strings, plucked by the first and second fingers of the right hand. Their tuning follows the cycle of fourths: *ab' eb' bb' . . . c♯' g♯'*, all within this one octave, and providing for every tonality a three-note major or minor chord in which two adjacent strings are plucked by one finger while the other strikes the third note. Beyond are the bass strings, also tuned cyclically: *Eb Bb F . . . C♯ G♯* (much as in a piano *accordion) bringing together the tonic, dominant, and subdominant in each key. Further bass strings may be added chromatically below. Through both these two sets of accompaniment strings, those for *F*, *A*, and *C♯* may be coloured red (thus every fourth string is a red one). The zither is played in its homelands in music of local character, often with a distinctive vibrato on the longer melody notes. It is also extensively exported for domestic music-making.

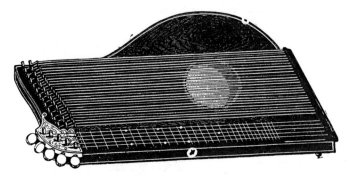

Little used in the orchestra, being not as loud as the harp or piano, it nevertheless appears solo in the introduction to Johann Strauss's *Tales from the Vienna Woods* (1868), the part being cued in small notes in the string parts for the sad occasions when no zither is available (Ex. 1).

For some by-products of the zither industry, see AUTOHARP; BOWED ZITHER.

2. *Older European zithers.* These are played, or were played up to the end of the 19th century, in many European regions, from the Alps and the Carpathians northwards to Scandinavia: mainly farmhouse instruments for dancing and accompanying old songs. Today they may be heard particularly in Hungary (*citara*), Norway (*langeleik*), Sweden (*hummel*), Belgium (*vlier*, also other names), and Alsace (*buche*, or *épinette des Vosges*, the smallest zither). The old Alpine *Scheitholt* is now rare, replaced by those of 'Kratzzither' types (Pl. 2) or by the more advanced zither described above.

The basic provision is a long narrow soundbox placed across the knees or on a table with the frets nearest the player. These are usually diatonic, and over them run two or more wire melody strings tuned in unison and characteristically stopped by pressing to the frets with a short metal or wooden rod held in the left hand (compare Appalachian dulcimer), but in some cases with the fingers. The other hand sweeps a plectrum (of bone, horn, etc.) back and forth across these strings and, in the same movement, the accompaniment strings which lie beyond and are tuned to sound a 'drone' on the keynote in different octaves and its dominant (compare BAGPIPE, HURDY-GURDY). The effect can be strong and rhythmic (the instrument seems always to have been played alone), with plectrum strokes fitted to the rhythm of a dance (see e.g. LANGELEIK, 1).

Some of these instruments have been traced in pictures back to the 15th century. The Medieval *monochord has been suggested as their source, though without any direct evidence of any such connection. The Swedish *hummel* is distinctive in that the strings and frets lie over a separate raised central part (as with an Appalachian dulcimer), while the main body widens in 'pear shape' towards the plucking end.

3. *'Zither' as an ethnomusicological term.* The instrument *classification of Hornbostel and Sachs adopts 'zither' to include a wide range of instruments over the world, from relatively simple forms (below) to *'long zithers' of the Far East such as the Japanese *koto.

(a) *Idiochord zither* (see IDIOCHORD). The narrow strips forming the 'strings' are raised from the fresh-cut epidermis of the bamboo or other plant-stem, using a metal or wooden needle or knife. The strips are then raised up by cane or wooden bridges, often after binding their ends to prevent the cuts running.

(i) *Raft zither.* Especially in tropical Africa and South-East Asia but a great traveller, made also in the Near East for children: a number of stems, each with one string cut in it, are placed side by side, as many as 17 of them, held together by the bridges (Pl. 3). Most typically the strings are tapped with a small stick. If at equal tension, a wider string gives a deeper note than a narrower (as a thicker actual string would), and a ready-made set of notes may be obtained on this basis alone, but more usual is tuning by small wedges, or wrapping a string with bast, or slanting the bridges, to make

Ex. 1. J. Strauss 'Tales from Vienna Woods'.

Pl. 2. The old Austrian *Kratzzither* played in a Tyrolean farmhouse, painting (1876) by F. Defregger; note the left hand pressing the melody strings and the right plucking these and the bass strings together.

the desired series of notes in a softly buzzing accompaniment to the player's song.

(ii) *Tube zither*. Corn-stalk fiddle (USA, a string cut along the length of the stem and plucked or bowed with a rolled leaf); as a toy in several parts of Europe, one or two 'strings' may be cut in two similar pieces of maize stem and one is 'bowed' with the other (both moistened) to make squeaking noises; French and other children used to call it a 'violon'. Of wider bamboo allowing many strings to be raised, *valiha* (Malagasy Republic), and many in South-East Asia, hit with a stick (the tube sometimes partly enclosed in a shell-like palm-leaf resonator).

(iii) *Half-tube zither*. Of bamboo sliced to make a trough, the strings raised along the convex side: especially South and East Asia, and reckoned to be, indeed in some cases traditionally believed to be, the form in which the family of long zithers originated (see also LONG ZITHER).

(iv) *Mvet*, a 'harp zither' (West Africa).

(b) *Board and trough zithers*. Of wood, with strings of plant fibre (or sinews) running from end to end, plucked with thumbs or fingers: East and Central Africa (*enanga, inanga*), where a single long length of string may be led through holes or notches at both ends to provide the required number of sounding string-lengths, tuned by pulling at their ends for the desired tensions to be held by frictional force (somewhat as the 'looped' strings of a modern piano).

(c) *Stick zither* (or 'bar zither'). A variable class, basically a bamboo or flat wooden stick with a string stretched from end to end. A half-gourd is fastened to the back of the stick at one end, its open mouth moved about by the player against the chest to vary the resonance. Held upright or slanting, one hand stops the string, the other plucks: *sese* (East and Central Africa, with high frets cut in the wood of the stick); *tuila* (India, on which the playing also makes use of harmonics).

Pl. 3. Raft zither, Africa (Oxford, Pitt Rivers Museum).

Zither banjo. See BANJO, 4.

Zuffalo (It.). A general term for a *whistle, e.g. tin whistle, or panpipe, or in former times the French *flageolet.

Zugtrompete (Ger.). See SLIDE TRUMPET, 3a.

Zukra. See BAGPIPE, 6.

Zummara. One of many names for the *reedpipe of the Near East with *idioglot reed, and typically a parallel double pipe: chiefly a folk instrument of shepherds and village boys: see REEDPIPE, Fig. 1a.

An *arghul* has, instead of the second fingerhole pipe, a long, softly humming drone pipe made in several lengths of cane, adjustable for tuning; it has sometimes been heard in Egyptian and Syrian classical ensembles in place of the flute *nay*, when playing, for example, at weddings for the wealthy.

Zurla (Yugoslavia). See SURNA.

APPENDIX: MAKERS OF INSTRUMENTS

Reference list of makers, manufacturers, and inventors cited in the articles in this work. (Included are certain names, found on instruments, that are, or are thought to be, those of suppliers, dealers, etc., of musical instruments.)

Acme: whistles
Adams: valves
Aeolian Co.: orchestrelle, player piano
Albert: clarinet
Albisi: alto and bass flute
Albrecht: square piano
Alexander: horn, Wagner tuba
Alexandre: harmonium, reed organ
Allen: valves
Almenraeder: bassoon, tenoroon
Amati: viola, violin
Antegnati: organ
Arnold: concertina

Babcock: piano, square piano
Bach, V.: trombone, trumpet
Badger: flute
Backers: piano
Baffo: harpsichord
Bainbridge: double flageolet
Band: concertina
Banks: violin
Barberi: barrel organ
Barker: organ
Barry: harp-lute
Baschet: sound sculptures
Bassano: bassanelli
Bazin: lap organ
Bechstein: piano
Bergonzi: violin
Besson: tenor cor, trumpet
Betts: violin
Bizey: oboe
Blaikley: tuba
Blanchet: harpsichord
Blüthner: piano
Boehm: alto and bass flute, Boehm system, clarinet, flute
Boosey: ballad horn, bassoon, trumpet, tuba
Bösendorfer: piano
Boucher: banjo
Brackhausen: musical box
Bressan: recorder
Broadwood: harpsichord, piano, square piano
Brod: bass oboe, cor anglais, oboe
Bryceson: barrel organ
Buechenberg: chitarrone
Buffet: bass clarinet, bassoon, clarinet
Bull: trumpet
Buschmann: harmonica

Cahusac: oboe
Cathcart: reed organ
Catlin: bass clarinet, clarinet, tenoroon
Cavaillé-Coll: organ

Celestini: harpsichord
Ceruti: violin
Cerveny: tuba
Chandler: bass drum
Chickering: piano, square piano
Clemm: spinet
Cliquot: organ
Colgrass: rototom
Conn: duplex, mellophone, reed contrabass, sarrusophone, saxophone, sousaphone
Cook: bell harp
Cooper: flute
Cotter: bass horn
Couchet: harpsichord
Courtois: slide trumpet, trombone
Cousineau: harp
Crabb: concertina
Cramer: bow
Crehore: square piano
Cristofori: clavicytherium, piano
Culliford: harpsichord

Dallam: organ
Dallapé: accordion
D'Almaine: Tenor drum
Dautrich: viola
Da Vinci: timpani
Dawes & Rainden: harmonium
Deagan: angklung, marimba
Debain: harmonium
Demian: accordion
Denner: bass oboe, bassoon, chalumeau, clarinet, oboe, racket, recorder, shawm
Distin: ballad horn, euphonium, tenor cor, saxhorn
Dodd: bow
Dodds & Claus: square piano
Dolmetsch: clavichord, recorder, viol
Dopyera: guitar

Eardsley: pitchpipe
Egan: harp
Ehe: trumpet
Eichentopf: contrabassoon, cor anglais, oboe d'amore
Érard: harp, piano
Estey: reed organ

Fender: electric guitar, Hawaiian guitar
Ferrari: mandolin
Finke: clarino
Fitzpatrick: gemshorn
Forveille: serpent
Fox: bassoon
Franklin: glaas harmonica
Frei, C.: barrel organ

Frei, H.: lute
Frichot: bass horn

Gand: violin
Gasparo da Salò: cittern, double bass, viola, violin
Gautrot: sarrusophone
Gavioli: barrel organ
Geib: harpsichord, piano, square piano
Gibson: banjo, electric guitar, harp-lute, Hawaiian guitar, mandolin
Gillet: oboe
Giorgi: Giorgi flute
Goffriller: violin
Goodrich: harmonium
Graf: piano
Grancino: violin
Green: seraphine
Greenway: harp
Grenié: harmonium
Grenser: bass clarinet, bassoon
Grosset: pardessus de viole
Grotrian: piano
Grundmann: oboe
Guadagnini: violin
Guarneri: violin
Guerson: pardessus de viole
Guichard: clavicor

Haas: trumpet
Haiden: geigenwerk
Hainlein: trumpet
Halary: cornet, ophicleide
Haliday: keyed bugle
Hamilton: harmonium
Hamlin: reed organ
Harlan: recorder
Harrington: tubular bells
Harris, Renatus: organ
Harris, J.: spinet
Haseneier: contrabassoon
Hass: clavichord, harpsichord
Hastrick: double flageolet
Hattersley: harmonium
Hawkes: trombone
Hawkins: piano
Haynes: flute
Hayward: spinet
Hebenstreit: dulcimer
Heckel: bassoon, contrabassoon, heckelphone
Hemony: carillon
Hieronymus: harpsichord
Hill: organ
Hintz: English guitar
Hitchcock: spinet
Hoffmann: cello
Hohlfeld: geigenwerk
Hohner: harmonica, melodica
Holtkamp: organ
Hope-Jones: cinema organ, diaphone
Hotteterre: Écurie, musette, oboe, recorder
Hoyer: organ
Hunt: recorder
Hutchins: viola

Hyde: slide trumpet

Jaquet-Droz: mechanical instruments
Jaye: viol
Jeffries: concertina

Kaufmann: Geigenwerk
Keat: trumpet
Keene: spinet
Kerner: trumpet
Key: bass horn, serpent
Kimball: reed organ
Kirckman: harpsichord
Klosé: clarinet
Koenig: tuning fork
Köhler: slide trumpet, valves
Korg: pitch
Kram: cittern
Kruspe: horn
Ktesibios: hydraulis

Lachenal: concertina
Ladegast: organ
Landolfi: violin
Laurent: flute
Leblanc: contrabass clarinet
Leclerc: mélophone
Leedy: vibraphone
Leichamschneider: horn
Liessem: English guitar
Light: harp-lute
Lochman: musical box
Lorée: oboe
Lot: flute
Lott: violin
Ludwig: timpani
Lupot: violin
Lyon: harp
Lyon & Healy: dulcimer, harp

MacCann: concertina
Machell: celesta
Maetzel: barrel organ, metronome
Maendler: xylophone
Maggini: double bass, viola, violin
Mahillon: bassoon, oboe d'amore, reed contrabass, trumpet
Maler: lute
Marenghi: barrel organ
Marigaux: bass oboe, oboe
Martin, C. F.: guitar
Martin, L.: harmonium
Mason & Hamlin: reed organ
Mayrhofer: basset horn
Meares: viol
Meares & Stainbank: bell
Meikle: tenoroon
Milhouse: bassoon, oboe
Moeck: crumhorn
Monk: cornett
Montagnana: violin
Moritz: tuba
Mortier: barrel organ

Morton: contrabassoon
Muller, I.: alto clarinet, clarinet
Müller, M.: piano
Mustel: celesta, harmonium

Naderman: harp
Naldi: chitarrone
Nicole: musical box
Niemecz: barrel organ
Norman: viol
Northey: diaphone

Oberlender: recorder
Oehler: clarinet
Orsi: rothphone

Pace: clavicor, cornet, slide trumpet,
    trombone
Pages: guitar
Paiste: gong and tamtam
Palmer: orpharion
Panormo: guitar
Pape: harp, piano
Paul: electric guitar
Paxman: horn
Pelitti: duplex, 2
Pepper: sousaphone
Périnet: valves
Perry: cither viol, English guitar
Pique: violin
Pittrich: timpani
Pleyel: harp, harpsichord, piano
Porthaux: bassoon
Powell: flute
Presbler: mandolin
Prescott: lap organ
Pressenda: violin
Preston: English guitar
Proser: flute
Püchner: bassoon

Regina Co.: musical box
Renault: tromba marina
Rhodes: electric piano
Riedl: valves
Ritter: viola
Rocca: violin
Rodenbostel: trumpet
Rogeri: violin
Roosevelt: organ
Rose: bandora, oroharion, viol
Roth: rothphone
Ruckers: harpsichord
Rudall, Rudall Carte: ballad horn, flute
Ruggeri: violin

Sacher: square piano
Salò, see Gasparo
Samme: contrabassoon
Sarrus: sarrusophone
Sattler: trombone, valves
Sauer: piano
Saurle: trumpet
Savary: bassoon

Sax: bass clarinet, saxhorn, saxophone,
    valved trombone
Schelle: lute
Scherer: organ
Scherr: harp-guitar
Schimmel: piano
Schnitger: organ
Schnitzer: trombone
Schoenhut: glockenspiel
Schorn: viola d'amore
Schunda: dulcimer, tarogato
Sellas: lute
Selmer: contrabass clarinet, horn
Serafin: violin
Shaw: valves
Shore: tuning fork
Shudi: harpsichord
Silbermann: organ, piano
Simcock: bell harp
Simpson: double flageolet
Smith: chamber organ, organ
Snetzler: organ
Soprani: accordion
Stainer: violin
Stanesby: contrabassoon, oboe, recorder
Staufer: arpeggione
Stegher: bass lute
Steiber: recorder
Stein: piano
Steinkopf: crumhorn
Steinway: duplex, piano, square piano
Stodart: fortepiano, piano
Stoelzel: valves
Storioni: violin
Stowasser: helicon
Stradivari: cello, cittern, viola, violin
Stroh: Stroh violin
Stumpff: timpani

Tabel: harpsichord
Tannenberg: organ
Taskin: harpsichord
Taylor: bell
Testore: violin
Theewes: claviorgan
Tieffenbrucker: lute
Tielke: cittern
Torres: guitar
Tour, de la: siren
Tourte: bow, violin
Triebert: bassoon, oboe

Uhlig: concertina

Venere: lute
Ventura: harp-lute
Vicento: keyboard
Vinaccia: mandolin
Virchi: cittern
Votey: player piano
Vuillaume: double bass, viola

Walcker: organ

Wallis: Giorgi flute
Welte: Player piano
Wheatstone: concertina
Wieprecht: tuba, valves
Wier, crumhorn
Willis: organ
Winkel: barrel organ
Woeggel: trumpet
Wood: tenoroon

Wornum: piano
Wurlitzer: barrel organ, cinema organ, harp

Yamaha: flute, piano

Zenti: spinet
Zildjian: cymbal
Zuleger: oboe
Zumpe: square piano
Zwahlen: seraphine

WORKS CITED

Place of publication is London unless otherwise stated.

Abbott, Djilda, and Segerman, Ephraim (1974), 'Strings in the 16th and 17th Centuries', *GSJ* 27.

Adkins, C. J. (1974), 'Investigation of the Sound-Producing Mechanism of the Jew's Harp', *J. Acoustical Society of America*, 55.

—— *et al.* (1981), 'Frequency-doubling chordophones', *Musica Asiatica*, 3.

—— and Dickinson, Alis (1982), 'Towards an Etymology of the Trumpet Marine', *JAMIS* 8.

Adkins, Hector E. (1945), *Treatise on the Military Band*, (rev. edn. 1958).

Agazzari, Agostino (1607), *Del sonare sopra'l basso con tutti li stromenti* (Siena, repr. Milan, 1933).

Agricola, Martin (1528, 1545), *Musica instrumentalis deudsch* (Wittenberg, repr. 1969).

Alexandru, Tiberiu (1974), 'Die rumänische Panflöte', *Studia instrumentorum musicae popularis*, iii (Stockholm).

Altenburg, Johann E. (1795), *Versuch einer Anleitung zur . . . Trompeter- und Pauker-Kunst* (Halle, repr. 1911; trans. Edward H. Tarr, 1974).

Andersen, Paul G. (1969), *Organ Building and Design*.

Anderson, R. D. (1976), *Catalogue of Egyptian Musical Instruments in the British Museum*.

Andersson, Otto (1930), *The Bowed Harp*, trans. Kathleen Schlesinger.

Ankermann, Bernard (1901), *Die Afrikanischer Musikinstrumente* (Berlin; repr. Leipzig, 1976).

Anoyanakis, Fivos (1979), *Greek Popular Musical Instruments* (Athens).

Armstrong, R. B. (1908), *Musical Instruments, Part II: English and Irish Instruments* (Edinburgh).

Arnaut of Zwolle, Henri (1454): Le Cerf, G., and Labande, E. R., *Instruments de musique du xve siècle: 'Les Traités d'Henri-Arnaut de Zwolle et de divers anonymes.* (Paris, 1932).

Arnold, Frank T. (1931), *The Art of Accompaniment from a Thorough-bass* (rev. edn. 1965).

Aubry, Pierre (1908), *Cent motets du XIIIe siècle* (Paris).

Audsley, George A. (1905), *The Art of Organ-Building* (New York; rev. edn. 1965).

Bach, Carl Philipp Emanuel (1753–62, Berlin) trans. William J. Mitchell (1949), *Essay on the True Art of Playing Keyboard Instruments* (New York).

Bachmann, Alberto (1925), *An Encyclopedia of the Violin* (New York).

Bachmann, Werner (1964, Leipzig), trans. Norma Deane (1969), *The Origins of Bowing*.

Bachmann-Geiser, B. (1981), *Die Volksmusikinstrumente der Schweiz* (Leipzig).

Backus, John (1969), *The Acoustical Foundations of Music* (New York).

Bahnert, Heinz, Herzburg, Th., and Schramm, Herbert (1958), *Metallblasinstrumente* (Leipzig).

Baines, Anthony (1951), 'Two Cassel Inventories', *GSJ* 4.

—— (1952), 'Shawms of the Sardana Coblas', *GSJ* 5.

—— (1957), *Woodwind Instruments and their History*.

—— (1960), *Bagpipes* (Oxford).

—— (1961), *Musical Instruments through the Ages*.

—— (1966), *European and American Musical Instruments*.

—— (1976), *Brass Instruments: Their History and Development*.

Baines, Francis (1975), 'Introducing the Hurdy-Gurdy', *EM* 3.1 (Jan.).

Balfour, Henry (1890), 'The Old British "Pibcorn" or "Hornpipe" ', *Journal of the Anthropological Institute*, 20.

—— (1899), *The Natural History of the Musical Bow* (Oxford).

Banchieri, Adriano (1609), *Conclusioni nel suono dell' organo* (Bologna).

Barbour, J. Murray (1951), *Tuning and Temperament* (East Lancing, Mich.).

Barnes, John (1979), 'Bach's Keyboard Temperament', *EM* 7.2 (Apr.).

Baron, Ernst G. (1727), *Historisch-theoretisch und practische Untersuchung des Instruments der Lauten* (Nuremberg); trans. 1976.

Barrenechea, José M. (1976), *Alboka* (Lecaroz, Navarre).

Barry, Wilson (1985), 'Henri Arnaut de Zwolle's *Clavicordium* and the Origin of the Chekker', *JAMIS* 11.

Bartholomew, John (1980), *The Steel Band*.

Bartók, Béla (1976): *Essays*, selected and edited by Benjamin Suchoff.

Bartolozzi, Bruno (1967), *New Sounds for Woodwind*.

Bate, Philip (1956), *The Oboe*.

—— (1966), *The Trumpet and Trombone*.

—— (1969), *The Flute*.

Bedos de Celles, Dom François (1778), *L'Art du facteur d'orgues* (Paris; repr. 1936).

Bellow, A. (1970), *Illustrated History of the Guitar* (New York).

Benade, Arthur (1976), *Fundamentals of Musical Acoustics* (New York).

Bendinelli, Cesare (1614), *Tutta l'arte della trombetta* (MS., Verona, trans. Edward Tarr, Nashville, 1975).

Benoit, Marcelle (1971), *Musiques de cour* (Paris).

Bentzon, Andreas (1969), *The Launeddas* (Copenhagen).

Berger, Kenneth (1957), *The March King and his Band* (New York).

Berliner, P. F. (1978), *The Soul of Mbira* (Berkeley, Calif.).

Berlioz, Hector (1858), *Modern Instrumentation and Orchestration* (trans. of Paris, 1844).

Bermudo, Fray Juan (1555), *Declaración de Instrumentos musicales* (Osuna; repr. Kassel, 1957).

Bertini, Auguste (1837), *New System for Learning . . . All Instruments* (part trans. Arnold Myers, *GSJ* 39 (1986)).

Bessaraboff, Nicholas (1941), *Ancient European Musical Instruments* (Boston).

Bevan, Clifford (1978), *The Tuba Family*.

Bilson, Malcolm (1980), 'The Viennese Fortepiano of the Late 18th Century', *EM* 8.2 (Apr.).

Bismantova, Bartolomeo (1677), *Compendio Musicale* (MS, Ferrara; facs. edn. Florence, 1983).

Blades, James (1961), *Orchestral Percussion Technique*.

—— (1970), *Percussion Instruments and their History*.

Boalch, Donald H. (1956), *Makers of the Harpsichord and Clavichord* (rev. edn. 1974).

Boehm, Theobald (1871), *The Flute and Flute-Playing* (Munich; trans. Dayton C. Miller, Cleveland, 1922).

Bogoras W. (1909), *The Chukchee*.

Bonanni, Filippo (1722), *Gabinetto Armonico* (Rome).

Bonner, Stephen (1972), *The Classic Image* (Harlow).

Bonta, Stephen (1977), 'From Violone to Violoncello: A Question of Strings?', *JAMIS* 3.

Bowers, Jane (1977), 'New Light on the Development of the Transverse Flute', *JAMIS* 3.

Bowers, Q. David (1972), *Encyclopedia of Automatic Musical Instruments* (New York).

Boydell, Barra (1982), *The Crumhorn and Other Renaissance Windcap Instruments* (Buren, Netherlands).

Boyden, David, D. (1965), *The History of Violin Playing from its Origins to 1761*.

—— (1980), 'The Violin Bow in the 18th Century', *EM* 8.2 (Apr.).

Brand, Erick D. (1942), *Band Instrument Repairing Manual* (Elkhart, Ind.).

Brandel, Rose (1961), *The Music of Central Africa* (The Hague).

Brindley, Giles (1968), 'The Logical Bassoon', *GSJ* 21.

Bröcker, Marianne (1973), *Die Drehleier* (Düsseldorf).

Broholm, Hans C., *et al.* (1949), *The Lurs of the Bronze Age* (Copenhagen).

Brown, Clive (1988), 'The Orchestra in Beethoven's Vienna', *EM* 16.1 (Jan.).

Brown, H. Mayer (1967), *Instrumental Music Printed before 1600* (Cambridge, Mass.).

Brussels Museum of Musical Instruments (1976, 1978), 'The Bagpipes in Europe', *Bulletin*, ed. René De Maeyer, 6, 8.

Brymer, J. (1976), *The Clarinet*.

Buchner, Alexander (1957), *Musical Instruments through the Ages.*

—— (1959), *Mechanical Musical Instruments.*

Byrne, Maurice (1971), 'Instruments for the Goldsmiths Company', *GSJ* 24.

—— (1983), 'Pierre Jaillard, Peter Bressan', *GSJ* 36.

Camden, A. (1962), *Bassoon Technique.*

Cameron, L. C. R. (*c.* 1905), *The Hunting Horn.*

Campbell, Margaret (1980), *The Great Violinists.*

Campbell, Murray, and Greated, Clive (1987), *The Musician's Guide to Acoustics.*

Cannon, Roderick D. (1988), *The Highland Bagpipe and its Music.*

Carse, Adam (1939), *Musical Wind Instruments.*

—— (1940), *The Orchestra in the XVIIIth Century* (Cambridge).

—— (1948), *The Orchestra from Beethoven to Berlioz* (Cambridge).

Castallani, Marcello (1977), 'The *Regola per suonare il Flauto Italiano* by Bartolomeo Bismantova (1677)', *GSJ* 30.

Chao Mei-pa (1969), *A Guide to Chinese Music* (Hong Kong).

Chassaing, Jean-F. (1983), *La Tradition de Cornemuse en Basse-Auvergne et Sud-Bourbonnais* (Moulins).

Clack, John E. T. (1948), *Musical Boxes* (Birmingham).

Clutton, Cecil, and Niland, Austin (1963), *The British Organ.*

Coates, Kevin (1985), *Geometry, Proportion, and the Art of Lutherie.*

Cockaygne, Eric V. (1971), *The Fairground Organ* (Newton Abbot).

Cocks, William A., and Bryan, J. F. (1967), *The Northumbrian Bagpipes* (Newcastle upon Tyne).

Collaer, Paul (1965, [1967], 1976), *Musikgeschichte in Bildern*: I.1 *Ozeanien*, I.2 *Amerika*, I.3 *Südöstasien* (Leipzig).

Collinson, Francis (1975), *The Bagpipe.*

Colt, C. F. (1981), *The Early Piano.*

Coover, James (1981), *Musical Instrument Collections, Catalogues, and Cognate Literature* (Detroit).

Cowling, Elizabeth (1975), *The Cello.*

Crane, Frederick (1972), *Extant Medieval Musical Instruments* (Iowa City, Ia.).

Cyr, Mary (1982), '*Basses* and *Basse Continue* in the Orchestra of the Paris Opéra', *EM* 10.2 (Apr.).

Dahlquist, Reine (1973), 'Taille, Oboe da Caccia and Corno Inglese', *GSJ* 26.

—— (1975), *The Keyed Trumpet and its Greatest Virtuoso, Anton Weidinger* (Nashville).

—— (1980), 'Some Notes on the Early Valve', *GSJ* 33.

Danks, Harry (1976), *The Viola d'Amore* (Halesowen).

Dart, Thurston (1948), 'The Cittern and its English Music', *GSJ* 1.

—— (1953), 'The Mock Trumpet', *GSJ* 6.

—— (1960), 'Bach's 'Fiauti d'Echo', *Music and Letters*, 41.4.

—— (ed.) (1957), *The Consort Lessons Collected By Thomas Morley.*

Davison, Archibald T., and Apel, Willi (1947), *Historical Anthology of Music: Oriental, Medieval and Renaissance Music* (Cambridge, Mass.).

Del Mar, Norman (1987), *A Companion to the Orchestra.*

Densmore, Frances (1927), *Handbook of the Collections of Musical Instruments in the United States National Museum: Bulletin 136* (Washington, DC).

Devale, Sue C. (1988), 'Musical Instruments and Ritual: A Systematic Approach', *JAMIS* 14.

Dobson, Richard (1992), *A Dictionary of Electronic and Computer Music Technology: Instruments, Terms, Techniques* (Oxford).

Dolge, Alfred (1911), *Pianos and their Makers* (Covina, Calif.).

Dolmetsch, Nathalie (1962), *The Viola da Gamba.*

Donington, Robert (1973), *A Performer's Guide to Baroque Music.*

Downie, Margaret A. (1979–80), 'The Modern Greek Lyra', *JAMIS* 7.

Duchesne-Guillemin, Marcelle (1966), 'L'Aube de la théorie musicale', *Revue de musicologie* (Paris) 52.2.

—— (1969), 'La théorie babylonienne des métaboles musicales', *Revue de musicologie* 55.1.

Dudgeon, Ralph T. (1983), 'Joseph Haliday, Inventor of the Keyed Bugle', *JAMIS* 9.

Dureau, Th. (1905), *Cours théorique et pratique d'Instrumentation . . . à l'usage des Harmonies et Fanfares* (Paris).

Duriyanga, Phra Chen (1948), *Thai Music* (Bangkok).

Edmunds, Martin (1980), 'Venetian Viols of the Sixteenth Century', *GSJ* 33.

Ehrlich, Cyril (1976), *The Piano: A History* (rev. edn. Oxford, 1990).

Eisel, J. P. (1738), *Musicus antodidactos* (Erfurt).

Elgar, Raymond (1960), *Introduction to the Double Bass* (St Leonards-on-Sea).

—— (1963), *More about the Double Bass* (St Leonards-on-Sea).

Eliason, Robert E. (1970), 'Early American Valves for Brass Instruments', *GSJ* 23.

—— (1982, 1983), 'George Catlin, Hartford Musical Instrument Maker', *JAMIS* 8, 9.

Ellis, Alexander J. (1880), 'On the History of Musical Pitch', *J. Society of Arts*, 28.

EM = *Early Music* (from 1973).

Enslein, Carl F. (n.d.), *Theoretische-praktische Zither-Schule* (Vienna).

Erlanger, Rodolphe d' (1930), *La Musique arabe, i* (Paris).

Evans, Tom, and Evans, Mary Anne (1977), *Guitars: Music, History, Construction and Players from the Renaissance to Rock* (New York).

Farga, Franz (1950), *Violins and Violinists.*

Farkas, Philip (1962), *The Art of Brass Playing* (Bloomington, Ind.).

Farmer, Henry G. (1957), 'Ancient Mesopotamia'; 'Islam', *New Oxford History of Music*, i. chs. V, XI.

Fischer, Hans (1983), *Sound-Producing Instruments in Oceania* trans. from German by Philip W. Holzknecht, ed. Don Miles (Boroko, Institute of Papua New Guinea Studies).

Fitzpatrick, Horace (1970), *The Horn and Horn-Playing, 1680–1830.*

—— (1972), 'The Gemshorn: A Reconstruction', *PRMA* 99.

Fleischhauer, Günter (1964), *Etrurien und Rom (Musikgeschichte in Bildern, II/5;* Leipzig).

Floyd, Leela (1980), *Indian Music.*

Forsyth, Cecil (1914), *Orchestration.*

Fox Strangways, A. S. (1914), *The Music of Hindustan.*

Fruchtmann, E. (1962), 'The Baryton', *Acta Musicologica,* 34 (Basle).

Gai, V. (1969), *Gli Strumenti musicali della Corte Medicea e il Museo del Conservatorio 'Luigi Cherubini' di Firenze* (Florence).

Galpin, Francis W. (1903), 'The Whistles and Reed Instruments of the American Indians of the North-West Coast', *PRMA* 29.

—— (1910), *Old English Instruments of Music.*

—— (1937), *The Music of the Sumerians.*

Ganassi, Silvestro (1535), *Opera intitulata Fontegara* (Venice; repr. 1970).

—— (1542), *Regola rubertina* (Venice; repr. 1970).

Geiser, Brigitte (1974a), 'Cister und Cistermacher in der Schweitz', *SIMP* 3.

—— (1974b), *Studien zur Frühgeschichte der Violine* (Berne).

—— (1976), *Das Alphorn in der Schweiz* (Berne). See also Bachmann-Geiser.

Gellermann, Robert F. (1973), *The American Reed Organ* (New York).

Geminiani, Francesco (1751), *The Art of Playing on the Violin* (facs. edn. 1952).

Gerle, Hans (1532, 1546), *Musica Teusch* (Nuremberg; repr. 1977).

Gill, Dominic (ed.) (1981), *The Book of the Piano.*

Gill, Donald (1960), 'The Orpharion and Bandora', *GSJ* 13.

—— (1981), 'Mandores and Colachons', *GSJ* 34.

Gilliam, Laura E. (1961), *The Dayton C. Miller Flute Collection: A Checklist* (Washington, DC).

Ginzburg, Lev (1983), *History of the Violoncello* (trans. from Russian).

Goldman, R. Franko (1961), *The Wind Band* (Boston).

Goodman, W. L. (1974), 'Musical Instruments and their Makers in Bristol Apprentice Register, 1536–1643', *GSJ* 27.

Grace, Nancy (1983), *The Hammered Dulcimer in America* (Washington, DC).

Gray Birch, Walter de, and Jenner, Henry (1879), *Early Drawings and Illuminations* (London).

Green, Robert (1982), 'The *Pardessus de Viole* and its Literature', *EM* 10.3 (July).

Gregory, Robin (1961), *The Horn.*

—— (1973), *The Trombone.*

Grunfeld, Frederick V. (1969), *The Art and Times of the Guitar* (New York).

GSJ = *Galpin Society Journal* (from 1948).

Guizzi, Febo, and Leydi, Roberto (1985), 'La Zampogne in Italia', *Strumenti musicali popolari,* i (Milan).

Gurvin, O. (ed.) (1958–67), *Hardingsfeleslåttar (Norske Folkemusic,* Oslo).

Gusinde, Martin (1937), *The Yamana* (Vienna; Eng. trans. New Haven 1961).

Gwozda L. (1987), see Kool, Jaap (1931).

Hadaway, Robert (1973), 'The Cittern', *EM* 1.2 (Apr.).

—— (1978), 'Another Look at the Viol', *EM* 6.4 (Oct.).

Haddon, A. (c. 1898), *The Study of Man.*

Haefer, J. Richard (1975), 'North American Indian Musical Instruments', *JAMIS* 1.

Haine, Malou (1980), *Adolphe Sax, sa vie, son œuvre et ses instruments de musique* (Brussels).

Halfpenny, Eric (1949), 'The English 2- and 3-Keyed Hautboy', *GSJ* 2.

—— (1951), 'Musicians at James II's Coronation', *Music and Letters,* 32.2.

—— (1952), 'The "Tenner Hoboy"', *GSJ* 5.

—— (1954), 'Tantivy: An Exposition of the "Ancient Hunting Notes"', *GSJ* 80.

—— (1956), 'The English Baroque Treble Recorder', *GSJ* 9.

—— (1957), 'The Evolution of the Bassoon in England, 1750–1800', *GSJ* 10.

—— (1962), 'William Bull and the English Baroque Trumpet', *GSJ* 15.

—— (1965), 'Early English Clarinets', *GSJ* 18.

—— (1967, 1969, 1971), (further articles on British trumpets, *GSJ* 20–2, 24).

—— (1978), 'The Mythology of the English Harp', *GSJ* 31.

Hall, Donald E. (1980), *Musical Acoustics.*

Hall, Monica J. L. (1978), 'The "Guitarra española" of Joan Carles Arnat', *EM* 6.3 (July).

Hanks, Sarah E. (1969), 'Pantaleon's Pantalon: an 18th-Century Musical Fashion', *Musical Quarterly* 55.2.

Harcourt, R. and M. d' (1925), *La Musique des Incas de ses survivances* (Paris).

Harding, Rosamund (1933), *The Pianoforte: Its History Traced to the Great Exhibition of 1851* (Cambridge; rev. edn. 1978).

Harich-Schneider, Eta (1973), *A History of Japanese Music.*

Harris, Rice (1975), *The Piano: A Pictorial Account.*

Harrison, Frank, and Rimmer, Joan (1964), *European Musical Instruments.*

Harwood, Ian (1974), 'An Introduction to Renaissance Viols', *EM* 2.4 (Oct.).

—— and Edmunds, Martin (1978), 'Reconstructing 16th-Century Venetian Viols', *EM* 6.4 (Oct.).

Hayes, Gerald R. (1930), *Musical Instruments and their Music, 1500–1750,* ii.

Haynes, Bruce (1976), 'Making Reeds for the Baroque Oboe', *EM* 4.1, 4.2 (Jan., Apr.).

—— (1978), 'Oboe Fingering Charts, 1695–1816', *GSJ* 31.

—— (1985), 'Johann Sebastian Bach's Pitch Standards: The Woodwind Perspective', *JAMIS* 11.

Heartz, Daniel (1963), 'An Elizabethan Tutor for the Guitar', *GSJ* 16.

Hedlund, H. Jean (1958), 'Ensemble Music for Small Bassoons', *GSJ* 11.

Hellwig, Friedemann (1974), 'Lute Construction in the Renaissance and the Baroque', *GSJ* 27.

—— (1976), 'Strings and Stringing: Contemporary Documents', *GSJ* 27.

—— (1981), 'The Morphology of Lutes with Extended Bass Strings', *EM* 9.4 (Oct.).

Hellyer, Roger (1976), 'The Transcriptions for *Harmonie* of *Die Entführung aus dem Serail*'. *PRMA* 102.

Helmholtz, Hermann L. F. (1875), trans. Alexander J. Ellis, *On the Sensations of Tone* (repr. New York, 1954).

Henley, William (1959), *Universal Dictionary of Violin and Bow Makers* (Brighton).

Henríquez, Alejandro (1973), *Organología del Folklore Chileno* (Valparaiso).

Heron-Allen, Edward (1885), *Violin Making as it Was, and Is* (frequently repr.).

Heyde, Herbert (1986a), communication by Albert Rice in *JAMIS,* p. 176.

—— (1986b), *Musikinstrumentenbau* (Leipzig).

—— (1987a), *Das Ventilblasinstrument* (Wiesbaden).

—— (1987b), 'Contrabassoons in the 17th and early 18th Century', *GSJ* 40.

Hickmann, Ellen (1971), *Musica instrumentalis* (Baden-Baden).

Hickmann, Hans (1949), *Catalogue général des antiquités Égyptiennes du Musée du Caire* (Cairo).

—— (1961), *Ägypten* (Musikgeschichte in Bildern, II/1; Leipzig).

Higbee, Dale (1986), 'Bach's *Fiauti d'Echo*', *GSJ* 39.

Hill, John W. (1983), 'Realized Continuo Accompaniments from Florence c. 1600', *EM* 11.2 (Apr.).

Hill, W. Henry, Arthur F., and Alfred E. (1902), *Antonio Stradivari* (repr. New York, 1963).

Hiller, Albert (1985), *Das Grosse Buch vom Posthorn* (Wilhelmshaven).

Hillsman, Walter (1980), 'Instrumental Accompaniment of Plain-Chant in France from the late 18th Century', *GSJ* 33.

Hind, Harold (1934), *The Brass Band*.

Holland, James (1978), *Percussion*.

Hoover, Cynthia Adams (1981), 'The Steinways and their Pianos in the Nineteenth Century', *JAMIS* 7.

Hornbostel, Erich M. von, and Sachs, Curt (1914), 'Systematik der Musikinstrumente: Ein Versuch', *Zeitschrift für Ethnologie*, 4–5 (Berlin). Trans. Anthony Baines and Klaus P. Wachsmann (1961), 'Classification of Musical Instruments', *GSJ* 14.

Horwood, Wally (1980), *Adolphe Sax, His Life and Legacy*.

Hotteterre, Jacques (1707), *Principes de la Flûte traversière* (Paris; repr. Berlin, 1941).

Howell, Thomas (1974), *The Avant-Garde Flute* (Berkeley, Calif.).

Hubbard, Frank (1965), *Three Centuries of Harpsichord Making* (Cambridge, Mass.).

Hunt, Edgar (1962), *The Recorder and its Music*.

Hutchins, Carleen M. (1962), 'The Physics of Violins', *Scientific American*.

—— (1976), *Musical Acoustics* (Stroudsburg, Pa.).

Huws-Jones, Edward (1972), 'The Theorbo and Continuo Practice in the Early English Baroque', *GSJ* 25.

Hyatt-King, Alec (1945), 'Mountain, Music, and Musicians', *Musical Quarterly* 31.4.

—— (1946), 'The Musical Glasses and Glass Harmonica', *PRMA* 72.

Hyslop, Graham (1975), *Musical Instruments of East Africa*, i: *Kenya* (Nairobi).

Izikowitz, Karl G. (1934), *Musical and Other Sound Instruments of the South American Indians* (Göteborg; repr. East Ardsley, 1970).

Jaffrennou, Gildas (1973), *Folk Harps* (Kings Langley).

Jahnel, Franz (1963), *Die Gitarre und ihr Bau* (Frankfurt/Main).

Jalovec, Karel (1968), *Encyclopedia of Violin-Makers*.

Jambe-de-Fer, Philibert (1556), *Epitome musical* (Lyons; repr. F. Lesure, *Annales musicologiques* 6, (1958–63), Paris).

James, Philip (1930), *Early Keyboard Instruments* (repr. 1970).

JAMIS = *Journal of the American Musical Instrument Society* (Vermillion, S. Dak., from 1975).

Janetzky, Kurt, and Brüchle, Bernhard (1976), *A Pictorial History of the Horn* (Tutzing; trans. James Chater 1988).

Jeans, Susi (1986), 'The Psalterer' *GSJ* 39.

Jenkins, Jean (1977), *International Dictionary of Musical Instrument Collections* (Buren, Netherlands).

—— and Olsen P. R. (1976), *Music and Musical Instruments of the World of Islam*.

Jones, A. M. (1959), *Studies in African Music*.

Jones, Trevor A. (1983), 'Australia', *NOCM*.

Joppig, Gunther (1988), *The Oboe and the Bassoon*.

Junius, Manfred (1974), *The Sitar* (Wilhelmshaven).

Karomatov, F. (1972), *Uzbekskaja instrumental'naja muzyka* (Tashkent).

Karp, Cary (1973), 'Structural Details of Two J. H. Eichentopf Oboi da Caccia', *GSJ* 26.

Kartomi, Margaret J. (1985), *Musical Instruments of Indonesia* (Melbourne).

Kastner, Georges (1848), *Manuel général de musique militaire* (Paris; repr. Geneva 1973).

Kaudern, Walter (1927), *Musical Instruments in Celebes* (Göteborg).

Keepnews, Ozzin, and Grauer, Bill (n.d.), *A Pictorial History of Jazz* (repr. 1968).

Kessler, Dietrich M. (1982), 'Viol Construction in 17th-Century England', *EM* 10.3 (July).

Kettlewell, David (1974), 'First Steps on the Dulcimer', *EM* 2.4 (Oct.).

Kinsky, Georg (1930), *A History of Music in Pictures*.

Kirby, Percival R. (1934), *The Musical Instruments of the Native Races of South Africa*.

Kirkpatrick, Ralph (1981), 'On Playing the Clavichord', *EM* 9.3 (July).

Kool, Jaap (1931), *Das Saxophon* (Leipzig; trans. Lawrence Gwozda 4, 1987).

Koster, John (1980), 'The Importance of the Early English Harpsichord', *GSJ* 33.

Kothari, K. S. (1968), *Indian Folk Musical Instruments* (New Delhi).

Kottick, Edward L. (1985), 'The Acoustics of the Harpsichord', *GSJ* 38.

Krishnaswami, S. (1971), *Musical Instruments of India* (Boston).

Kroll, Oskar (1968), *The Clarinet*, trans. Hilda Morris.

Kunst, Jaap (1942), *Music in Flores* (Leyden).

—— (1949), *The Music of Java* (The Hague; 3rd edn., ed. E. L. Heins, *Music in Java*, 1973).

—— (1967), *Music in New Guinea: Three Studies* (The Hague).

Kunz, Ludvík (1974), *Die Volksmusikinstrumente der Tschechoslowakei*, i (Leipzig).

Lamaña, José M. (1969), 'Los instrumentos musicales de la dinastía . . . de Barcelona', *Anuario Musical*, 24.

Lanfranco, Giovanni M. (1533), *Scintille di musica* (Brescia).

Langwill, Lyndesay G. (1960), *An Index of Musical Wind-Instrument Makers* (Edinburgh; 4th edn., 1974).

—— (1965), *The Bassoon and Contrabassoon*.

—— and Boston, Noel (1967), *Church and Chamber Barrel-Organs* (Edinburgh).

Larsson, Gunnar (1979), 'Die estnisch-schwedische Streichleier', *SIMP* 6.

La Rue, Hélène (1982), 'The Problem of the Cymbala', *GSJ* 35.

Lasocki, David (1986), 'The Bassanos: Anglo-Venetian and Venetian', *EM* 14.4 (Nov.).

Lavignac, Albert, and De La Laurencie, Lionel (eds.) (1913, etc.), *Encyclopédie de la Musique et Dictionnaire du Conservatoire*, i (Paris).

Lawson, Colin (1981), *The Chalumeau in Eighteenth-Century Music* (Ann Arbor, Mich.).

Ledang, Ola (1974), 'Instrument—Player—Music on the Norwegian Langleik', *SIMP* 3.

Leng, Ladislav (1967), *Slovenské ľudové hudobné nástroje* (Slovak popular musical instruments) (Bratislava).

Libin, Laurence (1985), *American Musical Instruments in the Metropolitan Museum of Art* (New York).

Lichtenwanger, William, et al. (1974), *A Survey of Musical Instrument Collections in the United States and Canada* (Ann Arbor, Mich.).

Lindley, Mark (1977), 'Instructions for the Clavier Diversely Tempered', *EM* 5.1 (Jan.).

—— (1984), *Lutes, Viols, and Temperaments* (Cambridge).

Lindsay, Jennifer (1979), *Javanese Gamelan* (Kuala Lumpur).

Ling, Jan (1967), *Nyckelharpan* (Stockholm; with Eng. summary).

Loesser, Arthur (1955), *Men, Women and Pianos: A Social History* (New York).

Lolov, Athanas (1984), 'Bent Plates in Violin Construction', *GSJ* 37.

Longworth, Mike (1975), *Martin Guitars: A History*.

Loretto, Alec (1973), 'Recorder Modifications: In Search of the Expressive Recorder', *EM* 1.2–4 (Apr.–Oct.).

Lumsden, David (1953), 'The Sources of English Lute Music (1540–1620)', *GSJ* 6.

Lund, Cajsa S. (ed.) (1987), *The Bronze Lurs, Second Conference of the ICTM Study Group on Music Archaeology*, ii (Stockholm).

Lütgendorff, Willibald L. von (1958), *Die Geigen- und Lautenmacher* (Frankfurt/Main).

McBride, William (1982), 'The Early Saxophone in Patents 1838–1850 Compared', *GSJ* 35.

MacDonald, Joseph (1803), *A Compleat Theory of the Scots Highland Bagpipes* (Inverness; repr. East Ardsley 1971).

Mace, Thomas (1676), *Musick's Monument* (facs. repr. 1966).

McGeary, Thomas (1989), 'German–Austrian Keyboard Temperaments and Tuning Methods, 1770–1840', *JAMIS* 15.

McLean, Mervyn (1974), 'The New Zealand Nose Flute: Fact or Fallacy?', *GSJ* 27.

McNett, Charles (1960), 'The Chirimia: A Latin American Shawm', *GSJ* 13.

McPhee, Colin (1966), *Music in Bali* (New Haven, Conn.).

Mahillon, Victor-Charles (1983, etc.), *Catalogue descriptif et analytique du Musée Instrumental du Conservatoire Royal de Musique Bruxelles* (repr. 1978).

Majer, Joseph F. B. C. (1732), *Museum Musicum* (Schwäb. Hall; facs. repr. Kassel, 1954).

Malm, William P. (1959), *Japanese Music and Musical Instruments* (Rutland, V.).

Marcuse, Sibyl (1964), *Musical Instruments: A Comprehensive Dictionary* (New York).

—— (1975), *A Survey of Musical Instruments* (Newton Abbot).

Martin, Lynn W. (1984), 'The Colonna-Stella *Sambuca Lincea*, an Enharmonic Keyboard Instrument', *JAMIS* 10.

Marvin, Bob (1972), 'Recorders and English Flutes in European Collections', *GSJ* 25.

Marx, Josef (1951), 'The Tone of the Baroque Oboe', *GSJ* 4.

Meadows Taylor, Captain (1864), 'Catalogue of Indian Musical Instruments', *Proc. Royal Irish Academy*.

Mendel, Arthur (1968), *Studies in the History of Musical Pitch* (Amsterdam).

Mersenne, Marin (1636), *Harmonie universelle* (Paris; repr. 1963; the books on instruments trans. Roger Chapman, The Hague, 1957).

Meucci, Renato (1989), 'Roman Military Instruments and the *Lituus*', *GSJ* 42.

Meyer, Kenton T. (1983), *The Crumhorn* (Ann Arbor, Mich.).

Meylan, Raymond (1988), *The Flute* (trans. Alfred Clayton).

Michaelides, Solon (1978), *The Music of Ancient Greece: An Encyclopaedia*.

Minor, Andrew C., and Mitchell, Bonner (1968), *A Renaissance Entertainment* (Columbia, Mo.).

Mobbs, Kenneth (1984), 'Stops and Other Special Effects on the Early Piano', *EM* 12.4 (Nov.).

Moeck, Hermann (1974), 'Czakane, englische und Wiener Flageolette', *SIMP* 3.

Monk, Christopher (1975), 'First Steps towards Playing the Cornett', *EM* 13.2, 3 (Apr., July).

Montagu, Jeremy (1976), *The World of Medieval and Renaissance Musical Instruments* (Newton Abbot).

—— (1979), *The World of Baroque and Classical Musical Instruments* (Newton Abbot).

—— (1981), *The World of Romantic and Modern Musical Instruments* (Newton Abbot).

Montanaro, Bruno (1983), *Guitares hispano-américaines* (Aix-en-Provence).

Monteverdi, Claudio (1607), *L'Orfeo, Favola in Musica*, ed. G. Francesco Malipiero, 1923.

Morgan, Fred (1982), 'Making Recorders based on Historical Models', *EM* 10.1 (Jan.).

Morley-Pegge, Reginald (1959), 'The "Anaconda"', *GSJ* 12.

—— (1960), *The French Horn* (rev. edn. 1973).

Morris, E. (1951), *Bells of All Nations*.

Morrow M. (1979), 'The Renaissance Harp', *EM* 7.4 (Oct.).

Morton, David (1976), *The Traditional Music of Thailand* (Berkeley, Calif.).

Mountney, Hugh (1969), 'The Regal', *GSJ* 22.

Moyle, Richard M. (1976–7), 'Tongan Musical Instruments', *GSJ* 29, 30).

Mozart, Leopold (1756), Augsburg, trans. Editha Knocker (1951), *A Treatise on the Fundamental Principles of Violin Playing*.

Murphy, Sylvia (1968), 'Seventeenth-Century Guitar Music: Notes on *Rasgueado* Performance', *GSJ* 21.

—— (1970), 'The Tuning of the Five-Course Guitar', *GSJ* 23.

Muskett, Doreen (1982), *Method for the Vielle or Hurdy-Gurdy*.

Myers, Arnold (1986), 'Fingering Charts for the Cimbasso and Other Instruments', *GSJ* 39.

Myers, Helen (1983), 'African Music', 'American Indian Music', 'Pacific Islands', 'South-East Asian Music', in *NOCM*.

Nelson, Sheila M. (1972), *The Violin and Viola*.

Neupert, Hanns (1960), *Harpsichord Manual* (trans. of *Das Cembalo*, Kassel, 1933).

—— (1948), *The Clavichord* (Kassel; trans., 1965).

New Grove Dictionary of Musical Instruments, ed. Stanley Sadie (1984).

New Oxford History of Music, i, ed. Egon Wellesz (1957).

Nickel, Ekkehart (1971), *Der Holzblasinstrumentenbau in der freien Reichsstadt Nürnberg* (Munich).

Nketia, J. H. Kwabena (1974), *The Music of Africa* (New York).

NOCM = The New Oxford Companion to Music, ed. Denis Arnold (Oxford, 1983).

Norlind, Tobias (1936), *Systematik der Saiteninstrumente* i: *Geschichte der Zither* (Stockholm).

—— (1941), *Musikinstrumentens Historia* (Stockholm).

North, Nigel (1987), *Continuo Playing on the Lute, Archlute and Theorbo*.

North, Roger (c. 1728), *The Musicall Grammarian* (ed. Hilda Andrews, 1925).

O'Brien, Grant G. (1979), 'Ioannes and Andreas Ruckers', *EM* 7.4 (Oct.).

Oliveira, Ernesto V. de (1966), *Instrumentos musicais populares portugueses* (Lisbon).

O'Loughlin, Niall (1982), 'The Recorder in 20th-Century Music', *EM* 10.1 (Jan.).

Ongaro, Giulio M. (1985), '16th-Century Venetian Wind Instrument Makers', *EM* 13.3 (Aug.).

Ord-Hume, Arthur W. J. G. (1973), *Clockwork Music: An Illustrated Musical History of Mechanical Musical Instruments*.

—— (1978), *Barrel Organ*.

—— (1980), *Musical Box*.

—— (1984), *Pianola*.

—— (1986), *The Harmonium: The History of the Reed Organ*.

Page, Christopher (1977), 'Biblical Instruments in Medieval Manuscripts', *EM* 5.3 (July).

—— (1978), 'Early 15th-Century Instruments in Jean de Gerson's "Tractatus de Canticis"', *EM* 6.3 (July).

—— (1979), 'Jerome of Moravia on the *Rubeba* and *Viella*', *GSJ* 32.

—— (1980), 'Fourteenth-Century Instruments and Tunings: A Treatise by Jean Vaillant?', *GSJ* 33.

—— (1981), 'The 15th-Century Lute: New and Neglected Sources', *EM* 9.1 (Jan.).

—— (1982), 'German Musicians and their Instruments: A 14th-Century Account by Konrad of Megenberg', *EM* 10.2 (Apr.).

—— (1982-3), 'The Medieval Organistrum and Symphonia', *GSJ* 35-6.

—— (1987), *Voices and Instruments of the Middle Ages*.

Palmer, Frances (1983), 'Musical Instruments from the *Mary Rose*', *EM* 11.1 (Jan.).

Panum, Hortense (1941), *The Stringed Instruments of the Middle Ages*, trans. Geoffrey Pulver.

Parkinson, Andrew (1981), 'Guesswork and the Gemshorn', *EM* 9.1 (Jan.).

Partridge, J. K., and Jeal, Frank (1977), 'The Maltese *Zaqq*', *GSJ* 30.

Pascual, B. Kenyon de (1986), 'The Wind-Instrument Maker, Bartolomé de Selma (†1616)', *GSJ* 39.

Peate, Iowerth C. (1947), 'Welsh Musical Instruments', *Man*, 47.

Peery, Paul D. (1948), *Chimes and Electric Carillons* (New York).

Peinkofer, Karl, and Tannigel, Fritz (1976), *Handbook of Percussion Instruments* (New York).

Perrot, Jean (1971), *The Organ, from its Invention in the Hellenistic Period to the End of the 13th Century*.

Picken, Laurence (1955), 'The Origins of the Short Lute', *GSJ* 8.

—— (1957), 'The Music of Far Eastern Asia', i: 'China', in Egon Wellesz (ed.), *New History of Music*, i.

—— (1975), *Folk Musical Instruments of Turken*.

—— (1981), 'The "Plucked" Drums: *Gopíy antra* and *Ānanda Laharī*', *Musica Asiatica*, 3 (Oxford).

Piggott, Sir Francis (1893), *The Music and Musical Instruments of Japan*, (repr. 1971).

Pilling, Julian (1975), 'Fiddles with Horns', *GSJ* 28.

Pinnell, Richard T. (1979), 'The Theorboed Guitar', *EM* 7.3 (July).

Planyavsky, Alfred (1970), *Geschichte des Kontrabasses* (Tutzing).

Playford, John (1652), *Musick's Recreation on the Lyra Viol* (repr. 1960).

—— (1654), *A Breefe Introduction to the Skill of Musick* (repr. 1966, 1973).

—— (1666), *Musick's Delight on the Cithren*.

Pleeth, William (1982), *The Cello*.

Plumley, Gwendoline (1976), *El Tanbur* (Cambridge).

Pohlmann, Ernst (1968), *Laute-Theorbe-Chitarrone* (Bremen).

Pollens, Stewart (1984), 'The Pianos of Bartolomeo Cristofori', *JAMIS* 10.

—— (1985), 'The Early Portuguese Piano', *EM* 13.1 (Feb.).

Poole, H. Edmund (1982), 'A Catalogue of Musical Instruments Offered for Sale in 1839 by D'Almaine & Co.', *GSJ* 35.

Popley, Herbert A. (1921), *The Music of India*.

Portnoi, Stephen (n.d.), *The Tin Whistle and its Role in Irish Folk Music* (Brighton).

Praetorius, Michael (1618), *Syntagma Musicum*, ii: *De Organographia* (Wolfenbüttel; trans. Harold Blumenfield, New York, 1962; David Z. Crookes, Oxford, 1986).

Prelleur, Peter (1731), *The Modern Musick Master* (repr. 1965).

Price, Percival (1933), *The Carillon* (Oxford).

—— (1983), *Bells and Man* (Oxford).

Pringle, John (1978), 'John Rose, the Founder of English Viol-Making', *EM* 6.4 (Oct.).

PRMA = *Proceedings of the Royal Musical Association*.

Prynne, Michael W. (1949), 'An Unrecorded Lute by Hans Frei', *GSJ* 2.

—— (1963), 'A Surviving Vihuela de Mario', *GSJ* 16.

Quantz, Johann Joachim (1752), *Versuch einer Anweisung die Flöte traversiere zu spielen* (Berlin; trans. E. R. Reilly, *On Playing the Flute*, 1966).

Rastall, Richard (1964), 'The Minstrels of the English Royal Households, 25 Edward I–Henry VIII: an Inventory', *RMA Research Chronicle*, 4.

Rayleigh, John W. S. (Lord), (1877), *The Theory of Sound* (repr. New York, 1945).

Reblitz, Arthur, A. (1988), *Player Piano Servicing and Rebuilding* (New York).

Rehnberg, Mats (1943), *Säckpipan i Sverige* (Stockholm; with Eng. summary).

Reidermeister, Peter (ed.) (1981), *Basler Jahrbuch für historische Musikpraxis* v, *Das Zinkbuch* (Winterthur).

Remnant, Mary (1986), *English Bowed Instruments from Anglo-Saxon to Tudor Times* (Oxford).

—— (1989), *Musical Instruments: An Illustrated History from Antiquity to the Present*.

Rendall, F. Geoffrey (1954), *The Clarinet* (rev. edn. 1971).

Rensch, Rosalyn (1969), *The Harp: Its History, Technique and Repertoire* (London and New York).

Retford, W. C. (1964), *Bows and Bow-Makers*.

Rice, Timothy (1982), 'The *Surla* and *Tapan* Tradition in Yugoslav Macedonia', *GSJ* 35.

Rice, W. G. (1926), *Carillon Music* (New York).

Ricks, R. (1969), 'Russian Horn Bands', *Musical Quarterly* 55.3.

Riley, Maurice W. (1980), *The History of the Viola* (Ann Arbor, Mich.).

Rimmer, Joan (1964a), 'Harps in the Baroque Era', *PRMA* 90.

—— (1964b), 'The Morphology of the Irish Harp', *GSJ* 17.

—— (1965-6), 'The Morphology of the Triple Harp', *GSJ* 18-19.

—— (1969a), *Ancient Musical Instruments of Western Asia in the British Museum*.

—— (1969b), *The Irish Harp* (Cork).

Ripin, Edwin M. (ed.) (1971), *Keyboard Instruments: Studies in Keyboard Organology* (Edinburgh).

—— (1974), *The Instrument Catalogs of Leopoldo Franciolini* (New York).

Ritchie, Jean (1963), *The Dulcimer Book* (New York).

Roberts, Helen H. (1926), *Ancient Hawaiian Music* (Honolulu; repr. New York, 1967).

Rockstro, Richard S. (1890), *A Treatise on . . . the Flute* (repr. 1928, 1967).

Rossing, T. D. (1976-7), 'Acoustics of Percussion Instruments', *Physics Teacher* (New York).

Rothwell, Evelyn (1953), *Oboe Technique*.

Rowland-Jones, A. (1959), *Recorder Technique*.

Rowsome, Leo (1936), *Tutor for the Uilleann Pipers* (Dublin).

Rubsamen, Walter H. (1968), 'The Earliest French Lute Tablature', *Journal of the American Musicological Society* 21.3.

Russell, John F., and Elliott, John H. (1936), *The Brass Band Movement*.

Russell, Raymond (1959), *The Harpsichord and Clavichord* (repr. 1979).

Sachs, Curt. (1913), *Real-Lexikon der Musikinstrumente* (Berlin; repr. 1964).

—— (1914), 'Systematik der Musikinstrumente', see Hornbostel, Erich von, and Sachs, Curt (1914).

—— (1928), *Geist und Werden der Musikinstrumente* (Berlin); repr. Hilversum, 1965).

—— (1930), *Handbuch der Musikinstrumentenkunde* (Berlin).

—— (1940), *The History of Musical Instruments* (New York).

—— (1943), *The Rise of Music in the Ancient World* (New York).

—— (1950), 'Chromatic Trumpets in the Renaissance' *Musical Quarterly*, 36.1.

—— (1959), *Vergleichende Musikwissenschaft* (Wilhelmshaven; repr. 1974).

Sandberg, Larry (1979), *Complete Banjo Repair* (New York).

Sárosi, Bálint (1967), *Die Volksmusikinstrumente Ungarns* (Leipzig).

Schaeffner, André (1936), *Origine des Instruments de Musique* (Paris).

Schechter, John M. (1984–5), 'The Diatonic Harp in Ecuador', *JAMIS* 10, 11.

Schlick, Arnold (1511), *Spiegel der Orgelmacher* (Speyer; repr. 1959; trans. E. B. Baxter, Buren, Netherlands).

Schlosser, Julius (1920), *Die Sammlung alter Musikinstrumente* (Vienna; repr. 1970).

Schott, Howard (1971), *Playing the Harpsichord*.

—— (1974), 'The Harpsichord Revival', *EM* 2.2 (Apr.).

Schröder, Jaap, and Hogwood, Christopher (1979), 'The Developing Violin', *EM* 7.2 (Apr.).

Selfridge-Field, Eleanor (1976), 'Bassano and the Orchestra of St Mark's', *EM* 4.2 (Apr.).

Sendrey, Alfred (1969), *Music in Ancient Israel* (New York).

Shackleton, Nicholas (1987), 'The Earliest Basset Horns', *GSJ* 40.

Shann, R. T. (1984), 'Flemish Transposing Harpsichords: An Explanation', *GSJ* 37.

Shone, A. B. (1951), 'Coaching Calls', *Musical Times*, 92.

Shreffler, Anne C. (1983), 'Baroque Flutes and Modern: Sound Spectra and Performance Results', *GSJ* 36.

Silbiger, Alexander (1980), 'Imitations of the Colascione in 17th-Century Keyboard Music', *GSJ* 33.

Simonson, Linda (1987), 'A Burmese Arched Harp (*Saùng-gauk*) and its Pervasive Buddhist Symbolism', *JAMIS* 13.

SIMP = Studia Instrumentorum Musicae Popularis (Stockholm, from 1969).

Simpson, Christopher (1659), *The Division-Violist* (repr. as *The Division-Viol*, 1965).

Skeaping, Kenneth (1955), 'Some Speculations on a Crisis in the History of the Violin', *GSJ* 8.

Sloane, Irving (1966), *Classic Guitar Construction* (New York).

Slobin, M. (1969), *Kirgiz Instrumental Music* (New York).

Smirnov, B. (1959), *Iskusstro Vladimirskikh rozhechnikov* (Moscow).

Smith, Douglas A. (1979), 'On the Origin of the Chitarrone', *Journal of the American Musicological Society*, 32.3.

Smith Brindle, Reginald (1970), *Contemporary Percussion*.

Smithers, Don L. (1973), *The Music and History of the Baroque Trumpet before 1721*.

Söderberg, Bertil (1956), *Les Instruments de musiqui au Bas-Congo et dans les régions avoisinantes* (Stockholm).

Soyer, A. M. (1927), *Des Instruments à Vent*, separation from Lavignac 1913.

Speer, Daniel (1687), *Grund-richtiger . . . Unterricht der musikalischen Kunst* (Ulm; 2nd edn. 1697).

Spencer, Michael (1981), 'Harpsichord Physics', *GSJ* 34.

Spencer, Robert (1976), 'Chitarrone, Theorbo and Archlute', *EM* 4.4 (Oct.).

Springer, George H. (1976), *Maintenance and Repair of Wind and Percussion Instruments* (Boston).

Stainer, Cecil (1896), *A Dictionary of Violin Makers* (Oxford).

Steger, Hugo (1961), *David Rex et Propheta* (Nuremberg).

Stevenson, Robert M. (1959), 'Ancient Peruvian Instruments', *GSJ* 12.

Stowell, Robin (1948), 'Violin Bowing in Transition', *EM* 12.3 (Aug.).

Such, David G. (1985), 'The Bodhrán', *GSJ* 38.

Sumner, William L. (1952), *The Organ* (repr. 1973).

Talbot, James (*c.* 1695), Christ Church Library, Oxford, Music MS 1187; sections publ. in *GSJ*: Wind Instruments (1948) 1; Bowed Instruments (1950) 3; Bagpipes (1952) 5; Lutes (1961) 14; Other Fretted Instruments (1962) 15; Harps (1963); Harpsichords (1968) 21. [see also Unwin]

Tarr, Edward (1975), see Bendinelli, C. (1614).

—— (1988), *The Trumpet*.

Taylor, Charles A. (1976), *Sounds of Music*.

Terry, Charles Sanford (1932), *Bach's Orchestra*.

Teuchert, Emil, and Haupt, E. W. (1911), *Musik-Instrumenkunde in Wort und Bild* (Leipzig).

Theophilus (MS, 11th Century), *Diversarum artium schedula*.

Thomas, Bernard (1973), 'An Introduction to the Crumhorn Repertoire', *EM* 1.3 (July).

—— (1974), 'Playing the Crumhorn', *EM* 2.3 (July).

—— (1975), 'The Renaissance Flute', *EM* 3.1 (Jan.).

Thomas, William R., and Rhodes, J. J. K. (1967), 'The String Scales of Italian Keyboard Instruments', *GSJ* 20.

—— (1971), 'Schlick, Praetorius and the History of Organ-Pitch', *Organ Yearbook*, 2.

Tikhomirov, G. (1983), *Instrumenty Russkogo narodnogo orkestra* (Moscow).

Tilmouth, Michael (1957), 'Some Improvements in Music noted by William Turner in 1697', *GSJ* 10.

—— (1961), 'A Calendar of References to Music in Newspapers published in London and the Provinces (1660–1719)', *RMA Research Chronicle*, 1.

Tinctoris, Johannes (*c.* 1484), *De inventione et Usu Musicae* (Naples; MS, Regensburg); ed. K. Weinmann (Regensburg, 1917); section on instruments trans. Anthony Baines (1950), *GSJ* 3.

Titcomb, Caldwell, (1956), 'Baroque Court and Military Trumpets and Kettledrums', *GSJ* 9.

Tobischek, H. (1977), *Die Pauke* (Tutzing).

Toff, Nancy (1979), *The Development of the Modern Flute* (New York).

Töpfer, Johann G. (1888), *Die Theorie und Praxis des Orgelbaues* (Weimar; repr. Amsterdam 1972).

Tracey, Hugh (1948), *Chopi Musicians*.

Traficante, Frank (1970), 'Lyra Viol Tunings', *Acta Musicologica* 42.3–4.

Trân văn Khê (1962), *La musique Vietnamienne traditionelle* (Paris).

Trojano, Massimo (1569), *Dialoghi* (Venice).

Trowell, Brian (1957), 'King Henry IV, Recorder-player', *GSJ* 10.

Tucci, Roberta, and Ricci, Antonello (1985), 'The Chitarra Battente in Calabria', *GSJ* 38.

Turnbull, Harvey (1974), *The Guitar: From the Renaissance to the Present Day*.

Tyler, James (1974), 'Checklist of Music for the Cittern', *EM* 2.1 (Jan.).

—— (1975), 'The Renaissance Guitar', *EM* 3.4 (Oct.).

—— (1980), *The Early Guitar*.

—— (1981a), 'The Mandore in the 16th and 17th Centuries', *EM* 9.1 (Jan.).

—— (1981b), 'The Italian Mandolin and Mandola, 1589–1800', *EM* 9.4 (Oct.).

—— and Sparks, P. (1989), *The Early Mandolin* (Oxford).

Unwin, Robert (1987), '"An English Writer on Music": James Talbot 1664–1708', *GSJ* 40.

Usher, Terence (1956), 'The Spanish Guitar in the 19th and 20th Centuries', *GSJ* 9.

Van Aalst, J. A. (1884), *Chinese Music* (Shanghai; repr. New York, 1964).

Vance, Stuart-Morgan (1987), 'Carte's Flute Patents of the Mid-Nineteenth Century', *JAMIS* 13.

Van der Meer, John Henry (1974), 'Studien zum Cembalobau in Italien', *SIMP* 3.

—— (1978), 'A Contribution to the History of the Clavicytherium', *EM* 6.2 (Apr.).

—— (1987), 'The Typology and History of the Bass Clarinet', *JAMIS* 13.

—— and Webster, Rainer (1982), *Catalogo degli Strumenti Musicali dell'Accademia Filarmonica di Verona* (Verona).

Van der Straeten, Edmund S. J. (1915), *History of the Cello* (repr. 1971).

Vandor, I. (1973), 'La notazione musicale Strumentale del Buddismo Tibetano', *Nuova rivista musicale italiana* (Rome) 7.

Vannes, René (1951), *Dictionnaire universel des luthiers* (Brussels).

Vega, Carlos (1943), *Los Instrumentos musicales aboregenes y criollos de la Argentina* (Buenos Aires).

Vertkov, K. *et al.* (1963), *Atlas muzykalnykh instrumentov narodov SSSR* (Moscow).

Vinogradov, V. (1961), *Muzykalnoe naslednie Toktogula* (Moscow).

Virdung, Sebastian (1511), *Musica getutscht* (Basel; repr. 1970).

Virgiliano, Aurelio (*c.* 1600), *Il Dolcimelo* (MS, Milan: ed. Marcello Castellani, Florence, 1979).

Wachsmann, Klaus P. (1953): in Margaret Trowell, *Tribal Crafts of Uganda, Part II*, 'The Sound Instruments'.

—— (1961), 'The Primitive Musical Instruments', in Anthony Baines, *Musical Instruments through the Ages*, ch. 1.

Walls, Peter (1984), 'Violin Fingering in the 18th Century', *EM* 12.3 (Aug.).

Warner, Thomas E. (1967), *An Annotated Bibliography of Woodwind Instruction Books, 1600–1830* (Detroit).

Webb, Graham (1984), *The Musical Box Handbook* (New York).

Webb, John (1984), 'Notes on the Ballad Horn', *GSJ* 37.

—— (1985), 'Designs for Brass in the Public Record Office', *GSJ* 38.

—— (1988), 'The Billingsgate Trumpet', *GSJ* 41.

Weber, Gottfried (1825), 'Wesentliche Verbesserungen des Fagotts', *Caecilia*, ii, (Mainz; followed by another article in the same, 1828).

Weber, Rainer (1976), 'Recorder Finds from the Middle Ages, and Results of their Reconstruction', *GSJ* 29.

—— and Van der Meer, John Henry (1972), 'Some Facts and Guesses Concerning *Doppioni*', *GSJ* 25.

Wegner, Max (1963), *Griechenland (Musikgeschichte in Bildern II/4)* (Leipzig).

Weigand, George A. (1973), 'The Cittern Repertoire', *EM* 1.2 (Apr.).

Weinmann, Karl (1917), *Johannes Tinctoris (1445–1511) und sein unbekannter Traktat 'De inventione et usu musicae'* (Regensburg).

Welch, Christopher (1911), *Six Lectures on the Recorder*.

Wells, Elizabeth (1978), 'An Early Stringed Keyboard Instrument: The Clavicytherium in the Royal College of Music', *EM* 6.4 (Oct.).

Wells, Robin H. (1982), 'The Orpharion' *EM* 10.4 (Oct.).

Westcott, W. (1970), *Bells and their Music* (New York).

Westernhagen, K. Von (1973), *Die Entstehung des 'Ring'* (Zurich).

Weston, Pamela (1971), *Clarinet Virtuosi of the Past*.

—— (1977), *More Clarinet Virtuosi of the Past*.

Weston, Stephen (1983), 'Improvements to the Nine-Keyed Ophicleide' *GSJ* 36.

White, Paul (1984), 'Early Bassoon Reeds', *JAMIS* 10.

Whitworth, Reginald R. (1932), *The Cinema and Theatre Organ* (repr. 1981).

Wiant, Bliss (1965), *The Music of China* (Hong Kong).

Wick, Denis (1971), *Trombone Technique*.

Willaman, Robert (1949), *The Clarinet and Clarinet Playing* (Salt Point, NY).

Williams, Peter (1966), *The European Organ*.

—— (1980), *A New History of the Organ*.

—— and Owen, Barbara (1988), *The Organ*.

Wilson, Michael (1968), *The English Chamber Organ 1650–1859*.

Wilson, Wilfred G. (1965), *The Art and Science of Change Ringing*.

Winckel, Fritz (1959), *Music, Sound and Sensation* (New York).

Winston, Winnie, and Keith, Bill (1975), *Pedal Steel Guitar* (New York).

Witten II, Laurence C. (1974), 'Apollo, Orpheus and David: A Study of the Crucial Century in the Development of Bowed Strings in North Italy 1480–1581', *JAMIS* 1.

—— (1982), 'The Surviving Instruments of Andrea Amati', *EM* 10.4 (Oct.).

Wobersin, W. (n.d.), *Schule für di Thüringer Waldzither* (Frankfurt/Main).

Word A. B. (1930, etc.), *A Textbook of Sound*.

Woodfield, Ian (1977), 'The Early History of the Viol', *PRMA* 103.

—— (1978), 'Viol Playing Technique in the Mid-16th Century', *EM* 6.4 (Oct.).

—— (1984), *The Early History of the Viol* (Cambridge).

Wright, Laurence (1977), 'The Medieval Gittern and Citole: A Case of Mistaken Identity', *GSJ* 30.

Wright, Michael (1976), 'Bergeron on Flute-Making', *GSJ* 29.

Wulstan, David (1973), 'The Sounding of the Shofar', *GSJ* 26.

Wyn Jones, David (1982), 'Observations: Vanhal, Dittersdorf and the Violone', *EM* 10.1 (Jan.).

Wythe, Deborah (1984), 'The Pianos of Conrad Graf', *EM* 12.4 (Nov.).

Young, Phillip T. (1981), 'A Bass Clarinet by the Mayrhofers of Passau', *JAMIS* 7.

—— (1982), *Twenty-five Hundred Woodwind Instruments* (New York).

—— (1986), 'The Scherers of Butzbach', *GSJ* 39.

Zacconi, Lodovico (1592), *Prattica di musica* (Venice).

Zamfir, C. (n.d.), *Metodă de Cobză* (Bucharest).

Zemp, Hugo (1981), 'Melanesian Solo Polyphonic Panpipe Music', *Ethnomusicology* 25.3.

Zeraschi, Helmut (1976), *Drehorgeln* (Leipzig).

Ziegler, Christiane (1979), *Catalogue des instruments de musique égyptiens au Musée du Louvre* (Paris).

Zingel, Hans J. (1932), *Harfe und Harfenspiel* (Halle).

Zuckermann, Wolfgang J. (1969), *The Modern Harpsichord* (New York).

CPSIA information can be obtained at www.ICGtesting.com
Printed in the USA
LVOW081914181211

260024LV00002B/10/A